CISCO

Cisco:
A Beginner's Guide

TOM **SHAUGHNESSY**, with TOBY **VELTE**

Osborne/**McGraw-Hill**

Berkeley   New York   St. Louis   San Francisco
Auckland   Bogotá   Hamburg   London   Madrid
Mexico City   Milan   Montreal   New Delhi   Panama City
Paris   São Paulo   Singapore   Sydney
Tokyo   Toronto

Osborne/**McGraw-Hill**
2600 Tenth Street
Berkeley, California 94710
U.S.A.

For information on translations or book distributors outside the U.S.A., or to arrange bulk purchase discounts for sales promotions, premiums, or fund-raisers, please contact Osborne/**McGraw-Hill** at the above address.

Cisco: A Beginner's Guide

34567890 AGM AGM 019876543210

ISBN 0-07-212115-7

Publisher
  Brandon A. Nordin
**Associate Publisher
and Editor-in-Chief**
  Scott Rogers
Executive Acquisitions Editor
  Wendy Rinaldi
Project Editor
  Emily Rader
Editorial Assistant
  Monika Faltiss
Technical Editor
  Velte Systems
Copy Editor
  Judith Brown

Proofreader
  Linda Medoff
Indexer
  Rebecca Plunkett
Computer Designers
  Gary Corrigan
  Dick Schwartz
  Roberta Steele
Illustrators
  Robert Hansen
  Brian Wells
  Beth Young
Series Design
  Peter F. Hancik

This book was composed with Corel VENTURA™ Publisher.

To My Three Sons:
Julien, Mathieu, and Max.
Before any "discussions" break out,
Boyz, please take note that you're listed in alphabetical order.

—Pops

About the Authors . . .

Tom Shaughnessy, CCNA, is a consultant for Velte Systems. He has more than 17 years of computer industry experience. Tom has worked on both the technical and marketing sides as a software designer, project manager, and marketing consultant. Most of his experience has been with the design and implementation of enterprise computing solutions for businesses. He has extensive background in helping managers understand complex technical subjects in order to make informed decisions.

Toby J. Velte, Ph.D., MCSE+I, CCNA, is CEO of Velte Systems, Inc., an enterprise network consulting firm based in St. Paul, Minnesota. Dr. Velte is an experienced network consultant. He specializes in the design and integration of heterogeneous networking environments for large businesses. He also designs strategies that enable organizations to best use technology to meet their business needs. He can be reached at tjv@velte.com.

CONTENTS

Part II

Cisco Internetworking Tools

Part III

Designing Cisco Networks

ACKNOWLEDGMENTS

This is to gratefully acknowledge those who helped in the creation of this book. Our deepest thanks to the Velte Systems crew: Amy Hanson, John McManus, Terry Bjorke, Tony Velte and, yes, even that young greenhorn Jeremy Cheney. Special thanks goes out to Rex Hale, CCIE, for his excellent technical input. Their technical expertise, industry experience, and critical review skills helped so much in amassing and organizing all the information contained herein.

Also acknowledged is the team at Osborne/McGraw Hill. It is fair to say that without the creative and insightful executive editor, Wendy Rinaldi, this book would never have gotten off the ground. To project editor Emily Rader we say thank you very much. To the Osborne illustration team—Brian Wells, Bob Hansen, and Beth Young—we say thank you for your patience. Monika, thanks for keeping all things in order and gently reminding us of the schedule. And to copy editor Judith Brown (our provisional English Lit. professor operating in the blue screens of Microsoft Word) we say thank you so very much for your light but incisive touch with the wordsmith's ever necessary scalpel.

TS & TJV

INTRODUCTION

An emergency meeting had been called about the fact that the e-commerce project was late, over budget, and experiencing performance problems. As he entered the conference room, the VP surveyed the cast of characters already there, and worried.

Almost two million dollars spent already, thought the VP, and yet the board was forced to seriously contemplate pulling the plug. He'd been sent to identify what was wrong and how to fix it. "OK," he said as he took a seat at the head of the table, "I'm throwing open the agenda. I want to know what the project's major problems are, what's causing them, and how long and how much it'll take to fix them." Turning toward the CIO and his network manager, the VP went on, "We all know that this project is central to our corporate strategy, nothing else has had a higher priority or consumed more resources during the last year. Yet our two primary competitors have already successfully launched their Web sites and upgraded their business-to-business e-commerce. But we can't see the end of the tunnel on this project. Let me remind you that this isn't just another little departmental application, the board wants the Internet to become our primary place of business. Our competition has already cut their cost of sale by 15 percent or more, and we've lost 5 percent market share in the last quarter alone. We aren't thrilled with having a half-finished network that runs like a dog, not to mention being over budget, but this weekend's security breach may have been the last straw. What's wrong with this project?"

The CIO started with a complaint that the contractors weren't adhering to the three-level hierarchical design he'd requested, complaining that back doors and chains were choking performance. The consultant shot back that if the company had retained them for project management things would be under better control using their rigorous management methodology. A person from the Web programming team snidely noted that the context-based access control algorithm was "puking back hosed code every time the implicit deny rule hit bottom." Another complained that the so-called strong cryptography chosen for the VPN was using an overwrought DES key. The consultants disputed that statement, noting that RMONs were probably chewing up too many CPU clicks with MIB collection, and that the NMS was over-polling SNMP anyway. The Network Manager then took exception, pointing out that the original EtherChannel wirespeed benchmark could be attained only if "major upgrades" were at last made to the blades jacked into the backplanes of the various LAN switches, especially the ones feeding the ATM LANE adapters, because they were blocking broadcasts within VLANs. Sure, *now* they all agreed that the route switch processor modules on the "big honker" Cisco 7500 were grossly underconfigured, but that wasn't the story during the big "to route or to switch" debate during the design phase. Fact is, if the backbone routers had PIM sparse mode implemented, everything would be cool, but *now* multicasts were bringing the network to its knees because there were too many unknown groups, especially going through the IGX switch fabric. Without that humming, QoS—especially for traffic shaping and CAR—didn't have a snowball's chance in summer, at least not without a serious commitment finally being made to multilayer switching as had been recommended. This was especially the case given all the subnet masks, DHCP, and DNS to handle down at the access layer. The consultants begged to disagree, pointing out that propagation delays were spawning loops, especially in the RIP domains, which they had specifically recommended against. IGRP was the superior choice, or better yet EIGRP, and anyway once the routing metrics were properly tuned, the RIP versus IGRP thing would fall to the wayside. Then traps could at long last be set to alarm for out of band operations, freeing the team to tweak the CBAC and ASA algorithms to assure that last weekend's security debacle didn't repeat itself.

The VP was sick to his stomach, feeling trapped and, yes, very much alarmed. Sensing the VP's growing discomfort, the head consultant blurted out an offer to reduce the billing rate for the nine people engaged full-time on the project from $160 to $150 an hour. But the VP, at the end of his rope, said, "I must tell you that I've never heard so much bull in my entire life. I've been in data processing for over twenty years and I haven't understood a thing said in this meeting. It really rips me that you network people can't speak plain English. This project is caught in a loop, and I've gotta get a grip on things here. Let's adjourn for now and get together after lunch."

At the back of the room sat two young staffers who were in the meeting just in case the network performance statistics they'd gathered needed explanation. They hadn't understood much of what was said, either. But without saying a word, they looked at another and raised their eyebrows at the same thought: $160 per hour?

WHO SHOULD READ THIS BOOK

This book is designed for anybody new to internetworking. It covers what one might refer to as the Internet's technical infrastructure. The software on your desktop—the Web browser, FTP software, or ICQ messenger—is only the tip of the iceberg. Over the past 30 years, an ever-growing group of dedicated computer scientists, telecommunications engineers, and programmers have been busy designing and building a global infrastructure that is revolutionizing commerce and culture alike. As you saw in the earlier meeting scenario, internetworking has taken on a language all its own—separate even from that used by the computer industry at large.

This book is for aspiring professionals interested in learning about the networking giant, managers in the computing industry who are weak on internetworking (that would be 90 percent or more of such managers), computer platform and software pros, and even those in the general public with a taste for technology.

This book is for those interested in the Internet and internetworking, not just in Cisco. Technology basics are covered generically before delving into Cisco particulars. Cisco is used for all examples in this book because they have the biggest and most comprehensive product line in the industry and, frankly, they're by far the biggest, baddest, most important player in the field.

For those of you interested in pursuing Cisco certification, read this book to be introduced to industry background, concepts, terms, and technology. Then go on to a test preparation book to nail down your CCNA test. Indeed, the publisher of this book also publishes the best CCNA test prep book, *CCNA Cisco Certified Network Associate Study Guide*, by Syngress Media, Inc. (Osborne/McGraw-Hill, 1998).

WHAT THIS BOOK COVERS

Chapter 1, "Cisco and the Internet"—The Internet represents the biggest and fastest economic change in history, and sooner or later all our lives will be profoundly affected by it (if they haven't been already). This chapter surveys the Internet as a phenomenon, with a particular eye toward Cisco Systems and how its IOS operating software has vaulted the company to a position among the computer industry elite, alongside Microsoft, Intel, and IBM. The internetworking industry is outlined, and how Cisco's product line matches up to industry niches is explained.

Chapter 2, "Networking Primer"—Modern internetworking is the culmination of dozens of sophisticated technologies. This chapter explains things from the wire up, starting first with electrons passing over cables up through binary bits and bytes. The major LAN technologies such as Ethernet and Token Ring are explained, right down to how they differ, including high-speed backbone technologies such as ATM and Gigabit Ethernet. The seven-layer Open Systems Interconnection (OSI) reference model is explained, including the inner workings of the TCP/IP protocol suite—the software used to run the

Internet. You'll learn the difference between connection-oriented and connectionless networking, and how domain names are translated to numerical IP addresses. The important networking fundamentals of IP addressing and subnet masks are explained in detail. Dial-in technologies such as DSL and ISDN are covered, as are WAN trunk technologies such as T1 and T3, Frame Relay, and ATM.

Chapter 3, "Cisco Certifications"—Like Microsoft and Novell, Cisco has a full-fledged certification program for technicians working on their products. This chapter details the three tracks—Routing & Switching, WAN Switching, and ISP Dial—and sorts out how the new Cisco certifications for design differ from the ones already in place for network support. Complete explanations are given of exam objectives for each certification. A must read for anyone interested in pursuing a career in internetworking, or faced with recruiting and managing Cisco certified personnel.

Chapter 4, "Router Overview"—This chapter focuses on Cisco router basics. We cover router hardware components from the printed circuit board up through the CPU, and explain how network administrators can log into Cisco routers to work on them, even rebooting to perform such basic tasks as password recovery. The major software components in Cisco routers are also surveyed, including the Cisco IOS command interface and feature sets. Cisco's router product line is reviewed here, including some tips on how to select the best router to solve a particular internetworking problem.

Chapter 5, "Configuring Routers"—Now it's time to delve into the heavier stuff, especially the configuration file. This chapter goes into the Cisco IOS operating mode, command hierarchy, utilities, and how to use the IOS help subsystem. But most of the focus is on the all-important configuration file, and how it's used to set up Cisco routers and configure internetworks. Reading this chapter introduces you to essential Cisco router commands, command syntax, how to read device status, and how to configure key router parameters. Cisco's ConfigMaker and FastStep configuration software tools are reviewed.

Chapter 6, "Switches and Hubs"—The so-called *access layer* is where host devices such as PCs and servers plug into internetworks. This chapter explains internetwork topology basics, cabling specifications, what bandwidth is, what distinguishes collision and broadcast domains, and how hubs and access switches differ. High-end LAN backbone switches are also covered, from the perspective of one of the most important subjects in the industry today—whether to design routed or switched networks. The more technical dimensions of switched networking are introduced, including switching protocols, virtual LANs (VLANs), and multilayered switching. Cisco's hub and switch product lines are reviewed.

Chapter 7, "Internet Access Products"—There are three types of technologies through which internetworks can be accessed: firewalls, access servers, and virtual private networks (VPNs). This chapter explains each of the three, with a particular focus on firewalls. The access list is explained, as are adaptive firewall security algorithms, the technology at the heart of internetwork security at the packet level. Cisco sells two firewall products: the Cisco PIX Firewall hardware/software combination and the IOS Firewall software feature set, and both are explained in detail. The VPN—the wide area network (WAN) of the future—is covered. How access servers work, and the role they play is also surveyed. Further, the Cisco access server product line is reviewed.

Chapter 8, "Routing Protocols"—Large internetworks, or for that matter the Internet, wouldn't be possible without routing protocols. This chapter covers fundamental problems confronting any internetwork, and how routing protocols are used to adapt to shifting traffic patterns, emerging problems, and topology changes. Basic routing protocol technology is covered here, as are the various major routing protocols in use today—both open standard protocols (RIP, OSPF, BGP) and Cisco-proprietary protocols (IGRP and EIGRP). Cisco's routing protocols are overviewed, down to the command level where routing metrics are set to modify network behavior to meet enterprise requirements.

Chapter 9, "Network Management"—Network management has become a major issue, as internetworks have grown in size and complexity. This chapter covers the standards and technologies that underlie network management systems: the Simple Network Management Protocol (SNMP), remote monitor instrumentation (RMON), and the management information base (MIB). Issues surrounding network management standards are covered, as is Cisco's approach to implementing them. SNMP configuration is introduced at the command level. Cisco's suite of network management software products—Resource Management Essentials, CWSI Campus, and NetSys Baseliner—are also reviewed.

Chapter 10, "Cisco Security"—A second type of network security that exists beyond firewalls is user-based security, used to set and enforce passwords to access networks and authorizations to use network resources. This chapter first covers the underlying industry standards for security, especially the AAA (Authentication, Authorization, and Accounting) standard. AAA is covered at the command level, then the CiscoSecure ACS product suite is reviewed. Cisco offers two user-based security products: RADIUS, an industry standard, and its proprietary TACACS+. Both are reviewed in detail.

Chapter 11, "Building Cisco Networks"—There are basics that must be covered when considering any network design decision, whether for a whole new internetwork or a modest expansion of an existing one. This chapter reviews what's been learned—routed versus switched networking, VLANs, the need for redundancy, and so on—and puts them to use in solving network design problems. The classic three-layer hierarchical design model is reviewed in terms of what to look for in the access, distribution, and backbone layers. Key design subjects such as topology meshing, load balancing, and Quality of Service (QoS) are reviewed. How to perform a comprehensive network needs analysis and how to translate it into design solutions using Cisco products is explained, covering such design factors as routing protocols, address design, routing versus switching, WAN services, and traffic load balancing.

Chapter 12, "Troubleshooting Cisco Networks"—You've arrived as a network pro when you can troubleshoot an internetwork. This chapter surveys typical internetwork problems, and the proper methodology for diagnosing and fixing them. Key Cisco IOS troubleshooting commands are reviewed in terms of how to handle connectivity problems, performance bottlenecks, and other problems. Particular attention is paid on how to track down and isolate configuration problems, how to tune routing protocol metrics, and how to troubleshoot WAN services such as serial line links.

Appendix A, "Configuring Switches and Hubs"—We feel that the routing versus switching debate is so critical that this appendix is included to give you a hands-on feel for how Cisco's connectivity products are configured and maintained. A complete review of Cisco's Visual Switch Manager and Hub Management Console user interfaces is given to let you know which parameters to set in order to properly configure and manage Cisco switches and hub devices.

HOW TO READ THIS BOOK

This book can be picked up and read from the beginning of any chapter. Chapters covering technology start out with the basics and give explanations from the standpoint of the technology's historical background, how it developed, and what the issues and trends surrounding it are. Only then is Cisco specifically covered in terms of IOS commands, Cisco software tools, and Cisco hardware and software products.

This book doesn't try to reinvent the wheel by publishing yet another new glossary on internetworking terms and acronyms. Every term introduced in this book is defined and explained in context. But the book should be read with the reader's browser pointed to Cisco's Web site at http://www.cisco.com. While this book stands on its own, it never hurts to browse around to help reinforce newly learned subject matter. Cisco's Web site contains a wealth of product illustrations, white papers, and other materials. In particular, someone reading this book should use the Universal Resource Locator (URL) for the following pages, three excellent online glossaries to complement this book:

http://www.cisco.com/warp/public/779/edu/academy/curriculum/demo/glossary-f.html
http://www.cisco.com/univercd/cc/td/doc/cisintwk/ita/index.htm
http://www.zdwebopedia.com/

Finally, as you'll learn in this book, nearly all of modern computer networking springs from either de facto or de jure standards. The single best source for information on internetworking standards and technologies is the Internet Engineering Task Force, whose URL is http://www.ietf.org/. The IETF publishes Requests for Comments, called RFCs for short, that go into painful technical detail on almost any conceivable internetworking subject. As you read this book and become more comfortable with technical subject matter, browse these RFCs at http://www.ietf.org/rfc.html. The RFCs may help you envision some of the technologies being discussed.

PART I

Cisco Overview

CHAPTER 1

Cisco and the Internet

he Internet is amazing. There's just no other word to describe a technology that few had even heard of ten years ago, yet now dominates so much of our collective consciousness. The gold fever surrounding the Internet makes the 1849 California gold rush seem insignificant in comparison. You've no doubt heard the analogies and the clichés—the Internet is the fastest growing market in history; the fastest growing technology in history; the first truly global, real-time marketplace of goods, services, and ideas. The Internet will bring profound change to all sectors, from business to education to entertainment. The Internet is the information superhighway that's our road to the future. The Internet will revolutionize society, and so on.

The most surprising thing about all the breathless Web hype is that most of it's true. Consider the numbers: total Internet user accounts are projected to grow from under 200 million now to a half *billion* over the next few years, putting onto one system a population nearly twice the size of the U.S. population. The number of registered Internet domain names more than doubles annually. There are now about 10 million Web sites, up from a million just two years ago. In 1998, U.S. businesses alone spent over $10 billion upgrading their internetworks. A thousand American households sign up for Internet access every *hour*. Over $3 billion was spent on Internet advertising last year, and some project that figure will grow to over $30 billion in the next few years. Many pundits seriously expect the "Internet economy" to exceed a trillion dollars by 2005. No matter how tired we are of hearing this litany, the numbers are awesome.

Although most press coverage dotes on visible technologies such as browsers and WebTV, the real action is in Internet infrastructure. Billions are being invested by serious players who foresee a day when virtually all mass media—radio, telephone, television—converge onto the Internet. This convergence will use the Internet as a single "pipe" through which virtually all communication travels. There's disagreement about whether the Internet pipe will run over telephone lines, cable TV wires, or even satellites. The bets are large because winning the Internet infrastructure game promises untold riches.

But there's trouble in paradise. As more people have hopped onto the bandwagon, the diameter of the pipe—called *bandwidth*, a measure of how much data can be moved over a link—has come under increasing scrutiny. New users and bigger applications are chewing up bandwidth as fast as additional network equipment can be added to the Internet's infrastructure, the global maze of telecommunications links and internetworking devices that makes it all go. The Internet has undergone perennial bandwidth scares, with pundits worrying that additional loads finally may bring the whole thing to a grinding halt. That hasn't happened yet, but a huge amount of money and attention is focused on Internet infrastructure.

    Wire speed x efficiency =
Available bandwidth

Device
speed

Device
speed

Users connect to servers over this Internet infrastructure, yet few are aware of how it works. Bandwidth isn't just a matter of telecommunications media running over high-speed fiber-optic cable. The networking devices sitting at each end of the cables are every bit as important. In many situations, the speed of these devices is as big a factor in the Internet's bandwidth as telecom media.

This book surveys internetworking's infrastructure from the ground up, starting with underlying technology up through the product level. If you're a beginner, read this book and you'll know the basics of internetworking. It's written from the perspective of the premier manufacturer of internetworking technology, Cisco Systems. Because the technologies are covered generically, you'll understand the technologies and components needed to make any internetwork run, not just one built from Cisco products. But make no mistake, this book is about *infrastructure*; that is, about the devices over which internetworks operate:

▼ **Routers**   These devices route data between local area networks (LANs). Routers put the *inter* in internetworking; without them, the Internet would not be possible. Routers use Internet Protocol (IP) addresses to figure out how to best route packets through internetworks.

■ **Switches**   These devices also forward data between LANs. Switches are faster than routers, but they don't use IP addresses and, therefore, don't have the capability routers do for finding paths through large internetworks.

■ **Firewalls**   These are basically routers that are specially outfitted for filtering packets to secure data processing assets within an enterprise's internal internetwork.

■ **Access servers**   These dedicated devices answer phone calls from remote users and connect them to the internetwork. Most access servers are used by Internet service providers (ISPs) to connect home users and small businesses to the Internet.

▲ **Hubs**   The lowly hub accepts cables from PCs and servers to create individual LANs called *LAN segments*, the basic building blocks of internetworking.

Collectively, these five types of devices make up the Internet's infrastructure. The only other major ingredient is telecommunications links to make wide area network (WAN) connections. In this book we'll cover all five device types as they exist within Cisco's product line, and review WAN technologies also. Doing so from the perspective of Cisco's product line will give you a more detailed look at the inner workings of internetwork devices.

CISCO'S POSITION IN THE COMPUTER INDUSTRY

We all know that Microsoft Windows is the world's most important computer operating system. But here's a pop quiz: can you name the second most important OS? Choose one:

▼ **MVS**   IBM's proprietary OS used to run mainframe computers. MVS still has a stranglehold on the central corporate and government data centers that handle financial accounting and other sensitive transactions.

- **UNIX**   There are actually about a dozen proprietary versions of UNIX from such computer manufacturers as Sun, HP, Compaq, Novell, and IBM. Nevertheless, UNIX is the predominant server OS in enterprise class client-server applications.

▲ **IOS**   Short for Internetwork Operating System, this is Cisco System's proprietary OS for its line of internetworking hardware.

IOS is the second most important operating system, and by a wide margin. We assert this partly because UNIX and MVS have both lost some of their edge—UNIX having lost market share to Microsoft Windows NT, and MVS still a mission-critical technology but one that has stopped growing altogether. But the main reason IOS is so important is that Cisco has over an 80 percent share of the Internet router market, and the Internet is the fastest growing market in history.

To put that in perspective, Cisco has about the same market share in router technology as Intel enjoys in Windows, or *Wintel*, hardware platforms. The Wintel regime has been attacked as a monopoly by competitors, and both Microsoft and Intel were recently charged by the U.S. Department of Justice with antitrust violations for alleged monopolistic practices. But there's a twist: Wintel is a duopoly, with the two companies dividing the hardware and software.

Not so with Cisco. IOS is their proprietary OS architecture, and it runs on their hardware only. This means that Cisco's 80 percent share garners both hardware and software revenues, and gives the company total architectural control over its products. Cisco's management team might wince at the thought, but the whispering has already started that Cisco is the industry's next monopoly. The company has earned its dominant market share fair and square, but some fear that IOS could become to internetworking what Windows became to desktop computing. Cisco makes no bones about the fact that they're aiming for the $50 billion mark, or higher.

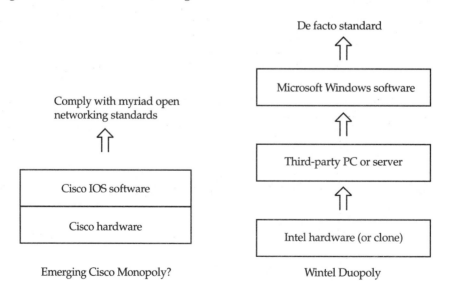

Emerging Cisco Monopoly?   Wintel Duopoly

Cisco's present position has its strengths and weaknesses compared to the Wintel duopoly. On the negative side of the ledger, Cisco products are largely used to run truly open-standard protocols, which reduces the extent to which they can leverage product architecture to assert market control. Cisco can't freeze any competitor out of design cycles to prepare products that implement emerging technologies, because the technologies implement open standards. On the positive side, Cisco is a single company that makes it's own products. This contrasts favorably to Wintel, a pair of companies that relies on hundreds of PC manufacturers to deliver their respective products to market.

None of this is lost on the investment community. They particularly like the fact that Cisco holds a first- or second-place share in every major internetworking hardware market niche, not just in routers. For example, the market for local data switches is one of the hottest segments in internetworking, and Cisco has a 40 percent share, with its nearest competitor holding less than 10 percent. Cisco is on such a roll, in fact, that CEO John Chambers claims Cisco is "the fastest growing and most profitable company in the history of the computer industry." Apparently his claim has some merit. At this writing in fall 1999, a time just after many Internet stocks got hammered, Cisco's total market capitalization holds steady at about $220 billion.

This book is not an endorsement of Cisco. Like any industry powerhouse, the company has its faults and is duly criticized in these pages when appropriate. But whether you're an individual mulling a career move or a manager weighing your company's Internet strategy, learning how Cisco technology works is your best possible introduction to the world of internetworking.

The Internet Landscape

The Internet isn't a single technology, it's a collection of related technologies that make internetworking possible:

- ▼ **Physical media** From connectors and cables to high-speed fiber-optic cables, the physical links that connect everything together are the foundation of networking.

- ■ **Network technologies** LAN protocols run what happens over the wire. The best known is Ethernet, but there are other important ones.

- ■ **TCP/IP** The Transmission Control Protocol/Internet Protocol is what binds the Internet together. IP handles addressing and TCP handles messaging.

- ■ **Operational technologies** Internetworks rely on a number of underlying standards and protocols to operate themselves, without which internetworking wouldn't be practical.

- ▲ **Application protocols** Network applications define the kinds of useful work internetworks can do, from file transfers to Web page downloads.

To engineer its products, the networking industry uses a seven-layer architectural guideline called the Open Systems Interconnection (OSI) reference model. It's no coincidence that the preceding list of enabling technologies more or less adheres to the OSI model, from the physical level up.

Before we proceed, a quick word to make sure our terminology is clear: the *Internet* is a global interconnection of individual internetworks. An *internetwork* is any collection of local area networks (LANs) under a single administrative regime—usually an enterprise or an ISP. A private internetwork is mechanically the same as the open Internet. A *host* is a user device such as a PC, server, mainframe, or printer. A *device* is a piece of networking equipment such as a router. The generic terms *node* and *station* refer to both hosts and devices. A *LAN segment* is a network medium that hosts share; most LAN segments are formed using a hub. An *application protocol* is a software standard to operate such things as Web browsers, file transfers, e-mails, and other useful functions. An *intranet* is an internal internetwork operating as a private Web, with enterprise applications software used through Web browsers instead of a more traditional graphical user interface (GUI) such as Microsoft Windows.

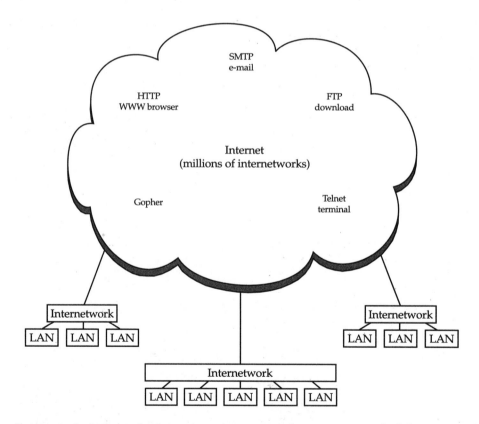

From a technical standpoint, private internetworks are composed of the same pieces as the Internet itself. The only thing that distinguishes the Internet from a large internetwork is its openness.

Internetworking's Five Major Device Types

A *hub* is a passive device that acts as a central connecting point by taking in cables from individual hosts—mainly PCs, servers, and printers—to form an individual LAN segment. Hosts connected to the same hub are members of that LAN segment, and they share the hub's bandwidth to do their communicating. This is because a hub simply repeats incoming signals to all devices attached to its ports.

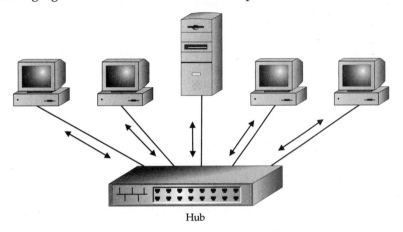

Hub

A *switch* connects hosts to the internetwork, much like a hub. But switches are fundamentally different in that they form a virtual circuit between the sending and receiving hosts. In other words, the switch's bandwidth is reserved for a single switched connection between two hosts as if it were 100 percent dedicated to that virtual circuit. Switches are able to do this by using better electronics than those used by hubs to "slice" bandwidth time into slivers—called *channels*—large enough to service each switch port. Switches are much faster than hubs, but they cost more and are more complicated to configure and manage.

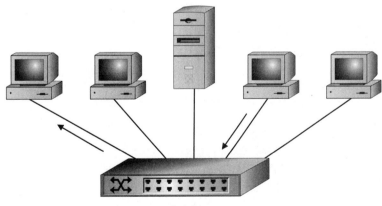

Switch

An *access server* is a specialized device that, stated roughly, acts like a modem on one side and a hub on the other. Access servers connect remote users to internetworks. The majority of the millions of access server ports in the world are operated by ISPs to take phone calls from Internet subscribers. Some perform more specialized functions, but the access server's main purpose is to connect remote dial-in users to an internetwork.

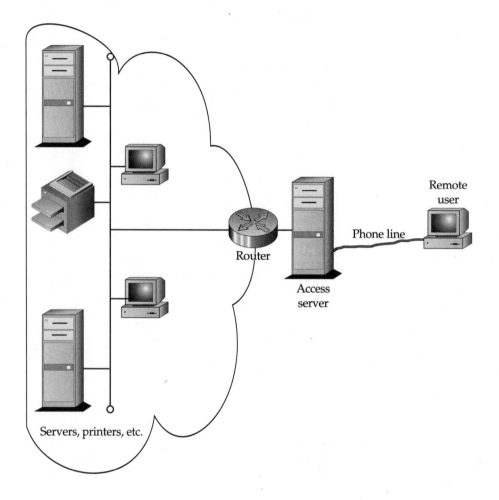

A *router* is an intelligent device that forwards traffic based on the IP address of a message. Whereas hubs and switches have ports into which individual hosts plug, routers have interfaces to which LAN segments attach. In simple terms, a router's job is to move *packets* of data between attached LAN segments.

The router is the single most important type of device in internetworking. It provides the flexibility and decision-making power that make it possible to run complicated internetworks. Without the logical capability routers provide, the Internet would be hundreds of times slower and much more expensive. As detailed in the next chapter, internetwork architectures have seven layers: hubs operate at layer 1, switches at layer 2, and routers at layer 3. Routers also have the capability to filter traffic based upon source and destination addresses, network application, and other parameters.

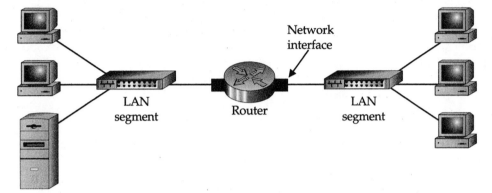

Firewalls are specialized routers that act as checkpoints between an internetwork and the outside. They work by checking each packet for compliance with security policies they have been programmed to enforce. A firewall forms an intentional traffic squeeze point and persistently monitors internal/external connections for security compliance. Any enterprise connected to the Internet should have a firewall configured.

The most powerful firewalls have specialized hardware, but they don't have to. A normal router can be programmed to perform many duties of a firewall, although a dedicated firewall device is preferred in most instances. Firewalls are increasingly being used internally, to safeguard assets from potential internal threats.

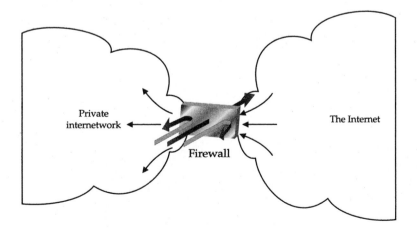

Basic Internetwork Topologies

A *topology* is the physical arrangement of nodes within an internetwork. Usually, a topology is expressed as a logical map that graphically represents each node and the media links connecting the nodes. In fact, topology maps are used as the GUI through which most network management software tools are operated.

Figure 1-1 depicts the basic network elements that are combined in one way or another to make up internetworks.

The LAN segment is the basic building block of internetworks. Put another way, LAN segments are the network units that internetworks link together. The Internet itself is a collection of millions of LAN segments. The reason we use the formal term LAN *segment* is that a local collection of individual segments are commonly referred to as "LANs," even though, strictly speaking, they are actually local internetworks. This may seem like nit-picking, but you'll be happy for the distinction in later chapters.

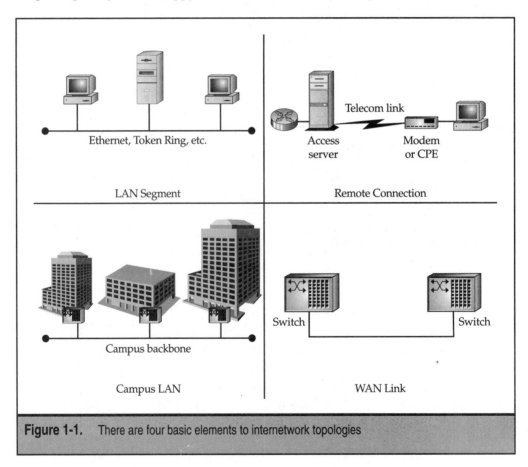

Figure 1-1. There are four basic elements to internetwork topologies

Remote connections use phone circuits to tie physically removed hosts into the LAN segment. The telecom link can be anything from a regular analog voice line to a Digital Subscriber Line (DSL), the hot new telecom technology for small office/home office (SOHO) users.

The *campus LAN* is a double misnomer, but get used to it. Cisco uses it as a generic term to describe local enterprise internetworks. Most exist within a single building, not over an office campus, and all are composed of multiple LAN segments, not a single LAN. But campus LANs are distinguishable by the use of a high-speed backbone segment to interconnect the other local LAN segments. Most LAN backbones run over fiber-optic cabling.

WAN links are long-distance telecom links between cities, although some are strung across ocean floors to connect continents. Virtually all new WAN links being installed run over ultra-high-speed fiber-optic links. The current state of the art is OC-48, with a data rate of 2.5 Gbps. (OC stands for optical carrier; Gbps stands for gigabits per second.) Slower WAN links run over technologies you've probably heard of—T1 and T3 (also called DS3), which run at 1.5 Mbps and 45 Mbps, respectively.

Internetwork Players

There is no "Internet network" as such. In other words, there is no separately owned dedicated trunk network operated under the auspices of some central management authority. The Internet is actually a free-for-all collection of individual networks bound together by two things:

▼ **Shared enabling technologies**   A complex of de facto standards and technologies that not only make the individual internetwork possible, but also enable internetworks to automatically interact with other internetworks.

▲ **IP**   The Internet Protocol is a globally accepted communication system that makes it possible to connect and exchange data with otherwise incompatible hosts anywhere on Earth. IP unifies virtually all computer systems into a unitary data format and addressing system.

Figure 1-2 lays out approximately how the Internet is formed. The prerequisite is that users need to be on a network of some kind, and nowadays, in an office or plant, this usually means some type of Ethernet LAN. Desktop protocols such as Novell NetWare IPX and AppleTalk implement Ethernet, but an increasing number of enterprises are running vanilla IP LANs.

ISPs play a central role in Internet connectivity for enterprises, not just for home users. From the Internet's standpoint, the key juncture is where you connect to the so-called peer network—a group of thousands of high-speed routers that pass IP routes and traffic among one another. Although some very large enterprises (big corporations, government agencies, and universities) have their own connections to the peer network, most tap in via ISPs.

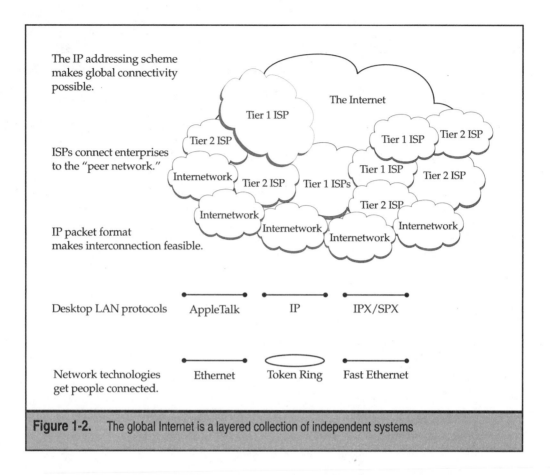

Figure 1-2. The global Internet is a layered collection of independent systems

Entry to the peer network almost always takes place via a very high-speed fiber trunk line, usually controlled by so-called Internet backbone providers (IBPs), such as UUNET, PSINet, MIC/WorldCom, Sprint, and others. Only Tier 1 ISPs such as AOL and EarthLink can afford to contract directly with the IBPs.

Internetworking Protocols

Protocols are the key to internetworking. A networking *protocol* is an agreed-upon data format and set of rules for message exchange to govern a specific process. The Internet's two most fundamental protocols exist at the lower layers of the OSI model, layers 2 and 3. These are the various network (or LAN) protocols and the IP protocol. (In case you're wondering, layer 1 covers cabling and other physical transport media.)

Layer 3	IP	Internetworking
Layer 2	Ethernet, Token Ring, etc.	LAN segment media access

Layers 2 and 3 are the primary focus of this book, because that's where Cisco and its competitors bring physical network infrastructures to life as internetworks. Layer 2 connects the host to its home LAN segment, and layer 3 interconnects LAN segments.

However, that's just the beginning of the protocol story. There are literally dozens of supplementary protocols large and small to do everything from checking whether a neighboring device is still running, to calculating the best path to send packets to the other side of the world. These supplementary protocols can be roughly divided into three groups: maintenance, management, and routing.

Routing protocols	Best paths	Exchange updates, calculate the best current routes
Management protocols	Health and security	Monitor performance, trip alarms, reconfigure
Maintenance protocols	Housekeeping	Discover devices, trace routes, notify neighbors

The maintenance protocols tend to be more proprietary (vendor specific) the closer they are to the network device hardware. For example, the Cisco Discovery Protocol keeps track of devices—but only Cisco devices. The management protocols are more generic. But Cisco is so big, they support the industry standard security protocol in addition to pushing their own proprietary security protocol. A third kind of maintenance protocols called routing protocols are what makes large, complicated networks possible.

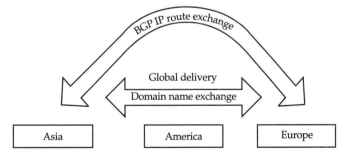

Routing protocols wring much of the labor and complexity out of very large networks by automatically tracking which routes to use between IP addresses. The Border Gateway Protocol (BGP) is the top-level routing protocol that connects everything within cities, between cities, and between continents. There are several other routing protocols used to track routes within private internetworks. Cisco supports industry-standard routing protocols in addition to pushing a couple of internal routing protocols of their own.

Routing vs. Switching

A technology war has emerged between routing and switching. As devices have become less expensive and more powerful, switching has emerged as a viable alternative to hubs on the low end and routers on the high end. Because switching is inherently faster, there's a push on to replace routed networks with switched networks. The battle is taking place at both ends of the internetworking landscape. At the low end—called the *access layer* because this is where hosts gain access to the internetwork—switches are replacing hubs as the device of choice to connect hosts because of switches' higher bandwidth. Switches are also beginning to displace routers as backbones that connect LANs within a building or a campus. Figure 1-3 shows the three different types of switching.

Switching has always been the norm over WAN trunks such as the fiber-optic links Internet backbone providers operate between cities. In fact, voice telephone systems are switched networks built over permanent physical circuits in the form of the telephone cables running to businesses and homes.

Data switches, of course, don't have dedicated cabling—the switched circuits they create are virtual. That is, they create temporary logical (not hard-wired) end-to-end circuits that are set up and torn down on an as-needed basis. But nonetheless, data switches are inherently faster than shared networks. The phrase "switch where you can, route where you must" has emerged as the industry motto—the translation being that wherever possible, you should use access switches in place of hubs for host access, and LAN switches instead of routers for internetwork connections.

Looking at Figure 1-3 tells you that the two technologies have their respective trade-offs. In a nutshell, routers are slower and more expensive, but are much more intelligent. Indeed, large internetworks will never be able to entirely do away with routing functionality of some sort. Thus, the industry is seeing the melding of switching's physical layer speed with routing's network layer intelligence. Hybrid devices have been rolled out that incorporate some IP routing intelligence into hardware. These hybrids are variously called layer-3 switches, multilayer switches, and so on.

Other Internetworking Trends

Beyond the routing versus switching technology war, a number of other trends are afoot in the internetworking industry:

▼ **Network management** A big push is under way to make large, complicated internetworks more reliable and manageable. Enterprises are adopting so-called management console or network management station (NMS)

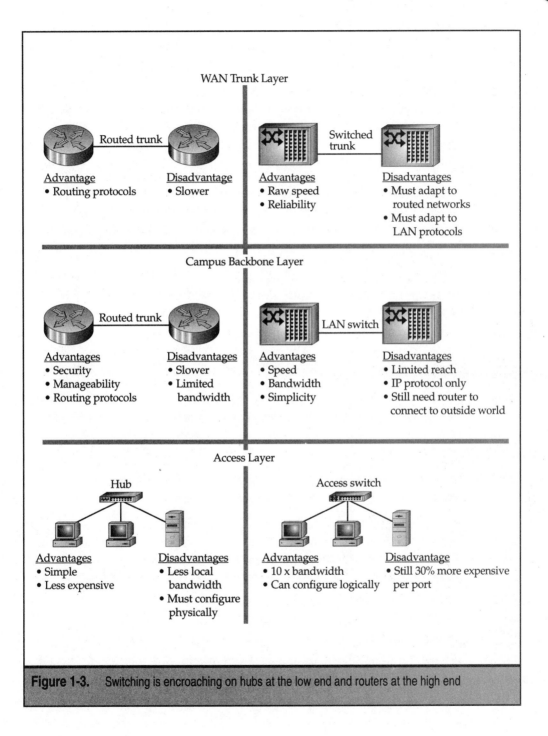

Figure 1-3.   Switching is encroaching on hubs at the low end and routers at the high end

software products from which their network teams can centrally monitor and troubleshoot internetworks. These NMS consoles are being fed by a couple of established but still-developing network management protocols.

■ **Network security** To date, most industry effort has been on securing access to network packets. The trend now is turning toward encrypting their contents to virtually guarantee data security and integrity. Tight security requires a harsh trade-off in expense or performance, however.

■ **Virtual private networks (VPNs)** It's projected that the majority of traditional leased-line WAN links will be replaced by 2003. VPNs use encryption to enable enterprises to operate private WANs over the Internet—at a fraction of the cost. Again, encryption exacts a trade-off in lowered performance.

■ **Faster dial-in links** Remote dial-in access technology to the home or small office is being upgraded by replacing plain-old telephone line circuits with digital circuits. At one time, Integrated Services Digital Network (ISDN) looked like the answer, but now Digital Subscriber Line (DSL) is viewed as the most likely way to travel the "last mile" from the local phone company switching office to the small home or office.

■ **Faster WAN trunks** Trunk lines running the Synchronous Optical Network (SONET) standard are advancing at a breakneck pace. The original 52 Mbps OC-1 has been improved over several increments to the present state-of-the-art 2.5 Gbps OC-48 standard. The 10 Gbps OC-192 is in the not-too-distant future.

▲ **Backbone technologies** A showdown is under way between two high-bandwidth network protocols to take ownership of the campus backbone market: ATM versus Gigabit Ethernet. Asynchronous Transfer Mode is a 622 Mbps non-IP standard that is ideal for multimedia traffic and has the ability to guarantee quality of service. However, it must be adapted for use with Ethernet networks. As the name implies, Gigabit Ethernet is the 1000 Mbps successor to the 100 Mbps Fast Ethernet specification.

These emerging technologies and standards have all the internetworking industry vendors jumping. Smaller competitors have tended to focus on a particular niche and choose sides, betting that one technology will prevail over the others. The big players have the resources and clout to take a more agnostic view of things, and this is true of Cisco in particular.

CISCO'S OFFERINGS

Cisco Systems has the broadest and deepest product line in the internetworking business. You'll be surprised the first time you hold their product catalog—so thick and heavy that it's reminiscent of a catalog from a big computer company like IBM or Hewlett-Packard.

The product line has been in a constant state of flux over the last several years. This is partly due to the industry's relentless introduction of new standards and technologies, causing perpetual product-line turnover. But the flux has as much to do with Cisco's fervid pursuit of technology by acquisition, having purchased over 30 companies since the mid-1990s. For example, when the speculation started as to whether ATM could or should take over as the backbone technology of choice, many observers assumed that Cisco—a company with deep roots in Ethernet—would side with Gigabit Ethernet. They instead went out and acquired StrataCom, the premier ATM technology company, in one of the largest technology mergers ever at that point. Cisco has also acquired software providers focused on providing solutions in such areas as network design and management. Cisco has spent years hyping itself as the industry's premier enterprise internetworking solutions vendor, and the company's willingness to adapt to technology trends instead of fighting them has impressed observers.

The Cisco product line can be broken down into two categories:

▼ **Devices**   Specific hardware products of the five types outlined at the beginning of this chapter

▲ **Solutions**   The combination of hardware, software, and services to fit certain customer requirements

The industry solutions piece is part hype, but it's a good indication of where and how Cisco sees its individual products put to use. For example, a strategic focus now is on voice over IP (VoIP). Should the much-touted data/voice convergence take hold, the potential exists for Cisco as the predominant IP device maker to become a key manufacturer of equipment used in telephone company back offices, and even of desktop data-phones.

As mentioned earlier, the salient feature of Cisco's product line is that every class of device runs the Internetwork Operating System. Cisco will tell you that this enables customers to do a better job of configuring and managing internetworks. Cisco's competitors will tell you that IOS makes devices more expensive and takes away customer options in making future technology decisions. Both sides are right, of course—everything's a trade-off.

What matters most, though, is that Cisco's IOS is far and away the most widely installed internetwork device operating system there is. This is leading many decision makers to view Cisco as the safe decision, given that the members of the internetworking labor market are more likely to be trained in IOS than another environment.

Cisco Hardware Devices

Cisco's product line is aligned according to customer scale. In other words, they package and price product models according to the size and sophistication of the customer market. For example, Tier 2 ISPs may not be that big in revenue, but the amount of traffic coursing through their internetworks rivals that of a Fortune 1000 company, and so does the sophistication of the members of their network teams. On the other hand, a small-office customer wants things kept simple and doesn't want to pay a premium for a product that's expandable when more capacity is unlikely to be needed.

SOHO Routers

SOHO is an industry term for very small network users. Typical SOHO customers have only one or two LAN segments in their facility and an ISP connection to the Internet.

The linchpin of Cisco's SOHO strategy is low-end routers. Allowing small companies to tap into ISPs router-to-router instead of as dial-in users saves money on telephone connections, performance is faster, and reliability is improved. Table 1-1 outlines Cisco's SOHO product series. The term *series* here means a chassis that is variously configured at the manufacturing plant into several product models—usually depending on the printed circuit cards installed in them. POTS stands for plain-old telephone system—analog phone circuits that must be used with modems.

SOHO products emphasize dial-in technologies (DSL and ISDN) because small offices and home offices don't have dedicated WAN links connecting them to their ISP or enterprise internetwork.

Midrange Cisco Routers

The small- to medium-sized network requires a wide variety of solutions. Cisco has several tiers of access router products designed to fit the customer's capacity needs and type of telecom link.

The series in Table 1-2 represent dozens of individual product numbers. Depending on the product series, various combinations of LAN technologies and WAN media can be configured. *Modular* means that the chassis can be upgraded in the field by inserting one or more modules. Nonmodular devices are fixed in configuration.

Backbone Routers 4000 and 7000 Series

When Cisco claims that over 70 percent of the Internet is run using its routers, these are the models they're talking about. The Cisco 4000 series is perhaps the most widely distributed router chassis there is. The 7000 and 12000 series are bigger, resembling dorm refrigerators in shape and size, and have data buses into which *blades* (whole devices on a board) can be installed.

Product Series	Description
Cisco 90	DSL access router to connect one user. Doesn't have user-configurable IOS.
Cisco 700 Series	ISDN access routers to connect up to 30 users. Doesn't have user-configurable IOS.
Cisco 800 Series	ISDN access routers to connect up to 20 users. Includes IOS and has VPN encryption capability.

Table 1-1.   Cisco Offers Three Series of SOHO Routers

Product Series	Description
Cisco 1000 Series	Ethernet access router to connect to either an ISDN or a serial WAN link.
Cisco 1401 Router	Ethernet access router to connect to either an ATM or a DSL trunk.
Cisco 1600 Series	Ethernet access router to connect to an ISDN or a serial WAN link. Includes VPN encryption capability.
Cisco 2500 Series	Ethernet or Token Ring router/hub or dial-access server models to connect one or two LAN segments to an ISDN or a serial link.
Cisco 2600 Series	Modular and cost-effective solution for duty as access router, voice/data gateway, or dial-access server. Connects one or two Ethernet or Token Ring LANs to ISDN, channelized T1, Ethernet, analog modems, or ATM links. Also supports voice/fax and Frame Relay.
Cisco 3600 Series	Modular high-density router for dial-access or router-to-router traffic. Supports ISDN, serial, channelized T1, digital modems, and ATM links. Also supports voice/fax and Frame Relay.

Table 1-2.   Cisco Has Several Midrange Routing Solutions

Because they're not access routers, Cisco's backbone routers can take as many users as they can handle packets. All three product series (described in Table 1-3) are modular, letting customers install modules according to the LAN technology being run and the ca-

Product Series	Description
Cisco 4000 Series	Three-slot routers supporting Ethernet, Fast Ethernet, Token Ring, FDDI, HSSI, serial, ISDN, channelized T1, and ATM.
Cisco 7000 Series	Four- to 13-slot central site routers supporting Ethernet, Fast Ethernet, Token Ring, FDDI, HSSI, serial, ISDN, channelized T1, packet over DS3, and ATM.
Cisco 12000 Series	Eight- or 12-slot Gigabit Ethernet switch router optimized for IP. Has special cards for OC-12 and OC-48 WAN links.

Table 1-3.   Cisco Has Three Series of Backbone Routers

pacity needed. In fact, these routers can operate more than one protocol simultaneously, such as Ethernet and Token Ring. A *slot* is an electronic bay into which a printed circuit board module is inserted.

HSSI stands for high-speed serial interface, a specialized I/O standard mainly used in conjunction with supercomputers. The behemoth Cisco 12000 router is a so-called carrier-class device, in that local equipment carriers' telecommunications network operators use them in their back-office data-switching operations.

All the backbone Cisco routers have extensive capabilities for VPN, security, quality of service (QoS), and network management.

Cisco Access Switches

Access switches, like hubs, have ports on their front into which individual host devices plug, and an "uplink" port on the back leading up the hierarchy to a router or a LAN switch. Cisco's access switches are outlined in Table 1-4. *Stackable* denotes the ability to cable individual boxes together and have them function as a single logical switch.

MicroSwitches are fixed-configuration devices with no access to the IOS command-line interface (they self-configure). As the popularity of access switches grows, some expect the low-cost MicroSwitch line to be expanded. Low-end Catalyst switches have more robust configurability.

Cisco Catalyst LAN Switches

A *LAN switch* is a high-speed layer-2 device that forwards traffic between LAN segments. They are not to be confused with access switches such as the MicroSwitch or a low-end Cata-

Product Series	Description
MicroSwitch 1548 Series	Eight-port Ethernet access switches with autosensing connectivity for both 10 Mbps Ethernet and 100 Mbps Fast Ethernet hosts. There are two models, one with sufficient electronics to support remote management.
Catalyst 1900 Series	Four models with 12 or 24 Ethernet ports and two uplinks for Fast Ethernet links. Not stackable.
Catalyst 2820 Series	Four models designed for aggregating hubs or servers. Has 24 Fast Ethernet ports plus two slots for a choice of high-speed modules—Fast Ethernet, FDDI, or ATM. Not stackable.

Table 1-4.   The Two-Model MicroSwitch 1548 Series Supports 10/100 Mbps Autosensing

lyst switch, which are devices that connect hosts to internetworks much like hubs. Put another way, access switches *form* LAN segments; LAN switches switch *between* them.

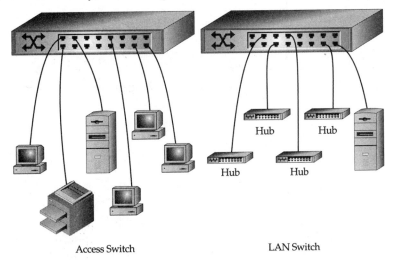

Access Switch   LAN Switch

Because hubs form LAN segments with multiple hosts attached to each segment, a switch powerful enough to connect hubs is regarded as a LAN switch. Keep in mind, though, that LAN switches can and do also connect such bandwidth-intensive hosts as servers and high-speed network printers.

The Cisco Catalyst Series family of LAN switches is the broadest in the industry. Catalyst models range from a four-port model all the way up to the carrier-class Catalyst 8500. The first tier of the Catalyst LAN switch line contains the 2900s, outlined in Table 1-5.

Multilayer switching (also called layer-2 switching) first appears in the middle range of the Catalyst switch line, as you see in Table 1-6. To reiterate, multilayer switches are devices with IP routing capability built into the switch hardware, thereby combining some of the logical capabilities of IP routing with the raw speed of switching.

Cisco offers two high-end backbone switches, one for Gigabit Ethernet and the other for ATM. Table 1-7 outlines them.

The Catalyst 6000 and 8000 are carrier-class switch devices. They have very high port density so as to interconnect hundreds of LAN segments. The 6000 has a special blade

Product Series	Description
Catalyst 2900 Series	Four models with 12–48 ports for Ethernet/Fast Ethernet 10/100 autosensing. Not stackable.
Catalyst 2900XL Series	Five models in two basic packages with 12 or 24 ports and two fiber-optic uplinks. Not stackable.

Table 1-5.   Midrange 2900 Catalyst Switches Have Higher Port Densities

Product Series	Description
Catalyst 3000 Series	Three models of multilayer switches with either 16 or 24 10BaseT ports in fixed configurations. Support for several Ethernet specifications and WAN link types. Stackable to eight switches in any combination of models.
Catalyst 3500XL Series	Three models, with 12 or 24 10/100BaseT Ethernet ports and 2 Gigabit Ethernet uplink ports. 3500XLs are stackable up to nine units running a swich fabric up to 10 Gbps. The 3500 Series is new, and is being positioned as Cisco's premier solution for low-end Gigabit Ethernet connectivity.
Catalyst 3900 Series	Two models with 20 fixed Token Ring ports and two slots for expansion modules, each with four ports for additional Token Ring user ports or one ATM or two Fast Ethernet uplinks. Stackable up to eight switches.
Catalyst 4000 Series	One model with three-slot modular chassis supporting 10/100/1000 Ethernet. One module has 48 10/100 ports and another, 32 10/100 ports with a variety of Gigabit Ethernet uplink options. Not stackable.
Catalyst 5000 Family	Two-series family with five models, with two- to five-slot modular chassis and 48–528 ports supporting 100BaseX, 1000X, ATM, FDDI, or Token Ring. Backplane of 1.2 Gbps–3.6 Gbps. Not stackable.

Table 1-6. Some Midrange Catalyst LAN Switches Incorporate Multilayer Switching

Product Series	Description
Catalyst 6000 Family	Four-model high-performance multilayer switch family with 6–9 slots supporting 384 10/100 ports and Gigabit Ethernet uplinks. Cisco's choice for gigabit backbones. Not stackable.
Catalyst 8500 Series	Two models with 5–13 slots supporting multiservice ATM switching, optimized for aggregating multiprotocol traffic. Not stackable. Cisco's choice for ATM backbone switches.

Table 1-7. Cisco's Two High-End Catalyst Switches Cover Gigabit and ATM Backbones

that handles multilayer switching functionality. The 8500 line is tuned for multimedia traffic types, such as VoIP, videocasting, and other specialized types.

Cisco Hubs

Cisco has two hub product lines: the MicroHub and the FastHub Series. The MicroHub 1538 is the sister product to the MicroSwitch 1548—a low-cost, simple-to-use alternative to higher-density, more configurable devices. Both lines are stackable up to four units per stack. Table 1-8 outlines Cisco's two hub lines.

The key thing to remember about hubs versus access switches is that hubs strictly connect hosts. To gain greater connectivity, a hub must connect either into a LAN switch or directly into a router.

Cisco Solutions

Cisco touts itself as the premier "end-to-end enterprise solutions provider" in internetworking. What this means in English is that they have the breadth of product line functionality to fulfill virtually any customer requirement, whether integrated voice/data, ATM backbones, integration to IBM SNA environments, and so on. In practical terms, Cisco has been able to do this because of its foresight and raw cash. Having over $200 billion in market capitalization has given the company the financial muscle to fill product-line gaps and enter emerging areas by either intensive internal R&D or going out and acquiring the best-of-breed provider. As mentioned, Cisco has acquired over 30 companies over the past several years. Each acquisition seems to have been made to acquire an emerging technology, not to buy the smaller company's installed customer base.

Not all of Cisco's solutions technologies were buyouts; some were developed in-house. However, many of their major technology additions were via acquisition. The key factor in each is whether Cisco can successfully integrate the new technology into their unifying IOS architecture. Despite the wishes of certain competitors, so far they've done fairly well at that, with some exceptions. Here's an overview of the major solutions areas:

▼ **IOS feature sets**   IOS can be purchased *a la carte* for many devices, to obtain the functionality needed to deal with the customer's installed environment, whether IBM SNA, Novell NetWare, AppleTalk, or vanilla IP.

Product Series	Description
Cisco MicroHub 1538	Eight-port 10/100 autosensing device that comes in managed and manageable variants, where one managed unit can be used to indirectly manage three other manageable units in a four-hub stack.
Cisco FastHub Series	Four models ranging from 12 to 24 ports with 10/100 autosensing ports per chassis.

Table 1-8.   The Cisco MicroHub and FastHub Lines Range from 32 to 96 Ports per Stack

■ **ATM**   Cisco has invested heavily in ATM technology, with the StrataCom buyout bringing a full line of ATM WAN switches, multiservice ATM switches, and edge concentrators. Cisco also purchased a company called LightStream to obtain the LightStream 1010 ATM module for connecting to ATM campus LANs.

■ **Voice/data integration**   To consolidate its position in the emerging VoIP market, Cisco offers the VCO/4K open programmable voice/data switch, Cisco-to-circuit switched gateways, and other voice integration products. Cisco now even sells two models of IP telephones.

■ **Network management**   Several disparate management software applications, both homegrown and acquired, are slowly being melded together under the CiscoWorks2000 banner. Right now things are still a bit of a mess, with three more-or-less stand-alone products: Resource Manager Essentials for managing routed networks, CWSI Campus for managing switched networks, and NetSys Baseliner for designing network topologies. CWSI and NetSys were acquisitions.

■ **ISP Connectivity**   Cisco offers "director" products for use by ISPs in managing their high-volume traffic loads. Cisco LocalDirector is a sophisticated server connection management system that manages traffic based on service requested, distribution method, and server availability. Cisco DistributedDirector is similar, but provides dynamic, transparent Internet traffic load distribution management between geographically dispersed servers.

▲ **Security**   CiscoSecure is the company's integrated client-server security management system. IOS itself incorporates many security commands at the client device level, and CiscoSecure keeps a central database of users, user authorizations, and security event history. Cisco offers the PIX Firewall for traffic-level security. Cisco also offers an IOS feature set called IOS Firewall, which is an expanded set of IOS commands that allows configuration of most midrange and high-end Cisco routers with firewall functionality.

These and other Cisco solutions are covered throughout this book. We won't go into them in any detail here; you need to get technical first. That process starts in the next chapter—a primer on internetworking technology basics.

CHAPTER 2

Networking Primer

E ver wonder how the Internet really works? Most of us at one time or another have wondered what happens behind the scenes when surfing Web pages, sending e-mail, or downloading files. You know instinctively that there must be many devices linking you to the other computer, but how exactly is the connection made? What makes up a message, and how does it find its way through the seemingly chaotic Internet back to your desktop? After all, it wasn't that long ago that incompatibility between various makes and models of computers made exchanging data a headache. Now everybody can connect to the Internet to share data and services without a second thought. How did the computer industry pull it off?

Most laypersons think the answer is technology, and to a point they're right. But the whole answer is that the Internet was brought together by a combination of technology and standards—specifically, du jour and de facto technical standards. Du jour standards are set by trade associations; de facto standards are set by brute economic force. All the routers and switches in the world couldn't form the Internet without standards to make hardware, software, and telecommunications equipment compatible.

The products fueling the Internet were introduced in Chapter 1. Now we'll cover the underlying architectures that made all that technology possible, from telecommunications infrastructure all the way up to inside your PC. An understanding of the technologies and standards underpinning an internetwork will give you a clear picture of what happens in the background when you click in your browser.

BITS AND BYTES

Before going into details on internetworking, it's necessary to cover the basic concepts that explain how computer technology works. We'll do this "from the wire up" to help you understand why systems work the way they do.

The Internet's infrastructure is composed of millions of networking devices—routers, switches, firewalls, access servers, and hubs—loosely hooked together through a sophisticated global address system. They're linked mostly by twisted-pair copper cable to the desktop and big trunk lines running over very high-speed fiber-optic cable. But mostly the Internet is a matter of millions of individual hardware devices loosely tied together by a global addressing scheme.

How Computers Understand Data

Networking devices are more or less the same as normal computer platforms such as your PC. The biggest differences are in configuration: most types of network equipment have no CRT or disks because they're designed to move data—not store it or present it. But all network devices are computers in the basic sense that they have CPUs, memory, and operating systems.

Bits Compose Binary Messages

Computing is largely a matter of sending electrical signals between various hardware components. In a normal computer platform, the signals shoot around tiny transistors inside the CPU or memory and travel over ultrathin wires embedded in printed circuit boards. Once on the outside, electrical signals travel over cables in order to move between devices.

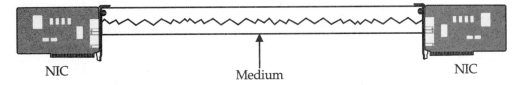

NIC   Medium   NIC

As signals are passed over the cable, network interface cards (NICs) at each end keep track of the electrical pulse waveforms and interpret them as data. The NIC senses each electrical pulse as either an On or Off signal. This is called *binary* transmission—a system in which each On pulse is recorded as the number 1 and each Off signal as the number 0. In machine language, these zeros and ones are *bits*, and a file of bits is a *binary* file.

Whether a signal represents a zero or a one is sensed by fluctuations in the voltage of electrical pulses (or light pulses, over fiber-optic media) during miniscule time intervals. These tiny time intervals are called *cycles* or Hertz (Hz) in electrical engineering circles. For example, the CPU in a 100 Mbps NIC can generate 100 million cycles per second. In practical terms, the payoff is that the computer can process 100 million pulses per second and interpret them as either zeros or ones.

How Order Is Maintained Among Bits

All computers use binary at the machine level. Bits are the basic raw material with which they work, usually as a collection of bits in a binary file. Binary is the stuff that gets put into memory, processed through CPUs, stored on disks, and sent over cables. Both data and software programs are stored as binary. If you were to look at a data file in any type of machine in binary format, you'd be staring at a page full of zeros and ones. Doing so might make your eyes glaze over, but machines can handle binary because of *ordinality*—a fancy term for knowing what piece of information is supposed to appear in a certain field position.

The computer doesn't keep track of ordinal positions one-by-one. It instead keeps track of the bit position at which a field begins and ends. A *field* is a logical piece of information. For example, the computer might know that bit positions 121 through 128 are used to store a person's middle initial.

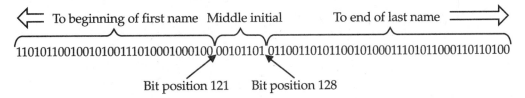

Computers are able to track bit orders with great precision by using clocks that time exactly where a CPU is in a stream of bits. By knowing where fields are, computers can build data from the wire up.

Computer Software Operates on Bytes

For simplicity, however, computers don't operate one bit at a time. There's an interim level one step up from bits called bytes—thus the expression "bits and bytes." A *byte* is a series of eight consecutive bits that are operated upon as a unit.

10110111	00110100	11001100	101110110	11000100
Byte	Byte	Byte	Byte	Byte

2-byte field   3-byte field

From a logical standpoint, the basic unit making up a data field is bytes. This not only makes systems run faster, but also makes them easier to program and debug. You'll never see a programmer declare how many bits long a field should be, but declaring byte lengths is routine. Keeping track of individual bit positions is left to the computer.

Computer Words

Unlike software, CPUs must deal in bits. At the lowest level, computer hardware deals with On/Off electrical signals pulsing through its circuitry in bits. It would take too long to perform bit-to-byte translations inside a CPU, so computers have what's called a *word size*. The step up from a byte is a *word*, which is the number of bytes a CPU architecture is designed to handle each cycle.

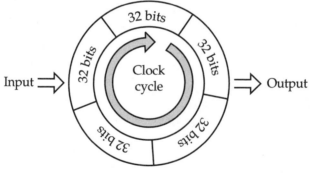

32-bit word CPU

For example, an Intel Pentium is a 32-bit word machine, meaning that it processes 32 bits per clock cycle. But as hardware miniaturization techniques have advanced—and the need to process data faster has grown—the industry has settled on 64-bit word architectures as the way to go. The Compaq Alpha architecture, the world's fastest single processor chip, is a 64-bit word architecture. Other 64-bit machines are available from IBM and Sun, and Intel's forthcoming Merced architecture will be a 64-bit machine also. Cisco devices use 32-bit CPUs.

Compiled Software

The last step up is from bytes to something we humans can understand. As you probably know, software takes the form of source code files written by computer programmers. The commands that programmers type into source code files are symbols instructing the computer what to do. When a program is written, it's changed into machine language—bits and bytes—by a *compiler*, which is a specialized application that translates software code into machine language files referred to as *executables* or *binaries*. For example, if code is written using the C++ programming language, it is translated through a C++ compiler.

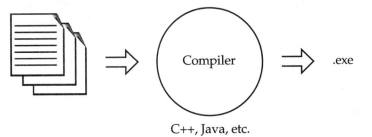

C++, Java, etc.

You may have noticed the .exe and .bin file extensions in your PC's directory. They stand for *executable* and *binary*, respectively. The Cisco Internetwork Operating System (IOS) is executable software. Actually, it's a package containing hundreds of executables that operate device hardware, forward packets, talk to neighbor network devices, and so on.

Computing Architectures

A *computing architecture* is a technical specification of all components that make up a system. Published computing architectures are quite detailed and specific, and most are thousands of pages long. But in certain parts they are abstract by design, leaving the exact implementation of that portion of the architecture up to the designer.

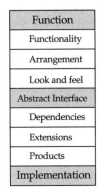

What separates an architecture from a regular product specification is the use of abstract layering. An *abstraction layer* is a fixed interface connecting two system components, and it governs the relationship between each side's function and implementation. If something changes on one side of the interface, by design it should not require changes on the other side. These layers are put in to help guarantee compatibility in two directions:

▼ Between various components within the system

▲ Between various products implementing the architecture

Abstraction between components stabilizes system designs, because it allows different development groups to engineer against a stable target. For example, the published interface between the layers in networking software allows hundreds of network interface manufacturers to engineer products compatible with the Fast Ethernet specification.

There are several important computing architectures at the turn of the twenty-first century—some more open than others. The Microsoft Windows/Intel 80x86 Wintel architecture is the stuff of legend. Other important computing architectures include RAID (random array of inexpensive disks), Java, CORBA, and dozens more. Yet perhaps the most important computing architecture ever devised is the one that created the Internet: the OSI reference model.

OSI REFERENCE MODEL

The International Standards Organization (ISO), an international engineering organization based in Paris, published the Open Systems Interconnect (OSI) reference model in 1978. This seven-layer model has become the standard for designing communication methods among network devices and was the template used to design the Internet Protocol (IP).

The goal of the OSI reference model was to promote interoperability. *Interoperability* means the ability for otherwise incompatible systems to operate together in such a way that they can successfully perform common tasks. A good example of interoperability would be an Ethernet LAN transparently exchanging messages with an IBM Token Ring LAN.

The Seven-Layer Stack

The OSI model divides networks into seven functional layers and thus is often called the *seven-layer stack*. Each layer defines a function or set of functions performed when data is transferred between applications across the network. Whether the network protocol is IP, Novell NetWare, or AppleTalk, if it adheres to the OSI model, more or less the same rules are applied at each of the seven layers. The seven layers are outlined in Figure 2-1.

As depicted in Figure 2-1, each layer is a protocol for communications between linked devices. Concerning network operations, the key thing to understand is that each layer on each device talks to its counterpart to manage a particular aspect of the network connection. Concerning interoperability, the key is the fixed interface sitting between each layer. Abstract layering reduces what would otherwise be daunting complexity.

▼ **Layer 1, the physical layer**   Controls the transport medium by defining the electrical and mechanical characteristics carrying the data signal. Examples include twisted-pair cabling, fiber-optic cabling, coaxial cable, and serial lines.

■ **Layer 2, the data-link layer**   Controls access to the network and ensures the reliable transfer of frames across the network. The best known data-link specification is Ethernet's Carrier Sense Multiple Access with Collision Detection. Token Ring and FDDI adhere to the token-passing data-link architecture.

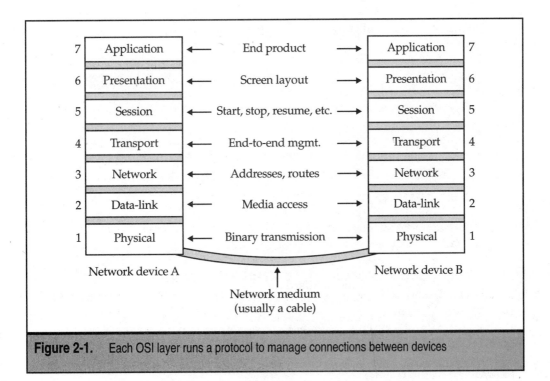

Figure 2-1.   Each OSI layer runs a protocol to manage connections between devices

■ **Layer 3, the network layer**   Manages the movement of data between different networks. Protocols at this layer are responsible for finding the device for which the data is destined. Examples include IP, IPX, and AppleTalk.

■ **Layer 4, the transport layer**   Makes sure that data reaches its destination intact and in the proper order. The Transmission Control Protocol (TCP) and User Datagram Protocol (UDP) operate at this layer.

■ **Layer 5, the session layer**   Establishes and terminates connections and arranges sessions between two computers. Example session layer protocols include Remote Procedure Call (RPC) and the Lightweight Directory Access Protocol (LDAP).

■ **Layer 6, the presentation layer**   Formats data for screen display or printing. Examples of presentation layer protocols include the Lightweight Presentation Protocol (LPP) and NetBIOS.

▲ **Layer 7, the application layer**   Contains protocols used to perform useful tasks over a network. Examples of network application protocols include the Simple Mail Transfer Protocol (SMTP) for e-mail, the Hypertext Transfer Protocol (HTTP) for Web browsers and servers, Telnet for remote terminal sessions, and hundreds of others.

Layer-7 network applications are the reason the bottom six layers exist. Many of these protocols saw their first use in UNIX systems, given that the UNIX operating system developed in parallel with the Internet.

Intensive effort is now under way to develop new network applications that more tightly integrate normal applications with the network. The goal is for all kinds of applications—PC, client-server, and mainframe—to transparently communicate with other computers over internetworks. For example, it would be nice if a UNIX server–based financial accounting software package could automatically query foreign exchange rate databases—sitting on IBM MVS mainframe computers in New York, London, and Hong Kong—in order to automatically recalculate hedge positions.

NOTE: Don't be misled by the name *application layer*. This layer runs network applications, not applications software such as spreadsheets or inventory. Network applications include e-mail, Web browsing (HTTP), FTP, and other useful network tasks.

Peer Layers Form Protocol-Independent Virtual Links

Each layer in the stack relies on the layers above and below it to operate, yet each operates independently of the others, as if it were having an exclusive conversation with its counterpart layer on the other computer. Each layer on the device is said to have established a *virtual link* with the same layer on the other device. With all seven virtual links running, a *network connection* (or *session*) is established, and the two devices are talking as if they were wired directly together.

For example, in Figure 2-2 the sending computer, the Wintel PC on the left, processes downward through the stack to send a message, and the IBM mainframe receives the message by processing the message upward through its stack to understand the data—an FTP download request, in this example. The computers then reverse the process by working through their stacks the other way, this time for the IBM mainframe to download a file to the Wintel PC via the FTP application.

In Figure 2-2, you begin to see how the Internet was able to interconnect the world's computers. Because the layers are abstracted and operate independent of one another, the FTP application can successfully run over different implementations of the OSI model—in this example, Ethernet and Token Ring. You can see that the FTP application doesn't care about the incompatibilities inherent between Windows 98 and IBM mainframes, or even those between the Ethernet and Token Ring network technologies. Its only concern is whether the connected devices are talking FTP in compliance with OSI rules.

OSI Implementation by Layer

Although the seven-layer stack is expressed in vertical terms, looking at things horizontally might help you understand how it works. This is because as a message is processed through the stack, its horizontal length changes.

At the wire level, a message is a series of pulses. The device works to encode or decode the pulses into binary zeros or ones to begin sorting out discrete message units. This signal processing is done in hardware on the network interface card, not in software.

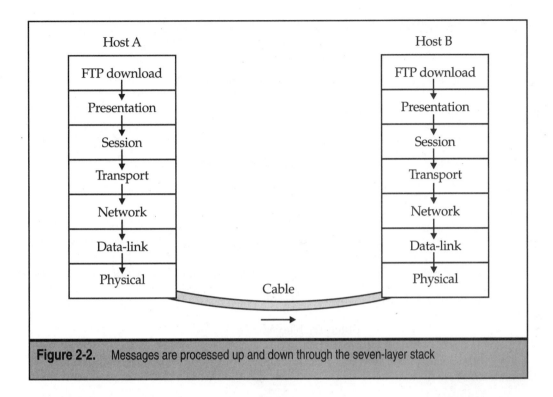

Figure 2-2.   Messages are processed up and down through the seven-layer stack

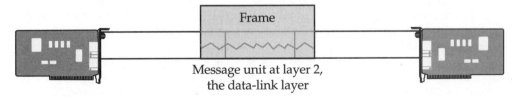

Message unit at layer 1,
the physical layer

At the data-link layer, the binary information is read and encased into a format called a *frame*. The precise format for a frame is specified by the network protocol on which the NIC is operating—Ethernet or Token Ring, for example. Each frame's header contains so-called media access control (MAC) addresses, which are unique identifiers that act as a kind of serial number for hardware devices.

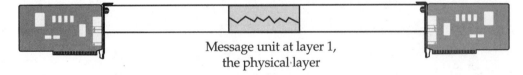

Message unit at layer 2,
the data-link layer

At the network layer, the message gets a bit wider and becomes a *packet* (also called a *datagram*). Each packet's header has a logical (not physical) network address that can be used to route the message through the internetwork. Network layer protocols include the IP portion of the TCP/IP protocol suite and the IPX layer of the Novell NetWare IPX/SPX protocol suite, among others.

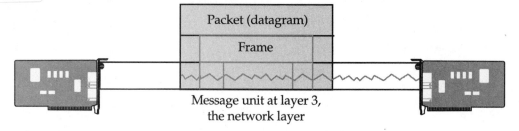

Message unit at layer 3,
the network layer

At the transport layer, the message is wider still. Tasks performed here include making sure the receiver knows the message is coming, ensuring that the receiver won't be overwhelmed with too many packets at a time, making sure that packets sent were indeed received, and retransmitting packets that were dropped. Transport protocols include the Terminal Control Protocol (TCP) and User Datagram Protocol in the TCP/IP suite, and the Sequenced Packet Exchange (SPX) layer of the NetWare IPX/SPX suite.

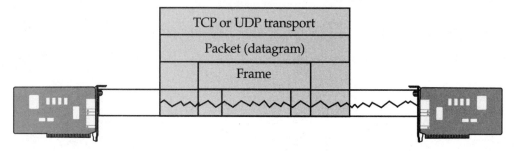

The remaining three layers handle connection logistics (session layer), data representation formats (presentation layer), and the network application to run (application layer). These final three layers add little to the width of the message unit. For example, which application to run is defined by a port number—the HTTP HTML Web page application is identified by port number 80.

Once all the message handling protocol information has been stripped away, you're left with payload data. There are many individual message units within a transmission. A network connection is made using a stream of packets, and each individual packet's data cargo contributes to the complete data file the connection needs—a Web page download, for example.

Payload data differs by application. For example, a Telnet session will send tiny data files to indicate a keystroke or a carriage return, maybe all contained in a packet or two. At the opposite extreme, an FTP file transfer may send millions of bytes of data spread across thousands of packets.

NOTE: The name *port number* was an unfortunate choice by the IETF engineers. It takes a while to get used to the fact that an IP port number refers to a software type, not a hardware port. On a related note, the term *socket* is an IP address paired with a port number.

NETWORK TECHNOLOGIES

Network technologies (also called LAN technologies or network specifications) are used to run the basic unit of all internetworks—the LAN segment. The most widely known network technology is Ethernet, but there are several others, including Token Ring, Asynchronous Transfer Mode (ATM), and Fiber Distributed Data Interface (FDDI).

Network technologies are implemented at the data-link layer (layer 2) of the seven-layer OSI reference model. Put another way, network technologies are largely characterized by the physical media they share and how they control access to the shared medium. This makes sense, if you think about it. Networking is connectivity; but to be connected, order must somehow be maintained among those users doing the sharing. For that reason, layer 2 (the data-link layer) is also called the *media access control* layer, or MAC layer for short. The message unit format at this level is the *data frame*, or frame.

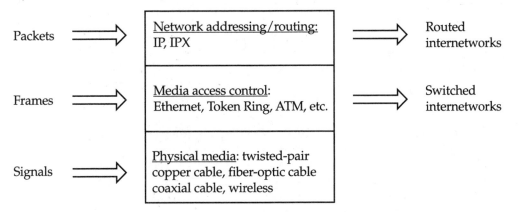

As such, network technologies in and of themselves can only deal with MAC addresses—those serial number–like device identifiers mentioned earlier. A network layer protocol such as IP is needed to route messages through the internetwork. Network technologies alone can only support switched internetwork operation—good only for local areas or simple paths over longer distances, where not much guidance is needed. Network technologies are used at opposite ends of the spectrum:

▼   **Access LANs**   Accept cabling from devices, tie workgroups together, and share resources such as departmental printers and servers

▲   **Backbone LANs**   Link access LANs, and share resources such as database servers, mail servers, and so on

Access LANs, formed by hubs or access switches, give users and devices connectivity to the network at the local level, usually within a floor in an office building. Backbone LANs, formed by routers or LAN switches, tie together access LANs, usually within a building or office campus. Routed internetworks are typically used to distribute traffic between the two.

Ethernet

Version 1 of Ethernet was developed by Xerox Corporation in 1970. Over the subsequent decade, Xerox teamed with Intel and Digital Equipment Corporation (now Compaq) to release Version 2 in 1982. Since that time, Ethernet has become the dominant network technology standard. Thanks mostly to economies of scale, the average cost per Ethernet port is now far lower than that of a Token Ring port. Indeed, it has become so much a de facto standard that many manufacturers are integrating Ethernet NICs into computer motherboards in an attempt to do away with the need for separate NIC modules.

Ethernet Architecture

Ethernet operates by contention. Devices sharing an Ethernet LAN segment listen for traffic being carried over the wire and defer transmitting a message until the medium is clear. If two stations send at about the same time and their packets collide, both transmissions are aborted and the stations back off and wait a random period of time before retransmitting. Ethernet uses the Carrier Sense Multiple Access with Collision Detection (CSMA/CD) algorithm to listen to traffic, sense collisions, and abort transmissions. CSMA/CD is the traffic cop that controls what would otherwise be random traffic. It restricts access to the wire in order to ensure the integrity of transmissions. Figure 2-3 illustrates the CSMA/CD process.

Because the medium is shared, every device on an Ethernet LAN segment receives the message and checks it to see whether the destination address matches its own address. If it does, the message is accepted and processed through the seven-layer stack, and a network connection is made. If the address doesn't match, the packets are dropped.

Ethernet is implemented as the IEEE 802.3 specification. The IEEE, the Institute for Electrical and Electronics Engineers, has been around since the 19th century and contributes to the computer industry by setting standards for layers 1 and 2 (the physical and data-link layers, respectively) of the OSI reference model. The IETF's work picks up at layer 3 and above.

▼

NOTE: An *algorithm* is a structured sequence of rules designed to automatically handle variable processes in an orderly manner. Algorithms are commonplace in computing and networking because things move so fast that there isn't time for a human to intervene.

Ethernet Implementations

Even apart from economies of scale, Ethernet is inherently less expensive, thanks to the random nature of its architecture. In other words, the electronics needed to run Ethernet

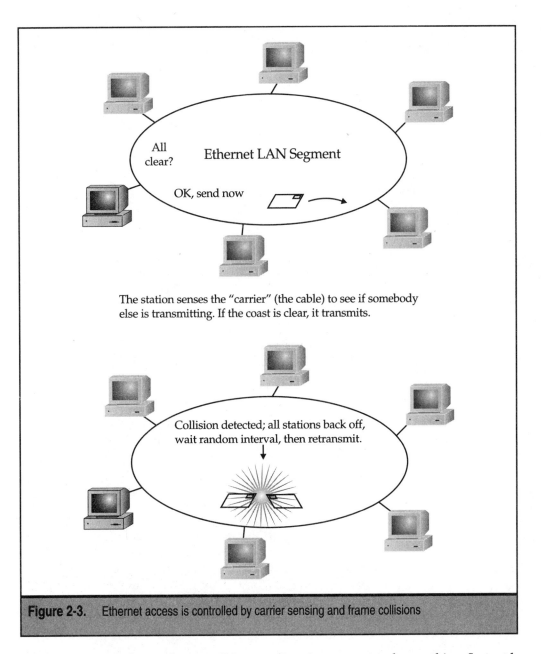

The station senses the "carrier" (the cable) to see if somebody else is transmitting. If the coast is clear, it transmits.

Collision detected; all stations back off, wait random interval, then retransmit.

Figure 2-3.   Ethernet access is controlled by carrier sensing and frame collisions

are easier to manufacture because Ethernet doesn't try to control everything. In rough terms, it only worries about collisions.

The obvious disadvantage of Ethernet is that a lot of raw bandwidth is sacrificed to aborted transmissions. Theoretical maximum effective bandwidth from Ethernet is estimated at only 37 percent of raw wire speed. However, the equipment is so inexpensive that Ethernet has always been on balance the cheapest form of effective bandwidth. In other words, its simplicity more than compensates for its inherent bandwidth inefficiency.

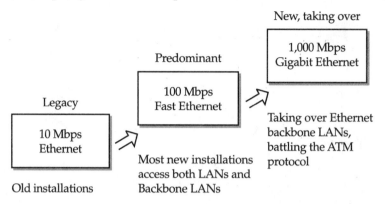

Ethernet has several implementation options. The original Ethernet specification ran at 10 Mbps over coaxial cable or 10BaseT twisted-pair cable (*T* stands for twisted-pair—we'll cover cabling specifications in Chapter 6). Fast Ethernet runs at 100 Mbps and runs over 100BaseTX or 100BaseFX fiber-optic cable (*F* stands for fiber). Gigabit Ethernet runs at 1000 Mbps (or 1 Gbps) over 1000BaseTX or 1000BaseFX cable. A popular configuration choice right now is Fast Ethernet access LANs interconnected through a Gigabit Ethernet backbone LAN.

Token Ring

Token Ring is Ethernet's main competition as a LAN (networking) standard—or it was. Token Ring differs sharply from Ethernet in its architectural approach. The IEEE has defined Token Ring as a published standard in the IEEE 802.5 specification (much as Ethernet is the 802.3 specification).

As its own LAN standard, Token Ring is incompatible with Ethernet in terms of the type of NICs, cable connectors, and software that must be used. Although Token Ring is widely installed in enterprises dominated by IBM, it hasn't caught on as an open standard.

Token Ring takes its name from the fact that it defines attached hosts into a logical ring. We use *logical* to describe Token Ring here because the LAN segment behaves like a ring by passing signals in a round-robin fashion as if the devices were actually attached to a looped cable. Physically, though, Token Ring LANs may be configured in a hub-and-spoke topology called a *star topology*. Figure 2-4 shows this. Note that in Token Ring parlance, the access concentrator is called a *media access unit* (MAU) instead of a hub.

Token Ring avoids contention over a LAN segment by a *token-passing* protocol, which regulates traffic flow by passing a frame called a token around the ring. Only the host in possession of the token is allowed to transmit, thereby eliminating packet collisions. Token Ring's architecture in effect trades wait-time for collisions, because each station must wait its turn before capturing the token in order to transmit. Nonetheless, eliminating packet collisions greatly increases Token Ring's effective utilization of raw bandwidth. Tests show that Token Ring can use up to 75 percent of raw bandwidth, compared to

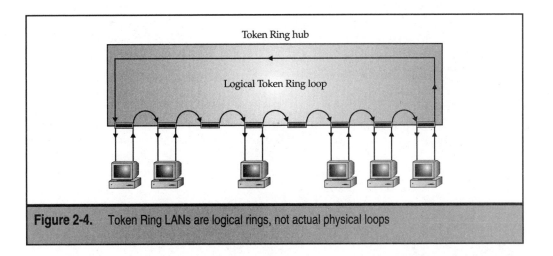

Figure 2-4.   Token Ring LANs are logical rings, not actual physical loops

Ethernet's theoretical maximum of about 37 percent. The trouble is that Token Ring only begins to pay off above certain traffic volumes.

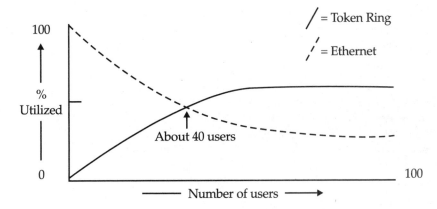

Persuading the market to accept a new technology as a de facto standard requires volume. Token Ring is a great technology, but it has lost out to Ethernet's immense edge in total number of LANs installed. From a market standpoint, Token Ring's need for large LAN sizes to pay off was probably fatal. Most LANs are small because most enterprises are small. Moreover, even big companies have mostly small LANs, whether in branch offices or even departments in large buildings. Remember, we're talking LAN *segments* in this context—the actual shared medium, not the "local network" that is a collection of all LAN segments attached to the LAN backbone.

Another problem is that Token Ring requires expensive electronics to operate its deterministic processes. If you think about it, it's only natural that manufacturing a NIC that transmits packets at will would be cheaper than making one to participate in an orderly regimen in which a token is required.

When Token Ring was introduced, it ran at 4 Mbps, but most LANs have since upgraded to 16 Mbps media. If this seems slow compared to Fast Ethernet's 100 Mbps speeds, keep in mind that Token Ring yields far more effective bandwidth from rated wire speed. A 100 Mbps Token Ring specification is now in the works.

ATM

ATM (Asynchronous Transfer Mode) is a data-link network technology that, like Ethernet, Token Ring, and FDDI, is specified at layer 2 of the OSI model. But that's where the similarities end. ATM transmissions send 53-byte cells instead of packets. A *cell* is a fixed-length message unit. Like packets, cells are pieces of a message, but the fixed-length format causes certain characteristics:

▼ **Virtual circuit orientation**   Cell-based networks run better in point-to-point mode, in which the receiving station is ready to actively receive and process the cells.

■ **Speed**   The hardware knows exactly where the header ends and data starts in every cell, thereby speeding processing operations. ATM networks run at speeds of up to 622 Mbps.

▲ **Quality of Service (QoS)**   Predictable throughput rates and virtual circuits enable cell-based networks to better guarantee service levels to types of traffic that are priority.

ATM doesn't have a media access control technology, per se. ATM is a switching technology, in which a so-called virtual circuit is set up before a transmission starts. This differs sharply from LAN technologies such as Ethernet and Token Ring, which simply transmit a message without prior notification to the receiving host, leaving it up to routers to figure out the best path to take to get there.

Compared to the tiny size of ATM cells, Ethernet packet size can range from 64 bytes to over 1,500 bytes—up to about 25 times larger per message unit. By being so much more granular, ATM becomes that much more controllable.

ATM is designed to run over fiber-optic cable operating the SONET (synchronous optical network) specification. SONET is an ANSI standard specifying the physical interfaces that connect to fiber-optic cable at various speeds. SONET specifications are set up for various cable speeds called *optical carrier levels*, or OC for short:

▼ **OC-1**   52 Mbps fiber-optic cable

■ **OC-3**   155 Mbps fiber-optic cable

■ **OC-12**   622 Mbps fiber-optic cable

■ **OC-24**   1.2 Gbps fiber-optic cable

▲ **OC-48**   2.5 Gbps fiber-optic cable

Like token-passing architectures, ATM's deterministic design yields high effective bandwidth from its raw wire speed. In fact, ATM's effective yield is said to be well above even Token Ring's 75 percent. Most ATM backbone LANs run OC-3 or OC-12. Most inter-city links run OC-12, although major Internet backbone providers are now wiring OC-48 to meet ever-increasing bandwidth demands.

Most intercity Internet trunks are OC-12 running ATM, with OC-48 taking over the heavier trunks. For example, UUNET—one of the largest Internet Backbone Providers—uses 622 Mbps fiber-optic cabling to connect Chicago with Atlanta, and 2.5 Gbps OC-48 to link New York with Washington D.C.

Latency and Sequence Sensitivity

Certain types of traffic need predictability more than others. For example, a phone conversation can't tolerate delays because each party would start talking before the other is finished. This is called *latency sensitivity*—the reason why wireless telephone systems are cellular. Another type of traffic sensitivity is *priority sensitivity*, where the order in which data is received is critical. For example, a video transmission's message units must be received in the proper order so that complete video frames can be displayed in sequence. Figure 2-5 depicts how latency and sequence problems harm service quality in priority-sensitive applications such as videocasting.

Videocasts are becoming a popular solution for such applications as distance learning and internal corporate communications. Many envision the day when Web TV will displace broadcast television. This brings up the important distinction between broadcast and multicast messaging.

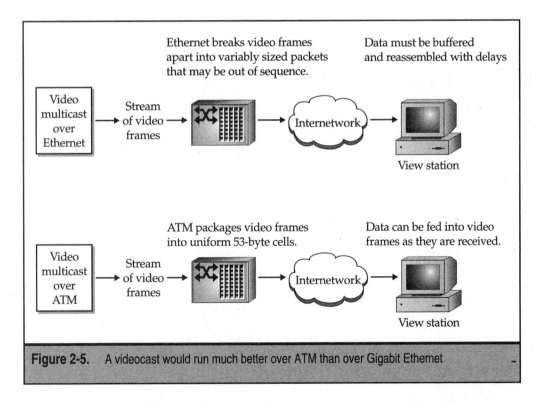

Figure 2-5. A videocast would run much better over ATM than over Gigabit Ethernet

Multicasting vs. Broadcasting

A *broadcast* message goes to every station within the broadcast domain. By default, a broadcast domain includes all stations attached to the shared medium of a LAN segment, although it can be purposely extended using routers.

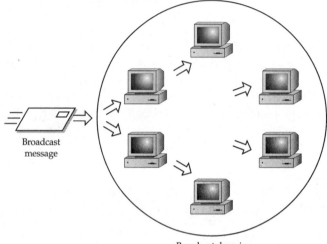

Broadcast domain

Each station must receive and examine the broadcast message, but can drop it at the interface if programmed to do so. For example, broadcasts can be beneficial to a network by keeping stations updated on such changes as new addresses or downed links. Too many broadcasts, however, can mire bandwidth in useless traffic.

A *multicast* message goes to a subset of stations within a broadcast domain. In basic terms, each station "signs up" for the types of multicasts it wishes to receive.

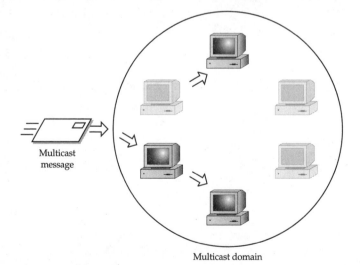

Multicast domain

The new classic example of multicasting is videocasting, in which a lot of bandwidth is used to move video images, so only those stations that want to participate receive it. It makes sense for bandwidth-intensive applications to use multicasting to avoid needless congestion. ATM is heavily identified with multicasting because it's fixed-cell format is ideal for multimedia applications.

If ATM is so much better than other network protocols, why aren't all networks running it? The answer lies in the fact that most traffic is not sensitive to transmission latency. The added expense and complexity of ATM can be hard to justify in the absence of a lot of multimedia traffic, because there is sufficient time to repackage messages at the receiving end. Figure 2-6 shows examples of both types of traffic.

Normal messages aren't particularly sensitive to intermittent delays or the sequence of delivery. For example, an e-mail with a document attached might be 20,000 bytes long (20K). The user doesn't care about the order in which various chunks of the message are received and wouldn't even be aware of any delays. Therefore, the network can deliver the e-mail as it sees fit.

Virtual Circuits

Because they're so small, ATM cells don't contain the amount of address information found in the header of an Ethernet packet. In fact, ATM uses an addressing scheme entirely different from other network technologies. This is why ATM needs to set up a virtual circuit to the remote end before communicating. A *circuit* is a connection between two points. For example, your home phone circuit is wired directly to the central switching office in your neighborhood. A *virtual circuit* behaves like a real one, but isn't hard-wired, passing instead through various network devices such as hubs, switches, and routers along its way, as shown here:

Internetwork

"Shall we connect?"

"I know you're there, and I'm ready to connect and conduct a session."

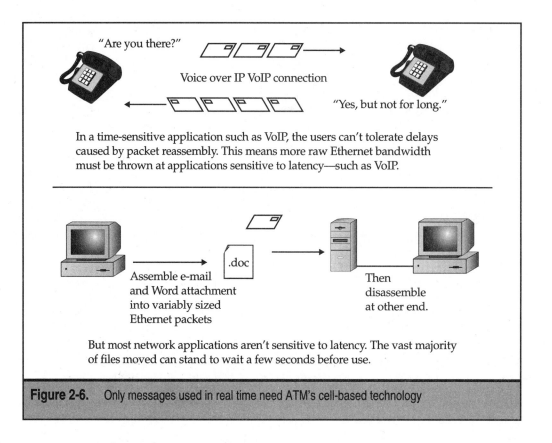

Figure 2-6.   Only messages used in real time need ATM's cell-based technology

Before transmission can begin over a virtual circuit, each end must agree to execute the transmission and the path over which it will travel. This is markedly different from internetwork messages that simply send off to a destination address, leaving the details about how to get it there up to one or more routers sitting between sender and receiver.

LAN Emulation (LANE)

Although it can be configured all the way out to the desktop, ATM is primarily used for backbones, either as backbone LANs within an office campus or long-haul Internet links between cities. ATM is a natural for backbone duty because its underlying cell switching technology is ideal for high-speed point-to-point links.

But at some point, a backbone must talk the same language as the access LANs it serves—usually Ethernet or Token Ring. Because ATM deals in cells instead of packets, it uses an encapsulation technique called LANE (for LAN emulation). In networking, *encapsulation* is the technique of placing a message unit of one format inside that of another format in order to let it traverse an otherwise incompatible network. LANE encapsulates frames at the data-link layer (layer 2) to set up so-called emulated LAN circuits, called

ELANs for short. In other words, LANE breaks down Ethernet or Token Ring packets into ATM cells on one side and reassembles them on the other.

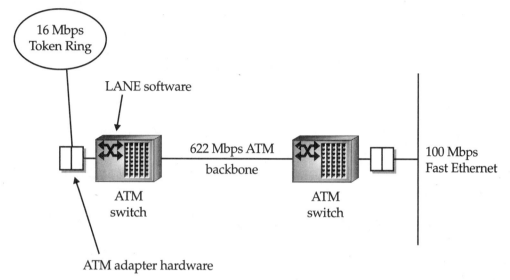

ATM is regarded by many as the answer to the Internet's bandwidth shortage. It's being installed by many enterprises to replace overtaxed FDDI backbones. Not only is ATM's 622 Mbps fast, but also its inherent predictability lends itself to guaranteeing Quality of Service (QoS)—especially for multimedia applications, which by nature cannot tolerate latency. However, because of the need for LANE adaptation, ATM has a relatively high cost per port. It also introduces a new protocol into the mix, thereby increasing complexity.

The ATM standard is coordinated by an international nonprofit industry group called the ATM Forum. The ATM Forum, based in Silicon Valley, publishes technical specifications and promotes the use of ATM products.

Gigabit Ethernet

Gigabit Ethernet is a 1000 Mbps extension of the Ethernet standard. Relatively new as a standard, the IEEE 802.3 committee adopted the Gigabit Ethernet 802.z specification in 1998. Gigabit Ethernet is sometimes also referred to as 1000BaseX in reference to the specification for the required copper or fiber-optic cabling. Gigabit Ethernet is being promoted by the Gigabit Ethernet Alliance, a nonprofit industry group much like the ATM Forum. The push for Gigabit Ethernet is largely motivated by its inherent compatibility with other Ethernet specifications (the original 10 Mbps Ethernet and 100 Mbps Fast Ethernet).

Gigabit Ethernet is ATM's main competition to replace FDDI as the backbone of choice. Its greatest advantage is familiarity, given that Ethernet is the pervasive technology. Originally designed as a LAN technology, at 1000 Mbps, Gigabit Ethernet can scale to WAN configurations. Because Ethernet uses variable frame sizing—ranging between 64 bytes and over 1400 bytes per frame—it does not enjoy the inherent QoS characteristics of ATM. However, many network managers are biased in favor of Gigabit Ethernet because their staffs are familiar with the technology, and it presumably doesn't introduce the added layer of complexity that LANE adaptation requires. Like ATM, Gigabit Ethernet backbones operate over a variety of fiber-optic cable types.

FDDI

FDDI stands for Fiber Distributed Data Interface, a 100 Mbps protocol that runs over fiber-optic cable media. Like IBM's Token Ring, FDDI uses a token-passing architecture to control media access, yielding high effective bandwidth from its 100 Mbps wire speed. If you've never heard of FDDI, you're not alone. FDDI has experienced a relatively low public profile because it has traditionally been used for backbones, not access LANs.

FDDI Was the Standard Backbone Network Technology

For years, FDDI was the network technology of choice for backbone LANs. This could be partially attributed to its speed. During the era of its introduction, FDDI was the first major fiber-based network technology, and its 100 Mbps speed set the standard.

But backbone LANs are mission critical. If the backbone goes down, the access LANs can't internetwork. For this reason, the FDDI specification was designed from the ground up for guaranteed availability, with a physical architecture configuring dual-redundant fiber-optic rings. Each station is connected to both rings, having two effects:

▼ The station can fail over to the backup ring if the primary ring fails.

▲ The station nearest the point of failure on the primary ring serves as a loop-back connector, effectively becoming a ring-connecting device that keeps the ring unbroken.

The FDDI Architecture Provides Dual-Ring Redundancy

FDDI's architecture made it attractive for use as backbone LANs, especially for office campuses and other large area applications. The dual rings provide redundant paths. Under normal operation, the secondary ring sits idle, passing only enough frames to keep itself running. The secondary ring goes into action when the primary ring fails (failures are usually caused by a break in the fiber or a faulty NIC somewhere in the network). As Figure 2-7 shows, FDDI isolates the damaged station by wrapping around to the secondary ring and looping back in the other direction—thus keeping the ring intact.

The first official FDDI standard was published by the American National Standards Institute (ANSI) in 1987. The current FDDI specification is ANSI X3T9.5. Because of its design, an FDDI can have as much as 100 kilometers (60 miles) in fiber-optic cabling configured—a scale sometimes referred to as a metropolitan area network (MAN). The distance reach comes from the combined use of fiber-optic cabling and token-passing media access—both of which inherently support longer distances. In reality, though, most FDDI

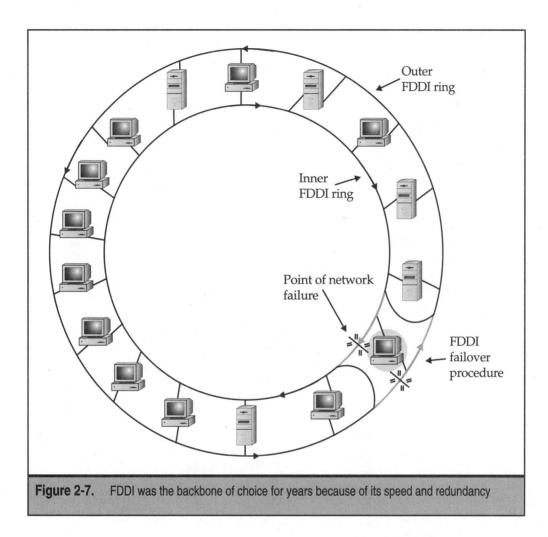

Figure 2-7.   FDDI was the backbone of choice for years because of its speed and redundancy

networks are located within a building or office campus. The few metropolitan area networks (MANs) that do exist generally belong to electrical utilities, which use them to centrally manage their power grids. FDDI is chosen for its fail-safe characteristics.

FDDI Can Now Be Run Over Copper as CDDI

In an attempt to expand market acceptance, FDDI was adapted to run over unshielded twisted-pair media using a technology called CDDI (for Copper Distributed Data Interface). CDDI is actually a trade name, not a standard, and Cisco acquired CDDI from Crescendo Communications in 1993. Even with Cisco's imprimatur, CDDI never really caught on as an alternative to Ethernet LANs. After a fairly long run of popularity as the backbone of choice with reliability-conscious large enterprises, FDDI itself has started to fade from the scene, with ATM and Gigabit Ethernet usurping it as the backbone technology of choice.

WAN TECHNOLOGIES

Most internetworks involve at least some remote users. Enterprises need to connect telecommuters and remote offices, ISPs need to take dial-ins from subscribers, and so on. There are two basic kinds of wide area networks (WANs):

▼ **Dial-ins**   A dial-in line establishes a point-to-point connection between a central location and one user, or a few at most. When the dial-in connection is no longer needed, the phone circuit is terminated.

▲ **Trunks**   A trunk is a high-capacity point-to-point link between offices. Usually, a trunk will connect a number of remote users to a central site. Most trunks run over T1 (1.5 Mbps) or T3 (45 Mbps) telephone lines, although new technologies have come on the scene.

Looked at another way, telephone networks exist on two planes: between telephone switching stations, and between the switching station and the home or office. The zone between the neighborhood switching station and the home or business is often called the *last mile* for its relatively slow telecommunications infrastructure. The term isn't meant literally, of course—the zone between endpoints and the switching station sometimes can be several miles.

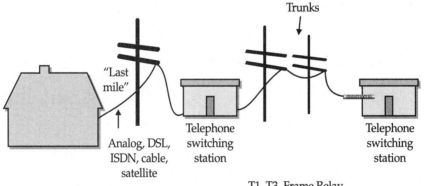

In case you didn't know, telephone switching stations are those small windowless buildings that sit inconspicuously in every neighborhood. Downtown switching stations are much bigger, usually taking up a few floors of the local telephone company building.

The so-called last mile has become a key battleground among internetwork vendors. This is because, with the boom in the Internet, more and more dial-ins are now individuals connecting to their ISPs from home. This includes telecommuters going to work in the corporate intranetwork, not just Web surfers. A huge technology battle has been joined to take over as the preferred medium for the last mile. The fray has largely been between DSL and ISDN—two digital telephony technologies. But cable TV operators and even satellite companies have joined the fray, bypassing the telephone grid altogether.

Dial-in Technologies

Two technologies have been introduced to bring digital bandwidth into the home and small office: ISDN and DSL. ISDN was introduced in the 1980s, but local telephone carriers have been slow in making it available. DSL is the hot new technology, promising even better speeds and wider availability.

Dial-in technologies differ from other WAN media in that connections made using them are temporary. In other words, once the computer user has finished with the session, the circuit is terminated by hanging up the telephone. To this day, most homes are connected via analog phone circuits. Because normal lines are analog, they require modems at each end to operate, and for that reason are referred to by some as *analog/modem* circuits.

The major problem with analog/modem circuits is that they're slow. What slows them down is that the acoustical signals use only a tiny fraction of the raw bandwidth available in copper telephone system cables, because they were designed for voice, not data. This is why the state-of-the-art analog home connection is now 56 Kbps—glacially slow compared to 100 Mbps Fast Ethernet now standard inside office buildings.

ISDN

ISDN, which stands for *Integrated Services Digital Network*, was proposed as the first digital service to the home. ISDN requires a special phone circuit from a local telephone carrier and is unavailable in many areas. The key improvement over analog/modem lines is that ISDN circuits are digital, and for that reason they use so-called CPEs (customer premise equipment) instead of modems—CPE is an old-time telephony term.

ISDN creates multiple channels over a single line. A *channel* is a data path multiplexed over a single communications medium (*multiplex* means to combine multiple signals over a single line). The basic kind of ISDN circuit is a BRI circuit (for Basic Rate Interface) with two so-called *B*, or bearer, channels for payload data. Figure 2-8 contrasts an analog/modem circuit with an ISDN BRI circuit.

Each B-channel runs at 64 Kbps for a total of 128 Kbps payload bandwidth. Having separate B-channels enhances throughput for symmetrical connections—in other words, sessions characterized by the bidirectional simultaneous flow of traffic. A third channel, called the *D*, or delta, channel, carries 15 Kbps. The D-channel is dedicated to network control instead of payload data. Separating control overhead signals enhances ISDN's performance and reliability.

A second kind of ISDN circuit is a PRI circuit (for Primary Rate Interface). PRI is basically the same as BRI, except that it packages up to 23 B-channels for up to 1.544 Mbps total payload bandwidth. Small businesses use PRI circuits to connect multiple users, competing at the low end of T1's traditional market niche.

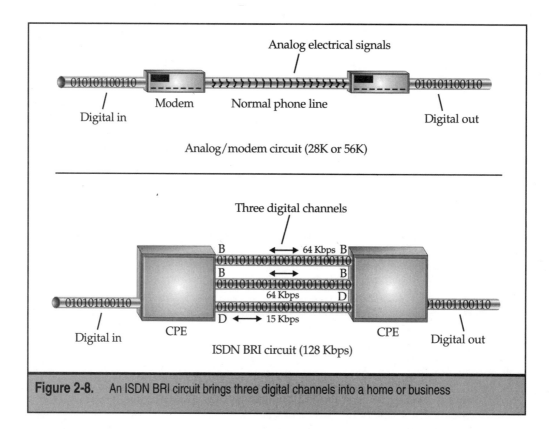

Figure 2-8. An ISDN BRI circuit brings three digital channels into a home or business

DSL

DSL stands for Digital Subscriber Line. As the name implies, DSL also runs digital signals over copper wire. DSL uses sophisticated algorithms to modulate signals in such a way that much more bandwidth can be squeezed from existing last-mile telephone infrastructure.

DSL is an inherently asymmetric telecommunications technology. What this means is that data can be moved much faster downstream (from the local phone carrier to your home) than upstream. There are several types of DSL; two are important to this discussion:

▼ **aDSL** Asymmetric DSL, a two-way circuit that can handle about 640 Kbps upstream and up to 6 Mbps downstream.

▲ **DSL Lite** Also called G.Lite, a slower, less expensive technology that can carry data at rates between about 1.5 Mbps and 6 Mbps downstream, and from 128 Kbps to 384 Kbps upstream. The exact speeds depend on the equipment you install.

DSL's inherent asymmetry fits perfectly with the Internet, where most small office/home office (SOHO) users download far more data than they upload.

The key fact to know is that DSL requires a special piece of equipment called a DSL modem to operate. It's the DSL modem that splits signals into upstream and downstream channels. The major difference with DSL Lite is that the splitting is done at the telephone switching station, not in the home or small office. Figure 2-9 depicts this.

Not requiring DSL signal splitting in the home makes DSL much more affordable than ISDN. To use most DSL circuits, you must be located no farther than about four or five miles from the telephone switching station.

Compaq, Microsoft, and Intel are cooperating on a new DSL standard in hopes that it will replace ISDN as the last-mile technology of choice. DSL's fat bandwidth is necessary

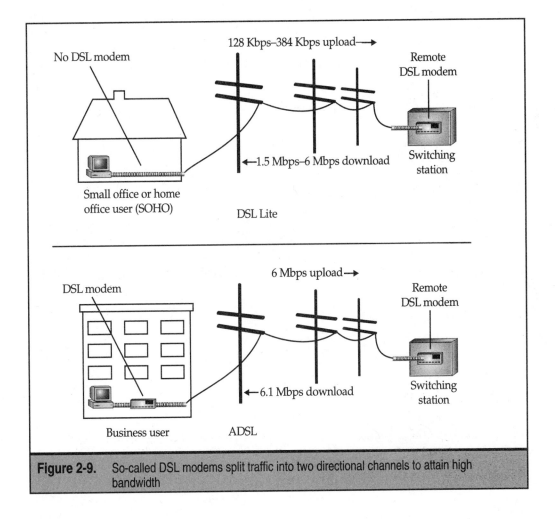

Figure 2-9. So-called DSL modems split traffic into two directional channels to attain high bandwidth

to realize the goal of continuous-transmission video, audio, 3-D animation, and other multimedia applications many envision for the Web.

WAN Trunk Technologies

A *trunk* is any high-capacity point-to-point data link. Trunks can exist within buildings and office campuses, but they're best known as wide area network links between buildings, cities, regions, and even continents.

WAN technology has evolved markedly over the past decade, and not just with the Internet boom. For example, Frame Relay packet-switching technology proved dramatically less expensive than dedicated leased WAN lines. We'll briefly review the WAN technologies in use today. They all share common characteristics in that they're dedicated circuits (not dial-in and hang-up) with high bandwidth used to connect locations with many users, as opposed to small office/home office sites with one or two users.

Most enterprises are replacing leased-line WAN services that shared infrastructure services. Their primary motive is to save money, but flexibility is also a big benefit.

T1 and T3 Leased Lines

T1 and T3 are the predominant leased-line technologies in use in North America and Japan today. (There are rough equivalents in Europe called E1 and E3.) A leased-line circuit (or part of a circuit) is reserved for use by the enterprise that rents it—and is paid for on a flat monthly rate regardless of how much it is used.

T1 is the most commonly used digital line technology. It uses a telecommunications technology called time-division multiplexing (TDM) to yield a data rate of about 1.5 Mbps. TDM combines streams of data by assigning each stream a different time slot in a set and repeatedly transmitting a fixed sequence of time slots over a single transmission channel. T1 lines use copper wire, both within and among metropolitan areas. You can purchase a T1 circuit from your local phone carrier or rent a portion of its bandwidth in an arrangement called fractionalized T1. Some Internet service providers (ISPs) are connected to the Internet via T1 circuits.

T3 is the successor to T1. T3 circuits are dedicated phone connections that carry data at 45 Mbps. T3 lines are used mostly by so-called Tier 1 ISPs (ISPs who connect smaller ISPs to the Internet) and by large enterprises. Because of their sheer bandwidth and expense, most T3 lines are leased as fractional T3 lines. T3 lines are also called *DS3* lines.

Frame Relay

Frame Relay switches packets over a shared packet-switching network owned by a carrier such as a regional telephone company, MCI, or AT&T. As depicted in Figure 2-10, Frame Relay uses local phone circuits to link remote locations. The long-distance hauls are over a telecommunications infrastructure owned by the Frame Relay provider, shared among a number of other customers.

The primary benefit of Frame Relay is cost efficiency. Frame Relay takes its name from the fact that it puts data into variable-sized message units called frames. It leaves

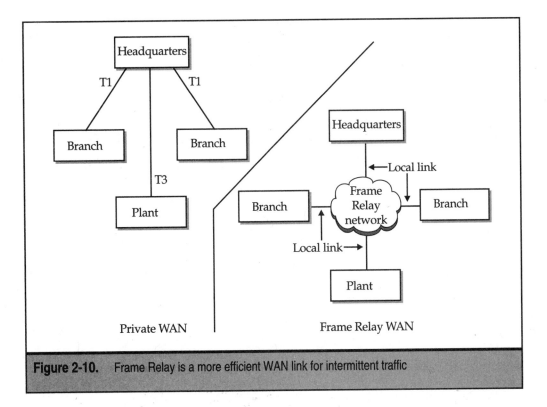

Figure 2-10. Frame Relay is a more efficient WAN link for intermittent traffic

session management and error correction to nodes it operates at various connection points, thereby speeding network performance. Most Frame Relay customers rent so-called permanent virtual circuits, or PVCs. A PVC gives the customer a continuous, dedicated connection without having to pay for a leased line, which uses dedicated permanent circuits. Frame Relay customers are charged according to level of usage. They also have the option of selecting between service levels, where QoS is programmed based on what priority the customer's frames are given inside the Frame Relay cloud.

Frame Relay networks themselves sit atop T1 or T3 trunks operated by the Frame Relay network operator. Use of Frame Relay makes economic sense when traffic isn't heavy enough to require a dedicated ATM connection.

VPN

VPNs, which stands for Virtual Private Networks, are enterprise internetworks operated over the Internet. VPNs work by using encryption to "tunnel" through switched virtual circuits (SVCs) that navigate over a number of intermediary LANs in order to reach remote enterprise locations. *Encryption* is the technique of scrambling data so that only a receiving station with the key to decode it can read it. Other techniques are applied to make sure data integrity is intact (all the contents are still there and unaltered) after a message has traversed a VPN tunnel. Figure 2-11 depicts how an enterprise might use a VPN to interconnect its sites.

A typical VPN scenario is for an enterprise to go to a Tier 1 ISP and purchase SVCs to each remote site. The SVCs assure that messages will be routed in such a way that performance and security are optimized, and that backup paths are available in case a primary SVC experiences a link failure. Routers must be configured at each enterprise site to perform the encryption and decryption operations.

VPNs are exploding in popularity because of their cost efficiency, geographical reach, and flexibility. The extra expense required to beef up router configuration to handle encryption is more than made up by money not spent for leased lines or even Frame Relay service.

TCP/IP

The Internet runs over TCP/IP, the Transmission Control Protocol/Internet Protocol. TCP/IP is actually a suite of protocols, each performing a particular role to let computers talk the same language. TCP/IP is universally available and is almost certainly running

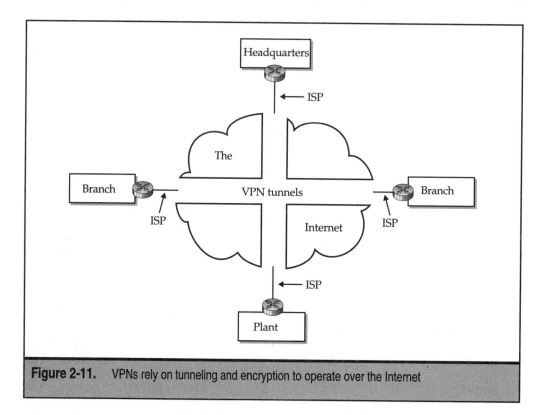

Figure 2-11.   VPNs rely on tunneling and encryption to operate over the Internet

on the computers you use at work and at home. This is true regardless of LAN protocols, because LAN vendors have implemented TCP/IP compatibility in their products. For example, the latest Novell NetWare product can talk TCP/IP, as can Microsoft Windows 98.

TCP/IP was designed by the Defense Advanced Research Projects Agency (DARPA) in the 1970s—the design goal being to let dissimilar computers freely communicate regardless of location. Most early TCP/IP work was done on UNIX computers, which contributed to the protocol's popularity as vendors got into the practice of shipping TCP/IP software inside every UNIX computer. As a technology, TCP/IP maps to the OSI reference model, as shown in Figure 2-12.

Looking at Figure 2-12, you can see that TCP/IP focuses on layers 3 and 4 of the OSI reference model. The theory is to leave network technologies to the LAN vendors. TCP/IP's goal is to move messages through virtually any LAN product to set up a connection running virtually any network application.

TCP/IP works because it closely maps to the OSI model at the lowest two levels—the data-link and physical layers. This lets TCP/IP talk to virtually any networking technology and, indirectly, any type of computer platform. Here are TCP/IP's four abstract layers:

▼ **Network interface**   Allows TCP/IP to interact with all modern network technologies by complying with the OSI model

■ **Internet**   Defines how IP directs messages through routers over internetworks such as the Internet

■ **Transport**   Defines the mechanics of how messages are exchanged between computers

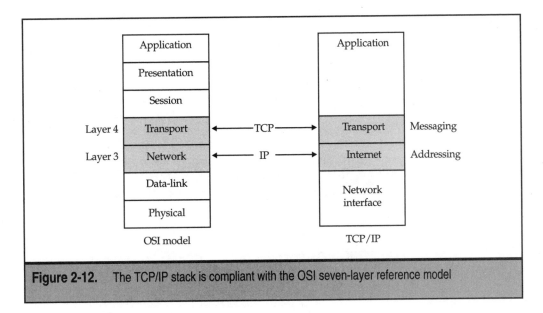

Figure 2-12.   The TCP/IP stack is compliant with the OSI seven-layer reference model

▲ **Application** Defines network applications to perform tasks such as file transfer, e-mail, and other useful functions

TCP/IP is the de facto standard that unifies the Internet. A computer that implements an OSI-compliant layer network technology such as Ethernet or Token Ring has overcome incompatibilities that would otherwise exist between platforms such as Windows, UNIX, MAC, IBM mainframes, and others. We've already covered layers 1 and 2 in our discussion of LAN technologies that connect groups of computers together in a location. Now we'll cover how computers internetwork over the Internet or private internetworks.

TCP/IP Messaging

All data that goes over a network must have a format so that devices know how to handle it. TCP/IP's Internet layer—which maps to the OSI model's network layer—is based on a fixed message format called the IP datagram—the bucket that holds the information making up the message. For example, when you download a Web page, the stuff you see on the screen was delivered inside datagrams.

Closely related to the datagram is the packet. Whereas a *datagram* is a unit of data, a *packet* is a physical message unit entity that passes through the internetwork. People often use the terms interchangeably; the distinction is only important in certain narrow contexts. The key point is that most messages are sent in pieces and reassembled at the receiving end.

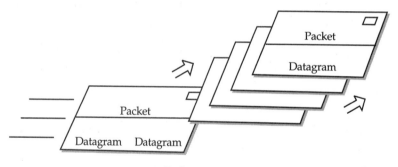

Packet stream

For example, when you send an e-mail to someone, it goes over the wire as a stream of packets. A small e-mail might be only ten packets; a big one may be split into thousands. At the opposite extreme, a request-for-service message might take only a single packet.

One advantage of this approach is that if a packet is corrupted during transmission, only that packet need be resent, not the entire message. Another advantage is that no single host is forced to wait an inordinate length of time for another's transmission to complete before being able to transmit its own message.

TCP vs. UDP as Transport Protocols

An IP message travels using either of two transport protocols: TCP or UDP. TCP stands for *Transport Control Protocol*, the first half of the TCP/IP acronym. UDP stands for *User*

Datagram Protocol, used in place of TCP for less critical messages. Either protocol provides the transport services necessary to shepherd messages through TCP/IP internetworks. TCP is called a *reliable* protocol because it checks with the receiver to make sure the packet was received. UDP is called *unreliable* because no effort is made to confirm delivery.

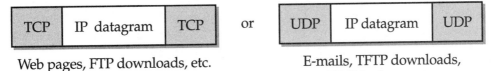

| TCP | IP datagram | TCP | or | UDP | IP datagram | UDP |

Web pages, FTP downloads, etc.   E-mails, TFTP downloads, DNS lookups, etc.

Don't let the name TCP/IP throw you. TCP has no involvement in a UDP message. And while we're at it, don't let the name User Datagram Protocol throw you either. An IP message sent via TCP contains an IP datagram just like a UDP message does.

A key point to know is that only one transport protocol can be used to manage a message. For example, when you download a Web page, the packets are handled by TCP with no involvement from UDP. Conversely, a Trivial File Transfer Protocol (TFTP) upload or download is handled entirely by the UDP protocol.

Which transport protocol is used depends on the network application—e-mail, HTTP Web page downloads, network management, and so on. As we'll discuss, network software designers will use UDP where possible, because it generates less overhead traffic. TCP goes to greater lengths to assure delivery and sends many more packets than UDP to manage connections. Figure 2-13 shows a sampling of network applications to illustrate the division between the TCP and UDP transports.

Figure 2-13's examples highlight a few good points. First, FTP and TFTP do essentially the same thing. The major difference is that TFTP is mainly used to download and back up network device software, and it uses UDP because failure of such a message is tolerable (TFTP payloads aren't for end users, but for network administrators, who are lower priority). The Domain Name System (DNS), the service that translates from URLs to IP addresses, uses UDP for client-to-server name lookups and TCP for server-to-server lookups. However, it may use only one of the two for a particular DNS lookup connection. Notice that FTP uses two port numbers—one to manage the request and the other to manage the download. This is because it can take hours to download a big file, so measures are taken to assure that FTP downloads are completed successfully.

The IP Datagram Format

The datagram is the basic unit of data inside IP packets. The datagram's format provides fields both for message handling and for the payload data. The datagram layout is depicted in Figure 2-14. Don't be misled by the proportions of the fields in the figure; the data field is by far the largest field in most packets.

You probably knew the shaded fields in Figure 2-14 were there without even thinking about it. When you connect to another computer, the packets making the connection contain your IP address in addition to the destination addresses and, obviously, a field con-

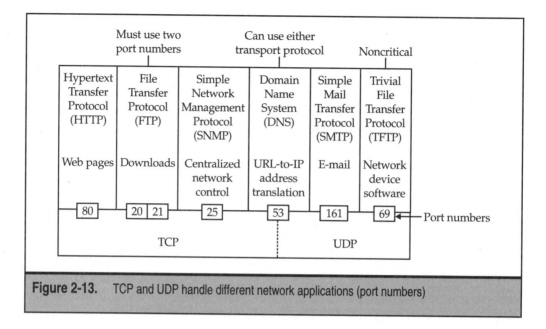

Figure 2-13.   TCP and UDP handle different network applications (port numbers)

taining any data being sent (such as an instruction to download a Web page). The other 12 packet fields are for handling purposes.

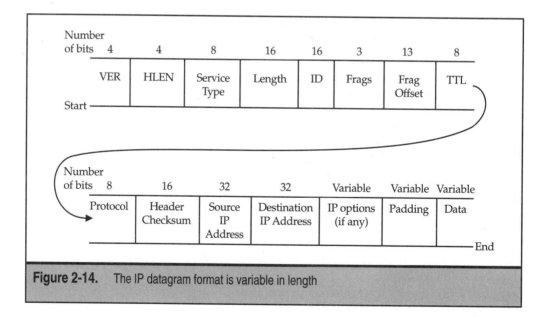

Figure 2-14.   The IP datagram format is variable in length

A key fact about IP packets is that they are variable in length. For example, in Ethernet LANs, one packet might be 200 bytes long, another 1400 bytes. IP packets can grow as large as 4000 bytes in Token Ring packets.

> **NOTE:** We're talking *bytes* instead of *bits* in this context because datagrams contain data, and computers prefer dealing with bytes. On the other hand, when discussing traffic streaming, say, over a cable, the unit of measure is bits—the preferred measure of networking.

Keep in mind that the CPU handling the packet needs to know where each field starts down to the exact bit position; otherwise, the entire thing is just a bunch of meaningless zeros and ones. Notice that the three fields that can vary in length are placed toward the right side of the format. If variable-length fields were to the left in the format, it would be impossible for machines to know where the subsequent fields begin. Here are the IP datagram fields:

- ▼ **VER** The version of IP being used by the station that originated the message. The current version is IP version 4. This field lets different versions coexist in an internetwork.

- **HLEN** For *header length*, this tells the receiver how long the header will be so the CPU knows where the data field begins.

- **Service Type** A code to tell the router how the packet should be handled in terms of level of service (reliability, precedence, delay, etc.).

- **Length** The total number of bytes in the entire packet, including all header fields and the data field.

- **ID, Frags, and Frags Offset** These fields identify to the router how to packet fragmentation and reassembly, and how to offset for different frame sizes that might be encountered as the packet travels through different LAN segments using different networking technologies (Ethernet, FDDI, etc.).

- **TTL** Stands for Time to Live, a number that is decremented by one each time the packet is forwarded. When the counter reaches zero, the packet is dropped. TTL prevents lost packets from endlessly wandering internetworks.

- **Protocol** The transport protocol that should be used to handle the packet. This field almost always identifies TCP as the transport protocol to use, but certain other transports can be used to handle IP packets.

- **Header Checksum** A *checksum* is a numerical value used to help assure message integrity. If the checksums in all the message's packets don't add up to the right value, the station knows that the message was garbled.

- **Source IP Address** The 32-bit address of the host that originated the message (usually a PC or a server).

- **Destination IP Address**   The 32-bit address of the host to which the message is being sent (usually a PC or a server).

- **IP Options**   Used for network testing and other specialized purposes.

- **Padding**   Fills in any unused bit positions so that the CPU can correctly identify the first bit position of the data field.

▲ **Data**   The payload being sent. For example, a packet's data field might contain some of the text making up an e-mail.

A packet has two basic parts: header information and data. The data portion of the packet holds the cargo—the payload that's being sent across the network. The header contains housekeeping information needed by routers and computers to handle the packet and keep it in order with other packets making up the whole message.

The Transport Layer

The way packets are handled differs according to the type of traffic. There are two techniques for sending packets over a TCP/IP internetwork: connection oriented and connectionless. In the strict sense, of course, a connection is made whenever a packet reaches its destination. *Connection-oriented* and *connectionless* refer to the level of effort and control that is applied to handling a message.

Every packet that goes over an internetwork consumes bandwidth, including overhead traffic. Connection assurance mechanisms are not used for certain types of TCP/IP traffic in order to minimize overhead packets where tolerable. Discrimination in packet handling is achieved by the choice of transport protocol:

▼ **TCP**   The connection-oriented mechanism to transport IP packets through an internetwork

▲ **UDP**   The connectionless mechanism for transporting packets

The primary difference between the two is that TCP requires an ACK message from the receiver that acknowledges the successful completion of each step of a transmission, while UDP does not. That's why UDP is often called the connectionless transport. Because UDP is connectionless, it's faster and more efficient than TCP. UDP is used for network applications where it is considered tolerable to retransmit should the message fail.

Both TCP and UDP operate at layer 4 of the OSI stack, just above the IP network layer. Internetworks run TCP and UDP traffic simultaneously, but an individual message may be sent using only one of the two. The difference between the two is manifested in the format of the IP datagram's transport wrapper, called a *segment*. When a stream of packets are sent over an IP network, they are wrapped in either a TCP segment or a UDP segment and handled according to the rules of that particular transport protocol. These segments hold the data used to transport the packet through the internetwork. Keep in mind that this is not payload data, but information used to manage transportation of the packets.

A packet sent via a TCP connection has a much longer header than one traveling via UDP. The extra fields in the TCP header contain information used for establishing connections and handling errors. TCP is the subsystem responsible for establishing and managing IP connections, and it uses a sophisticated handshake procedure to make sure the two end-stations are properly set up for the transmission. For example, when you click a hyperlink to jump to a new Web page, TCP springs into action to "shake hands" with that Web server so the page is downloaded properly. TCP also has procedures for monitoring transmissions and error recovery.

The TCP Segment Format

IP datagrams are placed inside TCP segments when transport is managed by the TCP protocol. The TCP segment format, depicted in Figure 2-15, holds certain pieces of data for establishing TCP connections and managing packet transport.

The data fields in the TCP segment reflect the protocol's focus on establishing and managing network connections. Each is used to perform a specific function that contributes to assuring that a connection runs smoothly:

▼ **Source port**   The application port used by the sending host.

■ **Destination port**   The application port used by the receiving host.

■ **Sequence number**   Positions the packet's data to fit in the overall packet stream.

■ **Acknowledgment number**   Contains the sequence number of the next expected TCP packet, thereby implicitly acknowledging receipt of the prior message.

■ **HLEN**   For *header length*, tells the receiver how long the header will be so the CPU knows where the data field begins.

■ **Reserved**   Bits reserved for future use by the IETF.

■ **Code bits**   Contains SYN (synchronize) bits to set up a connection or FIN (finish) bits to terminate one.

▲ **Window**   Contains the number of bytes the receiving station can buffer or the number of bytes to be sent. This field sets a "capacity window" to ensure that the sender does not overwhelm the receiver with too many packets all at once.

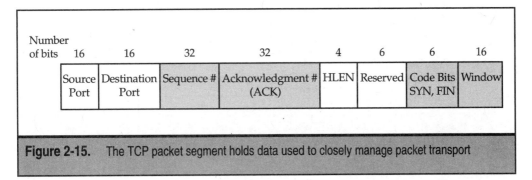

Figure 2-15.   The TCP packet segment holds data used to closely manage packet transport

Establishing a TCP Connection

The TCP connection process is often referred to as the "three-way handshake" because the second step involves the receiving station sending two TCP segments at once. The steps shown in Figure 2-16 show a couple of the TCP segment fields in action. The first TCP segment's sequence number serves as the initial sequence number—the base number used to keep subsequent packets in proper sequence. The Sequence field is used for reassembling out-of-sequence packets into a cogent message at the receiving end.

Figure 2-16's example shows a PC connecting to a Web server. But any type of end-stations could be talking—a server connecting to another server to perform an e-commerce transaction, two PCs connecting for an IRC chat session, or any connection between two end-stations over an IP network.

TCP Windowing

It's not enough just to establish the connection; the session must be dynamically managed to make sure things run smoothly. The major task here is to ensure that one station doesn't overwhelm the other by transmitting too much data at once.

This is done using a technique called *windowing*, in which the receiving station updates the other as to how many bytes it's willing to accept. Put another way, the station is saying how much memory buffer it has available to handle received packets. The TCP windowing process is depicted in Figure 2-17, with a too-small window size shown on the left, and a proper window size on the right.

Window size is communicated via the ACK messages. Looking at Figure 2-17, obviously, a 1000-byte window size is no good because it causes a one-to-one ratio between incoming packets and outgoing ACKs—way too much overhead in relation to payload

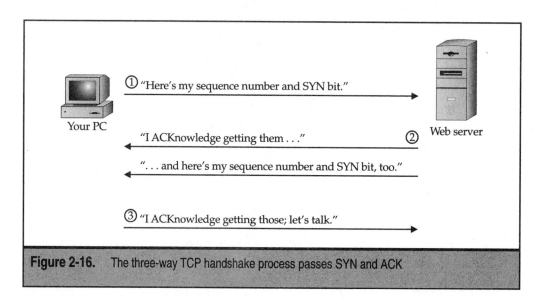

Figure 2-16. The three-way TCP handshake process passes SYN and ACK

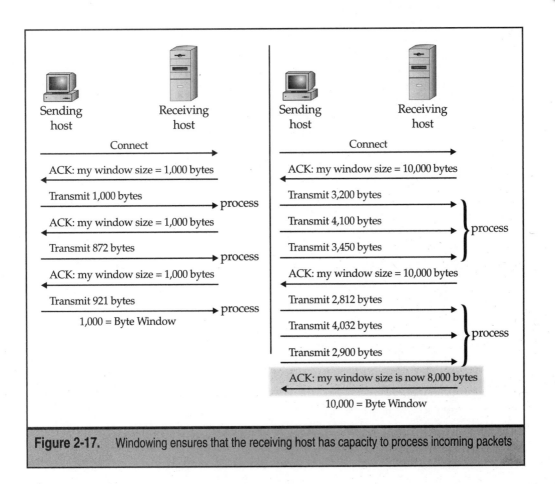

Figure 2-17. Windowing ensures that the receiving host has capacity to process incoming packets

traffic. The right half of Figure 2-17 shows a better window size of 10,000 bytes. As the illustration shows, this lets the sending station fire off as many packets as it wants as long as the cumulative total stays beneath the 10,000-byte window size limit. This permits a more favorable payload-to-overhead message ratio.

The message at the bottom right is shaded to highlight the fact that window sizes are adjusted dynamically during a session. This is done because of changing conditions within the receiving station. For example, if a Web server suddenly picks up connections from other sending hosts, it has less memory buffer available to process your packets, and it adjusts your window size downward.

Connectionless IP Packet Handling via UDP

The User Datagram Protocol is connectionless in that it doesn't use acknowledgments or windowing. Compared to TCP, UDP is a "best effort" transport protocol—it simply transmits the message and hopes for the best. The UDP segment format is shown in

Figure 2-18. Besides the port numbers to tell which network applications to run, UDP segments basically just declare packet size. The only reliability mechanism in UDP is the checksum, used to verify the integrity of the data in the transmission. The odds that the checksum of a received packet containing altered data will match the checksum of the sent packet are miniscule.

Port Numbers

A port number identifies the network application to the upper layers of the application. For example, each packet in an e-mail transmission contains the port number 25 in its header to indicate the Simple Mail Transfer Protocol (SMTP). There are hundreds of assigned port numbers. The Internet Assigned Numbers Authority (IANA) coordinates port number assignments according to the following system:

▼ **Numbers 255 and below**   Assigned to public applications (such as SMTP)

■ **Numbers 256 to 1023**   Assigned to companies to identify network application products

▲ **Numbers 1024 and above**   Assigned dynamically by the end-user application using the network application

Port numbers help the stations keep track of various connections being processed simultaneously. For example, for security reasons, most firewalls are configured to read port numbers in every packet header.

Many beginners are confused as to exactly how port numbers are used. For example, if you're trying to connect to a Web server from your PC, you might think that both end-stations would use port 80 (HTTP) to conduct a Web page download. In fact, the requesting client uses a random port number in the request packet's source port field and uses assigned HTTP port number 80 only in the destination port field. Figure 2-19 demonstrates how port numbers are used during a transmission.

The client uses a random port number to help keep track of conversations during a connection. A *conversation* is a discrete port-to-port transaction between end-stations. There can be any number of conversations within a single connection.

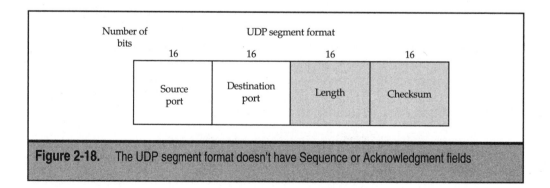

Figure 2-18.   The UDP segment format doesn't have Sequence or Acknowledgment fields

Looking at Figure 2-19, the page downloaded in step 2 may have included one of those annoying embedded HTML commands that automatically creates a new browser window without your asking for it (these are called pop-ups). The pop-up window requests that a new page be downloaded, thereby creating a whole new stream of HTML code, text, GIFs, and JPEGs to handle—a second conversation, in other words.

At the server end, however, a widely recognized port number such as 80 for HTTP must be used—otherwise, the thousands of hosts hitting the Web server would have no idea what application to ask for.

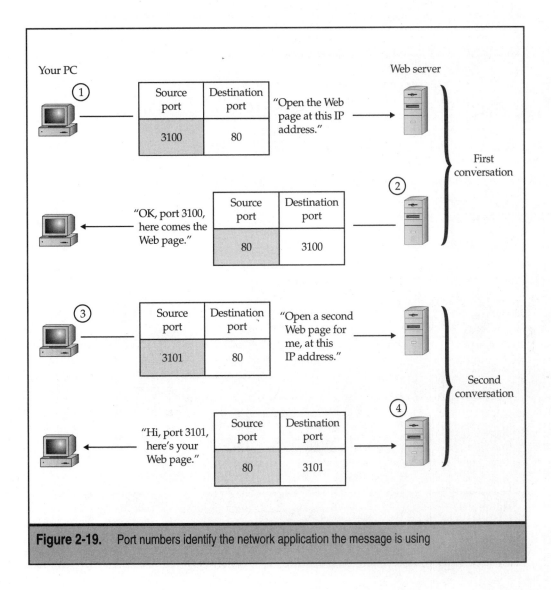

Figure 2-19. Port numbers identify the network application the message is using

IP ADDRESSING

To go somewhere on the Internet, you must type a Uniform Resource Locator (URL) into the Address field on your browser. A unique domain name combines with its organization category to form a URL such as velte.com. Actually, you seldom even have to type in a URL; you just click a hyperlink that has the URL stored in the HTML that makes up the Web page you're leaving.

URLs only exist to make surfing the Internet easier; they aren't true IP addresses. In other words, if you type the URL **velte.com** into your browser, a query is sent to the nearest Domain Name System (DNS) server to translate the URL to an IP address, as shown in Figure 2-20.

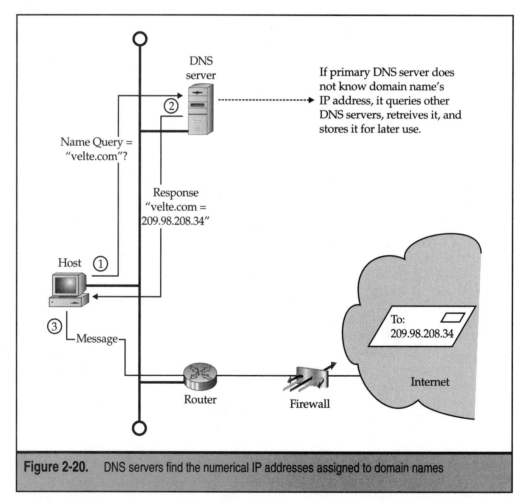

Figure 2-20.   DNS servers find the numerical IP addresses assigned to domain names

Translation to IP addresses is necessary because the routers and switches that run the Internet don't recognize domain names. Indeed, an IP address must be used just for your query to get as far as the DNS server.

All Internet addresses are IP addresses. The IANA issues IP addresses. Domain names are issued by an organization called InterNIC (for Internet Information Center). The primary responsibility of these organizations is to assure that all IP addresses and domain names are unique. For example, velte.com was issued by InterNIC; and its IP address, 209.98.208.34, was issued by the ISP, which for its part was issued the IP address from the IANA.

NOTE: A new organization called the Internet Corporation for Assigned Names and Numbers (ICANN) was started in early 1999 to take over assignment duties. ICANN, however, has run into industry resistance and financial difficulties. It remains to be seen whether they'll become the Internet's central registrar.

The IP Address Format

Every node on the Internet must have an IP address. This includes hosts as well as networks. There's no getting around this rule because IP addressing is what ties the Internet together. Even stations connected to a LAN with its own addressing system (AppleTalk, for example) must translate to IP in order to enter the Internet.

It's somewhat ironic that, despite the requirement that every IP address be unique to the world, at the same time they all must be in the same format. IP addresses are 32 bits long and divided into four sections, each 8 bits long, called *octets*.

Routers use IP addresses to forward messages through internetworks. Put simply, as the packet hops from router to router, it works its way from left to right across the IP address until it finally reaches the router to which the destination address is attached.

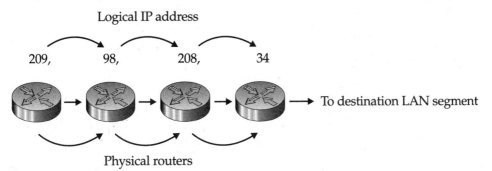

Of course, sometimes a message will go through several router hops before moving closer to its destination. More frequently, messages skip over entire octets and move to the destination LAN segment in just one or two hops. Sometimes hops are needed to find the next destination.

From Bits to Dotted-Decimal Format

As discussed earlier, machines only understand instructions and data in binary format. This goes for IP addresses, too, but the dotted-decimal format was invented so people could read binary IP addresses. *Dotted-decimal* takes its name from the fact that it converts bits to decimal numbers for each octet, punctuated with periods. Figure 2-21 shows the conversion of an IP address to dotted-decimal format.

Figure 2-21 also shows the two reserved addresses. All ones in an octet are for broadcast, where the router automatically forwards a message to all hosts attached to networks

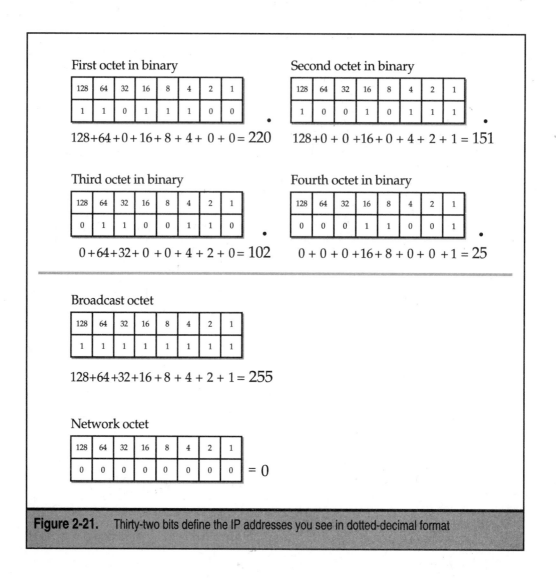

Figure 2-21. Thirty-two bits define the IP addresses you see in dotted-decimal format

addressed thus far in the address. For example, messages addressed to 220.151.102.255 will be forwarded to all interfaces whose first three octets are 220.151.102. The other reserved address—called the "this network" address—is used for technical purposes not discussed here. Just understand that an address like 220.151.102.0 is an abstract representation of all networks falling within the octet with address 0.

IP Address Classes

The IETF divides IP addresses into three general classes (plus two specialized ones). As mentioned earlier, IP addresses are divided into four dotted-decimal octets. Each class differs in the way the octets are designated for addressing networks as opposed to hosts. Figure 2-22 shows the first octet number ranges. The shaded octets show how much of the IP address space is reserved for addressing networks. As the shaded portion moves to the right, there are more possible networks, but fewer possible hosts.

This designation of ranges is called the *first octet rule*. Any router in the world can read the first octet of an IP address and know which bits to interpret as part of the network address versus the host address. If routers weren't able to make this distinction, the Internet couldn't work at all.

The majority of networks are numbered using either Class B or Class C IP addresses. The first octet ranges for each class are as follows:

▼   **1 to 126**   Class A, range of network numbers is 1.0.0.0 to 126.0.0.0 for 126 networks. There are 16,777,214 possible host addresses (16,777,216 minus 2).

■   **128 to 191**   Class B, range of network numbers is 128.0.0.0 to 191.254.0.0 for 16,256 networks. There are 65,534 possible host addresses (65,536 minus 2).

▲   **192 to 223**   Class C, range of network numbers is 192.0.0.0 to 223.254.254.0 for 2,064,512 networks. There are 254 possible host addresses (256 minus 2).

All network space calculations must use the "minus 2" calculation to deduct two reserved addresses: 0 for "this network" and 255 for broadcast. Addresses 1 through 254 may be assigned to hosts. In case you're wondering, first octet numbers 224 through 254 are reserved for two special classes not discussed here (multicasting and research).

As you look at the above list, you can imagine that only a few very large organizations have Class A addresses—only 126 of them, in fact. Most of us connect to the Internet via either Class B or Class C IP addresses.

NOTE: Don't forget that a *network* by strict definition is a LAN segment—an individual, shared access medium. That's what is meant by the word *network* in the context of IP addressing. A *network* (or LAN segment) is also identified as a *network interface* (or *interface*, for short), because only one network may connect to a router's interface. For example, Ford Motor Company's intranet is probably referred to as a network by its employees, but Ford's network manager must assign unique IP addresses to the tens of thousands of individual networks (LAN segments) connected to the company's router interfaces.

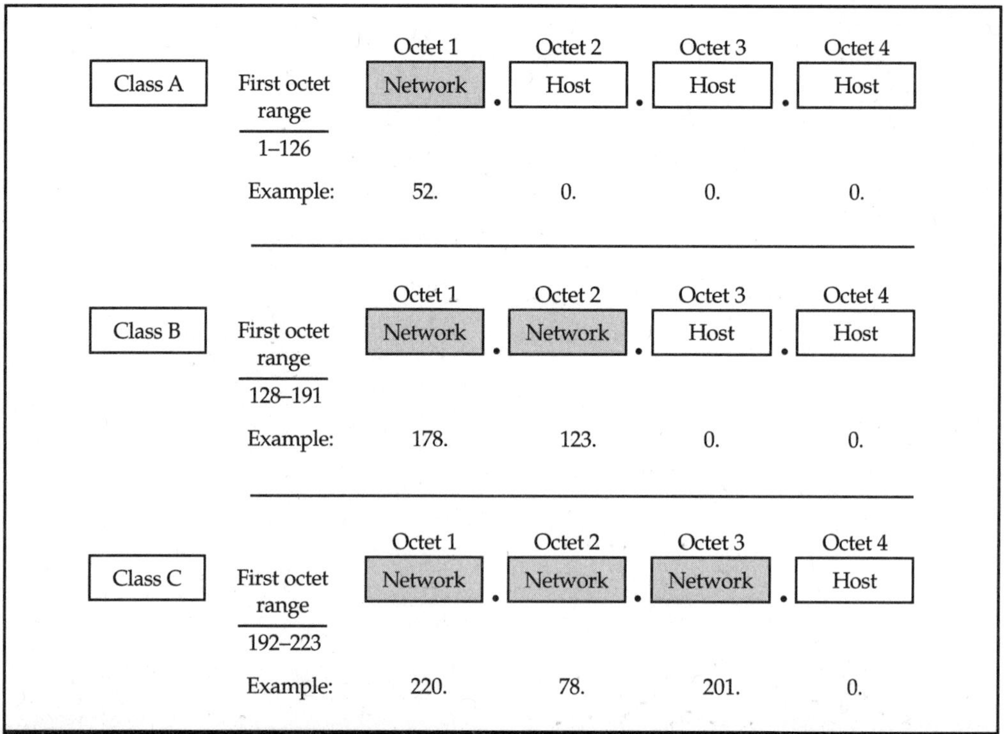

		Octet 1	Octet 2	Octet 3	Octet 4
Class A	First octet range	Network	Host	Host	Host
	1–126				
	Example:	52.	0.	0.	0.

		Octet 1	Octet 2	Octet 3	Octet 4
Class B	First octet range	Network	Network	Host	Host
	128–191				
	Example:	178.	123.	0.	0.

		Octet 1	Octet 2	Octet 3	Octet 4
Class C	First octet range	Network	Network	Network	Host
	192–223				
	Example:	220.	78.	201.	0.

Figure 2-22.   Three IP address classes differ by octets they use for network addresses

Private Addressing

The IANA reserved three blocks of IP addresses for private addresses. A private IP address is one that is not registered with the IANA and will not be used beyond the bounds of the enterprise's internetwork—in other words, not on the Internet. Privately numbered internetworks are also sometimes called *private internets*, but we term them internetworks in this book to avoid confusion. The three blocks of reserved private address space are as follows:

▼ **10.0.0.0 through 10.255.255.255**   The *10 block* is a single Class A network number.

■ **172.16.0.0 through 172.31.255.255**   The *172 block* is 16 contiguous Class B network numbers.

▲ **192.168.0.0 through 192.168.255.255**   The *192 block* is 255 contiguous Class C network numbers.

Edge devices, such as firewalls and boundary routers, must be assigned public IP addresses to conduct business with the outside. Private addresses are assigned only to hosts that make most or all of their connections within the private internetwork.

That's not to say, however, that a privately addressed host cannot connect to the outside. Two IP address translation services are used to temporarily assign valid public Internet IP numbers to hosts with permanent private IP addresses. One technique is Network Address Translation (NAT), and the other is Port Address Translation (PAT). How the two work is depicted in Figure 2-23.

Address translation is usually done by a firewall. Keep in mind that these private-to-public translations are temporary. In NAT, when the internal host terminates its connection to the outside, the public IP address is returned to the pool for reuse.

The obvious advantage of private addressing is to have virtually unlimited address space for numbering internal networks and hosts. With a properly configured firewall or edge router to perform NAT or PAT address translation, these privately addressed hosts are still afforded connectivity to the Internet. Moreover, because their actual addresses are "spoofed" by a temporarily assigned pool number, hackers see no indication of the private internetwork's topology.

Subnetting

Subnetting is the practice of squeezing more network addresses out of a given IP address than are available by default. As discussed, IP address classes define which bits, by default, will address networks versus hosts. What *by default* means here is that upon reading the first octet in an address, a router knows which bits to treat as network address bits. Taking a Class C address as an example, the router will, by default, see the first three octets as network bits, and the final octet as host bits.

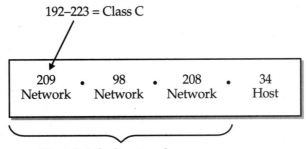

Class C default network space

But in the real world, most enterprises need more network address space than what they are assigned by their ISPs. This creates the need to "cheat" by claiming some of the default host bits for use in addressing networks. This is done by inserting a third zone between the default network and host addresses spaces. Figure 2-24 shows two IP ad-

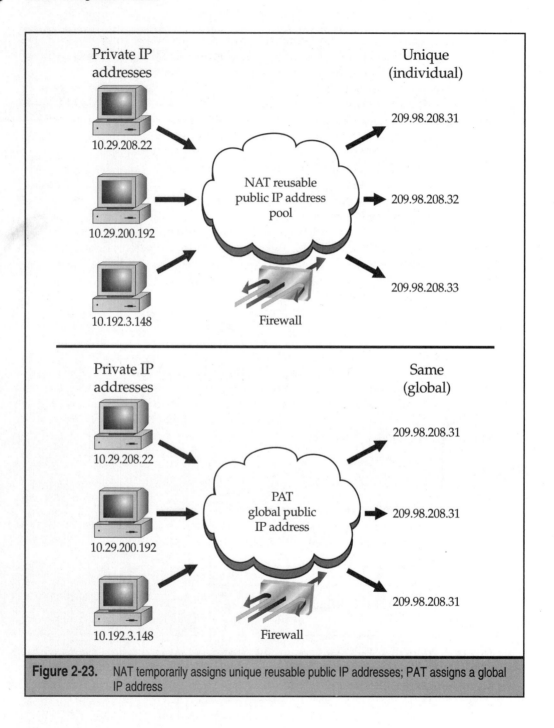

Figure 2-23. NAT temporarily assigns unique reusable public IP addresses; PAT assigns a global IP address

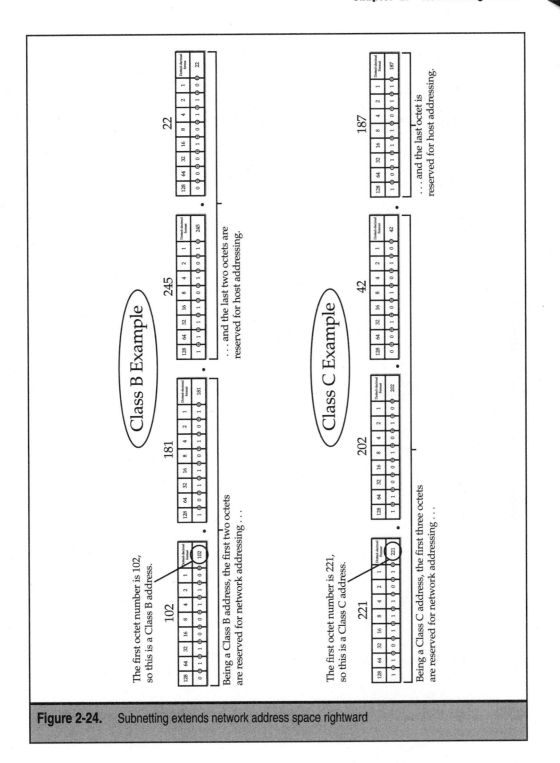

Figure 2-24. Subnetting extends network address space rightward

dresses, one a Class B and the other a Class C address. They're shown in both dotted-decimal and binary format.

Which class an IP address belongs to is important, because subnets extend to the right starting from the rightmost bit in the default network address space. In other words, only bit positions in the shaded portions of Figure 2-24 may be encroached for subnet addressing.

Be aware that the majority of enterprises are assigned Class C addresses, meaning that they have at most only eight bits with which to work. Indeed, most networks are assigned only a range of host numbers, for example, 221.198.20.32-48.

Whole Octet Subnet Example

Subnetting makes more efficient use of public IP addresses without changing them. Take the network in Figure 2-25 as an example. The enterprise was issued the Class B public IP address 151.22.0.0 and subnetted the entire third octet.

Looking at Figure 2-25's configuration, you can see that there is address space for 254 subnetworks, with space for 254 hosts per subnetwork. The shaded host at the bottom right shows a complete subnet address—in this example host number 1 attached to subnet number 2 within IP address 151.22.0.1. The key feature of this example is that an entire octet—the third octet—is subnetted.

As remote routers work their way rightward through Figure 2-25's subnetted addresses, the packets will automatically fall through the correct interface in the edge router at the bottom center of the cloud.

What Subnet Masks Look Like and Where They Exist

All subnet masks are 32 bits in length. Take note that masks are not addresses; they are overlays that define how an IP address is to be used. They differ from normal IP addresses in two key ways:

▼ **Form**   A subnet mask is represented as a string of ones in binary, or 255 in dotted-decimal format.

▲ **Location**   A subnet is applied to a specific network interface within the configuration file of the router to which the subnetwork is attached.

The configuration file sits inside the IOS software of the Cisco router. An attached LAN segment is subnetted by entering a statement like this:

```
MyRouter(config-if)#ip address 151.22.1.1 255.255.255.0
```

The MyRouter(config-if)# prompt means "configure this network interface on this router," where the command is being entered into a Cisco router named MyRouter. The **ip address** command is used to set the IP address for the network interface in question.

The interface's proper IP address is 151.22.1.1 (a Class B address), and the subsequent 255.255.255.0 tells the router to subnet the entire third octet, represented in bits as

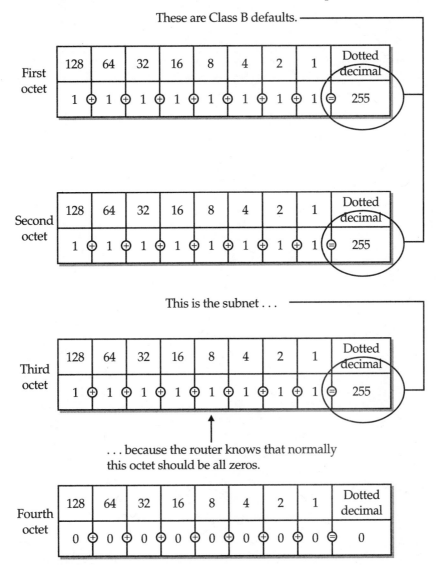

These are Class B defaults.

First octet

128	64	32	16	8	4	2	1	Dotted decimal
1 ⊕	1 ⊕	1 ⊕	1 ⊕	1 ⊕	1 ⊕	1 ⊕	1 ⊖	255

Second octet

128	64	32	16	8	4	2	1	Dotted decimal
1 ⊕	1 ⊕	1 ⊕	1 ⊕	1 ⊕	1 ⊕	1 ⊕	1 ⊖	255

This is the subnet . . .

Third octet

128	64	32	16	8	4	2	1	Dotted decimal
1 ⊕	1 ⊕	1 ⊕	1 ⊕	1 ⊕	1 ⊕	1 ⊕	1 ⊖	255

. . . because the router knows that normally this octet should be all zeros.

Fourth octet

128	64	32	16	8	4	2	1	Dotted decimal
0 ⊕	0 ⊕	0 ⊕	0 ⊕	0 ⊕	0 ⊕	0 ⊖	0	0

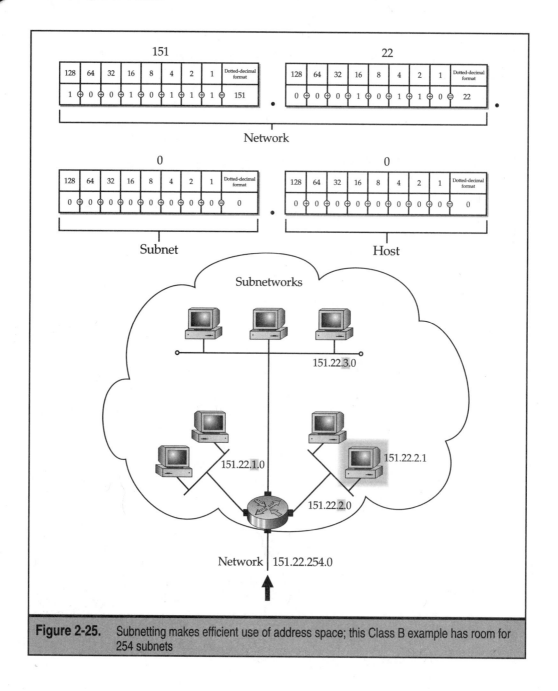

Figure 2-25. Subnetting makes efficient use of address space; this Class B example has room for 254 subnets

That's not too complicated. A subnet mask is the contiguous string of 1-bits extending from the end of the network address space into the host portion. Where that point is depends on the address class (the preceding example is a Class B). The subnet mask is entered into the router's config file using the **ip address** command to append the subnet mask to the normal IP address and apply it to a specific network interface—and in so doing, a specific LAN segment.

Partial Octet Subnetting

In most cases, however, subnets aren't quite so simple. This is because most enterprises are issued Class C IP addresses, where only the fourth octet is reserved by default as host address space. In these cases, the subnet mask extends only partway into the host address space, and is thus represented by some dotted-decimal number less than 255.

The shaded portion in Figure 2-26 represents the bits claimed for subnetting from the fourth octet. Notice that only half the bits were claimed, not all eight. This is the so-called .240 mask, which permits up to 16 subnets, each subnet with enough address space for 14 hosts—for a total of 224 possible hosts. This example would be input into the router's config file as follows:

```
MyRouter(config-if)#ip address 209.98.208.34 255.255.255.240
```

This command instructs the router that the interface is a subnet with 28 network ID bits and 4 host ID bits. From there, packet delivery into the subnet is automatic.

There are several subnet masks from which to choose, as illustrated in Table 2-1. The farther right a mask extends into the host address space, the lower the number of possible

Subnet Mask	Network ID Bits	Host ID Bits	Example Notation	Number of Subnets	Number of Hosts per Subnet
.192	26	6	209.98.208.34/26	4	62
.224	27	5	209.98.208.34/27	8	30
.240	28	4	209.98.208.34/28	16	14
.248	29	3	209.98.208.34/29	32	6
.252	30	2	209.98.208.34/30	64	2

Table 2-1.   Subnet Masks Listed by Number of Network ID Bits

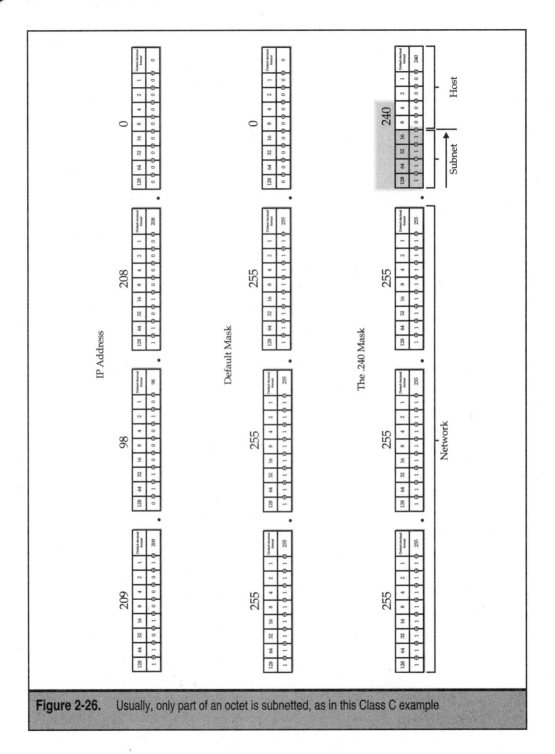

Figure 2-26. Usually, only part of an octet is subnetted, as in this Class C example

hosts per subnet. Which mask to use depends entirely on the application. For example, if a network interface on a router is attached to a point-to-point connection with a remote office, only two host addresses are required—one for each end. In this scenario, it would make sense to use the .252 mask, which has only two host addresses.

PUTTING IT ALL TOGETHER

So, what happens behind the scenes when you make a connection across the Internet? Let's take the most common scenario of all, a Web page download.

Your PC sends UDP packets to your local DNS server to translate the domain name into an IP address, and returns the results. If there's a problem, the DNS lookup will time out and the browser will complain that the server was not found.

The destination IP address is inserted into the header of your packets, along with your IP address and the port number for HTTP (80). Your request is sent over the TCP transport to the destination host to set up a connection. The route taken to the destination is left up to the routers, who read the IP address and hop from router to router to get there. If the packets can't find the destination host, you will likely see a "destination un-reachable" error, or if there is a routing loop in the network, the Time-to-Live (TTL) counter will reach zero and the connection attempt will be timed out.

If the routers find the router on which the destination host resides, the packets go through the network interface to enter the host's LAN segment, using the destination IP address's subnet mask, if there is one.

The receiving host reads your message and decides whether to respond. To answer your service request, it answers using the TCP three-way handshake and windowing techniques, the connection is established, and the requested Web page download is executed under the management of TCP windowing.

In simplified terms, that's what happens when you click a hyperlink in your browser.

CHAPTER 3

Cisco Certifications

The boom in internetworking has created an urgent need for more technical talent to install and manage network infrastructure. Growth in the industry's sheer size is the biggest factor. The number of installed routers, switches, and other internetworking devices has grown explosively over the last few years, and more qualified technicians are needed to take care of them. But industry growth isn't the only factor driving the talent shortage; another driver of the shortfall is that internetworking technology itself has become a lot more complicated. What used to be a fairly straightforward proposition of hubs and routers has given way to switched networks, virtual LANs, ATM emulated LANs, virtual private networks (VPNs), optical telecommunications media, firewalls, management tools, and more. The onslaught of new and better internetworking technology is coming so fast that it's even hard for established pros to stay current.

If you're considering a career move into a technical area, the advice here is to take a serious look at network engineering. Internetworking professionals—often referred to as *wireheads* or *networkers*—are the people who work with the infrastructure that's largely invisible to network users. This is an entirely different group from the people who code HTML pages or write Java applets. Wireheads are the people who work with routers, switches, firewalls, access servers, and other internetworking devices. Some of them help run office or campus networks, and others work with wide area networks (WANs). A growing number of wireheads work for ISPs and other provider organizations instead of end-user enterprises. In addition, an increasing number of them are with internetwork consulting firms, not as full-time, permanent employees.

Talent shortages are nothing new to the computer business, and they're recognized as a threat. If demand for a vendor's products is hot but customers can't find anybody to install and maintain them, the vendor's growth is curtailed. Another pitfall is having unqualified personnel working on the vendor's equipment. This inevitably leads to technical disasters large and small, and the vendor often ends up taking the brunt of customer dissatisfaction.

The industry response has been vendor certifications. A *certification* is a stamp of approval that a person has a certain level of technical competency with the vendor's products. They're obtained by passing a battery of tests specifically geared to the vendor's product line. These tests sometimes include hands-on lab exercises in addition to written exams. Vendors typically farm out their certification programs to approved training organizations who must adhere to the vendor-designed curriculum. Most vendor certification programs are arranged into a career track with certifications by level (beginner, intermediate, and expert) and sometimes also by area of specialization.

Interestingly, the first well-known certification program came from a network company, not a computer company—the major LAN software vendor Novell. Novell's theory was that not only are networks quite complicated, but one that malfunctions is highly visible within the customer organization. So, in the 1980s, Novell instituted their Certified Network Administrator (CNA) and Certified Network Engineer (CNE) programs. The idea was a huge success, and soon the want ads were filled with the CNA and CNE acronyms. The certifications became such a standard job requirement that even veteran Novell technicians were forced to qualify.

Other vendors followed Novell's lead with programs of their own to the point that now the computer section of the Sunday want ads is an alphabet soup of certification acronyms. Perhaps the best-known certification program is Microsoft's, ranging from the Microsoft Certified Professional (MCP) to the high-end Microsoft Certified Systems Engineer (MCSE)—a hot credential that virtually guarantees high-paying employment.

Certification programs work both ways for the vendor. On one hand, they help keep customers happy; on the other, the vendor's market position is enhanced by having a qualified workforce ready to install and maintain its products. A certification program is a way for vendors to reduce risk and secure market position, and some even make money off their programs. For these reasons, all the major computer companies now have certification programs of one type or another.

But certifications make just as much sense for the individual. Even the lowest ranking certification is a virtual pass to a good job with lots of opportunity. For example, a person holding a Cisco Certified Network Associate (CCNA) with little or no real-world experience can get an entry-level job paying $35,000 or more. A CCNA with some hands-on Cisco experience can expect to make around $50,000. These figures vary according to region and the type of employer, of course, but that kind of money at the bottom rung speaks to how important certifications have become. Some observe that nowadays the right certification carries more weight than a college degree.

CERTIFICATIONS OVERVIEW

Cisco has one of the most extensive certification programs in the computer industry. This may surprise you; but as you read this book, you'll come to understand just how big and complicated the field of internetworking is. Cisco's program certifies three tiers of expertise: Associate, Professional, and Expert. Within these tiers, you can be certified in any of several specialties. The overall program is called Cisco Career Certifications, although sometimes the company uses the term "CCIE pathway" as a generic reference to all three program tiers.

Cisco Career Paths Overview

Cisco offers and recommends training courses for its Career Certifications program. Recommended courses are taught by Cisco Training Partners, who must use a standardized college-level instruction curriculum designed by Cisco. The training companies may not deviate from the approved curriculum. Cisco Training Partners are authorized on a country-by-country basis, but they may not administer certification exams or issue Cisco certifications. A company called Sylvan Prometric is retained by Cisco as the exclusive test administrator in the United States. Most tests cost $100 or $200 to take. Because many people don't have access to Cisco equipment to use for practice, the company sponsors a number of practice labs. However, there are a limited number of them, and they cost $500 to $1,000 per day to use.

Three Cisco Certification Tiers

The certification program is designed to encourage participants by offering a progressive learning path:

▼ **CCNA** Cisco Certified Network Associate—the entry-level certificate requires proficiency in basic internetworking concepts, terminology, technologies, products, and rudimentary configuration skills.

■ **CCNP** Cisco Certified Network Professional—the intermediate certificate requires working proficiency in the Cisco product line, advanced technologies, device configuration, troubleshooting, and management.

▲ **CCIE** Cisco Certified Internetwork Engineer—the top-level certificate requires best-of-breed proficiency that only years of experience and sustained training can bring.

Cisco touts the CCIE as better than other computer industry certification programs. Some wags call it the black belt of network certifications. Cisco claims that "experience is the number one factor" in earning a CCIE certification. And they have a point, in that the CCIE exam is a grueling two-day hands-on lab exam that is very difficult. The train-cram-test routine so many use to qualify for top-rung technical certifications isn't an option with the CCIE. Much of the exam can only be learned from extensive job experience. Cisco emphasizes that the CCIE certification is "experience based, not training based" as are most other certifications. This shouldn't dissuade the beginner, however, because the CCNA requires only one written exam, and that's a start.

Certain other top-level vendor certifications have been criticized for failing to assure quality. The loudest complaining has been about Microsoft's top-of-the-line MSCE certification. Many employers complain that because the MSCE is only a battery of multiple-choice written exams with no hands-on proof, tens of thousands of inexperienced people are cramming their way through to certification with little or no applied knowledge and poor knowledge retention after the tests.

CCIE Overview

A CCIE is the most respected certification in the networking industry, affording its holder status among the elite in practitioners of advanced internetworking technology. There are only about 5000 CCIEs worldwide, but thousands are now working their way through the CCIE program, hoping to cash in on the benefits the certification brings.

The CCIE program was instituted in 1993. The intermediate CCNA and CCNP certifications were created in 1998 in response to customer demand for more Cisco talent. Each certification requires passing a supervised test. The candidate is not required to have a CCNA or CCNP before attempting to become a CCIE, but the intermediate certificates are intended as stepping-stones to that status. Given the intensive long-term training and experience required to pass the CCIE, most candidates earn their CCNA and CCNP certifications anyway as they work through the CCIE learning track. Doing so boosts the person's employability and market value, so why not take the tests?

Employers can verify a person's certification by e-mailing the CCIE program at www.cisco.com. Once certified, individuals must requalify every two years to help assure that they have stayed current with technology and product developments.

Support vs. Design Disciplines

To provide candidates with learning programs that fit their needs, career paths are divided into network support and network design disciplines. Each discipline tracks through all three tiers, offering a candidate the opportunity to specialize in one side of the business. Most candidates pursue Support certifications because the biggest job pool is there, but the Design option is becoming more popular.

Presumably, Cisco is offering Design certifications because customers are increasingly aligning their network teams along Design and Support disciplines out of necessity. On one hand, they must keep up with the relentless demand for network expansion and incorporate more advanced technologies; but on the other, they must maintain and optimize the installed infrastructure.

Figure 3-1 charts how the Design track maps to the Support track. The Design track is new, and Cisco is pushing it as a way to help relieve the shortage of qualified network designers (and in so doing, they hope their products will fill up all these newly designed networks). Cisco uses pyramids to depict their certification program, so we will too.

In case you're wondering, the variable number of tests required for some certifications depends on the technology track being taken.

The CCIE Pathway

Cisco's term for the certification program, CCIE pathway, is partly marketing hype to encourage those earning a CCNA or CCNP to think of themselves as partway through the process of earning a CCIE. That's not necessarily the case, of course. Many generalists will take one or both of the intermediate certifications to round out their credentials, with no intention of going for the CCIE.

Internetworking technology is an expansive subject area, which is why several areas of specialization have emerged. The field has grown so big and complicated that it's no longer feasible for even a motivated industry veteran to maintain expertise in all areas. This is especially the case for technicians working with Cisco's product line, by far the biggest in the business. For that reason, Cisco has instituted so-called technology tracks that represent fields of study much like a college major:

▼ **Routing and Switching**   Deals with traditional Cisco internetworking, covering the skills needed to work with local routing and switching and wide area routing.

■ **WAN Switching**   Concentrates on the skills needed to work with wide area networks. Subjects include telecommunications, wide area protocols such as ATM and Frame Relay, and service provider technologies such as network-to-network connections.

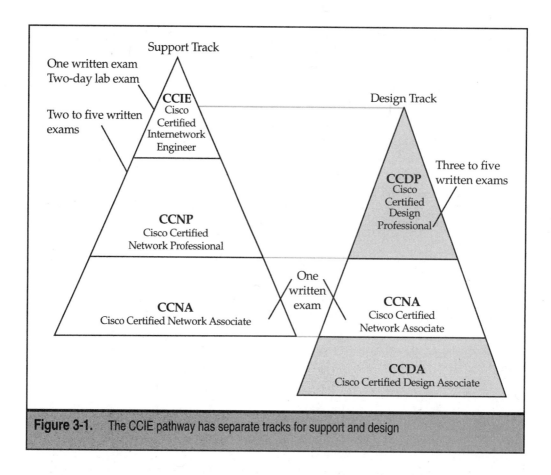

One written exam
Two-day lab exam

Two to five written exams

Support Track

CCIE
Cisco Certified Internetwork Engineer

CCNP
Cisco Certified Network Professional

CCNA
Cisco Certified Network Associate

One written exam

Design Track

Three to five written exams

CCDP
Cisco Certified Design Professional

CCNA
Cisco Certified Network Associate

CCDA
Cisco Certified Design Associate

Figure 3-1.   The CCIE pathway has separate tracks for support and design

▲ **ISP Dial**   Covers IP routing, dial-up remote access, and WAN technologies used by engineers to design and manage the kind of configurations typical to ISPs.

The Routing and Switching and WAN Switching career paths represent the two halves of internetworking. As you'll learn in this book, the WAN field deals with its own set of technologies and products. Almost everything is different on the WAN side: topology configurations, problems, tools—so much so that WAN Switching is almost an industry unto itself. By contrast, Routing and Switching represents the mainstream of the internetworking industry and is the certification path taken by the majority of aspiring CCIEs.

Once a person earns a CCNP within a chosen technology track, the option exists to take a certification in one of seven specialties. This is the Cisco Career Specialization program—a grouping of several specialty certifications in such niche areas as Cisco Security and Cisco Network Management. Specialization certificates aren't stand-alone; you must possess either a CCNP or CCIE to qualify for one. The various certification tracks are depicted in Figure 3-2.

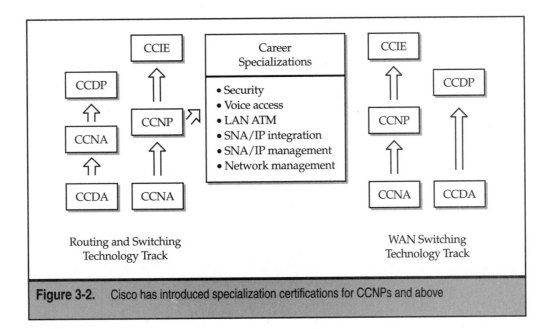

Figure 3-2. Cisco has introduced specialization certifications for CCNPs and above

These specializations are meant to assure solid knowledge within a narrow skill area, as opposed to having only a passing familiarity, perhaps obtained by working occasionally with a particular subset of the technology. Acute talent shortages exist in each of the areas. For example, CCNPs with some real-world experience and a Cisco Security certification are among the hottest recruits in any sector of the computer business.

There are dozens of standard tests in the Cisco Career Certifications program. The tests you must take depend on the career path and specialization (if any). The course work is matched to the certification's required exams. Cisco also offers so-called beta exams, which are tests under development by the company. Cisco encourages candidates to take the beta exams at no charge. They want to use you as a guinea pig, in effect, to "test the test" before releasing it for use by Sylvan Prometric. Many candidates like taking the tests for practice.

NOTE: Out of necessity, the exam outlines in this chapter introduce many acronyms, technologies, and products without defining or explaining them. Don't worry about the technical details here; most will be covered in later chapters. The exam outlines are intended to give you a flavor of the nature and scope of each certification.

ROUTING AND SWITCHING TECHNOLOGY TRACK

The Routing and Switching technology track, taken by most candidates, covers the internetworking mainstream, dealing with office and campus LANs and routing. You can take either Support or Design certifications within the Routing and Switching track. This track is also where all the career specializations are offered.

Support Certifications for Routing and Switching

The Routing and Switching technology track is what most candidates certify in because most jobs involve supporting building and campus internetworks. There are three tiers within this track: the CCNA, CCNP, and CCIE.

Routing and Switching CCNA

One written exam must be passed in order to earn a CCNA certification in the Routing and Switching track. Cisco recommends alternative training options to prepare for the CCNA exam. Training option 1 is meant for individuals who are familiar with internetworking concepts and may even have some technical skills in the area, but are unfamiliar with configuring Cisco products. Option 2 is for those new to the industry, with courses covering the fundamental concepts of internetworking in addition to Cisco configuration. Figure 3-3 shows the Routing and Switching CCNA track.

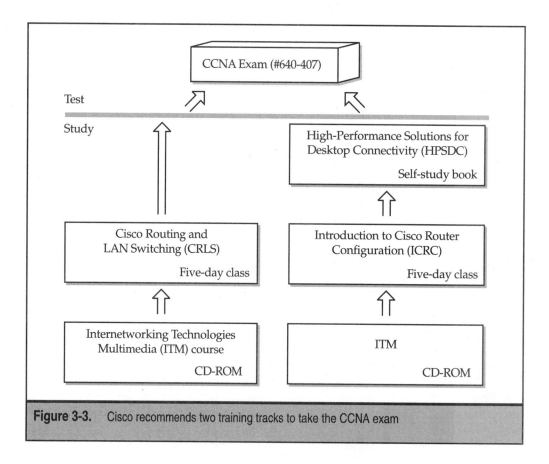

Figure 3-3.   Cisco recommends two training tracks to take the CCNA exam

CCNA Routing and Switching Exam	Exam #640-407
Overview	Understand the OSI reference model, LAN and WAN networking protocols, the basic features and functions of Cisco products; demonstrate the ability to use IOS command language and CiscoWorks to configure a Cisco router.
Objectives	Demonstrate a grasp of basic internetworking concepts and terminology, networking protocols, and the seven-layer OSI reference model. Identify features and functions of Cisco products and how to use IOS commands to configure Cisco routers, switches, and hubs. Understand multiprotocol internetworks composed of IP, IPX, and AppleTalk protocols; perform basic configurations of multirouter internetworks using various LAN and WAN interfaces. Understand network management options, describe Fast Ethernet and switching concepts, describe and demonstrate Cisco Fast Hubs and low-end Catalyst switches. Create VLANs and configure a family of routers using the CiscoWorks2000 tool.

Table 3-1.   Most Candidates Take the CCNA for Routing and Switching Exam

The ITM course is a self-paced multimedia tutorial on CD-ROM, not an instructor-led classroom training offering. HPSDC is a self-study book. CRLS is a five-day instructor-led classroom course. Table 3-1 outlines the CCNA for Routing and Switching exam.

The CCNA for Routing and Switching exam differs from that for the WAN Switching technology track. Because most individuals follow the Routing and Switching track, this is the most frequently taken test. Most think of it as the entry into the Cisco Career Certifications program.

Routing and Switching CCNP

To earn a CCNP in the Routing and Switching technology track, you must pass what amounts to four written exams. As can be seen in Figure 3-4, the Foundations of Routing and Switching Exam (FRS) is actually three tests in one: the ACRC, CLSC, and CMTD. Test Track 1 is favored by those with a higher comfort level with the subject material, because by taking the FRS they're able to qualify for three tests in a single sitting. The FRS is about three hours long, but it saves you about $100 in test fees.

Looking at the training offerings and tests, you can readily see that the CCNP is more in-depth than the CCNA. Whereas the CCNA deals mainly with concepts, terminology, and underlying technologies, the CCNP drills down into the technical details. The content requires a working knowledge of configuration, monitoring, and troubleshoot-

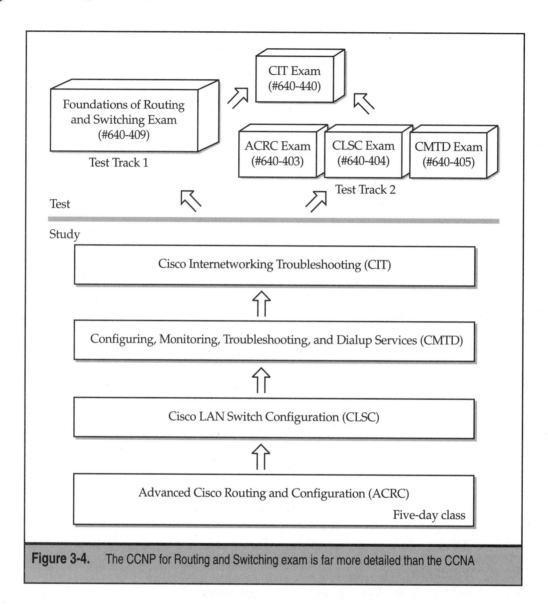

Figure 3-4.   The CCNP for Routing and Switching exam is far more detailed than the CCNA

ing—subjects that require a lot more practice and know-how than that required for the CCNA's overview focus. To see what's involved, the four CCNA for Routing and Technology exams are outlined in Tables 3-2 to 3-5.

Design Certifications for Routing and Switching

Although most candidates pursue Support certifications because that's where the bulk of the jobs are, over the past few years the trend has been toward breaking off network de-

Advanced Cisco Router Configuration Exam (ACRC)	Exam #640-403
Overview	Understand how to configure Cisco routed internetworks for access control and traffic management, and how to configure routing protocols.
Objectives	Configure internetwork access controls; configure solutions to traffic congestion in IP networks using access lists and other tools; manage traffic in Novell IPX/SPX networks; configure queuing to manage traffic; understand routing protocol basics; configure the OSPF routing protocol in single and multiple areas; configure the EIGRP routing protocol; optimize routing updates; understand WAN technologies; configure an enterprise connection to an ISP.

Table 3-2. The ACRC Exam Closely Covers the Ins and Outs of Cisco Routers

sign into a stand-alone discipline. This is not to say that the two don't share a lot of technical subject matter—they do. But the Design certifications emphasize needs analysis and architecture in lieu of troubleshooting.

Cisco LAN Switch Configuration Exam (CLSC)	Exam #640-404
Overview	Understand basic LAN switching technology; demonstrate a basic working knowledge of Cisco Catalyst switches.
Objectives	Describe the architecture and major features of Cisco Catalyst switches; design a topology with Catalyst switches placed for optimum performance; use IOS commands to configure a series of switches and switch modules, and to configure a trunk, VLAN, and ATM LAN emulation. Describe benefits of LAN segmentation; name and describe two switching methods; describe full versus half duplexing; define VLAN and describe reasons for using VLANs; describe the five components of VLANs and how they can be used with hubs; differentiate static versus dynamic VLANs; describe the entire Cisco Catalyst switch product line; demonstrate the ability to configure and troubleshoot networks based on Catalyst switches.

Table 3-3. The CLSC Exam Goes into Depth on LAN Switching Technology and Configuration

Configuring, Monitoring, and Troubleshooting Dialup Services Exam (CMTD) | Exam #640-405

Overview | Understand access server technologies and how to configure, monitor, and troubleshoot dial-up services using Cisco products.

Objectives | Describe the access server's enabling technologies and what's driving change in dial-up technology; describe and configure PPP connections; explain ISDN concepts such as BRI versus PRI lines; explain the ISDN call setup and tear-down process; describe T1 carrier technology, 56 Kbps lines, and xDSL technology. List Cisco's Access Server product lines and the features of each product; describe IOS dial-up features, line types, password facilities, and error logging capability; describe terminal emulation services; describe modem concepts and configure an external modem to work with a Cisco Access Server; describe and configure dial-on-demand routing (DDR); specify cost management methods for dial-up connectivity.

Table 3-4. The CMTD Covers Configuring and Troubleshooting Cisco Dial-Up User Connections

Cisco Internetwork Troubleshooting Exam (CIT) | Exam #640-440

Overview | Understand the methodology and steps of identifying and diagnosing the source of a problem, and demonstrate basic Cisco troubleshooting skills.

Objectives | Describe tools available for troubleshooting Cisco routers and switches; list Cisco troubleshooting support resources; describe trouble escalation procedures; demonstrate basic troubleshooting skills for problems at the data-link and network layers, and also with connectionless versus connection-oriented transports. Describe how to use the LANWatch protocol analyzer to diagnose a problem; demonstrate working knowledge of IOS commands used to troubleshoot Cisco devices; obtain routing protocol information for diagnosis; troubleshoot a campus network running TCP/IP and Windows hosts; analyze symptoms and device resolution strategies for TCP/IP, IPX, AppleTalk, Frame Relay, ISDN, and Catalyst Switch VLAN configurations in test exercises.

Table 3-5. The CIT Exam Tests You on the Toughest Skill of All: Troubleshooting

Routing and Switching CCDA

The first-rung design certification in the Routing and Switching track is the Cisco Certified Design Associate. The CCDA is designed to qualify the candidate as having solid knowledge in the design issues and in the methods used to gather design information and solve design problems. Figure 3-5 shows the two-step DCN track.

The CCDA must demonstrate a working knowledge of such higher level technical subjects as network layer addressing, routing protocols, and traffic control techniques. Softer subjects such as customer needs analysis, design documentation, and network capacity planning are also covered. Table 3-6 outlines the DCN exam.

Routing and Switching CCNA—Design Certification

The CCNA certification is required before you can receive the Cisco Certified Design Professional (CCDP) certification. The CCNA exam is the same as the one for Support certification, covered earlier (refer back to Table 3-1).

Routing and Switching CCDP

The CCDP seeks to assure that the certificate holder has as sound a background in Cisco internetworking technology as the CCNP. The same base-level exams are required—the FRS, or the ACRC, CLSC, and CMTD individually—but the final exams differ. Whereas the CCNP requires you to pass the Cisco Internetwork Troubleshooting (CIT) exam, the CCDP requires the Cisco Internetwork Design (CID) exam instead. The CCDP study and exam tracks are outlined in Figure 3-6.

Cisco is confusing the market somewhat by positioning the CCDP as a top-tier certification on par with the CCIE. This probably has mostly to do with the company's desire for more qualified Cisco designers in the marketplace. After all, three of the four CCDP exams are the same as for the CCNP.

Nonetheless, the CCDP is an important certification. The three base tests put the individual on par with most CCNPs, and the CID test swaps design expertise for the CCNP's

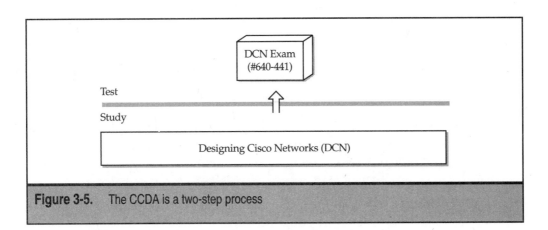

Figure 3-5.   The CCDA is a two-step process

Designing Cisco Networks Exam (DCN) | **Exam #640-441**

Overview   Understand the concepts and methodology of internetwork design, typical design problems, and trade-offs; demonstrate the skills needed to design effective small- to medium-sized internetworks.

Objectives   Gather and document customer requirements for capacity, performance, security, and scalability; characterize an existing network; produce a network topology diagram that meets these requirements; design network-layer addressing scheme and naming model; select routing protocols; provision LAN and WAN devices and network media; produce a written network design specification document; describe how to build a prototype using Cisco products to build an end-to-end configuration that is within customer budget and can pass technical edit.

Table 3-6.   The DCN Exam Ranges from Customer Needs Analysis Through Design Validation

---

troubleshooting exam. The CID forces the qualifier to demonstrate solid technical knowledge as applied to design issues, outlined in Table 3-7. Remember, don't worry about acronyms you don't yet know; they'll be covered later in this book.

Cisco Internetwork Design (CID) Exam | **Exam #640-025**

Overview   Demonstrate an in-depth understanding of the methodology of designing internetworks.

Objectives   Define internetwork design goals; list issues confronting designers; analyze and document an enterprise's technical and business requirements; define the hierarchical topology model; construct an internetwork design that fits those requirements; define switches, VLANs, and LANE; identify addressing issues and produce an addressing scheme for the enterprise; select the proper routing protocol; design an OSPF configuration; demonstrate a working knowledge of the IGRP routing protocol; design an IPX network topology that controls RIP and SAP overhead traffic; list major factors in choosing WAN links; configure resource-efficient WAN connectivity.

Table 3-7.   The CID Exam Gets into Much Tougher Subject Matter Than the DCN

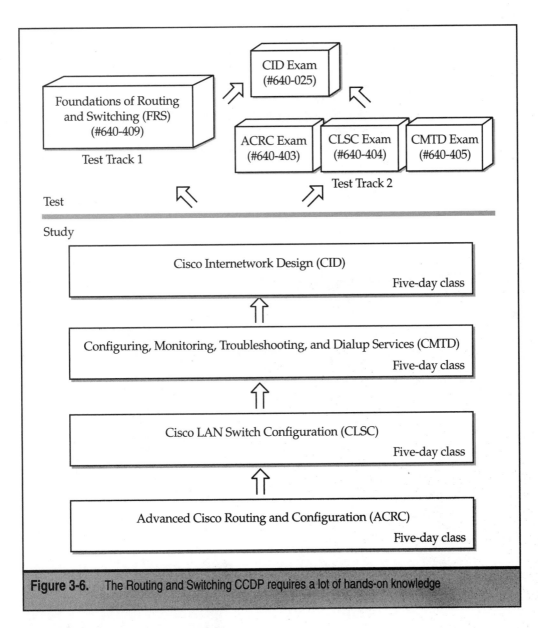

Figure 3-6.   The Routing and Switching CCDP requires a lot of hands-on knowledge

Routing and Switching CCIE

A two-hour, 100-question written exam must be passed in order to qualify for the CCIE lab exam. The lab exam lasts two full days. It covers IP and IP routing, non-IP desktop protocols such as IPX and AppleTalk, and other technologies. The CCIE exam content is too expansive to enumerate here. The CCIE Qualification exam is administered by Sylvan Prometric, but the lab exam is supervised by Cisco at one of its facilities.

The lab exam works this way: the candidate is presented with a complex design scenario to implement using an array of Cisco hardware available in the lab. The candidate must design a solution and physically configure it using actual Cisco hardware. Once the candidate has the configuration up and running, the Cisco lab engineer administering the test will insert faults into the candidate's internetwork. The candidate must recognize, find, and resolve each fault. Figure 3-7 depicts the Routing and Switching CCIE lab exam.

The candidate is responsible only for the network devices on the internetwork, not end-user hosts such as PCs and servers. There is a preassigned point value for each scenario and problem. (More than one scenario is assigned.) A passing score on the CCIE lab exam is 80 percent.

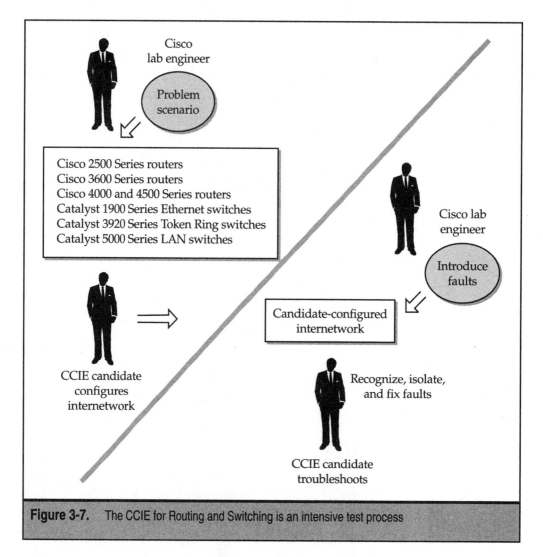

Figure 3-7.   The CCIE for Routing and Switching is an intensive test process

WAN SWITCHING TECHNOLOGY TRACK

As mentioned, WANs are a world all their own. The WAN field has its own technologies and Cisco products. That's not to say there isn't a lot of shared technology; it's just used differently. The main reason WAN switching is its own discipline is that long lines are typically point-to-point connections. That's why they're switched—not a lot of addressing intelligence is necessary to find a port on a behemoth switch sitting at the other end of a fiber-optic cable a couple hundred miles long. However, WAN switching *does* require special technologies to keep data moving at lightning speeds through those big pipes. The Asynchronous Transfer Mode (ATM) protocol, in particular, differentiates WAN Switching from the Routing and Switching field. For that and other reasons, WAN Switching also means working with a different lineup of Cisco products.

Support Certifications for WAN Switching

There are three WAN Switching Support certifications: the CCNA, CCNP, and CCIE. It can be a tough area to break into if you don't have access to WAN equipment. That's why you'll see WAN Switching candidates coming from ISPs and large enterprises supporting internal WAN links. However, the CCNA can be achieved with little or no hands-on experience, thereby affording an ambitious person the opportunity to join a WAN team and get the real experience necessary for the CCNP and beyond.

WAN Switching CCNA

The WAN Quick Start (WQS) preparatory course is a self-study CD-ROM. The materials deal directly with the Cisco IPX, IGX, BPX, and AXIS product lines, which are high-end trunk switch products used by ISPs and large enterprises to move large volumes of data over long distances. Figure 3-8 shows the WAN Switching CCNA track.

The subject matter in the WAN Switching technology track differs sharply from that in the Routing and Switching track. As you read this book, you'll come to understand why this is so; but for now, suffice it to say that WAN switches form point-to-point connections that funnel very large amounts of data between sites—often between cities or even continents. Table 3-8 outlines the CCNA WAN Switching exam, the first step in the WAN track.

WAN Switching CCNP

The CCNP for WAN Switching certification qualifies for skills in configuring, operating, and managing switched networks running over Cisco BPX, MGX, and AXIS switches. The technical skills focus on ATM and FastPacket high-speed trunk technologies, Frame Relay, voice, and data services, and skills with SNMP and ForeSight network management tools. Figure 3-9 shows the track for the WAN Switching CCNP.

ATM is a hot area in internetworking. Gigabit Ethernet is vying with ATM for control of the long-line data trunk market; but for now at least, ATM is in the lead. Most of the Internet trunk providers who connect the Internet between cities and continents use

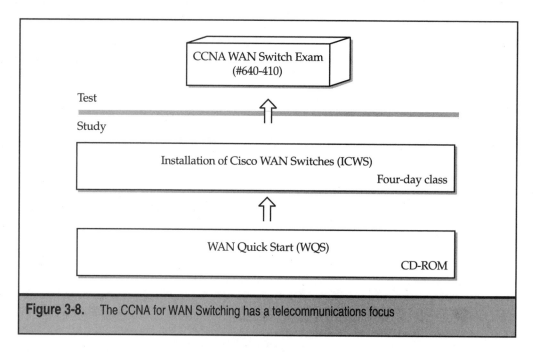

Figure 3-8.   The CCNA for WAN Switching has a telecommunications focus

ATM to run traffic. The ATM talent pool is perennially tight because there are few ATM LANs from which technicians can migrate to become WAN operators (most LANs are run using Ethernet). The demand for ATM talent is being further driven by the looming

Cisco Certified Network Associate WAN Switching Exam (CCNA WAN Switching)		Exam #640-410
Overview	Understand WAN switching fundamentals, and know how to work with IGX, BPX, and AXIS devices.	
Objectives	Demonstrate working knowledge of T1 and E3 narrowband and T3, E3, and OC-3 broadband transports; identify Cisco WAN switching devices and their functions; identify them on a network map; install and set up Cisco WAN switching devices; troubleshoot installation problems; replace defective parts; perform a formal preinstallation site survey; log into and configure Cisco WAN switching devices; monitor device operations; understand how to use StrataView Plus and StrataView Lite software; know how to install and use the latter on a laptop; diagnose alarm conditions; repair failed hardware on IGX, BPX, and AXIS devices.	

Table 3-8.   The WAN Switching Technology Track Has Its Own Acronyms and Product Names

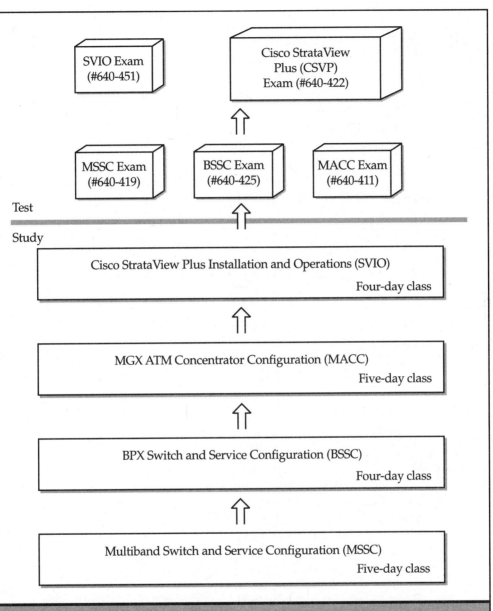

Figure 3-9. The CCNP for WAN Switching requires heavy skills with high-end Cisco switches and ATM

prospect of voice over IP (VoIP) taking voice traffic away from the telephone companies. The WAN Switching CCNP exams are outlined in Tables 3-9 to 3-13. As you can see, it's a highly technical field that requires a substantial amount of training.

Multiband Switch and Service Configuration Exam (MSSC) | **Exam #640-419**

Overview   Understand the Cisco BPX switch and its services, how to configure trunks, data channels and lines, how to configure voice over IP (VoIP), and how to connect networks running Frame Relay and ATM protocols.

Objectives   Describe capabilities of IGX/IOX nodes and interfaces to Cisco StrataCom transport for voice, data, Frame Relay, and ATM traffic; define the FastPacket format; list the StrataCom network types; perform an inventory of interface modules within an IGX cabinet; describe how the IGX system data bus works. Configure and activate trunks; modify trunk parameters; configure and activate lines; add VoIP connections; work with data channel configurations; monitor EIA data channel states; create logical Frame Relay ports and add Frame Relay connections. Add serial connections; add ATM connections; add Frame Relay-to-ATM connections; identify and describe trunk model used to route traffic; test connections and interpret results; monitor IGX/IOX alarm and event log.

Table 3-9.   The MSSC Exam Deals with Cisco IGX Switch Configuration

---

BPX Switch and Service Configuration Exam (BSSC) | **Exam #640-425**

Overview   Understand how to configure BPX switch nodes into a variety of ATM environments.

Objectives   Identify the five types of ATM services; describe ATM cell characteristics; identify BPX features; describe ATM traffic flow processes; describe BPX hardware; know how to log into and use BPX systems. Configure RMON alarm thresholds; configure BPX by activating lines and trunks; configure ATM connection classes; monitor ATM ports and channels; describe impact of ATM statistics. Manipulate routes; predict routing protocol decisions; describe trunk load models; analyze trunk utilization statistics; identify type and location of alarms; monitor BPX alarm and event log; monitor trunk, line and slot alarms and errors. Find and fix card failures; find causes of port connection failures; configure network clocks, and monitor and resolve clocking alarms.

Table 3-10.   The BSSC Exam Covers Using a BPX Network as the ATM Backbone

MGX ATM Concentrator Configuration Exam (MACC) | **Exam #640-411**

Overview   Understand how to configure MGX concentrators into an ATM backbone network, and know how to configure and monitor Cisco MGX concentrator devices.

Objectives   Configure MGX 8220 edge concentrators from isolation into a network using BPX as the ATM backbone; identify MGX cards, features, and user services; inventory MGX lab hardware; configure card redundancy. Modify the MGX BNM trunk; modify the BPX BXM or BNI trunk; monitor an MGX from a BPX switch; activate lines; identify and modify MGX configuration parameters; configure inverse multiplexing and monitor ATM inverse multiplexing statistics. Verify network continuity; monitor circuit emulation; create logical Frame Relay ports; identify port alarms; add Frame Relay channels; add BPX ATM-to-Frame Relay connections; identify Frame Relay port and channel statistics. Activate ATM ports; configure ATM port queuing and signaling protocols; describe traffic policing parameters; modify ATM channels; monitor ATM port and channel statistics; identify and monitor line alarms; find cause of port and channel failures; add line and channel test loops.

Table 3-11.   The MACC Exam Focuses on Cisco MGX ATM Concentrators

Cisco StrataView Plus Exam (CSVP) | **Exam #640-422**

Overview   Understand how to install and configure the StrataView Plus (SV+) switched network management software, and how to use it.

Objectives   Identify SV+ installation features, identify system requirements; partition disks and install the SV+ database management system; verify installation; identify and resolve SV+ installation failures. Describe network management cycle; describe SV+ features for planning, deployment, and monitoring; describe SV+ components in a sample network; match a SV+ version with the proper HP OpenView and IBM NetView versions.

Table 3-12.   The CSVP Exam Covers StrataView Plus Basics

StrataView Plus Installation and Operations (SVIO)	Exam #641-451
Overview	Understand how to install and run the StrataView Plus (SV+) switch management software.
Objectives	Identify major SV+ features; identify requirements for installing SV+; install and configure switches using SV+; configure Cisco switches to participate as clients in switched network management system; use SV+ to discover devices and inventory assets. Configure SV+ security and accounting; gather statistics using the Statistics Agent application; use SV+ to document a switched network topology; configure and test network connections with Connection Manager; perform device management for MGX AXIS shelves using SV+.

Table 3-13.   The SVIO Exam Goes into Greater Detail on How to Use StrataView Plus

Design Certification for WAN Switching

The WAN Switching technology track has no design certification for the CCNA tier; the track's only design certification is the CCDP. Myriad issues affect decisions on how to design WAN switching topology. The field has a strong emphasis on quality of service (QoS), where providers attempt to guarantee minimum service levels to users. This can be seen especially in ATM configurations, where measures for available bit rates (ABR), constant bit rates (CBR), and the like are honed to keep traffic moving according to sophisticated priority schemes. This is the type of thing that requires sophisticated design skills. The two-step WAN Switching CCNP track is depicted in Figure 3-10.

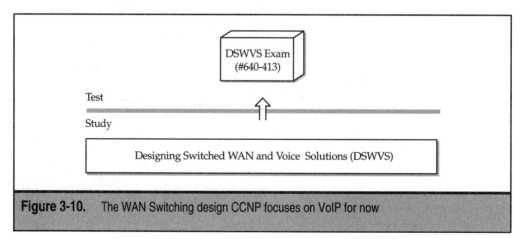

DSWVS Exam (#640-413)

Test

Study

Designing Switched WAN and Voice Solutions (DSWVS)

Figure 3-10.   The WAN Switching design CCNP focuses on VoIP for now

The focal point of this certification is on VoIP. Cisco regards VoIP as one of the strategic vehicles that can take the company to the $50 billion plateau, and they're pushing for more VoIP design talent to help take them there. The DSWVS Exam is outlined in Table 3-14.

WAN Switching CCIE

The qualification exam and lab exam structure for the WAN Switching CCIE is largely the same as that for Routing and Switching. There are small differences: the qualification exam has a passing score of 65 percent instead of 80 percent, although the lab exam is 80 percent. Naturally, the equipment list is very different from the Routing and Switching lab exam, as shown in Figure 3-11.

ISP Dial CCIE

The ISP Dial CCIE track focuses on technologies and skills most needed in the service provider environment. The ISP Dial track covers IP routing, dial-up, remote access, and WAN technologies. It's the same as the other two tracks in that a written Qualification exam must be passed in order to attempt the lab exam. The ISP Dial CCIE Qualification exam is 100 questions long.

The ISP Dial certification is aimed specifically at the problems typical to Internet service providers. ISPs differ from other internetwork operators in that their topologies are top-heavy with technologies needed to support large numbers of remote dial-up users. Technologies on which ISPs are focused include access servers, firewalls, dial-up protocols, ISDN and DSL digital phone circuits, and so on.

Designing Switched WAN Voice Solutions (DSWVS)	Exam #640-413
Overview	Understand the full cycle of tasks involved in designing a switched WAN voice over IP (VoIP) solution using Cisco products.
Objectives	List and describe major steps of designing a switched WAN VoIP solution; be able to identify customer profiles most likely to benefit from VoIP solutions; list deliverables in a VoIP design; recognize customer business goals in network design. Inventory and accommodate installed WAN; gather customer VoIP requirements criteria; design a preliminary VoIP solution that meets requirements for installed equipment, capacity, functionality, reliability, and budget; design a total switched WAN VoIP solution for a customer in a case study.

Table 3-14. The DSWVS Exam Qualifies Competency in Designing Cisco VoIP Solutions

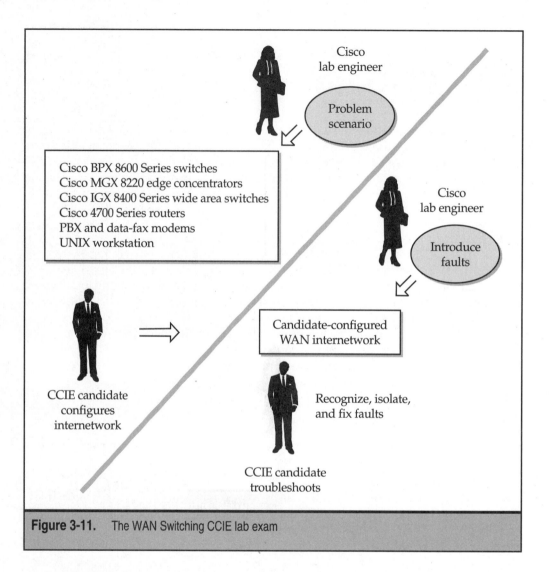

Cisco
lab engineer

Problem
scenario

Cisco BPX 8600 Series switches
Cisco MGX 8220 edge concentrators
Cisco IGX 8400 Series wide area switches
Cisco 4700 Series routers
PBX and data-fax modems
UNIX workstation

Cisco
lab engineer

Introduce
faults

Candidate-configured
WAN internetwork

CCIE candidate
configures
internetwork

Recognize, isolate,
and fix faults

CCIE candidate
troubleshoots

Figure 3-11.   The WAN Switching CCIE lab exam

The ISP Dial is a mixture of subjects taken from both the Routing and Switching and WAN Switching tracks. As Internet portals, ISPs are intensively focused on routing on one hand, but as operators of banks of access servers answering thousands of dial-up phone calls every hour, telecom technology and user account administration is also emphasized. The ISP Dial CCIE lab exam is charted in Figure 3-12.

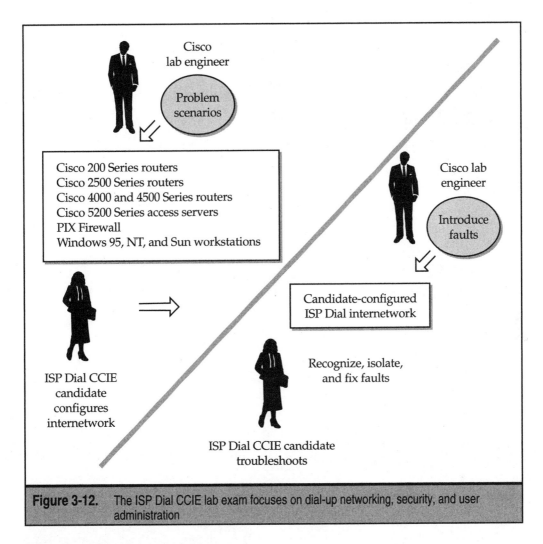

Figure 3-12.   The ISP Dial CCIE lab exam focuses on dial-up networking, security, and user administration

CAREER SPECIALIZATIONS

Cisco currently offers certifications in seven niche areas. These are meant to alleviate the shortage of personnel qualified to handle specialty areas. The reasoning is that certain functions are so complicated (or mission critical) that an individual must be fully dedicated to that field, not a part-timer who works the technology from time to time in addition to other duties. A candidate must be a certified CCNP or CCDP in order to qualify for any of the seven Cisco Career Specialization certifications.

Once an individual has reached the CCNP level, it makes sense to take a specialty certification. Doing so is a good way of enhancing his or her market value and obtaining a focused career path. The jack-of-all-trades wirehead is dying out as internetwork technology becomes more varied and complicated.

Security Certification

Cisco Security is a popular specialization. After having installed billions of dollars of internetworks, enterprises are now trying to figure out how to secure them, especially in light of the rise of hackers and viruses. The Security certification is earned by taking the Managing Cisco Network Security (MCNS) exam.

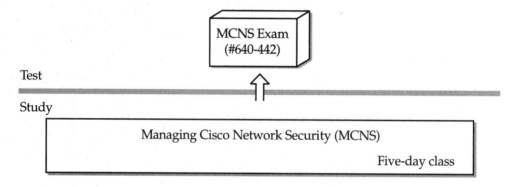

The Cisco Security certification requires knowledge that ranges from IOS security commands, access list controls, the TACACS+ and RADIUS dial-up security protocols, to the CiscoSecure ACS security and firewalls. Virtual private networks (VPNs) and the encryption technology that enables them are driving demand for security expertise even higher. The MCNS exam is outlined in Table 3-15.

Network Management Certification

The Network Management specialization focuses on the skills needed to implement and operate Cisco's network management station (NMS) products. Cisco has two major NMS products now packaged under the CiscoWorks2000 moniker: Resource Manager Essentials for routed networks and CiscoWorks for Switched Internetworks (CWSI). There is also a small tool called CiscoView for working with individual devices. Two tests must be passed, one each for routed and switched Cisco networks.

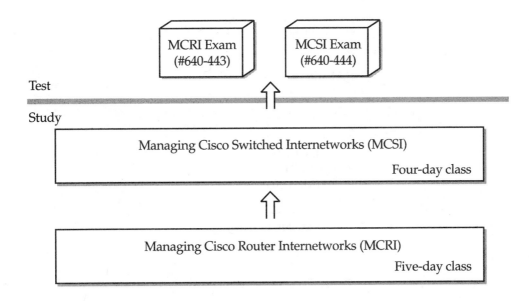

Test

Study

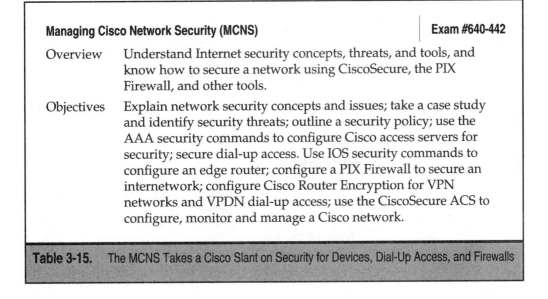

Managing Cisco Network Security (MCNS)	Exam #640-442

Overview   Understand Internet security concepts, threats, and tools, and know how to secure a network using CiscoSecure, the PIX Firewall, and other tools.

Objectives   Explain network security concepts and issues; take a case study and identify security threats; outline a security policy; use the AAA security commands to configure Cisco access servers for security; secure dial-up access. Use IOS security commands to configure an edge router; configure a PIX Firewall to secure an internetwork; configure Cisco Router Encryption for VPN networks and VPDN dial-up access; use the CiscoSecure ACS to configure, monitor and manage a Cisco network.

Table 3-15.   The MCNS Takes a Cisco Slant on Security for Devices, Dial-Up Access, and Firewalls

Managing Cisco Routed Internetworks (MCRI)	Exam #640-443
Overview	Understand how to install and operate the CiscoWorks and Cisco Resource Manager NMS products for routed networks.
Objectives	Explain network management concepts, strategies, and tasks; explain the SNMP and other management protocols; prepare and install CiscoWorks onto a UNIX platform; explain how to install and configure Resource Manager and HP OpenView. Prepare Cisco devices for configuration management; discover devices; inventory assets; manage device config files; identify key SNMP commands; set passwords and SNMP community strings. Use CiscoView to gather and interpret switched port statistics; describe and use Cisco's fault management applications; use CWSI to monitor and troubleshoot by isolating, analyzing, and resolving problems; use technical resources on Cisco's CCO Web page.

Table 3-16. The MCRI Exam Covers Some Basics and What's Required to Run a Routed Cisco Network

Most networks nowadays are multilayered, in that traffic is directed both by switches and routers, depending on the place in the internetwork topology. The two required exams are outlined in Tables 3-16 and 3-17.

LAN ATM Certification

The LAN ATM specialization qualifies technicians to design, implement, and manage campus ATM networks. ATM is a switching protocol with roots in the telephony industry. It's an entirely separate protocol from TCP/IP and other networking architectures based on the seven-layer OSI reference model. ATM is booming in popularity because it's so much faster than Ethernet. The drawback for enterprises is that it takes a different set of skills to deal with its radically different underlying technologies. But it is a big employment market advantage for an individual qualified in the ATM area. A single test must be passed to qualify for the LAN ATM certification.

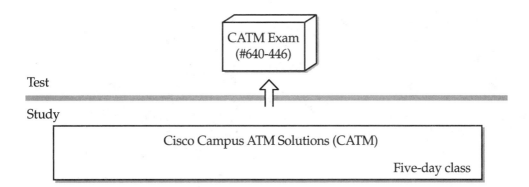

Take note here that the CATM focuses on campus networks where ATM trunks are used for local network backbones. Many of the CATM skills have to do with traffic adaptation between ATM trunks and campus Ethernet LANs using a technology called ATM LAN emulation (LANE). On a side note, ATM has become the dominant long-line networking protocol for moving internetworked data between cities, requiring a different

Managing Cisco Switched Internetworks (MCSI)	Exam #640-444
Overview	Understand how to install and operate the CiscoWorks for Switched Internetworks (CWSI) and Resource Manager NMS products.
Objectives	Prepare and install CWSI and Resource Manager; prepare Cisco switches for configuration management; discover devices; inventory devices; manage device config files; use tools to monitor and troubleshoot by isolating, analyzing, and resolving problems. Use VLAN Director to create Ethernet VLANs and ATM VLANs (LANE); use CWSI and CiscoView to manage switched networks; inventory switch devices; use Traffic Director to monitor and manage network traffic; use ATM Director to mange ATM networks, PNNI topology, and LANE services.

Table 3-17. The MCSI Exam Covers Fewer Basics, but Goes In-Depth on Switched Networks

skill set handled in the WAN Switching technology track, not in CATM. The CATM exam is outlined in Table 3-18. Again, don't worry about terms you don't know here; they're covered later.

Voice Access Certification

Cisco regards voice as one application that can take the company to massive size and profitability. Voice/data integration—often referred to as *convergence*—requires a special set of technical skills.

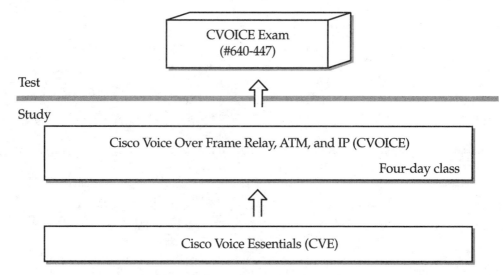

It remains to be seen who will win out in the convergence war—cable TV operators, phone companies, wireless services, internetworking vendors—but it's a sure bet that having a certification in the area will pay off at least to some extent. The CVOICE exam is outlined in Table 3-19.

SNA/IP Integration Certification (for CCNPs)

The majority of the world's most important networks operate both SNA and IP protocols. SNA stands for Systems Network Architecture, IBM's proprietary technology introduced in the 1970s. SNA is complicated and expensive, but very secure and reliable. This is why most large organizations still use it for their core applications. Figure 3-13 shows the track for the SNA/IP CCNP.

Cisco Campus ATM Solutions (CATM) | Exam #640-446

Overview — Understand Asynchronous Transfer Mode (ATM) basics and Cisco's ATM implementations, and be able to configure various Cisco ATM solutions.

Objectives — Describe Cisco ATM products and the basic components of an internetwork built from Cisco ATM products; describe the ATM lower and higher layers; explain the principles of ATM signaling; identify Cisco-supported transmission media; explain how ATM cells are carried over SONET media; explain Cisco's campus ATM implementation. Configure the ATM interface on a Cisco router; configure the ATM on a Cisco LightStream 1010 switch; configure a LANE ELAN; describe LANE version 2 and MPOA; identify the interfaces that support AIP; describe AIP PVC and SVC operations; describe NPM's features and how they compare to AIP.

Table 3-18. The CATM Exam Illustrates How Different (and Complicated) ATM Can Be

Cisco Voice Essentials (CVOICE) | Exam #640-447

Overview — Understand digital telephony basics and how voice traffic operates over Frame Relay, ATM, and voice over IP (VoIP).

Objectives — Explain and compare analog and digital telephony; identify Cisco voice products and their features and benefits; select the optimum service to fit customer needs (Frame Relay, ATM, or VoIP); design branch and regional office voice connectivity in a case study; configure Cisco 3620/3810 multiservice equipment; configure Cisco 2600, Cisco 3600, and AS5300 devices for voice connectivity.

Table 3-19. The CVOICE Exam Emphasizes Practical Knowledge Applied to Digital Telephony

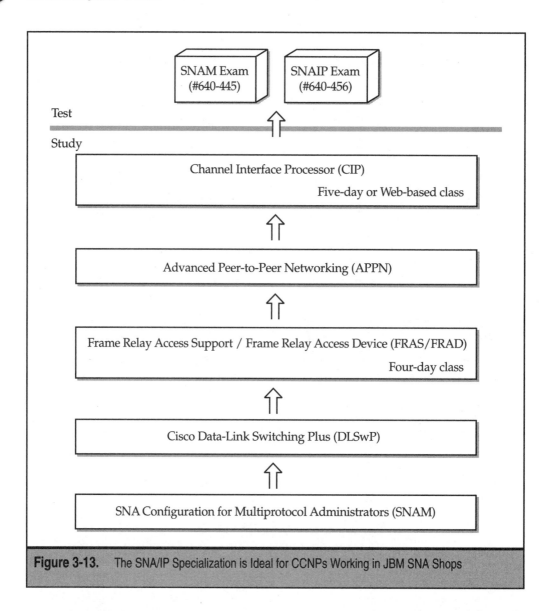

Figure 3-13.   The SNA/IP Specialization is Ideal for CCNPs Working in JBM SNA Shops

As IP has taken over the marketplace, Cisco has invested heavily in making its products integrate with IBM networks. You must pass two exams to earn the SNA/IP Integration certification: the SNAM and the SNAIP. Table 3-20 outlines the SNAM exam (the SNAIP exam was objectives weren't available at this writing).

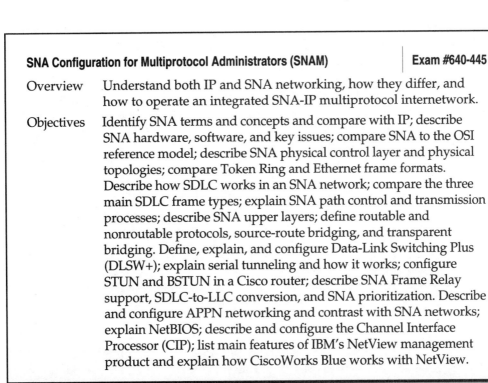

SNA Configuration for Multiprotocol Administrators (SNAM)	Exam #640-445

Overview   Understand both IP and SNA networking, how they differ, and how to operate an integrated SNA-IP multiprotocol internetwork.

Objectives   Identify SNA terms and concepts and compare with IP; describe SNA hardware, software, and key issues; compare SNA to the OSI reference model; describe SNA physical control layer and physical topologies; compare Token Ring and Ethernet frame formats. Describe how SDLC works in an SNA network; compare the three main SDLC frame types; explain SNA path control and transmission processes; describe SNA upper layers; define routable and nonroutable protocols, source-route bridging, and transparent bridging. Define, explain, and configure Data-Link Switching Plus (DLSW+); explain serial tunneling and how it works; configure STUN and BSTUN in a Cisco router; describe SNA Frame Relay support, SDLC-to-LLC conversion, and SNA prioritization. Describe and configure APPN networking and contrast with SNA networks; explain NetBIOS; describe and configure the Channel Interface Processor (CIP); list main features of IBM's NetView management product and explain how CiscoWorks Blue works with NetView.

Table 3-20.   The SNAM Exam Qualifies for Expertise on Integrating SNA and IP

SNA/IP Network Management Certification

The SNA/IP Network Management certification qualifies an individual as capable of operating an internetwork on which SNA and IP coexist. The technology scope covers multilayered networks with both switched and routed areas.

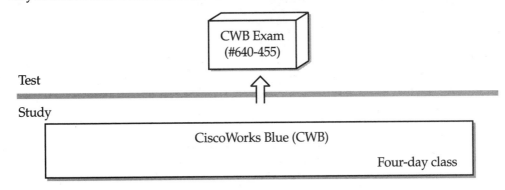

CiscoWorks Blue Exam (CWB)	Exam #640-455
Overview	Understand the SNA concepts and terminology, and know how to use CiscoWorks to manage SNA network links and devices.
Objectives	List the six CiscoWorks Blue software modules; be able to install and configure CicsoWorks Blue; list common operational problems and explain how to resolve them; use Native Service Point (NSP); establish security for NSP; demonstrate ability to service and troubleshoot NSP. Generate topology maps for SNA and APPN networks; work with DLSw maps; use SNA View to monitor and troubleshoot an SNA/IP network; explain the CWB Internetwork Performance Monitor (IPM); configure and operate IPM; use IPM for troubleshooting.

Table 3-21.   The CWB Exam Focuses on Managing SNA and Related Technologies

CiscoWorks Blue (CWB) is a variant of the CiscoWorks network management station software for managing IBM networks. By learning CWB, the candidate should be able to step in and work with integrated SNA/IP networks. Table 3-21 outlines the CWB.

SNA/IP Integration Certification (for CCDPs)

Cisco is so intent on consolidating its position as the preferred infrastructure vendor for large enterprises that they offer a third IBM SNA-related certification. SNA/IP Integration focuses on the interoperation between the two network architectures, with an eye toward migrating nodes from SNA to IP—Cisco's stronghold.

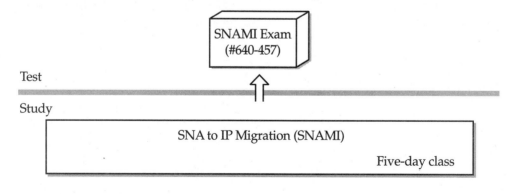

SNA-to-IP Migration Exam (SNAMI)	Exam #640-457
Overview	Understand how to integrate SNA and IP networks using Cisco products.
Objectives	Explain SNA and APPN concepts and terminology; explain SDLC technology; explain NetBIOS; explain how to consolidate bridged and switched SNA networks to IP; demonstrate an understanding of Data-Link Switching Plus (DLSw+); demonstrate a working knowledge of IBM data centers and of TCP/IP on IBM mainframes; understand serial tunneling (STUN and BSTUN); understand how to migrate SNA networks to IP.

Table 3-22.   The SNAMI Exam Specifically Focuses on Connecting SNA to IP

Passing a single exam, the SNAMI, earns the Cisco SNA/IP Integration certification. The SNAMI test is outlined in Table 3-22. SNA-related concepts are advanced subjects not covered in this book.

NOTE: CCIE certification progress is documented in the Cisco Career Certification Tracking System administered by Galton Technologies, Inc., at www.galton.com/~cisco_s/login.html. Inconsistencies have crept into the documentation of CCIE programs. For example, at this writing Galton's site indicates that one must take a CCIE Qualification Exam in order to qualify for the CCDP, which is not a stated requirement at the Cisco Learning Connection page. Also, Galton shows a CCIE Qualification Exam for SNA/IP Integration, while the Cisco Learning Connection makes no mention that a SNA/IP CCIE even exists. These examples make one wonder whether the Cisco Learning Connection page is being kept up to date.

PART II

Cisco Internetworking Tools

CHAPTER 4

Router Overview

A dizzying array of hardware, software, telecommunications media, and technical expertise goes into internetworking. Switches, hubs, firewalls, packets, gateways, ports, access servers, interfaces, layers, protocols, serial lines, ISDN, frames, topologies—the list can seem endless. But there is a way to simplify things. A single, tangible entity makes sense of it all: the router.

In the most basic terms, internetworking is about nothing more than linking machines and people through a maze of intermediary telecommunications lines and computing devices. This takes routing, which in essence involves just two fundamental missions: determine a path along which a link can be made, and transmit packets across that path. It is within these two functions—which take place inside the router—that internetworking becomes easier to understand. This is because the router itself must cut all the complexity down to a level it can deal with. The router does this by working with everything, one IP packet at a time.

Looked at in this way, the router is the basic fabric of internetworks. Indeed, without the router, the Internet as we know it couldn't even exist. This is because of the router's unique and powerful capabilities:

▼ Routers can simultaneously support different protocols (such as Ethernet, Token Ring, ISDN, and others), effectively making virtually all computers compatible at the internetwork level.

■ They seamlessly connect local area networks (LANs) to wide area networks (WANs), which makes it feasible to build large-scale internetworks with minimum centralized planning—sort of like Lego sets.

■ Routers filter out unwanted traffic by isolating areas in which messages can be "broadcast" to all users in a network.

■ They act as security gates by checking traffic against access permission lists.

■ Routers assure reliability by providing multiple paths through internetworks.

▲ They automatically learn about new paths and select the best ones, eliminating artificial constraints on expanding and improving internetworks.

In other words, routers make internetworks possible. They do so by providing a unified and secure environment in which large groups of people can connect. But there are obstacles to bringing users together on internetworks, whether on a corporate intranet, a Virtual Private Network, or the Internet itself. Figure 4-1 depicts how routing technology is the key to overcoming these obstacles.

The router's ability to simultaneously support different protocols is probably its most important feature, because this capability lets otherwise incompatible computers talk with one another regardless of operating system, data format, or communications medium. The computer industry spent decades and billions of dollars struggling to attain compatibility between proprietary systems and met with limited success. Yet, in less than a decade, TCP/IP internetworking has built a common platform across which virtually all computer and network architectures can freely exchange information.

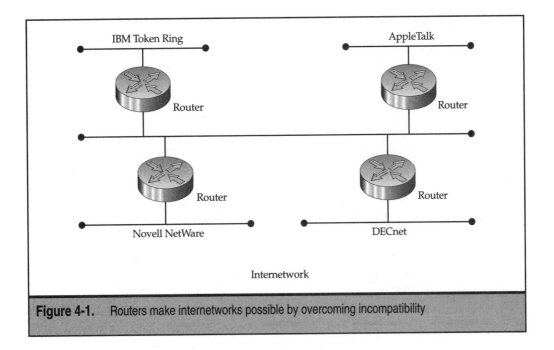

Figure 4-1.   Routers make internetworks possible by overcoming incompatibility

The router's ability to filter out unwanted traffic is also important to internetworking. If users are bombarded with volumes of unwanted messages, or if they feel their systems can be easily broken into, they will resist linking up to internetworks. Traffic filtering and access control provided by routers give users sufficient privacy and confidence to participate in internetworks.

There are other important types of network devices besides the router, but understanding how a router works will go a long way toward your understanding the whole of internetworking. But before you can learn how to configure and manage routers, you need to know the basics of what makes one up. This chapter gives a general review of Cisco router hardware and software.

COMMUNICATING WITH A ROUTER

Most users of internetworks don't communicate with routers, they communicate *through* them. Network administrators, however, must deal directly with individual routers in order to install and manage them.

Routers are purpose-built computers dedicated to internetwork processing. They are important devices that individually serve hundreds or thousands of users—some serve even more. When a router goes down, or even just slows down, users howl and network managers jump. As you might imagine, then, network administrators demand foolproof ways to gain access to the routers they manage in order to work on them.

But routers don't come with a monitor, keyboard, or mouse, so you must communicate with them in either of two other ways:

▼ From a terminal that's in the same location as the router and is connected to it via a cable (the terminal is usually a PC or workstation running in terminal mode)

▲ Via the network on which the router sits

In large networks, network administrators are often physically removed from routers and must access them via a network. However, if the router is unreachable due to a network problem, or if there is a problem with the router itself, someone must go to its location and log directly into the router. The three ways to gain administrative access to routers are depicted in Figure 4-2.

Even when network administrators manage routers in the same building, they still prefer to access them by network. It doesn't make sense to have a terminal hooked up to each router, especially when there are dozens of them stacked in a data closet or com-

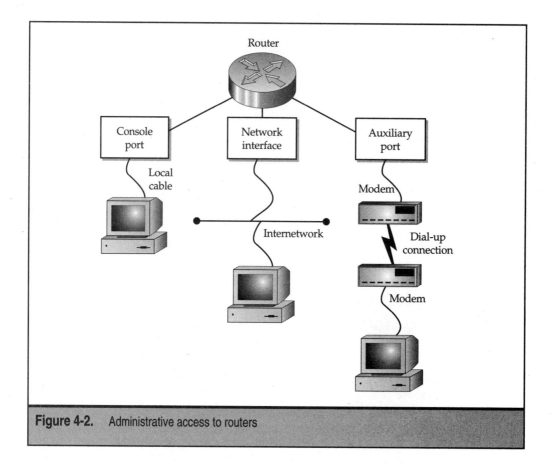

Figure 4-2. Administrative access to routers

puter room. Also, it's much more convenient to manage them all from a single PC or workstation.

There are several ways to communicate with a router, each made possible by a particular communications protocol. Table 4-1 lists each method, the protocol, and how each is used.

The Console Port

Every Cisco router has a console port on its back. It is there to provide a way to hook up a terminal to the router in order to work on it. The console port (sometimes called the management port) is used by administrators to log into a router directly—that is, without a network connection. The console must be used to install routers onto networks because, of course, at that point there is no network connection to work through.

But long term, the console's role is to be there as a contingency in case of emergency. When a router is completely down—in other words, when it is no longer able to process network packets—it cannot be accessed via the network. Or if the router is up and processing packets, but the network segment through which the technician must access it is down, going over a network to fix the router is not an option. This is when the console port provides a sure way to log into the router to fix things. The drawback, of course, is that someone must be in the same physical location as the router in order to connect to it.

Console Terminal Types

A standalone CRT, PC, or workstation can be used as a console. Console terminals must run a character-based user interface. They cannot run a graphical user interface (GUI)

Access Method	Protocol	Communication Method
Console port	EIA/TIA-232	Serial line connection from local terminal.
Auxiliary port	EIA/TIA-232	Serial line terminal connection via modem.
Telnet	Telnet	Virtual terminal connection via TCP/IP network.
HTTP Server	HTTP	Web browser connection via TCP/IP network.
SNMP	SNMP	Simple Network Management Protocol, virtual terminal connection made via a TCP/IP network. (SNMP is covered in Chapter 9.)

Table 4-1.   How Network Administrators Access Routers

such as Microsoft Windows, Mac, or X-Windows. In order to use a PC or workstation as a console, you must use terminal emulator software. For example, one of the best-known terminal emulators is HyperTerminal from Hilgraeve, Inc., which ships with all versions of Windows. Start up HyperTerminal (or one of the many other terminal emulator products) and log into the router from there.

Console Connector Types

Console ports in Cisco routers use a variety of connector types (25-pin, RJ-45, 9-pin, etc.), but all provide a single terminal connection. A word of warning: make sure you have the proper cable before trying to hook up a console terminal to work on a router. Many a network administrator has spent a half hour fiddling with cables to finally find one that could connect to a router just to do 15 minutes of productive work.

> **NOTE:** Console ports on Cisco devices are usually labeled "Console"—but not always. On some products, console ports are labeled "Admin," and on others they are labeled "Management." Don't be confused by this; they are all console ports.

The Auxiliary Port

Most Cisco routers have a second port on the back called the auxiliary port (usually called the AUX port, for short). Like the console port, the AUX port makes possible a direct, non-network connection to the router.

How does the AUX port differ from the console port? The AUX port uses a connector type that modems can plug into (console ports have connectors designed for terminal cables). If a router in a faraway data closet goes down, the network administrator asks somebody in the area to go to the router and plug in a modem so it can be serviced remotely. In more critical configurations, a modem is often left permanently connected to a router's AUX port. Either way, the AUX port affords "console like" access when it isn't practical to send a technician to the site to work on a router through a local console.

Figure 4-3 shows the console and AUX ports on the back of a Cisco 4500 router.

> **NOTE:** Cisco's smaller routers do not have AUX ports, only console ports. These devices support remote management logins by connecting a modem to the router using an auxiliary/console cable kit.

Telnet

Once a router is installed on a network, access to it is almost always made via Telnet sessions, not via the console or AUX ports. Telnet is a way to log into a router as a virtual terminal. "Virtual" here means that a real terminal connection is not made to the device via a direct cable or a modem, as with the console or AUX ports. Telnet connections are instead made through the network. In the most basic terms, a real terminal session is composed of bits streaming one-by-one over a serial line. A virtual terminal session is composed of IP packets being routed over a network, pretending to be bits streaming over a serial line.

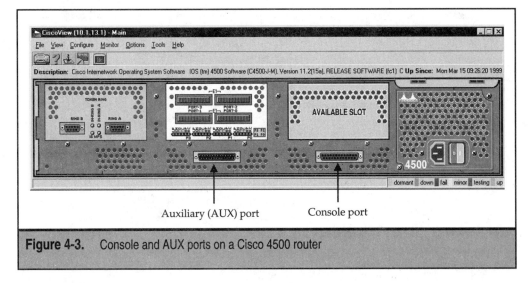

Figure 4-3.   Console and AUX ports on a Cisco 4500 router

Telnet is a network application, not a terminal emulator. It was developed in the early days of the UNIX operating system as a way to log into remote computers to manage them. Later, internetwork pioneers incorporated Telnet directly into the TCP/IP networking protocol as a way to get to and manage internetwork devices. Telnet ships with every copy of Cisco's IOS software and most computer operating systems.

When using Telnet to access a router, you do so over a virtual line provided by the Cisco IOS software. These are called *VTY lines.* Don't let the word *line* confuse you. It does not refer to an actual communications circuit; it means a virtual terminal session inside the IOS software. IOS supports up to five virtual terminal lines (numbered VTY 0–4, inclusive), making it possible to have up to five virtual terminal sessions running on a router at the same time. This is probably design overkill, however. It's rare to have more than one virtual terminal session running on a router at the same time.

Cisco's IOS software is used mostly in character-based interface mode, which is to say that it's not a point-and-click GUI environment we've grown accustomed to using on our Microsoft Windows PCs, Apple Macs, or X-Windows UNIX workstations. Whether logging into a router via the console port, AUX port, or Telnet, you are delivered to the character-based IOS software interface. The following shows character-based IOS output:

```
!
line con 0
 exec-timeout 0 0
line aux 0
 transport input all
line vty 0 2
 exec-timeout 0 0
 password 7 1313041B
 login
line vty 3
```

```
 exec-timeout 5 0
 password 7 1313041B
 login
line vty 4
 exec-timeout 0 0
 password 7 1313041B
 login
!
```

The preceding example is a listing of the seven IOS lines *con* for console, *aux* for auxiliary, and *vty* for the virtual terminal. The seven lines are

▼ The console port, accessed through a local cable connection

■ The AUX port, accessed through a modem connection

▲ Five VTY lines, accessed through TCP/IP network connections

The HTTP Server User Interface

A more recent router access method is HTTP Server. Don't be misled by the name; no computer server is involved in using HTTP Server. The "server" in HTTP Server refers to a small software application running inside the Cisco IOS software. HTTP Server first became available with IOS Release 10.3. HTTP Server makes it possible to interact with the router through a Web browser. Figure 4-4 shows an HTTP Server screen.

Using HTTP to handle IOS command-line input and output isn't particularly ergonomic. The majority of network administrators still prefer using the IOS software in character-based mode because it's faster and more direct than pointing and clicking. This is not unlike those old hands who jump into Microsoft Windows' MS-DOS Prompt window to type in system-level commands. But Cisco may gradually move IOS toward a graphical user interface for a couple of reasons. The most obvious reason to at least offer a GUI-based alternative to working with IOS is that Cisco devices are increasingly being tended to by nonexperts. The other is that as complexity increases, the need for system visualization even inside a single router grows. Using visualization tools (to show load conditions, isolate errors, etc.) will, of course, require a browser instead of the old-fashioned "green screen" character-based command-line interface.

NOTE: To use the command-line interface, you must know what commands to type. You may want to use HTTP Terminal to get started and phase over to character-based mode as you become comfortable with the IOS command structure.

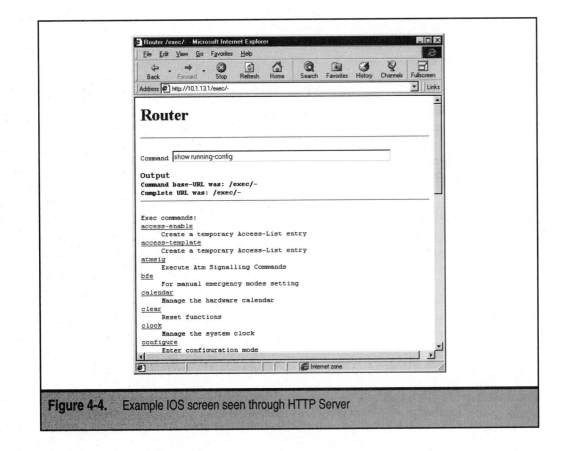

Figure 4-4.   Example IOS screen seen through HTTP Server

ROUTER SECURITY

Routers aren't very visible on internetworks, mainly because they don't have Uniform Resource Locators (URLs) such as www.yahoo.com or www.amazon.com. Routers don't need to have human-friendly addresses, because normal internetwork users never need to know that a router is there; they just need the connectivity it provides them.

The only people who ever need to log directly into a router are members of the network team responsible for managing it. In TCP/IP networks—the protocol on which most internetworks run—routers identify themselves to internetworks only with their IP addresses. For this reason, to log into a router you must first know that it exists and then what its IP address is. The network administrators responsible for the router will, of course, know this information.

But the potential for abuse by hackers still exists. As you will learn in Chapter 8, routers constantly send messages to one another in order to update and manage the internetworks on which they operate. With the proper skills and enough determination, a hacker could discover a router's IP address and then attempt to establish a Telnet connection to it. Given that routers are the links that stitch internetworks together, it's easy to understand why Cisco and other internetwork equipment manufacturers design many security measures into their products. As shown in Figure 4-5, security must restrict access to areas within an internetwork and to individual devices.

NOTE: Router passwords only control entry to the router devices themselves. Don't confuse router passwords with passwords normal internetwork users must type in to enter certain Web sites or to gain admittance to intranets (private internetworks). Restrictions put on normal users are administered through firewalls and access lists, which are covered in Chapters 7 and 10, respectively.

Router Passwords

Router passwords aren't intended only to keep out hackers. Password protection is administered on a router-by-router basis. Passwords to get into a router are stored inside the router itself in most cases. Large internetworks have dozens or even hundreds of

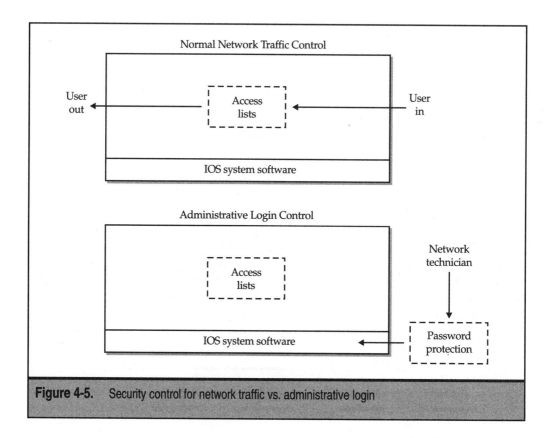

Figure 4-5.   Security control for network traffic vs. administrative login

routers—some more critical to network operations than others—so it's a common practice for network managers to allow only select network team members access to certain routers, or even to command levels within routers. Table 4-2 lists router passwords and what they do.

In Cisco routers, passwords are used to restrict access to

▼ The router device itself

■ The Privileged EXEC (enable mode) portion of the IOS software environment

▲ The use of specific IOS commands

Line Passwords

Line passwords are used to control who can log into a router. They are used to set password protection on the console terminal line, the AUX (auxiliary) line, and any or all of the five virtual terminal (VTY) lines.

You must set at least one password for the router's VTY lines. If no Line password is set, when you attempt to log into the router via Telnet, you will be stopped by the error message "password required but none set." Remember, anyone on the Internet can conceivably Telnet into any router, so setting Line passwords will stop all but the best hackers from getting a foothold. Below, IOS is prompting for a password:

```
User Access Verification

Password:
Router>
```

Control Point	Password Type	What's Restricted
Console port	Line	Logging into router via a local line connected via the console port
AUX port	Line	Logging into router via a modem (or local) line connected via the auxiliary port
Network login	Virtual Terminal	Logging into the router via a network connection using Telnet on a VTY line
Privileged EXEC	Enable or Enable Secret	Entry into the more powerful Privileged EXEC level of IOS environment

Table 4-2. Overview of Router Passwords and Their Uses

When you enter passwords into IOS, no asterisks appear to mask the letters typed—something to which most of us are accustomed. In the preceding example, at the prompt Router> (the router's host name in this example), the correct password was entered, the host Router was successfully logged into, but no asterisks appear to the right of the Password prompt. This might throw you off at first, but you'll grow accustomed to it.

> **NOTE:**   You may have noticed that the password examples in this chapter are not made person-specific with usernames. While it is possible to have usernames with Enable and Enable Secret passwords, it is rarely done. This is because Enable and Enable Secret passwords are stored in router configuration files. Network managers find it more practical to simply issue generic passwords to avoid the administrative nightmare of maintaining username/passwords across dozens or even hundreds of routers. Refer to Chapter 10 on how user accounts and passwords can be centrally maintained using TACACS+ and CiscoSecure.

Enable and Enable Secret Passwords

Once you get past the Line password, you are logged into the router's IOS software environment. IOS is divided into two privilege levels, EXEC and Privileged EXEC (which is usually called enable mode).

The EXEC level contains only basic, nondestructive commands. Being in enable mode provides access to more commands. EXEC-level commands basically allow you to view a router. Enable mode commands are more powerful in that they let you reconfigure the router's settings. These commands are potentially destructive commands, the **erase** command being a good example.

Two types of passwords can be used to restrict access to Privileged EXEC (enable mode): the Enable password and the Enable Secret password. The idea of a "secret password" seems silly at first. *Of course* all passwords are secret, or at least they should be. What the Cisco engineers are alluding to here is the level of encryption used to mask the password from unauthorized users.

THE PRIVILEGED EXEC LEVEL OF IOS   Enable and Enable Secret passwords both do the same thing: they restrict access to Privileged EXEC (enable mode). The difference between the two is in the level of encryption supported. *Encryption* is a technique used to scramble data, making it incomprehensible to those who don't have a key to read it. Enable Secret passwords are scrambled using an advanced encryption algorithm based on 128 bits for which there is no known decoding technique. Encryption for the Enable password relies on a less powerful algorithm. Cisco strongly recommends using Enable Secret instead of the Enable password.

Enable Secret was introduced in 1997, so a lot of hardware and software that can support only Enable passwords is still in use, and servers storing backup IOS images frequently service both old and new routers. When both are set, the Enable Secret password always takes precedence over the Enable password. IOS will only put the Enable password to use when running an old version of IOS software.

IOS passwords are stored in the configuration file for a router. Configuration files routinely cross networks as routers are updated and backed up. Having an Enable Secret password means that a hacker using a protocol analyzer (a test device that can read packets) will have a tougher time decoding your password. The following sample configuration file illustrates this:

```
version 11.2
service password-encryption
service udp-small-servers
service tcp-small-servers
!
hostname Router
!
enable secret 5 $1$C/q2$ZhtujqzQIuJrRGqFwdwn71
enable password 7 0012000F
```

Note that the encryption mask of the Enable password on the last line is much shorter than the encryption mask of the Enable Secret password (on the second-to-last line).

THE SERVICE PASSWORD-ENCRYPTION COMMAND   Certain types of passwords, such as Line passwords, by default appear in clear text in the configuration file. You can use the **service password-encryption** command to make them more secure. Once this command is entered, each password configured is automatically encrypted and thus rendered illegible inside the configuration file (much as the Enable/Enable Secret passwords are). Securing Line passwords is doubly important in networks on which TFTP servers are used, because TFTP backup entails routinely moving config files across networks—and config files, of course, contain Line passwords.

ROUTER HARDWARE

At first glance, routers seem a lot like a PC. They have a CPU; memory; and, on the back, ports and interfaces to hook up peripherals and various communications media. They sometimes even have a monitor to serve as a system console.

But there's one defining difference from a PC: routers are diskless. They don't even have floppy disks. If you think about it, this makes sense. A router exists to do just that: route. They don't exist to create or display information or to store it, even temporarily. Routers have as their sole mission the task of filtering incoming packets and routing them outbound to their proper destinations.

Another difference is in the kind of add-on modules that can be plugged into routers. Whereas the typical PC contains cards for video, sound, graphics, or other purposes, the modules put into routers are strictly for networking (for obvious reasons). These are called *interface modules*, or just plain *interfaces*. When people or documents refer to a router interface, they mean an actual, physical printed circuit board that handles a particular networking protocol. E0 and E1, for example, probably mean Ethernet interface numbers 1 and 2 inside a router. Interface modules are always layer-2 protocol specific. There is one protocol per interface.

Interfaces are added according to the network environment in which they will work. For example, a router might be configured with interface modules only for Ethernet. A router serving in a mixed-LAN environment, by contrast, would have interfaces for both the Ethernet and Token Ring protocols. And if that router were acting as a LAN-to-WAN juncture, it might also have an ISDN module.

There is one last difference between routers and general-purpose computers—a more subtle one. Computer product lines are almost always based on a common central processor (CPU) architecture, for example, Wintel PCs on the venerable Intel x86 architecture, Apple's Motorola 68000 variants, Sun's SPARC, and so on.

In contrast, Cisco routers use a variety of CPUs, each chosen to fit a particular mission. Cisco 700 Series routers, for example, employ 25 MHz 80386 CPUs (remember those?). Cisco probably made this selection because the 700 Series is designed for small office or home office use, where activity loads are light. The Intel 80386 CPU is reliable; capable of handling the job; and, perhaps most important, inexpensive. Moving up the router product line, Cisco uses progressively more powerful general-purpose processors from Motorola, Silicon Graphics, and other chip makers.

Router Memory

Routers use various kinds of memory to operate and manage themselves. Figure 4-6 depicts the layout of a motherboard in a Cisco 4500 router (a good example because it's one of the most widely used routers in the world today). All Cisco router motherboards use four types of memory, each dedicated to performing specific roles.

Each Cisco router ships with at least a factory default minimum amount of DRAM and flash memory. Memory can be added at the factory or upgraded in the field. As a general rule, the amount of DRAM can be doubled or quadrupled (depending on the specific model), and the amount of flash can be doubled. If traffic loads increase over time, DRAM can be upgraded to increase a router's throughput capacity.

RAM/DRAM

RAM/DRAM stands for random access memory/dynamic random access memory. Also called working storage, RAM/DRAM is used by the router's central processor to do its work, much like the memory in your PC. When a router is in operation, its RAM/DRAM contains an image of the Cisco IOS software, the running configuration file, the routing table, other tables (built by the router after it starts up), and the packet buffer.

Don't be thrown by the two parts in RAM/DRAM. The acronym is a catch-all. Virtually all RAM/DRAM in Cisco routers is DRAM—dynamic random access memory. Nondynamic memory, also called static memory, became obsolete years ago. But the term RAM is still so widely used that it's included in the literature to avoid confusion on the subject.

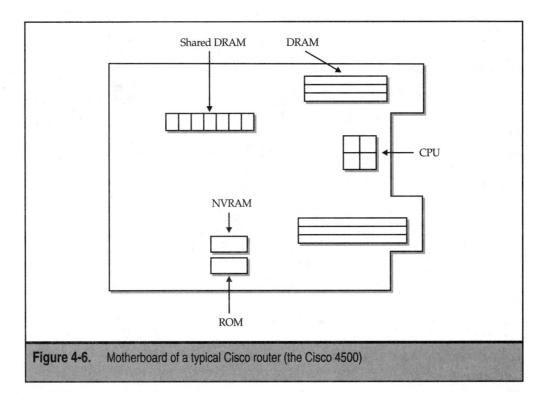

Figure 4-6. Motherboard of a typical Cisco router (the Cisco 4500)

Cisco's smallest router, the 700 Series, ships with a minimum of 1.5MB of DRAM and can be expanded to a maximum of 2.5MB. At the other end of the spectrum, the 12,000 gigabit switch router, Cisco's largest, ships with 32MB minimum DRAM and 256MB maximum.

> **NOTE:** Shared memory *(also called* packet memory*) is a specialized type of DRAM. Shared memory DRAM is dedicated to handling the router's packet buffer. Cisco's designers separate out shared memory to help assure I/O throughput. Shared memory is even physically nearer to the interface modules to further boost performance.*

NVRAM

NVRAM stands for nonvolatile RAM. Nonvolatile means memory that will retain information after losing power. Cisco routers store a copy of the router's configuration file in NVRAM (configuration files are covered later in this chapter). When the router is intentionally turned off, or if power is lost, NVRAM enables the router to restart in its proper configuration.

Flash Memory

Flash memory is also nonvolatile. It differs from NVRAM in that it can be erased and re-programmed as needed. Originally developed by Intel, flash memory is in wide use in computers and other devices. In Cisco routers, flash memory is used to store one or more copies of the IOS software. This is an important feature because it enables network managers to stage new versions of IOS on routers throughout an internetwork and then upgrade them all at once to a new version from flash memory.

ROM

ROM stands for read-only memory. It, too, is nonvolatile. Cisco routers use ROM to hold a so-called bootstrap program, which is a file that can be used to boot to a minimum configuration state after a catastrophe. ROM is also referred to as ROMMON. In fact, when you boot from ROM, the first thing you'll see is the rommon> prompt. ROMMON (for ROM monitor) harks back to the early days of the UNIX operating system, which relied on ROMMON to reboot a computer to the point where commands could at least be typed into the system console monitor. In smaller Cisco routers, ROM holds a bare-bones subset of the Cisco IOS software. ROM in some high-end Cisco routers holds a full copy of IOS.

Router Ports and Modules

A router's window to the internetwork is through its ports and modules. Without them, a router is a useless box. The ports and modules that are put into a router define what it can do.

Internetworking can be intimidating, with the seemingly endless combinations of products, protocols, media, feature sets, standards—you name it. The acronyms come so fast and so hard that it might seem hopeless to learn how to properly configure a router. But choosing the right router product can be boiled down to manageable proportions. Table 4-3 lays out five major requirement areas that, if met, will lead you to the best router solution.

Cisco obviously can't manufacture a model of router to match every customer's specific requirements. To make them more flexible to configure, routers come in two major parts:

▼ **The chassis**   The actual box and basic components inside it, such as power supply, fans, rear and front faceplates, indicator lights, and slots

▲ **Ports and modules**   The printed circuit boards that slide into the router box

Cisco's router product-line structure tries to steer you to a product—or at least to a reasonably focused selection of products—meeting all five requirement areas in Table 4-3.

Area		Configuration Requirement
1	Physical	It must be hardware compatible with the physical network segment on which the router will sit.
2	Communication	The router must be compatible with the transport medium that will be used (Frame Relay, ATM, etc.).
3	Protocol	It must be compatible with the protocols used in the internetwork (IP, IPX, SNA, etc.).
4	Mission	The router must provide the speed, reliability, security, and functional features the job requires.
5	Business	It must fit within the purchase budget and network growth plans.

Table 4-3.   Five Major Factors in Selecting a Router

Finding the right router for your needs is basically a three-step process. The following illustrates the process of selecting a router for a large branch office operation:

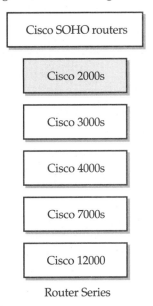

Cisco SOHO routers

Cisco 2000s

Cisco 3000s

Cisco 4000s

Cisco 7000s

Cisco 12000

Router Series

First, Cisco's routers are grouped into product families called series. Choosing a router product series is usually a matter of budget, because each series reflects a price/performance tier. Models within series are generally based on the same chassis, which is the metal frame and basic components (power supply, fans, etc.) around which the router is built. We'll select the Cisco 2000 Series because it fits both the purchase budget and performance requirements for our large branch office.

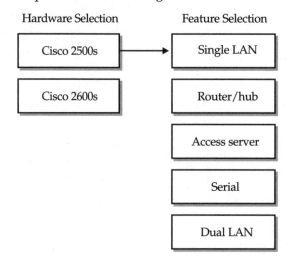

From the 2000 Series, we'll take the Cisco 2500 Series. The 2500 chassis is versatile enough to fit a lot of situations, making it the world's most popular brand of branch office router.

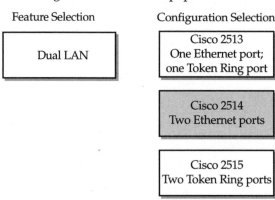

Third, we'll select the Cisco 2514 because it has two Ethernet ports; and our imaginary branch office will operate two subnets, one for the customer service office and another for the front office. The two Ethernet ports will let us separate the two departments, thereby isolating traffic.

NOTE: The term *port* can cause confusion if you're not careful. When speaking of hardware, port means a physical connection through which I/O can pass (a serial port, for example). But there are also so-called ports at the transport layer of network protocols. These "ports" are actually port numbers used to identify what network application packets contain. These ports (port numbers) are also referred to as TCP ports or "listeners," because they inform the receiver what's inside the message. Example TCP-defined port numbers include Port 25 for Simple Mail Transfer Protocol and Port 80 for HTTP. Refer to Chapter 2's section, "The Transport Layer," for more on TCP ports.

Router Packaging

Three major categories of modules can be configured into Cisco routers to support either LAN or WAN connectivity:

▼ **Ethernet modules**   To support any of the many Ethernet LAN variants on the market, including Novell NetWare, Banyan VINES, and AppleTalk.

■ **Token Ring modules**   IBM's LAN technology, which is well established in banks, insurance companies, and other Fortune 1000 corporate environments.

▲ **WAN connectivity modules**   To support a wide variety of WAN protocols, some old and some new. Example WAN technologies include newer protocols such as ISDN; Frame Relay; Asynchronous Transfer Mode (ATM); and legacy protocols, such as SDLC and X.25.

Configuration options depend mainly on the specific Cisco router:

▼ Lower-end routers tend to be "fixed configuration" in that the modules are factory integrated only (preconfigured).

■ Midrange routers, such as the Cisco 4500, are "modular" in that they can accept a variety of modules, often packaging different protocols in the same box. Interface modules are plugged into this class of routers' motherboards.

▲ High-end routers, the Cisco 7000 Series and Cisco 12000 Series, have buses (also called *backplanes*). Bus-based routers accept larger modules—usually referred to as *blades* or *cards*—that are effectively self-contained routers (they have their own CPUs, memory units, etc.).

Figure 4-7 is a view of the back of a Cisco 4500 configured with two Token Ring modules (Ring A and Ring B) and four serial ports. Notice that an empty slot is available on the right. It's a common practice to purchase a router model with room for adding an interface as network traffic grows.

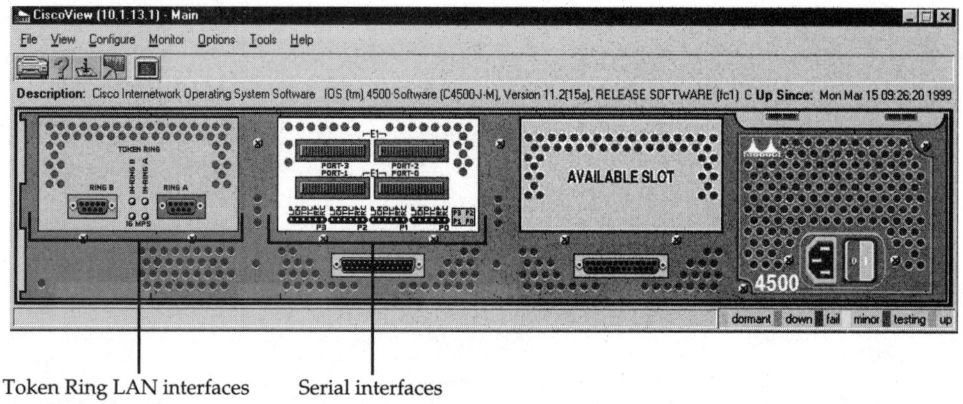

Figure 4-7. Interfaces on a Cisco 4500 router

ESSENTIAL FILES

In contrast to normal computers, Cisco routers have just two main files:

▼   The configuration file

▲   The Cisco IOS (Internetwork Operating System) software

Cisco IOS software contains instructions to the router. IOS acts as the traffic cop directing activity inside the router. IOS manages internal router operations by telling the various hardware components what to do, much like Windows 95 or UNIX with a general-purpose computer. Customers cannot alter the contents of the IOS file.

The configuration file contains instructions to the router input by the customer, not Cisco. It contains information describing the network environment in which the router will run and how the network manager wants it to behave. In a phrase, the configuration file tells it *what* to do; IOS tells the router *how* to do it.

As will be covered in the next chapter, routers also use dynamic files, which are not stored in the router's flash memory, NVRAM, or ROM. Dynamic files instead are built from scratch when a router is booted and are strictly reactive in the sense that they only hold live information, not operational instructions.

IOS: The Internetwork Operating System

We usually don't think of an operating system as a file. After all, your PC's operating system is made up of many thousands of files (they sit in your directory with file extensions such as SYS, EXE, DRV, and DLL).

But IOS is indeed contained in a single file. When you ship an IOS file somewhere, it holds everything necessary to run a router. Depending on the version, an IOS software image will have a footprint from 3MB to over 10MB in size.

> **NOTE:**   Less sophisticated Cisco internetworking devices, such as hubs, get their intelligence in the form of factory-installed software called firmware. *Firmware* is a subset of IOS itself. It can be field up-graded to keep the device's software current with the rest of the network.

IOS needs to be tightly constructed because copies of it, referred to as *system images*, are routinely shipped across internetworks. System images are uploaded and downloaded over routers in order to back up routers, upgrade their capabilities, and restart them after a fail-ure. It wouldn't be practical to send thousands of 50MB files. Being able to send a single, small, self-contained IOS file makes effective network management possible.

IOS Feature Sets

Feature sets are packages that try to simplify configuring and ordering IOS software. There is no single IOS software product, per se. IOS is actually a common software plat-form on which a suite of IOS implementations is based, each packaged to fulfill a specific mission. Cisco calls these IOS packages feature sets (also called *software images* or *feature packs*). When you order a Cisco router, you choose an IOS feature set that contains all the capabilities your particular situation requires. Most of these requirements have to do with maintaining compatibility with the various hardware devices and network proto-cols in the environment in which the router will operate.

As depicted in Figure 4-8, variants of the Cisco IOS software are defined two ways: by feature set and by release. Feature sets define the job a version of IOS can do; releases are used to manage the IOS software through time.

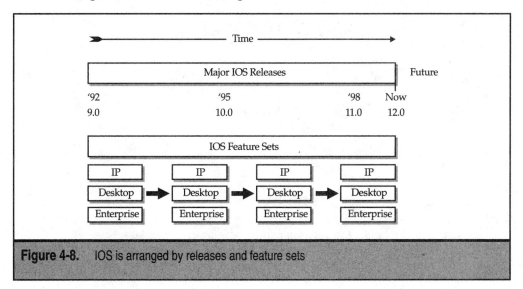

Figure 4-8.   IOS is arranged by releases and feature sets

Cisco IOS feature sets are designed to

▼ Be compatible with certain router platforms

■ Enable interoperability between disparate networking protocols (Novell NetWare, IBM SNA, AppleTalk, etc.)

▲ Provide functional features in the form of network services and applications for such things as network management, security, and multimedia

Packaging and selling IOS software in this way simplifies things for Cisco and customers alike. For the customer, having a single part number to order simplifies figuring out what software to buy. For Cisco, it helps the company's product engineers to figure out what goes where so that their support personnel figure out who has what. Remember, internetworking can get hopelessly complicated because the nature of the business is to enable disparate computer platforms and networking protocols to interoperate and coexist.

HOW FEATURE SETS ARE CONSTRUCTED   Because IOS feature sets have dependencies to the router hardware on which they run, two rules of thumb apply:

▼ You can't run all feature sets on all router platforms.

▲ Sometimes, specific features within a feature set will or will not run, depending on the router platform.

If you look at a Cisco product catalog, understanding Cisco's feature sets can seem tough at first glance. Feature sets do nothing more than put functionality groupings into logical packages that customers can use. All feature sets, in one way or another, derive their functionality from about a dozen categories, listed in Table 4-4.

Don't worry about the examples on the right side of this table, or all the acronyms you don't know. The important thing here is to understand that IOS software's myriad features and functions can be grouped into about a dozen categories.

Cisco IOS feature sets try to combine features into groups most likely to match real-world customer requirements. Cisco offers dozens of point-product feature sets in the form of IOS software product numbers you can put on a purchase order. They are grouped by general characteristics into the four general feature set families shown in Table 4-5. Notice in Tables 4-4 and 4-5 that proprietary computer platforms, such as IBM, DEC, and Apple, and proprietary networking platforms, such as Novell and SNA, drive much of the need for feature sets. Each Cisco router must deal with the customer's real-world compatibility requirements, which means being able to run with legacy hardware and software. Nearly all legacy architectures exist at the "network's edge." Which is to say most of the proprietary equipment with which IP must maintain compatibility sits either on LANs or on computers sitting on the LANs. This is where compatibility issues with proprietary legacy computer architectures or specialized platforms are manifested.

Tables 4-4 and 4-5 also show which software functionality groupings go into what IOS feature set products. For example, multinational enterprises are likely to be interested in IBM functionality, such as NetBUI over PPP and Frame Relay for SNA, and

Category	Examples of Features
LAN support	IP, Novell IPX, AppleTalk, Banyan VINES, DECnet
WAN services	PPP, ATM LAN emulation, Frame Relay, ISDN, X.25
WAN optimization	Dial-on-demand, snapshot routing, traffic shaping
IP routing	BGP, RIP, IGRP, Enhanced IGRP, OSPF, IS-IS, NAT
Other routing	IPX RIP, AURP, NLSP
Multimedia and QoS	Generic traffic shaping, random early detection, RSVP
Management	SNMP, RMON, Cisco Call History MIB, Virtual Profiles
Security	Access lists, extended access lists, lock and key, TACACS+
Switching	Fast-switched policy routing, AppleTalk Routing over ISL
IBM support	APPN, Bisync, Frame Relay for SNA, SDLC integration
Protocol translation	LAT, PPP, X.25
Remote node	PPP, SLIP, MacIP, IP pooling, CSLIP, NetBUI over PPP
Terminal services	LAT, Xremote, Telnet, X.25 PAD

Table 4-4.   IOS Software Feature Categories

would probably be interested in one of the Enterprise/APPN feature sets. By contrast, an advertising agency heavy into Apple and NT would focus on the Desktop feature sets.

Feature Set Family	Target Customer Environments
IP	Basic IP routing
Desktop	IP, Novell NetWare IPX, AppleTalk, DECnet
Enterprise	High-end functionality for LANs, WANs, and management
Enterprise/ APPN	Same as Enterprise, but with many IBM-specific features added

Table 4-5.   IOS Feature Set Families

Grouping feature sets into families is Cisco's way of bringing a semblance of order to pricing policies and upgrade paths. Ordering a single IOS part number instead of dozens helps everybody avoid mistakes. Figure 4-9 depicts the process of feature set selection.

Last, feature sets are further grouped into software product variants:

▼ **Basic** The basic feature set for the hardware platform

■ **Plus** The basic feature set and additional features, which are dependent on the hardware platform selected

▲ **Encryption** The addition of either a 40-bit (Plus 40) or a 56-bit (Plus 56) data encryption feature atop either the Basic or Plus feature set.

The ultimate goal of feature sets is to guide you through the process of ordering, say, IOS Feature Set Enterprise 56 for a Cisco 7500/RSP running Release 11—without making a mistake that costs your network upgrade project a two-week delay.

THE ANATOMY OF CISCO RELEASE NUMBERS Cisco IOS software release numbers have four basic parts, as shown in Figure 4-10.

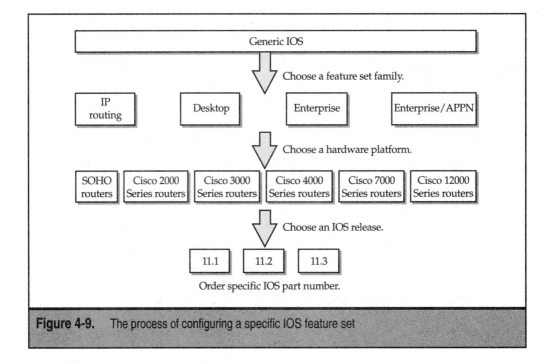

Figure 4-9.   The process of configuring a specific IOS feature set

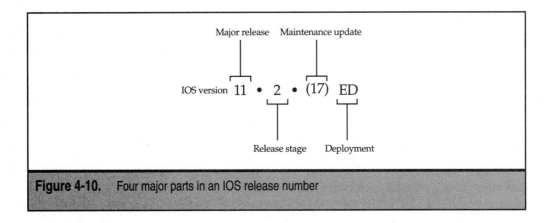

Figure 4-10. Four major parts in an IOS release number

The first part is a major release—the "11" in Figure 4-10—which marks First Customer Shipments (FCS) of an IOS version of stable, high-quality software for customers to use in their production networks. Major releases are further defined by the following:

▼ **Stage**   The "2" in Figure 4-10, which marks FCS of various major release stages (first release, general deployment release, short-lived release, etc.). Stage releases are often referred to in the future tense, when they are still planned but have not yet taken place.

▲ **Maintenance update**   The "(17)" in Figure 4-10, which denotes support for additional platforms of features beyond what was available in the major release's FCS.

The fourth part of the release number is the deployment. A general deployment (GD) release is for unconstrained use by all customers. Early deployment (ED) releases are to deliver new functionality or technologies to customers to deploy in a limited manner in their networks. Limited deployment (LD) denotes a limited life cycle between FCS and GD.

At any given time there can be several major releases in use in the field. For example, during 1999 two versions of IOS 12 are available, but almost everybody is using either 11.2 or 11.3. Most network managers are content to stick with a release they know works for them. Early adopters use advanced IOS releases because they need platform or feature support not before available. Most users are happy to let the early adopters help Cisco shake things out before general release.

NOTE: The terms *version* and *release* are sometimes used interchangeably in connection with editions of IOS software. In this book, version is used to specify a particular release of a particular IOS feature set.

Using TFTP for IOS Backups and Updates

In the event of a network catastrophe, it is possible for a router's IOS system image to be corrupted or erased from flash memory altogether. Standard procedure is to maintain a backup image of every IOS version in use in the network being managed. These backup IOS images are maintained on TFTP servers or within network management applications such as CiscoWorks 2000 (covered in Chapter 9).

TFTP stands for Trivial File Transfer Protocol. TFTP is a TCP/IP application derived from the early days of the UNIX operating system. As you may have guessed, TFTP is a stripped-down version of FTP, the command many of you have used to download files over the Internet. IOS uses TFTP instead of FTP because it's speedier and uses fewer system resources.

So-called TFTP servers are computer platforms on an internetwork that store and download IOS system images and configuration files. It is recommended that more than one TFTP server be used to back up a network. This is in case the TFTP server itself goes down or the network segment connecting it to the devices it backs up becomes unavailable.

To load a new IOS image to a router's flash memory, use the **copy tftp flash** command following the procedure, shown here:

```
Router#copy tftp flash

System flash directory:
File  Length    Name/status
  1   4171336   c4500-j-mz_112-15a.bin
[4171400 bytes used, 22904 available, 4194304 total]
Address or name of remote host [10.1.10.40]? 10.1.10.40
Source file name? c4500-j-mz_112-15a.bin
Destination file name [c4500-j-mz_112-15a.bin]? yes
Accessing file 'c4500-j-mz_112-15a.bin' on 10.1.10.40...
Loading c4500-j-mz_112-15a.bin from 10.1.1.12 (via TokenRing1): [OK]

Erase flash device before writing? [confirm]yes
Flash contains files. Are you sure you want to erase? [confirm]yes

Copy 'c4500-j-mz_112-15a.bin' from server
  as 'yes' into Flash WITH erase? [yes/no]yes
Erasing device... eeeeeeeeeeeeeeee ...erased
Loading c4500-j-mz_112-15a.bin from 10.1.1.12 (via TokenRing1): !
!!!!!!!!!!!!!!!!!!!!!!!!!!!!!!!!!!!!!!!!!!!!!!!!!!!!!!!!!!!!!!!!!!!!!!!!
!!!!!!!!!!!!!!!!!!!!!!!!!!!!!!!!!!!!!!!!!!!!!!!!!!!!!!!!!!!!!!!!!!!!!!!!
!!!!!!!!!!!!!!!!!!!!!!!!!!!!!!!!!!!!!!!!!!!!!!!!!!!!!!!!!!!!!!!!!!!!!!!!
!!!!!!!!!!!!!!!!!!!!!!!!!!!!!!!!!!!!!!!!!!!!!!!!!!!!!!!!!!!!!!!!!!!!!!!!
!!!!!!!!!!!!!!!!!!!!!!!!!!!!!!!!!!!!!!!!!!!!!!!!!!!!!!!!!!!!!!!!!!!!!!!!
!!!!!!!!!!!!!!!!!!!!!!!!!!!!!!!!!!!!!!!!!!!!!!!!!!!!!!!!!!!!!!!!!!!!!!!!
```

```
!!!!!!!!!!!!!!!!!!!!!!!!!!!!!!!!!!!!!!!!!!!!!!!!!!!!!!!!!!!!!!!!!!!!!!!!!!!
!!!!!!!!!!!!!!!!!!!!!!!!!!!!!!!!!!!!!!!!!!!!!!!!!!!!!!!!!!!!!!!!!!!!!!!!!!!
!!!!!!!!!!!!!!!!!!!!!!!!!!!!!!!!!!!!!!!!!!!!!!!!!!!!!!!!!!!!!!!!!!!!!!!!!!!
!!!!!!!!!!!!!!!!!!!!!!!!!!!!!!!!!!!!!!!!!!!!!!!!!!!!!!!!!!!!!!!!!!!!!!!!!!!
[OK - 4171336/4194304 bytes]

Verifying checksum...  OK (0x29D5)
Flash copy took 00:00:30 [hh:mm:ss]
Router#
```

You can see that the TFTP server confirmed that it had the IOS system image before overwriting the one in the router's flash memory. Each exclamation point in the display indicates that a block of the file was successfully copied over the network from the server to the router.

NOTE: If you are copying a file to a TFTP server, be sure the name of the file that you are attempting to transfer already exists in the TFTP directory. Create the file on UNIX systems using the **touch** command. On Microsoft platforms, open Notepad to create the file and save it under the filename.

The Configuration File

Managing a router involves installation, upgrades, backups, recovery, and other event-driven tasks. But the biggest part of router management is the care and feeding of a router's configuration file. The configuration file is the cockpit from which the network administrator runs the router and all the traffic going through it. As will be detailed in the next chapter, configuration files contain access lists, passwords, and other important router management tools.

Viewing the Configuration File

The most common way to examine the status of a router is to view its configuration file. To view most anything in IOS is to ask for a view of the configuration. The main IOS command for viewing such information is the **show** command.

The following example uses the **show running-config** command to view a router's running configuration. There are two types of configuration files. The *running* configuration file is an image running in DRAM (main memory) at a given time. The *backup* configuration file is stored in NVRAM and is used to boot the router.

```
Router#show running-config
Building configuration...
Current configuration:
!
version 11.2
service password-encryption
service udp-small-servers
```

```
service tcp-small-servers
!
hostname Router
!
enable secret 5 $1$C/q2$ZhtujqzQIuJrRGqFwdwn71
enable password 7 0012000F
!
vty-async
!
interface Serial0
 no ip address
 no ip route-cache
 no ip mroute-cache
 shutdown
! interface Serial1
 no ip address
 .
 .
 .
 .
```

In the next chapter we will go into greater depth on what the configuration file does and how to edit it.

Using TFTP for Configuration File Backups and Updates

As with IOS system image backups and updates, TFTP servers are used to back up and update configuration files. For example, the **copy config tftp** command is used to back up the router's running configuration file (named tomtest in this example) to a TFTP server, using the following procedure:

```
Router#copy running-config tftp
Remote host []? 10.1.10.40
Name of configuration file to write [router-confg]? tomtest
Write file tomtest on host 10.1.10.40? [confirm]yes
Building configuration...

Writing tomtest !! [OK]
Router#
```

The other TFTP commands to back up or update configuration files are

▼ **copy tftp running-config**   Configure the router directly by copying from the TFTP directly into the router's DRAM.

■ **copy startup-config tftp**   Back up the startup configuration from the router's NVRAM to the TFTP server.

▲ **copy tftp startup-config**   Update the router's startup configuration file by downloading from the TFTP server and overwriting the one stored in the router's NVRAM.

Note that **tftp** goes *in front of* the file type—**running-config** or **startup-config**—to download (update from the server) and *behind* the file type to upload (back up to the server). Think of the **copy** command as copying *from* somewhere *to* somewhere.

PASSWORD RECOVERY

Sometimes situations occur that make it necessary to recover a router's password. Two of the most common such situations are

▼ A password is forgotten, and a record of it cannot be found.

▲ A router is bought used, and it came with passwords on it.

Password recovery naturally involves somehow getting into the router's configuration file to find the lost password, change it, or erase the entire configuration file and reconfigure the router from scratch.

The trouble is that the configuration file sits inside the Privileged EXEC (enable mode) level of IOS, which itself is password protected. For that reason, recovering a password means getting to the base level of the IOS software. This is why password recovery procedures are so involved.

There are several procedures for recovering passwords from Cisco routers, depending on whether a Line or Enable password was lost, the model of router hardware, and the version of IOS software. All the procedures involve resetting settings that tell the router how to boot. Older Cisco routers use physical hardware jumpers, so you need to go inside the router box to reset them. Newer Cisco routers have "soft jumpers," called the *configuration register,* where settings can be changed. An example configuration register setting is 0x2102. The third character position (the one after the x) is the key:

▼ When 0 is in the first character position after the x, this indicates the router will enter rommon> mode upon reboot.

■ When 1 is in the first character position after the x, this means the router will boot from the IOS system stored in ROM.

▲ When 2 is in the first character position after the x, this indicates the router will look to the configuration file in NVRAM to find which IOS system image to boot from.

Recovering Enable Passwords

Two procedures are used to recover Enable passwords (Enable and Enable Secret). The one to use depends on the router model, and sometimes the CPU or IOS software version the router runs on.

To recover a password, you must somehow get to a base level of IOS: the rommon> prompt to recover Enable or Enable Secret passwords; the test-system> prompt to recover a Line password. This is done by sending a Break signal from the console terminal to the router to interrupt the normal boot process.

> **NOTE:** The router may not respond to the Break signal sent from PC terminal emulators. You must understand how the terminal emulator you're using generates Break signals. In some emulators, Break is generated with the ALT-B key combination; in others, CTRL-B. Check the help documentation for your emulator if you have problems interrupting the router's boot process with Break.

Getting to the rommon> Prompt

The first part of the two procedures to recover Enable/Enable Secret passwords—getting to the rommon> prompt level of IOS—is the same:

1. Attach a terminal, or a PC running terminal emulation software, to the router's console port.

2. Go to the > prompt and type the **show version** command. (Remember, you lost either the Enable or Enable Secret password, which only locks you out of enable mode, not out of the IOS entirely.)

```
TN3270 Emulation software.
2 Token Ring/IEEE 802.5 interface(s)
4 Serial network interface(s)
128K bytes of non-volatile configuration memory.
4096K bytes of processor board System flash (Read/Write)
4096K bytes of processor board Boot flash (Read/Write)

Configuration register is 0x2102
```

The last line of the **show version** display is the configuration register. The factory default setting is usually 0x2102; sometimes it is 0x102. Write down the settings in your router for later use.

3. Reboot the router by turning off the power and then turning it back on.

4. Press the BREAK key on the terminal (or combination of keys required to send Break from your terminal emulator) within 60 seconds of having turned the router back on.

5. The rommon> prompt—without the router's name showing—should appear.

Now that you've gotten to the rommon> prompt, the battle of password recovery is half won. From this point on, what to do is a matter of the model of router from which you need to recover the password (in some cases, the IOS version and CPU also come into play). Look at Tables 4-6 and 4-7 to determine which procedure to follow, and pick up step 6 from there.

Recovery Procedure	Platforms Using Procedure 1
Enable Password Recovery Procedure 1	Cisco 2000 Series Cisco 2500 Series Cisco 3500 Series Cisco 4000 Series with Motorola 680x0 CPU Cisco 7000 Series running IOS Release 10.0 or later in ROMs installed on the RSP card IGS series running IOS Release 9.1 or later in ROMs

Table 4-6. Platforms Using Enable Password Recovery Procedure 1

ENABLE PASSWORD RECOVERY PROCEDURE 1   Use this procedure for routers that belong to the Cisco router series listed in Table 4-6 (and its CPU and/or IOS release, if applicable).

At the rommon> prompt, enter o/r0x42 to boot from flash memory or o/r0x41 to boot from ROM.

6. Boot from flash if you can—that way you have the option to change the password. If flash memory has been erased, you must boot from ROM, and you can only view the configuration.

7. Still at the rommon> prompt, enter the **reload** command to reboot the router. This command makes the router reboot from the image in flash memory and ignore the saved configuration file (and the passwords it holds).

8. At the system configuration display, answer **no** to each prompt in the System Configuration dialog box until you reach the "Press Return to get started!" prompt.

9. Press ENTER at the "Press Return to get started!" prompt. The Router> prompt will then appear ("Router" is a default name that IOS assigns to routers during initialization).

10. Enter the **enable** command at the prompt. The Router# prompt will then appear. This step is, of course, taken to enter Privileged EXEC (enable mode) of the IOS software, just as you would during a normal IOS session.

11. If you are recovering an Enable password, enter the **more nvram:startup-config** command to view the password and thereby recover it. If the lost password is an Enable Secret password, it will be displayed in encrypted format, so you must create a new one using the **configure memory** and **write memory** commands.

ENABLE PASSWORD RECOVERY PROCEDURE 2   Use this procedure for routers that belong to the Cisco router listed in Table 4-7 (and its CPU, if applicable).

12. Enter the **confreg** command at the rommon> prompt. (Note that **confreg** is not a typographical error where **config** is actually meant, but **confreg** stands for *configuration register*). When the "do you wish to change configuration?" prompt appears, answer **yes**.

13. Answer **no** to each of the prompts until the "ignore system config info?" prompt appears; then answer **yes**.

14. Answer **no** to all prompts until the "change boot characteristics?" prompt appears; then answer **no**. The "enter to boot" prompt will then appear.

15. If flash memory is still good (if it hasn't been erased), enter the number 2 in order to boot from the configuration file in flash memory. If flash memory is erased, enter the number 1 in order to boot from the raw IOS software image stored in ROM.

Boot from flash if you can. That way you have the option to change the password. If flash memory has been erased, you must boot from ROM, and you can only view the configuration. When the "do you wish to change configuration?" prompt appears, answer **no**.

NOTE: If flash is erased and the router is a Cisco 4500, it must be returned to Cisco in order to recover the password.

Recovery Procedure	Platforms Using Procedure 2
Enable Password Recovery Technique 2	Cisco 1003 Series Cisco 1600 Series Cisco 3600 Series Cisco 4500 Series Cisco 7500 Series AS-5200 and AS 5300 platforms IDT running Orion-based routers

Table 4-7.   Platforms Using Enable Password Recovery Procedure 2

16. Enter the **reload** command to reboot. If the router is a Cisco 4500 or Cisco 7500, instead of entering this command, reboot by turning the router off and on again (a step sometimes called *power-cycle* in Cisco product documentation).

17. Answer **no** to all prompts during the boot sequence.

18. Once you arrive at the Router> prompt, enter the **enable** command to enter Privileged EXEC (enable mode).

19. Once at the Router> prompt, follow one of these three procedures:

    ■ If the password is not encrypted (if it is an Enable password), view it by entering the **more nvram:startup-config** command.

    ■ If the password is encrypted, create a new one using the **configure memory** and **write memory** commands.

    ■ To erase the entire configuration file and start over, enter the **write erase** command.

20. Enter the **config term** (configure terminal) command at the Router# prompt.

21. Enter the **config-register** (configure the configuration register) command, and type in the settings you recorded after having used **show version** at step 2. This tells the router to boot normally—from NVRAM, as it did before being reset for the password recovery procedure.

22. Press CTRL-Z to leave the configuration editor you entered in step 18. The Router# prompt will reappear.

23. Enter the **write memory** command to save the new configuration to NVRAM.

Recovering a Line Password

The router must be forced into factory diagnostic mode in order to recover a lost Line password. Refer to the hardware installation/maintenance publication for the router product for specific information on configuring the processor configuration register for factory diagnostic mode. Table 4-8 summarizes the hardware or software settings required by the various products to boot into factory diagnostic mode.

Once the router has been forced into factory diagnostic mode, follow these steps:

1. Answer **yes** when asked if you want to set the manufacturer's addresses. The test-system> prompt appears.

2. Enter the **enable** command to get the test-system> enable prompt.

3. Type **config term**, then **show startup-config**. You're now looking at the system configuration file. Find the password and write it down. Do not attempt to change the password.

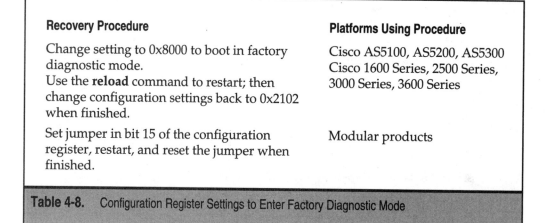

Recovery Procedure	Platforms Using Procedure
Change setting to 0x8000 to boot in factory diagnostic mode. Use the **reload** command to restart; then change configuration settings back to 0x2102 when finished.	Cisco AS5100, AS5200, AS5300 Cisco 1600 Series, 2500 Series, 3000 Series, 3600 Series
Set jumper in bit 15 of the configuration register, restart, and reset the jumper when finished.	Modular products

Table 4-8. Configuration Register Settings to Enter Factory Diagnostic Mode

4. Restart the router.

5. Use the recovered Line password (the one you wrote down) to log into the router.

Recovering Passwords from Older Cisco Routers

To recover passwords from legacy Cisco routers—and there are millions of them still out there, installed and running—it is necessary to change the configuration register setting using a hardware jumper switch. Those procedures are not covered here. Refer to http://www.cisco.com to find password recovery procedures for legacy products listed in Table 4-9.

Recovery Procedure	Legacy Cisco Platforms Using Procedures
Technique 3	IG routers running software earlier than Cisco IOS 9.1
Technique 4	CGS, MGS, AGS, AGS+, and any Cisco 70x0 Series running ROMs earlier than Cisco IOS 10.0
Technique 5	500-CS Communication Servers
Technique 6	Cisco 1020

Table 4-9. Cisco's Password Recovery Procedures for Legacy Router Products

CHAPTER 5

Configuring Routers

The router is the centerpiece of internetworking. It's the device that stitches networks together into internetworks and makes them useful. So if you can learn how to manage routers properly, you can pretty much manage an internetwork. The network administrator's single point of control over router behavior is the configuration file, called the *config file* for short. The config file is one of only two permanent files on a router. The other is the IOS software, which is general in nature and cannot be altered by customers. The config file, then, is the network administrator's single point of control over the network. It's at the center of the router operations, with IOS referring to it hundreds of times per second in order to tell the router how to do its job.

Although the config file is the key tool, at first it can seem hard to understand. This is because the config file is unlike the kinds of files most of us are used to. You can't put a cursor inside one and edit it in real time like you would, say, a word processor document. You can't compile it and debug it the way computer programmers turn source code into executable code. Config files are modified by entering IOS commands and then viewing the new configuration to see if you achieved the desired results.

THE CONFIGURATION FILE'S CENTRAL ROLE

Most network problems are caused by configuration problems, not by glitches in hardware or errors in telecommunications circuits. This is not surprising if you think about it. The config file is where all the network administrator's input goes and, by implication, where human error is most likely to be manifested. As we saw in the previous chapter, a router in and of itself is a sophisticated device. But put one on an internetwork—where a router interacts with other routers—and you understand how the average router's config file is rife with interdependencies. Every router added to an internetwork increases complexity exponentially. If follows, then, that each time you make a change to a config file, the complexity becomes that much harder to track.

And configuration mistakes don't necessarily make themselves immediately apparent in the form of operational problems. Many problems are harder to see (and thus harder to avoid) because they remain latent—lying in config files across a network waiting to rear their ugly heads at the worst possible moment.

So when internetworking people talk about "configuring" a router, the subject isn't what parts to put into the box. They're talking about making a change to a router's behavior and considering everything that might flow from that change. Internetworks, by their very nature, tend to magnify things by passing them down the line. This is why network administrators put a lot of thought and planning into what might seem inconsequential to the uninitiated. Network administrators spend most of their time either changing or reviewing config files because that's where the action is.

Further magnifying the importance of config file design is the fact that the average config file controls more than one router. By and large, network management isn't performed one router at a time. Config files are generally maintained for groups of routers *en masse.* Mass distribution of config files is done as much for design control as for convenience. It's a way of assuring consistency that internetworks need to run smoothly.

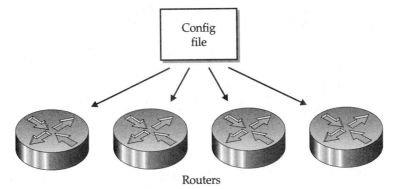

Routers

Network designers typically divide router populations into subgroups—or classes—with common characteristics having to do with network areas, equipment software version levels, or security requirements. Therefore, it makes sense to implement network policy changes, upgrades, tests, and so on en masse in config file downloads and uploads. A router's config file is usually dealt with individually only when there is a problem with that particular machine.

Three Types of Cisco Router Files

Three types of files are used to run a Cisco router: the two permanent files—the IOS image and config file—and files created and maintained by the router itself. It's important to have an idea about how they fit together.

Like any operating system, IOS is dedicated to running the machine on which it sits. But it differs from other operating systems in that its predominant focus is moving transient packets in and out of the box. Where other kinds of operating systems are concerned with interacting with users, crunching numbers, printing output, and the like, IOS is almost solely concerned with forwarding packets unchanged to their next destination. It cares about supporting a user interface only insofar as one is necessary to let network administrators perform housekeeping chores.

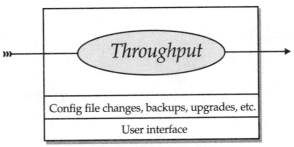

Priorities of IOS Operations

The config file is where management instructions are put to tell IOS how to properly function in the internetwork. The config file defines the network interface hardware in the router box, the protocols to support, what packets get through, and so on. In short, the config file is where network administrators store all their work. Once you learn to work well with config files, you've mastered the basics of internetwork management.

Config file	External (network behavior)
IOS	Internal

But the router creates a number of files on its own. These files—as a class sometimes called *dynamic files*—come into existence only after the router is turned on. Turn the router off and the dynamic files disappear (only the IOS image and config file are permanently stored).

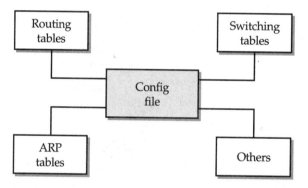

Dynamic files are created and maintained by the router in order to adapt on a moment-by-moment basis, which is why it wouldn't be practical for a person to keep them updated. But while network administrators cannot put instructions into dynamic files, they can control behavior of dynamic files indirectly by setting parameters in the config file. Also, administrators frequently examine dynamic file contents in order to troubleshoot network problems. The ins and outs of how the various dynamic files work will be covered in later chapters. For now, just remember the following:

▼ You cannot put things directly into dynamic files.

■ The contents of dynamic files change minute by minute in response to trends in network traffic—that's why they're called "dynamic."

▲ Control over dynamic files is indirect, through parameters set in the config file.

IOS	Config file	Dynamic files
Releases, feature sets	Operational instructions	Temporary info

Taken together, IOS, the config file, and dynamic files make up the router's operational environment. The config file is the focal point of control over routers and, by implication, control over whole networks. IOS is left to the Cisco software engineers; you control it only by loading new versions every year or so. Dynamic files you control only indirectly. Thus, all network management changes go into the config file.

Given that you cannot edit config files directly, the process of administering Cisco routers tends to be more indirect than what most of us are accustomed to. Figure 5-1 depicts the typical process of modifying a config file.

To some, the combination of a character-based user interface and the indirect management process routers involve seems complicated. But internetworking is simpler than it seems. Understanding these basic facts will help the beginner get started in analyzing and troubleshooting network problems:

▼ IOS is your interface; you use IOS commands to interact with the router.

■ The config file and the various dynamic files hold the information you need to analyze network problems.

■ The config file tells you how a router is set up, dynamic files show how the setup is working in the network environment.

■ The config file is your single point of control.

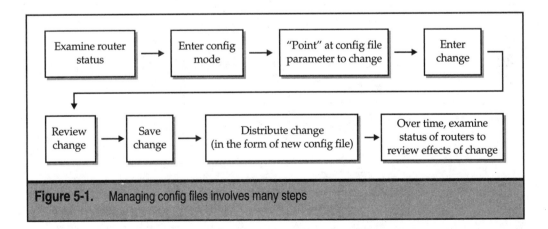

Figure 5-1. Managing config files involves many steps

▲ You can't directly edit the config file; you change it through IOS commands and then review the results.

Now that you know your way around a router, it's time for some hands-on work. If you have access to a Cisco router, log in and follow along.

GETTING STARTED WITH CISCO ROUTERS

To configure and manage Cisco routers, you need to be able to interact with them through some kind of connection. First, you must somehow communicate with a router, either by logging into it or by downloading and uploading files to and from it. Once you're successfully hooked up to a router, you must then be able to speak its language, which in Cisco routers is IOS commands.

Communicating with IOS

You can gain access to a router either directly through the console or AUX ports, or via a network using either the Telnet or HTTP protocol. Network pros generally use Telnet for convenience. Whatever method is used, you need to get into the IOS environment in order to review files and enter commands. Telnet is distributed with all Microsoft Windows operating systems. You can run it by clicking the Start button (in the Microsoft Windows desktop), then Run; then enter **telnet** at the command prompt, and a blank Telnet screen will appear. Click on Connect at the far left of the menu bar, and then enter the IP address of the router you want to log into under the Remote System option. This brings you to the Line password prompt of the target router.

Notice in Figure 5-2 that either remote or local hosts can be accessed. The IP address highlighted in Figure 5-2 is for a router on the local area network (LAN) in the same office

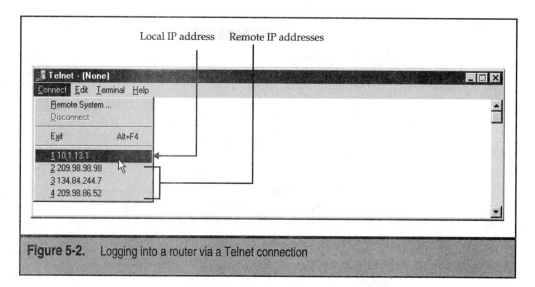

Figure 5-2. Logging into a router via a Telnet connection

as our imaginary network administrator. One of the remote IP addresses would be used if the router were located at a remote site (that is, beyond the LAN). But even if you are on the same network with the router, a valid password must be entered in order to gain entry into the router.

Just in case you ever encounter it, Figure 5-3 shows an error condition that commonly befuddles beginners typing in their first IOS commands.

What's happening in Figure 5-3 is this: when you enter text that IOS cannot interpret as a command, it assumes that it's a symbolic name for an IP address. IOS has no choice in the matter. After all, one purpose of a router is to communicate with other routers, and no single router has all existing addresses on file. Here, the router attempts to send the symbolic address name to all addresses within its broadcast domain. Broadcasts are always addressed 255.255.255.255 (as you no doubt remember from Chapter 2). After ten seconds or so, the router gives up, displays an error message, and returns to the prompt.

NOTE: If you enter a bad command into most computer operating systems, you get an error message. Give IOS a bad command and it assumes the input is a network address and tries to Telnet to it. Normal operating systems know all possible input values that can go into them, but IOS doesn't have that luxury. It deals in network addresses, and routers never assume they know all possible addresses because networks change constantly.

Using IOS Commands

Any computer software environment has its quirks, and IOS is no exception. On one hand, IOS is a purpose-built operating system that has been stripped of all but the bare essentials in order to keep things simple and fast. That's a good thing, but you won't see the plush conveniences that a Mac, X-Windows (UNIX), or Microsoft Windows graphical

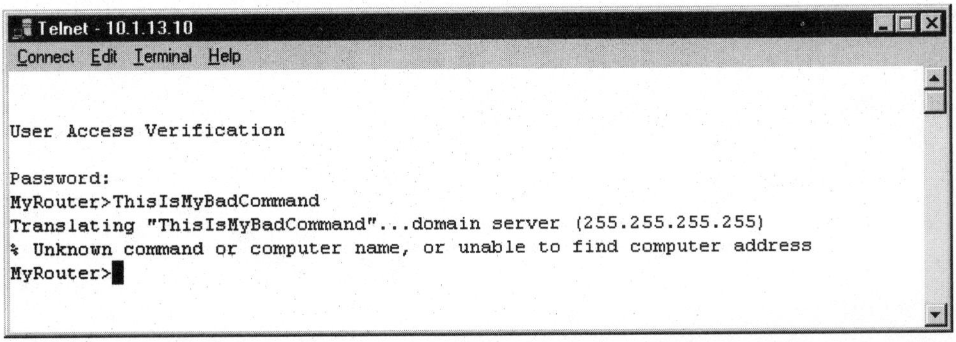

```
 Telnet - 10.1.13.10                                              _ □ ×
Connect   Edit   Terminal   Help


User Access Verification

Password:
MyRouter>ThisIsMyBadCommand
Translating "ThisIsMyBadCommand"...domain server (255.255.255.255)
% Unknown command or computer name, or unable to find computer address
MyRouter>█
```

Figure 5-3.   Entering a bad command results in inadvertent broadcast message

user interface (GUI) offers. On the other hand, IOS is one of the world's most widely distributed and important operating systems; so everything you need to operate is inside if you look.

The IOS Command Hierarchy

IOS has hundreds of commands. Some can be used anywhere in IOS, others only within a specific area. Even Cisco gurus haven't memorized all IOS commands. So, like any good operating system, IOS arranges its commands into a hierarchy. Figure 5-4 is an overview of how IOS commands are structured.

The first division within IOS is between the user EXEC and privileged EXEC levels of IOS. User EXEC, of course, contains only a subset of privileged EXEC's commands. The less powerful user EXEC mode is where **connect**, **login**, **ping**, **show**, and other innocuous commands reside. These are in privileged EXEC too. But privileged mode is where the more powerful, and potentially destructive, commands **configure**, **debug**, **erase**, **setup**, and others are exclusively available.

Depending on the IOS feature set installed, there are about twice as many commands in privileged EXEC as in user EXEC. The commands in user EXEC mode tend to be "flat."

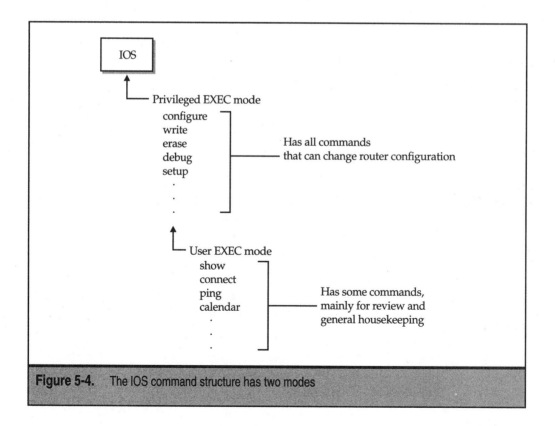

Figure 5-4.   The IOS command structure has two modes

In other words, they don't have branches leading to subset commands underneath, as the following example shows:

```
Router>connect ?
WORD  IP address or hostname of a remote system
  <cr>
```

As a rule, user EXEC mode commands go at most just two levels deep. Being more powerful, privileged EXEC mode commands can go deeper, as the following example sequence shows:

```
MyRouter#show ip ?
  access-lists        List IP access lists
  accounting          The active IP accounting database
  aliases             IP alias table
  arp                 IP ARP table
  .
  .
  .
```

The **ip** root command has many available arguments (subcommands):

```
MyRouter#show ip arp ?
H.H.H                 48-bit hardware address of ARP entry
Hostname or A.B.C.D   IP address or hostname of ARP entry
  Null                Null interface
  Serial              Serial
  TokenRing           IEEE 802.5
  <cr>
```

And arguments can be modified by other arguments still deeper in the root command's "subcommand" tree:

```
My Router#show ip arp serial ?
  <0-3>  Serial interface number
  <cr>
```

The end of the branch is announced with the <cr> symbol, which is IOS telling the user to enter the completed command with a carriage return. For example, after you've pieced together a full command from the preceding options—**ip access-lists serial2**, for example—you would enter a carriage return after the "2" for serial line number two.

Piecing together straightforward command lines is one thing. The real trick is knowing where to find arguments to root commands so you can put together complete and correct command lines. This is where the IOS help system comes into play.

Traversing IOS with the Help System

IOS has a built-in context-sensitive help system. *Context-sensitive* means the help system responds with information based on where you are in the system at the time. You can get the broadest kind of context-sensitive help by simply entering a question mark at the prompt. Here, for example, is a listing of all the root commands available in the user EXEC level of IOS:

```
Router>?
Exec commands:
  <1-99>          Session number to resume
  access-enable   Create a temporary Access-List entry
  atmsig          Execute Atm Signalling Commands
  clear           Reset functions
  connect         Open a terminal connection
  disable         Turn off privileged commands
  disconnect      Disconnect an existing network connection
  enable          Turn on privileged commands
  exit            Exit from the EXEC
  help            Description of the interactive help system
  lat             Open a lat connection
  lock            Lock the terminal
  login           Log in as a particular user
  logout          Exit from the EXEC
  .
  .
  .
```

You can also get what some call "word help" by entering part of a command you don't know followed immediately by a question mark:

```
Router>sh?
show
```

Word help is a great way to get definitions and is especially handy for figuring out what truncated commands are, as with *show* in the preceding example. Another way to get help on a partial command is to simply enter it, whereupon the system will come back with an instruction on how to obtain complete help on the command:

```
Router>sh
% Type "show ?" for a list of subcommands
```

Notice that in help's suggested command **show ?** there is a space between the command and the question mark. As you've by now noticed, there is always a space between a command and its modifier (called an *argument*). Doing this in a help request is the way to ask for a list of arguments available for the command. In the following example, the question mark asks for all arguments available for the **show** command:

```
Router>show ?
  bootflash    Boot Flash information
  calendar     Display the hardware calendar
  clock        Display the system clock
  context      Show context information
  dialer       Dialer parameters and statistics
  history      Display the session command history
  hosts        IP domain-name, lookup style, nameservers, and host table
  kerberos     Show Kerberos Values
  location     Display the system location
  .
  .
  .
```

Sometimes using help in this way is called *command-syntax* help, because it helps you properly complete a multipart command. Command-syntax help is a powerful learning tool because it lists keywords or arguments available to you at nearly any point in IOS command operations. Remember, the space must be inserted between the command and the question mark in order to use command-syntax help.

In IOS, help plays a more integral role than help systems in normal PC or business application software packages. Those help systems, also context sensitive, are essentially online manuals that try to help you learn a whole subsection of the application. IOS help is terse: it just wants to get you through the next command line. That's refreshing. Most help systems nowadays seem to assume that you're anxious to spend hours reading all about an entire subsystem when, in fact, you just want to know what to do next.

> **NOTE:** Don't be confused by the **show** command's name. **show** displays running system information. It is not an all-purpose command to "show" help information; the **?** command does that. The **show** command is used to examine router status.

Command Syntax

There's more to operating IOS commands than simply "walking rightward" through the root command's subcommand tree. To run IOS, you must learn how to combine different commands, not just modify a single command, in order to form the command lines it takes to do the heavy lifting network administration requires. But IOS isn't rocket science, as the following example sequence demonstrates:

```
MyRouter#config
Configuring from terminal, memory, or network [terminal]?
```

In the preceding prompt, we're entering config mode, and IOS wants to know if the configuration will be delivered via network download, copied from an image stored in the router's NVRAM memory, or typed in from the terminal. We just as easily could have bypassed the prompt by concatenating the two commands into one command line:

```
MyRouter#config terminal
```

Don't let this throw you: we're not configuring a terminal as IOS's phrasing seems to imply. In IOS command shorthand, **config terminal** means we're "configuring from a terminal." The next step is to "point" at the thing to be configured. We'll configure an interface:

```
MyRouter(config)#interface
% Incomplete command.
```

But instead of asking, "What interface would you like to configure?," IOS cruelly barks back that our command is no good. This is where some user know-how is required:

```
MyRouter(config)#interface tokenring1
MyRouter(config-if)#
```

IOS wanted to know what physical interface module was to be configured. Told that port number one of the Token Ring interface module was the one to be configured, the IOS prompt changes to MyRouter(config-if)#, where the **if** is shorthand for "interface." (Configuration modes will be covered later in this chapter.)

NOTE: Always keep track of the device you're pointing at when configuring. The IOS config prompt is generic and doesn't tell you at which network interface the (config-if)# prompt is pointed. IOS does not insert the interface's name into the prompt.

Once pointed at the network interface to be configured, from there router configuration is simply a matter of supplying IOS the configuration parameters for that interface, which we'll cover in a few pages.

An understanding of how IOS syntax works, combined with the help system, is enough for anyone to begin entering correct command lines—with some time and hard work, of course.

Command Completion

Sooner or later you'll encounter IOS command lines filled with seemingly cryptic symbols. Don't be intimidated by them; they are only commands that expert users have truncated (cut off at the end) to speed the process of typing commands—and maybe to impress people a bit. IOS is like DOS and most other editors in that it will accept truncated commands. But if the truncated command is not a string of letters unique to the command set, it will generate an error message. For example, if you type the first two letters of a command that another command starts with, you'll get an error message, such as

```
Router#te
% Ambiguous command:  "te"
```

This error is displayed because IOS has three commands beginning with the letter string *te*: **telnet, terminal**, and **test**. If the intent was to Telnet somewhere, one more character will do the job:

```
Router>tel
Host:
```

> **NOTE:**   If you run across a truncated command you don't understand, simply look it up by using word help in the online help system. Type in the truncated command followed immediately by a question mark. Unlike command-syntax help, when using word help no space should precede the **?** command.

Recalling Command History

IOS keeps a running record of recently entered commands. Being able to recall commands is useful for

▼   Avoiding having to type commands that are entered repeatedly

▲   Avoiding having to remember long, complicated command lines

The history utility will record anything you enter, even bad commands. The only limit is the amount of buffer memory you dedicate to keeping the history. Here's an example:

```
Router#show history
   test
   tel
   exit
   enable
```

More recently entered commands are toward the top of **show history** lists. They are not listed in alphabetical order.

Arrow keys can also be used to display prior commands. Using arrow keys saves having to enter the **show history** command, but only shows prior commands one at a time. Press the UP ARROW (or CTRL-P) to recall the most recent commands first. If you're already somewhere in the sequence of prior commands, press the DOWN ARROW (or CTRL-N) to recall the least recent commands first.

Overview of Router Modes

Cisco routers can be in any one of seven possible operating modes, illustrated in Figure 5-5. Three of them are startup modes. In the other four, network administrators are in either user EXEC mode or privileged EXEC (enable) mode. You must go through the password prompt in user EXEC to enter privileged EXEC. Once inside privileged EXEC, configuration changes can be made either to the entire device or to a specific network interface.

You must keep track of what router mode you are in at all times. Many IOS commands will execute only from a specific mode. As can be seen in Figure 5-5, router modes get more specific—and powerful—as the user traverses toward the center of IOS. It pays to keep an eye on IOS prompts because they'll always tell you which mode you're in.

Three Types of Operating Modes

Cisco router operating modes exist to handle three general conditions:

▼ Boot a system.

■ Define what commands can be used.

▲ Specify which part(s) of the router will be affected by changes made to the config file.

Table 5-1 outlines the various IOS modes and what they are used for. As you become more familiar with Cisco internetworking in general, and the IOS software in particular, you will see that most of the action takes place inside the various configuration modes.

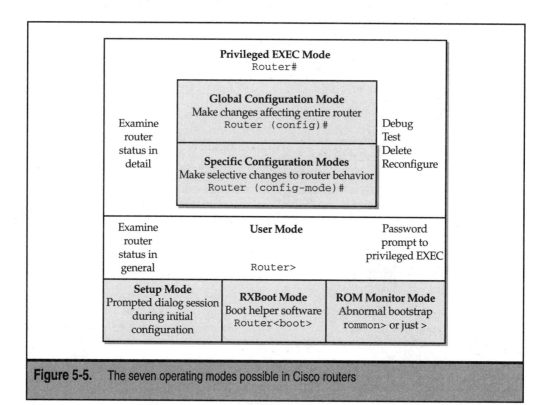

Figure 5-5. The seven operating modes possible in Cisco routers

Mode Type	Purpose
Boot	*Setup mode* is used to make a basic working configuration file.
	RXBoot mode assists router boot to rudimentary state when a working IOS image can't be found in Flash memory.
	ROM monitor mode is used by the router if the IOS image can't be found or the normal boot sequence was interrupted.
User	*User EXEC mode* is the first "room" one enters after login; it restricts users to examining router status.
	Privileged EXEC mode is entered using an Enable password; it allows users to change the config file, erase memory, etc.
Configuration	*Global config mode* changes parameters for all interfaces.
	Config-command mode "targets" changes at specific interfaces.

Table 5-1.   Three General Kinds of IOS Software Modes

Configuration Modes

Configuration modes differ from user modes by nature. The two EXEC "user modes" define what level of IOS commands you may use. By contrast, configuration modes are used to target specific network interfaces—physical or virtual—to which a configuration change applies. For example, you would go into configure interface mode—identified by the **(config-if)#** prompt—in order to configure a specific Ethernet interface module. There are eight configuration modes in all, each targeting different parts of the configuration file, as enumerated in Table 5-2.

A look at Table 5-2 tells you that configuration mode is all about instructing IOS what to do with packets flowing through the device. Some modes apply to packets flowing through specific connection points such as interfaces, lines, and ports. The other IOS configuration modes deal with routing protocols and tables needed to handle that flow.

The Two Types of Config Files

There are two types of config files for every router:

▼ Running-config file

▲ Startup-config file

As their names imply, the basic difference is that the running-config file is "live" in the sense that its image is in RAM. Any changes made to the running-config file go into

Configuration Mode	Router Port Targeted	Applies To
Global	Router(config)#	Entire config file
Interface	Router(config-if)#	Interface module (physical)
Subinterface	Router(config-subif)#	Subinterface (virtual)
Controller	Router(config-controller)#	Controller (physical)
Line	Router(config-line)#	Terminal lines (virtual)
Router	Router(config-router)#	IP routing (protocol)
IPX-Router	Router(config-ipx-router)#	IPX routing (protocol)
Route-Map	Router(config-route-map)#	Routing tables

Table 5-2.   Each Config Mode Targets a Part of the Router

effect immediately. The startup-config file is stored in the router's NVRAM, where the IOS bootstrap program goes to fetch the router's running configuration parameters when starting up.

The **copy** command is used to save and distribute config file changes. As can be seen at the bottom of Figure 5-6, a master config file can be distributed to other routers via a TFTP server.

ESSENTIAL ROUTER COMMANDS

A few major root commands handle most tasks associated with configuring routers:

▼ **show**   Examine router status.

■ **configure**   Make changes to config file parameters.

■ **no**   Negate a parameter setting.

▲ **copy**   Put config file changes into effect.

The **show** command is the bread-and-butter command of IOS. It's used to examine nearly everything about a router. The following example shows who's logged into the router, which is moment-to-moment information:

```
Router>show users
    Line      User      Host(s)           Idle Location
*   2 vty 0             idle                 00:00:00
```

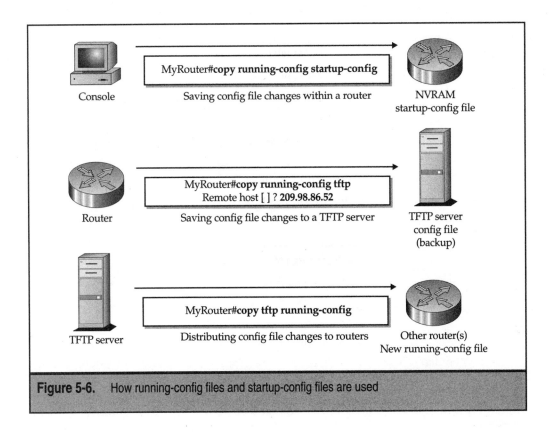

Figure 5-6.   How running-config files and startup-config files are used

The **show** command can also be used to show information that might change once every year or so, such as the version of IOS software installed:

```
MyRouter>show version
Cisco Internetwork Operating System Software
IOS (tm) 4500 Software (C4500-J-M), Version 11.2(15a), RELEASE
 SOFTWARE (fc1)
Copyright (c) 1986-1998 by cisco Systems, Inc.
Compiled Mon 24-Aug-98 01:47 by tmullins
Image text-base: 0x600088A0, data-base: 0x607C4000

ROM: System Bootstrap, Version 5.2(7b) [mkamson 7b], RELEASE SOFTWARE
 (fc1)
BOOTFLASH: 4500 Bootstrap Software (C4500-BOOT-M), Version 10.3(7)
 .
 .
 .
```

Command	Purpose
Enable	Move from user EXEC to privileged EXEC mode.
Disable	Return to user EXEC mode from privileged EXEC mode.
Exit	Terminate a login session.
CTRL-A	Move to the start of a command line.
CTRL-B	Move backward one character position.
CTRL-F	Move forward one character position.
CTRL-Z	Quit a process (such as a login or a multipage display.
ESC-B	Move to the beginning of the prior word (good for making corrections).
ESC-F	Move to the beginning of the next word.

Table 5-3. IOS Navigation Commands

The **no** command is used to reverse an existing parameter setting. For example, if we turned on IP accounting for Token Ring port number one and now want to turn it off, we point to that interface in configure interface mode—indicated by the MyRouter(config-if)> prompt—and then simply precede the command used to turn it on (**ip accounting**) with the **no** command, as shown here:

```
MyRouter(config-if)#no ip accounting
```

Any IOS command can be turned off using the **no** command syntax.

Knowing how to navigate within an operating system environment is always half the battle. This is especially so in command-line interfaces because there are no graphical icons to show the way. Table 5-3 lists commands used to move around within the IOS environment.

"Hot key" commands are useful because some config file command lines can get long and complicated.

STEP-BY-STEP ROUTER CONFIGURATION

A router can be configured by

▼ Entering changes directly to a router's running-config file

■ Downloading a new config file from a TFTP server

▲ Setting up the config file from scratch

The best way to learn how to configure a router is to set one up from scratch. We'll step through setup mode here, not because the procedure is performed that often, but because it's an excellent way to review the fundamentals of router configuration.

Setup Mode

Setup is run to get the router up to a basic level of operation. If the device is new (and therefore has never been configured) or the config file in NVRAM has been corrupted, the IOS software defaults into setup mode to rebuild the config file from scratch. Once that's accomplished, setup mode can be exited and the router rebooted in normal IOS mode, whereupon a complete config file can be built. Setup mode doesn't run by itself; a network administrator must be present to respond to setup's long sequence of questions about how to configure the router. Also, given that the router isn't configured, you cannot run setup via a network connection. Setup must be run through either the console or AUX port.

A router doesn't have to be new or corrupted to run setup. Setup can also be useful in nonemergency situations. Network administrators sometimes use setup when a config file has become so jumbled that it makes more sense to start anew—sort of like a blank sheet of paper. Used in this way, the parameter settings given as answers during a setup session overwrite the existing config file.

Setup mode is entered using the **setup** command. But before starting, hook your PC's COM port to the router's console port. Then start whatever terminal emulator software you prefer to use (remember, you'll be logged into the router's operating system, not your PC). The following instructions assume you're running on a Microsoft Windows PC. If you're not, you'll need to know how to start your terminal emulator. This shouldn't be a problem, because if you're running Apple, you're a survivor; if you're running X-Windows from a UNIX computer, you don't need our advice on such a trifling technical issue in the first place:

1. Click the Start button.

2. Select Programs, then Accessories, then HyperTerminal.

3. A HyperTerminal window will open, with the a blinking cursor in the upper-left corner.

4. Press ENTER, and you should be looking at the router's prompt.

5. Go into privileged EXEC mode by entering **enable** and then the enable secret password (**setup** is essentially a configuration command, and config files cannot be modified from the user EXEC level of IOS).

6. Type **setup**, and setup mode is started.

Once setup is started, a banner appears with command instructions, an option to quit, and an option to review a summary of the interface modules on the router. Figure 5-7 shows the System Configuration Dialog banner.

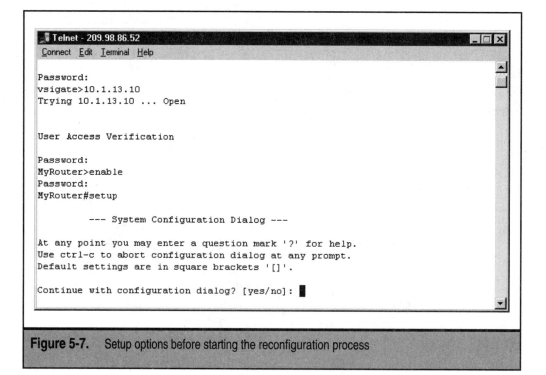

Figure 5-7. Setup options before starting the reconfiguration process

If you decide to proceed, setup starts by configuring global parameters. This is basic information, such as giving the router a name and passwords. If it's a new router or the config file in NVRAM has been corrupted, you must enter new parameters for these things.

```
Configuring global parameters:

  Enter host name [MyRouter]: MyRouter

The enable secret is a one-way cryptographic secret used
instead of the enable password when it exists.

  Enter enable secret [<Use current secret>]: test

The enable password is used when there is no enable secret
and when using older software and some boot images.

  Enter enable password [02101752]: test1
  Enter virtual terminal password [02101752]: test1
```

Once the fundamentals are covered, setup takes you through a list of protocols that you might want to globally configure. This gives a picture of the protocols supported in the IOS feature set on our example router. But if, for example, this router had an image of the Enterprise/APPN IOS feature set in its Flash memory, setup would present a list including many IBM SNA protocols at this point.

Several prompts ask whether you want to configure legacy protocols. For example, LAT (local area terminal) is an old-time protocol for wiring terminals into a DECnet LAN using terminal servers. In today's world, the protocols you're most likely to use are IP, Novell IPX, AppleTalk, and VINES, in about that order.

```
Configure LAT? [no]:
  Configure AppleTalk? [no]:
  Configure DECnet? [no]:
  Configure IP? [yes]:
    Configure IGRP routing? [yes]:
      Your IGRP autonomous system number [1]:
  Configure CLNS? [no]:
  Configure IPX? [no]:
  Configure Vines? [no]:
  Configure XNS? [no]:
  Configure Apollo? [no]:
  Configure bridging? [no]:
```

If an existing config file is being replaced, setup isn't completely ignorant of the router's current configuration. In the preceding example, you can see from the **[yes]** default prompts that setup senses that the preexisting global config file is configured with IP using the IGRP routing protocol configured to use the IGRP autonomous system number 1. If, however, the router were new or the existing config file had been corrupted, no pre-existing parameter settings would be sensed, and all prompts would have **[no]** as the default. (Don't sweat the IGRP terminology here; we'll cover it in Chapter 8.)

After these global configuration parameters are done, setup turns to interface-specific configuration and begins prompting for settings for specific interface modules.

Looking at the following example, setup automatically detects interface modules physically present in the router's slots. One by one, it asks whether each "interface is in use," as shown in the following example. Don't be confused by the phrase "in use" here. It doesn't mean whether a cable is attached to the port; it means whether the port's administrative status setting is turned on inside the config file.

```
Configuring interface Serial1:
  Is this interface in use? [no]:

Configuring interface Serial2:
  Is this interface in use? [no]:
```

```
Configuring interface Serial3:
  Is this interface in use? [no]:

Configuring interface TokenRing0:
  Is this interface in use? [no]:

Configuring interface TokenRing1:
  Is this interface in use? [yes]:
  Tokenring ring speed (4 or 16) ? [16]:
```

By answering yes to any of these prompts currently showing a [no] default answer, you are opting to change that parameter setting from "administratively down" to up. The last prompt in the preceding example is for the router's second Token Ring port, which is administratively up. This demonstrates that setup can sense not only presence and up/down status but also interface settings (for Token Ring speed, in this case), which it senses as being set to 16 Mbits per second.

NOTE: The reason interfaces are set to administratively down is that if you leave one administratively up but physically unused, IOS will sense that it's not signaling and assume there's a problem with it. This will cause the router to repeatedly generate alerts of the apparent error until the interface port is either reset to administratively down or properly cabled so it can begin signaling.

When an interface is detected, setup wants its parameters to be set:

```
Is this interface in use? [yes]:
  Tokenring ring speed (4 or 16) ? [16]:
  Configure IP on this interface? [yes]:
    IP address for this interface [10.1.13.1]:10.1.13.254
    Number of bits in subnet field [24]:
```

Parameters are changed by simply typing in a new value instead of taking the default with a carriage return. In the preceding example, the IP address of Token Ring interface number one was changed from 10.1.13.1 to 10.1.13.254.

When all the interfaces have been dealt with, setup will present the user with a "script" recapping the router's new config file, including any changes, and ask you whether to go ahead and put the just-completed config file into force.

```
Use this configuration? [yes/no]: yes
Building configuration...
```

If you go ahead, setup then takes a few seconds to "build" the config file (as we said earlier, config files are not edited interactively like a word processor file). Once the build is done, you're delivered to IOS in "normal mode," and advised that if you want to continue configuring, do so using the **config** command:

```
[OK]
```

Once the setup session is done, a basic configuration file has been created. From there you would follow normal procedure and enter the privileged EXEC mode and use the **configure** command to input a complete configuration file.

Giving a Router an Identity

Taking the time to properly name and document each router helps make networks easier to manage. Identifying information can be given by

▼ Giving the router a meaningful name

■ Individually documenting router interfaces

▲ Putting a message-of-the-day (MOTD) on the router

You will frequently see the example name "Router" used in configuration examples. Don't let that confuse you; "Router" is not a mandatory part of the Cisco IOS prompt. A router could just as easily be named "MainOffice" or "R23183" or anything else. Routers should be given meaningful names that inform network administrators where the router is and what it does. You must be in global configuration mode and use the **hostname** command to change the device name, as shown here:

```
Router(config)#hostname MyRouter
MyRouter(config)#
```

Because the new name was input into the running-config file, the new router name MyRouter is used immediately in the next command prompt. However, unless you use the **write** or **copy** command to store the new name (or any other change) in NVRAM, if the router were rebooted, IOS would come back up using the old name.

NOTE: The term *host* can confuse computer industry veterans new to internetworking. In the computer applications world, a host is a full-fledged computer system acting as a server, and network devices are *nodes*. In the internetworking context, host can mean any networked device, including routers, switches, and access servers, in addition to servers. We try to keep all this clear by referring only to computers as hosts and calling network equipment *devices*—but beware, the term host can take on different meaning in internetworking documents.

A router interface can be specifically documented using the **description** command. Using descriptions is a great way to keep track of the network (and users) serviced by an interface. This may not sound like much, but big networks have thousands of interfaces, and they are reconfigured frequently. To enter an interface-specific description, you must first go to that interface, in this example TokenRing0:

```
MyRouter(config)#interface TokenRing0
MyRouter(config-if)#
```

Then enter the **description** command followed by the description:

```
MyRouter(config-if)#description TokenRing for finance department
MyRouter(config-if)#
```

Descriptions can be up to 80 characters in length. To close the loop, the description can be seen in the part of the config file for the interface:

```
MyRouter(config-if)#
MyRouter#show running-config
.
.
.
interface TokenRing0
 description TokenRing for finance department
```

Router names and interface descriptions are only seen by network administrators. A third router identification tool—the message-of-the-day banner—is a way to announce information to all terminals connected to a router. MOTD banners are a good way to make sure housekeeping announcements are seen by all users on the network. Banners are commonly used to warn against unauthorized use, announce scheduled system downtime, and make other types of announcements. Use the **banner motd** command to put a banner on a router:

```
MyRouter(config)#banner motd $MyRouter will be down tonight$
```

The dollar sign was arbitrarily chosen for use here as the delimiter marking the start and end of the banner message. Any character can be used; just make sure to use a character that will not appear in the banner text itself.

The banner will display whenever someone either logs directly into the router or hits the router from a Web browser:

```
MyRouter will be down tonight
User Access Verification
Password:
```

Fancy multiline banners can be built using extended mode commands for VT terminals. VT is a de facto standard for terminal programming from Digital Equipment Corporation (now part of Compaq Computer). A note of caution: do not put any sensitive information in

MOTD banners, because anybody can see them. And there could be legal implications if a "Welcome to…" message greets a hacker while breaking into your network.

Examining Device Status

Examining network interfaces is a basic technique for getting critical status information. The **show interface** command does this. Figure 5-8 shows example output.

Keepalive messages are sent by interfaces to one another at the data link layer to confirm that the virtual circuit between them is still active.

Table 5-4 summarizes what the various status reports mean (using an interface named TokenRing1 as an example).

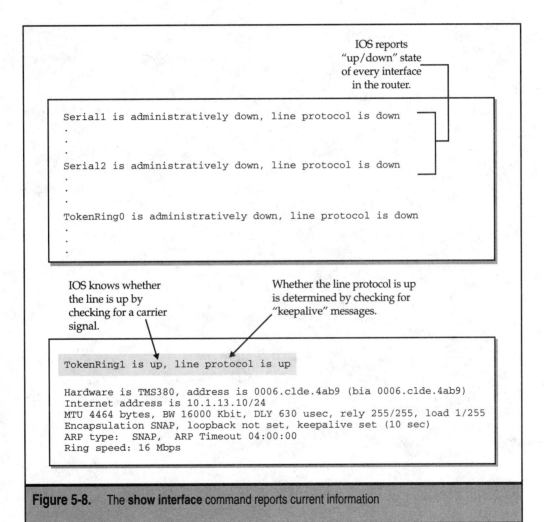

Figure 5-8.   The **show interface** command reports current information

Message	Meaning
TokenRing1 is up, line protocol is up	Running OK
TokenRing1 is down, line protocol is down	Interface problem
TokenRing1 is administratively down, line protocol is down	Disabled

Table 5-4.   Interface Status Report Definitions

Cisco Discovery Protocol

Cisco has a proprietary troubleshooting tool called the Cisco Discovery Protocol (CDP). It ships with all Cisco equipment, including routers. CDP is used by devices to discover and learn about one another. It is media and protocol independent. Cisco devices use CDP as a way to advertise their existence to neighbors on a LAN or on the far side of a WAN connection. Think of CDP as a sort of "show configuration" command for a neighborhood of Cisco routers and other devices.

CDP runs at the data link layer in order to be compatible with devices running different network layer protocols (IPX, IP, AppleTalk, etc.). CDP can communicate with any physical media supporting the Subnetwork Access Protocol (SNAP), including LANs, Frame Relay, and ATM media. SNAP is a protocol designed to let devices pass messages within a subnetwork as a way to let them keep track of what's operating in the neighborhood.

CDP is automatic. You can connect any combination of Cisco devices, power them up, stand back, and let them automatically identify one another—even prior to being assigned network addresses. CDP is able to do this using a proprietary standard called the Cisco Proprietary Data-Link Protocol. Figure 5-9 shows how CDP spans otherwise incompatible protocols.

CDP is enabled by default in all Cisco devices. CDP works by having all Cisco devices in a directly connected network pass CDP frames to one another. The key to understanding CDP's outer limit lies in the words "directly connected." CDP can discover devices beyond a LAN, but only as long as the WAN connection does not go through any non-Cisco (and therefore non-CDP) devices to make the connection. CDP frames must be able to pass through internetwork connections in order to keep extending its map of what's connected to its home LAN.

Use the **show CDP** command to see what its current operating settings are.

```
MyRouter>show CDP
Global CDP information:
        Sending CDP packets every 60 seconds
        Sending a holdtime value of 180 seconds
```

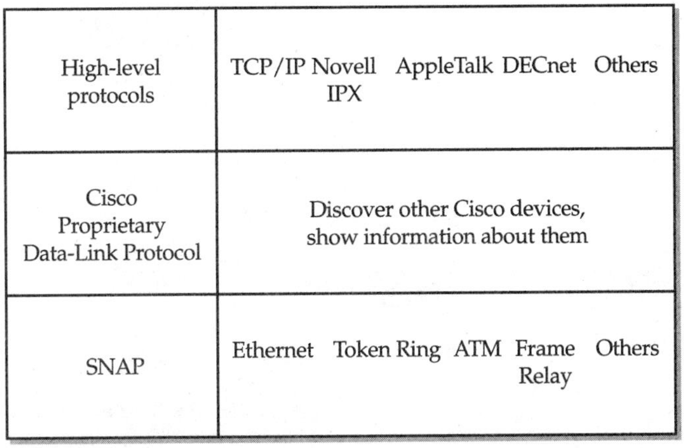

High-level protocols	TCP/IP Novell AppleTalk DECnet Others IPX
Cisco Proprietary Data-Link Protocol	Discover other Cisco devices, show information about them
SNAP	Ethernet Token Ring ATM Frame Others Relay

Figure 5-9. CDP bypasses incompatible protocols to keep track of networks

Asking for command-syntax help for the **show CDP** command displays the kind of information CDP can provide:

```
MyRouter>show CDP ?
  entry      Information for specific neighbor entry
  interface  CDP interface status and configuration
  neighbors  CDP neighbor entries
  traffic    CDP statistics
  <cr>
```

The most common usage of CDP is probably to show other devices directly connected to the device requesting the CDP information:

```
vsigate>show cdp neighbors
Capability Codes: R - Router, T - Trans Bridge, B - Source Route
Bridge, S - Switch, H - Host, I - IGMP, r - Repeater

Device ID          Local Intrfce    Holdtme     Capability
Platform               Port ID
tacacsrouter           Tok 0            168           R
4500                   Tok 0
Switch.velte.com       Eth 1            129           S
WS-C2924M              Fas 0/1
vsitest7               Tok 1            169           R
RSP2                   Tok 6/0
```

To look in greater detail at a specific neighbor, use the **show cdp entry** command:

```
vsigate>show cdp entry vsitest7
-----------------------
Device ID: vsitest7
Entry address(es):
  IP address: 10.1.12.2
Platform: cisco RSP2,  Capabilities: Router
Interface: TokenRing1,  Port ID (outgoing port): TokenRing6/0
Holdtime : 138 sec

Version :
Cisco Internetwork Operating System Software
IOS (tm) RSP Software (RSP-JSV-M), Version 11.2(12a)P, RELEASE
SOFTWARE (fc1)
Copyright (c) 1986-1998 by cisco Systems, Inc.
Compiled Sun 15-Mar-98 22:14 by dschwart
```

As you can see, CDP is able to remotely gather fairly detailed configuration information on devices. CDP was designed to be an efficient, low-overhead protocol so as not to gobble precious bandwidth and thereby render Cisco's entire product line slow. Because CDP is proprietary, it is able to gather a lot of information using a tiny amount of overhead. Other tools exist for discovering "locally connected" devices. The SNMP network management tools are great for centralized management, but gather less granular configuration information than CDP can on Cisco devices (SNMP is covered in Chapter 7).

USING APPLICATIONS TO HELP CONFIGURE ROUTERS

Thus far in this chapter, we've dealt with configuring routers by hand. Cisco makes two software applications to serve as tools:

▼ **ConfigMaker** A midrange tool that runs on Windows 95, 98, and NT 4.0—a tool for configuring Ethernet LANs and WAN connectivity, targeted for use by reasonably proficient network managers or consultants

▲ **Fast Step** A low-end tool that runs on Windows 95, 98, and NT—used to configure and install small Cisco routers and access servers, targeted for use by less sophisticated users.

We'll quickly run through configuring a router using each tool. In doing this, we'll cover some router configuration concepts not covered during the setup procedure.

Both tools use a graphical user interface to assist with the task of getting routers up and running. Neither tool addresses large or complex internetworking problems. A separate product called NetSys Baseliner is used for enterprise internetwork modeling and management. ConfigMaker and Fast Step are meant for use by intermediates and beginners only.

ConfigMaker

ConfigMaker is a Microsoft Windows–based tool used to design and configure small networks. It works both for LAN configurations and WAN connectivity, with support for a wide range of Cisco devices and protocols. ConfigMaker provides a clean and intuitive desktop work environment that strikes a good balance between ease of use and functionality. But it isn't intended for power users, as it has no support for high-end devices such as Cisco 7000 Series routers or high-end switches. Nor does ConfigMaker support the Token Ring LAN protocol.

ConfigMaker runs on Windows 95, 98, and NT 4.0. Cisco makes it available at no charge. To try it out, download a copy from Cisco's Web site at www.cisco.com/public/sw-center/sw-netmgmt.shtml. For the growing number of technical staff in small- and medium-sized enterprises who want to handle their own network configurations, ConfigMaker is probably the solution—as long as their networks are made up of all or nearly all Cisco devices.

The ConfigMaker Desktop Environment

At the center of ConfigMaker's desktop is a network diagram area into which network "objects" are placed, configured, and linked together. At the outset, the network diagram area is empty, like a sheet of drafting paper before the first line is drawn. The network diagram area is surrounded by three windows, each put there to help you build a network through to completion:

▼ **Device window**   Source for devices to drag and drop into Network Diagram

■ **Connections window**   Source for wide area network connections to drag and drop into Network Diagram

▲ **Task List**   Checklist of the chronological steps that must be completed in network configuration

The first step is to drag and drop devices from the Device window onto the Network Diagram area. It's a simple proposition; just choose whatever devices are to be part of the network: routers, hubs, LAN cables, and so on. As each device is put into the diagram, ConfigMaker prompts for settings needed to make it functional. The prompt routines are similar to the Add New Hardware routine in the Microsoft Windows Control Panel.

Once the devices have been put into the diagram, it's time to connect them into a network. This is done by dragging one or more connections into the diagram from the Connections window. To connect a device to the network, first click on the connection, then on the device to be connected. Figure 5-10 shows the ConfigMaker desktop with the beginnings of an Ethernet network displayed in the network diagram area, with two Cisco

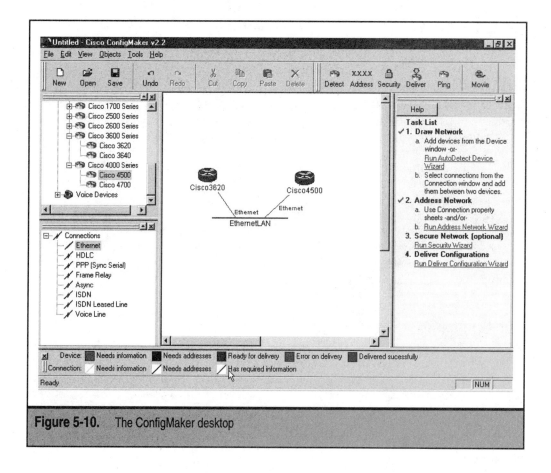

Figure 5-10.   The ConfigMaker desktop

routers connected to an Ethernet LAN. The user keeps adding devices and connections until the entire network is depicted in the diagram.

ConfigMaker's Methodology

Building a network through this graphical interface is great for conceptualizing network topology, but ConfigMaker is more than merely a network diagramming program. Every item put into the diagram drawn in the Device window has intelligence behind it. As each network object (device or network connection) is put in, ConfigMaker asks for line item details such as settings, names, and so on. This information is stored in a database hidden behind the diagram and is used by ConfigMaker to check for completeness and internal consistency. ConfigMaker enforces a quality assurance methodology over the network design process:

1. As a device is added to the network, information is collected about it.

2. The information is checked for consistency with the rest of the database.

3. If an error is made, ConfigMaker prompts the user to correct it right away.

4. ConfigMaker's rules-based logic keeps checking the entire network for correctness as each new object (device or connection) is added.

> **NOTE:** As the perceptive beginner you are, you're probably wondering why Ethernet is in both the Device and Connections windows. If you drag the Ethernet icon from the Device window, it's defined to your diagram as a local area network segment; drag Ethernet from the Connections window, and it becomes a wide area network link. In other words, the Ethernet LAN segment—a cable or a hub box—is treated as a physical device, while the Ethernet connection logically represents an internetwork link.

To see the database kept by ConfigMaker, right-click on any device and bring up Properties. This seven-tab dialog box presents all the information known about a device. Figure 5-11, for example, shows the hardware configuration tab. The tab's left window contains all the possible modules that can be plugged into the device. The right window shows the current configuration. In this example, the Cisco 4500 is configured with one six-slot Ethernet module and a 1-port T1/ISDN module. ConfigMaker has the logic to catch most configuration errors before they happen: the user is prevented from inserting a network module into an incompatible device, and a proper interface must be in a device before it can be connected to the network. Glancing at our example in Figures 5-10 and 5-11, the Cisco 4500 router was allowed to connect to the Ethernet network because it was first configured with its six-port Ethernet interface, and it could also be hooked up to a T1/ISDN connection.

The boxes along the bottom of the ConfigMaker screen (Figure 5-10) make up a legend of color-keyed status conditions. Table 5-5 gives a legend for the color keys. A device icon or connection line will change colors on the screen as the configuration status of the object changes.

Building a Network with ConfigMaker

The Task List is a help system and checklist in one. The Task List window is to the right of the network diagram. It uses wizards to guide the user through the four major steps of network configuration. Once any of the four major network configuration tasks is completed, a check mark displays to its left. (In Figure 5-10, the Draw Network and Address Network tasks are checked as done.) The Task List window is divided into four parts, each with a wizard dedicated to a particular job:

▼ **AutoDetect Device Wizard**   A series of "Add New Hardware" dialog box prompts that gather necessary description and settings information for network devices

■ **Address Network Wizard**   The part of the "Add New Hardware" prompt sequence that collects addressing information for devices and their connections

■ **Secure Network Wizard**   Helps apply security settings to restrict connections between network segments

▲ **Deliver Configurations Wizard**   Automatically downloads config files to devices

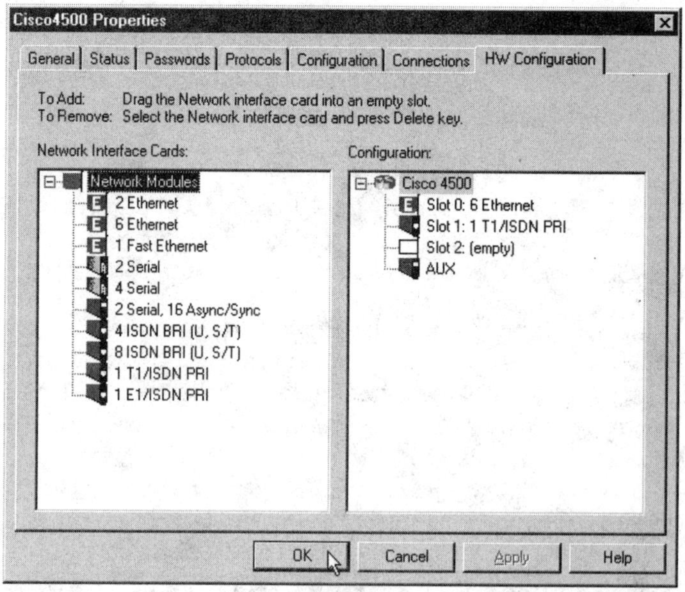

Figure 5-11.   ConfigMaker Properties dialog box for a Cisco 4500 router

Color	Configuration Status
Gray	Additional information is needed on the device or connection.
Black	Addresses (IP addresses, submasks, etc.) are needed for the device.
Blue	The device config file is ready for delivery (or the connection has the required information).
Red	The device config file was delivered and encountered an error.
Green	The device config file was delivered successfully.

Table 5-5.   Color Keys Track Configuration Status

THE AUTODETECT DEVICE WIZARD   Using the AutoDetect Device Wizard is optional. If you use it, it will automatically sense and identify the type of hardware to be configured. AutoDetect Device is handy if you're configuring devices remotely and aren't there to physically inspect hardware components for model numbers, installed interface modules, and so on. The AutoDetect Device Wizard supports both network and virtual terminal (VTY) connections to the devices being configured.

THE ADDRESS NETWORK WIZARD   If addresses have been preassigned to devices in your network, they can be entered manually. If not, the Address Network Wizard will automatically assign a block of addresses to selected or all devices in your network. If part of the network being designed already exists (and therefore already has addresses you'd like to keep), you can select the new part of the network diagram and use automatic addressing for those devices only. Figure 5-12 shows the Address Network Wizard prompting for a range of IP addresses and a subnet mask.

Looking at Figure 5-12's IP subnet mask inset, you can see the inverse relationship between the number of subnets and the maximum possible number of hosts (routers). As the decimal value in the rightmost octet of the subnet mask (0 at first, then 248) gets higher,

▼   The maximum number of subnets increases.

▲   The maximum number of hosts per subnet decreases.

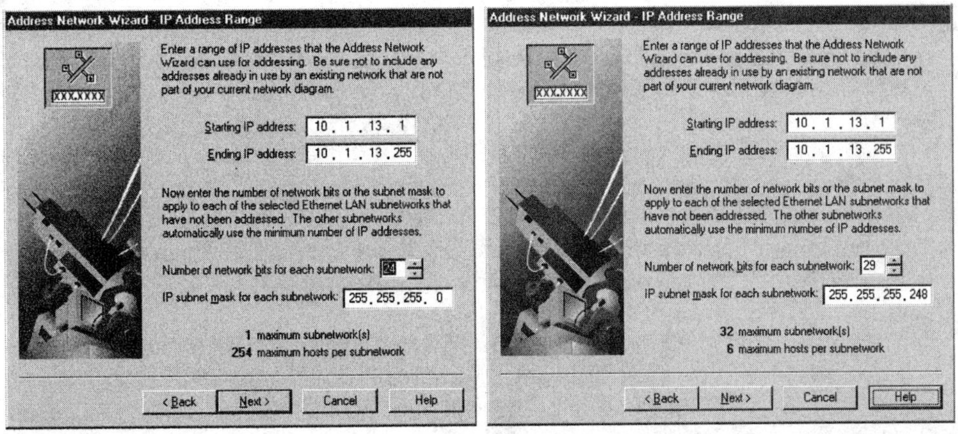

Figure 5-12.   Two subnet mask scenarios within an IP address range

A company with a lot of offices and few devices per office to connect would be happy with the subnet mask 255.255.255.248. Conversely, one with a few offices but many devices per office would want to use the subnet mask 255.255.255.0.

THE SECURITY WIZARD The Security Wizard is used for internetworking only. For example, the Security Wizard cannot be used to set security parameters for the local network being configured in Figure 5-12 because that network is a single LAN segment, not an internetwork. If a network diagram includes the Internet or an intranet, the Security Wizard helps set policies about which LANs can access them, and which internal LANs can access each other. The Security Wizard uses prompts to help establish policies for basic security, firewalls, and even so-called DMZs. *DMZ* stands for "demilitarized zone"—a term taken from the Korean and Vietnam wars. A DMZ is a LAN to which the public—the whole Internet or an enterprise's intranet—is given access, but is a cul-de-sac beyond which public users cannot go. Network operators use DMZs to make part of their operations available to the public without letting users inside the rest of the private network. Web servers and FTP servers are the most common examples of DMZ hosts.

THE DELIVER CONFIGURATION WIZARD The Deliver Configuration Wizard does just that: it automatically downloads config files created by ConfigMaker into the target devices. To use this, the devices must be connected (via the console port or network) to the PC on which ConfigMaker is running.

ConfigMaker Product Review

An important benefit of ConfigMaker is that users will find it hard to make mistakes. Many configuration mistakes involve wrong choices for particular devices. In ConfigMaker—which is Cisco specific—if you try to put an incompatible device in a particular router, an error message will stop you. If you leave out something necessary, ConfigMaker will prompt you. This capacity for quality assurance not only helps avoid mistakes, but also helps keep the user up-to-date on product options (which change constantly).

But perhaps the most important benefit of ConfigMaker is that you don't need to know the Cisco IOS software command-line interface to be able to configure network devices and connections. When you need to input something, the correct choices are right there in front of you. The Windows-based GUI makes that possible. The use of Windows conventions (the "Add New Hardware" prompts, the menu bar, etc.) and color keys makes it easy to learn and use.

ConfigMaker strikes a good enough balance between capability and ease of use that both nonexperts and those with internetworking expertise can use it. It's a godsend for the uninitiated, not only for getting a network up and running, but also for learning internetworking basics.

ConfigMaker has limits, however. It's not meant for designing and managing large or complicated networks. For example, only routers up through the Cisco 4000 Series are supported, not the high-end router series. And its functionality won't let you simulate network behavior.

Fast Step

Cisco Fast Step is a configuration utility that ships with low-end routers and access servers. It is targeted for use by the novice network user to configure end-to-end connections between a PC and an Internet service provider (ISP) or corporate intranets. Fast Step runs on Microsoft Windows 95, 98, or NT 4.0. It ships on a CD-ROM for installation on a Windows PC. Fast Step can be used two ways:

▼   To configure the router interactively while connected to the router either over a serial cable from its PC COM port to the router console port, or via an Ethernet link

▲   To build a configuration file for later download to the router, or as a base to configure other routers (the file can be read by Fast Step's Setup Wizard)

After installing Fast Step, clicking the icon starts a sequence of dialog boxes prompting the user to input the information needed to configure and install the router. The sequence can go over a dozen dialog boxes, depending on the options taken. To help sort things out, every Fast Step screen has a Tasks window on the left side. You can see where you are in the process by finding which task is highlighted in the Task window on the left side of any Fast Step screen. As outlined in Table 5-6, Fast Step groups configuration tasks into four major steps.

Step	Description of Tasks
Find and Connect	Provide router number; select setup mode (interactive or download); define connection type (ISP or corporate); give settings; access provider IP address and phone numbers, user name, password, etc.
Security	Specify router name, router read-only password, and router enable secret password; specify the types of services (Web server, mail server, FTP server)
Local Addressing	Specify IP address for LAN connection provided by ISP or corporate intranet
Setup and Test	Save config file to router and run, save config file for use with other routers

Table 5-6.   Fast Step Divides Configuration Tasks into Four Parts

Find and Connect

Fast Step starts by asking for general information about the configuration session, such as the model of the router to be configured and whether a new config file is to be created or a preconfigured file will be used.

Then more specific information is requested. Fast Step asks you to enter your PPP (Point-to-Point Protocol) username issued to you by the ISP or your corporate intranet administrator. The PPP username is case sensitive, so be sure to type it in exactly as it appears on the information given by your ISP or network administrator.

Next, enter your PPP password. This isn't your network login password. The PPP password is only for dial-in remote access over a router-to-router connection. Be sure that the password complies with the requirements set by your ISP or corporate network (minimum number of characters, etc.). This password is sometimes called a "PAP" or "CHAP" password and is also case sensitive. Last, enter the central router or PPP name of the router to which you'll be connecting (not the name of the router you're configuring). PPP, CHAP, and PAP are covered in Chapter 10.

The second half of the Find and Connect step is to provide the information and settings needed to hook the router up to the Internet. To do this, Fast Step prompts for more involved parameters such as switch type, ISDN SPIDs, and access phone numbers. (SPID stands for service provider ID, usually an ISP.)

Then things get really involved—at least by a beginner's standards. Figure 5-13 shows Fast Step prompting for IP address information.

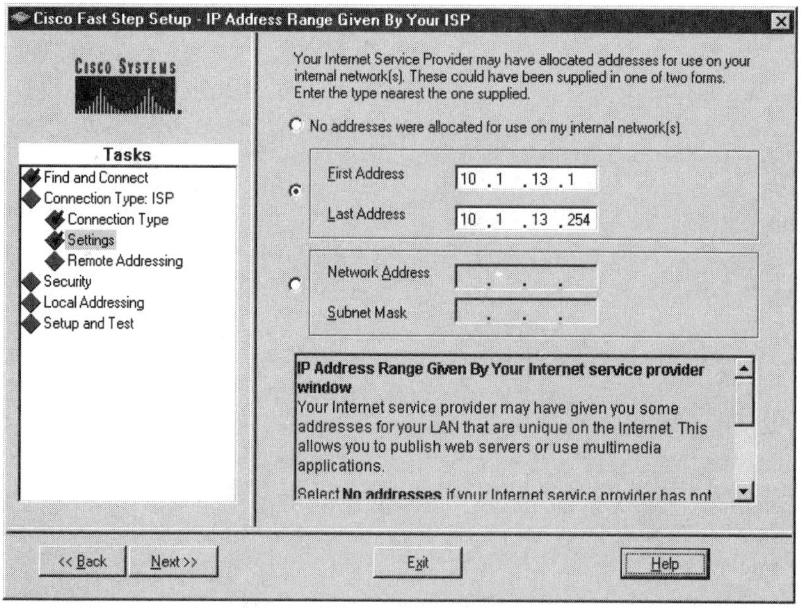

Figure 5-13.   Fast Step prompting for IP address information

Only one of the three options can be taken:

▼ Don't provide any address because you don't have them yet.

■ Give a range of addresses provided to you by your ISP or corporate network administrator.

▲ Give an IP network address and subnet mask.

This information is meant to identify the LAN segment the user will be connected to with an address unique to the Internet. Fast Step needs this information to make the connection to the Internet. These settings are in essence the user's address as it is presented to the rest of the Internet (or corporate intranet community). Fast Step can automatically discover the address but lets the user input it directly if desired.

Security

Next, Fast Step asks for parameters having to do with router security and router server publishing. Figure 5-14 shows the user being prompted to give the router a name, a read-only password, and an enable password.

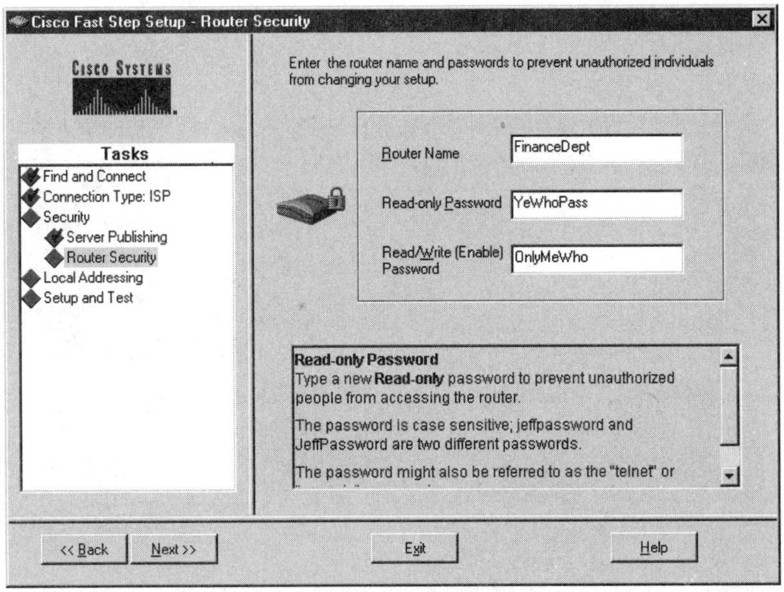

Figure 5-14.   Fast Step prompts for a router name and administrative passwords

A number of rules apply to the names and passwords here—violate one and an error message stops you. The online help system tells the user what the rules are. These passwords apply to gaining access to the router itself for administrative purposes. Fast Step then lets the user configure one or all of four Internet services options:

▼ Single Server (both a Web server and mail server—the most common option)

▪ Web server (a Web page but with no e-mail service)

▪ Mail server (only Internet e-mail services)

▲ FTP server (the ability for Internet users to download information from your site)

Internetworking pros often call these options "servers." For example, if the parameter to offer FTP downloads from the user's LAN was set to yes, that LAN is running an FTP server. Don't be put off by this; it's just a fancy term for a service.

Local Addressing

Finally, Fast Step prompts for the IP addresses of the wide area network to which the user's LAN is connected. These addresses, shown in Figure 5-15, identify the ISP or corporate network on the Internet.

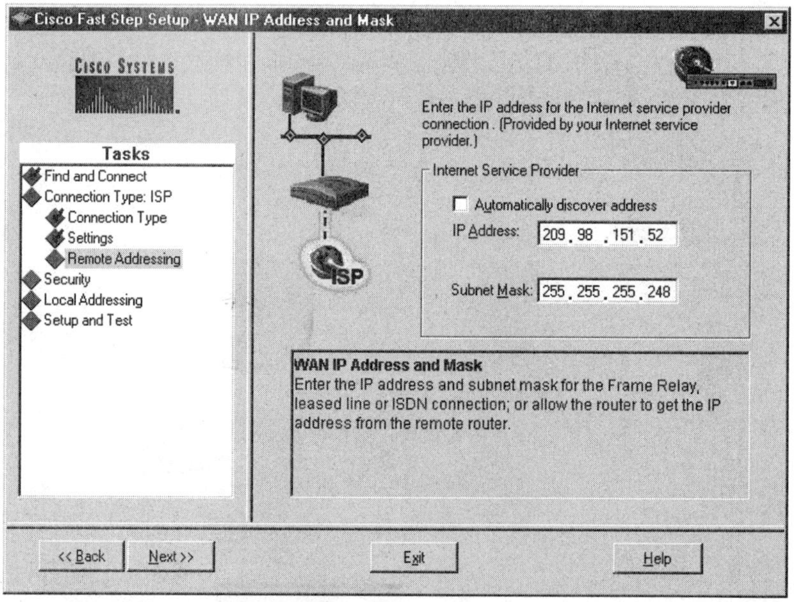

Figure 5-15. Fast Step prompting for the ISP's address information

Looking at Figures 5-13 and 5-16, we see that Fast Step wants two sets of addresses, which are used to identify two separate network segments to be involved in connecting the user's remote LAN to the Internet. This can confuse the beginner. Keep in mind here that the router will connect to the ISP/intranet by way of a point-to-point, router-to-router connection—not over some nebulous Internet IP address. The address information provided in Figure 5-13 is used to identify the router being configured using Fast Step. This router is what connects the user's LAN to the Internet. Because that LAN will presumably have more than one user operating on the Internet at any given time, Fast Step asked for a range of IP addresses—one per user (Figure 5-13). On the other hand, the *remote* address prompted for in Figure 5-15 will be used to identify the network segment identifying the ISP/intranet through which the user will connect.

Figure 5-16 helps sort these addresses out. The LAN local to the user (and the router being configured using Fast Step here) is usually issued a block of IP addresses. The example in Figure 5-13 has a block of 254 addresses issued for the user's internal network (10.1.13.1–10.1.13.254, inclusive).

The ISP or corporate intranet has an IP address to identify its network segment, and a subnet mask for that IP address—255.255.255.248—allows for up to six possible host addresses within that subnetwork.

If the scenario calls for hooking up to a corporate intranet, a third network segment comes into play: the corporation's main network segment, which is on the left side of Figure 5-16. To the user configuring the router, the internetwork cloud in the middle is the

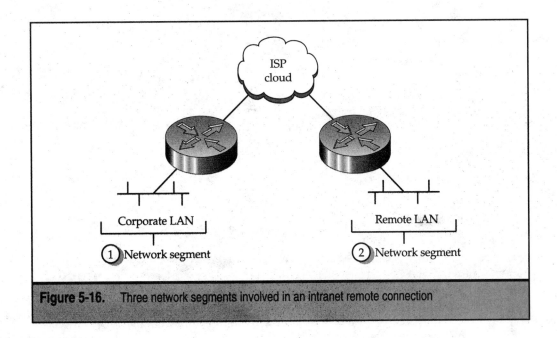

Figure 5-16.   Three network segments involved in an intranet remote connection

same service whether the connection is made through a private corporate network or an ISP, and the corporate network segment on the left side likely can be reached only by passing through a firewall.

Setup and Test

In the last part of the configuration, Fast Step lets you complete the router configuration process by either

▼ Loading the config file into the router

▲ Making a separate copy of the config file

If the user opts to make a separate copy, the file must of course be given a name. The choice exists either to save the file as is in Fast Step's CFG format for use on other routers, or save it in IOS command format for use as a template from which to build slightly different config files for other routers. Here's the top portion of a Cisco 801 router config file created using Fast Step:

```
! Cisco IOS router configuration file
! Automatically made by Cisco Fast Step v2.0
! Designed for Cisco C801
! March 31, 1999
! Cisco Fast Step Template

no service udp-small-servers
no service tcp-small-servers
service password-encryption
hostname shaughee
username shaughne password Password
enable secret SuperSecret
no ip source-route
isdn switch-type basic-5ess
.
.
.
```

Fast Step Product Review

Fast Step's series of dialog boxes prompt the user to give all the information required to configure an end-to-end connection between a home or small office PC and an ISP (or corporate intranet). And that's good because, like it or not, network configurations can get complicated.

But compared to ConfigMaker, the prompts leave more room for omission and error. This is largely because Fast Step's job is different from ConfigMaker's. For example, to decide which interface to configure into a slot in a Cisco router, ConfigMaker gives you a window containing only interfaces compatible with the router being configured. By contrast, Fast Step asks mostly for opened-ended answers that come from outside sources—rather than providing an input selection window inside the Fast Step screen. The user must refer to outside documents for such things as phone numbers, control numbers, usernames, IP addresses, and so on. Cisco knows this, which is why they provide worksheets in the Quick Start Guide to help users gather required configuration parameters before starting.

Extensive input edits are in force throughout Fast Step. This helps the user catch mistakes as they happen. If the user tries to input something illegal, an exclamation point will appear to the right of the field, and an error message will appear in the prompt box. The edits can be both a blessing and a curse. For example, if you try to input a bad PPP password, the prompt box informs you that it "does not meet the accepted rules." Fair enough, but what are the rules? Push the Help button, and your answer is "Password is a login password given to you by your Internet service provider or network administrator," when what you really need to know is what the syntax rules are. The Fast Step help subsystem is generally good, but at times uneven.

However, with Fast Step's prompts and abundant choices, as well as a little effort, a novice can configure and install a low-end router to the Internet. Without Fast Step, a layperson would have little chance of configuring and rolling out a router. Fast Step may not be perfect, but it gives you more than a fighting chance.

CHAPTER 6

Switches and Hubs

The two previous chapters discussed routers, which operate between networks. An internetwork is by definition a collection of local area networks (LANs) connected by routers. To travel across an internetwork, a message hops from router port to router port until it at last arrives at the IP address it's looking for.

But what then? At that juncture, the message has gotten past the last router and must worm its way through the destination network's wiring. In other words, it must drop out of the internetwork cloud and look not for yet another router interface, but for the specific connection port into which the destination host is plugged.

Hosts—PCs and servers, for example—need to hook up to networks somehow. The router is designed to connect networks to other networks, so it is of little use when it comes to physically connecting hosts. That's where hubs and switches come in. They provide local connectivity to hosts. Hubs and switches are the building blocks with which LANs are pieced together.

The last leg of a message's journey takes place inside a building or within an office campus. Here, the transition must be made from the internetworking cloud's telecom lines, down into the cabling strung through the walls and ceilings of the building, all the way out to a wall plate, and finally to the host device itself. This final stage requires making the transition to the destination host's physical address. This address is called the media access control address, or MAC for short. The IP address gets you to the neighborhood, and the MAC address identifies the actual NIC (network interface card) connecting the destination device to its LAN. MAC addresses are always unique. They serve as a kind of serial number for a physical device, such that any device on any network in the world can be uniquely identified.

But a one-step shift from a worldwide IP address down to an individual host's MAC address would be too abrupt. There needs to be an intermediary step separating the high-speed router level from slow-speed NICs. Having no buffer zone would in effect put side-street traffic onto the interstate highway. Even if NICs and hosts were lightning fast, a middle level would still be necessary just to make things manageable. That intermediary step is either a hub or a switch. Figure 6-1 shows where they fit in.

In this chapter, we delve into that local zone sitting between the desktop and the router that links it to the LAN. This is the realm of cables and connectors. We realize eyes tend to glaze over when talk turns to cable plants and patch panels, as if these things are for some reason best left to the building janitor. But the subject of local connectivity is not as mundane as you might think. As high-tech networking equipment inches outward from the backbone toward the desktop, deciding how to connect individual hosts and workgroups has become strategic to the big picture of enterprise internetworking. Technology advances are coming fast in the field of local connectivity. You should understand the basics of this subject area, including some specifics on how Cisco hubs and switches work.

NETWORK TOPOLOGIES

The physical layout of a network is referred to as its *topology*. Fifteen or twenty years ago, there was little if any choice in designing a network's topology. To build a LAN, you ran a

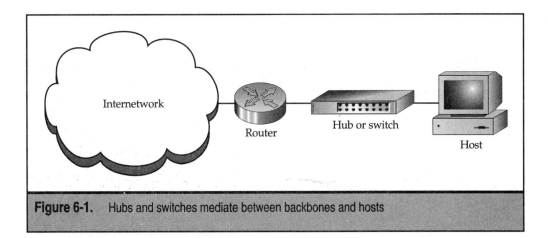

Figure 6-1.   Hubs and switches mediate between backbones and hosts

fat coaxial cable called a *Thicknet* through your building and tapped hosts directly into it. The Thicknet cable was the network backbone. Connecting hosts directly to the network backbone resulted in a so-called bus topology. A *bus* is a cable (or a printed circuit board acting like a cable), and a bus topology is where most or all of a network's devices are connected to a single cable—which is like having everybody's driveway empty into one major thoroughfare instead of side streets. Two typical early network topologies are depicted in Figure 6-2.

As network technology developed, topologies evolved a bit with the introduction of terminal servers, which made it possible to indirectly connect dumb terminals to the LAN. This was a good thing because it gave individual users easy access to more than one minicomputer or mainframe. Another advance was the introduction of a thinner kind of coaxial cable called *Thinnet*, which was cheaper and far easier to work with than Thicknet cabling. But these improvements were only incremental; network layouts were still basically a bus topology.

The trouble with bus topologies was that if something failed along the trunk, the whole network went down (or at least a big part of it). Another drawback was that connecting hosts meant crawling into the ceiling plenum, finding the trunk cable, making the tap, dropping a second cable from the tap down to the device, and then testing the connection to see if it worked. Not only were early networks prone to failure and hard to install, but the equipment was also bulky and expensive.

Things have changed a lot since then. Nowadays, most hosts are connected to networks through either hubs or switches. Hubs and switches give network administrators more choices in both the physical and logical layout of networks. They are modular in the sense that devices and hosts can be added without having to change anything on the network backbone. But above all, hubs and switches do away with bus topologies by allowing the easy installation and management of multiple LANs. Network designers use star topologies in place of one overtaxed LAN.

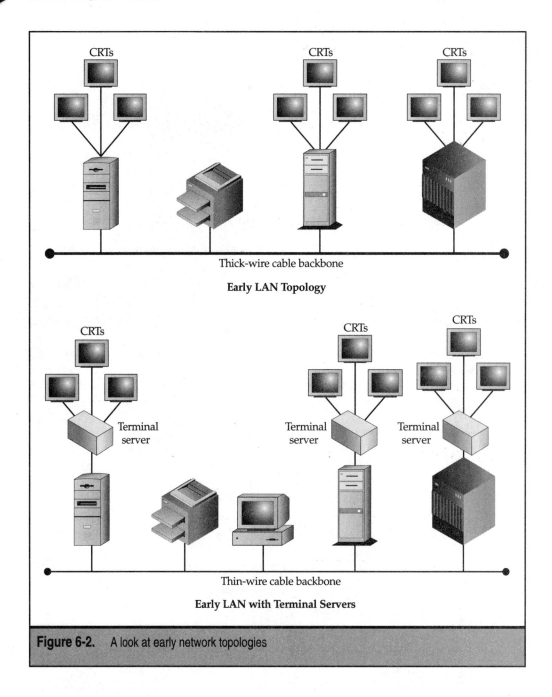

CRTs

CRTs

CRTs

Thick-wire cable backbone

Early LAN Topology

CRTs

CRTs

CRTs

Terminal server

Terminal server

Terminal server

Thin-wire cable backbone

Early LAN with Terminal Servers

Figure 6-2. A look at early network topologies

NOTE: The term *LAN* can be confusing. In the old days, a LAN was a central trunk running through a building with everything on the network connected directly to it. Now, that same building might have dozens of hubs serving as host connection points, with the hubs in turn connected to a backbone. Any shared network medium is a LAN. A hub is a shared medium, and so is the backbone's central trunk cable. Even experts use the term LAN, or local area network, to loosely describe a local network comprised of multiple LANs. To avoid confusion, in this book we use the term LAN segment to describe a shared network medium, which is the basic building block of network topologies. A LAN segment is defined by a hub, switch, or cable. Nowadays, the term LAN most often refers to a collection of LAN segments within a building or campus.

Breaking things up into smaller LANs makes it easier to meet current needs and still leave room for future change and growth. Network segmentation improves network performance by isolating traffic. Users within a workgroup or department are most likely to send messages to one another, so putting them on their own LAN segment means others won't get caught in their traffic. Reliability is better because what happens on one LAN segment doesn't affect the overall network; the fault is isolated within the segment where the trouble started. Network administrators can better identify where the trouble is because of the transition points between LAN segments—an important feature in complicated networks. Also, the modularity of hierarchical networks naturally enhances security and manageability because devices can be grouped in ways that best fit management needs.

For all these reasons, networks today use hubs and switches to concentrate multiple hosts into a single network connection point—an approach called the *star configuration*. Star configurations are the building blocks with which hierarchical networks are constructed. Figure 6-3 shows common variations on the basic star topology.

In stark contrast to the bad-old-days of trunk pulling and cable dropping, connecting a host to a network now is as simple as plugging in a phone-style jack. Each star-topology building block meets certain needs:

▼ A small business or department might use just one hub or switch to form a LAN—in effect putting the entire network inside a box—which is called a single-star topology. With hubs or switches, backbone cabling is no longer necessary to form small networks.

▲ A star-hierarchy topology is used to make more connection ports available within an office. Plugging outlying hubs into a master switch or hub gives more hosts a place to plug in without having to pull additional cable into the area.

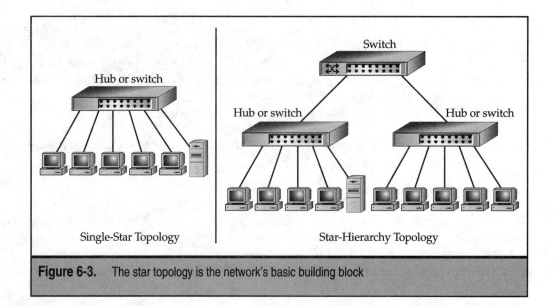

Figure 6-3.   The star topology is the network's basic building block

NOTE: The terms *backbone* and *central trunk* evoke the image of a single, unbroken span of cable. In reality, most backbones are made up of many cable spans spliced together. At the other extreme, some backbones aren't made up of cable at all, but instead are contained inside a box entirely on circuit boards, which is called a collapsed backbone. By definition, though, a backbone is the part of a network that acts as the primary path routing traffic between LAN segments. In general, only hubs, switches, and routers are connected directly to backbones. In large networks, a backbone usually runs at a higher speed than the LAN segments it connects.

The topology of a network is of course most closely tied to the enterprise's geography—who's on what floor, which server sits where, and so on. But other considerations also come into play. Table 6-1 lists network design factors and how they affect decisions about what to do when designing a network.

Network design decisions are most often constrained by the amount of money to be spent and such logistical issues as how long the enterprise plans to stay in a building. Platforms, on the other hand, are always strategic and usually an overriding circumstance over which network designers have little or no control. If the enterprise is heavily invested in Novell NetWare or IBM SNA or Apple, the network equipment must adapt to the hardware and software platforms already installed.

Nowadays, however, no matter what your budget is or which platforms you're using, segmenting networks is not only an option but is the preferred design approach.

The Importance of Network Domains

The *domain* is one of the most fundamental concepts in internetworking. Although the term has many uses, for our purposes what's important are the two most basic kinds of domains:

▼   The collision domain (or the token domain in Token Ring LAN segments)

▲   The broadcast domain

Factor	Network Design Consideration
Preexisting cable plant	To save time and money, network designers frequently try to run networks over wiring already installed in the walls and ceiling spaces of a building. Sometimes they have no choice and the type of network devices that can be used is dictated by preexisting cabling.
Performance goals	Projected network traffic loads and end-user "need for speed" can influence the class of network devices and cabling plant used.
Platforms	The installed base of network operating systems and computer platforms frequently dictates network design decisions.
Security	Topology layout is often used as a way to help enforce security.

Table 6-1.   Topology Design Factors (Besides Geography)

LAN segments run over shared media. In physical terms, member hosts in a LAN segment share a cable, hub, or switch. To stave off the electronic chaos that would otherwise ensue from sharing a medium, some form of control must be enforced over access to it. This is called media access control (from whence the MAC address takes its name).

> **NOTE:** For the literal-minded out there thinking that the name should be *medium access control* because LANs by definition share only a single cable, hub, or switch, you're right—to a point. But keep in mind that MAC addresses are routinely exchanged between segments. Besides, somehow medium access control sounds half-hearted in the world of strict networking rules.

Ethernet and Token Ring are both shared media LAN technologies, but they use sharply contrasting access control methods:

▼   Ethernet's CSMA/CD method (Carrier Sense Multiple Access/Collision Detection)

▲   Token Ring's token-passing method

Ethernet Collision Domains

Ethernet lets network hosts randomly contend for bandwidth. A host may send a message at will; but if it collides with a message sent by another host, both must back off and retry after a random wait period. An Ethernet collision domain is any segment in which collisions can take place—the LAN's shared medium in the form of a hub, switch, or cable. The more traffic there is on a collision domain, the more likely it is that collisions will occur. Increased collisions in turn result in hosts spending more and more time futilely attempting to retransmit.

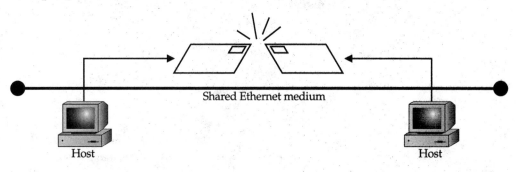

Shared Ethernet medium

Host   Host

Token Domains

A token domain is a Token Ring LAN's shared medium. Token Ring uses a deterministic method for controlling media access called *token passing*. In token passing, each host must wait for the token to be passed around the LAN's ring to grab it and transmit. Although they have no packet collisions, Token Ring LANs are not immune to traffic congestion. The more hosts connected to a ring, the longer each must wait for the token to come back around to be able to transmit. A good analogy to help understand Token Ring technology is a traffic light at the top of a highway on-ramp. You're forced to wait for a green light before entering the highway; thus, the heavier the traffic, the longer the wait. You're not going to be stuck in a jam down on the highway, but if traffic's heavy you still must do your waiting up on the ramp.

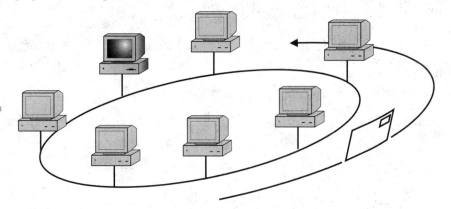

The majority of new LAN installations are Ethernet, so through the remainder of this chapter we'll focus on Ethernet hubs and switches and refer to Token Ring only where appropriate.

NOTE: There are three kinds of messages in IP-based networks, all ending in "cast": (1) a *unicast* message is a message sent to a single network address, (2) a *multicast* is a single message copied and sent to a specific group of network addresses, and (3) a *broadcast* message is sent to all nodes on a network.

Broadcast Domains

A broadcast domain is a set of all stations (network devices and hosts) that will receive any broadcast message originating from any device or host within the set. The key differentiation between broadcast and collision domains is that they are defined by the type of message they encompass: collision domains encompass messages of any kind; broadcast domains encompass only broadcast messages. As the lower-left part of Figure 6-4 illustrates, for two hubs to join in the same broadcast domain, they must somehow be internetworked (routers usually block broadcasts).

The right side of Figure 6-4 shows how broadcast domains can be very different switched networks. Using switch technology, a broadcast domain can be specifically con-

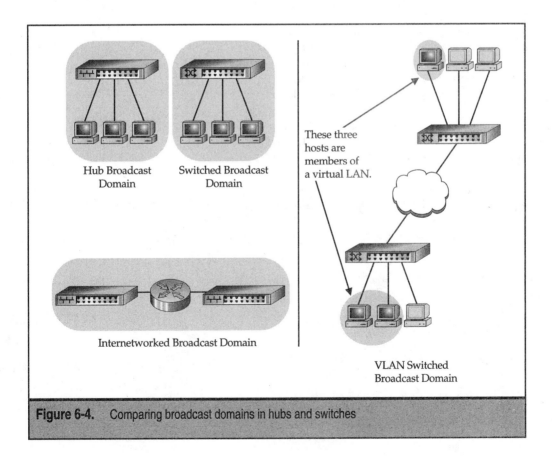

Figure 6-4. Comparing broadcast domains in hubs and switches

figured through logical connections instead of physical ones. This is called a *virtual LAN*, or VLAN for short. The *virtual* in VLAN means that the LAN's domain is not defined by a physical connection. In fact, VLANs usually aren't even local at all (more on that later).

Collisions waste bandwidth because they abort transmissions. In contrast, broadcast messages indeed reach their destinations, but are still wasted bandwidth if the receiving hosts discard them as irrelevant. Obviously, then, broadcasts also play a central role in traffic congestion. Think of broadcast domains as internetworking's version of the ZIP code: the more addresses within a ZIP code, the longer it takes to deliver all the mail. Internetworking is no different. The larger the broadcast domain is, the slower the network tends to be.

The Need to Segment Networks

LAN segments should be kept small in order to help guarantee throughput speed by limiting the frequency of collisions. Small is also good when it comes to network flexibility, security, and maintainability. The trend is to divide networks into more and more LAN segments as network bandwidth comes under increasing strain. More users are becoming members of networks, and on average individual users are generating more network traffic. In addition, the mix is changing to more bandwidth-intensive applications such as graphics, voice, and video. All this has combined to push network managers to deliver more bandwidth by

▼ Installing faster networking media

▲ Breaking up networks into ever smaller segments

Network managers are doing both. But demand for bandwidth is outstripping the ability of network manufacturers to create faster technology, so network infrastructures are being reconfigured to incorporate more hierarchy and segmentation. This trend is reinforced as the cost of the hardware needed to segment networks plummets. But the trend's greatest reinforcement is that the tools needed to integrate and manage heavily segmented networks have improved so much. These tools are so good, in fact, that switches are being used to "microsegment" networks into tiny LAN segments.

Cabling Defines Network Speed and Distance

You can't appreciate traffic management without understanding the basics of road building. So, before we go into how Cisco hubs and switches address these problems, it's necessary to learn about the physical media over which networks operate: the cabling.

The most fundamental fact about networks is that they run over either of two kinds of physical transport media:

▼ Copper wire

▲ Fiber-optic cable

The vast majority of all LANs installed in the world today are on some form of copper wire. Fiber-optic cabling—often called *fiber* or *glass* for short—is mostly used for high-speed backbones.

The proliferation of network users and bandwidth-hungry applications has driven the industry to introduce a steady stream of newer and faster transport technologies. A review of network cabling and terminology will help you keep things straight.

A Brief History of LAN Cabling

As mentioned, the earliest LANs ran over Thicknet coaxial cables. Thicknet was costly and hard to work with, so in the mid-1980s it was replaced by Thinnet coaxial cable (which is also called Cheapernet). When used to run 10 Mbps Ethernet, Thinnet has a maximum length of 185 meters. Thinnet LANs can be extended beyond that distance using repeaters to link segments. (*Repeaters* are devices placed along a LAN cable to amplify electrical signals and extend maximum operating length. Simple repeaters are rarely used now.) Also, coaxial cable requires that there be a certain minimum amount of spacing between connections, which cramps topology design choices.

Hubs were introduced in the late 1980s. Also called concentrators, hubs make hierarchical network topologies possible and simplify the installation and management of a cable plant. Hubs hastened the introduction of a new type of cabling called twisted-pair, which is inexpensive and very easy to work with. One of the reasons using twisted-pair became possible is that its relatively short operating limit of 100 meters is extensible using hubs. For example, an office space 300 meters in length could be wired with twisted- pair by placing two hubs into the topology.

LAN Cabling Today

Most larger networks today use a combination of fiber and twisted-pair. Twisted-pair is used to connect hosts to hubs; fiber is used for network backbones. Thanks to technological advances, even though twisted-pair uses less copper and shielding than Thinnet coaxial cable, it supports faster data rates. About the same time twisted-pair was taking over desktop connectivity, fiber-optic cabling established itself as the preferred medium for high-speed network backbones. Fiber is used to connect floors or major areas within an office building; twisted-pair is used to connect LAN segments spanning from the backbone. As Figure 6-5 depicts, hubs and switches funnel the LAN segments into the backbone via various star-hierarchy configurations. *Backbone* is a relative term, however. For example, the fiber trunk interconnecting the buildings of a campus LAN is referred to as its backbone, while the fiber-optic cable connecting the floors of one of the buildings is referred to as a *riser*.

Twisted-pair cable comes in two basic types:

▼ **STP (shielded twisted-pair)**   A two-pair cabling medium encased in shielded insulation to limit electromagnetic interference of signals.

▲ **UTP (unshielded twisted-pair)**   A four-pair cabling medium not encased in shielding. UTP is used in most networks.

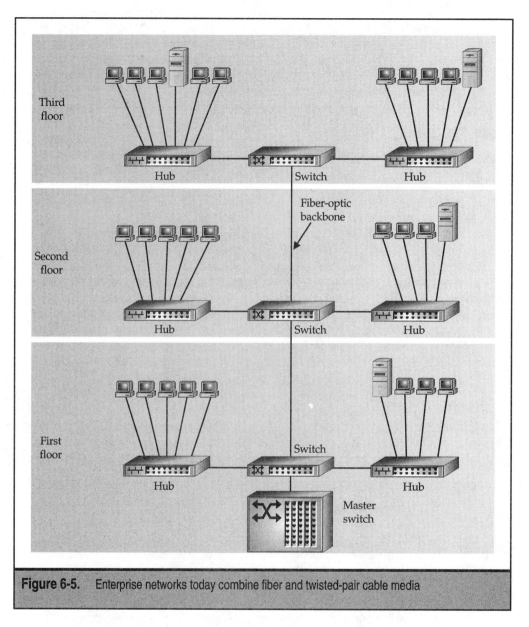

Figure 6-5.   Enterprise networks today combine fiber and twisted-pair cable media

The more tightly twisted the copper wire strands are, the less likely it is there will be interference or signal loss. STP has only two twisted pairs, but compensates with its shielding. UTP has no shielding, but compensates with an extra pair of wires. Because UTP is fast, reliable, and inexpensive, it has become the predominant type of cabling used in networking today. Use of the more expensive STP is limited to environments made hostile by high levels of electromagnetic interference.

CABLING SPECIFICATIONS Table 6-2 explains the five categories of unshielded twisted-pair specified by an international standards organization called TIA/EIA (Telecommunications Industry Association/Electronics Industry Association). These cabling specifications are important in that the rate at which data can be reliably transmitted is determined by a combination of factors:

▼ How tightly twisted the copper wire is

■ The quality of the cable's copper

■ The type of insulation used to encase the cable

▲ The design and quality of the cable connectors

In Table 6-2, Categories 3 and 5 represent the lion's share of twisted-pair networks today—especially Cat 5.

Category	Cable Description	Cable Application
Cat 1	Traditional telephone cable	Not usable for networking; no longer installed for telephones
Cat 2	Four twisted-pairs	4 Mbps, not recommended for networking
Cat 3	Four twisted-pairs with three twists per foot, rated up to 16 MHz	10 Mbps Ethernet and 4 Mbps for Token Ring, also used for new telephone cabling
Cat 4	Four twisted-pairs, rated up to 20 MHz	16 Mbps, used for Token Ring
Cat 5	Four twisted-pairs with eight twists per foot, rated up to 100 MHz	100 Mbps, used for Fast Ethernet, fast becoming ubiquitous in networked buildings
Enhanced Cat 5	Four twisted-pairs with eight twists per foot, but made of higher-quality materials and rated up to 200 MHz	(Forthcoming) Rated up to twice the transmission capability of regular Cat 5
Cat 6	Four twisted-pairs with each pair wrapped in foil insulation; whole bundle wrapped in polymer	(Forthcoming) Rated up to six times the transmission capability of regular Cat 5

Table 6-2. TIA/EIA Unshielded Twisted-Pair (UTP) Specifications

Note that higher category numbers indicate higher speeds. Most new LAN installations use Cat 5 in order to accommodate 100 Mbps Fast Ethernet, but many still run on older Cat 3 because it's so widely installed in network infrastructures.

The alternative to copper cabling is fiber-optic cabling. Although it's used mostly as a backbone medium, it's sometimes used all the way out to the desktop for demanding applications such as high-end graphics. The advantage of fiber is that it can sustain very high speeds over long distances, but its use is constrained by relatively high costs. Even so, many envision that one day all new installations will be over fiber.

NETWORK TECHNOLOGIES   Cabling specifications such as Cat 5 describe the physical medium. *Network specifications* describe what is to happen over a medium and are built around the capabilities and limitations of one or more cabling specifications.

There are several Ethernet specifications, each designed to guarantee efficacy on the physical medium over which it's designed to operate. Any networking technology's ability to function properly depends on how well matched it is to the physical medium. The faster a network must run—or the greater the distance over which it will operate—the better the underlying cable plant must be.

Network specification names seem mysterious until you've been introduced to the logic behind them. The following illustration breaks down the name of the most widely installed network specification in the world today, Ethernet 10BaseT.

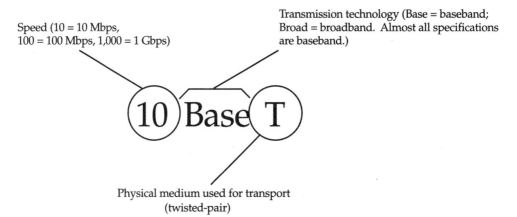

Sorting out the various network specifications shows that some media are used only for certain speeds, some are legacy specs no longer used in new installations, and others are specs that never quite caught on. Table 6-3 lists network specifications (mostly Ethernet) in their approximate order of importance based on

▼ Percentage of new LANs being installed

■ Percentage of all installations

▲ Probable future importance as a technology

The specifications reflect the worldwide trend toward Ethernet technologies. The two major exceptions are FDDI and ATM.

LAN Spec	Description
10BaseT	10 Mbps Ethernet using UTP Cats 3, 4, or 5 cabling; most new installations during the 1990s; in the process of being eclipsed by 100BaseT; 100-meter limit
100BaseTX	100 Mbps Fast Ethernet using UTP Cat 5 cabling; most new installations going in now are 100BaseT; 100-meter limit
100BaseFX	100 Mbps Fast Ethernet using two strands of multimode fiber-optic cable per link; most new high-speed backbones are 100BaseFX; 400-meter limit
FDDI	100 Mbps Fiber Distributed Data Interface token-passing LAN using either single-mode or multimode fiber-optic cabling (or sometimes either STP or UTP copper, called CDDI, for Copper Distributed Data Interface); 100-kilometer limit over fiber, 100-meter limit over copper
ATM	622 Mbps Asynchronous Transfer Mode over fiber-optic cabling; popular as a backbone for its sustained throughput and its proven ability to move multimedia applications at speed
1000BaseFX	1 Gbps Gigabit Ethernet over fiber-optic cabling; although 1000BaseX is now being reengineered to run over Cat 5 copper (to be called 1000BaseTX)
100VG-AnyLAN	100 Mbps Fast Ethernet and Token Ring using UTP Cats 3, 4, or 5 cabling; developed by Hewlett-Packard; can be run over any existing 10BaseT networks
10Base2	10 Mbps Ethernet using Thinnet coaxial cabling; widely installed in the 1980s; eclipsed by 10BaseT; 185-meter limit
10Base5	10 Mbps Ethernet using Thicknet coaxial cabling; widely installed in 1970s and 1980s; 500-meter limit
100BaseT4	100 Mbps Fast Ethernet using four pairs of UTP Cats 3, 4, or 5 cabling; 100-meter limit
10BaseFB	10 Mbps Ethernet using fiber-optic cabling; used as a LAN backbone (not to connect hosts directly); 2-kilometer limit

Table 6-3. LAN Specifications with Cable Types and Distance Limits

LAN Spec	Description
10BaseFL	10 Mbps Ethernet using fiber-optic cabling; 2000 kilometer limit, 1 kilometer with FOIRL (Fiber-Optic Inter-Repeater Link, a precursor signaling methodology that FL replaces)
10BaseFP	10 Mbps Ethernet using fiber-optic cabling; used to link computers into a star topology without using repeaters; 500-meter limit
10Broad36	10 Mbps Ethernet using broadband coaxial cable cabling; 3.6 kilometer limit

Table 6-3. LAN Specifications with Cable Types and Distance Limits *(continued)*

Table 6-3 shows that many network specifications are either old or are contending standards meeting with limited market acceptance. The trend in networking technology is of course toward ever-faster speeds running over cheaper cabling plant. Not including high-speed backbones, most new LANs today use 100BaseTX Fast Ethernet running over Cat 5 cabling.

Things are less clear about which technology is winning out as the backbone medium of choice. As this book is being written, ATM is supplanting FDDI, probably in part due to the recent sharp increase in the demand for multimedia applications. ATM's competition as the backbone of the future is 1000BaseX, commonly called Gigabit Ethernet. Planners not only like Gigabit Ethernet's rated speed of 1000 Mbps, but they also like its compatibility with most installed Ethernet networks. Chapter 2 discusses competing network technologies in detail.

NOTE: Ever wonder how data travels over a cable? In simple terms, electrical pulses going over a wire are measured for plus or minus voltages to track signals. Special encoding schemes—for example, the Institute of Electrical and Electronics Engineers (IEEE) schemes for Fast Ethernet and Gigabit Ethernet—are used to translate data from identifiable bit patterns represented by the voltage fluctuations. Fast Ethernet uses a three-level encoding scheme to track data; Gigabit Ethernet uses a five-level encoding scheme. The two major problems facing network communications are return-loss and far-end crosstalk. Without getting bogged down in engineering details: *return-loss* is when a signal echoes back to the transmitter, confusing it; *crosstalk* is when signals leak between wire pairs, creating electrical noise. Network engineers are always looking for improved encoding schemes to squeeze more bandwidth into smaller wires. It ain't like connecting two tin cans with a baling wire, is it?

WHAT HUBS AND SWITCHES DO, AND HOW THEY DIFFER

Hubs and switches have many similarities—so much so that the technical name for a switch is switched-hub. Both contain banks of connection ports into which twisted-pair cables can be plugged (usually with RJ-45 connectors, which are similar to phone jacks). Hubs and switches both compose a LAN domain, both can be used to funnel messages into network backbones, and both support remote management. Figure 6-6 depicts their similarities.

The essential distinction between hubs and switches is that a switch can create a private connection between hosts on a network. In other words, they split bandwidth. Instead of contending for a shared medium as hosts connected to a hub-based LAN must do, hosts on a switched-based LAN are given full use of the medium's bandwidth for the split second it takes to complete the transmission.

Switches create network domains based on administrative parameters, not on physical connections. Put another way, using switches, an administrator can sit down and create broadcast domains at will, whereas rearranging domain memberships in a shared hub network requires physically reconnecting hosts. Figure 6-7 draws out the differences between hubs and switches.

The defining difference between the two is how they handle signals from hosts connected to them.

A hub simply takes frames received from one attached host and retransmits them to all other hosts attached to it. A switch looks at the frames coming into its ports and immediately transfers—or switches—them over to one or more other switch ports. Because the process is so fast, switches allow multiple data streams to pass simultaneously. This is how switches are able to support dozens of hosts funneled into a single switch port. Only

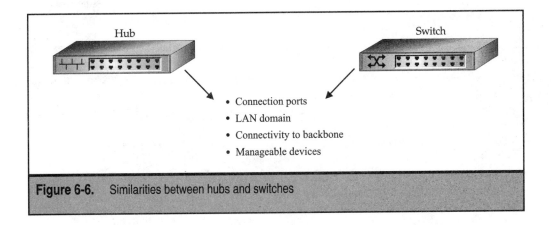

Figure 6-6. Similarities between hubs and switches

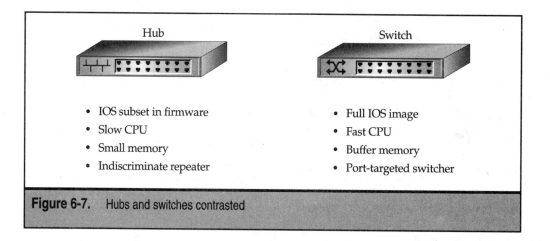

Figure 6-7.　Hubs and switches contrasted

one frame is actually being switched between ports at any given instant. But the process is so fast that it's transparent to the hosts involved.

NOTE:　Usually this book talks about messages when referring to network transmissions because it's a common-sense term that's generic at any level of internetworking. The term *frame* is used because part of being network savvy means knowing the subtleties. Messages are not transmitted over networks as whole entities any more than a word goes over a phone line as a single sound wave. A frame is the message subunit at layer 2—the data-link layer—of the OSI reference model. A *packet* is a subunit of a message at layer 3—the network layer. Switches operate at layer 2 and thus move frames. Routers operate at layer 3 and deal in packets. Don't be confused if you see frame and packet used interchangeably; it doesn't necessarily mean you're misunderstanding, because by their strict definitions these terms are often used incorrectly, even by networking experts.

Because their mission is so much more sophisticated than a hub's, switches run full-blown images of IOS software that can be operated through the IOS command-line interface. Cisco hubs have only cut-down IOS functionality loaded in firmware and operated through a menu-driven interface called the Hub Management Console. Indeed, a low-end hub has no interface at all. You simply turn it on and let it set itself up. These are often called *dumb hubs*.

Switches have more powerful hardware and software capabilities that make it possible to create and manage domains. At the extreme, each physical switch port can be made into a collision domain of one. Buy a 16-port switch and you get 16 collision domains right out of the box.

Switches overcome most of the trade-offs that come with shared media and LAN segmentation. They eliminate unnecessary network delays by letting administrators specify broadcast domains on a case-by-case basis. For these reasons and others, the world is moving from hub-based hierarchical topology networks to switched networks, in which unwanted randomness is removed at minimal cost to connectivity.

But, as Figure 6-8 depicts, the hub's ability to provide cheap and simple device connectivity has carved out a role in switched networks. For cost reasons, switched ports are rarely dedicated to a single device. The majority of switched ports service a group of hosts, and those hosts are connected to the shared switch port through a hub.

As the price gap narrows, switches will eventually replace hubs altogether, much as routers replaced bridges over the past decade. But that hasn't happened yet. For its part, the hub has gotten smarter and less expensive over the years. Hubs continue to be used for enterprise work groups and small companies. Even computer rooms at the center of sophisticated enterprise networks use hubs as an easy and inexpensive way to make

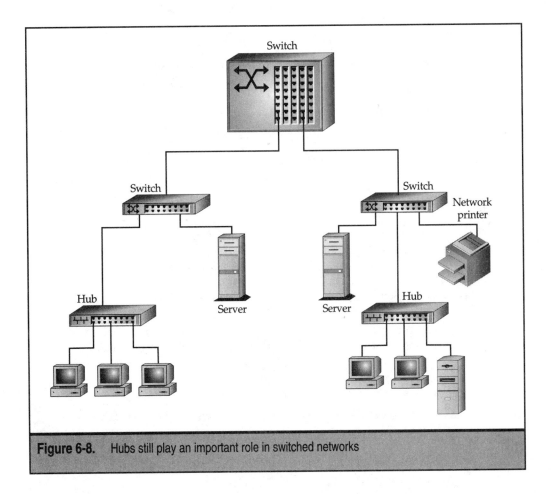

Figure 6-8. Hubs still play an important role in switched networks

ports available to low-volume servers, administrative PCs, computer room printers, network monitor hosts, and other equipment.

Another reason hub technology persists is that as the world of internetworking booms, an ongoing stream of new LANs are created. Most of these new networks are small, and their users want the kind of low-cost, simple-to-manage connectivity hubs provide.

Picking the Right Tool

Most LANs should be segmented using some form of star-configured hierarchy. This should be done if for no other reason than to simplify the network's wiring. Beyond that, LAN connectivity then becomes a two-level question:

▼ Whether to use hubs or switches, or some combination of the two

▲ Which model of hub or switch to use and what options to configure

Deciding how to configure a LAN is largely a matter of analyzing network traffic patterns:

1. The first factor to review is whether the network is performing at sufficient speed. Don't fall into the trap of useless statistics here; measure the LAN's performance at peak periods, say, during month-end accounting closings or seasonal sales peaks.

2. Forecast growth of the user community. Firm up projections to about two years out. If you're a lowly technician, don't be shy about getting well-considered projections from senior management—after all, they'll be the first to howl if the network slows to a crawl a year from now. If you're in a big enterprise, try to make sure the projections you're given are in line with other planning baselines being used by finance.

3. Project change in the application mix. Are any new computer applications planned that are likely to affect bandwidth consumption? The most likely suspects are videoconferencing, computer telephony, and anything graphical. Network planners should take special care if any extranet projects are in the works. An *extranet* is a sort of intranet, but open to preferred trading partners, usually by interfacing the intranets of two or more enterprises. In an extranet, cooperative business partners are allowed to tap into your enterprise's intranet to perform tasks—and when they do this, they'll be consuming resources. Extranet projects can blindside planners if they forget to factor in resource demand driven by users outside the organization.

4. Forecast changes in "enterprise geography." The movement of users and resources within the enterprise can strain networks, even in the absence of overall growth. Security, logistics, and network management must respond to organizational flux. And remember that network planning is not just a matter of switches, routers, and firewalls; the expertise and human resources must be there to implement and support technology.

Generally speaking, hub-based networks will suffice if user demand for bandwidth is growing slowly and there are no special security requirements. However, if bandwidth demand, organizational change, or new security and/or network management requirements are on the horizon, serious consideration should be given to using switched networks instead of hubs.

CISCO HUBS

If you take a close look at Cisco's product documentation, you'll see the description of each Cisco hub as a Class II repeater. Virtually all modern hubs are Class II repeaters—all the ones discussed in this book are. But you should know about Class I repeaters in case you encounter them somewhere.

An active hub is an IEEE Class I repeater, which uses an analog-to-digital conversion of the electrical signal coming into the hub in order to allow passing it between different Ethernet implementations (for example, from 10BaseT to 100BaseTX). The conversion introduces a time delay, which puts a limit of one or two Class I hosts per segment. A *passive hub* is a Class II repeater, which performs no signal conversion and simply retransmits the signal. Because Class II repeaters introduce virtually no delay, additional repeaters can be put on a single LAN segment. Therefore, for speed and simplicity almost all hubs are of the lower-tech Class II variety. All Cisco hubs are Class II repeaters.

NOTE: In the Ethernet space, the hub is still sometimes referred to as a *concentrator* or *repeater*. In Token Ring environments, the hub is referred to as an *MSAU (multi-station access unit)*. In FDDI networks, hubs are called concentrators.

Cisco Hub Basics

Cisco manufactures several hub product models. The Cisco product line isn't covered in detail here. Refer to Chapter 1 of this book for how the Cisco hub product line is positioned, or browse cisco.com to find catalogs of information on hubs and other Cisco products. Major features can be used to differentiate hubs:

▼ Can the hub be stacked, or is it standalone only?

■ Is the hub model's chassis modular or fixed configuration?

■ Can the hub be managed?

▲ What LAN protocol(s) can the hub support?

Stackable Hubs vs. Standalone Hubs

Stacks create a single logical hub from multiple hubs, electronically linking them together. Stack connections are not high-level links made when a router talks to another router. A hub stack is integrated using special cables running between IN and OUT stack ports in each hub. The level of integration in stacks takes place at a lower level closer to the electronics and so is very fast. Stacks daisy-chain hubs in this way to create logical hub units like the one depicted here:

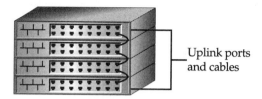

Uplink ports and cables

Stack-member hubs must be assigned Hub ID numbers according to the following numbering regimen:

▼ The hub with no hub connected to its OUT uplink port and with another hub connected to its IN uplink port is always assigned the highest Hub ID number (any number from 2 to 5).

▲ The lowest Hub ID number in a stack (number 1) is always the hub with another hub connected to its OUT uplink port and with no hub connected to its IN uplink port.

Generally, there can be up to four Cisco hubs in a stack. Stacks are truly integrated in the sense that all connection ports within a stack operate under a single IP address, and all the hubs within the stack's logical hub can be managed as a unit. For all practical purposes, once a hub is integrated into a stack, it becomes just another part within a logical hub. If a hub cannot be stacked, it's referred to as a *standalone hub*.

Cascaded Hubs vs. Stackable Hubs

Sooner or later you'll encounter the term *cascaded hubs*. How are cascaded hubs different from stacked hubs? Cascaded hubs don't have uplink port connections via special cables; instead, a second hub is connected to the first hub as if it were a normal host such as a PC or a server. Where stacked hubs create a single logical unit and one collision domain, each cascaded hub is its own collision domain, as depicted in Figure 6-9.

Cascading hubs is a stop-gap practice. A cascaded hub is usually put out in the work space as a quick-and-dirty way to get more connection ports in the area in lieu of proper wall plate end points. Cascading one hub is OK, but daisy-chaining two or more hubs to a master hub is a definite no-no, both because manageability goes out the window and because the electronics are slow (hub connection ports are designed to handle a single host, not a hub bringing in traffic from several hosts).

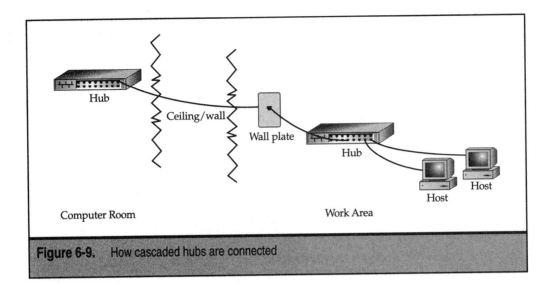

Figure 6-9. How cascaded hubs are connected

Modular Hubs vs. Fixed-Configuration Hubs

Modular means that additional modules (printed circuit boards, sometimes also called *cards* or *line-cards*) can be inserted into the chassis in order to expand its configuration. Some Cisco FastHubs are able to incorporate up to four modules per box. Low-end FastHubs are fixed in configuration; you cannot add modules.

Most often, modules are added to increase the number of ports. Some Cisco documentation calls this increasing the device's *port density*. The overall port density of a network composed of fixed-configuration hubs can be increased by stacking.

Two other kinds of Cisco hub modules are the NMMs (network management modules) and BMMs (bridge management modules). Each fulfills a dedicated role. An NMM provides on-board intelligence for RMON, SNMP, and Telnet, which together make possible per-port, per-hub, and per-stack management. A BMM provides all the NMM functionality plus the ability to maintain a MAC address table.

Managed Hubs vs. Unmanaged Hubs

Some hubs are manageable and others are not. Cisco refers to the two types as *managed* and *unmanaged* hubs, as shown in the following illustration. As with fixed-configuration models, unmanaged hubs are offered to save money. A second kind of managed hub is called a *manageable* hub, which must be in a stack with a managed hub in order to be remotely managed.

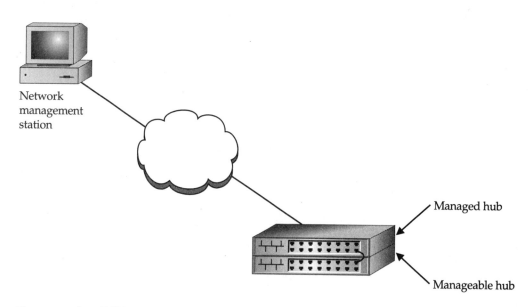

Network
management
station

Managed hub

Manageable hub

Support for Different LAN Specifications

Another differentiating feature is that some Cisco Ethernet hubs are dual speed, in that they can automatically sense whether 10BaseT or 100BaseT is being received and operate accordingly. These hubs are marketed to the world's huge installed base of 10 Mbps 10BaseT networks now in the process of migrating to the 100 Mbps specification. Keep in mind that large internetworks don't cut over from a legacy standard to a newer standard all at once. It's more practical (and safer) to phase over gradually to the new technology, converting the more bandwidth-hungry hosts first. The Cisco 1528 Micro Hub 10/100, for example, was introduced for just this market.

All Cisco hub models are specific to layer 2 of the seven-layer OSI model. Hubs must be purchased to match the networking technology implemented in the network in which they are meant to operate. In other words, if you want to connect hosts to an Ethernet, not only must you buy an Ethernet-compatible hub, but the hub must also be of the same Ethernet implementation as your network (for example, you must have a 10BaseFX-compatible hub to connect hosts in a 10BaseFX network).

Sometimes you may want to uplink into the larger network through a faster medium than that used for host ports. An *uplink* port is generally used to carry signals from the hub to another device nearer the LAN backbone (uplinks are used in switches, too). To satisfy this need, some Cisco devices are dual specification (as contrasted with dual speed). Figure 6-10 shows a 16-port hub with 15 100BaseTX ports and one 100BaseFX uplink port so as to carry traffic *up* to a faster device over a fiber-optic cable.

Straight-Through vs. Crossover Cables and Devices

Network hardware documentation frequently refers to *straight-through* cables and *crossover* cables. Network devices have transmitter (TX) pins and receiver (RX) pins. In a

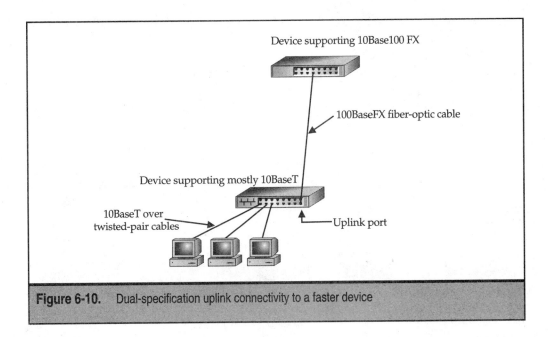

Figure 6-10.   Dual-specification uplink connectivity to a faster device

straight-through cable, the wire pair does not cross from TX to RX between interfaces. In a crossover cable, wire pairs are crossed over from TX to RX between connections. You must use crossover cables to connect hosts with identical interfaces. If a straight-through cable is used, one of the two devices must perform the crossover function. If neither device has a crossover connector, then a straight-through cable must be used. In other words, signals must be crossed over either in one of the devices or in the cable. Figure 6-11 illustrates the two ways.

Think of a signal traveling RX-to-RX or TX-to-TX as being like a conversation in which two persons mouth words, but no sound reaches their ears. Crossing over signals between devices makes networking possible by moving the signal from "mouth to ear."

Cisco Hub Products

As with routers, choosing a Cisco hub model should be a straightforward process. There are three general classes of Cisco hubs, as explained in Table 6-4. Developments in hub technology in the future will focus on making them low cost and simple to manage.

Configuring and Managing Cisco Hubs

Hubs are relatively straightforward devices. To put a host on a hub-based LAN is a matter of simply plugging its cable into one of the hub's ports.

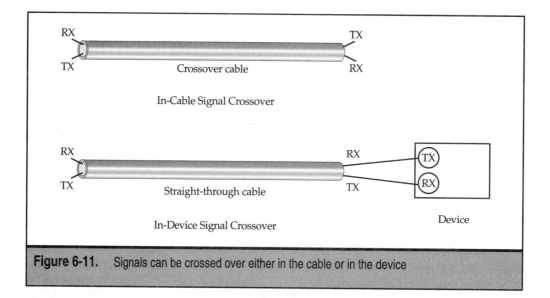

Figure 6-11. Signals can be crossed over either in the cable or in the device

Series	Description
Cisco FastHub 400 Series	High-performance Fast Ethernet 10/100 hubs in both modular and fixed-configuration models, with 12 or 24 ports per module and up to hundreds of ports per stack. All models are stackable in either managed or manageable versions. (Note: As of this writing, the FastHub 100, 200, and 300 Series models are being consolidated into the 400 Series.)
Cisco Mirco Hub 1500 Series	Low-cost Fast Ethernet 10/100 hubs in fixed 8-port configuration desktop models for the small office or home office. Both Micro Hub models are stackable; one is managed, the other is manageable.
10BaseT Hub	Developed with Hewlett-Packard, this is a Fast Ethernet 10/100 fixed-configuration managed hub optimized for use with Cisco Catalyst 1900 and 2820 Series switches. It is not stackable but can be cascaded.
Specialty Hubs	Concentrators used in specialized environments such as FDDI.

Table 6-4. General Classes of Cisco Hub Products

Proper configuration, of course, involves more than just plugging a host into a hub. Much like when configuring a router interface, the network administrator must configure a host into a shared hub LAN by setting many parameters.

If the device is a manageable hub, the first step is to use the Console port in order to assign an IP address; then you can Telnet to it. Cisco hubs have an interface called the Hub Management Console. The Hub Management Console is menu driven, and there is no command-line interface as there is with IOS images running on a router or switch. Hubs contain only a stripped-down version of IOS deployed in firmware loaded at the factory (or downloaded to the hub to update the revision level). Instead of typing in complex commands, you navigate using menu selections and the TAB key, much like the setup menus in a PC's BIOS. The interface doesn't need to be fancy or powerful because configurable hubs only have a limited number of parameters the user can set. Mostly the Management Console is used to review hub status and activity statistics in order to troubleshoot problems.

Configuration parameters can be set at both the port level and the unit level (*unit* here means the entire hub instead of just one of its ports). Figure 6-12 shows the IP Configuration screen.

```
 Telnet - 10.1.1.3                                                  _ □ ×
Connect  Edit  Terminal  Help
qqqqqqqqqqqqqqqqqqqqqqqqqqqqqqqqqqqqqqqqqqqqqqqqqqqqqqqqqqqqqqqqqqqqqqqq
                          FastHub 200 Series
qqqqqqqqqqqqqqqqqqqqqqqqqqqqqqqqqqqqqqqqqqqqqqqqqqqqqqqqqqqqqqqqqqqqqqqq
                           IP Configuration

                Ethernet Address:   00-C0-1D-83-EC-07

       IP address of system              [010.001.001.003]
       IP subnet mask                    [255.255.255.000]
       IP address of default gateway     [010.001.001.001]
       IP address of DNS server 1        [010.001.001.100]
       IP address of DNS server 2        [000.000.000.000]
       DNS domain name                   [velte.com              ]
       Use Routing Information Protocol  [Disabled]




                            < Exit >




    Press F3 or ? for help on the selected item
```

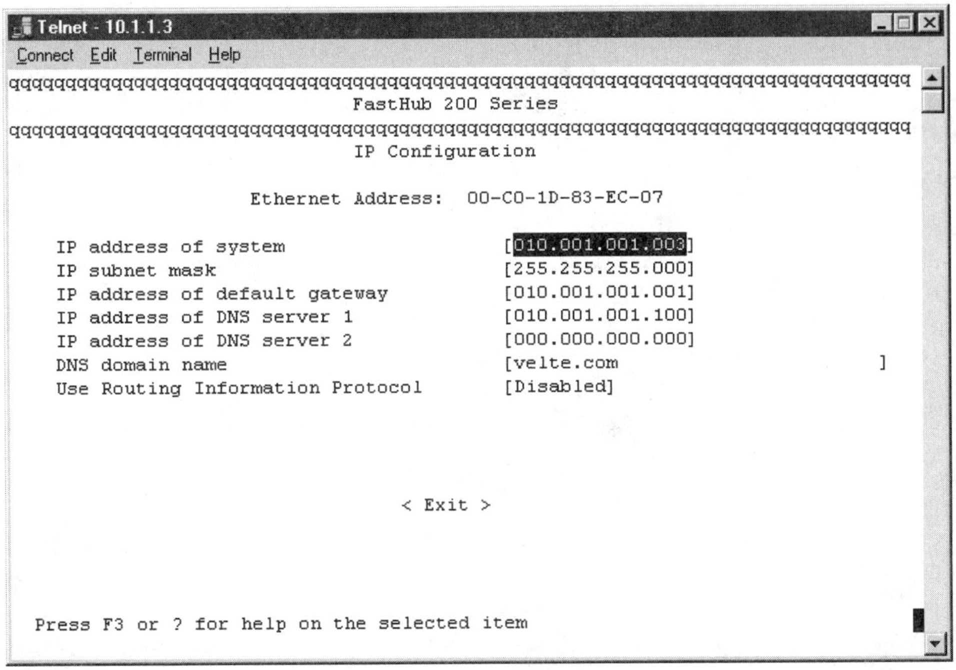

Figure 6-12. Cisco FastHub 200 Series IP Configuration screen

The IP address, subnet mask, and default gateway addresses are assigned to the hub in order to be able to access the hub via Telnet or SNMP. The DNS (Domain Naming System) server addresses attach the hub to the network's domain name.

> **NOTE:** Always prepare before starting to configure a device. Scrambling to find information (such as the IP addresses in Figure 6-12) during a configuration session wastes time and can lead to mistakes. Cisco provides users with configuration worksheets to help avoid this pitfall and make configuration a more pleasant experience.

Other configuration parameters to be configured include such mundane but important things as giving the hub a name, setting up password control, and making the hub active in the LAN (by setting its Port Status to enabled). Most of the options available in the Hub Management Console are ways to review status reports on the hub's operations. Hub status can be reported on a per-unit and per-port basis.

Refer to Appendix A for a complete review of Hub Management Console screens. We suggest you flip through these to get a flavor of how Cisco hubs are managed. A discussion on how hubs can be configured and managed using SNMP and CiscoWorks is in Chapter 9.

CISCO SWITCHES

It's no exaggeration to say that switched network technology is revolutionizing how internetworks are designed and what they can do for users. Over the last 15 years, hubs helped the world build millions of reliable and effective LANs. Over the past 5 years, switches have begun pushing internetworks to size scales and service levels many considered unfeasible not long ago.

This is because switches operate in a fundamentally different way than hubs. To illustrate: while a 26-port hub would have a collision domain of 16, a 16-port switch would have a collision domain of 1 (both would have a broadcast domain of 16). Switched networks are faster for the simple reason that bandwidth loss from collisions is virtually eliminated. With that kind of efficiency, it's not outlandish to state that one day in the future many Ethernet hosts will have a collision domain of one—and still have full connectivity to all other hosts on a network.

But what exactly are switched networks? How do they work? As Cisco likes to put it: hubs deliver shared media; switches deliver shared bandwidth. How can the switch do this? The answer is in the electronics.

▼ They run at very high speeds because they operate at the data-link layer (layer 2) instead of at the network layer (layer 3) where routers operate. This enables switches to process traffic without creating bottlenecks.

▲ They have many of the capabilities of a router, but sit between the host and the backbone, instead of between backbones as routers do. Switches can take control over traffic at or near its source, whereas the router usually doesn't take over until the message is ready to begin its trek to a remote LAN. Taking control at the source takes much of the randomness out of network operations.

How an Individual Switch Works

Almost all computer advances in one way or another come down to miniaturization and speed, and the network switch is no different. What separates a switch from a hub is its electronics. Signals entering a hub port are indiscriminately repeated to the hub's other ports. Not so with the switch, which is smart and fast enough to read both the source port and the destination port of each frame and "switch" messages between the two (thus the name). This is shown in Figure 6-13.

Much like routers, switches examine destination and source addresses as messages pass through. Switches differ from routers in that they're looking at layer-2 MAC addresses instead of layer-3 IP addresses.

The switch like the hub provides a shared media LAN into which hosts can connect. But the switch is at the same time able to assume router-like duties, for two reasons:

▼ Switches have more powerful electronics than hubs (they have more transistors crammed onto their printed circuit boards).

▲ They operate at the data-link layer (layer 2), which means they don't have to dig as deep into messages as layer-3 routers.

Beefed-up electronics gives the switch the ability of a speed reader. But while switches are smart, they're not nearly as smart as routers. The switch is in effect assigned a lighter reading assignment than routers because it handles traffic at layer 2.

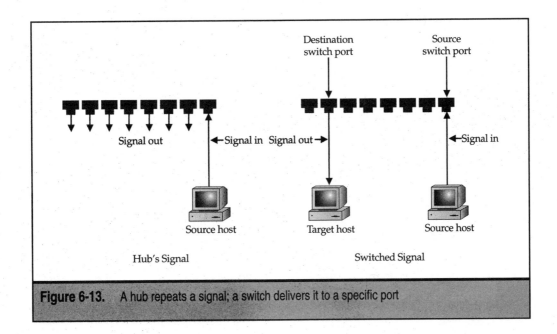

Figure 6-13. A hub repeats a signal; a switch delivers it to a specific port

To illustrate this, Figure 6-14 traces a message through a hypothetical switched network. The first step takes place between the host sending the message and its switch port. To do this the switch reads the incoming message's destination MAC address and instantly moves it to the outbound port it associates with that destination MAC.

Because the message is switched to a targeted outbound port instead of being replicated to all ports (as in a hub), it encounters no collisions. This makes more bandwidth available and moves messages at faster throughput speeds.

The same process holds for the message's second step. As the message pours out of the outbound port on Switch 1, it has dedicated bandwidth (no collisions) over the cable connecting it to the port in Switch 2. The switching process again repeats itself through the third step all the way out to the destination host.

When a switch receives a message seeking an address it doesn't know, instead of dropping the message, the switch broadcasts the message to all its ports. This process is called *flooding*, which is necessary for discovery-type messages. For example, DHCP (Dynamic Host Configuration Protocol) is used by a host when it boots up to locate nearby services such as network printers. Without flooding, switches could not support broadcast messages sent by DHCP and other utilities.

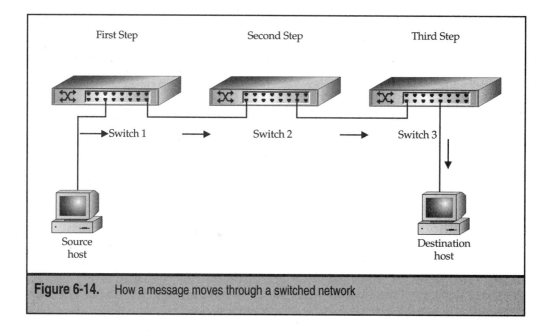

Figure 6-14.   How a message moves through a switched network

Switched Networking Basics

How is it possible to have dedicated bandwidth all the way through a multiple device network connecting hundreds of hosts? The answer is that switched networks balance intelligence with raw power.

In simplified terms, routers move messages through an internetwork to their destinations by working from left to right across the destination's IP address, as depicted here:

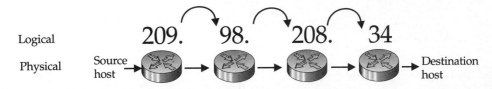

As the message hops between routers, it checks the routing table maintained in each new router, trying to match the next part of the destination IP address. When it finds a more complete match, the message physically moves through the internetwork to the router whose location is represented by that matched IP address information. Sooner or later all the IP address parts are matched, and the message arrives at the router serving as the gateway to the destination host.

In sharp contrast, a message must find its way through a switched network without the luxury of hierarchical IP addresses. Switched networks operate using MAC addresses, which are considered to be flat in topology. A MAC address—also called a physical address—is a sort of network serial number assigned to a host's NIC. The first half of every MAC address is a vendor code signifying the manufacturer of the NIC; the second half is the serial number of the actual device. If you move a device to the other side of the world, its MAC address remains unchanged. Switched networks are completely flat in that because they rely solely on MAC addresses, they in effect think all devices and hosts are attached to the same cable. Beyond the friendly confines of the home LAN, a MAC address is a small clue. How, then, do switched networks manage to deliver messages?

When a switch is turned on, it begins building a dynamic address table. It does so by examining the source MAC address of each incoming frame and associating it with the port through which it came. In this way, the switch figures out what hosts are attached to each of its ports. Figure 6-15 shows a dynamic address table.

The switch also discovers and maps the surrounding neighborhood using CDP (Cisco Discovery Protocol), which was covered in the preceding chapter. The switch uses CDP to discover nearby switches and begins sharing dynamic address table information with them. CDP only talks to those switches it can ping directly; but as Figure 6-16 shows, that doesn't matter. MAC addresses are passed back through a chain of cooperating switches until they reach the switch building its dynamic address table.

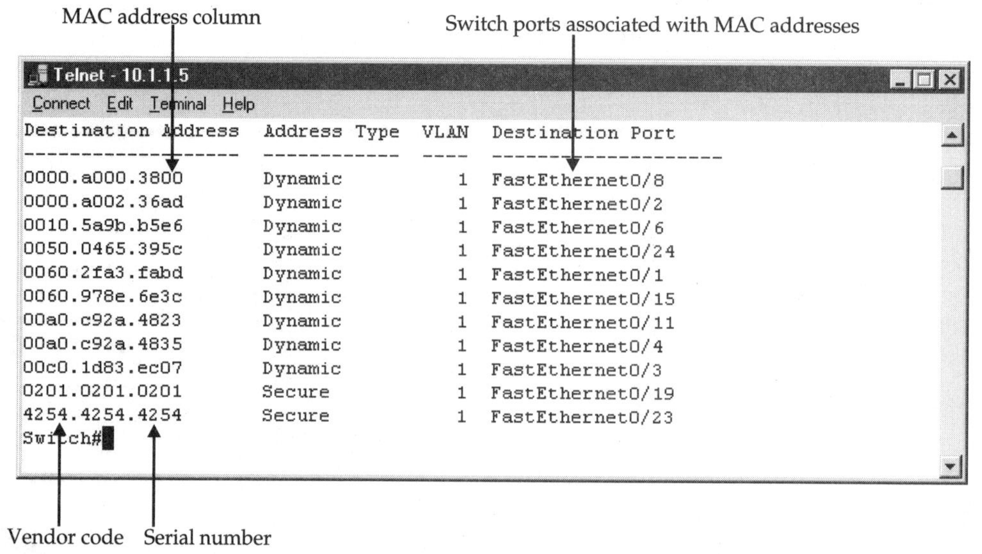

MAC address column   Switch ports associated with MAC addresses

```
Telnet - 10.1.1.5                                                    _ □ ✕
Connect  Edit  Terminal  Help
Destination Address    Address Type   VLAN   Destination Port
------------------     ------------   ----   ----------------
0000.a000.3800         Dynamic          1    FastEthernet0/8
0000.a002.36ad         Dynamic          1    FastEthernet0/2
0010.5a9b.b5e6         Dynamic          1    FastEthernet0/6
0050.0465.395c         Dynamic          1    FastEthernet0/24
0060.2fa3.fabd         Dynamic          1    FastEthernet0/1
0060.978e.6e3c         Dynamic          1    FastEthernet0/15
00a0.c92a.4823         Dynamic          1    FastEthernet0/11
00a0.c92a.4835         Dynamic          1    FastEthernet0/4
00c0.1d83.ec07         Dynamic          1    FastEthernet0/3
0201.0201.0201         Secure           1    FastEthernet0/19
4254.4254.4254         Secure           1    FastEthernet0/23
Switch#
```

Vendor code   Serial number

Figure 6-15.   The contents of a switch's dynamic address table are topologically flat

Theoretically, a switch could eventually compile a list containing the MAC addresses of every switch in the world. To prevent that from happening, switches drop unused MACs after a default period of five minutes. The dynamic address table isn't as smart as routing tables, which use all types of costing algorithms to choose optimal paths. A switch simply places the most frequently used MACs toward the top of its dynamic address table. Together, these two procedures guarantee that the switch's network path–finding intelligence is at least fresh and more likely to be reliable.

Designing Switched Internetworks

Even if a switch's dynamic address table could identify a path through a very large switched internetwork, if that path required hundreds or even just dozens of hops, it would be too slow. Two technologies have been developed to solve this problem:

▼   Switched backbones

▲   Multilayer switching

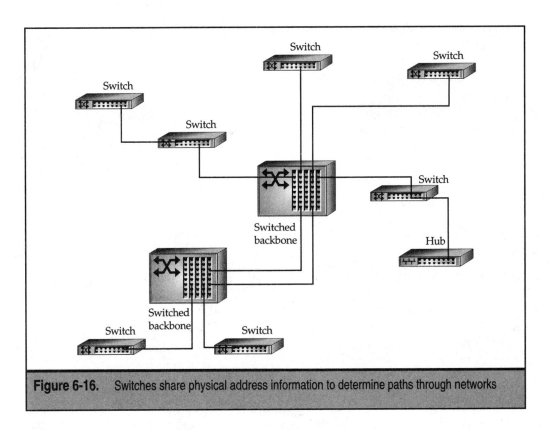

Figure 6-16. Switches share physical address information to determine paths through networks

Switched Backbones

Switched backbones are high-end switches used to aggregate bandwidth from other switches. The idea of a switched backbone is for it to have the biggest dynamic address table of all. Switched backbones are frequently configured with multiple high-end switches, both for purposes of redundancy and in order to attain blazingly fast throughput rates.

It'd be neat to tell you that switched backbones are fat high-tech cables strung atop towering pylons in electrical utility power grids, or that they're meshed networks of very fast and expensive T3 high-speed phone circuits. But they're not. Even the biggest of the big switched backbones is an unglamorous collection of refrigerator-like boxes cabled together, quietly humming away in a computer room somewhere.

A switched backbone's job is to concentrate what would otherwise be many hops into a single hop through a single backbone LAN. This is what's meant by bandwidth aggregation. Switched backbones pack large amounts of memory and throughput into a single configuration. Not all switched backbones are behemoths. A switched backbone might be a device about the size of a pizza box sitting in a rack in a data closet. Remember, a backbone by definition is a relatively fast LAN interconnecting other LANs.

While switched backbones aren't absolutely necessary in smaller networks, they probably are in very large ones. You probably remember when AOL's network collapsed. After the headlines faded, gurus lambasted AOL for having stuck with its mostly router-based topology too long.

Switched backbones are implemented using any of four technologies:

▼ ATM (Asynchronous Transfer Mode)

■ Fast Ethernet or Gigabit Ethernet

■ FDDI

▲ Token Ring

Many large internetworks inevitably have subnets implementing a variety of technologies. For this reason Cisco's Catalyst 5000 family of switches features any-to-any switching between ATM, Gigabit, Fast Ethernet, Token Ring, and FDDI.

Aggregating bandwidth of course means rolling up messages from a large number of subsidiary switches. Because switched networks deal only in MAC addresses, this cannot be done by hierarchical routing. The workaround is to create levels of switches through uplink ports. Figure 6-17 depicts how this configuration funnels the traffic from many hosts through the host switch out to the backbone switch.

This configuration technique enables designers to create power hierarchy in lieu of a logical hierarchy. Switched networks aggregate traffic into the bandwidth of a single switch to help the message find its way. Described in basic terms, this is accomplished by a switched backbone machine having more switches connected directly to it and thus building a much larger dynamic address table.

Each Cisco switch's ability to aggregate bandwidth into high-speed intelligent backbone relies on most or all of the advanced switching technologies introduced in Table 6-5.

The technology central to Cisco's switched backbone strategy is something called EtherChannel, which is a bus technology. Strictly speaking, a bus is a cable (or a printed circuit board functioning like a cable). What makes EtherChannel a full-blown technology is that it's an integrated package of high-speed cabling, connectors, controllers, software, and management tools designed to sustain high switching throughput rates. EtherChannel provides bandwidth scalability in increments from 200 Mbps to 800 Mbps.

EtherChannel works by setting up logical groups of ports to serve as high-speed connections between switches sitting in the same location—in effect letting multiple switch devices function as a single machine. An EtherChannel group can have up to 12 member ports. Ports are usually grouped to service a specific VLAN, which is why EtherChannel is central to Cisco's switched network strategy: aggregating bandwidth means interconnecting switches to switch servers holding ever larger dynamic MAC address tables.

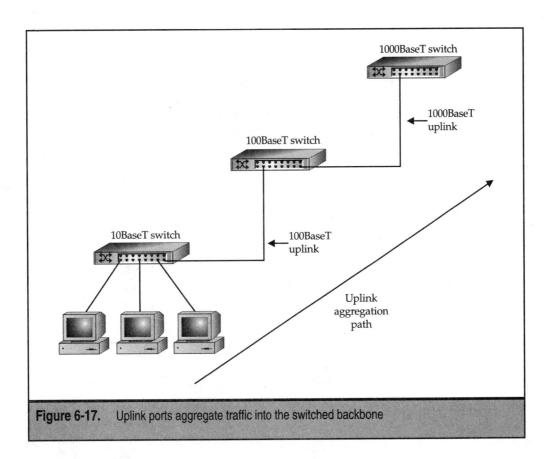

Figure 6-17. Uplink ports aggregate traffic into the switched backbone

Large-volume streams of switched messages flow within VLANs. EtherChannel is where the logical meets the physical. It funnels a VLAN's traffic through a dedicated high-speed bus into a collapsed switched backbone running at about the same speed. Balanced bus-to-switch throughput speed is increasingly referred to as a *switch fabric*, where ports and even stack units share a common dynamic address table.

An added benefit is that EtherChannel groups provide load balancing and redundancy. If one port is overloaded or fails, traffic loads are transparently shifted to other ports in the group. EtherChannel is a design architecture Cisco plans to use to deliver multi-gigabit capacity in the future. The technology implements IEEE 802.3 100BaseX and 1000BaseX standards as Fast EtherChannel and Gigabit EtherChannel products, respectively.

Multilayer Switching

Multilayer switching is a hybrid of routing and switching technologies. Even the best-designed switched networks must still use routers at some level. The hierarchical topology

Technology	Description
Address Cache	Also called MAC cache—the maximum number of MAC addresses a switch can maintain in its dynamic address table, which is a function of a combination of factors, including DRAM and CPU capacity.
Wirespeed	Also called forwarding rate—the rate at which a switch can pick up a stream of packets from an incoming cable, usually expressed in packets per second (pps).
Backplane (Switch Fabric)	The data rate of the switch's bus, which services CPU, memory, and I/O controllers, expressed in megabits per second (Mbps) or gigabits per second (Gbps).
IP Multicast	Certain message types tend to be multicast, where, for example, one copy of a message is sent to 1000 hosts instead of 1000 copies being sent. Doing this through a switched network requires a switch with sufficient processing power, memory capacity, bus speed, and software to handle such large MAC addressing transactions. IP Multicast is becoming an important switch technology as the world moves to the type of traffic lending itself to multicast messaging, such as video on demand.

Table 6-5.   Key Switching Technologies

of layer-3 IP addressing has much better "aim" than do switched network schemes, given that routers use hierarchical addresses instead of flat MAC addresses. This is why smart network designers are using multilayer switches to augment switched networks with the capabilities of a router to identify optimal paths to destinations. Depending on the manufacturer, multilayer switching is also called *IP switching, layer-3 switching, shortcut routing,* and *high-speed routing*.

Operators of very large internetworks—mainly corporations running big intranets—are offering services where users can click a hyperlink in one place and suddenly create a message demanding information or services from a faraway server. As users increasingly move about an internetwork to use its remote services, strain is put on the capacity of its routers. Properly implemented, multilayer switching can deliver tenfold throughput improvements at heavily traveled connection points. It's a relatively new and immature technology.

Multilayer switching works by first determining the best route or routes through an internetwork using layer-3 protocols and storing what it finds for later reference. Users who come along later wanting to travel that route do so via switches, bypassing the router (and the bottleneck it would cause).

Even if multilayer switching technology is not integrated into a switched network, some routing should still be used to provide some form of hierarchical topology to the network. This is necessary not only to maintain networkwide performance, but also to enhance security. Switches will not displace routers from internetworks in the foreseeable future. However, multilayer switching could be the industry's first step toward melding what are now two technologies into one—much like the bridge was subsumed by the router five to ten years ago.

VLANs

In a switched network, a host can participate in a VLAN. Much as a group of hosts become members of a physical LAN by plugging into a shared hub, they become part of a virtual LAN by being configured into it using switched network management software. In switched networks built using Cisco equipment, VLANs are created and maintained using the Visual Switch Manager software.

Within a VLAN, member hosts can communicate as if they were attached to the same wire, when in fact they can be located on any number of physical LANs. Because VLANs form broadcast domains, members enjoy the connectivity, shared services, and security associated with physical LANs.

Basing LANs on logical parameters instead of physical topology gives network administrators the option to align domains to parallel, geographically dispersed work groups. Even temporary exigencies can be accommodated using VLANs. For example, if two computer programmers needed to run a week's worth of tests involving heavy upload and download activity, they could be temporarily configured into a VLAN so as not to drag down the network's performance for other members of the normal VLAN.

Domains are usually arranged by department or work group. However, the trend toward dynamic organizational structures in the business world has made planning and maintaining modern networks somewhat tougher than it would otherwise be. Contemporary business phenomena such as virtual offices, distributed teams, reorganizations, mergers, acquisitions, and downsizing cause near constant migration of personnel and services within networks. Figure 6-18 outlines what a VLAN topology might look like.

But VLANs are more than just an organizational convenience. They are a necessity in switched networks in order to contain broadcast domains. Don't forget that using only MAC addresses causes flat network topology. VLANs ameliorate most flat topology problems by creating virtual hierarchies.

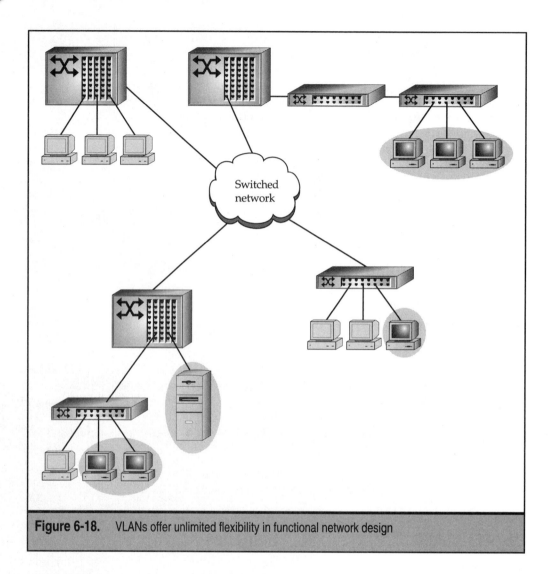

Figure 6-18.   VLANs offer unlimited flexibility in functional network design

Cisco's Switched Network Products

Cisco's product line of switch platforms is divided into two product groups:

▼   **Micro Switches**   A relatively new product family targeted at the branch office/small-business market niche. Micro Switches are desktop eight-port 10/100 devices that are part of what Cisco calls the Cisco Networked Office (CNO) stack family of products. CNO is designed to deliver high-performance networking in low-cost, simple-to-operate packages.

▲   **Catalyst Switches**   Cisco's main line of switched network solutions delivered in the form of no less than ten series of products amounting to over twice as many orderable product models. The Catalyst line is similar to Cisco routers in that it includes fixed-configuration desktop models, configurable plug-and-play modular chassis models, all the way up to "dormitory refrigerator" packages with high-speed buses into which many cards can be inserted—each card packing as much as do other fully configured Catalyst models.

In keeping with well-established trends in the networking marketplace, most Cisco LAN switches are Ethernet products. The lineup of Catalyst switched backbone products incorporates the diversity of technologies competing at that level, with support for Fast Ethernet, Gigabit Ethernet, FDDI, and ATM.

Most Cisco switches run a full-blown image of the IOS software, different only in that it's tuned for switching rather than routing. Most Catalyst switches offer the regular command-line interface, but some have a menu-driven interface similar to the Hub Management Console.

Cisco switched network products are packaged to

▼   Deliver seamless migration from legacy technologies with tools such as 10/100 autosensing and high-speed uplink ports.

■   Enable interoperation between diverse technologies such as ATM, FDDI, Token Ring, and Ethernet.

■   Facilitate bandwidth aggregation through scalable configurations and powerful switch fabric technologies.

▲   Be manageable using remote monitoring, configuration, and security tools.

Table 6-6 outlines the Cisco switch product line, which at the time this book is being written is composed of 11 product series. Refer to cisco.com for catalogs of information on Cisco switches and other products.

Configuring and Managing Cisco Switches

Cisco Catalyst switches can be configured using either the IOS command-line interface or the Visual Switch Manager, a tool operated through Web browser interface. Which to use is a matter of user preference; neither configures anything the other doesn't. If you use the command-line interface, the normal rules apply as far as using Telnet to log in through the Console port. For simplicity's sake, we'll use Visual Switch Manager to explain Cisco switch configuration and management. (Micro Switches are plug-and-play devices that self-configure after being turned on.)

Visual Switch Manager has six configuration management areas that lead to a combined total of 18 pages (browser screens). Figure 6-19 shows the Visual Switch Manager home page and a list of pages by area. The home page itself handles such housekeeping chores as naming the switch and setting its Line password.

Product Series	Description
Micro Switches	Two models with 8 ports—a desktop device designed to create high-performance LANs. The only Cisco switch series with an unmanaged model.
Catalyst 1900 Series	Four models with 12 or 24 10BaseT ports and 2 uplink ports for 100BaseTX or 100BaseFX. All models have 1K MAC address cache. Not stackable.
Catalyst 2820 Series	Four model series designed for aggregating 10BaseT hubs to 100BaseT, FDDI, or ATM backbones or servers. Contains 24 10BaseT ports plus 2 slots to accommodate a choice of high-speed modules (100BaseT, FDDI, or ATM). 1 Gbps backplane. 2K or 8K MAC address cache. Not stackable.
Catalyst 2900 Series	Four models with 12–48 ports for 10/100BaseTX or 100BaseFX with uplinks to 1000BaseX. 1.2 Gbps–2.4 Gbps backplane. Not stackable.
Catalyst 2900XL Series	Five models in two basic packages with 12 100BaseFX or 24 ports for 10/100BaseT and two uplinks to 100BaseFX. Up to 16K MAC address cache. 3.2 Gbps backplane. Not stackable.
Catalyst 3000 Series	Three models of multilayer switches with either 16 or 24 10BaseT ports in fixed configurations. Models differ by having either 1, 2, or 6 expansion slots for modules with ports supporting coaxial cable, twisted-pair cable, or fiber cable types and support for several Ethernet specifications or WAN connectivity. 480 Mbps backplane. Stackable to eight switches in any combination of models.
Catalyst 3500XL Series	Three models, with 12 or 24 10/100BaseT Ethernet ports and 2 Gigabit Ethernet uplink ports. 3500 XLs are stackable up to nine units running a switch fabric up to 10 Gbps. The 3500 Series is new, and is being positioned as Cisco's premier solution for low-end Gigabit Ethernet connectivity.
Catalyst 3900 Series	Two models with 20 fixed Token Ring ports and 2 slots for expansion modules, each with 4 ports for additional Token Ring user ports or 1 ATM OC-3 or 2 100BaseX uplink(s). 520 Mbps backplane. Stackable up to eight switches.

Table 6-6.   Cisco's Switch Product Line Is Made Up of 12 Series

Product Series	Description
Catalyst 4000 Series	One model with 3-slot modular chassis supporting 10/100/1000 Ethernet. One module has 48 10/100 ports and another 32 10/100 ports with a variety of 1000BaseX uplink options. Powerful 24 Gbps backplane. Not stackable.
Catalyst 5000 Family	Two series family with five models, with 2-to-5 slot modular chassis with 48–528 ports supporting 100BaseX, 1000X, ATM, FDDI, or Token Ring. 1.2 Gbps–3.6 Gbps backplane. Not stackable.
Catalyst 6000 Family	Four-model multilayer switch family with 6–9 slots supporting 384 10/100 ports, 192 100BaseFX ports, or 130 1000BaseX ports. 150 Mbps throughput. 32 Gbps backplane scalable to 256 Gbps. Not stackable.
Catalyst 8500 Series	Two models with 5–13 slots supporting multiservice ATM switching, optimized for aggregating multiprotocol traffic. 6–24 Mbps throughput. 10 Gbps or 40 Gbps backplane. Not stackable.

Table 6-6. Cisco's Switch Product Line Is Made Up of 12 Series *(continued)*

An outstanding feature of Visual Switch Manager is that a device's status can be viewed by looking at a live image of it on the home page. Figure 6-20 shows the graphical image of a Cisco 2924XL switch. You can't see the color keys in this black-and-white book,

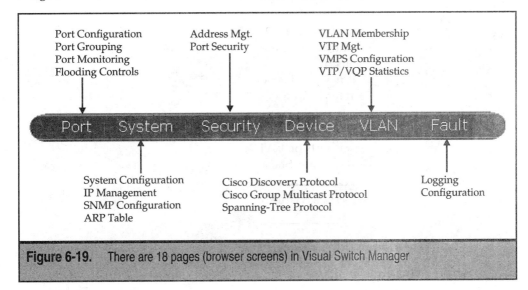

Figure 6-19. There are 18 pages (browser screens) in Visual Switch Manager

but if the port is colored green, its status is Link Up, blue means No Link Status, and red indicates Link Faulty or Port Disabled.

Notice in Figure 6-20 that Visual Switch Manager makes the distinction between a port and a link. A *port* is the physical connection where the cable is plugged in. A *link* is the logical connection taking place over that port to a port on some other device—which could be another switch, hub, router, server, or other device. A port could be operating OK, and at the same time the link running through it could be malfunctioning. You can see how Visual Switch Manager helps network administrators isolate and solve problems quickly.

The Port Configuration pages (or commands, if you're in the IOS command-line interface) allow you to enable or disable specific switch ports and to set duplex mode to full, half, or automatically selected, according to the capability of the host device making a link to the port. If the switch device being configured is 10/100, speed mode can be set in the same way. If a switch is participating in an EtherChannel, individual ports would be assigned to EtherChannel groups in the Port Grouping page.

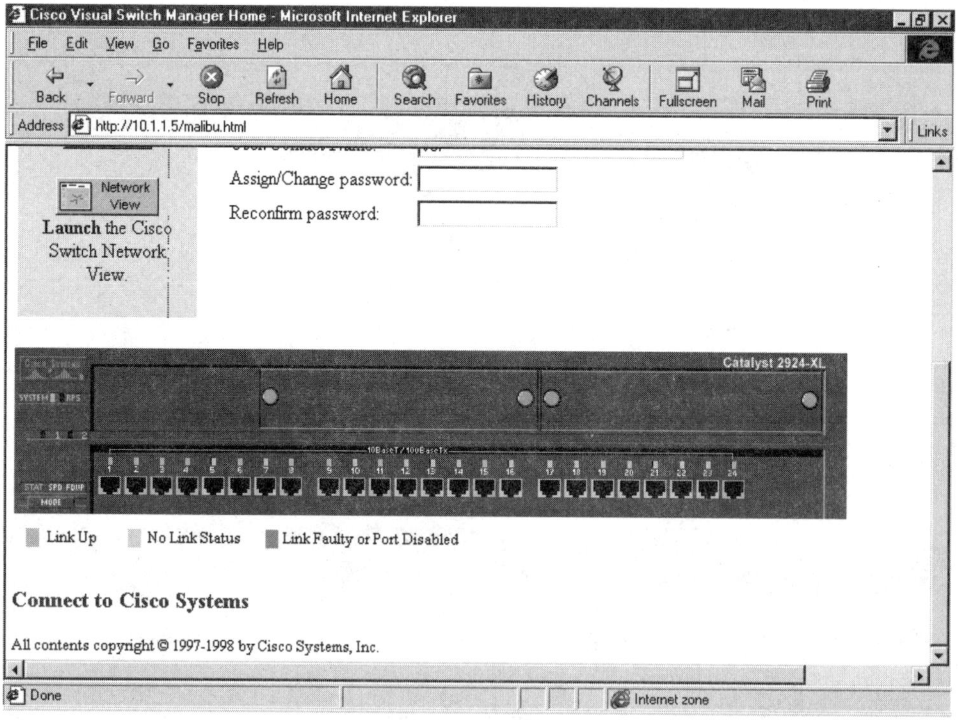

Figure 6-20.   A "live" graphical image reports a Cisco switch's status

The System area pages cover basic systemwide configuration parameters such as the version of IOS software installed, booting procedure, system console baud rate, and memory configuration options.

For brevity's sake, Visual Switch Manager is not covered fully here. Refer to Appendix A for a complete review of Visual Switch Manager pages. Review it to get a flavor of how Cisco switches are managed. Also, several features and functions of Cisco switch technology not discussed here are outlined on the example Visual Switch Manager pages.

For example, perhaps the most important area of switch configuration and management has to do with VLANs. Visual Switch Manager has four pages. The first is to assign ports VLAN memberships. The other three pages are to set parameters for such specialized VLAN services as

▼ **STP (Spanning Tree Protocol)**   A link management protocol that allows advertisement of redundant paths through switched networks, while at the same time preventing paths from looping back to their source. STP does for switched networks what routing protocols do for routed networks.

■ **VTP (VLAN Trunk Protocol)**   A way to create pathways serving a number of switches in a VLAN, accomplished by dynamically sharing MAC addresses and other information from a VTP server and VTP clients.

■ **VMPS (VLAN Membership Policy Server)**   A client-server based protocol that dynamically tracks the VLAN (or VLANs) to which a particular MAC address belongs.

▲ **VQP (VLAN Query Protocol)**   A protocol that continually runs statistics on VMPS queries sent by the VMPS server to its clients.

In case you need to know a bit more about advanced VLAN specifics, each of these is briefly explained in Appendix A. How switches can be configured and managed using SNMP and CiscoWorks is covered in Chapter 9.

CHAPTER 7

Internet Access
Products

The last few chapters showed how data moves over internetworks. Starting with the twisted-pair cable running from the desktop, messages travel through hubs, switches, and routers to destinations across buildings or on the other side of the world. All this technology has made it possible to do some amazing things. It's now routine for businesses to sell and support entire product lines from Web sites—unthinkable just a few short years ago. Just as impressive, whole companies are now being managed within internetwork management platforms. It's even possible to operate private networks over the public Internet. But there's a catch to all this technology: networks are two-way streets. If good things can happen over internetworks, it follows that bad things can, too.

Hooking a computer up to any kind of network necessarily incurs risk. Hooking up an entire enterprise, as you might imagine, brings a boatload of security issues. Network security is a broad subject that encompasses policies, safeguards, techniques, standards, protocols, algorithms, and specialized hardware and software products. Security has been paramount in computing since the early years of central mainframes and green screen terminals. Experts now regard security as the single biggest hurdle to the Internet becoming the all-encompassing business environment that so many envision. Indeed, network security is such an important subject that it's an entire industry unto itself.

Good security is tougher to attain now because systems are so interconnected. In the old days, you either had a terminal hooked up to the mainframe or you were out. But in this era of connectivity, anybody with sufficient resources and time conceivably can break into any system. Vulnerability is a fact of life in internetworking, and the industry's response is a phalanx of security technologies.

All security starts with *access*. Even back in the misty days of cavemen, having good security meant not letting bad things in or valuable things out. Internetworking is no different. Running an internetwork is like running a storefront business; it's in your interest to let strangers freely enter and exit the store, but doing so inevitably means giving thieves and vandals a shot at your goods. You have to keep access open; all you can do is try to weed out the bad guys. Three network access technologies try to balance the conflicting needs for access and security:

▼ **Firewalls**   Special routers that intercept and control traffic between a private network and public networks (especially the Internet)

■ **Virtual private networks (VPNs)**   Private networks operating over a public network (usually the Internet)

▲ **Access servers**   Dedicated devices used with modems connecting remote users to internetworks over normal telephone lines

Of the three technologies, only the firewall is solely concerned with security, and it doesn't provide access so much as permit it. The other two—VPNs and access servers—exist primarily to deliver cost-effective connectivity. Access servers provide remote persons a way to enter internetworks. The mission of a VPN is to run a wide area network (WAN) over the Internet. But both access servers and VPNs restrict unauthorized access and attempt to ensure data integrity.

This chapter covers Cisco access technology from both functional and security perspectives. Integrated security management tools are covered in Chapter 10.

FIREWALLS

A *firewall* is a checkpoint between a private network and one or more public networks. It's a gateway that selectively decides what may enter or leave a private network. To do this, a firewall must be the sole gateway between the network it protects and the outside. If traffic can go around a firewall, the security it provides is worthless. A basic tenet is that all external traffic must pass through the firewall. A normal router could serve as a firewall if it were configured as a choke point. Figure 7-1 shows how a firewall acts as a funnel through which all traffic must pass.

There is a necessary trade-off between security and network performance. If you substituted cars and trucks for IP packets in Figure 7-1, you'd see traffic from several high-

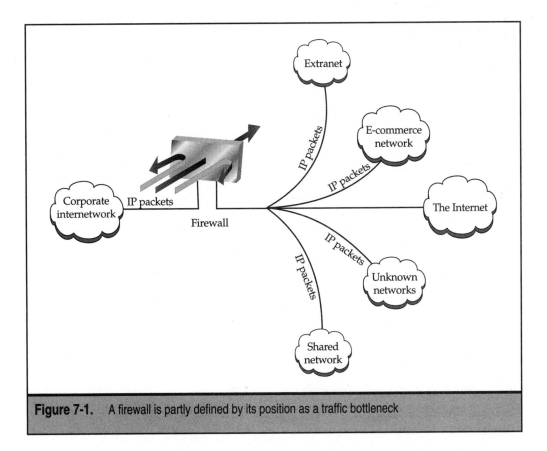

Figure 7-1.   A firewall is partly defined by its position as a traffic bottleneck

ways squeezed through a single on-ramp. If security weren't a concern, to boost access private internetworks would be surrounded on all sides by routers.

Firewall Basics

The firewall, in fact, is a kind of router. Traffic enters through one network interface, leaves through another, and messages are handled at the network layer (layer 3) of the 7-layer OSI model.

Firewalls operate by intercepting and inspecting each packet that enters any of their network interfaces. The inspections vary according to the firewall's sophistication and how tight security policy is. But the goal is always to identify a match between each packet's contents and the security rules the firewall has been programmed to enforce. The basic steps of intercepting and inspecting packets are shown in Figure 7-2.

There's nothing fancy about how a firewall intercepts traffic. It does so by funneling all traffic entering its network interfaces over a single path (called a *data bus* in computer terminology). By having all traffic pass through the firewall's internal data bus and memory, the central processing unit (CPU) is given the opportunity to check each packet against the security rules it's been programmed to enforce.

The actual inspection is done by reading the packet's header for conditions that match rules set up in security tables. Security tables usually include dozens of rules, each designed to explicitly accept or reject specific kinds of traffic by applying a pass/fail test to

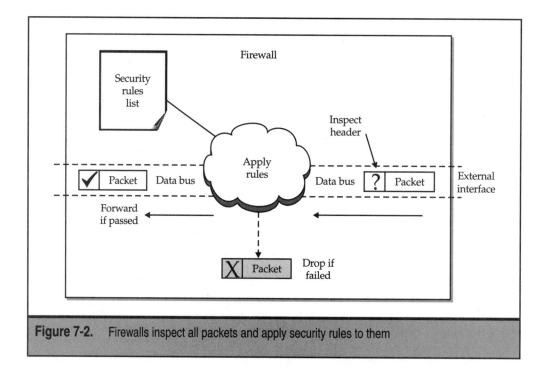

Figure 7-2.   Firewalls inspect all packets and apply security rules to them

the packet. If the packet passes, it's forwarded to its destination. If it fails, the packet is dropped at the network interface and ceases to exist.

Firewalls Map Out a Defensive Landscape

Routers tend to take a friendly view of the world. They focus on addresses and the best routes to deliver messages to them. By contrast, firewalls take a militaristic view of things where addresses are still important, but for inspection and clearance instead of delivery. Firewalls define the world as either inside networks or outside networks, with the division made according to what lies beyond the security perimeter. The security perimeter itself is established by one or more firewalls placed between the secured network and the outside. The firewall places every network it encounters into one of three classifications:

▼ **Trusted network** Inside the security perimeter and under complete administrative control of the enterprise

■ **Untrusted network** Outside the security perimeter and known to the firewall, but beyond the enterprise's administrative control

▲ **Unknown network** Unknown networks that the firewall has received no information or instructions about—basically almost the entire Internet

The security perimeter is drawn right down the middle of the firewall, with the physical configuration of the device itself defining what's internal and external. The network interfaces on the firewall are designated as either *inside* or *outside* interfaces. The network attached to each interface in turn takes on its interface's designation as either an *inside network* or *outside network*. In Figure 7-3, for example, network 10.1.13.0 is attached to an inside interface, and thus is defined as being inside the security perimeter, and therefore a trusted network.

In terms of network security, *administrative control* is the ability to do such things as assign IP addresses, issue user accounts and passwords, and maintain network device configuration files. Usually the network media—local area networks (LANs) and WANs—over which a secured network operates are owned and controlled by the enterprise. The major exception to this is the VPN, which runs mostly over intermediate network segments operated by somebody else, but are still regarded as trusted networks.

Security Is a Matter of Policy, Not Technology

Internetwork security isn't just a matter of how much control you can exert, it's also how much you *choose* to exert. Much like the trade-off between security and performance, one also exists between security and connectivity. In theory, any LAN could have impenetrable security by simply unplugging all routers, switches, and modems leading to the outside.

But enterprises are compelled to connect to the outside because the benefits of connectivity outweigh the risk it brings. In fact, almost all businesses are now connected to the most unknown and dangerous public network of all: the Internet. Every time you hit a company's Web site to look up information, download software, or place an order, that enterprise has taken a calculated risk by letting you access some part of its system. Most

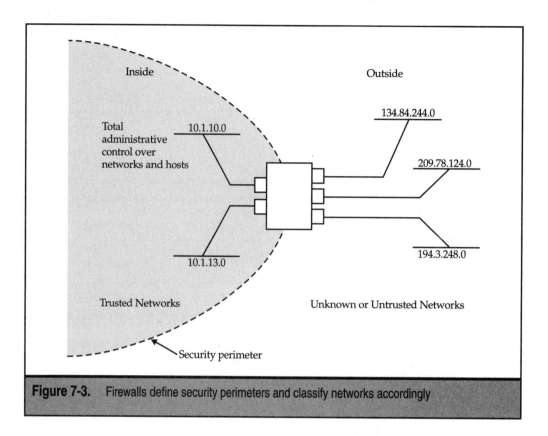

Figure 7-3. Firewalls define security perimeters and classify networks accordingly

enterprises need to open their internal networks to the public to at least some degree. Businesses do it to sell and support, governments to serve, and educational organizations to teach. Firewalls try to help accommodate this intentional security compromise by defining a middle ground called a *demilitarized zone*, or DMZ for short. Figure 7-4 shows a typical DMZ configuration.

LAN segments on the firewall's outside are called the *external perimeter networks*, and ones on the inside are called *internal perimeter networks*. Usually each perimeter network has a router attached, and access lists on these routers handle the bulk of traffic flow duties, allowing the firewall to focus on packet inspection and rules enforcement. The outside router is often referred to as the *shield router*, which usually has an Internet service provider (ISP) attached to at least one of its interfaces. In addition to normal router duty, the shield router also protects the servers in the DMZ from attack by acting as an alarm system for the firewall. The router on the inside, called the *inside shield router*, is the last line of defense between the firewall and the inside networks. The key point to understand is that a firewall is defined as much by its physical configuration (what's connected to what) as the security rules it's programmed to enforce.

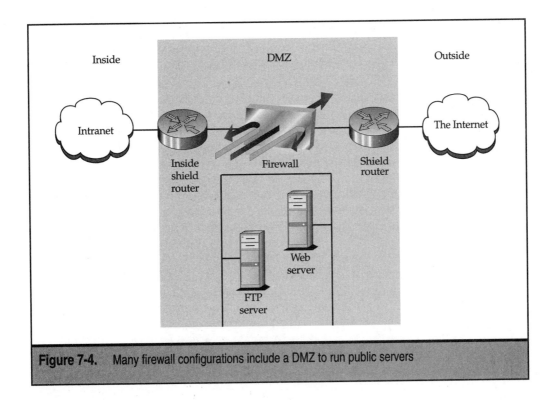

Figure 7-4.   Many firewall configurations include a DMZ to run public servers

How Firewalls Work

Security rules are defined for each firewall network interface. This is true whether the firewall is a router trying to serve as a firewall or a high-tech dedicated device such as the Cisco PIX Firewall. Each packet is filtered based on rules applied to the specific network interface card through which it entered the firewall. The act of configuring a firewall, then, is largely a matter of assigning security rules to each firewall interface.

The Access List Is the Most Basic Internetwork Security Tool

The simplest form of network security technology is the access list. Also called *access control lists*, or *filters*, the access list is a basic component of any router's configuration. As the name implies, access lists restrict certain traffic from gaining access to a network. Access lists can provide a basic level of network security by filtering packets according to three criteria:

▼ **Source address**   The IP address from which the packet originated

■ **Destination address**   The IP address (or addresses) to which the packet is addressed

▲ **Port number**   The application-layer (layer 7) protocol the packet will use

Cisco calls these *extended access lists*—the extension being the port number. Early Cisco products used only source/destination addresses, which were referred to as *standard access lists*. But don't be misled by this terminology; extended access lists are the basic type of access list being used now.

> **NOTE:**   Port numbers (also called *network ports* or just *ports*) aren't physical interface ports like S0 or E3. Messages sent using the TCP or UDP transport-layer protocols (layer 4) use port numbers to identify which application protocol the transmission will run. For example, the number for HTTP (WWW) is port 80, SMTP's is port 25, and FTP's is port 21.

Network administrators create access lists in the router's configuration file. One access list is created for each network interface. If an interface handles traffic in multiple network protocols—for example, IP, IPX, and AppleTalk—each network protocol has its own access list format. Therefore, a separate access list must be created for each protocol to run over that network interface. Regardless of the network protocol used, each criterion (access rule) occupies a line on the list. Figure 7-5 depicts how access lists work. This example uses a router restricting the flow of traffic between departments within an organization.

As each packet attempts to enter an interface, its header is examined to see if anything matches the access list. The router is looking for positive matches. Once it finds a match, no further evaluations are performed. If the rule matched is a *permit* rule, the packet is forwarded out a network interface on the other side of the router. If the matched rule is a *deny*, the packet is dropped right there at the interface.

If a packet's evaluation runs all the way to the bottom of the access list without a match, it is dropped by default. This mechanism is called the *implicit deny rule*, which provides an added measure of security by dealing with conditions not anticipated in the access list.

The router evaluates the packet one rule at a time, working its way from the top line to the bottom. The bottom part of Figure 7-6 is an example taken from a router's access list. Each line in the list is a rule that either permits or denies a specific type of traffic. The top of Figure 7-6 charts the parts of a rule's statement, starting with the **access-list** command followed by various modifiers. Keep in mind that this example is for IP, and syntax varies slightly for IPX, AppleTalk, and other non-IP network protocols.

A cohesive access list is created by using a common access list name at the beginning of each statement for an IP access list. Each statement must declare a transport protocol: the Transmission Control Protocol (TCP), the User Datagram Protocol (UDP), or the Internet Control Messaging Protocol (ICMP). If the rule involves a network application, the statement must first declare a transport protocol and end with the application protocol. In the example rule at the top of Figure 7-6, the transport protocol is TCP, and the application protocol is HTTP.

To apply a rule to incoming traffic, you must put the outside host's IP address in the *from* position, which always precedes the *to* position. This order is reversed in order to re-

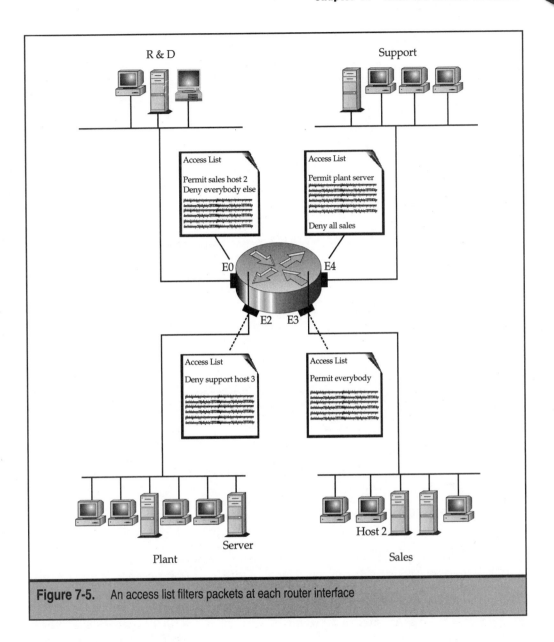

Figure 7-5. An access list filters packets at each router interface

strict outbound traffic. The modifier **any** is used to indicate all networks. The statement at the top of Figure 7-6, then, is saying "permit host 209.98.208.25 to access any network in order to run the HTTP application over TCP."

The access list is activated on an interface by using the **access-group** command, as shown in the following code snippet. The first line "points" the IOS at serial0 interface,

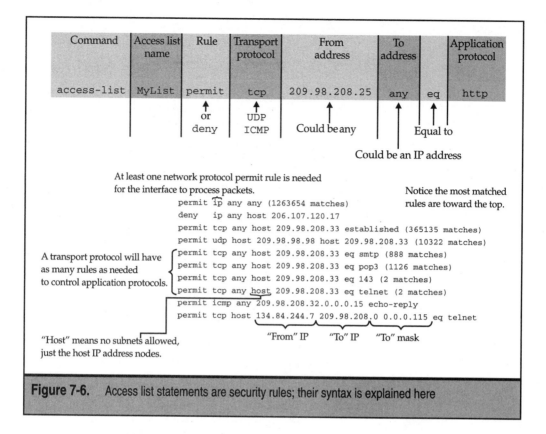

Figure 7-6. Access list statements are security rules; their syntax is explained here

and the second line applies access list 100 to all incoming traffic trying to enter through serial0:

```
MyRouter(config)#interface serial0
MyRouter(config-if)#tcp access-group 100 in
```

Routers look for matches between packet header content and the interface's access list. A catch would be a source address, destination address, or port number. If the matched rule is a permit rule, the packet is forwarded. If, however, a deny rule is matched, the packet is dropped without evaluating against any rules further down the list.

An access list can have as many filtering rules as desired, with the practical limit being the amount of router memory you wish to use for security filtering instead of productive routing. Because access list rules are evaluated from top to bottom, the most frequently encountered matches should be put toward the top of the list so as not to waste router CPU cycles.

Keep in mind that an access list alone doesn't turn a router into a firewall. The majority of standard access lists are used for basic traffic management within internetworks. However, you could physically configure a router as a choke point so that all traffic must pass an access list, thereby making it into a lightweight firewall. This is frequently done to restrict access between networks making up an internetwork. In fact, standard IOS has dozens of security-oriented commands beyond the **access-list** command that are also used in Cisco's firewall products. But relying on the access list as the centerpiece of a firewall configuration results in questionable security.

Access lists make lousy security gateways because they're stateless. *Stateless* means that access rules are applied without the benefit of understanding the context of each connection made between hosts (called *sessions*). Simple packet filters have no idea which sessions packets belong to, so decisions to forward or block them are based strictly on source address, destination address, or port number. Knowing which conversation a packet belongs to makes for better security.

Firewalls Track Internetwork Sessions

Firewall technology builds on access lists by keeping track of sessions. This technology is called *stateful* or *context-based* packet filtering because an individual packet can be handled based on the larger context of its connection. This type of filtering uses what some call *reflexive access lists*, so named because their contents dynamically change in reflexive response to the state of individual sessions (whether the session was initiated from an inside host, how long it's been running, etc.). Figure 7-7 shows how context-based firewalls track sessions.

> **NOTE:**   TCP and UDP are protocols running at the transport layer (layer 4) of the 7-layer OSI reference model. TCP stands for Terminal Control Protocol, a connection-oriented protocol designed to deliver full-duplex communications with guaranteed delivery. The bulk of IP traffic goes via TCP connections. UDP stands for User Datagram Protocol, a no-frills, low-overhead, connectionless protocol that has no guaranteed delivery or error correction. UDP is used by relatively simple and noncritical applications like TFTP (Trivial File Transfer Protocol). A third transport protocol is ICMP (Internet Control Message Protocol), a specialized protocol used by the **ping** and **traceroute** troubleshooting commands. Transport protocols are covered in Chapter 2.

The astute reader might wonder how a firewall can track UDP sessions, given that UDP is a so-called connectionless transport protocol lacking the formal handshakes and acknowledgments of TCP. UDP filtering works by noting the source/destination address and port number of the session, and then guessing that all packets sharing those three characteristics belong to the same session. Because timeout periods are so brief for UDP sessions (usually a fraction of maximum times set for TCP sessions), the firewall almost always guesses right.

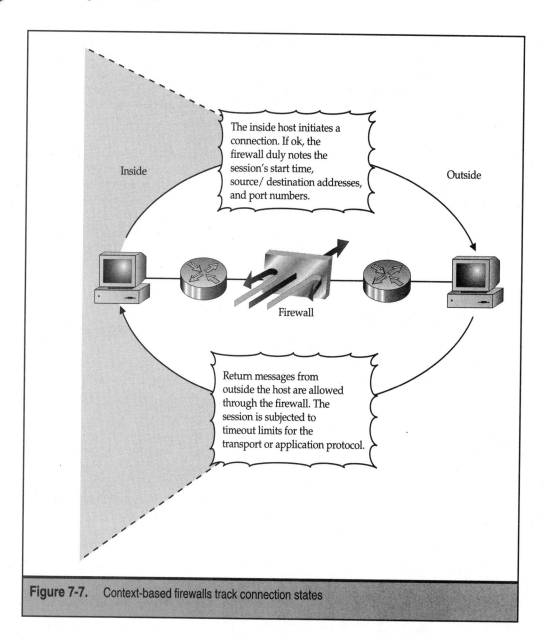

Figure 7-7. Context-based firewalls track connection states

Using Global Addresses to Hide Internal Network Topology

Cisco's IOS software has a capability called Network Address Translation (NAT) used by routers and firewalls to mask internal network addresses from the outside world. As discussed in Chapter 2, IP allows the use of private addresses instead of registered IP addresses—for example, 10.1.13.1 instead of 209.78.124.12. This is done for a variety of reasons, but mainly it's done to conserve addresses (sometimes called *address space*) because there simply aren't enough IP addresses to uniquely number all the hosts, devices, and LANs in most internetworks. It's possible to run an internetwork without private addresses, but it's rarely done.

As packets are forwarded to the outside, NAT overwrites the internal network address in the source address field with a full IP address. This is done from a pool of registered IP addresses made available to NAT, which then assigns them to outbound connections as they're established. NAT maps the inside local address to the pool address, deletes the mapping when the connection is terminated, and reuses the pool address for the next outbound connection that comes along. As you can see at the top of Figure 7-8, NAT translation takes place on a one-to-one basis. Therefore, although NAT hides internal addresses, it does not conserve address space.

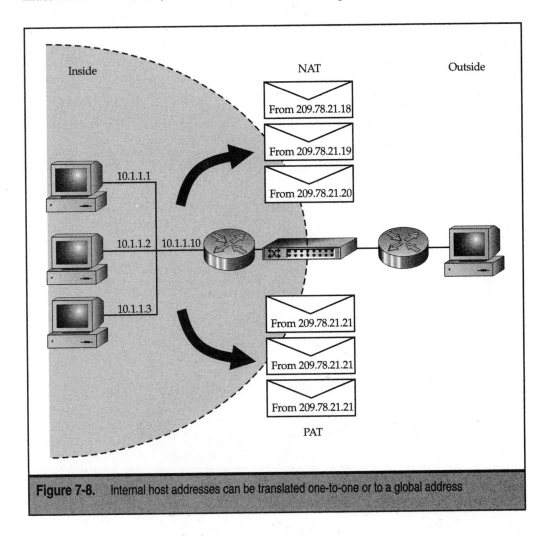

Figure 7-8.   Internal host addresses can be translated one-to-one or to a global address

The bottom of Figure 7-8 shows NAT can also be configured to use just one registered address for all internal hosts making outside connections. This function is called Port Address Translation (PAT), which differs from NAT by translating to one global outside address instead of to individual outside addresses. PAT provides additional security by making it impossible for hackers to identify individual hosts inside a private internetwork because everybody appears to be coming from the same host address. Beyond enhancing security boost, PAT also conserves address space.

Address translation is an example of the value of context-based session tracking. Without the ability to keep track of which session each packet belongs to, it wouldn't be possible to dynamically assign and map internal addresses to the public addresses.

Proxy Servers

A *proxy server* is an application that acts as an intermediary between two end systems. Proxy servers operate at the application layer (layer 7) of the firewall, where both ends of a connection are forced to conduct the session through the proxy. They do this by creating and running a process on the firewall that mirrors a service as if it were running on the end host. As Figure 7-9 illustrates, a proxy server essentially turns a two-party session into a four-party

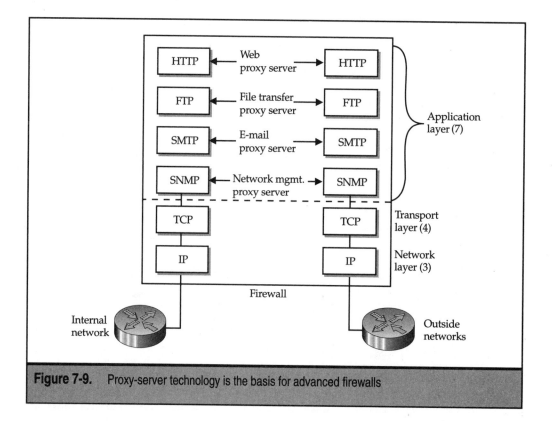

Figure 7-9.   Proxy-server technology is the basis for advanced firewalls

session, with the middle two processes emulating the two real hosts. Because they operate at layer 7, proxy servers are also referred to as *application-layer firewalls*.

A proxy service must be run for each type of Internet application the firewall will support—a Simple Mail Transport Protocol (SMTP) proxy for e-mail, an HTTP proxy for Web services, and so on. Proxy servers are almost always one-way arrangements running from the internal network to outside networks. In other words, if an internal user wants to access a Web site on the Internet, the packets making up that request are processed through the HTTP Server before being forwarded to the Web site. Packets returned from the Web site in turn are processed through the HTTP server before being forwarded back to the internal user host. As with NAT, the packets go to the external Web server carrying the IP address of the HTTP server instead of the internal host address. Figure 7-9 depicts a firewall running several proxy servers at once.

Because proxy servers centralize all activity for an application into a single server, they present the ideal opportunity to perform a variety of useful functions. Having the application running right on the firewall presents the opportunity to inspect packets for much more than just source/destination addresses and port numbers. This is why nearly all modern firewalls incorporate some form of proxy-server architecture. For example, inbound packets headed to a server set up strictly to disburse information (say, an FTP server) can be inspected to see if they contain any write commands (such as the **PUT** command). In this way, the proxy server could allow only connections containing read commands.

Proxy server is another technology possible only in context-based firewalls. For example, if a firewall supports thousands of simultaneous Web connections, it must of course sort out to which session each of the millions of incoming packets with port number 80 (HTTP) belong.

Dual-Home Configurations

A *dual-homed* firewall configuration turns off routing between the network interface cards. Doing this forces all traffic to go through a proxy service before it can be routed out another interface, which is why proxy-server firewalls use dual-homed configurations, as depicted on the left side of Figure 7-10. Another use of dual homing is when you want users on two networks—say, the R&D and sales departments—to access a single resource, but don't want any traffic routed between them. The configuration on the right of Figure 7-10 shows this.

Using a dual-homed configuration this way doesn't create a firewall gateway, per se, because inbound traffic isn't headed anywhere beyond the server. It's just an easy way to have one server take care of two departments that shouldn't exchange traffic. It's also a way of making sure traffic isn't exchanged, because routing services are turned off inside the router.

Event Logging and Notification

Record keeping is an important part of a firewall's overall role. When a packet is denied entry by a firewall, the event is duly recorded into a file called *syslog* (industry shorthand for system log). Most firewalls can be configured to upload log information to a security

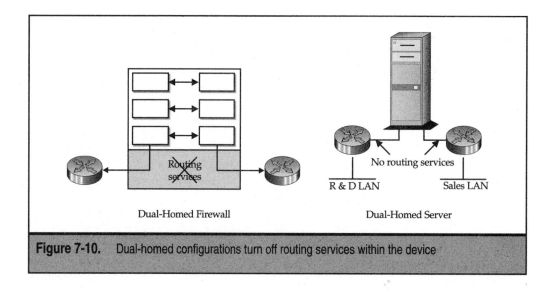

Figure 7-10.   Dual-homed configurations turn off routing services within the device

server elsewhere on the network, where it's analyzed to better inform the enterprise's security policy.

Firewalls can also be configured to generate alert messages if specified thresholds are surpassed. In more sophisticated network operations, these alerts are immediately directed to a manned console so that the network team can respond to the event by any number of measures (usually shutting down the network interface where the apparent security breach is taking place).

The IOS Firewall Feature Set

The IOS Firewall is a value-added option to the Cisco IOS software. It is purchased as a so-called IOS feature set (feature sets are covered in Chapter 5). IOS Firewall is used to turn a standard Cisco router into a fairly robust firewall by adding several security functions over and above the basic traffic filtering of standard IOS software:

▼ **Context-Based Access Control (CBAC)** An advanced form of traffic filtering that examines application-layer (layer 7) information such as HTTP to learn about the state of TCP or UDP connections.

■ **Address translation (PAT and NAT)** Disguises internal IP addresses by inserting disguised source addresses on packets sent outside the firewall. PAT and NAT hide internal network topology from hackers.

■ **Security server support** The router can be configured as a client to TACACS+, RADIUS, or Kerberos security servers, where usernames and passwords can be stored in such a server's user authentication database.

- ■ **Denial-of-service attack detection**   Detects the traffic patterns characteristic of so-called *denial-of-service* attacks and sends alert messages. (Denial-of-service attacks attempt to deny service by overwhelming a network with service requests such as illegal e-mail commands or infinite e-mails.)

- ■ **Java blocking**   The ability to selectively block Java messages from a network (Java applets are downloadable self-operating programs, and applets can be programmed to harm any host system unfortunate enough to execute them.)

- ■ **Encryption**   The ability to make a packet's contents incomprehensible to all systems except those provided with a cipher (key) to decipher it.

- ■ **Neighbor router authentication**   A command by which a router can force a neighboring router to authenticate its identity or all packets routed from it are blocked.

- ▲ **Security alerts and event logging**   Messages alerting network administration of a security problem, and the logging of all security events for later collation and analysis.

Most of these capabilities are enabled by Context-Based Access Control, which is the central technology in the IOS Firewall software.

How Context-Based Access Control Works

Context-Based Access Control is a set of IOS commands that can be used to inspect packets much more closely than using normal access lists. CBAC works by tracking outside connections initiated from inside the firewall. CBAC identifies sessions by tracking source/destination IP addresses and source/destination port numbers gleaned from the packets. When a response returns from the session's remote host in the form of inbound traffic, CBAC determines the session to which the inbound packets belong. CBAC in this way maintains a dynamic list of ongoing sessions and is able to juggle security exceptions on a moment-by-moment basis. This dynamic list, called the *state table*, tracks the state of valid sessions through to termination. The CBAC state table maintains itself by deleting sessions when concluded by users or dropping them after a maximum allowable period of inactivity called a *timeout*. Timeout values are specified by the network administrator for each transport protocol. Figure 7-11 depicts the CBAC process.

CBAC uses the state table to make dynamic entries and deletions to the access list of the interface. Source/destination address or port numbers normally blocked by the access list are momentarily allowed, but only for a session CBAC knows to be a valid session initiated from inside the firewall security perimeter. CBAC creates openings in the firewall as necessary to permit returning traffic and thus is bidirectional. Once the session shuts down, the access list's prohibition is put back in effect until another session calls from the CBAC state table asking for a temporary exception of its own.

If it seems as if the router would be overwhelmed by the sheer complexity of it all, remember that state tables and access lists are maintained on a per-interface basis. Each interface on a Cisco router running IOS Firewall has its own access list, inspection rules,

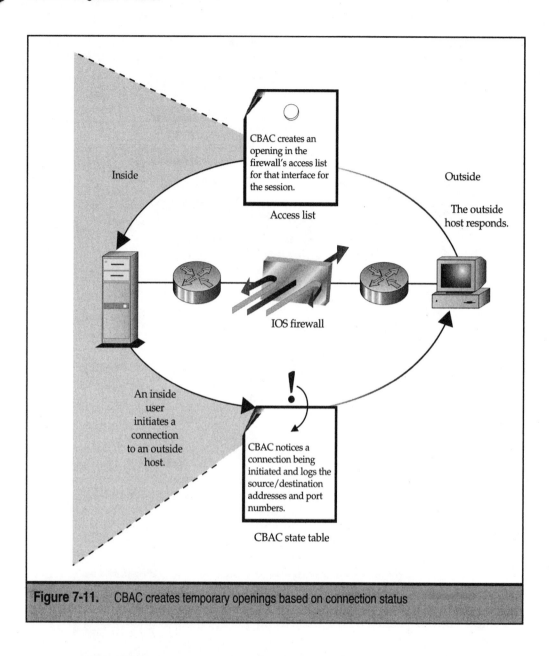

Figure 7-11. CBAC creates temporary openings based on connection status

and valid sessions. Good firewall configuration design can cut down a big part of the complexity you must deal with, by grouping similar traffic types or sources onto specific network interfaces.

Major IOS Firewall Functions

IOS Firewall selectively enforces security rules based on the context of each session. To pull this off, IOS Firewall must inspect packets much more closely than simple access lists do. For this reason, the IOS Firewall software is granular in its application of inspection rules. *Granular* here means inspection rules are applied much more selectively than the "all-or-nothing" permit/deny scheme used in access lists. This makes the firewall more flexible and a tougher security barrier to crack. We won't delve into IOS Firewall inspection features too deeply since this is a beginner's book, but a quick review will illustrate how firewall technology works at the packet inspection level:

▼ **SMTP inspection**   Many of the worst virus attacks inject themselves into secured internetworks via e-mail. Beyond just inspecting each packet for the SMTP port number, IOS Firewall inspects SMTP packets for illegal commands. Any SMTP packet containing a command other than the 15 legal SMTP commands will be discarded as subversive.

■ **Java inspection**   Some network security policies prohibit downloading Java applets from outside networks because of their potential destructive power. A security policy mandating that all internal users disable Java in their Web browsers is unenforceable. IOS Firewall allows you to block incoming Java applets at the firewall and also to designate a list of trusted (friendly) external sites from which downloaded Java applets will not be blocked (or you could permit applets from all sites except sites explicitly defined as hostile).

■ **H.323 inspection**   NetMeeting is a premier H.323 protocol application that requires use of a second channel (session) in addition to the H.323 channel maintained in the CBAC state table. IOS Firewall can be configured to inspect for a generic TCP channel in addition to the H.323 channel to allow NetMeeting connections to operate through the firewall.

▲ **RPC inspection**   The IOS Firewall RPC (Remote Procedure Call) inspection command accepts the entry of program numbers. For example, if the program number for NFS (Network File System Protocol) is specified in an RPC command, then NFS traffic may operate through that firewall interface.

Configuring IOS Firewall

Address translation is configured in the IOS Firewall using the **nat** and **pat** commands. The first step of configuring an IOS Firewall is to set up translation to mask internal IP addresses from the outside world. Example configurations for NAT and PAT (Port Address Translation) are given in the next part of this chapter, which covers the PIX Firewall.

Context-based security is configured in the IOS Firewall by creating inspection rules. Inspection rules (also called *rule sets*) are applied to access lists governing specific firewall network interfaces. Configuring an IOS Firewall, then, is done mostly using two variations of two commands:

▼ **access-list**   A command used to define the basic access rules for the interface

▲ **ip inspect**   A command used to define what CBAC will look for at the interface

The access list specifies which normal rules apply to traffic entering the interface. The access list is used to tell the interface which network applications (port numbers) are prohibited, which destination addresses are blocked, and so on. CBAC inspection rules dynamically modify the access list as necessary to create temporary openings in the IOS Firewall for valid sessions. CBAC defines a valid session as any TCP or UDP connection that matches its access list criteria.

In addition to creating temporary openings in the firewall, CBAC applies inspection rules to detect various kinds of network attacks and generate alert messages, which are usually sent to the network management console.

NOTE: One of the best-known denial-of-service attacks is SYNflood, so named for the SYN bit used to consummate a three-way handshake used to set up TCP connections. SYNflood attacks try to drown the target network in a flood of connection attempts—thereby denying legitimate hosts network service. A command called **synwait-time** is used by the network administrator to tell IOS Firewall how long an unrequited SYN bit is retained before being discarded. By not letting SYN bits pile up, the **synwait-time** command can be used to thwart this type of denial-of-service attack.

The IOS Firewall can be configured either of two ways, depending on whether the firewall configuration includes a DMZ. Figure 7-12 depicts this. The configuration on the right of Figure 7-12 shows the access list pulled back to the inside of the firewall.

Configuring CBAC on the internal interface relieves the firewall from having to create and delete context-based rule exceptions for traffic hitting the DMZ's Web (HTTP) Server and DNS (Domain Name System) Server. With this arrangement, CBAC can still selectively control access to HTTP and DNS services by internal users, but it doesn't have to worry about connections hitting the DMZ servers.

NOTE: IOS Firewall is a version of Cisco IOS software, so normal IOS conventions therefore apply. To configure IOS Firewall, you must first gain access to the router via Telnet or the Web browser interface, enter Privileged Exec command mode, and then enter configuration mode with the firewall(config-if)# prompt pointing to the interface to which the CBAC configuration will apply.

The first step in configuring the IOS Firewall interface is to create an access list. To define an access list, use the following command syntax:

```
Firewall(config)#ip access-list standard access-list-name-or-number permit
```

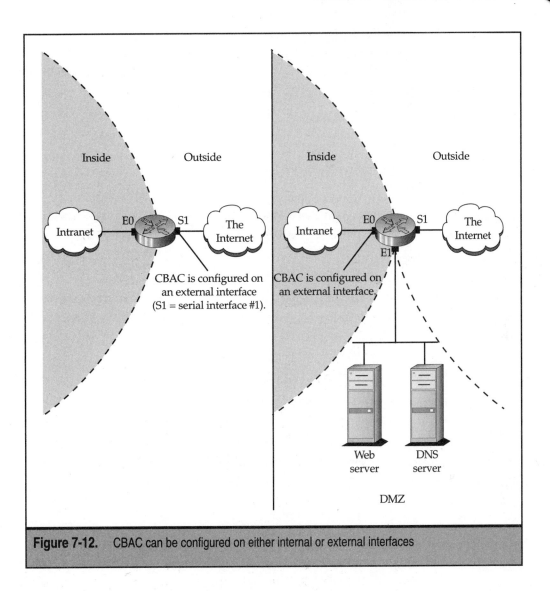

Figure 7-12.   CBAC can be configured on either internal or external interfaces

If a permit rule is matched, the packet is forwarded through the firewall. Deny rules are defined using the same syntax:

```
Firewall(config)#ip access-list standard access-list-name-or-number deny
```

If a deny rule is matched, the packet is dropped. Figure 7-13 shows an example access list 100. This access list will be applied to the Ethernet0 firewall interface. Access list 100 permits all traffic that should be CBAC inspected. The last line of the access list is set up to deny unknown IP protocols that a hacker might attempt to use.

The second step in configuring CBAC is to create inspection rules with the **ip inspect** command, using the following syntax:

```
Firewall(config)#ip inspect name inspection-name protocol [timeout seconds]
```

This command syntax tells IOS Firewall what to inspect packets for and the maximum period of inactivity to keep open any session that was created using the inspection rule. Timeout periods are important in CBAC configurations. If timeout limits are set too high, the state table could become bloated, which could hurt router performance and even security. On the other hand, if timeouts are set too low, users could become frustrated at having to frequently reset connections made to Internet hosts.

A set of inspection rules is created by using the same *inspection-name* in all the commands to be included in the set. The following code snippet shows an inspection rule set being built under the name Rulz. By sharing the name Rulz, the seven **ip inspect** commands included in this set can be invoked in a single statement. Table 7-1 gives the keywords used for protocol inspection commands.

```
Firewall(config)#ip inspect name Rulz ftp timeout 2000
Firewall(config)#ip inspect name Rulz smtp timeout 3000
Firewall(config)#ip inspect name Rulz tftp timeout 60
Firewall(config)#inspect name Rulz http java-list 99 timeout 3000
Firewall(config)#ip inspect name Rulz udp timeout 15
Firewall(config)#ip inspect name Rulz tcp timeout 2000
```

The timeout limits in the preceding example allow TCP applications about three to five minutes to respond and UDP applications a minute or less. This reflects the fact that UDP applications are more concerned with causing minimal network overhead than

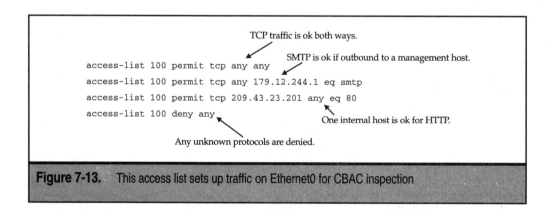

Figure 7-13.   This access list sets up traffic on Ethernet0 for CBAC inspection

Transport-Layer Protocols	Keyword
Terminal Control Protocol (TCP)	tcp
User Datagram Protocol (UDP)	udp
Application-Layer Protocols	
CU-SeeMe	cuseeme
FTP	ftp
Java	http
H.323	h323
UNIX R commands (r-login, r-exec, r-sh)	rcmd
RealAudio	realaudio
RPC	rpc
SMTP	smtp
SQL*Net	sqlnet
StreamWorks	streamworks
TFTP	tftp
VDOLive	vdolive

Table 7-1. Keywords in IOS Firewall's **inspect** and **access-list** Commands

with session integrity. The timeouts set for TCP and UDP are overridden in sessions running an application protocol. For example, any TFTP backup session running through this firewall would have the 60-second timeout limit set for TFTP in force (preempting the 15-second limit set for UDP-only sessions).

While it's true that timeouts help conserve system resources, the primary reason for configuring them in a firewall is security. The less time you give a hacker's attack program to try to worm through the firewall's interface, the better your internetwork security is. However, timeouts can't be set at too tight of a tolerance or legitimate users will have to make several attempts to connect. Like everything else in internetworking, timeout strategy is a balancing act.

The last step in configuring an IOS Firewall interface is applying an inspection rule set to the access list. The following snippet taken from the config file for firewall interface Ethernet0 shows the inspection set Rulz has been invoked for access list 89. The rules have been applied to inspect and filter inbound traffic.

```
interface Ethernet0
  description VelteSystems Extranet Gateway
  ip address 209.78.124.12 255.255.255.248
  ip broadcast address 209.78.124.1
  ip inspect Rulz in
  ip access-list 89 in
```

Without inspection rules to modify access lists, IOS Firewall behavior would revert to that of a normal router running normal access lists.

IOS Firewall Session Management Features

By now you've seen how important time is to firewalls. This is not unlike the head of security in a bank maintaining strict control over how long the safe door may stay open as people enter and leave it. For obvious reasons, the security chief would frown on employees loitering about the safe door.

THE MAX-INCOMPLETE SESSION COMMANDS   Like the bank's security chief, network administrators fret over connections pending at the firewall's interfaces—especially the outside interfaces. These incomplete connections are called *half-open sessions*. A rising number of half-open sessions at the firewall indicates that a denial-of-service attack is under way. IOS Firewall has several commands, called TCP intercept commands, that intercept denial-of-service attacks before they can overwhelm a firewall's network interface.

IOS Firewall uses the **ip inspect max-incomplete** command to track and control half-open sessions. For TCP, *half-open* means that a session has not yet reached the established state (in fact, it's entered into the CBAC state table as a pending request to start a session). A UDP session is deemed half-open when traffic is detected from one direction only (remember, UDP is a connectionless protocol).

CBAC monitors half-open sessions both in absolute numbers and in relative trends. Once every minute, CBAC totals all types of half-open sessions and weighs the total against an allowable threshold specified in the config file (500 half-open requests is the default limit). Once the threshold is exceeded, CBAC begins deleting half-open requests from its state table. It will continue deleting them until it reaches a minimum threshold, whereupon operations are returned to normal. The following code snippet shows a typical configuration of the **max-incomplete high** command. It's a good practice to keep the high-low spread narrow to let CBAC make frequent use of this control feature.

```
Firewall(config)#ip inspect max-incomplete high 1000
Firewall(config)#ip inspect max-incomplete low 900
```

THE INSPECT ONE-MINUTE COMMANDS   The other command to control half-open sessions is the **inspect one-minute** command. Instead of acting on the number of half-open connections, the rate of change in half-open sessions is what's measured. It works much like the **max-incomplete** command. Here's an example configuration (using the default values):

```
Firewall(config)#ip inspect one-minute high 900
Firewall(config)#ip inspect one-minute low 400
```

OTHER TCP INTERCEPT COMMANDS   CBAC has other commands to thwart denial-of-service attacks. As mentioned earlier, the **inspect synwait-time** command controls SYNflood attacks by deleting connection requests with SYN bits that have been pending longer than a specified time limit (the default is 30 seconds). The **inspect finwait-time** command similarly controls FINflood attacks (FIN bits are exchanged when a TCP connection is ready to close; its default is 5 seconds). The **inspect max- incomplete host** command is used to specify threshold and timeout values for TCP host-specific denial-of-service detection. It limits how many half-open sessions with the same host destination address are allowed and how long CBAC will continue deleting new connection requests from the host (the defaults are 50 half-open sessions and 0 seconds). Finally, generic protection is given by configuring the maximum idle times for connections with the **inspect tcp idle-time** and **inspect udp idle-time** commands (with default limits of 1 hour and 30 seconds, respectively).

The Cisco PIX Firewall

The PIX Firewall is Cisco's premier product for firewall duties. The IOS Firewall feature set is targeted at more price-sensitive customers or for duty in cordoning off access within enterprise networks. PIX is a total package positioned by Cisco to compete head-to-head with the major firewall products on the market today. The PIX Firewall differs from the IOS Firewall in these ways:

▼ **Integrated hardware/software**   The PIX Firewall is an integrated package on a hardware platform purpose-built for heavy-duty firewall service. It doesn't come as a separate software package.

■ **Adaptive Security Algorithm (ASA)**   Neither a packet filter nor an application proxy firewall, PIX implements a cut-through proxy architecture that delivers higher performance.

▲ **Integrated VPN option**   A plug-in processor card configures virtual private networks supporting the advanced Internet Security (IPSec) encryption and Internet Key Exchange (IKE) standards.

Network administrators are increasingly turning to purpose-built devices such as the Cisco PIX Firewall to meet their network security needs. The electronics and software in the PIX Firewall are tuned specifically to balance advanced security functionality with the need for high-throughput performance. The PIX Firewall and dedicated products like it are called *network appliances*—the hip new term for devices built to serve a narrowly defined networking function. The most obvious advantage of using a firewall appliance is that the IOS software doesn't have to split its time between filtering and routing.

NOTE: *Cut-through* processing is the technique of forwarding the beginning of a message before its last packet has been received.

Beyond the appliance versus firewall-enabled router debate, Cisco is positioning PIX as a real-time embedded system against competitors' firewall appliances based on UNIX platforms. The argument is that UNIX-based firewall appliances must pay a price in performance and in security. The reasoning is that a general-purpose operating system kernel like UNIX not only has latencies and overheads inappropriate for firewall duty, but also has inherent security holes that hackers could use to break into the firewall itself.

The PIX Firewall's Adaptive Security Algorithm

The Adaptive Security Algorithm is roughly equivalent to the IOS Firewall's Context-Based Access Control. Both serve as the central engine for their respective firewall products. Both PIX and IOS Firewall run a version of IOS software, which is beneficial because network administrators are familiar with the environment and its basic commands (**configure**, **debug**, **write**, etc.). But ASA has a very different set of firewall-specific commands, and its architecture is radically different from that of IOS Firewall. ASA enables the PIX Firewall to implement tighter security measures and to scale to higher capacity gateway sizes.

NOTE: What's an *algorithm*? The term makes it sound as if writing one would involve quantum physics with a dash of quadratic equations thrown in. But algorithms aren't anything mysterious. An algorithm is nothing more than a carefully crafted set of rules rigorously applied to a repetitive process, and logically able to handle variable conditions. Yes, some algorithms contain mathematical equations, but most don't. Computers make heavy use of algorithms because nearly everything in computing is repetitive and driven by variables.

THE NAMEIF COMMAND   The cliché is that the world is painted not in black and white, but in shades of gray. So, too, for the world of internetwork security, where the "good guys versus bad guys" model falls short because almost *everybody* is regarded as suspect. The trend in truly powerful network security, then, is the capability to designate networks and hosts as a spectrum of security levels instead of merely as "inside" or "outside."

The PIX Firewall's **nameif** (name interface) command lets you specify relative security levels for interfaces both inside and outside of the firewall. Applying relative security levels on an interface-by-interface basis lets you draw a far more descriptive security map than you would be able to by defining all networks as either inside or outside.

To configure a firewall's interfaces with relative security levels, you enter a **nameif** command for each interface. You can choose any value for a security level between 0 and 99, and no two interfaces on a PIX firewall may have the same level. The common practice is to assign levels in tens, as shown in the following code snippet, which identifies eight interfaces in three security zones:

```
Firewall(config)#nameif ethernet0 outside security0
Firewall(config)#nameif ethernet1 outside security10
Firewall(config)#nameif serial0 outside security20
Firewall(config)#nameif ethernet2 dmz security50
```

```
Firewall(config)#nameif ethernet3 dmz security30
Firewall(config)#nameif ethernet4 inside security100
Firewall(config)#nameif ethernet5 inside security90
Firewall(config)#nameif serial1 inside security70
```

The way security levels work is that each host on a network takes on the security level assigned to it. A connection being made from a higher level to a lower network is treated by the software as outbound; one headed from a lower-level interface to a higher level would be treated as inbound. This scheme enables the network administrator to apply rules on a much more granular basis.

Because each zone has its own security scale, the option exists to implement intrazone security checks. For example, access lists could apply restrictions on traffic flowing between hosts attached to the two DMZ networks. Some possible uses of security levels are depicted in Figure 7-14.

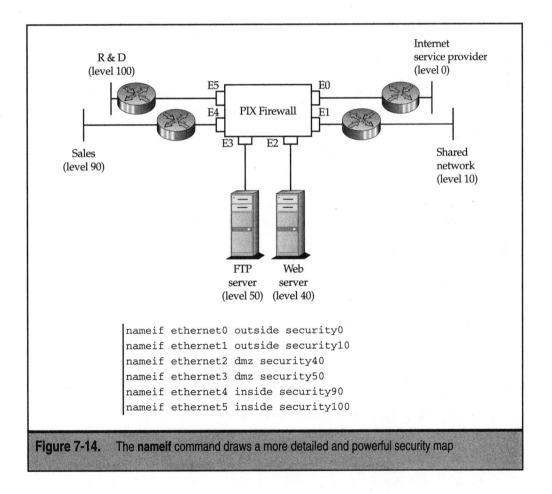

Figure 7-14.   The **nameif** command draws a more detailed and powerful security map

As with the IOS Firewall and other firewalls, packets may not traverse the PIX Firewall without a connection and a state. The Adaptive Security Algorithm checks inbound packets using these rules:

▼ All inbound connections must be explicitly configured by a **conduit** command. *Conduits* specify which external IP addresses are allowed to connect to which internal addresses behind the PIX Firewall.

■ All outbound connections are permitted except those configured as denied in outbound access lists.

▲ Static outbound connections can be configured using the **static** command, bypassing the dynamic translation pools created using the **global** and **nat** or **pat** commands.

PIX FIREWALL TRANSLATION SLOTS   As with the IOS Firewall, address translation and session tracking are at the center of the architecture. But the PIX Firewall uses a more formal system to implement IP address translation. Instead of simply creating a new translation and dynamically entering it into a reflexive access list like IOS Firewall, ASA assigns a *slot* to the new connection.

PIX Firewalls are sold with connection licenses that limit the total number of connection slots that can be used simultaneously. Each session consumes a slot. Slots configured with both the **global** or **static** commands are sometimes referred to as *xlates* (as in *translates*), although they're usually just called slots. When a connection is initiated, ASA takes a slot from the license pool and enters the session into the state table. The slot is returned to the pool when the session terminates.

If an internetwork needs more simultaneous connections than it's licensed for, the operator must buy a bigger software license from Cisco. Table 7-2 shows the increments in which PIX Firewall slots may be licensed.

To help manage slot consumption, you can specify a slot limit when configuring interfaces with the **nat** command. In this way, network administrators can prevent individual network users from consuming too many translation slots.

DRAM	Maximum Connections (Slots)
8MB	16,384
16MB	32,768
32MB	65,536
64MB	131,072

Table 7-2.   The Number of Maximum Simultaneous Connections Is a Function of Firewall Memory

> **NOTE:** Did you know that some applications use more than one connection at a time? For example, FTP takes two connections. A Web browser (which runs the HTTP application protocol) can take up to four or more connections, depending on whether it's in the process of loading a page or some other objects such as Java applets. So don't think of Internet connections in terms of something the user consciously decides to start and stop. Sessions are launching and quitting without our even knowing it. Microsoft Internet Explorer is said to consume up to 20 TCP connections per user!

We'll run through a simple PIX Firewall configuration to showcase some of the commands. Whole books have been written about firewalls, so we'll only cover those commands that will help you understand basic PIX Firewall operations. The PIX Firewall runs a special version of IOS, so the usual IOS command conventions apply. Figure 7-15 shows a three-interface PIX configuration with one shield router, one inside shield router, and one DMZ server attached. The configuration incorporates global address translation, restrictions on outbound traffic, and an outbound static route with an inbound conduit.

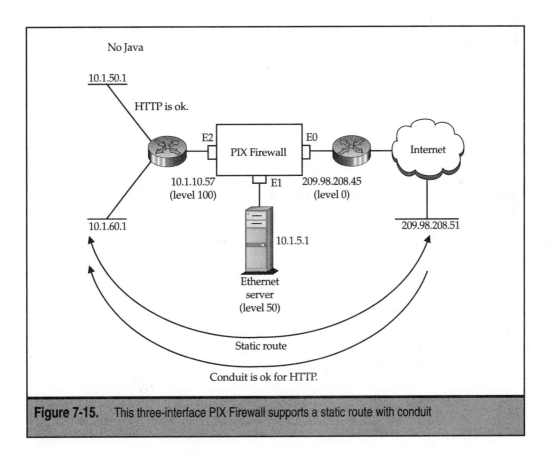

Figure 7-15. This three-interface PIX Firewall supports a static route with conduit

The first step is to go into configure interface mode, pointing at each interface as it's being configured:

```
Firewall>enable
Password:******
Firewall#config t
Firewall(config)#
```

Then **interface** commands are used to give the interfaces security zones and levels:

```
Firewall(config)#nameif ethernet0 outside security0
Firewall(config)#nameif ethernet1 Extranet security50
Firewall(config)#nameif ethernet2 inside security100
```

Next, **interface** commands specify the Ethernet specification that the interfaces will operate (autosensing 10/100 Mbps):

```
Firewall(config)#interface ethernet0 auto
Firewall(config)#interface ethernet1 auto
Firewall(config)#interface ethernet2 auto
```

The interfaces must be identified with IP addresses and masks, which is done using **ip address** commands. Notice that the names you just gave to the interface (outside, Extranet, and inside) are put to use, and the private internal IP addresses are used for the Extranet and inside interfaces (10.1.5.1 and 10.1.10.57):

```
Firewall(config)#ip address outside 209.98.208.45 255.255.255.240
Firewall(config)#ip address Extranet 10.1.5.1 255.255.255.0
Firewall(config)#ip address inside 10.1.10.57 255.255.255.0
```

The **nat** command is used to let all users in two inside user groups make outbound connections using translated IP addresses. The number following the **(inside)** arguments of the two statements is a NAT ID number or NAT reference number (1 and 2), used to link groups to global address pools:

```
Firewall(config)#nat (inside) 1 10.0.0.0 255.0.0.0
Firewall(config)#nat (inside) 2 10.0.0.0 255.0.0.0
```

Statements using the **global** command create two global address pools. They're assigned to users by way of the NAT ID numbers (1 and 2 here). The middle statement is the PAT address pool. What's happening here is that the system is being told to assign NAT addresses and, when they're all in use, to begin applying the PAT global address to sessions. All connections assigned a PAT address will show a source address of 1 209.98.208.50:

```
Firewall(Config)#global (outside) 1 209.98.208.46-209.98.208.49 netmask 255.255.255.240
Firewall(Config)#global (outside) 1 209.98.208.50 netmask 255.255.255.240
Firewall(Config)#global (outside) 2 209.98.210.1-209.98.210.254 netmask 255.255.255.240
```

A **static** statement is used to create an externally visible IP address. An accompanying **conduit** statement permits a specified host or network—a business partner, for example—through the PIX Firewall. The following example statement permits users on an outside host access through the firewall to server 10.1.60.1 via TCP connections for Web access. The **eq 80** clause specifies that the TCP connection must be running (equal to) port 80—the port number for the HTTP application protocol. The **any** modifier lets any external host attach to 10.1.60.1.

```
Firewall(config)#static (inside, outside) 209.98.208.51 10.1.60.1
                netmask 255.255.255.0
Firewall(config)#conduit permit tcp host 10.1.60.1 eq 80 any
```

This statement using the **outbound** command creates an access list that permits an inside host Web access (port 80), but forbids it from downloading Java applets. PIX uses the **outbound** command to create access lists and the **apply** command to apply them. Notice that the port number for Java is represented by the text string **java** instead of a port number. Using names instead of numbers is possible for some newer application-layer protocols like Java. It's obviously a lot easier to remember names instead of a cryptic number. The outgoing_src option denies or permits an internal address the ability to start outbound connections using the services specified in the **outbound** command.

```
Firewall(config)#outbound 10 permit 209.98.208.22 255.255.255.255 80
Firewall(config)#outbound 10 deny 209.98.208.22 255.255.255.255 java
Firewall(config)#apply (Extranet) 10 outgoing_src
```

There are many other commands to use when configuring a PIX Firewall. Indeed, in most internetworking environments there are several more that *must* be configured to get the firewall working properly. Properly configuring a PIX firewall with multiple servers, protocols, access lists, and shield routers would take days. The possible configurations are endless. But the simple statements we just went through demonstrate that configuring even a firewall—one of internetworking's most complex devices—isn't rocket science. It can get pretty deep, but doing it is just a matter of taking things one interface at a time, one command at time.

There are many other major elements of firewall configuration. One example is configuring two firewalls—one as the primary gateway server and the other as a hot backup box to which traffic will go if the primary server fails (configured using the **failover** command). Another is configuring the firewall to integrate with a security server such as TACACS+, which we cover in Chapter 10.

VIRTUAL PRIVATE NETWORKS (VPNs)

What is a VPN? As so often happens in the computer business, marketing hype can muddle an otherwise clear term. In the case of VPNs, some confusion exists over what's *virtual* in a VPN—the privacy or the network? Here's the two-part definition of a virtual private network:

▼ VPN topology runs mostly over *shared* network infrastructure, usually the Internet, and has at least one private LAN segment at each end point.

▲ VPN sessions run through an encrypted connection.

To operate through encrypted connections across the Internet, the network segments at each end of a VPN must be under the administrative control of the enterprise (or enterprises) running the virtual network. In practical terms, this means that the end point routers must be under a common security and operational regimen. Above all, the end point routers in a VPN must operate a common encryption scheme.

What Composes a VPN

Think of VPNs as wide area networks that operate at least partly over the Internet. Like most WANs, a VPN could provide a mixture of access types, as shown in Figure 7-16.

VPNs are steadily taking over the role of WANs in enterprise networking. All or part of a VPN can be an intranet, an extranet, or a remote access vehicle for telecommuters or mobile workers. A significant number of new VPNs are owned and operated by Internet service providers, who parcel out VPN bandwidth to enterprises. Outsourcing VPNs is becoming a standard practice for all but the largest enterprises because it's less expensive, and the enterprise can rely on the ISP to manage VPN infrastructure for them.

Encryption and other security measures largely define a VPN. This is for the simple reason that running enterprise WANs over the Internet is easy and inexpensive, but not feasible without appropriate security. Thus, security is only part of what makes up a VPN. It is also defined by a suite of Internet-compatible access servers, network appliances (such as firewalls), and internetwork management techniques.

> **NOTE:** *Encryption* is a technique that scrambles the format of data in such a way that it can only be read by a system holding an authorized key with a mathematical formula needed to unscramble the payloads (packet headers are left unscrambled so that they can be routed). Encryption and decryption take place between two peer encrypting routers, called *peer routers* (note that firewalls can also handle encryption). Peer routers share a secret algorithm key used to unscramble the payload. Peer routers must authenticate each other before each encrypted session, using Digital Signature Standard (DSS) keys (unique character strings). When a signature is verified, the peer router is authenticated and the encrypted session begins. The actual scrambling is done using a temporary Data Encryption Standard (DES) key, which must be exchanged in the connection messages between the peer routers. When the encrypted session is over, the DES key is discarded.

The components making up a VPN are

▼ **Tunneling**   Point-to-point connections over a connectionless IP network—in essence, a set of predetermined router hops taken through the Internet to guarantee performance and delivery.

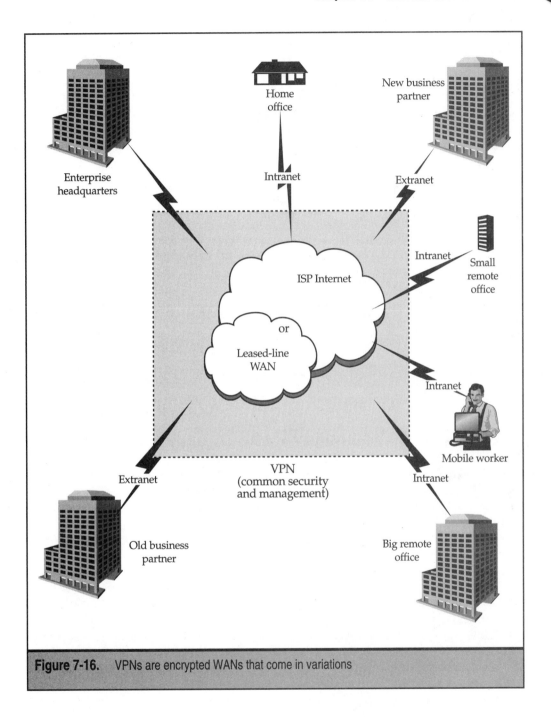

Figure 7-16. VPNs are encrypted WANs that come in variations

- ■ **Encryption**   The scrambling of an IP packet's contents (but not the header) to render it unreadable to all but those with a key to unscramble it (keys are held by authorized VPN senders and receivers only).

- ■ **Encapsulation**   Placing a non-IP frame inside an IP packet to bridge dissimilar networks (the IP is unpacked on the other side), effectively allowing tunneling to take place across otherwise incompatible VPN network segments.

- ■ **Packet authentication**   The ability to ensure the integrity of a VPN packet by confirming that its contents (payload) weren't altered en route.

- ■ **User authentication**   User authentication, authorization, and accounting (AAA) capabilities enforced through security servers such as TACACS+, RADIUS, or Kerberos.

- ■ **Access control**   Firewalls, intrusion detection devices, and security auditing procedures used to monitor all traffic crossing VPN security perimeters.

- ▲ **Quality of Service (QoS)**   Cisco's QoS is a set of internetwork management standards and functions to assure interoperability of devices and software platforms, and to leverage the platform to guarantee end-to-end network performance and reliability.

This list shows how a VPN is as much about *seamlessness* as security. Forcing network administrators or users to go through multiple steps to accomplish simple tasks would make using a VPN as infeasible as poor security. In practical terms, therefore, a VPN must be configured using hardware and software devices with these required characteristics.

Why Most WANs Will Soon Be VPNs

VPNs are reliably estimated to be from 30 percent to 80 percent less expensive than private WANs. This is mainly due to the very low cost of Internet connectivity compared to leased data lines and dial-up remote telephone connections. But it's also due to the economies of scale the Internet obviously has. For example, the cost of Internet connection equipment tends to be less expensive than, say, X.25 or IBM SNA gear. In the same way, the operational and management infrastructures available from ISPs cost a lot less than internal WAN operations teams.

Most infrastructure investments take several years to pay for themselves. It's widely accepted that converting from a WAN to a VPN can pay for itself in months—maybe in a year or so if the existing WAN is really cost effective. In addition to the dramatic cost savings, running a WAN over the Internet as a VPN also affords an enterprise nearly instant connectivity to anybody else, even on the other side of the world. This is why some gurus predict that private WANs will virtually disappear from the networking scene by the year 2003.

But most enterprises have invested significant amounts of money and effort in their WANs, and they know they work. So companies are adopting a strategy of peaceful coexistence—operating their internetworks over a hybrid of WAN and VPN links. They can do this in an orderly and secure way, until the last remaining private WAN leased line is removed from the internetwork topology.

The Cisco 1720 VPN Access Router is used to connect small remote sites to a VPN. The 1720 is packaged to perform high-speed encryption and deliver tunnel routing services in a single package. A conduit must be configured to operate a VPN through a PIX Firewall.

ACCESS SERVERS

Access servers connect users to internetworks over normal telephone lines. They are the Internet's version of front-end processors used in WANs. The mission of access servers is to deliver to remote enterprise users internetwork-ready connections. The users might be mobile workers, home workers, a small branch office, or even a remote LAN. *Access servers* (also called *communication servers* or *network access servers*) are equipped with hardware and software specially designed to behave like normal internetworking devices, but over modems connected to serial telephone lines.

Access servers can be configured to perform any or all of four types of duty:

▼ **Terminal service**   Connecting asynchronous devices using terminal emulation software such as IBM's TN3270, UNIX rlogin, or Digital Equipment's Local-Area Transport (LAT). Such a device could be a PC running terminal emulation software.

■ **Protocol translation service**   The conversion from the remote user's virtual terminal protocol to another virtual terminal protocol, used when connecting to an internetwork with hosts running various protocols.

■ **Telecommuting service**   Connections made mostly using the Point-to-Point Protocol (PPP) or its predecessor, the Serial Line Interface Protocol (SLIP). PPP connections can be router to router or host to router, and this protocol is used by Internet service providers to connect most home users.

▲ **Routing service**   The same full-featured IP routing functionality as if the remote host were sitting in the enterprise's campus network, its key feature is the ability to provide dial-on-demand routing (DDR) over low-cost dial-up phone lines.

NOTE: What's the big deal about internetworking over normal phone lines? Most phone lines support asynchronous transmission, which means digital signals are transmitted without the precise clocking services present on LANs. Asynchronous transmission encapsulates individual message characters in control bits (called start and stop bits) that designate the beginning and end of each character. Synchronous transmission also uses start and stop bits, but has precise clocking.

Cisco offers three basic access server platforms:

▼ **Cisco Universal Access Servers** A three-model line of high-end access servers with a 9-slot chassis that supports 16 to 120 asynchronous lines and some combination of Ethernet, Token Ring, synchronous serial, or ISDN PRI network interface modules.

■ **Cisco 500-CS** Eight to 16 asynchronous ports and 1 Ethernet port.

▲ **Cisco AS2500 Series** Five models, each with some combination of 8 or 16 asynchronous ports, 1 or 2 synchronous serial ports, and 1 Ethernet or Token Ring interface.

Whatever the package, though, access servers by nature have an internetwork side and a remote side. In other words, logical access to the internetwork is made within the access server box. Figure 7-17 depicts this.

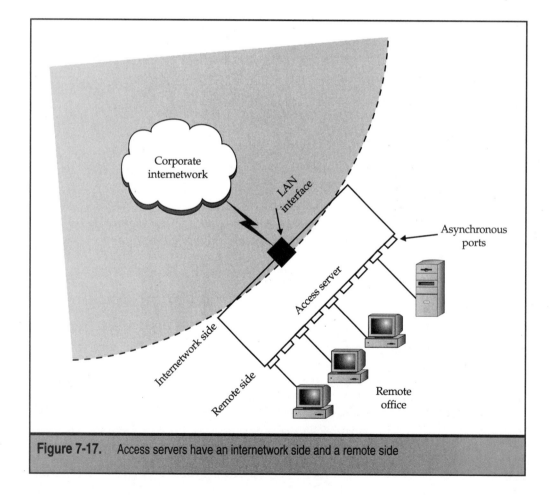

Figure 7-17. Access servers have an internetwork side and a remote side

Although telecommuting and DDR are the remote access services of the future, tens of millions of remote CRTs are still in use. Terminals will continue to play an important (if peripheral) role in internetworks until every desktop has a PC. Most terminals in the world run either IBM TN3270 or DEC LAT when connecting remotely. Many hosts still rely on the X.25 protocol. Nowadays, almost everybody needs connectivity to the Internet's IP protocol. Figure 7-18 depicts an access router running remote terminal services.

Most UNIX and PC hosts support Telnet for virtual terminal sessions. But many devices still rely on LAT or the X.25 protocol. Figure 7-19 shows how an access server can support multiple protocol translations.

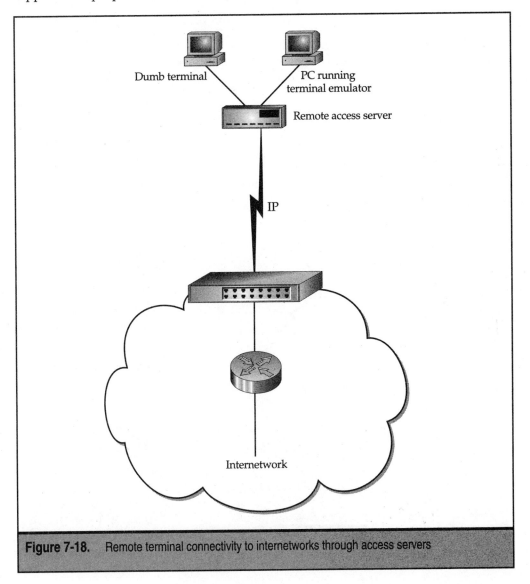

Figure 7-18.   Remote terminal connectivity to internetworks through access servers

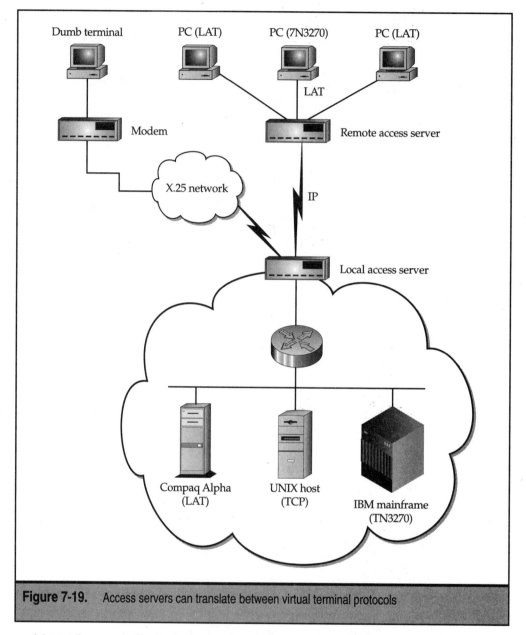

Figure 7-19.   Access servers can translate between virtual terminal protocols

Most telecommuting is done via the Point-to-Point Protocol, although some older configurations still use SLIP. And some hard-core UNIX shops have what are called X-terminals, which are a kind of thin client running the UNIX X-Windows interface on a stripped down desktop that connects via the X-Remote protocol. Figure 7-20 shows how they might connect through access servers.

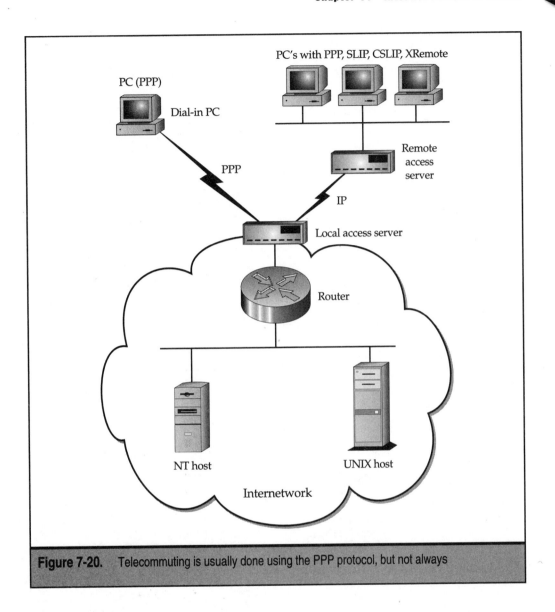

Figure 7-20.   Telecommuting is usually done using the PPP protocol, but not always

Dial-on-demand routing (DDR) effectively makes a remote site appear to an internetwork as if it had a direct full-time router connection. DDR is a hot technology because it brings significant phone-line savings for small offices by letting them connect through dial-up lines instead of costly leased lines. It's important to get a DDR router's configuration right so that network overhead traffic (pings, routing protocol updates, etc.) don't tie up phone lines. Figure 7-21 depicts DDR.

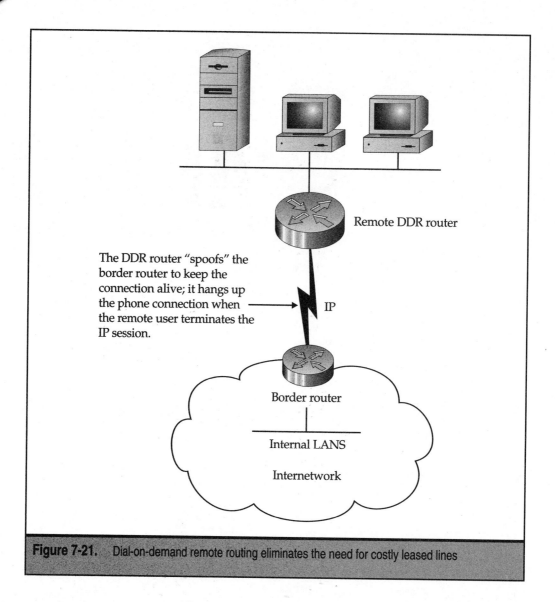

The DDR router "spoofs" the
border router to keep the
connection alive; it hangs up
the phone connection when
the remote user terminates the
IP session.

Remote DDR router

IP

Border router

Internal LANS

Internetwork

Figure 7-21.   Dial-on-demand remote routing eliminates the need for costly leased lines

Together, these four types of remote access make IP-based internetworking a viable
option for dial-up users. Like a chain that's only as strong as its weakest link, an
internetwork becomes less viable as the number of users unable to access it grows. With
the explosion in telecommuting and mobile workforces, the future of internetworking as
a total solution hinges on Internet-enabling remote access services. Dial-on-demand routing and PPP connectivity are especially vital to successful internetwork configurations.

PART III

Designing Cisco Networks

CHAPTER 8

Routing Protocols

Over the past four chapters, we've covered the gamut of network devices. The hub, usually sitting in a data closet, takes in twisted-pair cables from host devices and forms a LAN-in-a-box. Switches perform the same modest duty, but also pack the power to support VLANs. A third inhabitant of the data closet is the access server, used to link remote users into internetworks via dial-in telephone lines. If a packet moves beyond its source LAN segment, it flows onto a backbone LAN where it encounters a router and (if it's a secured internetwork) a firewall. After that point is the Great Beyond. Once the packet goes past the local network, it enters a realm of seemingly infinite complexity.

Internetworks are complex because they're big and subject to endless fluctuation. An internetwork's topology is altered whenever a new hub or switch is added, or when a router is inserted to help direct growing internetwork loads. As usage patterns evolve, traffic congestion seems to pop up in different spots every day. If network devices crash, they take their connected LAN segments down with them, and traffic must be immediately diverted—and then redirected once the downed device is brought back online. More frequently, the network device is up but one of its network interfaces has gone down, or the interface is OK but a cable was accidentally knocked from its port. To top it all off, sometimes all the physical network equipment is running fine but things *still* go awry because a rotten config file was somehow introduced into the mix!

The point here is that large internetworks are simply too complicated to be managed by people alone. Imagine a roomful of network administrators trying to manually control each and every network event in a Fortune 500 company, and you'd see a portrait of creeping disorganization. Now imagine that same room—or even a building—filled with people attempting to corral the Internet itself, and you see unmitigated chaos. There's just too much complexity and change to handle without a constant source of reliable help—automated help.

So how does it all work? How do packets find their way across internetworks with the reliability we've come to take for granted? The answer is routing protocols.

OVERVIEW OF ROUTING PROTOCOLS

As you've learned, a *protocol* is a formalized system for exchanging a specific type of information in a certain way, and an *algorithm* is a system of rules carefully crafted to control a process that must contend with varying factors.

In our context, a *routing protocol* formalizes the ongoing exchange of route information between routers. Messages called *routing updates* pass information used by routing algorithms to calculate paths to destinations. A *routing algorithm* is a system of rules that controls an internetwork's behavior in such a way that it adapts to changing circumstances within the internetwork's topology. Ongoing changes include such things as which links are up and running, which are fastest, whether any new equipment has appeared, and so on. Each router uses its own copy of the algorithm to recalculate a map of the internetwork to account for all the latest changes from its particular perspective.

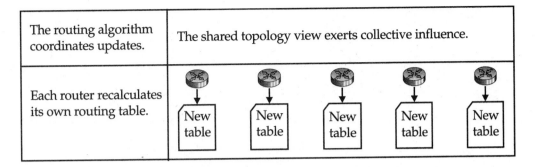

The routing algorithm coordinates updates.	The shared topology view exerts collective influence.
Each router recalculates its own routing table.	New table New table New table New table New table

Routing protocols use a peer arrangement in which each router plays an equal role. Those new to internetworking often think that routes are somehow coordinated by a centralized management server, maybe an SNMP server. They are not. There is no routing protocol server to centrally manage routing processes. Ongoing routing table maintenance is handled in real time through an arrangement in which each router makes its own route selection decisions. To configure a routing protocol for an internetwork, the routing protocol process must be configured in each router that will be involved in the arrangement. In practical terms, the IOS config file for every router must have parameters set to send and receive routing updates, run the algorithm, and so forth. Properly configured, the routing protocol is able to collectively influence all these machine-made decisions so that they work in harmony. The area within which routing information is exchanged is called a *routing domain*.

NOTE: The terms *path* and *route* are synonymous. *Path* is widely used for no other reason than it's hard to discuss routing protocols that use routing algorithms to calculate new optimal routes for distribution in routing updates sent to all routers for use in recalculating their respective routing tables. You get the point.

Routing Protocol Basics

Of the many routing protocols, some are standards based and others are proprietary. Several are old and fading from use, a few are used only within narrowly defined market niches, and others are in such wide use that they are de facto standards (this last group we'll briefly review later). Routing protocols also differ in the type of internetworks they're designed to manage, and in the size of internetworks they can handle. Naturally, these differences are manifested in each routing protocol's algorithm. Yet all their algorithms share these two basic processes:

▼   Routers send one another update messages advising of changes in internetwork topology and conditions.

▲   Each router recalculates its own routing table based on the updated information.

Updating one another helps each individual router know what's going on. More important, it helps orchestrate an internetwork's routers by maintaining a common set of information with which to operate.

The Routing Table's Central Role

A *routing table* is a list of routes available to forward traffic to various destinations. Every router in an internetwork maintains its own routing table, the contents of which differ from those maintained by other routers. Each router maintains a single routing table (not one per interface). The majority of routers run just one routing protocol, although specialized border routers run two in order to pass routes between areas using different protocols (more on that later).

A routing table constitutes the router's self-centered view of the internetwork's topology—sort of its personal formula for conducting business. Every time an update is received, the routing protocol takes the information and mashes it through its algorithm to recalculate optimal paths to all destinations deemed reachable from that router. Figure 8-1 illustrates the routing table update process.

Each router must have its own routing table to account for conditions specific to its location in the internetwork. In a routing domain, the routers collectively share the same news about any change, but then each puts that information to use individually.

The Routing Protocol Is an Internetwork's Intelligence

The goal of routing protocols is to let an internetwork respond to change. They do this by providing routers a common framework for decision making about how to respond to topology changes within the internetwork. The routing protocol coordinates the passing of updates between routers; then each router recalculates optimal routes in its own table. If, after recalculation, all the routing tables have arrived at a common view of the topology—albeit each from its self-centered perspective—the internetwork is said to have reached *convergence* (so called because the router community has converged on a singular view of the topology). A converged topology view means all the routers agree on which links are up, down, running fastest, and so on.

Routing protocols are the quintessence of high-tech internetworking. They represent the ability of individual devices and even whole networks to help manage themselves. One could say that internetworks have become organic in the sense that routing protocols make them self-aware and self-correcting. As topologies grow from day to day or circumstances change from moment to moment, internetworks can respond because routing protocols enable the router community to converse intelligently about what to do.

A trendy marketing cliché holds that "the network is the system." If that's true, then routing protocols serve as the network's operating system. Routing protocols raise the limit on what is practical in terms of internetwork size and complexity. It's no exaggeration to state that the development of sophisticated routing protocols is what has made the Internet's explosive growth possible.

Figure 8-1. Routing update messages coordinate routing tables

> **NOTE:** Cisco Discovery Protocol (CDP), the Hot Standby Routing Protocol (HSRP), and other specialized protocols are sometimes also referred to as routing protocols. For our purposes, a routing protocol is a protocol that coordinates the exchange of routing updates to notify other routers of topology changes and applies an algorithm to recalculate optimal routes through an internetwork.

Comparing Routed Networks to Switched Networks

A good way to explain routing protocols is by comparison. Remember switching tables from a couple of chapters ago? To refresh: Switches keep track of switched network topology by brute force. Every time a message arrives, the switch associates the frame's source MAC address (layer-2 physical address) with the switch port it came in on and then makes an entry into its MAC address table. In this way, the switch builds a list of destination MAC addresses for each switch port. Here's the basic layout of a switch's address table:

Destination MAC Address	Destination Switch Port
0060.2fa3.fabc	Fast Ethernet0/8
0050.0465.395c	Fast Ethernet0/4
0010.5a9b.b5e6	Fast Ethernet0/12
.	.
.	.
.	.

This isn't a particularly intelligent way to map routes because the switch's MAC address table only sees one step ahead. The table says nothing about the complete route to the destination; it merely shows you out the next door. The only way a switch can reduce the number of hops a frame must take between switches is to compile bigger and bigger MAC address tables, thereby increasing the odds that the best path will be encountered. Switch designers call this "aggregating bandwidth," but what's really being aggregated is MAC addresses. (In case you're wondering how switches choose between alternative paths, they favor those most frequently used, which appear higher in the MAC address list.)

Routers, by contrast, *can* see more than one step ahead. Routing tables give routers the ability to see farther into an internetwork without expanding their lists. Where switches substitute quantity for quality, routers apply intelligence. Here's the basic layout of a simple type of routing table:

Destination	Next Hop	Hop Count
209.98.134.126	209.126.4.38	3
	127.197.83.128	5
	202.8.79.250	9
.	.	.
.	.	.

This example may not look like much, but it's superior to the switch table in a fundamental way. The switch plays the odds, but the router plays it smart, because the Hop Count column gives routers information about the entire route. Knowing how many routers a packet must hop through to reach its destination helps the sending router choose the best path to take. This kind of measurement is called a *routing metric*, or *metric* for short. Metrics such as hop count are what separate routing from the switch's abrupt "out this door please" approach. Metrics supply the intelligence needed by routing algorithms to calculate best paths through internetworks.

Routing Updates Are Control Messages

Routed networks carry an undercurrent of specialized traffic that exchanges routing update messages. Switched networks do no such thing; they guess at what's going on by looking only at the source MAC address and incoming port of payload packets. A *payload message*, by the way, is one that carries content useful for an application instead of for the internetwork's internal operations. Figure 8-2 outlines the difference.

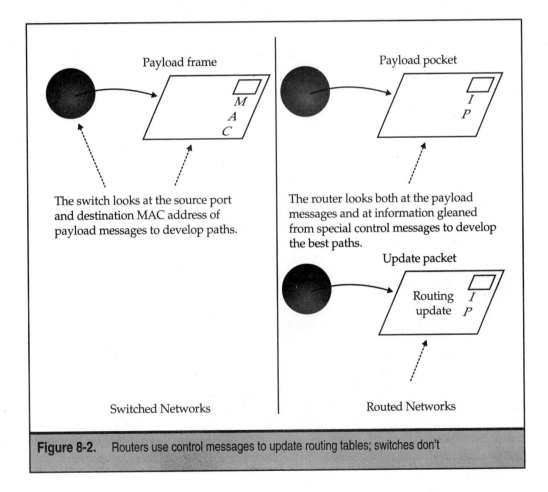

Payload frame

M
A
C

The switch looks at the source port and destination MAC address of payload messages to develop paths.

Payload pocket

I
P

The router looks both at the payload messages and at information gleaned from special control messages to develop the best paths.

Update packet

Routing   I
update   P

Switched Networks

Routed Networks

Figure 8-2.   Routers use control messages to update routing tables; switches don't

Routing updates aren't payload messages, they're *control messages*. The content they deliver is used by the internetwork for internal operations. This second type of traffic carrying routing updates is the lifeblood of internetworking, delivering the intelligence an internetwork must have to act in a unitary fashion and survive in the face of change. Given their importance, to reach a basic understanding of routing protocols you need to know what routing updates contain, how and where they're sent, and how they're processed.

Dynamic vs. Static Routing

Before we go further, a little background is in order. There are two basic types of routing:

▼ **Static routing**   A static route is a fixed path preprogrammed by a network administrator. Static routes cannot make use of routing protocols and don't self-update after receipt of routing update messages; they must be updated by hand.

▲ **Dynamic routing**   The type of routing made possible by routing protocols, which automatically calculate routes based on routing update messages. The majority of all internetwork routes are dynamic.

This distinction is made here to drive home a key point. Not all routes are automatically (dynamically) calculated by routing protocols, and for good reason. In most situations, network administrators will opt to retain direct control over a minority of routes.

The best example of how static routes are used is the default gateway. A router can't possibly know routes to all destinations, so it's configured with a *default gateway* path to which packets with unknown destinations are sent. Default gateways are entered as static routes to make sure undeliverable traffic is steered to a router that has routing table entries leading outside the internetwork. Figure 8-3 shows a default gateway in action.

The ability of routing protocols to automate routing table selection is a good thing, but only in measured doses. The use of static routes as default gateways to handle unanticipated messages exemplifies this.

Routers Collaborate to Attain Convergence

Convergence is when all routers in an internetwork have agreed on a common topology. For example, if a particular network link has gone down, the internetwork will have converged when all the routers settle on new routes that no longer include that link. Yet, each router must have its own routes to account for its unique position in the network topology. Thus the routers act collectively by sharing updates, yet take independent action by calculating their own routes. When the process is complete, they have converged in the sense that all the routes were calculated based on a common set of assumptions about the network's current topology.

This collaboration is orchestrated by the internetwork's routing protocol. Having routers work collectively gives internetworks their strength because it may take more

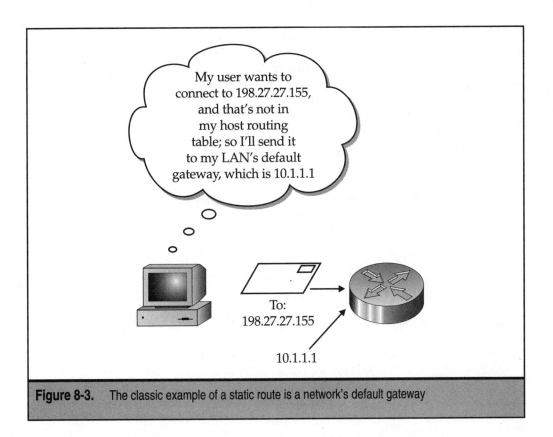

Figure 8-3. The classic example of a static route is a network's default gateway

than one router to isolate a network problem. And, until a problem is isolated, no router has the information needed to calculate new routes around the problem.

How Routers Sense Topology Change

Routers use gateway discovery protocols to keep track of one another. A *gateway discovery protocol* is a system that coordinates the exchange of small "are you still there?" messages between routers in an internetwork, mainly as a way of sensing downed links.

▼ Each router broadcasts "hello" messages to its immediate neighbor routers at a fixed interval (say, once every 90 seconds).

■ If no "ACK" acknowledgment message is received back within a specified period (3 minutes), the route is declared invalid.

▲ If no ACK has returned within a longer period (7 minutes), the router and its routes are removed from the sending router's table, and a routing update is issued about all routes that incorporated the nonresponding router as a link.

Gateway discovery protocols are low overhead control protocols that in IP networks are sent via the UDP transport protocol. Figure 8-4 illustrates how they work.

In addition to sensing problems, gateway discovery protocols detect the appearance of new equipment. The four types of gateway discovery messages in Figure 8-4 are collectively referred to as *timers*.

How Routing Updates Converge

Sensing a topology change is only the first step. From the point of discovery, routing updates must be passed until all routers can converge on a new topology by incorporating the change.

Let's take an example. Figure 8-5 shows a relatively simple four-router topology with route redundancy, in that messages have alternative paths to destinations. A message sent from Manufacturing to Accounting could travel via either the R&D or Marketing

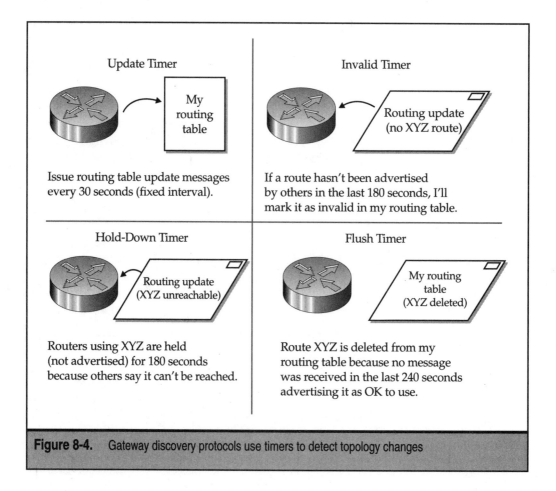

Update Timer

Issue routing table update messages every 30 seconds (fixed interval).

Invalid Timer

If a route hasn't been advertised by others in the last 180 seconds, I'll mark it as invalid in my routing table.

Hold-Down Timer

Routers using XYZ are held (not advertised) for 180 seconds because others say it can't be reached.

Flush Timer

Route XYZ is deleted from my routing table because no message was received in the last 240 seconds advertising it as OK to use.

Figure 8-4.   Gateway discovery protocols use timers to detect topology changes

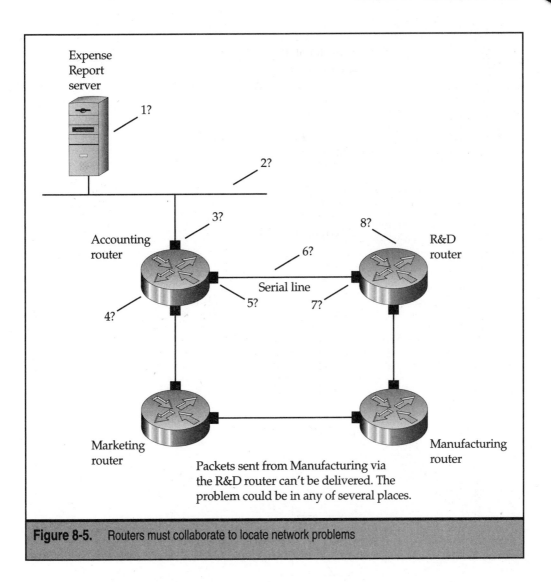

Expense
Report
server

1?

2?

3?

Accounting
router

8?

R&D
router

6?

Serial line

5?   7?

4?

Marketing
router

Manufacturing
router

Packets sent from Manufacturing via
the R&D router can't be delivered. The
problem could be in any of several places.

Figure 8-5.   Routers must collaborate to locate network problems

router. If packets sent from Manufacturing via the R&D router to the Expense Report
server suddenly become undeliverable, the Accounting router can't be relied upon to diagnose the problem on its own. This is because there are so many potential sources for the
problems, as depicted by the question marks in Figure 8-5. Here's a roundup of the most
likely suspects of what caused the problem:

1. The Expense Report server has crashed.

2. The LAN connection to the Expense Report server has failed.

3. The Accounting router's interface to the Expense Report server's LAN segment has failed.

4. The Accounting router has totally failed.

5. The Accounting router's serial interface to the R&D router has failed.

6. The serial transmission line connecting Accounting with R&D is down.

7. R&D's serial interface to the Accounting router has failed.

8. The R&D router has totally failed.

The Accounting router can't have definitive knowledge as to problems 1, 2, 7, or 8 because it's not directly responsible for these network devices. And the Accounting router would be of no use at all in the event of problem 4.

Packets can't be routed to detour around the failure until the problem has been located. Also, the problem must be located in order for the routers to converge on a new (post-failure) network topology.

If, in our example topology, the serial line between Accounting and R&D has failed, both routers would sense this at about the same time and issue updates. Figure 8-6 tracks the routing update as it flows from the Accounting and R&D routers. Once the router has sensed the problem, it deletes the failed path from its routing table. This in turn causes the routing algorithm to calculate a new best route to all destinations that had incorporated the failed link. When these new routes are calculated, the router issues them in a routing update message sent out to other routers in the internetwork.

Updated routing tables are sent from the Accounting and R&D routers to announce they are no longer using the serial line in their routes. These are routing update messages. The Manufacturing and Marketing routers in turn replace any routes they have using the serial link. In the Figure 8-6 example, it took two routing updates for the internetwork to converge on a new topology that's minus the serial line. When the serial line is brought back online, the connected routers will also sense the topology change, and the whole route update process will repeat itself in reverse.

Short convergence time is a primary design goal when laying out an internetwork's topology. In big networks it can take several updates to converge. The length of convergence time depends on the routing protocol used, the size of the internetwork, and where in the topology a change takes place. For example, if the problem in Figure 8-5 had occurred behind the Accounting router's gateway (say, with the Expense Report server or its LAN segment), only the Accounting router would have originated a routing update, which would have resulted in a convergence time of three updates.

Long convergence time is a symptom of a poorly functioning internetwork. Many factors can slow convergence, but the major factor in convergence times is propagation delay.

Propagation Delay

A network phenomenon called *propagation delay* is the delay between the time a packet is sent and when it arrives at its destination. Propagation delay isn't a simple matter of geo-

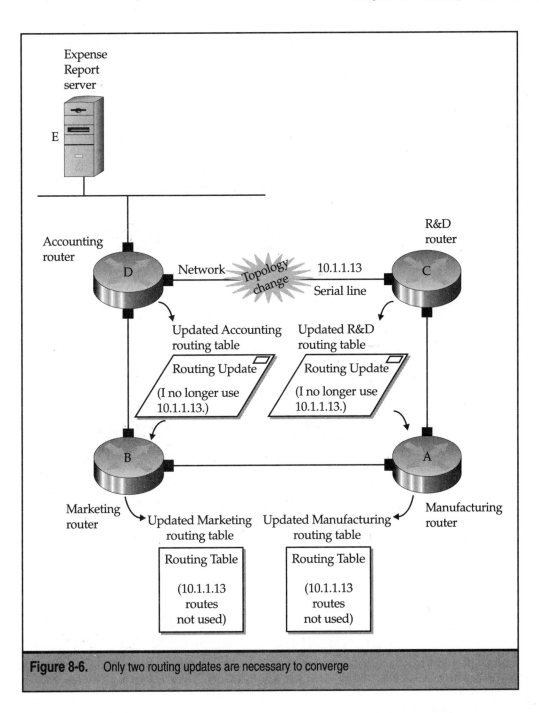

Figure 8-6.   Only two routing updates are necessary to converge

graphical distance or hop count; other factors can also have an influence. Figure 8-7 shows various propagation delay factors.

Obviously, something as basic as the time required for data to travel over a network is important to all areas of internetworking. But propagation delay is a huge factor for routing protocols, because all routers receive a routing update at the same moment. No matter how fast the network medium, convergence takes time as a routing update is passed from router to router until it arrives at the farthest router.

The importance of propagation delay grows with an internetwork's size. Big internetworks have dozens of routers, hundreds of connected LAN segments, and thousands of hosts—each a potential source of topology change. All other things being equal,

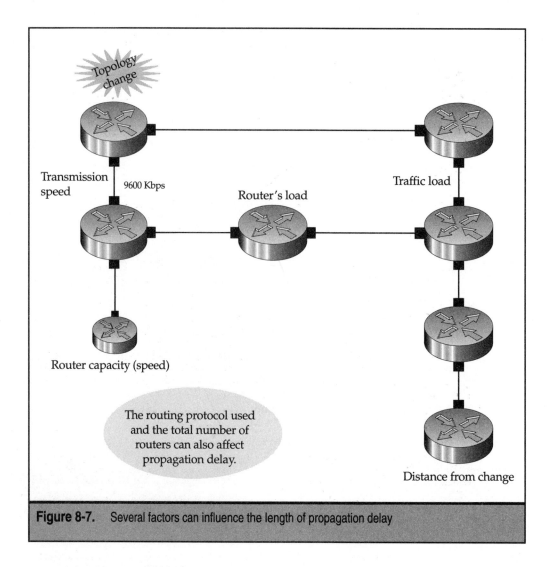

Figure 8-7.   Several factors can influence the length of propagation delay

the bigger the network, the greater its propagation delay; and the more redundant paths are used, the greater the potential for confusion.

Routing Loops

Propagation delay wouldn't pose a problem to routing protocols if routers always converged before any new changes emerged. But they don't. The longer propagation delay is in an internetwork, the more susceptible it is to something called a routing loop. A *routing loop* is when payload packets can't reach their destinations because of conflicting routing table information. This happens in large or change-intensive internetworks when a second topology change emerges before the network is able to converge on the first change.

Taking the example shown in Figure 8-8, the R&D router senses that network 10.1.1.13 has gone down and issues a routing update. But before the Manufacturing router receives the update it issues a routing update indicating that network 10.1.1.13 is still good (because the update has paths that incorporate this network). The updates from R&D and Manufacturing conflict and, depending on how the timing works out, can confuse the other routers and even each other, throwing the internetwork into a routing loop.

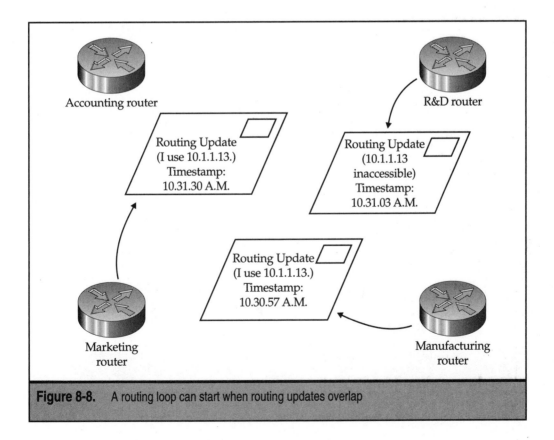

Figure 8-8.   A routing loop can start when routing updates overlap

Routing loops can be self-perpetuating. If the conflicting routing updates are persistent enough, each repeatedly nullifies the other in route decisions made by the affected routers. If the router's primary route vacillates each time it receives an update, the internetwork has become unstable. If things go too far out of balance (for example, there are too many loops in progress and primary route selections are flapping), the protocol's collective topology can begin to disintegrate altogether. The downward spiral goes like this:

▼ Two or more conflicting routing updates cause messages to be routed via downed routes, and thus they are not delivered.

■ As the loop persists, more bandwidth is consumed by inefficiently routed payload packets and routing updates trying to fix the problem.

▲ The diminishing bandwidth triggers still more routing updates in response to the worsening throughput.

The vicious circle of a routing loop is depicted in Figure 8-9.

Mechanisms to Keep Internetworks Loop Free

A scenario like the one just described is unacceptable to effective network operations. Routing protocols incorporate a number of sophisticated mechanisms to thwart the onset of routing loops:

▼ **Hold-downs**   Suppression of advertisements about a route that's in question long enough for all the routers to find out about its true status

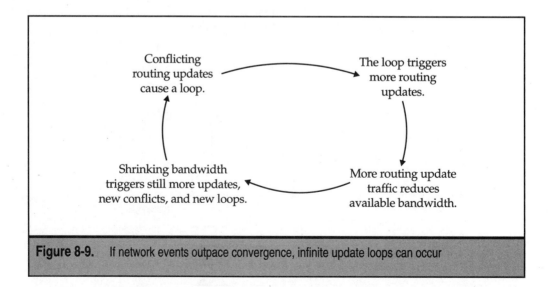

Figure 8-9.   If network events outpace convergence, infinite update loops can occur

- ■ **Split horizons**   The practice of not advertising a route back in the direction of the route itself
- ▲ **Poison reverse updates**   A routing update message that explicitly states a network or subnet is unreachable (instead of a nearby router merely dropping it from its routing table for lack of use)

HOLD-DOWNS   A *hold-down* is a way to help prevent bad routes from being reinstated by mistake. When a route is placed in a hold-down state, routers will neither advertise the route nor accept advertisements about it for a specific interval called the hold-down period. Hold-downs have the effect of flushing information about a bad route from the internetwork. It's a forcible way to take a bad apple from the barrel to help reduce the chances of it starting a routing loop. At the extreme, a hold-down period would be an interval slightly longer than it normally takes for the entire network to learn of a routing change—its average convergence time.

But holding back the release of routing updates obviously slows convergence, so there's a harsh trade-off between the loop prevention benefit of hold-downs and the quality of network service. This is because delaying release of an update leaves a bad route in play for a longer period. In internetworks of any size, setting hold-down intervals to match average convergence time results in frequent timeout messages to end users. In the real world, hold-down times are often set to an interval far less than the network's average convergence time to partially ameliorate loop risk, but at the same time avoid most network timeouts for users. This trade-off is depicted in Figure 8-10.

SPLIT HORIZONS   A *split horizon* is a routing configuration that stops a route from being advertised back in the direction from which it came. The theory is that it's basically useless to send information back toward its source. An example of this is outlined in Figure 8-11. Router B, in the middle, received a route to network 10.1.99.1 from Router A on the left. The split-horizon rule instructs Router B not to include that route in updates it sends

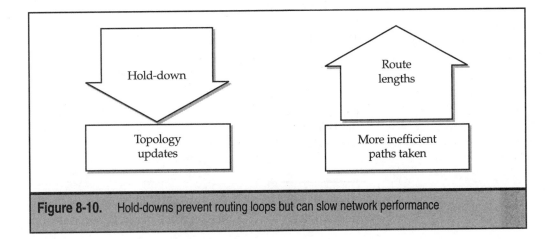

Figure 8-10.   Hold-downs prevent routing loops but can slow network performance

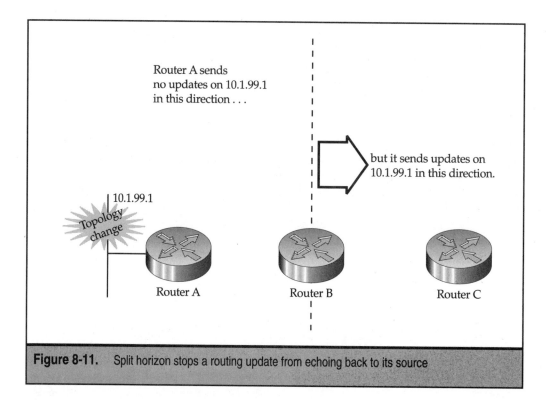

Router A sends
no updates on 10.1.99.1
in this direction . . .

but it sends updates on
10.1.99.1 in this direction.

10.1.99.1

Topology
change

Router A

Router B

Router C

Figure 8-11. Split horizon stops a routing update from echoing back to its source

back toward Router A. The assumption is that Router A was probably the source of the route (given that it is in the direction of network 10.1.99.1) and therefore doesn't need to be informed of the route. If Router A's interface to network 10.1.99.1 went down and it didn't have enough built-in intelligence, it might take its own routing update back from Router B and try to use it as a way around the downed interface.

Hold-downs can normally prevent routing loops on their own, but split horizons are generally configured as a backup measure because there's no particular trade-off in doing so.

POISON REVERSE UPDATES By now you've probably noticed that routing protocols work implicitly. In other words, they steer traffic around a bad link by not including routes involving that link in routing updates. *Poison reverse updates*, by contrast, explicitly state that a link is bad. Poison reverse works by having a router check for overlarge increases in metrics. Routing metrics are designed such that an increase reflects deterioration. For example, an increase in the number of hops a route must take makes it less desirable. A router compares an incoming routing update's metric for a route against what it was when the router itself had issued an earlier update including that same route. The routing protocol is configured with an acceptable increase factor that, if exceeded, causes the router to assume the route is a looping ("reversing") message. Figure 8-12 depicts the process.

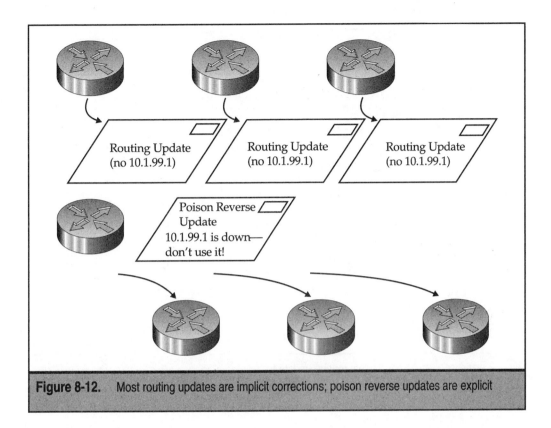

Figure 8-12.   Most routing updates are implicit corrections; poison reverse updates are explicit

In Cisco routing protocols, the default maximum increase for a routing metric is a factor of 1.1 or greater. In other words, if a route returns in an update with a metric that is 110 percent or more of what it was on the way out, it's assumed that a loop is in progress. For example, if a router sends out an update with a route with a hop count metric of 1 and it returns in someone else's update with a hop count of 2, the assumption is that a loop is under way. When this happens, the router places the router into a hold-down state where it neither sends nor receives updates on that route. The hold-down state stays on for a period deemed sufficiently long to flush the problem from the update system. Thus the name poison reverse: the loop is a bad metric "reversing" onto the router; the hold-down is a way of "poisoning" (or killing) updates that could contain the bad metric.

Split horizons are a good way to prevent routing loops among adjacent routers. But in large internetworks in which routing updates are passed between routers far removed from one another, poison reverse updates help prevent bad routes from starting to loop before update convergence can take place. Both techniques use hold-downs.

Routing Metrics

A routing metric is a value used by a routing protocol to influence routing decisions. Metric information is stored in routing tables and is used by routing algorithms to determine optimal routes to destinations. The terminology takes some getting used to, but here are the most widely used metrics:

▼ **Cost** Not financial cost, but a theoretical "cost" number used to represent the time, difficulty, risk, and other factors involved in a route.

■ **Distance** Not physical distance in miles or cable feet, but a theoretical "distance" number. Most distance metrics are based on the number of hops in a route.

■ **Bandwidth** The bandwidth rating of a network link (100 Mbps, for example).

■ **Traffic load** A number representing the amount of traffic (such as the number and size of packets) that traveled over a link during a specified period of time.

■ **Delay** In this context, the time between the start of a routing update cycle and when all routers in an internetwork converge on a single topology view (also called *propagation delay* or *latency*).

■ **Reliability** A relative number used to indicate reliability of a link.

▲ **MTU** The maximum packet size (maximum transmission units) that a particular network interface can handle, usually expressed in bytes.

> **NOTE:** Sometimes *cost* is used as a general term for the result calculated by an equation inside the routing protocol algorithm. For example, someone might state that the overall cost of one route was more than another's, when actually the routing algorithm used metrics for distance, bandwidth, traffic load, and delay.

Some simple routing protocols use just one metric. However, usually more than one routing metric goes into determining optimal routes. For example, a two-hop route traversing a 9600 Kbps serial line is going to be much slower than a three-hop route going over T3 circuits at 44 Mbps. You don't have to be Euclid to figure out that moving bits 4000 times faster more than compensates for an extra hop.

Sophisticated routing protocols not only support multiple metrics, they also let you decide which to use. In addition, you can assign relative weights to metrics to more precisely influence route selection. If the network administrator sets the metrics properly, the overall behavior of the internetwork can be tuned to best fit the enterprise's objectives. Figure 8-13 shows some routing metrics in action.

All Cisco routing protocols come with default settings for metrics. These default settings are based on design calculations made in Cisco's labs and real-world experience gained in the field. If you ever get your hands on a routing protocol, think long and hard before you start changing routing metric default settings. The domino effect of a bad routing metric decision can be devastating. Out-of-balance metric settings can be manifested in the form of poor network performance and routing loops.

Network Blueprints

Table of Contents

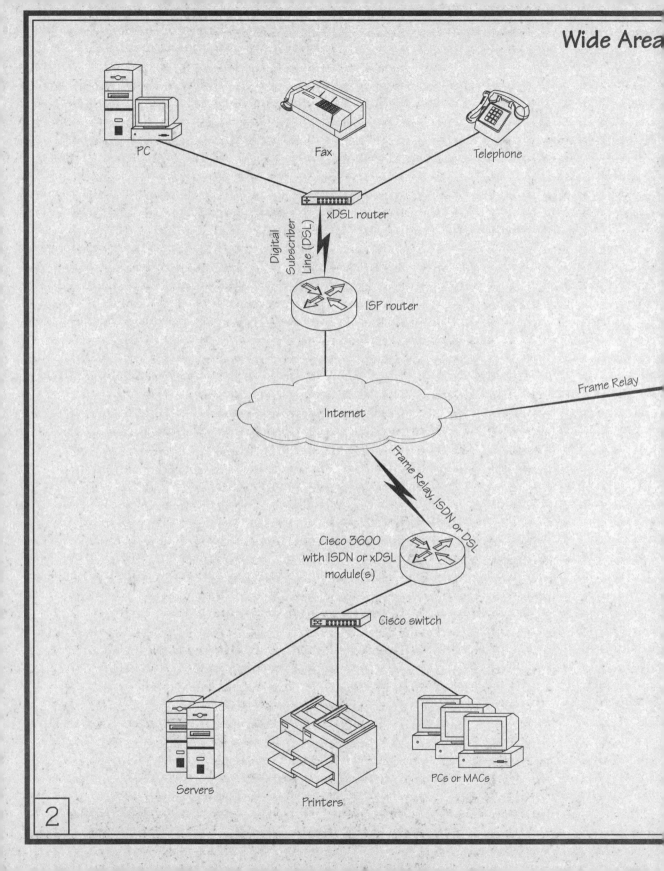

PC

Fax

Telephone

xDSL router

Digital
Subscriber
Line (DSL)

ISP router

Internet

Frame Relay

Frame Relay, ISDN or DSL

Cisco 3600
with ISDN or xDSL
module(s)

Cisco switch

Servers

Printers

PCs or MACs

2

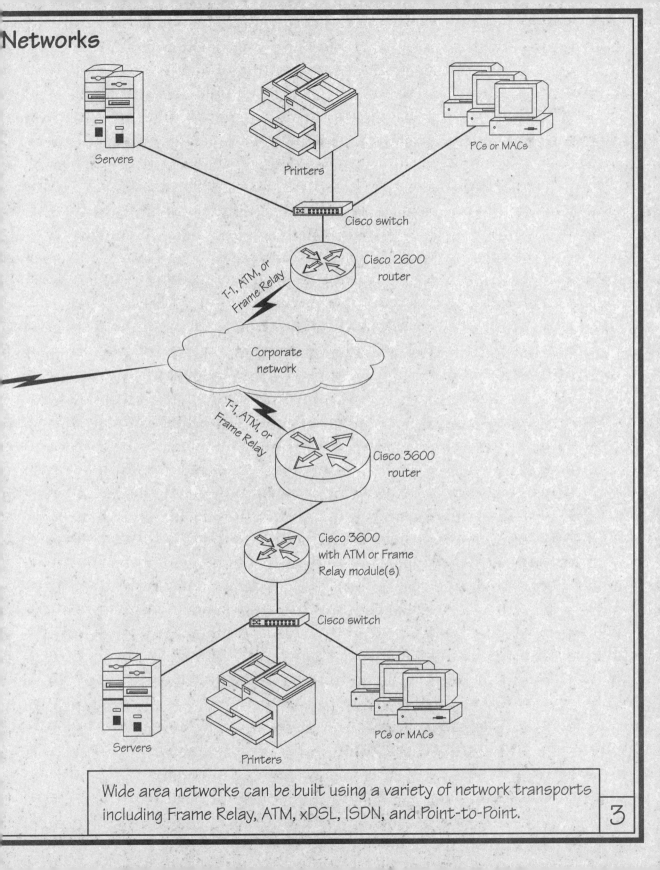

Wide area networks can be built using a variety of network transports including Frame Relay, ATM, xDSL, ISDN, and Point-to-Point.

3

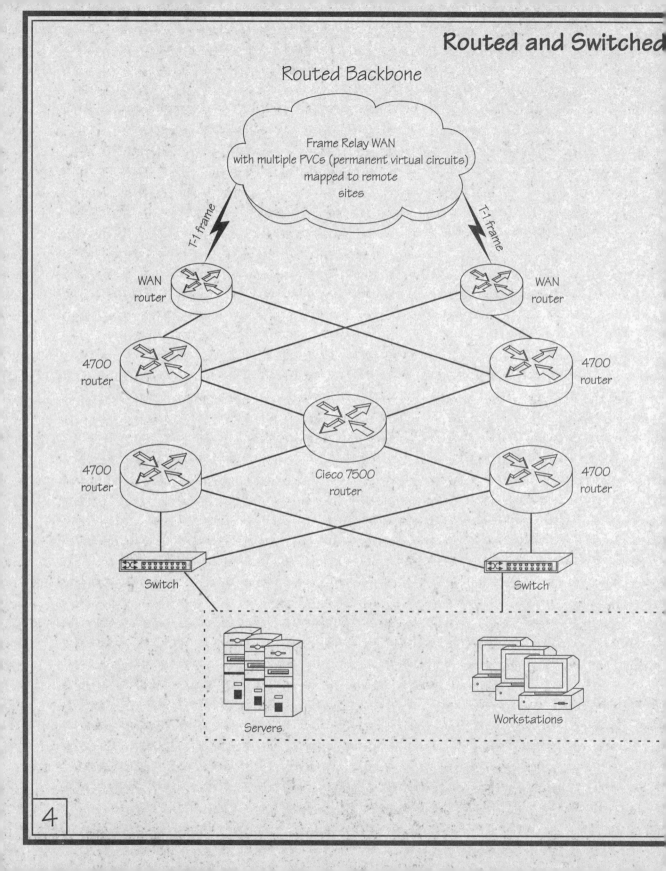

Routed Backbone

Frame Relay WAN
with multiple PVCs (permanent virtual circuits)
mapped to remote
sites

T-1 frame

T-1 frame

WAN
router

WAN
router

4700
router

4700
router

Cisco 7500
router

4700
router

4700
router

Switch

Switch

Servers

Workstations

LAN Backbones

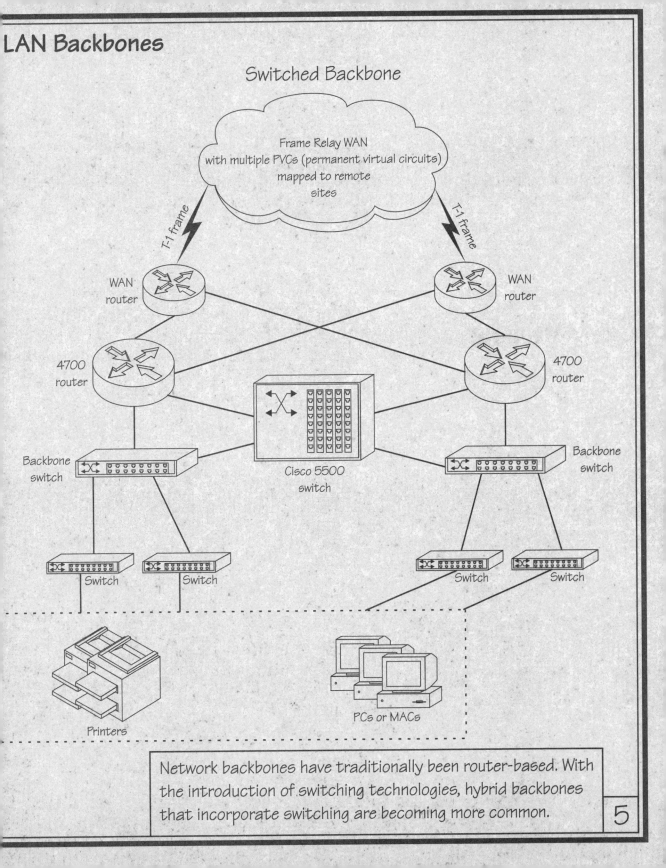

Switched Backbone

Frame Relay WAN
with multiple PVCs (permanent virtual circuits)
mapped to remote
sites

T-1 frame

T-1 frame

WAN router

WAN router

4700 router

4700 router

Cisco 5500 switch

Backbone switch

Backbone switch

Switch

Switch

Switch

Switch

Printers

PCs or MACs

Network backbones have traditionally been router-based. With the introduction of switching technologies, hybrid backbones that incorporate switching are becoming more common.

5

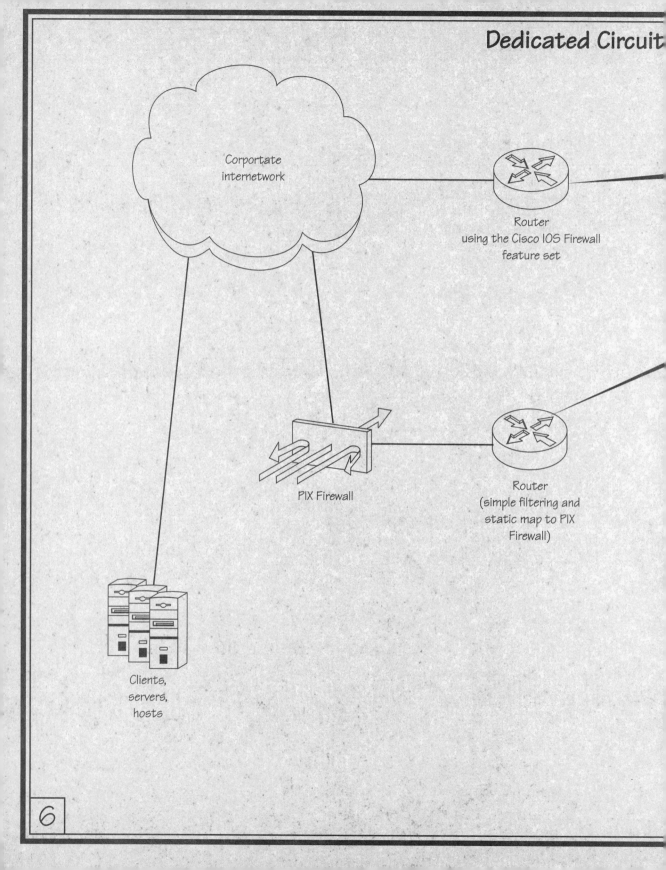

Corportate
internetwork

Router
using the Cisco IOS Firewall
feature set

PIX Firewall

Router
(simple filtering and
static map to PIX
Firewall)

Clients,
servers,
hosts

Internet Connectivity

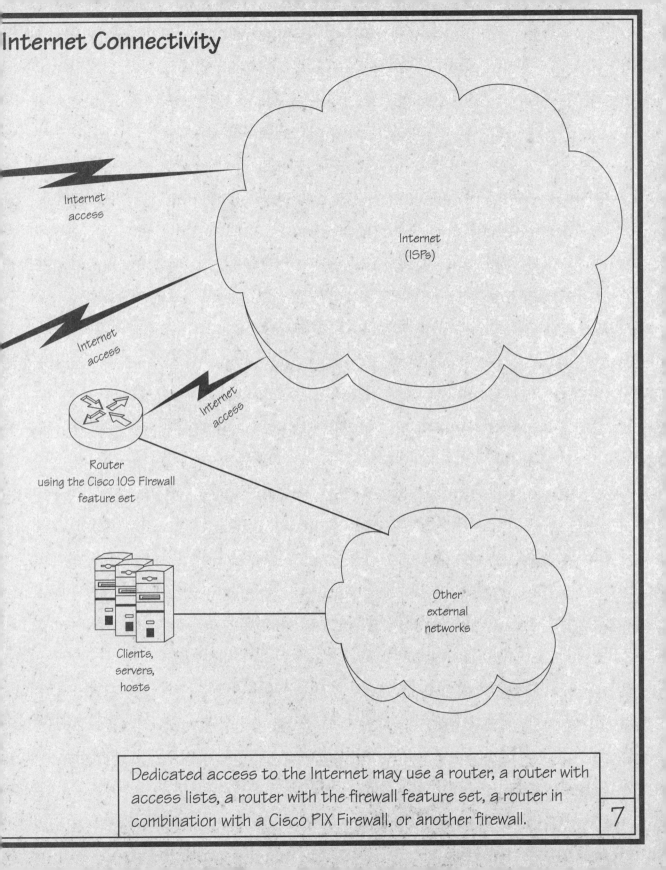

Internet
access

Internet
access

Internet
(ISPs)

Internet
access

Router
using the Cisco IOS Firewall
feature set

Other
external
networks

Clients,
servers,
hosts

Dedicated access to the Internet may use a router, a router with access lists, a router with the firewall feature set, a router in combination with a Cisco PIX Firewall, or another firewall.

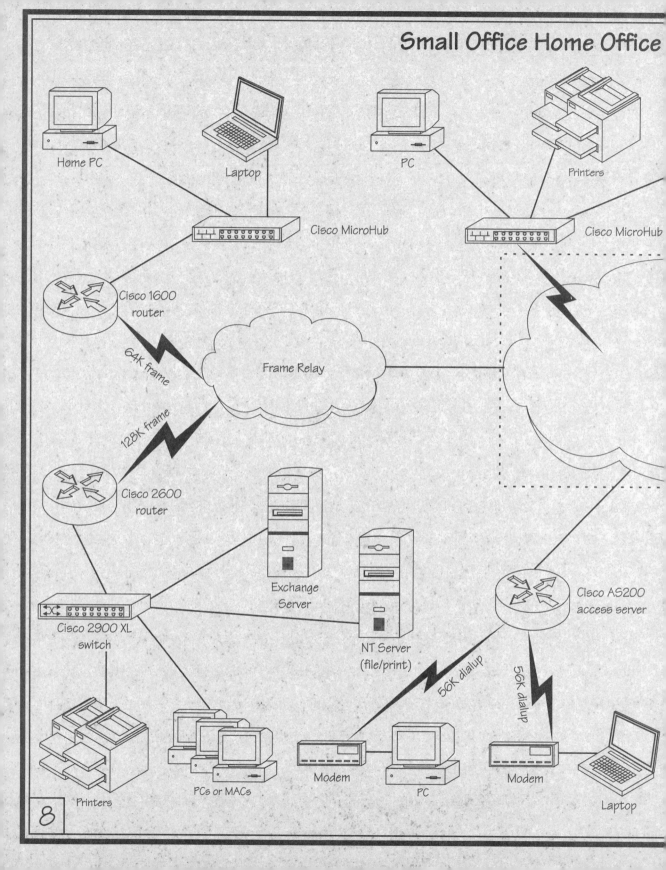

(SOHO) Office Connectivity

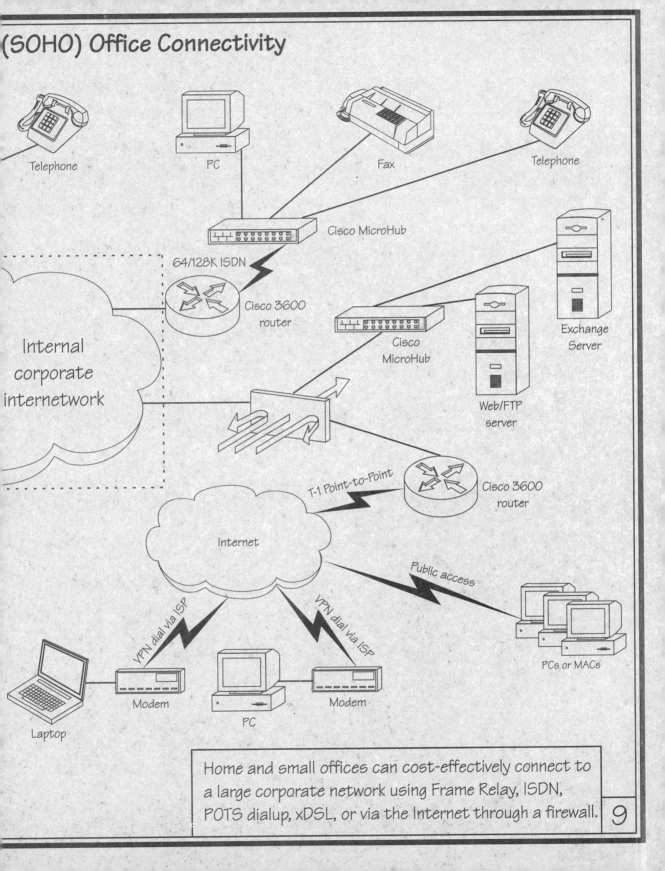

Home and small offices can cost-effectively connect to a large corporate network using Frame Relay, ISDN, POTS dialup, xDSL, or via the Internet through a firewall.

9

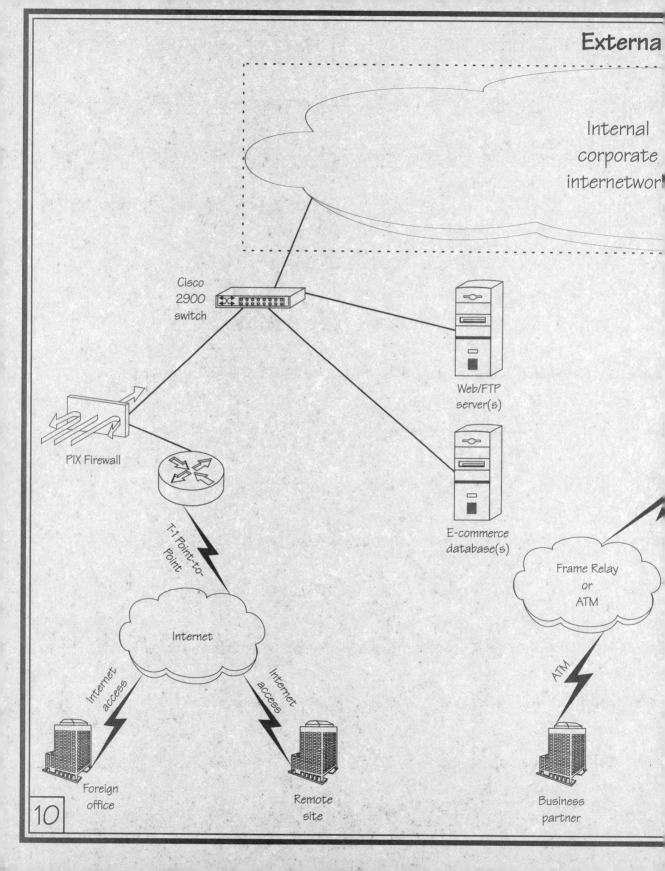

Internal
corporate
internetwor

Cisco
2900
switch

Web/FTP
server(s)

PIX Firewall

E-commerce
database(s)

T-1 Point-to-
Point

Frame Relay
or
ATM

Internet

Internet
access

Internet
access

ATM

Foreign
office

Remote
site

Business
partner

10

Corporate Connections

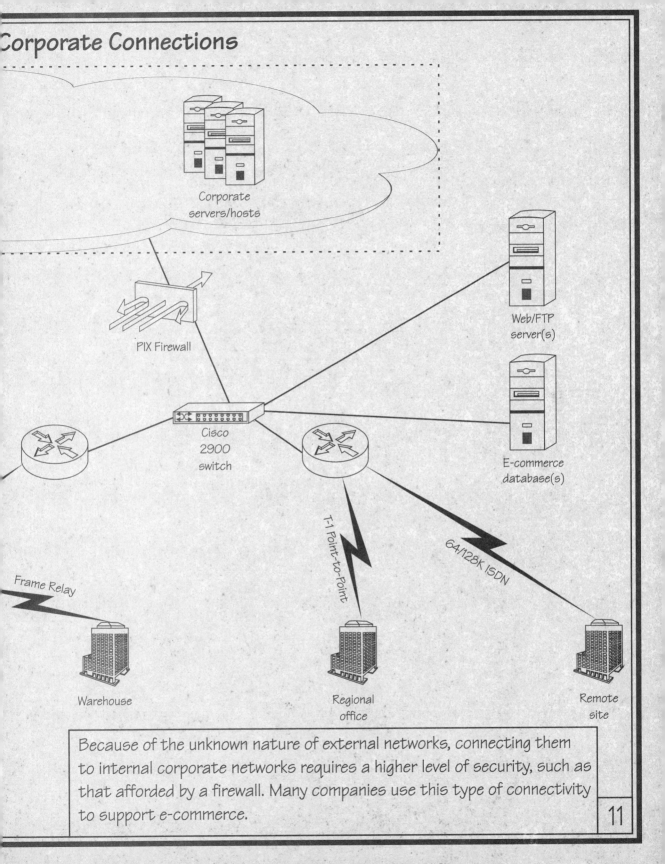

Corporate
servers/hosts

PIX Firewall

Cisco
2900
switch

Web/FTP
server(s)

E-commerce
database(s)

T-1 Point-to-Point

64/128K ISDN

Frame Relay

Warehouse

Regional
office

Remote
site

Because of the unknown nature of external networks, connecting them to internal corporate networks requires a higher level of security, such as that afforded by a firewall. Many companies use this type of connectivity to support e-commerce.

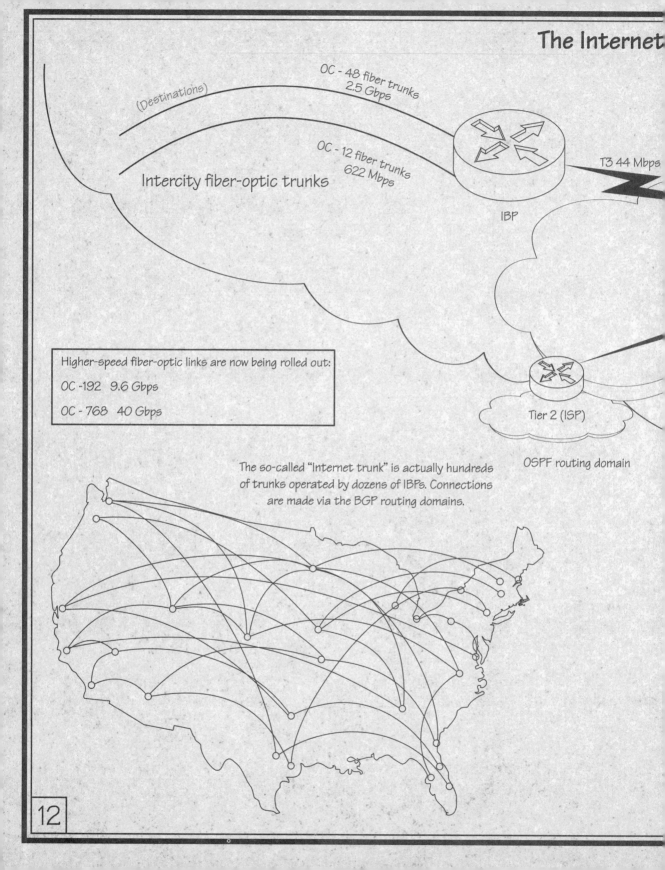

OC - 48 fiber trunks
2.5 Gbps

(Destinations)

OC - 12 fiber trunks
622 Mbps

Intercity fiber-optic trunks

T3 44 Mbps

IBP

Higher-speed fiber-optic links are now being rolled out:

OC -192   9.6 Gbps

OC - 768   40 Gbps

Tier 2 (ISP)

OSPF routing domain

The so-called "Internet trunk" is actually hundreds
of trunks operated by dozens of IBPs. Connections
are made via the BGP routing domains.

Backbone

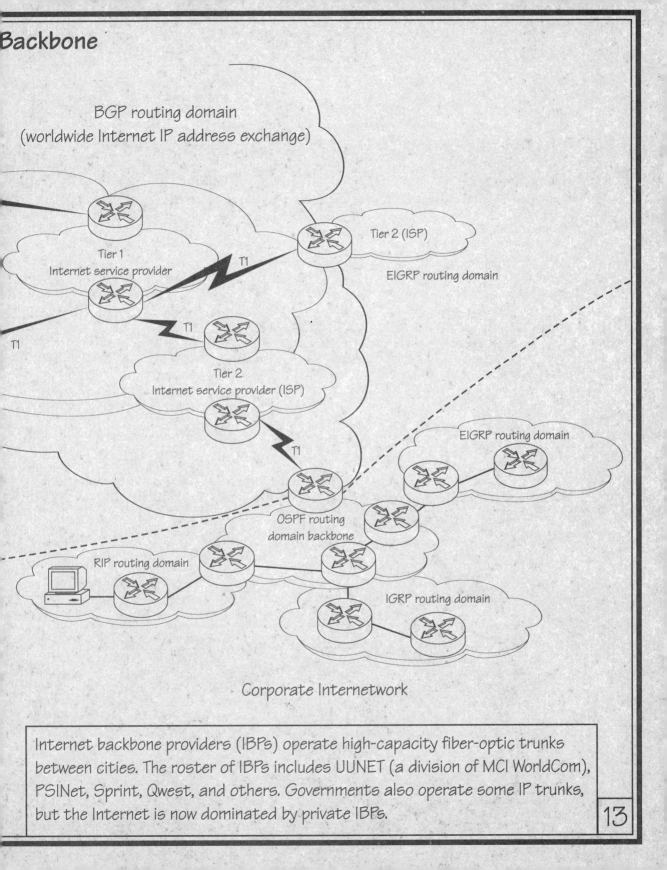

BGP routing domain
(worldwide Internet IP address exchange)

Tier 1
Internet service provider

Tier 2 (ISP)

EIGRP routing domain

T1

T1

T1

Tier 2
Internet service provider (ISP)

T1

EIGRP routing domain

OSPF routing
domain backbone

RIP routing domain

IGRP routing domain

Corporate Internetwork

Internet backbone providers (IBPs) operate high-capacity fiber-optic trunks between cities. The roster of IBPs includes UUNET (a division of MCI WorldCom), PSINet, Sprint, Qwest, and others. Governments also operate some IP trunks, but the Internet is now dominated by private IBPs.

13

214.96.117.[2 2 0]

1 1 0 1 1 1 0 0 (220 in binary)

128 64 32 16 8 4 2 1 = 255

1 + 1 + 0 + 1 + 1 + 1 + 0 + 0 = 220

214	96	177	220

128 64 32 16 8 4 2 1 | 128 64 32 16 8 4 2 1 | 128 64 32 16 8 4 2 1 | 128 64 32 16 8 4 2 1

1 1 0 1 0 1 1 0   0 1 1 0 0 0 0 0   0 1 1 1 0 1 0 1   1 1 0 1 1 1 0 0

1 1 1 1 1 1 1 1   1 1 1 1 1 1 1 1   1 1 1 1 1 1 1 1   1 1 1 1 1 1 0 0

24 bits default to network ID bits (Because this example is a class C IP address,
class B has 16 default network ID bits; class A has only 8.)

Subnetwork bits   Host bits

128 + 64 + 32 + 16 + 8 + 4 = 252

.252 mask network ID bits

128	64	32	16	8	4
0	0	0	0	0	0
0	0	0	0	0	1
0	0	0	0	1	0
0	0	0	0	1	1
0	0	0	1	0	0
0	0	0	1	0	1

How a .252 mask is applied

A .252 mask has up to 64 subnet addresses

.252 mask host ID bits

2	1	Host ID
0	0	
0	1	
1	0	
1	1	

Two possible host ID names

.1
.2

Each subnet defined using the .252 mask can have up to two host addresses (addresses of all 0's or all 1's are reserved).

Using the .252 subnet mask, up to 64 LANs with up to two hosts each yields a maximum of 128 IP host addresses.

.192 mask → 4 subnets
.224 mask → 8 subnets
.240 mask → 16 subnets
.248 mask → 32 subnets
.252 mask → 64 subnets

Destination IP Address	Subnet Mask	
11010110011000000111010111011100	11111111111111111111111111111100	← .252 mask
10101101100101110001001111001110	11111111111111111111111111110000	← .240 mask

Mask	Number of Network ID Bits	Example Notation	Number of Host ID Bits	Number of Subnets	Total Number of Host IP Addresses
.192	26	195.211.12.1/26	6	4	62
.224	27	195.211.12.1/27	5	8	30
.240	28	195.211.12.1/28	4	16	14
.248	29	195.211.12.1/29	3	32	6
.252	30	195.211.12.1/30	2	64	2

Addressing

This is an IP address shown in dotted decimal format. IP addresses are composed of four octets.

Machines work only with bits, not decimal numbers. Bits are set to either 0 or 1. An octet contains 8 bits, an IP address 32 bits.

Each column in an IP octet has a fixed value. A column value is counted only when the bit in the column is set to 1. The octet's decimal number is the total of all bits set to the value of 1; the maximum is 255.

A subnet mask tells the router which of the IP address's bits to use for subnetworks. The mask is indicated by a string of all 1-bits.

Usually, subnet masks end within an octet. The decimal total of all 1-bits in the subnet option gives it its number. The 1-bits in this example total to the .252 mask.

The subnet mask's length determines how many network and host addresses are possible. Each subnet mask has its use. For example, the .252 mask has two hosts per network, and therefore is used for point-to-point WAN connections.

Depending on which mask is used, between 4 and 64 subnets can be squeezed from a single class C block of addresses.

The router stores the mask alongside the IP address in its routing table. It tells which bits identify subnetworks instead of hosts.

There is a direct trade-off between subnets and hosts. The more you have of one, the fewer you can have of the other. As shown in this table, each subnet mask strikes a different trade-off. Cisco refers to masks both by number and by notation.

Firewall and Router VPNs

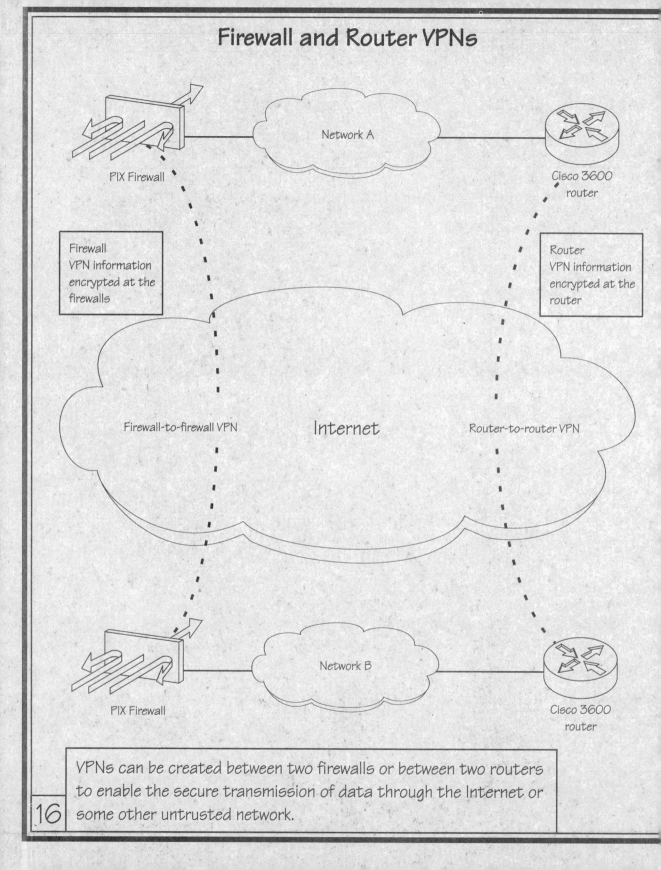

Network A

PIX Firewall

Cisco 3600
router

Firewall
VPN information
encrypted at the
firewalls

Router
VPN information
encrypted at the
router

Firewall-to-firewall VPN

Internet

Router-to-router VPN

PIX Firewall

Network B

Cisco 3600
router

VPNs can be created between two firewalls or between two routers
to enable the secure transmission of data through the Internet or
some other untrusted network.

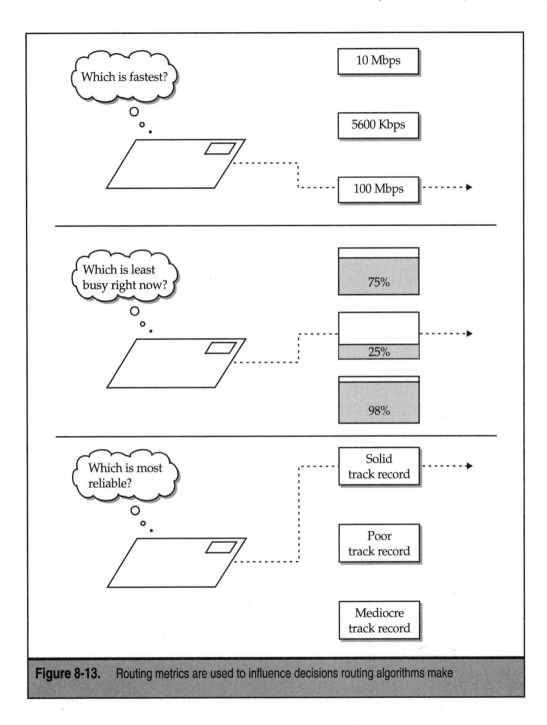

Figure 8-13.   Routing metrics are used to influence decisions routing algorithms make

Routing Protocol Architectures

There are three basic types of routing protocol architectures:

▼ **Distance-vector routing protocols**   Simple algorithms that calculate a cumulative distance value between routers based on hop count.

■ **Link-state routing protocols**   Sophisticated algorithms that maintain a complex database of internetwork topology.

▲ **Hybrid routing protocols**   A combination of distance-vector and link-state methods that tries to incorporate the advantages of both and minimize their disadvantages.

Distance-Vector Routing

Early distance-vector routing protocols used only a so-called distance metric to calculate the best route to a destination. The distance is the number of router hops to the destination. Distance-vector algorithms (also called Bellman-Ford algorithms) operate a protocol in which routers pass routing tables to their immediate neighbors in all directions. At each exchange, the router increments the distance value received for a route, thereby applying its own distance value to that route. The updated table is then passed further outward where receiving routers repeat the process. The fundamental theory is that each router doesn't need to know all about other links, just whether they are there and what the approximate distance is to them. Figure 8-14 depicts the distance-vector routing update process.

Distance-vector routing can be slow to converge. This is because routing updates are triggered by timers to take place at predetermined intervals, not in response to a network event that causes a topology change. This makes it harder for distance-vector protocols to respond quickly to the state of a link's current operating condition. If a network link goes down, the distance-vector system must wait until the next timed update cycle sweeps past the downed link to pick it up and pass an updated routing table—minus the downed link—through the internetwork.

NOTE: The name *distance-vector* can be confusing because some advanced distance-vector protocols use routing metrics other than theoretical distance. In fact, some newer so-called distance-vector installations only partially rely on the hop count metric. The best way to think of distance-vector protocols is that they update routing topologies at fixed intervals.

Relying on fixed-interval updates renders distance-vector protocols slow to converge on topology changes and therefore more susceptible to routing loops. Also, most distance-vector protocols are limited to 16 hops and are generally used in internetworks with fewer than 50 routers.

Despite their unsophisticated ways, distance-vector protocols are by far the most widely used. The distance-vector method is simple and easy to configure. Because it doesn't do a lot of calculating, it consumes little router CPU or memory resources. Generally,

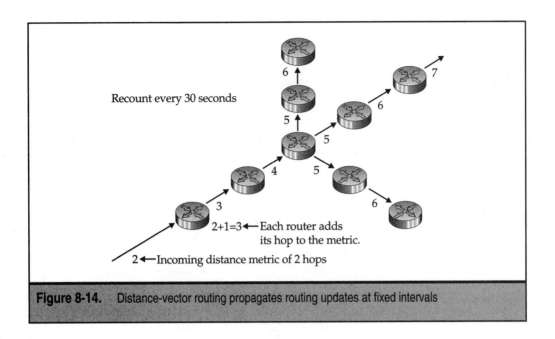

Recount every 30 seconds

6

7

5

6

5

4

5

3

6

2+1=3←Each router adds
its hop to the metric.

2←Incoming distance metric of 2 hops

Figure 8-14.   Distance-vector routing propagates routing updates at fixed intervals

distance-vector algorithms are good enough to adapt to topology changes encountered in smaller internetworks. The most widely installed distance-vector routing protocols are RIP and IGRP.

Link-State Routing

Link-state routing is event driven. Also known as *shortest path first (SPF)*, link-state routing protocols focus on the state of the internetwork links that form routes. Whenever a link's state changes, a routing update called a *link-state advertisement (LSA)* is exchanged between routers. When a router receives an LSA routing update, the link-state algorithm is used to recalculate the shortest path to affected destinations. Link-state routing attempts to always maintain full knowledge of the internetwork's topology by updating itself incrementally whenever a change occurs. Figure 8-15 depicts the link-state process.

The link-state algorithm does much more than just have a router add its local distance value to a cumulative distance. After an LSA update is received, each router uses the algorithm to calculate a *shortest path tree* to all destinations. Link-state calculations are based on the Dijkstra algorithm (loosely referred to as *shortest path first* or *SPF* algorithm for short). This process yields entirely new routes instead of merely applying new distance values to preexisting routes. Think of it this way: distance-vector routing places a new value on the same old route; link-state routing's SPF algorithm builds whole new routes piece by piece, from the link up. SPF is able to do this because the link-state database contains complete information on the internetwork's components and its topology.

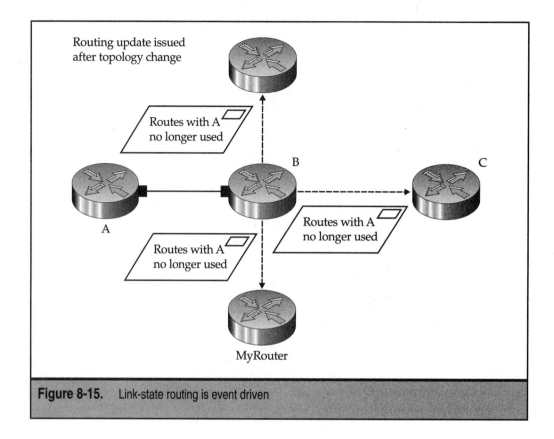

Figure 8-15. Link-state routing is event driven

New routes calculated by SPF are entered into the updated routing table. These entries include recalculated values for all metrics configured for use in the link-state implementation. Possible metrics include cost, delay, bandwidth, reliability, and others, with their values updated to reflect the new route. This is done by rolling up metric information for each link incorporated into the newly calculated route. Figure 8-16 shows how the SPF algorithm picks the best route.

There are two other advantages to link-state routing; both have to do with bandwidth conservation. First, because LSA updates contain only information about affected paths, routing updates travel faster and consume less bandwidth. Second, in distance-vector routing, most update cycles are wasted because they take place even though there was no topology change. Unnecessary update cycles not only increase bandwidth overhead but also boost the odds that conflicting routing updates will be converging simultaneously. By issuing LSA updates only when required, link-state protocols diminish the opportunity for the self-perpetuating conflicts of routing loops.

By being event driven, in link-state protocols adaptation to topology change need not wait for a series of preset timers to go off before the convergence process can begin. This

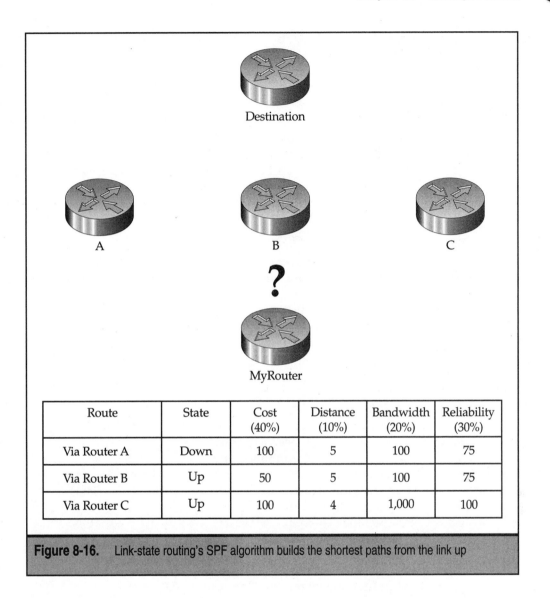

Figure 8-16.   Link-state routing's SPF algorithm builds the shortest paths from the link up

not only makes link-state protocols less prone to loops but also makes them more power-ful in that there is no limit on the number of hops in routes they calculate.

The drawbacks to link-state routing protocols mainly have to do with logistics and ex-pense. During the initial stages of implementation, LSA traffic tends to flood an internetwork with database-building control messages, making implementation expensive. Because it does so much more calculating, link-state routing also can consume considerable router CPU and memory resources when recalculation is necessary. This means that those considering an upgrade to a link-state routing protocol must face the prospect of spending big money on equipment upgrades. Yet perhaps the biggest hurdle to link-state protocols is that they're complicated. These are sophisticated routing protocols that can be intimidating to network administrators, especially those set in their ways.

Hybrid Routing

Hybrid routing protocols use more accurate distance-vector metrics in a protocol designed to converge more rapidly. Although open standards have been developed for so-called hybridized routing, the only Cisco product based on the concept is the Enhanced Interior Gateway Routing Protocol (EIGRP).

How Routing Protocols Are Implemented

Much like firewalls, routing protocols take their own particular view of the internetwork landscape. To a firewall, networks are either *inside* or *outside*, and connections are controlled accordingly. Routing protocols have as their overriding concern the gathering and dissemination of updated topologies, not connections. Thus routing protocols define the networking landscape in terms of *interior* and *exterior*, where one routing domain ends and another begins. This is because a router needs to know which other routers are part of its own routing domain—are in the interior—and therefore should share routing updates.

Autonomous Systems

Administrative control is defined as who controls the configuration of equipment in a network. Because the Internet interconnects so many organizational entities, it has developed the concept of an autonomous system. An *autonomous system* is defined as a collection of networks that are under the administrative control of a single organization and that share a common routing strategy. Most autonomous systems are internetworks operated by corporations, Internet service providers (ISPs), government agencies, and universities.

Looking at the three autonomous systems in Figure 8-17, each regards the other two as exterior (or external) autonomous systems. This is because the other two are under the administrative control of someone else, and they are running a separate routing strategy. A *routing strategy* is a term used to describe the fact that routing updates are being exchanged under a common routing protocol configuration. Thus a routing strategy implies running a single routing process to exchange updates and sharing other configuration parameters, such as the relative settings of each path's metrics.

The three autonomous systems in Figure 8-17 could be running the same routing protocol software—even the same *version* of the same routing protocol—but because the autonomous systems aren't within the same routing process of update messages and relative metrics settings, they don't share a common routing strategy. In other words, they're in the same autonomous system, but in different routing domains.

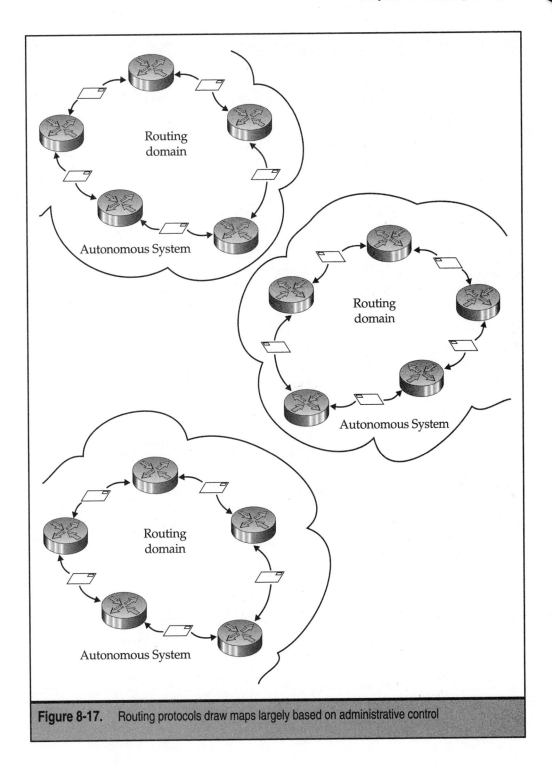

Figure 8-17.   Routing protocols draw maps largely based on administrative control

The Difference Between Interior and Exterior Gateway Protocols

So what we have, then, is a nice neat little package where routing domains and administrative domains overlay one another, right? Well, as always seems to be the case in internetworking, things aren't quite so tidy. If routing strategy were as simple as configuring one routing protocol for every administrative domain, there could be no Internet. After all, if everything were internal, who or what would coordinate routing updates between the millions of autonomous systems making up the Internet?

The answer is exterior gateway protocols. An *exterior gateway protocol* runs on routers sitting at the edge of an autonomous system and exchanges routes with other autonomous systems. These edge routers are also called *border routers, boundary routers,* or *gateway routers*. A routing protocol that operates within an autonomous system is an *interior gateway protocol*. Figure 8-18 shows the two side by side.

In practical terms, the most obvious difference between the two is where in the topology the routers running the protocol sit. Exterior routers sit at the edge of autonomous systems; interior gateway routers sit toward the middle. A closer inspection of how the exterior protocols are implemented brings out more fundamental differences:

▼   An exterior protocol lets an autonomous system designate certain other routers as peers. The border router exchanges updates with its peer routers and ignores other routers (in interior protocols, all routers participate in router updates).

■   Routing tables maintained by exterior protocols are lists of autonomous systems (interior protocols keep lists of LAN segments).

▲   Exterior protocols simply insert a new route received for a destination into the routing table; no recalculation of new best paths is computed after an update is received (interior protocols recalculate new routes based on weighted metrics).

Methods That Let Autonomous Systems Interconnect

Reaching beyond an autonomous system invites potential trouble. For a firewall the potential trouble is a security breach. For an exterior gateway protocol, the trouble can be either bad information about routes to other autonomous systems—or even just too much information to handle. The problems inherent in connecting to the outside also hold for exterior and interior protocols alike:

▼   Without some way to filter route exchanges, exterior protocols would be overwhelmed by a torrent of traffic flowing in from the Internet.

▲   Interior protocols could be confused about the best connections to take to the outside without being able to identify and select from various sources providing new routes.

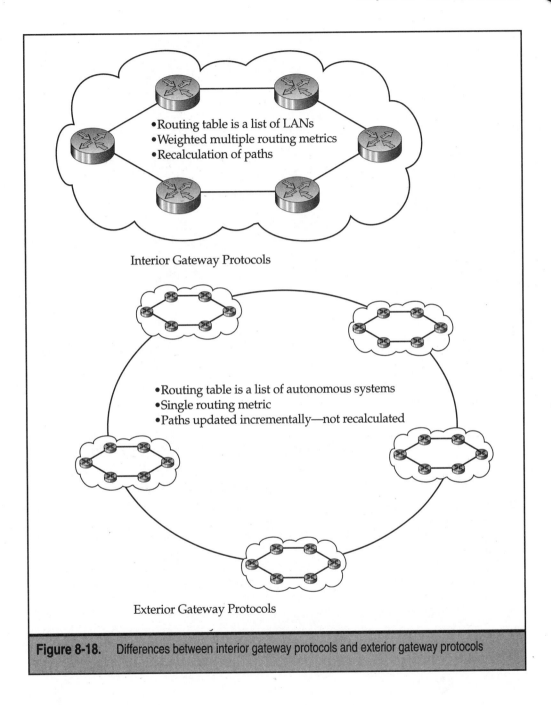

Interior Gateway Protocols

- Routing table is a list of LANs
- Weighted multiple routing metrics
- Recalculation of paths

- Routing table is a list of autonomous systems
- Single routing metric
- Paths updated incrementally—not recalculated

Exterior Gateway Protocols

Figure 8-18. Differences between interior gateway protocols and exterior gateway protocols

Interior and exterior gateway routing protocols use a set of techniques to handle these problems. As a group, these techniques are intended to cut down on the volume of routing information and to boost the reliability of new route information that is received:

▼ **Route summarization**   A technique that divides an internetwork into logical areas, with the area's border router advertising only a single summary route to other areas, thereby cutting down on the size of routing tables.

■ **Route filtering**   Also called *administrative distance*, an add-on metric that rates the relative trustworthiness of individual networks as a source from which to learn optimal routes.

■ **Route tagging**   A technique that tags a route in a number of ways to identify the source from which it was learned. Tags can include router ID, autonomous system number, exterior protocol ID, and exterior protocol metric.

▲ **Router authentication**   In effect, this requires a communicating router to present a password before the receiving router will accept routing updates from it.

It's notable that some of the techniques are implemented in both internal and external systems, not just one or the other. This is done to enable interior and exterior routing domains to act in concert as messages flow between the autonomous system and outside world. Another notable fact is that some of these techniques are applied between interior routing domains where differing routing protocols are being run within the same autonomous system (for example, route summarization between OSPF and RIP routing processes).

Routing Domains, Routing Areas, and Administrative Domains

A *routing domain* is a group of end systems within an autonomous system. An autonomous system, in turn, is defined as an administrative domain, where there exists singular administrative control over network policy and equipment.

Most routing protocol architectures coordinate the exchange of *complete* route information between all routers in the routing domain. However, this practice can become inefficient as internetworks grow, because that means more update traffic traveling longer distances.

State-of-the-art routing protocols use the concept of routing domain areas. A *routing area* is a subdivision of a routing domain into logically related groups, with each area uniquely identified by an area name or number. The primary benefit of areas is that route information can be summarized when exchanged between areas, cutting down on network overhead and enhancing control over traffic flow. Routing domain areas are also used to unify several smaller routing domains into a single, larger routing process.

Routing area	Routing area	Routing area
Routing domain		

The typical global enterprise implements a single routing domain worldwide. This is done so that employees on one continent can connect to company colleagues and resources anywhere in the world. So it would follow, then, that there is always a one-to-one relation between a routing domain and an administrative domain. And, until recently, this was the case.

A new phenomenon called external corporate networks extends routing domains across administrative domains. An *external corporate network* is a configuration in which two or more enterprises build a unified routing domain to share routes between their respective organizations. The shared routing domain is the subset of each enterprise's overall autonomous system, and contains the resources and users that are to participate in the shared business process. Figure 8-19 illustrates how such a configuration is set up.

The thing to focus on with external corporate networks is that routes are being freely exchanged between enterprises—at least within the shared routing domain area in the middle. The external corporate network configuration enables routers within two or more enterprises to keep up an ongoing dialog on how to route cross-border connections. This is a relatively new internetworking practice. Not that long ago, the idea of directly trading route information between autonomous systems was unthinkable, not only out of concern for system security, but also for competitive reasons.

This is the most advanced form of extranet, in that one *system* is allowed behind another's firewall. Think of it this way: Most extranets involve a person logging through a firewall by entering a username and password. In the Figure 8-19 example, the system of one enterprise is able to freely conduct business behind the firewall of another, system to system (not person to system). Harking back to the last chapter's coverage on firewalls, in an external corporate network the extranet is *route* based, not *connection* based. Put another way, routes are shared between enterprises for long-term use; in the traditional extranet relationship, a user is allowed to connect to a resource on a per-session basis.

OVERVIEW OF CISCO ROUTING PROTOCOLS

When internetworking started to take off during the mid-1980s, internetworks were smaller and simpler. The interior gateway protocol of choice back then was RIP (Routing

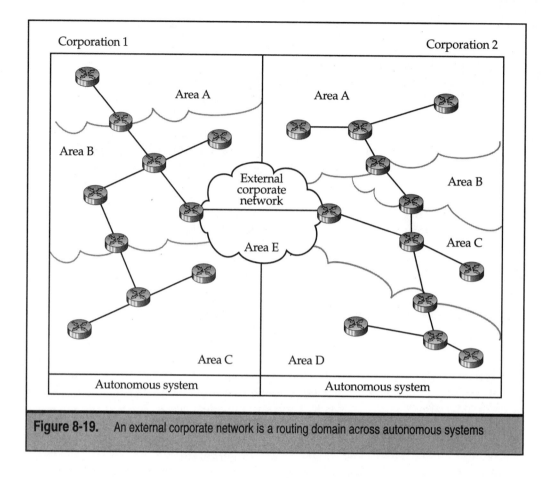

Figure 8-19. An external corporate network is a routing domain across autonomous systems

Information Protocol). At that time the two predominant proprietary networks were IBM SNA and Digital Equipment's DECnet implementation of Ethernet, each with its own routing scheme. But at the time, the "open" networking market was booming, with UNIX servers connecting to Novell's NetWare IPX LANs. RIP shipped with most UNIX server systems and emerged as the de facto standard. Thus, RIP is an open standard, not a Cisco proprietary technology.

RIP is simple to understand, easy to configure, and works well enough for small, homogenous networks. To this day, RIP is still the most widely installed routing protocol in the world.

But the early versions of RIP were limited to just the hop count metric. This didn't provide the routing flexibility needed to manage complex environments. Also, RIP was slow to converge and thus limited to a maximum hop count limit of 16. Configure a longer route and the user will encounter a "destination unreachable" message. As a distance-vector protocol, RIP issues routing updates at a fixed interval (the default update interval for most RIP products is every 90 seconds).

Cisco's Interior Gateway Routing Protocol (IGRP)

It gradually became apparent that RIP was a roadblock to continued internetwork expansion. The 16 hop limit, single-metric scheme constrained network size and capacity. Cisco seized the opportunity by devising a replacement routing technology that did away with most of RIP's disadvantages: a more robust distance-vector protocol named IGRP (Interior Gateway Routing Protocol).

IGRP, a company-proprietary extension of the open RIP standard, was first released by Cisco in 1986 for IP only. In the succeeding years, IGRP implemented support for other network layer protocols (IPX, AppleTalk, etc.), and it became the standard in customer shops using only Cisco equipment. By around 1990, RIP's limitations had become apparent, and IGRP was positioned as its general replacement for client-server networks.

Many observers regard IGRP as the single most important factor behind Cisco's explosive growth. The competition had devised OSPF as their primary replacement to RIP—but it was (and still is) limited to IP-only networks. IP-only compatibility is acceptable in some enterprises, but the reality is that most internetworks still run multiple protocols (IPX, AppleTalk, DECnet, etc.). Cisco was able to couple IGRP's superior functionality with the 1990's UNIX/Internet juggernaut to attain the market dominance it enjoys today.

IGRP was a major departure in that it used multiple metrics: distance, delay, bandwidth, reliability, and load. This advance was a big deal because it enabled network administrators to get a handle on increasing network complexity and provide better service. Figure 8-20 compares IGRP's features with RIP's.

A big virtue of IGRP is the granularity of its metrics. For example, being able to set parameters for reliability or load to any value between 1 and 255 gives administrators the granularity needed to finely tune IGRP route selection. IGRP's ability to specify alternate routes boosts reliability and performance. This provides redundancy, so that if a link goes down, the IGRP routing algorithm dynamically begins to steer traffic to the secondary route. Multipath routing also introduced *load balancing*—the ability to dynamically shift traffic between alternate routes depending on how busy each is. These were important benefits during a period when most internetworks were in their infancy and prone to slowing to a crawl or going out altogether.

In 1994, Cisco augmented IGRP with a product called EIGRP (Enhanced Interior Gateway Domain Protocol). EIGRP is a substantial advance over its predecessor—so much so that Cisco touts it as a hybrid routing protocol instead of a mere distance-vector protocol. Although competitors might disagree, most observers now regard EIGRP as the new de facto standard for interior gateway protocols.

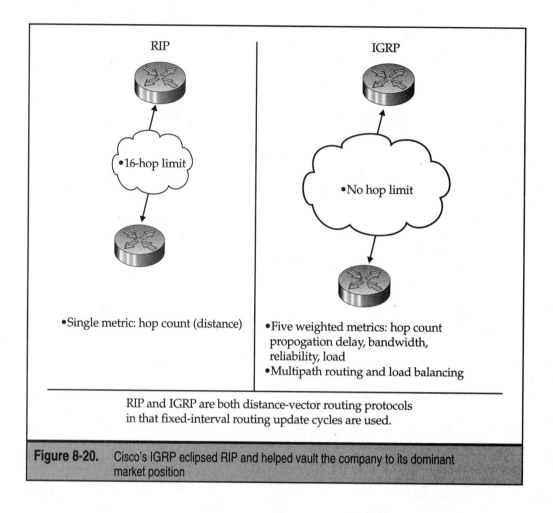

RIP

IGRP

•16-hop limit

•No hop limit

•Single metric: hop count (distance)

•Five weighted metrics: hop count
propogation delay, bandwidth,
reliability, load
•Multipath routing and load balancing

RIP and IGRP are both distance-vector routing protocols
in that fixed-interval routing update cycles are used.

Figure 8-20.   Cisco's IGRP eclipsed RIP and helped vault the company to its dominant
market position

EIGRP combines the advantages of link-state protocols with those of distance-vector
protocols. It provides superior convergence properties and operating efficiency. Here are
the key EIGRP features:

▼   **DUAL finite state machine**   The software engine used by the EIGRP
algorithm. DUAL (Diffusing Update Algorithm) is used to provide loop-free
operation at every instant throughout a route computation. DUAL allows
routers to synchronize route changes and does not involve routers unaffected
by the change. The key architectural feature is that routers running DUAL store
all of their neighbors' routing tables (called *neighbor tables*) so that they can
more intelligently recalculate alternate paths in order to speed convergence.

- ■ **Variable-length subnet masks (VLSM)**   The ability to automatically summarize subnet routes at the edge of a subnet. Before VLSM, routing protocols such as RIP could not build routes with subnet addresses included. All subnets had to be the same.

- ■ **Partial updates**   Also called *event-triggered updates*, this means routing updates are issued only when the topology has changed. This saves control message overhead.

- ■ **Bounded updates**   The method whereby routing update messages are sent only to those routers affected by the topology change. This saves overhead and helps speed convergence.

- ▲ **Reliable Transport Protocol (RTP)**   A protocol guaranteeing the orderly delivery of priority update packets to neighbor routers. RTP works by classifying control message traffic into four priority groups: Hello/ACKs, updates, queries and replies, and requests. Only updates and queries/replies are sent *reliably*. By not sending Hello and ACKs or requests reliably, resources are freed to guarantee the delivery of message types more critical to EIGRP's internal operations.

It is commonplace for enterprises using Cisco hardware to migrate their internetworks from IGRP to EIGRP over time. EIGRP routers can be operated as compatible with IGRP routers. The metrics between the two are directly translatable. EIGRP does this by treating IGRP routes as external networks, which allows the network administrator to customize routes to them. EIGRP advertises three types of routes:

- ▼ **Internal routes**   Routes between subnets in a network attached to a router's interface. If the network is not subnetted, no interior routes are advertised for that network.

- ■ **System routes**   Routes to networks within the autonomous system. System routes are compiled from routing updates passed within the internetwork. Subnets are not included in system routing updates.

- ▲ **External routes**   Routes learned from another routing domain or those entered into the routing table as static routes. These routes are tagged individually to track their origin.

Figure 8-21 shows the interplay between these three types of EIGRP routes. Breaking down routes into these three categories facilitates advanced functions within the EIGRP algorithm. The internal routes designation enables EIGRP to support variable-length subnet masks; external routes make it possible for EIGRP to exchange routes that are discovered outside the autonomous system.

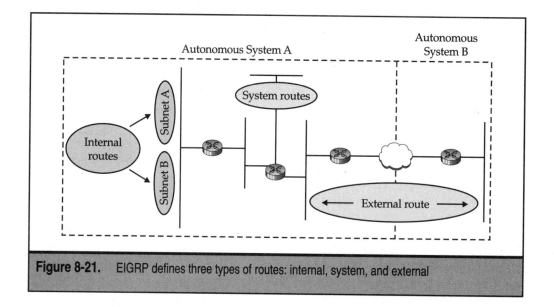

Figure 8-21.   EIGRP defines three types of routes: internal, system, and external

General Cisco Routing Protocol Configuration Steps

Configuring any Cisco routing protocol is largely a matter of setting its options. The number of steps is a function of how many options the routing protocol has for you to set. The more options a routing protocol has to set, the more commands there are for you to use. Because all Cisco routing protocols are implemented within IOS software, the initial steps of configuring Cisco routing protocols are the same. Table 8-1 explains the standard IOS routing protocol configuration steps.

Configuration Step	Description
Initialize and number the routing process.	The routing protocol must be turned on in a router so it can begin exchanging routing updates with other routers. This is done using the **router** command and giving the new routing domain an autonomous system number.
Configure LANs into the routing domain.	The **network** command is used to configure networks into the routing domain.
Set other routing protocol parameters.	Once the routing domain is constructed, its behavior is specified by using the routing protocol's various commands from the (config-router)# prompt.

Table 8-1.   The Initial Steps to Configure Cisco's Various Routing Protocols Are the Same

Routing domains are built router by router. In other words, because routing protocols are peer arrangements, the routing process must be configured in each router that will be included in the routing domain. This is done by working with each router's configuration file individually. Once all the routing processes are configured on all the routers in the internetwork, the routing domain is complete.

Configuring EIGRP

The **router** command initializes the routing process on a router. In this example, an EIGRP for autonomous system 999 is turned on in a router called MyRouter:

```
MyRouter(config)#router eigrp 999
MyRouter(config-router)#
```

An autonomous system number must be given in order to start a routing process. IOS uses the autonomous system number to distinguish one routing process from others. Notice that the IOS prompt changed to MyRouter(config-router)# when the **eigrp 999** routing process was invoked. All routing protocol parameters are set from this prompt.

The **network** command is used to start the routing protocol running over specific networks. Sticking with our example, the following command would make network 10.1.13.0 part of the routing process:

```
MyRouter(config-router)#network 10.1.13.0
```

The preceding command initializes EIGRP across network 10.1.13.0. If MyRouter is a four-port router and the other three LAN segments are also to run EIGRP, the **network** command must be used to make them part of the **eigrp 2** routing process also:

```
MyRouter(config-if)# network 10.1.14.0
MyRouter(config-if)# network 10.1.15.0
MyRouter(config-if)# network 209.168.98.32
```

Now the EIGRP routing process is running across all four of MyRouter's LAN segments, subnets 10.1.13.0–10.1.15.0, and network 209.168.98.32.

Each routing protocol has its own command set. These commands reflect the protocol's particular capabilities. Once a routing protocol is initialized, its commands are used to set various parameters in the configuration file to tune the behavior of the routing process as it operates in that router. EIGRP's command set is listed in Table 8-2.

Given that this is an introductory guide, we won't go into the commands for EIGRP or the other Cisco protocols—each one has its own complete command reference manual. But looking at the commands in Table 8-2 gives you a notion of how the concepts introduced in this chapter are implemented. Let's take one example of an advanced command to give you an idea of how things work:

```
MyRouter(config-router)#metric maximum-hops 25
```

What the preceding command does is set a maximum network diameter for the routing domain. *Network diameter* is a limit on how many hops a route may have before the

EIGRP Command	Description
auto-summary	Enable automatic network number summarization.
default	Set a command to its defaults.
default-information	Control distribution of default information.
default-metric	Set metric of redistributed routes.
distance	Define an administrative distance.
distribute-list	Filter networks in routing updates.
maximum-paths	Forward packets over multiple paths.
metric	Modify IGRP routing metrics and parameters.
neighbor	Specify a neighbor router.
network	Enable routing on an IP network.
offset-list	Add or subtract offset from IGRP or RIP metrics.
passive-interface	Suppress routing updates on an interface.
redistribute	Redistribute information from another routing protocol.
timers	Adjust routing timers.
traffic-share	Algorithm for computing traffic share for alternate routes.
variance	Control load balancing variance.

Table 8-2.   EIGRP's Command Set (Each Routing Protocol Has Its Own)

routing protocol stops advertising it. The setting in this use of the **maximum-hops** command will enforce a limit of 25 hops. Should the router receive a routing update with 26 or more hops indicated in its distance metric, the router will decline to enter it into its routing table. The **maximum-hops** command is an easy way to limit the kind of traffic a router will carry.

Configuring RIP 2

Although the severe limitations of early RIP versions opened the door for EIGRP, the competition fought back. The IETF (Internet Engineering Task Force) oversaw the release of the RIP 2 open standard in 1997. RIP 2 has most of the advanced functionality of other state-of-the-art interior gateway protocols such as EIGRP and OSPF. None of the improvements are unique to RIP 2, but they go a long way toward catching RIP's functionality up with other routing protocols. The IETF felt this was a good thing because RIP has such a huge installed base and is still quite useful for small internetworks.

But even with its advances, the use of RIP 2 is still limited to smaller internetworks by its 16 hop limit. Also, RIP 2 still issues routing updates on a fixed-interval cycle, causing it to converge more slowly than EIGRP or OSPF.

Configuring RIP 2 involves the same generic commands as other Cisco routing protocols, where the commands must be used to initialize the routing process on the router and its networks:

```
MyRouter(config)#router rip
.
.
.
MyRouter(config-if)#network 209.11.244.9
.
.
.
```

You'll notice that no autonomous system number was entered (as in **router rip 999**), because neither RIP nor RIP 2 supports autonomous system numbers. Also, the command to initialize RIP 2 is **router rip** (not **router rip2**), because the version of RIP you can run is a function of the version of IOS the router has loaded.

Once the RIP 2 process is launched, configuring it is a matter of setting its other parameters. In RIP 2, these include router authentication using the **rip authentication** commands, route summarization using the **auto-summary** command, and validation of the IP addresses of routers sending routing updates using the **validate-update-source** command.

Let's take a look at an example RIP 2 command that's more generic in nature. The **timer basic** command is used to set the routing update intervals within a RIP routing domain. The default is 30-second intervals. If you wanted to change routing update frequency to every 25 seconds, you'd enter the following command:

```
MyRouter(config-router)#timer basic 25
```

Changing basic metrics such as this is discouraged. Making updates five seconds more frequent will help speed convergence, but will increase network overhead by causing more routing messages.

Configuring Open Shortest Path First (OSPF)

In 1991, the industry moved to establish an open standard replacement for RIP. The result was OSPF (Open Shortest Path First), which, as the name implies, is an open standard used to seek out shortest path routes just like RIP. But that's where the similarities end. OSPF is a link-state, not distance-vector, routing protocol. OSPF converges faster than RIP and operates under the link-state concept, in which each router keeps a database of all links in a network and information on any delays it might be experiencing. In addition,

OSPF saves control message overhead by issuing routing updates only on an event-driven basis.

OSPF Routing Areas

Most OSPF features are designed to help cope with internetwork size. The central concept behind OSPF is internetwork areas. An *area* is a zone within an autonomous system that is composed of a logical set of network segments and their attached devices. The areas are used by the routing system as a strategy to control traffic flow and sieve out unwanted routing table details. Every OSPF domain must have a backbone area with number 0. Areas are created by using the keyword **area** as an argument with the **network** command, as follows:

```
MyRouter(config-router)#network 10.0.0.0  0.255.255.255 area 0
```

This command puts the subnet 10.0.0.0 into OSPF area 0. It's possible to run a one-area OSPF network, having only an area 0. Figure 8-22 shows a three-area OSPF network.

A key functionality of OSPF is that it can redirect routing updates between areas. *Redirect* is a routing update that passes through one or more areas of a routing domain, usually through a number of filters designed to cut down routing update traffic.

Variable-Length Subnet Masks (VLSMs)

OSPF networks are frequently used to tie together preexisting routing domains such as RIP internetworks. This is done by creating an OSPF area for each RIP domain and passing

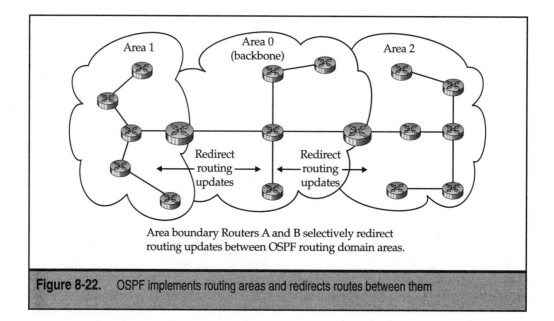

Figure 8-22. OSPF implements routing areas and redirects routes between them

routing updates between them through the OSPF backbone (area 0). The routers at the edges of the areas are called autonomous system boundary routers (or ASBRs for short). The ASBRs sit between the OSPF autonomous system and the RIP networks, and run both OSPF and RIP protocols.

Variable-length subnet mask (VLSM) support is a critical feature for OSPF. Respective areas often have their own subnet scheme to fit their particular needs. In Figure 8-23, all the serial line–based networks in Area 0 use the .252 subnet mask, typical for long-distance connections. This is because the .252 mask allows up to 64 subnets but only 2 hosts per subnet. This is ideal for networks composed of a serial line connection because only two hosts are needed: one at each end of the line.

Each of the other end-system areas uses its own scheme. Area 1 uses the .248 mask (yielding a maximum of 32 subnets and 6 hosts each), Area 2 uses the .192 mask (up to 4 subnets with 62 hosts each), and Area 3 uses the .224 mask (up to 8 subnets with 30 hosts each).

VLSM support means that the routes exchanged in updates passed between the OSPF areas can include the subnet addresses (instead of just the network address). This is an important feature because it allows complete routes to be shared across areas using differing subnet schemes, which means each area can use only the amount of address space required for its needs. For example, in Figure 8-23's Area 0, there are only a few hosts connected to the serial lines, and being able to use the .248 masks lets Area 0 use up only a few addresses (a .248 mask has only 6 hosts per subnet).

Even with all of OSPF's power, it would be hard to scale internetwork size very much without VLSM. This is because most LANs use subnetted addressing schemes in order to conserve precious IP address space. OSPF areas make possible large-scale expansion of routing domains and, therefore, internetwork size. VLSM enables routers to have full address visibility between areas and thus route traffic within internetworks with much greater efficiency.

Border Gateway Protocol (BGP)

The Border Gateway Protocol (BGP) is the high-level routing protocol that makes the Internet possible. Optimized to coordinate internetworking between autonomous systems, BGP is at this point virtually the only exterior gateway protocol in use today. The Exterior Gateway Protocol (EGP) is still used to run MILNET, the unclassified portion of the United States Defense Data Network.

EIGRP and OSPF let network operators scale their internetworks to large capacities, but it is BGP that ties them all together along so-called Internet trunks, or peer networks. Most networking types will never work with BGP; its use is mainly left to ISP administrators concerned with discovering routes across high-speed backbones. But it's helpful to briefly review how BGP fits in.

The predominance of a single exterior routing protocol is unsurprising in light of the fact that the world's network operators need a single standard to integrate the millions of autonomous systems operating in the world. If the industry hadn't settled on BGP as the common platform, some other exterior gateway protocol would be the de facto standard instead.

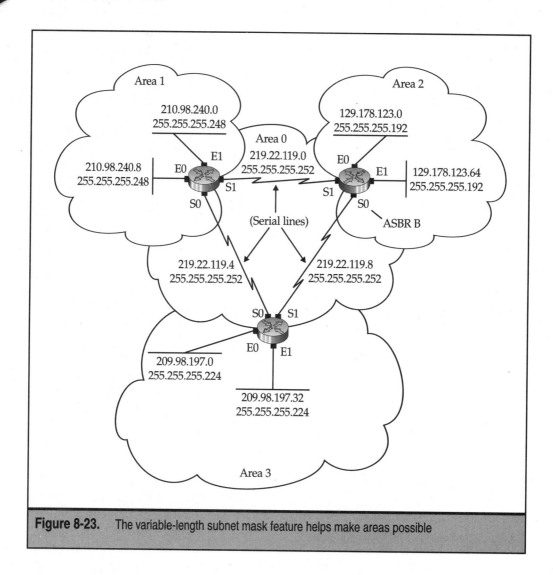

Figure 8-23. The variable-length subnet mask feature helps make areas possible

BGP Routing

Like interior gateway protocols, BGP uses routing update messages and metrics to maintain routing tables. BGP is a modified link-state architecture routing protocol, but obviously is radically different in architecture to be able to scale to Internet growth. BGP's architecture is characterized by the use of route aggregation and the ability to work with interior gateway protocols. BGP supports three types of routing:

▼ **Inter-autonomous system**   Inter-autonomous system routing is the basic function of BGP in the Internet routing operations.

- ■ **Intra-autonomous system**   Intra-autonomous system routing is performed by BGP when two or more BGP routers operate inside the same autonomous system. This is generally seen in cases where it's necessary to cross a large internetwork from one edge to the other.

- ▲ **Pass-through autonomous system**   Sometimes it is necessary for BGP traffic to traverse a non-BGP autonomous system in order to connect to another BGP autonomous system.

As an exterior gateway routing protocol optimized to scale to Internet size, BGP differs sharply from interior protocols in some fundamental ways:

- ▼ **Peer routers**   The network administrator specifies a list of BGP routers representing other autonomous systems (usually other ISPs or large internetwork portals). This is done because it isn't feasible to pass routing updates through a worldwide routing domain.

- ■ **Routing table contents**   A table entry in BGP is an autonomous system (not a LAN, as it is in an interior gateway protocol). Each route consists of a network number and a list of autonomous systems that must be passed through, called an *AS path*.

- ■ **Single routing metric**   BGP uses a single metric to determine the best path to a given network. This metric consists of an arbitrary number to weight the degree of preference to a particular link. It's not dynamic; it must be input and updated by a network administrator.

- ▲ **Incremental route updates**   When a routing update is received, BGP simply replaces the old route with the new one. No best path recalculation is done, because to maintain a link-state database on the Internet's topology is not feasible.

Cisco's implementation of BGP supports each router establishing a set of neighbors, or peers, with which to exchange reachability information. A variety of techniques are used to aggregate routes to help simplify route processing and to reduce the size of routing tables. One is the use of *route maps*—a practice that restricts the dissemination of routing updates to certain routers. Another is the use of a simplified form of administrative distance where, instead of having the choice between 255 relative weightings, a route can take on any of three trustworthiness ratings depending on the topology position of the router.

BGP's key facet is its ability to filter, reduce, and simplify the routing information it gathers from the Internet.

Cisco's Routing Protocol Strategy

The move around 1990 to replace RIP with a more robust interior gateway protocol was a key moment in the history of the internetworking industry. (Keep in mind that 1990 is ancient history in Internet time.) The ability to scale beyond 16 hops or a network diameter of 50 routers was sorely needed. Faster convergence was also on the critical list because loops were becoming a pressing problem.

Cisco exploited the moment by promoting IGRP as a RIP replacement. This was a risk because IGRP was (and is) a proprietary standard. But the strategy was wildly successful because it solved customers' needs to continue internetwork expansion, and at the same time persuaded network managers to standardize on Cisco equipment. Most of those that did have since migrated to EIGRP.

OSPF is an IP-only routing protocol. The technology planners on the OSPF Working Group were right to promote a RIP replacement. And they were probably right that one day all networks will be based on the Internet Protocol. But that won't happen for another ten years. It was only ten short years ago that many were pointing a finger at Novell and complaining that Novell held a monopoly on client-server LAN operating systems. There are millions of IPX LANs to this day. The reality is that most enterprises still have a mix of network-level protocols and need to support them using an interior gateway technology like EIGRP. This was the marketing window Cisco exploited.

Cisco supports an OSPF product as a complement to its EIGRP strategy. OSPF is a powerhouse in its own right. Most ISPs (and an increasing number of enterprises) are running large IP-only routing domains; and given the standards-setting clout of the Internet, many think that one day everybody will be IP only. OSPF has built the mission-critical infrastructure surrounding and sustaining the BGP peer networks. Without OSPF, BGP peer networks probably wouldn't be possible. Both are enabling technologies that made the explosive growth of internetworks and the Internet possible.

Comparing the functionality of current routing protocols can be confusing. Although RIP is the lowliest of the interior gateway protocols, it has been so heavily enhanced that it now shares much of the advanced functionality available with EIGRP and OSPF. Further confusing the routing protocol landscape is that RIP and other protocols are being subsumed into OSPF domains as routing domain areas. Things get more clouded because OSPF is so scalable that it has a lot of the size-scaling functionality associated with BGP.

Suffice it to say that today's routing protocols overlap so much that they're hard to keep straight. Just keep in mind that the essential distinctions are distance-vector versus link-state architectures and interior gateway protocols versus exterior gateway protocols.

CHAPTER 9

Network Management

We've now covered the major technology pieces of internetworks. Routers, switches, firewalls, and access servers are cabled together to form network topologies. Most configurations run over twisted-pair copper feeding into fiber-optic backbones that move data at speeds from 100 Mbps up to a mind-boggling 2.5 Gbps. While network devices vary in type and size, most look like PCs or servers in that they have memory, CPUs, and interface cards. But they're diskless, seldom have monitors, and use their interfaces to connect networks instead of peripherals.

Cisco's software infrastructure to make it all go is the Internetwork Operating System (IOS). IOS is a lean package of commands, protocol software, and the all-important config file. IOS software images differ greatly depending on the type of device. The lowly hub has but a stripped-down version of IOS without even a command-line interface, while the behemoth Cisco 12000 Series Gigabit Router is loaded with protocols and specialized management software packages. Yet, regardless of device type or IOS functionality, network behavior is controlled by setting parameters in the config file.

As we saw in the previous chapter, perhaps the most sophisticated internetworking technology of all is the routing protocol. Routing protocols give internetworks a level of self-awareness and self-adaptation without which large-scale configurations wouldn't be practical. They do this by constructing a hierarchy of LANs and autonomous systems to find optimal paths to get across the office campus—or to the other side of the world.

But it takes more than optimal routes to run an internetwork. The ability to self-operate is only part of the network management equation. Routing protocols may be able to handle most minute-to-minute issues, but internetworks still require constant management effort from people. Without persistent review and intervention from administrators, an internetwork's ability to self-operate will be overwhelmed by a progressive deterioration in operating conditions. Internetworks must be constantly updated and even upgraded to accommodate problems, growth, and change. Network teams need tools for managing change and anticipating problems (and, hopefully, avoiding them).

If left alone, even a perfectly configured internetwork will degrade under the strain of added users, increased loads, shifting traffic, new hardware and software versions, and new technology. Network administrators must monitor, reconfigure, and troubleshoot without end. The recent boom in users—and the increase in the amount of traffic generated per user—has left network teams scrambling to keep up. Routing protocols and other automated features only make effective internetwork management feasible, they don't make it easy. Network management tools are needed also.

The industry's response has been a stream of standards, technologies, and products focused on the configuration and operation of internetworks.

OVERVIEW OF NETWORK MANAGEMENT

Network management can be confusing to newcomers. By its nature, the field involves a daunting list of tasks. Figure 9-1 outlines the range of tasks performed by the typical network management team. Internetworks must be planned, modeled, budgeted, designed,

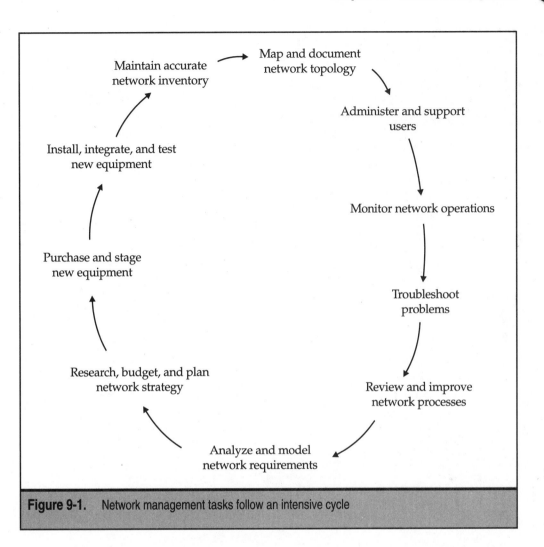

Figure 9-1.   Network management tasks follow an intensive cycle

configured, purchased, installed, tested, mapped, documented, operated, monitored, analyzed, optimized, adjusted, expanded, updated, and fixed. That's a lot. No single tool can do all these things, at least not yet. Suffice it to say that network management products and services is an industry unto itself, composed of a complex array of technologies, products, and vendors providing everything from simple protocol analyzers that measure a single link to worldwide network command centers.

NOTE: You may have noticed that the term *network management* is used in connection with internetworks (almost nobody manages just one LAN any more). The term has held on since the rise of internetworking and is still in universal use. There is no real difference between network management and internetwork management.

The Evolution of Management Tools

Historically, the problem with computer management tools has been delivering true multivendor support. In other words, it's hard to find a single tool that can handle equipment from different manufacturers equally well. Multivendor configurations—the norm in virtually all enterprise IT (information technology) infrastructures today—are tough to manage using a single tool because of subtle differences in each manufacturer's equipment.

Computer management tools have evolved from opposite poles of the computing industry: systems and networks. The goal is to bring all computing assets under the management control of a single tool, and the prevalence of placing host systems on networks is driving existing system and network management tools into one another's arms.

Traditional System Management Consoles

Sophisticated computing management systems called *system consoles* have been around for decades. These consoles were generally hooked up to mainframes sitting in a data center and used to schedule jobs, perform backups, and fix problems. Over time, they developed more and more capabilities, such as managing remote computers.

The best-known product from the data center mold is Unicenter from Computer Associates (CA). Unicenter is actually an amalgamation of products that CA has woven into a single management solution. Unicenter evolved from a sophisticated console for managing IBM mainframes and disk farms to an integrated management system with support for all the important hardware and software platforms. Most Unicenter product growth has been achieved by acquisition, understandable given the product scope.

The key to Unicenter and other system consoles is the ability to handle the various computer architectures that enterprises are likely to put into a configuration.

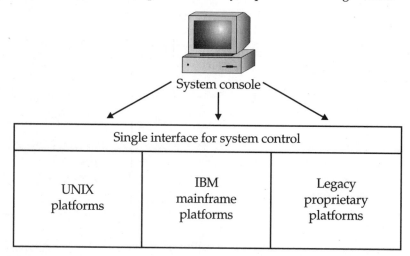

Single interface for system control		
UNIX platforms	IBM mainframe platforms	Legacy proprietary platforms

Network Management Systems

Over the past decade, a second breed of management tool emerged in the form of network management systems. These tools focus on network infrastructure instead of the data center. They use the networks they manage as the platform for monitoring events and are controlled from a console referred to as the network management station (NMS).

The leading NMS is OpenView from Hewlett-Packard (HP). There's a bit of history as to how HP ended up in this enviable position. HP had committed to UNIX as its strategic operating system in the mid-1980s—years earlier than other enterprise platform vendors. (Don't give HP too much credit; they did so out of desperation because their proprietary 16-bit operating system had run out of gas.) By that time, UNIX and IP had become closely linked in the market, mostly because IBM and other big system vendors were still pushing their proprietary networking schemes. Around 1990, HP seized the moment and OpenView rode the UNIX bandwagon to become the predominant network management tool. There are now over 100,000 OpenView installations.

As with Unicenter, the key to OpenView's success is its ability to work with devices from various manufacturers. But HP had a built-in design advantage in the form of a then-new IP network management standard called SNMP (Simple Network Management Protocol). Instead of having to design to dozens of proprietary interfaces, HP was able to let the network equipment vendors design products to the SNMP standard. OpenView was the first major management product to implement SNMP.

Network management station (e.g., HP OpenView or IBM NetView)					
Device inventory	Configuration	Topology mapping	Device monitoring	Troubleshooting	Analysis
SNMP/RMON					
Routers	Switches	Hubs	Access servers		Servers
CiscoWorks 2000		Bay Network's Optivity		Others (e.g., Castle Rock, NetScout, etc.)	
Resource mgr. essentials	CWSI				

The defining difference between system and network consoles is the level at which they operate. System management tools focus on operating systems, transactions, data files, and databases as they exist across servers, storage controllers, and disks. Network management tools focus on packets and connections as they exist over network devices, network interfaces, and transmission links.

System and network consoles are now converging into a single technology class some call enterprise system management (ESM) tools. Convergence into ESM is inevitable as the line between network and computer blurs and enterprises complete the shift to client-server architectures that move resources from the data center out into their internetwork topologies.

The focus of this book is internetworking, so we'll cover only the networking components of ESM.

Network Management Tools Today

It has proven to be very difficult to manage an internetwork using a single tool. The problem has been the inability to collect consistent data from the variety of devices that exist in most enterprise IT infrastructures. The problem isn't so much old versus new equipment, although that's part of it. The major hang-up is that most network management systems are shallow in their implementations; in other words, they can manage only a few aspects of device operation, and leave some devices unmanaged altogether.

This is so despite the fact that all major network equipment makers bundle SNMP into their device operating systems. The base SNMP infrastructure is there, but device manufacturers seldom implement it fully in their products. There are a variety of reasons for this:

▼ **Consumption of resources by network management**   Every CPU cycle spent gathering a measurement or sending an SNMP message is a cycle not used for payload traffic. Network management extracts a cost either in slower performance or extra hardware.

■ **Spotty standards support by manufacturers**   It would be expensive for device makers to build complete compliance into their products. Device hardware would need to be beefed up to handle the additional SNMP work, pushing up prices in the process. In addition, some manufacturers prefer a dash of SNMP incompatibility to steer customers toward standardizing on their product line because implementing SNMP from one manufacturer is easier than bringing devices of different manufacturers under the same management regime.

■ **Labor**   A lot of time and attention is required for enterprises to implement and operate a network management system. Management teams are hard pressed just to keep up with network growth. Few have the manpower to make greater use of SNMP-based systems.

▲ **Price-conscious customers**   Customers are fixated on low price points. The network half of IT shops is regarded as infrastructure, and managers demand commodity pricing. The relentless focus on driving down the cost per port looks good on paper, but incurs hidden costs in the form of poorly utilized assets.

For these reasons, most SNMP implementations gather only high-level information. Fewer processes—called *objects*—are monitored, samples are smaller, polling cycles are less frequent, and so on.

Often, even when an enterprise *does* want more network management controls, blind spots are still created by noncompliant devices. Blind spots occur when a policy cannot be enforced in part of a network because a device doesn't support it. Blind spots often occur at backbone entryways, especially to switched backbones. Take the scenario depicted in Figure 9-2. The part of the topology on the bottom has implemented a policy to manage traffic usage between a pair of communicating hosts. But the switch in the middle is not configured to monitor that, leaving that SNMP policy unenforced beyond the switch.

The IETF (Internet Engineering Task Force) is responsible for the SNMP standard, and it has a tough job. The implementation of any standard requires coordinated acceptance from both manufacturers and users. This is difficult to pull off because manufacturers are wary of market acceptance and the potential loss of competitive advantage. Understandably, then, standards setting is always a tricky process. Yet the goal of an integrated NMS console has proved to be particularly elusive for these reasons:

▼ **Hardware dependencies**   Any computer standard must contend with various architectures used for CPUs, buses, device interfaces, drivers, and the like. This both complicates the standards-setting process and makes it more expensive for manufacturers to comply. The problem is exacerbated by the internetworking industry's habit of using so many different parts in their product lines. Remember all the different CPU architectures that go into Cisco's router line?

■ **Converging technology**   Telecommunications, data networking, and computing until recently were viewed as separate and distinct industries, with their own industry bodies, standards, and so on. But nowadays, all of the equipment they make falls under the purview of network managers, increasing the scope of the standards and bringing together different engineering fields has been a strain.

▲ **Technology onslaught**   Relentless technology advances in all quarters of computing (telecommunications, operating systems, CPUs, cabling, etc.) has presented the IETF with a constantly moving target. And a manufacturer that has won a hard-earned advantage is often reluctant to fall into line with standards and make life easier for competitors.

Progress has been slow. Yet the lack of integrated management hasn't impeded the explosive growth in the size and use of networks. To accommodate this conflict, management teams use several products to track different parts of their internetworks. Most big enterprises have an ESM, but they augment it with dedicated tools to manage critical parts of internetworks. Figure 9-3 illustrates a typical scenario, with OpenView used to watch the overall network and manufacturer-specific tools to manage critical assets.

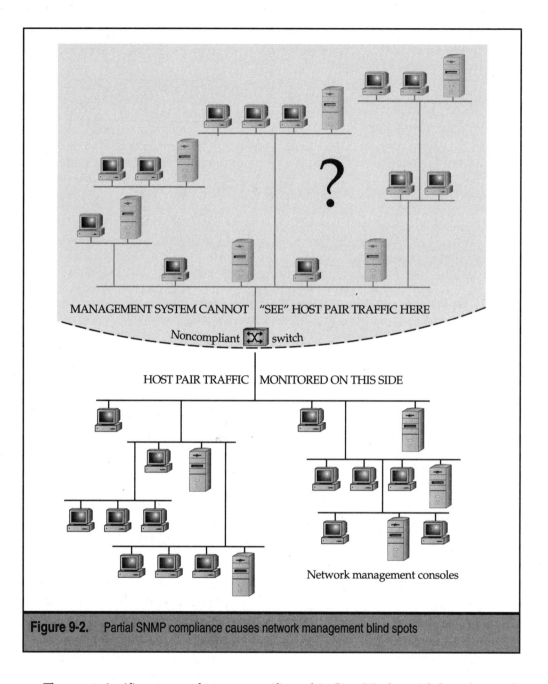

MANAGEMENT SYSTEM CANNOT   "SEE" HOST PAIR TRAFFIC HERE

Noncompliant switch

HOST PAIR TRAFFIC   MONITORED ON THIS SIDE

Network management consoles

Figure 9-2.   Partial SNMP compliance causes network management blind spots

The most significant manufacturer-specific tool is CiscoWorks, with broad enough functionality to be considered an ESM unto itself—but only as long as you're strictly running Cisco gear. For that reason, CiscoWorks is usually snapped into an ESM suite like OpenView or NetView.

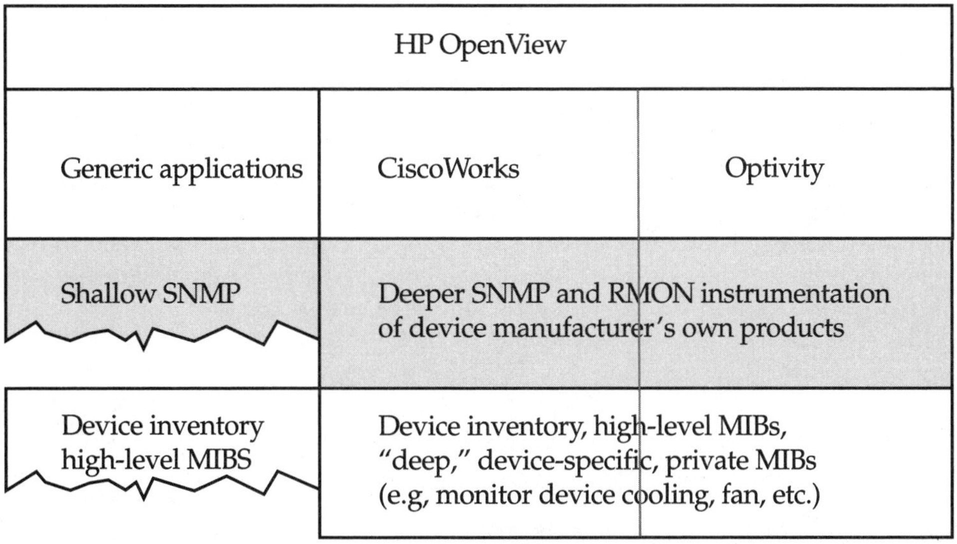

HP OpenView		
Generic applications	CiscoWorks	Optivity
Shallow SNMP	Deeper SNMP and RMON instrumentation of device manufacturer's own products	
Device inventory high-level MIBS	Device inventory, high-level MIBs, "deep," device-specific, private MIBs (e.g, monitor device cooling, fan, etc.)	

Figure 9-3.   Most network teams use several tools to manage their internetworks

NOTE: Management standards aren't just a problem in internetworking. An industry group called the Distributed Management Task Force (DMTF) has been trying for years to get a standard called the Desktop Management Interface (DMI) implemented. The purpose of DMI, aimed at distributed PCs and small servers, is to let consoles monitor inventory—disks, drivers, BIOS versions, memory configurations, and so on—and to perform remote upgrades. DMI 2.0 products include Compaq's Insight Manager, IBM's Universal Management Agent, Intel's LANDesk Manager, HP's TopTools, and others. Trouble is, these products pretty much work only with platforms of their own manufacture. Microsoft has weighed in with an open standard called WBEM (Web-Based Enterprise Management), now under the auspices of the DMTF. Intel is working on a complementary standard at the hardware level called WfM (Wired for Management). For now, you either restrict the number of vendor product lines you use, or use individual tools to manage each of them. Sound familiar?

Trends in Enterprise System Management

ESM tools have been criticized as difficult to implement, labor intensive, expensive, slow, and ineffective. They're priced at up to $250,000 and cost at least that much again to implement. As far as specialized management hardware, RMON probes can cost over $10,000 each. The expense has left most small- to medium-sized internetworks relying on multiple tools of more or less equal importance, each usually specific to the major equipment manufacturers used in the configuration. A second result is that fewer things are monitored, diminishing proactive network management.

But the market for tools is robust anyway, because the potential for savings from NMS tools is enormous. Some estimate that during a typical IT infrastructure's life cycle, 75 percent or more of all costs are spent on operations. There is a double benefit of enabling network administration personnel to be more productive and getting better results in available bandwidth. NMS tools help enterprises reduce costs and boost service at the same time.

Competition is heating up in the NMS arena. There are now over a dozen major NMS tools. In addition to OpenView and Unicenter, other notables are IBM's Tivoli NetView (IBM acquired Tivoli Systems a few years ago), Platinum Technology's ProVision, Cabletron System's Spectrum, Bay Network's Optivity, Loran Technologies' Kinnetics, Bull Worldwide's OpenMaster, and Sun's SunNet Manager.

Microsoft has tentatively entered the fray with the introduction of Microsoft Management Console (MMC) in its Windows 2000 release (formerly dubbed Windows NT 5.0). MMC is a key to the company's NT server strategy in that corporate computing must have management capability. It's just a bare-bones framework for a few Microsoft applications for now, but rest assured that Microsoft will be pushing hard to get vendors to snap their management applications into the Microsoft Management Console. Figure 9-4 charts how different management tools interrelate.

The cast of contenders comes from three sources: computer platform makers such as HP and IBM, network device manufacturers Cisco and Bay Networks, and software com-

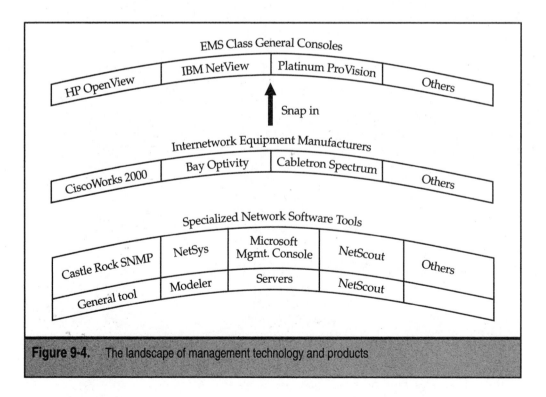

Figure 9-4.   The landscape of management technology and products

panies in the form of Microsoft, Castle Rock, and others. Who prevails will tell which is most important: the wire, the desktop, or the mainframe. Regardless of vendor, NMS technology is headed toward these goals:

▼ **More coverage**   Where greater management control is placed on devices and network processes, doing this will require faster device hardware.

■ **Simplicity**   As internetworking has exploded in popularity among small- and medium-sized enterprises, more networks are being operated by nonexperts.

■ **Automation**   As underlying network management technologies improve, more management tasks are being automated to improve Quality of Service (QoS).

▲ **Proactive management**   A new breed of tools helps isolate emerging problems and avert major network problems by taking early corrective action.

Nearly all progress in computing results directly or indirectly from industry standards. Internetworking ushered in the era of open computing with the help of several standards: the seven-layer OSI reference model, IP, Ethernet, UNIX, Wintel (the Windows + Intel desktop standard), HTTP, SQL, and others. Now it's time to bring it all under control with integrated management technology driven by SNMP.

SNMP IS IP'S COMMON MANAGEMENT PLATFORM

Almost all modern internetwork management suites are built atop the Simple Network Management Protocol. Before discussing the Cisco management applications, a look at their underlying network management technology is in order.

What Is SNMP?

SNMP is a TCP/IP protocol purpose-built to serve as a communications channel for internetwork management operating at the application layer of the IP stack. Although SNMP can be directly operated through the command line, it's almost always used through a management application that uses the SNMP communications channel to monitor and control networks. As Figure 9-5 shows, SNMP has two basic components: a network management station and agents.

Agents are small software modules that reside on managed devices. They can be configured to collect specific pieces of information on device operations. Most of the information consists of totals, such as total bytes, total packets, total errors, and the like. Agents can be deployed on the panoply of devices:

▼ Routers
■ Switches
■ Access servers
■ Hubs

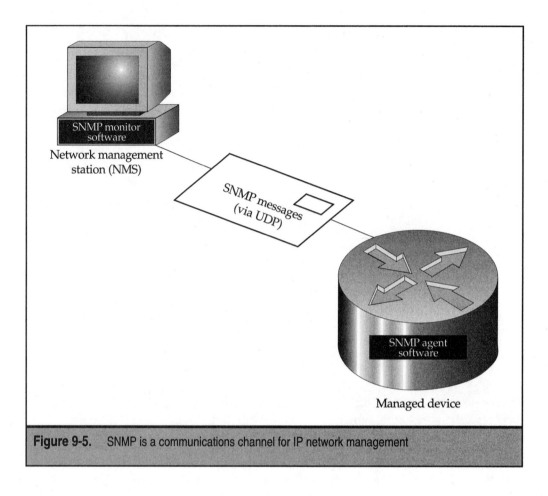

Figure 9-5.   SNMP is a communications channel for IP network management

- Servers (NT, UNIX, Linux, MVS, VMS, etc.)
- Workstations (PCs, Macs, and UNIX desktops)
- Printers
- ▲ UPS power backup systems

The idea is to place agents on all network devices and manage things according to the status information sent back. A piece of equipment with an SNMP agent loaded onto it is referred to as a *managed device* (also called a *network element*).

The NMS is the internetwork's control center. Usually, there's just one NMS for an autonomous system, although many large internetworks use more than one NMS—usually arranged in a hierarchy. Most NMSs today run on dedicated UNIX or Microsoft NT servers.

SNMP Polling and Managed Objects

SNMP is a fairly simple request/response protocol. It works by having the NMS periodically poll managed devices for fresh information. The polling frequency is a matter of configuration choice, but it usually takes place once every few minutes or so. There are three types of polling:

▼ **Monitor polling** To check that devices are available and to trigger an alarm when one is not

■ **Threshold polling** To detect when conditions deviate from a baseline number by a percentage greater than allowed (usually plus or minus 10 percent to 20 percent) and to notify the NMS for review

▲ **Performance polling** To measure ongoing network performance over longer periods and to analyze the data for long-term trends and patterns

The agent responds to the poll by returning a message to the NMS. It's able to do this by capturing and storing information on subjects that it has been configured to monitor. These subjects are usually processes associated with the flow of packets. A process about which the agent collects data is called a managed object. A *managed object* is a variable characteristic of the device being managed. The total number of UDP connections open on a managed device, for example, could be a managed object. One open UDP session on a specific interface is an *object instance*, but the total number of simultaneously open UDP sessions on the device (say, a router) is a managed object. Figure 9-6 shows our example UDP connections as managed object and instances.

Managed objects are usually operating characteristics of managed devices. The managed devices can be anywhere in the topology—backbone devices, servers, or end systems. Most objects are physical pieces, such as a network interface. But a managed object isn't necessarily a physical entity. An object could also be a software application, a database, or some other logical entity.

The MIB

The agent stores the information about objects in specialized data records called *MIBs* (*management information bases*). A MIB is the storage part of the SNMP agent software. Information stored in MIBs is referred to as *variables* (also called *attributes*). MIBs usually collect information in the form of totals for a variable during a time interval, such as total packets over five minutes. Figure 9-7's example shows variables being extracted from instances and processed through managed MIBs and the managed object—in this example, a count of total Ethernet packets going through a router's interface. Again, the packet count from each interface is a managed object instance; the count for all three interfaces is the managed object.

By collating data from multiple objects, the MIB lets the agent send the NMS information concerning everything on the device that is being monitored.

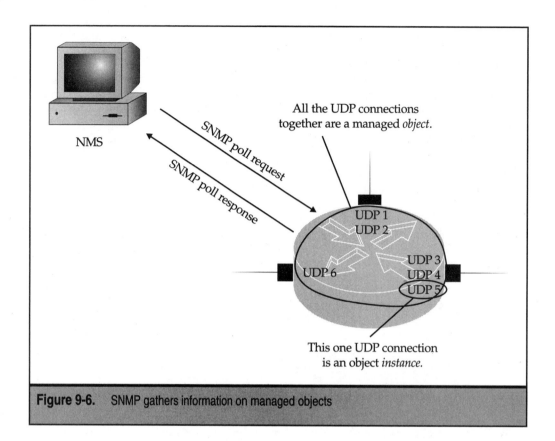

All the UDP connections together are a managed *object*.

NMS

SNMP poll request

SNMP poll response

UDP 1
UDP 2
UDP 3
UDP 4
UDP 5
UDP 6

This one UDP connection is an object *instance*.

Figure 9-6.   SNMP gathers information on managed objects

Types of MIBs

MIBs are prefabricated to perform specific jobs. They're often called MIB objects. Basic MIBs usually come packaged inside the network device operating system. For example, IOS comes packaged with MIB objects for most network management jobs.

Generally, MIBs are named using a convention that indicates the MIB category. For example, a Cisco MIB object that deals with a specific network interface will have *if* in its name (from the letters *i* and *f* in *interface*). The ifInErrors MIB object monitors incoming packet errors on an interface, ifOutErrors the outgoing errors. sysLocation reports a device's network location, and so on. In and Out specify whether the MIB object is to measure incoming or outgoing traffic. Table 9-1 shows five basic MIB categories used in most SNMP systems.

It is possible to set a MIB to gather information on a single object instance only, called a *scalar* object. Most managed objects, however, are composed of several related instances. This practice, called *tabular* objects, is the rule in most MIBs because it's more efficient to manage as much as possible from a single data collection point. As the name implies, a tabular MIB keeps the information straight by storing it in rows and tables.

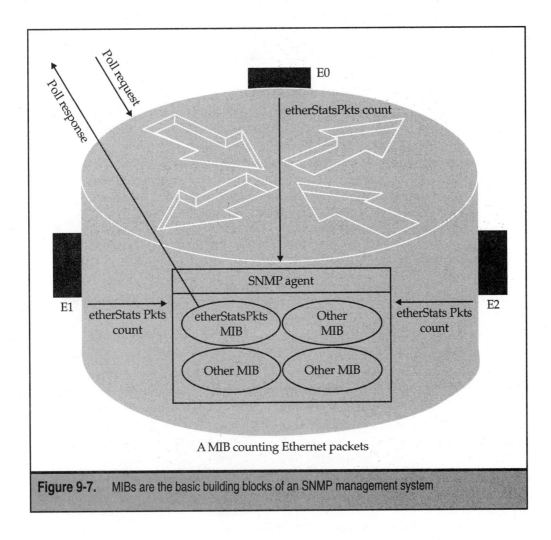

A MIB counting Ethernet packets

Figure 9-7. MIBs are the basic building blocks of an SNMP management system

NOTE: MIB lingo can be confusing. You'll hear references to *the MIB* as if it were a single MIB object. But that's not the case. For example, the Cisco MIB is not a MIB as such; it's actually the root of about 400 private Cisco MIB objects.

What Makes SNMP Machine Independent

We don't want to get too technical in this book, but you should understand how the SNMP standard makes itself machine independent. In other words, how is it able to run on different brands of equipment, each with its own proprietary operating system?

Category	Description and Examples
Configuration	MIBs that report basic management information such as device name, contact person, device location, and uptime. MIB configuration objects are sysName, sysDescr, sysContact, sysLocation, sysUpTime, ifNumber, romID, and others.
Interface error rates	MIBs that monitor specific interfaces. Packet errors are a normal condition, but watching their trends indicates device health and helps isolate faults. For Ethernet interfaces, use ifInErrors, ifOutErrors, locifCollisions, locIfInRunts, or locIfInGiants, locIfCRC, and others. For serial interfaces, use locIfInFrame, locIfInAbort, locIfInIgnored, locIfResets, locIfRestarts, and others.
Bandwidth	ICMP is a layer-3 protocol that reports on IP packet processing. It's best known for its **echo** command used to verify the presence of other devices by pinging them. Timed pings are used to determine how far away a device is (much like in the submarine movies). SNMP sends ping input and output messages to measure available bandwidth. Cisco's MIB objects for this are icmpInEchos and icmpInEchoReps, and icmpOutEchos and icmpOutEchoReps. Generally speaking, these are the only SNMP messages not sent as UDP messages.
Traffic flow	Performance management is largely a matter of measuring traffic flow. There are Cisco MIBs to measure traffic rates both as bits per second and packets per second: locIfInBitsSec, locIfOutBitsSec, locIfInPktsSec, and locIfOutPktsSec.
Unreachable address	The object to measure how often a router is asked to send messages to an unreachable address is icmpOutDesUnreachs.
SNMP data	There are even objects to measure how much time the router spends handling SNMP messages. The objects include snmpInGetRequests and snmpOutGetRequests, snmpInGetResponses and snmpOutGetResponses, and others.

Table 9-1.   Basic Cisco MIB Objects Commonly Used in SNMP Implementations

The SNMP standard requires that every MIB object have an object ID and a syntax. An object ID identifies the object to the system, and tells what kind of MIB to use and what kind of data the object collects. Syntax means a precise specification a machine can understand in binary form.

To understand a field's contents, IOS must know whether the field contains a number, text, a counter, or other type of data. These are called data types. *Data types* specify the syntax to be used for a data field. A *field* is any logical piece of data, such as a model number or temperature reading. In the same way that a field has its own box on an input screen, it has its own position in a computer file. A file represents data in binary (zeros and ones), and a set of binary positions are reserved for each field within the file. All fields must be declared as some data type or another, or else the machine cannot process the data held there.

Computer hardware architectures, operating systems, programming languages, and other environmentals specify the data types they're willing to use. A data type represents the layer where software meets hardware. It tells the machine what syntax to use to interpret a field's contents. A different syntax is used for floating-point numbers, integer numbers, dates, text strings, and other data types.

SNMP makes itself independent by declaring its own data types. It does so in the form of the Structure of Management Information (SMI) standard. SMI is a standard dedicated to specifying a machine-independent syntax for every data type. These data types are independent of the data structures and representation techniques unique to particular computer architectures. SMI specifies the syntax for data types such as object IDs, counters, rows, tables, octet strings, network addresses, and other SNMP elements.

MIBs are programmed by vendors using an arcane programming language called ASN.1, created just for programming SMI data types. ASN.1 (for Abstract Systems Notation One) is an OSI standard, from the same people that brought us the seven-layer reference model. Figure 9-8 shows how SMI data types universalize MIB information.

SMI tries to let vendors code "write-once, run anywhere" MIB objects. In other words, someone should be able to write a single piece of MIB software—a packet counter, for example—and the counter MIB should be able to run on any device that supports the SMI syntax definition for a counter.

SMI data types are SNMP's building blocks at the lowest level. They are used to construct MIB object formats in a syntax any machine can understand. From there, object instances are measured and rolled up into managed objects, which in turn are reported by the SNMP agent to the NMS. This is how NMSs can operate across disparate device architectures.

Standard MIBs and Private MIBs

The current MIB standard is MIB-II, which has nearly 200 standard MIB objects. The standard is implemented as a hierarchy that starts from a root and continues to branch down from the source MIB to the root Internet MIB. Looking at Figure 9-9, you see that each branch is marked both by a name and a number (the numbers are used to build object IDs).

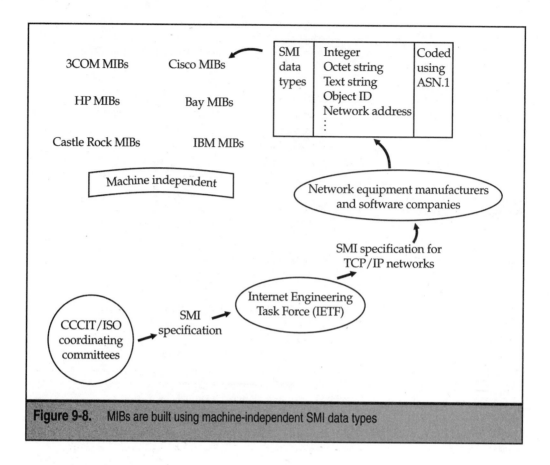

Figure 9-8. MIBs are built using machine-independent SMI data types

Figure 9-9 also shows the players in the history of the Internet. ISO is the International Standards Organization, and DoD is the U.S. Department of Defense (which started it all with ARPANET). CCITT is the Consultative Committee for International Telegraph and Telephone. The CCITT is only a distant cousin of the Internet, handling telephony and other communications standards. The CCITT is now known as the ITU-T (for Telecommunication Standardization Sector of the International Telecommunications Union), but you'll still see the CCITT acronym attached to dozens of standards.

Because they're more user friendly, text strings are usually used to describe MIB objects in directories. Object IDs are mainly used by software to create compact, encoded representations of the names.

Working from the tree structure in Figure 9-9, the Internet root's object ID is 1.3.6.1, named iso.org.dod.internet. The two main branches beyond the Internet root are the management and private MIBs. Industry-standard MIBs go through the management branch to become iso.org.dod.internet.mgmt.mib with the object ID 1.3.6.1.2.1. Private

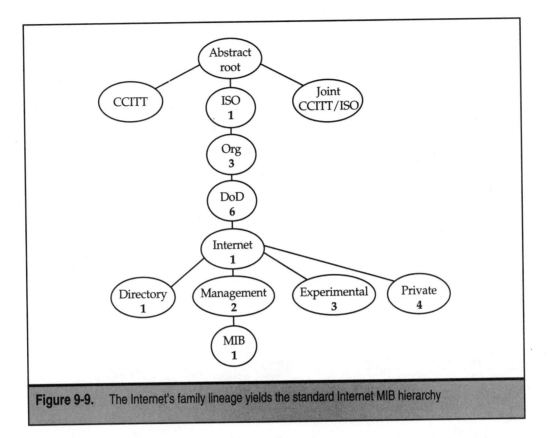

Figure 9-9.   The Internet's family lineage yields the standard Internet MIB hierarchy

MIBs become iso.org.dod.internet.private and 1.3.6.1.4. Cisco's private MIB is represented as iso.org.dod.internet.private.enterprise.cisco, or object ID 1.3.6.4.1.9.

Vendors can build private MIBs by extending standard MIB branches. In this way, they can customize MIBs to better fit their particular needs. Figure 9-10—Cisco's private MIB hierarchy—shows how private MIBs extend from the standard Internet MIB.

Many of the object groups within the Cisco Management, Temporary Variables, and Local Variables subgroups measure Cisco proprietary technology. For example, the Cisco Environmental Monitor group in the Cisco Management subgroup—object ID 1.3.6.4.1.9.9.13—looks after such things as operating temperature inside the device. This type of information is the "deep" stuff we were talking about that management applications from other manufacturers have trouble getting at.

Another important thing to see in Figure 9-10 is support for legacy desktop protocols. Novell NetWare IPX, VINES, AppleTalk, DECnet, and even Xerox XNS networks can be managed using Cisco MIBs. These are legacy in that the IP LAN specification seems to be steamrolling the market, but the others are still in use and therefore important to their customers.

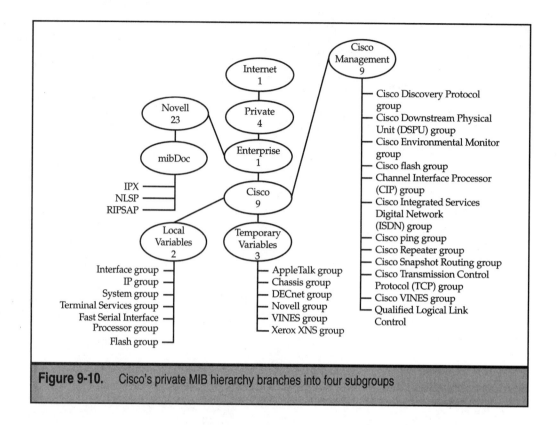

Figure 9-10. Cisco's private MIB hierarchy branches into four subgroups

Polling Groups and Data Aggregation

MIBs are frequently placed into polling groups to facilitate SNMP data collection. A *polling group* is a set of logically related managed objects that are reported and analyzed as a cohesive entity. For example, Figure 9-11 shows polling groups for three different classes of equipment in an internetwork: the backbone switches, routers, and application servers. Different MIB variables are likely to be collected for each type, so each gets its own polling group. In this way, logically related management information is compiled and stored into the SNMP database under group names.

Grouping simplifies the network administrator's job. In the Figure 9-11 example, thresholds can be set to fit tolerances appropriate for each group. For example, a network team is likely to set alarm variables to be more sensitive for the backbone switches, because trouble with them could bring the entire internetwork down. Polling similar MIBs en masse simplifies SNMP operations and helps assure data that's consistent, trustworthy, and easier to assimilate.

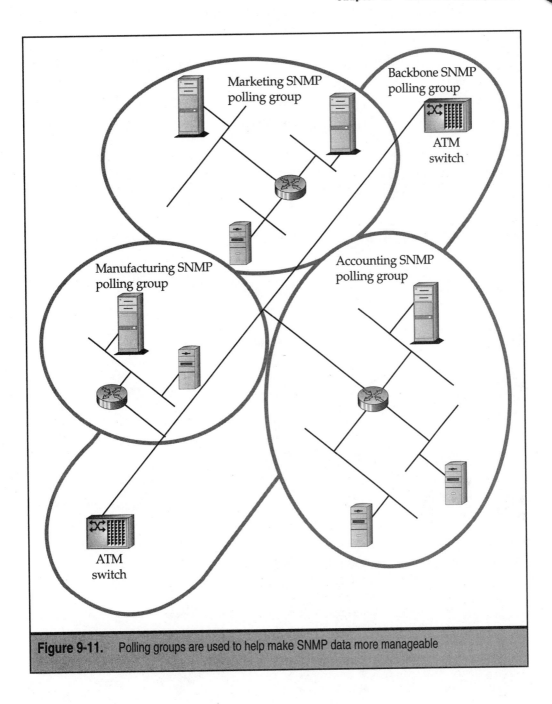

Figure 9-11.   Polling groups are used to help make SNMP data more manageable

Groups also make it easier to limit the amount of information stored in the NMS database. SNMP could build mountains of data on every device in a network, but doing so would be neither practical nor worthwhile. Storing information on related MIB groups facilitates the movement of raw data through a cycle of aggregation and purging. Figure 9-12 shows a typical scenario, in which MIB variables in a group are polled and stored in the NMS database every five minutes. Each midnight, the data is aggregated into minimums, maximums, and averages for each hour, and stored in another database. The data points are purged from the database weekly, leaving behind only the aggregated data.

The collect-aggregate-purge cycle has several benefits. It keeps disk space open on the NMS server for storing new MIBs and maintains statistical integrity of the data record, but at the same time also keeps a consistently fresh picture of network operations.

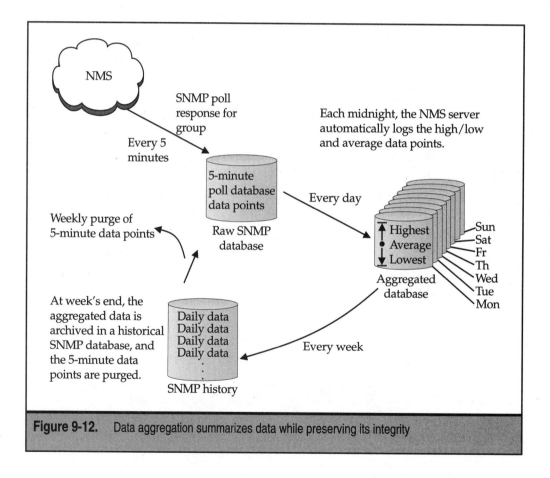

Figure 9-12.   Data aggregation summarizes data while preserving its integrity

SNMP Commands

The *simple* in Simple Network Management Protocol comes from the fact that the protocol has just six root commands. They're used to set SNMP parameters within the device's config file. Here are the root SNMP commands:

▼ **Get**   Used by the NMS to retrieve object instances from an agent.

■ **GetNext**   Used to retrieve subsequent object instances after the first instance.

■ **GetBulk**   New for SNMP version 2, only one **GetBulk** operation is necessary to retrieve both the first and all subsequent instances in a managed object (replaces the need for iterative **GetNext** operations).

■ **Set**   Used to set values for object instances within an agent (such as a threshold).

■ **Trap**   Used to instruct an agent to unilaterally notify the NMS of an event (without being polled).

▲ **Inform**   New for SNMP version 2, this command instructs one NMS to forward trap information to one or more other NMSs.

NOTE: Most of the time, SNMP commands are used by computer programs rather than by people directly. For example, if an administrator enters the location of a router in an inventory screen in the Essentials console, a process is launched from Essentials that invokes the **set snmp location** command in IOS inside that router.

SNMP's two basic commands are **get** and **set**. The **set** command is used to set managed parameters in managed objects. The following code snippet shows a command that configures the managed device to supply its geographical location if polled for it.

```
MyRouter>set snmp location St. Paul
```

The **get** command is used to fetch stored variables from agents and bring them back to the NMS. This example requests a specific MIB object be reported by calling out a specific object ID of a private Cisco MIB:

```
MyRouter>getsnmp 1.3.6.1.4.1.9.9.13
```

SNMP needs to be simple in order to make itself supportable by disparate architectures. Doing so is a practical requirement for SNMP interoperability.

Thresholds

A *threshold* defines an acceptable value or value range for a particular SNMP variable. When a variable exceeds a policy, an *event* is said to have taken place. An event isn't necessarily an either/or situation, such as a switch going down. Events are usually operational irregularities that the network team would want to know about before service is affected. For example, a network administrator may set a policy for the number of packet errors occurring on router interfaces in order to steer traffic around emerging traffic bottlenecks. Thresholds can be set either as a ceiling or as a range with upper and lower bounds. The two types of thresholds are depicted in Figure 9-13.

The shaded portions of the graph in Figure 9-13 are called *threshold events*. In other words, an event is when something has taken place in violation of the set policy. A *sampling interval* is the period of time during which a statistic is compiled. For example, a MIB object can store the total number of packet errors taking place during each five-minute period. Intervals must be long enough to gather a representative sample, yet short enough to capture events before they can substantially affect network performance.

Events and Traps

When an event occurs, the network administrator can specify how the SNMP agent should respond. The event can either be logged or an alarm message can be sent to the

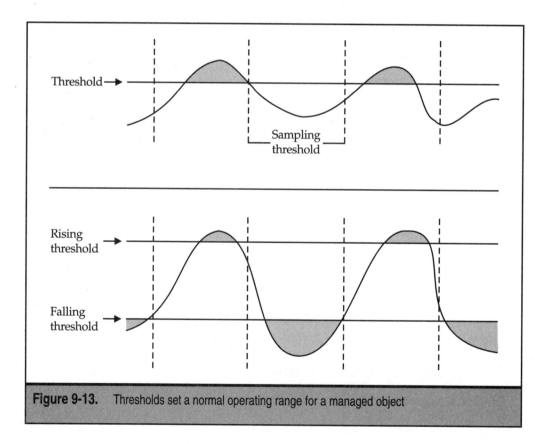

Figure 9-13.   Thresholds set a normal operating range for a managed object

NMS. An SNMP alarm message is called a *trap*, so named because it catches (or traps) the event at the device. A trap contains information about the event. Figure 9-14 shows the course of events leading up to an alarm.

Alarms can take many forms. They're often configured to show themselves as a blinking icon on the NMS console, but you could have a noise generated. Networks that don't have administrators present at the NMS all the time have the trap dial a pager or send a priority e-mail to alert the person on response duty at the time.

Traps aren't used just to send alarms. As an internetwork grows in size, SNMP overhead traffic will increase along with it. Network managers can reduce SNMP overhead by stretching the polling frequency, but doing that makes the NMS less responsive to emerging network problems. A better way to limit SNMP overhead is to use traps. Given that they're unsolicited messages instead of SNMP poll responses, traps consume a negligible amount of bandwidth.

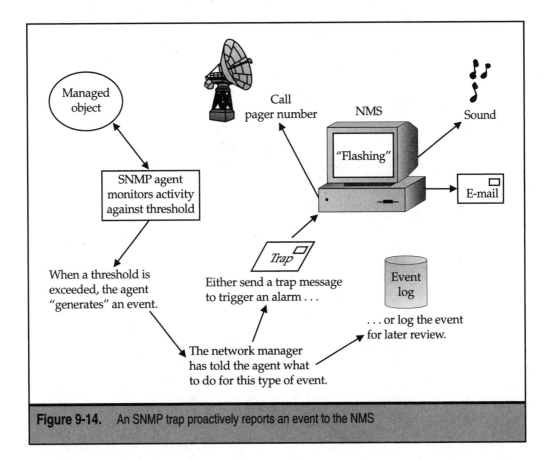

Figure 9-14.   An SNMP trap proactively reports an event to the NMS

The following code snippet is from a Cisco router's config file. It shows the SNMP settings made for the device. RO and RW are the read-only and read-write community strings that make the device a member of a particular management group.

```
MyRouter(config)#snmp-server community yellow RO
MyRouter(config)#snmp-server community blue RW
MyRouter(config)#snmp-server enable traps snmp
MyRouter(config)#snmp-server enable traps isdn call-information
MyRouter(config)#snmp-server enable traps config
MyRouter(config)#snmp-server enable traps bgp
MyRouter(config)#snmp-server enable traps frame-relay
MyRouter(config)#snmp-server enable traps rtr
MyRouter(config)#snmp-server host 10.1.1.13 traps vsi
```

A number of SNMP traps are enabled in this config file. This tells the SNMP agent on the device to send trap messages if anything changes. The last line gives the IP address of the NMS, so the agent knows where to send the trap messages.

RMON: Hardware Probes for Switched Networks

RMON (short for *remote monitoring*) is a separate but related management standard that complements SNMP. RMON is similar to SNMP in several ways: it is an open standard administered by the IETF, it uses SMI data types and the root MIB format, and it collects device data and reports it to an NMS. But RMON differs from normal SNMP in these fundamental ways:

▼ RMON is instrument based, in that it uses specialized hardware to operate.

■ RMON proactively sends data instead of waiting to be polled, making it bandwidth efficient and more responsive to network events.

▲ RMON allows much more detailed data to be collected.

RMON instrumentation is more powerful, but more expensive. Consequently, RMON probes tend to be placed on critical links such as network backbones and important servers.

RMON and Switched Networking

The movement toward RMON-based network management is closely linked to the rise of switched networking. While LAN switching is on the rise as the way to improve network performance, it poses special problems for conventional SNMP management methods. In a network formed using hubs, a LAN analyzer has full visibility because the medium is shared by all nodes. But a switched LAN isn't a shared medium; so to maintain the same level of visibility, the analyzer would have to be placed on each switched port. The solution is to incorporate the analyzer (or at least the sensor part of it) directly into the switch's hardware. That's what an RMON probe is. Figure 9-15 shows a switched network managed with and without RMON.

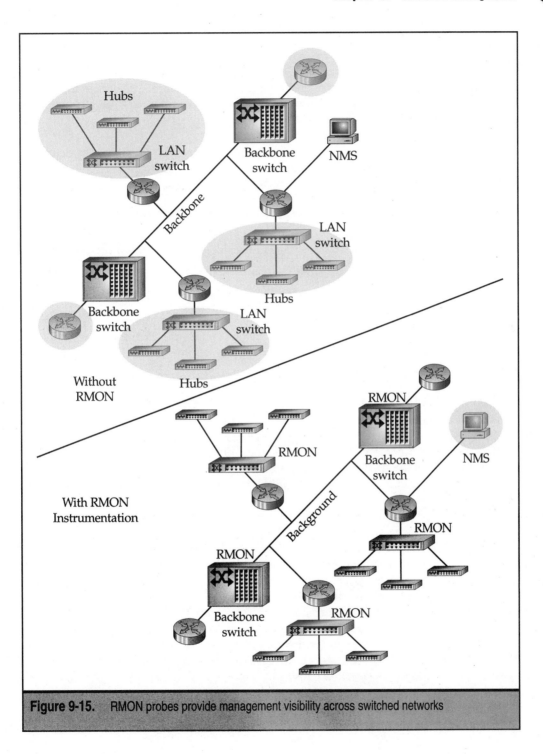

Figure 9-15. RMON probes provide management visibility across switched networks

RMON became a standard in 1992 with the release of RMON-1 for Ethernet. The RMON-2 standard, the current version, was completed in early 1997. While RMON-1 operated only at the physical and data link layers (layers 1 and 2) of the seven-layer OSI reference model, RMON-2 adds the capability to collect data at higher layers, giving it more reporting capability. The ability to monitor upper layer events has been a boon to the popularity of RMON. For example, RMON-2 can report what's happening with IPX traffic as opposed to IP on a multiprotocol LAN segment.

RMONs replace expensive network analyzer devices that must be physically attached to the approximate area of a network problem. RMON probes come in different forms, depending on the size and type of device to be monitored:

▼ An RMON MIB that uses the monitored device's hardware (called an *embedded agent*)

■ A specialized card module inserted into a slot within the monitored device

■ A purpose-built probe externally attached to one or more monitored devices

▲ A dedicated PC attached to one or more monitored devices

Having specialized hardware remotely located with a monitored device brings advantages. RMON probes can yield a much richer set of measurement data than that of an SNMP agent. The dedicated hardware is used as a real-time sensor that can gather and analyze data for possible upload to the NMS.

The Nine RMON MIB Groups

Another advantage RMON enjoys is its freedom as a separate standard. The root RMON MIB defines nine specialized MIB groups (and a Token Ring group). The nine groups let RMON collect more detailed and granular management information than can be collected using SNMP. Figure 9-16 charts the RMON MIBs.

RMONs, at a minimum, come with the Events and Alarm groups. Most come with four groups needed for basic management: Events, Alarms, Statistics, and History. Because of hardware expense and response time concerns, resource-intensive groups such as the Traffic Matrix group are infrequently deployed.

The Alarm RMON MIB is a more powerful mechanism for event management than SNMP. For example, because there's a separate MIB just to keep track of events, RMON can adjust itself to avoid sending too many alarms. In addition, the Matrix MIB can monitor traffic on a "conversation" basis. In other words, it can be set up to monitor connections between pairs of MAC addresses and report on what's happening with each connection. For example, if a Matrix MIB was set up to watch an expensive link, say, between New York and London, and someone was using it to play a transatlantic game of Doom, the MIB could see that and alert the NMS that valuable bandwidth was being wasted.

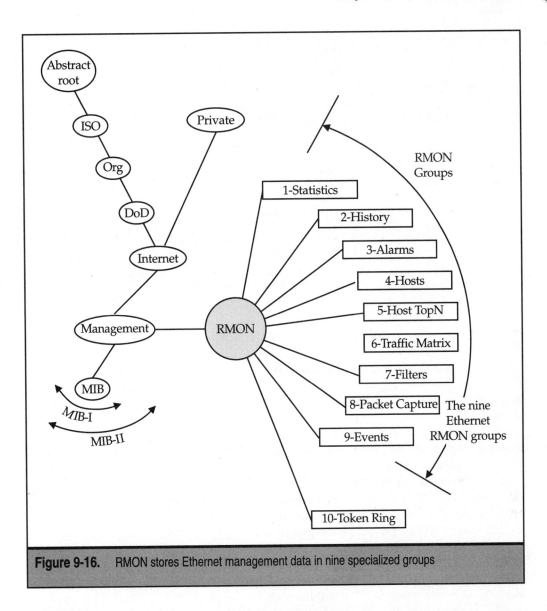

Figure 9-16. RMON stores Ethernet management data in nine specialized groups

The problem with RMON is that it's expensive. It takes extra hardware to store and analyze packets in real time, and that costs money. Consequently, RMON is being put to use to manage links that are mission critical or expensive.

Trends in Network Management Technology

SNMP compliance issues have left new versions of the standard mired in political infighting. In addition, the fast development of powerful RMON-based tools is pushing the approach to network management in a new direction. The technology underpinnings of network management applications exhibit these trends:

▼ More powerful data collection (more information reported faster)

■ More proactive management

■ Improved built-in hardware support for management

▲ Better security for protecting management tools themselves

The trend toward more intensive management of internetworks is coming up against the same old problem: every management message is overhead that consumes precious bandwidth. This dilemma is what's pushing the industry toward RMON, because that technology captures better information and works locally (instead of via NMS polling).

The other trends have to do with making management systems more efficient and providing SNMP itself with better security.

Advanced SNMP Commands

The evolution of SNMP can be seen in the **GetBulk** and **Inform** commands. **GetBulk** makes it easier for the agent to fetch MIB information from multiple object instances. **Inform** makes it easier to use a hierarchy of NMSs to manage complex internetworks, as shown in Figure 9-17.

SNMP's support for protocols beyond IP is a substantial change. Doing this will extend the reach of SNMP into non-IP topologies. This is a very important advance for network managers overseeing multiprotocol internetworks. Don't forget that big parts of many sophisticated internetworks run legacy network architectures, such as Novell NetWare IPX, AppleTalk, and DECnet, and will continue to do so for the foreseeable future. Extended SNMP protocol support will help bring these topologies under the control of centralized NMSs.

SNMP Version 1 vs. SNMP Version 2

Keeping track of standards can be confusing because they overlap. For example, right now the majority of all SNMP implementations are of version 1 (SNMPv1). Improvements have been incorporated in SNMPv2, which is just now being implemented by the major vendors. Yet the security pieces of version 2 were found wanting, so a third version of SNMP is under active consideration even before most have implemented SNMPv2! Whatever the version, here are the components of the basic SNMP message format:

▼ **Version**   The SNMP version being used.

■ **Community string**   The equivalent of a group password used by all devices in the same administrative domain. The SNMP message is ignored without the proper community string.

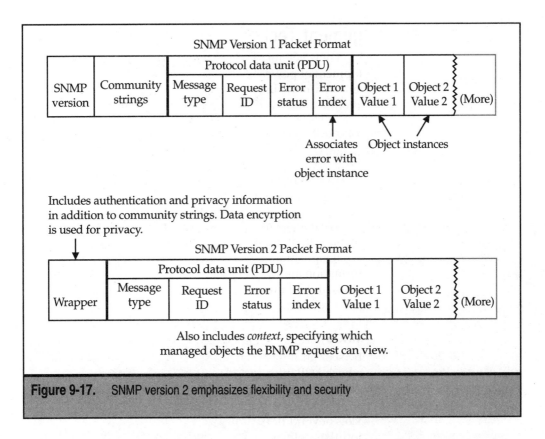

Figure 9-17.   SNMP version 2 emphasizes flexibility and security

■ **Protocol data unit (PDU) type**   The instructions about what to do. The PDU specifies the operation to be performed (**GetBulk, Trap,** etc.) and the object instances on which to perform the operation.

■ **Error status**   This field defines an error and error type.

■ **Error index**   This field associates the error with a particular object instance.

▲ **Variable bindings**   Don't be intimidated by the fancy name; a variable binding is the data collected on the object instance—it's the SNMP packet's payload.

SNMPv2 enhances the message format with these changes:

▼ **Wrapper**   This includes destination and source party identifiers for SNMP message authentication and privacy, and also identifies context in the form of the managed objects on which the PDU is to perform its operation.

■ **Enhanced PDU**   The **GetBulk** and **Inform** operations.

▲ **Multiple transport protocols**   Originally, all SNMP packets were transmitted via UDP (User Datagram Protocol). SNMPv2 supports Novell NetWare IPX, AppleTalk DDP, and OSI CLNS.

The enhancements in SNMPv2 reflect the demand for more powerful controls and better security.

Better Security for SNMP Messages

Support for SNMP has been hindered by security concerns. A smart hacker armed with a protocol analyzer would like nothing more than to intercept SNMP messages. Instead of just getting some user's file download, hacking an SNMP system could yield a virtual blueprint of the internetwork topology.

Today, most networks rely on a combination of access lists and SNMPv1 community strings to secure their management systems. If a hacker somehow obtains the community string for an SNMP system, he might navigate around the access list controls and retrieve data on all network devices. Worse, knowing the Read-Write community strings would allow a hacker to alter config file settings on the community's network devices. This would be a devastating security breach, especially if community strings on **set** operations were stolen, because that would hand over control of all devices configured for remote management.

Both customers and manufacturers called for more stringent SNMP security. Keep in mind that a *user* here doesn't necessarily have to be a person; it could just as easily be an automated process such as a **get** request as part of an SNMP poll. In SNMPv2 format, the wrapper contains authentication information that identifies approved destination and source parties to the SNMP transaction. The authentication protocol is designed to reliably identify the originating party. Beyond authentication, SNMPv2 makes it possible to specify which managed objects can be included in a message. Figure 9-18 outlines measures taken to secure SNMPv2 messages.

Setting standards is difficult, however. The security pieces of the SNMPv2 specification proposed by the IETF were found unsatisfactory, and a new SNMPv3 standard is now under review to address these concerns. SNMPv3 will go beyond just the two levels of protection (unsecured and authenticated) by adding a third level, authenticated with encryption, that scrambles SNMP message contents.

Cisco's SNMP and RMON Implementations

Cisco claims unparalleled SNMP and RMON capability. Virtually all the company's devices ship with SNMP agents and most switches with RMON. As the internetworking industry's powerhouse, Cisco sits on the major standards-setting committees and is among the first to release products supporting new standards.

Cisco and SNMP

Cisco includes SNMP support in the form of agent software on every router and communications server it makes. According to the company, its SNMP agents can communicate successfully with OpenView and NetView. Cisco supports over 400 MIB objects. Cisco's private MIB objects feature support for all the major LAN protocols, including IP, Novell NetWare IPX, Banyan VINES, AppleTalk, and DECnet.

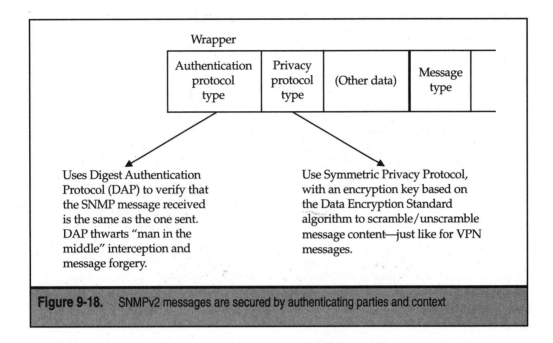

Wrapper

Authentication protocol type	Privacy protocol type	(Other data)	Message type	

Uses Digest Authentication
Protocol (DAP) to verify that
the SNMP message received
is the same as the one sent.
DAP thwarts "man in the
middle" interception and
message forgery.

Use Symmetric Privacy Protocol,
with an encryption key based on
the Data Encryption Standard
algorithm to scramble/unscramble
message content—just like for VPN
messages.

Figure 9-18.   SNMPv2 messages are secured by authenticating parties and context

Cisco uses its private MIB to enhance system monitoring and management of Cisco devices. For example, Cisco routers can be queried both by interface and by protocol. You can query for the number of runt packets on a network interface or query for the number of IPX packets sent or received from that interface. This kind of information is invaluable to baselining the traffic profile of a network. Average CPU usage statistics are sampled by five-second, one-minute, and five-minute intervals to ascertain whether a router is being properly utilized. Physical variables are also measured. Air temperature entering and leaving a device or voltage fluctuations can be monitored to assure continued device operation. Cisco's private MIB includes chassis objects to report the number of installed modules, module types, serial numbers, and so on. Figure 9-19 depicts some of Cisco's advanced SNMP features.

To help secure SNMP messages, IOS provides the ability to prohibit SNMP messages from traversing certain interfaces. SNMP is further secured by the option to designate certain community strings as read-only or read/write, thus restricting the ability to remotely configure certain devices. Also, a device can be assigned more than one community string, enabling key routers or switches to fall under multiple SNMP regimes (sometimes used in large internetworks).

Cisco has committed to making their routers "bilingual" in their simultaneous support of both SNMPv1 and SNMPv2. The coexistence strategy uses two techniques—a proxy agent that translates messages between versions, and the support of both versions in a single NMS platform.

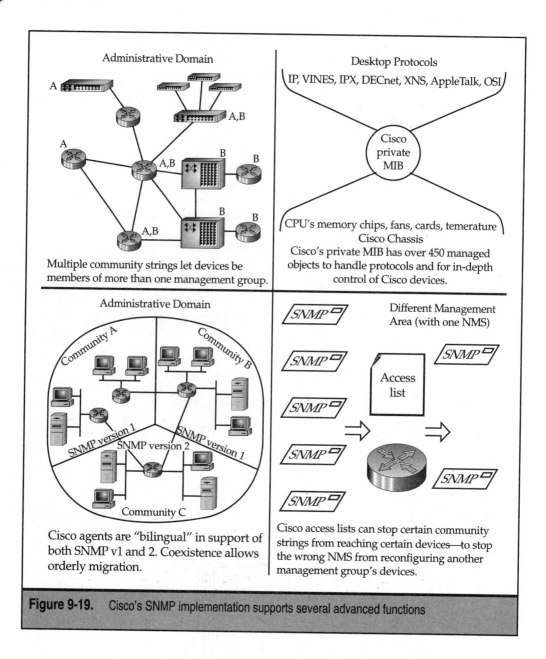

Administrative Domain

A

A,B

A

A,B

B   B

B   B

A,B

A,B

Multiple community strings let devices be members of more than one management group.

Desktop Protocols

IP, VINES, IPX, DECnet, XNS, AppleTalk, OSI

Cisco private MIB

CPU's memory chips, fans, cards, temerature
Cisco Chassis
Cisco's private MIB has over 450 managed objects to handle protocols and for in-depth control of Cisco devices.

Administrative Domain

Community A

Community B

SNMP version 1

SNMP version 2

SNMP version 1

Community C

Cisco agents are "bilingual" in support of both SNMP v1 and 2. Coexistence allows orderly migration.

Different Management Area (with one NMS)

SNMP

SNMP

SNMP

SNMP

SNMP

SNMP

SNMP

Access list

Cisco access lists can stop certain community strings from reaching certain devices—to stop the wrong NMS from reconfiguring another management group's devices.

Figure 9-19.   Cisco's SNMP implementation supports several advanced functions

Cisco and RMON

Cisco integrates RMON into all its platforms. The greatest RMON capabilities are packaged into the high-end Catalyst 5000, but RMON capability is built into the LightStream ATM switch line cards also.

RMONS FOR CATALYST SWITCHES   The Catalyst simultaneously acts as a LAN switch and a network probe because of its multiprocessor design. One CPU does the switching, and the other handles management data collection and forwarding duties. The Catalyst can be configured to collect traffic data in either of two modes:

▼   **Standard RMON mode**   The RMON agent collects data for up to all nine RMON groups across all attached switch ports.

▲   **Roving RMON mode**   A focused mode that collects more detailed data for just one or two RMON groups across all eight ports, and then focuses on a single LAN when an event takes place there.

In either mode, the RMON follows a structured course of action to enforce thresholds, generate events, and send alarms. Figure 9-20 depicts the structure.

The concurrent RMON configuration is the normal mode. Its ability to see across all connected LANs is particularly valuable for troubleshooting, especially client-server applications in which the communicating hosts are on different LANs.

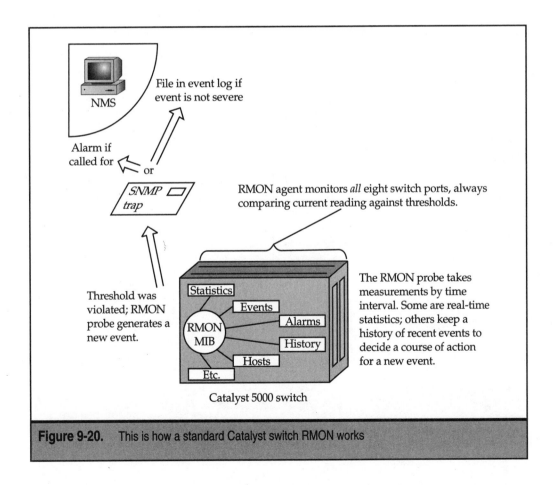

Figure 9-20.   This is how a standard Catalyst switch RMON works

Catalyst's roving RMON is as advanced as it gets. Normally, it works at collecting detailed historical information on a per port and even per host level. But when a trap is sent, the stripped-down, two-group RMON spawns a fully configured nine-group RMON probe that automatically begins collecting troubleshooting data just from the offending connected LAN. Figure 9-21 depicts how a roving RMON changes to handle an event.

By the time the administrator responds to the alert, the roving RMON has already reconfigured itself and started intensive monitoring of the LAN segment in which the problem emerged.

Cisco offers a complete line of RMON probes for various situations. Fast EtherChannel configurations are instrumented using so-called Mini-RMONs, which are built-in agents that monitor channel utilization and launch SNMP traps when necessary. Mini-RMON agents are also packaged into Catalyst Token Ring ports.

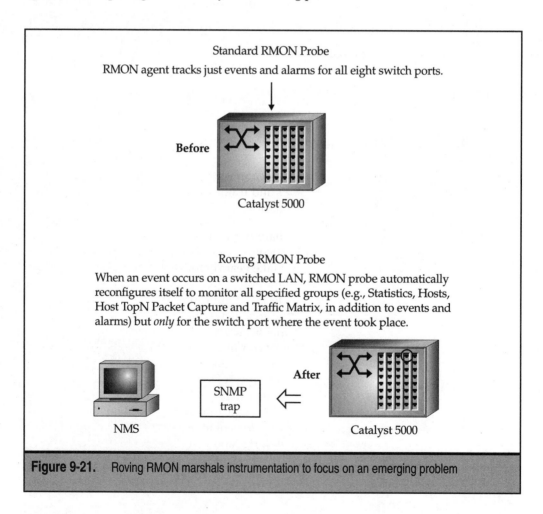

Standard RMON Probe

RMON agent tracks just events and alarms for all eight switch ports.

Before

Catalyst 5000

Roving RMON Probe

When an event occurs on a switched LAN, RMON probe automatically reconfigures itself to monitor all specified groups (e.g., Statistics, Hosts, Host TopN Packet Capture and Traffic Matrix, in addition to events and alarms) but *only* for the switch port where the event took place.

After

SNMP trap

NMS

Catalyst 5000

Figure 9-21.   Roving RMON marshals instrumentation to focus on an emerging problem

Cisco offers a family of stand-alone RMONs called SwitchProbes. These are physical devices with hardware tuned to serve as instrumentation. Usually customers attach them to critical links or diagnostic ports. The SwitchProbe product line comes in either a small or a large chassis, ranging from 1 to 12 ports and 4MB to 32MB. There are SwitchProbe models for Fast Ethernet, FDDI, WAN or HSSI (High-Speed Serial Interconnect), Ethernet, and Token Ring.

CISCOWORKS2000

CiscoWorks2000 is Cisco's NMS suite. It contains over a dozen network management applications based on SNMP and RMON infrastructure. CiscoWorks2000 to some degree is more packaging than a cohesive product because it comes in four pieces, each with its own user interface:

▼ **Resource Manager Essentials** A Web browser–based suite of seven applications designed for managing switched networks, operated through a topology map.

■ **CWSI Campus** A Windows-based suite of four applications operated through a network topology map.

■ **CiscoView** A Windows-based application in which you interact with a lifelike color image of the actual device.

▲ **Netsys Baseliner** A Windows-based application also operated through a topology map that displays VLANs and traffic over the physical network, used to model what-if configuration scenarios.

Except for Baseliner, the applications share common device inventory database and other background processes. Baseliner was acquired by Cisco and is just now being integrated into the larger product suite. It may take years before Cisco gets everything integrated into a single Web browser GUI. Right now, Cisco's NMS must be regarded as a work in progress. The inconsistent user interfaces and functional overlaps between the four pieces are confusing and inefficient. The good news, though, is that CiscoWorks2000 packs a lot of powerful tools that are invaluable once you learn how to use them.

Although it boasts full SNMP and RMON compliance, CiscoWorks2000 is used only for Cisco products. And don't let the name fool you, CiscoWorks2000 runs on UNIX platforms in addition to Microsoft Windows 2000 (née NT).

Given Cisco's dominance of the world router market, CiscoWorks2000 should be regarded as the most important manufacturer-specific tool in the industry. This isn't surprising, given that routers are the most critical element in internetworks. Network teams use a variety of tools to manage big internetworks, and Cisco's tools are front and center more often than not. The most common management scenario these days is to use HP

OpenView as the base enterprise system management (ESM) platform, CiscoWorks2000 to manage Cisco routers and switches, Bay Network's Optivity to manage the hub stacks, and several smaller tools for narrower duties.

CiscoWorks2000 Overview

CiscoWorks2000 is a product family, not a point product. In other words, it's a common software platform that serves as a framework from which optional applications can be operated. Some call the applications that plug into suites *snap-ins*. The goal of product suites is to integrate snap-in applications by letting them share data. The suite's infra-structure shares a database and various background processes such as SNMP polling, configuration checking, and so on. CiscoWorks2000 can import data from the HP OpenView, IBM NetView, Sun Microsystem's SunNet, and other ESM suites.

Browser	Windows	
Essentials	CiscoView	CWSI Campus
Device inventory database		

CiscoWorks has been around for a few years. The original incarnation—called CiscoWorks for Windows—featured only two snap-in applications:

▼ **CiscoView** An interactive graphical tool in which a screen image of the actual device is used to monitor and configure the device.

▲ **Configuration Builder** A GUI-based tool that prompts the user through the process of configuring network devices.

Configuration Builder is an older, cruder version of Cisco ConfigMaker, covered in Chapter 5. The only plus to Configuration Builder is that it handles Token Ring devices. We anticipate that Configuration Builder will be phased out as ConfigMaker matures.

CiscoWorks2000, released in 1999, is more than a mere replacement for CiscoWorks for Windows—it's a full-fledged management environment. It is so big that it would take a vet-eran network administrator weeks to learn all its applications. With CiscoWorks2000, Cisco's management tools are finally catching up with its burgeoning product line. CiscoView and Netsys Baseliner are stand-alone applications that will eventually be inte-grated into Cisco's premier management suites:

▼ **Resource Manager Essentials**   Called Essentials for short, these are the foundation applications for monitoring, controlling, and managing Cisco devices. Essentials has tools for remote device installation, SNMP monitoring, configuration management, software deployment, path analysis, device inventory, and so on.

▲ **CiscoWorks for Switched Internetworks (CWSI)**   Pronounced "swizee" and usually called CWSI Campus, this is a suite of integrated applications for management of Cisco switched networks. CWSI handles VLAN configuration, real-time device management, RMON-based traffic analysis, and ATM connection and performance management.

CiscoWorks2000 installs and operates on a normal computer platform—not a specialized network device. The platform must have a minimum of 256MB memory and at least 4GB of disk storage. In addition to the Microsoft Windows NT Server platform, CiscoWorks2000 can be installed on the IBM AIX, HP PA-RISC, and Sun Solaris operating systems. The software ships with a run-time version of the Sybase database management system.

CiscoWorks2000 Resource Manager Essentials

Resource Manager Essentials (we'll call it Essentials hereafter) provides the CiscoWorks2000 environment and several tools for everyday network management chores. The centerpiece is the device inventory database that keeps a record on individual Cisco devices. The inventory database is kept up-to-date via SNMP polling, and it serves as the basis for network management. Essentials is composed of several applications:

▼ **Inventory Manager**   Maintains an up-to-date database of Cisco devices. Can import device records from HP OpenView, IBM NetView, CWSI, or a flat file. From there, polls for additional SNMP data such as chassis type, installed memory, interfaces, IOS version, and so on.

■ **Configuration Manager**   Archives router and switch configurations. Configuration Manager is *active* in that it senses device changes and keeps a running file of who did what. Configuration Manager passes change information to the Change Audit Service application and others. Configuration Manager is frequently used to automatically compare config files in different devices.

■ **Change Audit Service**   Provides a central view of all configuration changes. It records who changed what, how, and when, and whether the change was made from the device console, Telnet, or CiscoWorks.

■ **Software Manager**   Simplifies version management and deployment of IOS software images. Provides a wizard-assisted planning tool that validates proposed changes. Software Manager can reduce time to do software upgrades from hours to minutes.

- **Syslog Analyzer** Filters syslog messages logged by routers, switches, access servers, and Cisco IOS firewalls. Syslog Analyzer displays probable causes and recommends corrective actions.

- ▲ **CCO Connection** CCO stands for Cisco Connection Online, the name of the www.cisco.com Web site. CCO Tools is an online service where registered customers can tap into Cisco resources. Several Essentials applications have an option to connect to a related application at cisco.com. For example, you can select an option in the Software Manager application, log into CCO, and have a special server analyze a device's IOS image and recommend upgrades.

These applications share the Essentials management console (user interface) and work from the same device inventory.

NOTE: There are dozens of screens and hundreds of options in CiscoWorks2000—far too many to cover here. We'll cover key items and concepts in this chapter and show other CiscoWorks2000 features in Chapter 13.

The User Interface for Resource Manager Essentials

Essentials provides one user environment through which several management applications can be operated. The management console is Web based, which is to say that it's used through a browser. Shown in Figure 9-22, the key to the console is the login window in the left pane, where you select which applications to run. At any given moment, the login window only displays the navigation tree for one of three option groups: Tasks, Tools, and Admin.

In Figure 9-22, the login window is pointed to the Tasks group. The console uses a Microsoft Windows Explorer–style navigation tree interface with drawers and folders. Essentials' three menus are organized as follows:

- ▼ **Tasks** Applications used to perform various management tasks: Daily Reports, Availability Manager, Change Audit, Device Configuration, Inventory, Software Management, and Syslog Analysis

- ■ **Tools** Support mechanisms to research problems. Tools that connect to www.cisco.com are Case Management, CCO Tools, Contract Connection, and Management Connection Certification. Local tools are Connectivity Tools and Device Navigator.

- ▲ **Admin** Basic tools for the applications in the Tasks menu. This is where you select application options. For example, Syslog Analysis is in both the Tasks and Admin drawers. Tasks is where you see data logged about network events; Admin is where you go to tell Essentials what you want Syslog to collect.

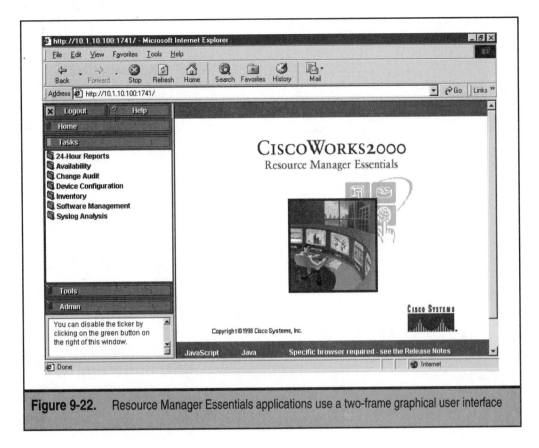

Figure 9-22.   Resource Manager Essentials applications use a two-frame graphical user interface

Each menu group is a drawer in the login window. Inside each drawer there is a folder for each application. Click a folder and the application's options pop out, as Figure 9-23 shows for the Availability reporting option.

If you look closely at Figure 9-23, you'll notice three different icons to the left of the application functions: the one with the folded upper-right corner indicates a program; the icon with horizontal lines is for reports; the icon with three vertical bars is for graphs.

Double-click an option to start it. As a Web application, Essentials responds by downloading the information into your browser or starting a background process to gather the information. Essentials is a slow-running application because it is implemented as Java applets that must download from the NMS server to your PC. It's made even slower by the fact that it needs to gather the necessary data. When using Essentials, you'll find yourself looking at the hourglass cursor a lot, so be patient. Response time depends on the size of the network you're managing, your LAN connection speed, and the configuration of your PC.

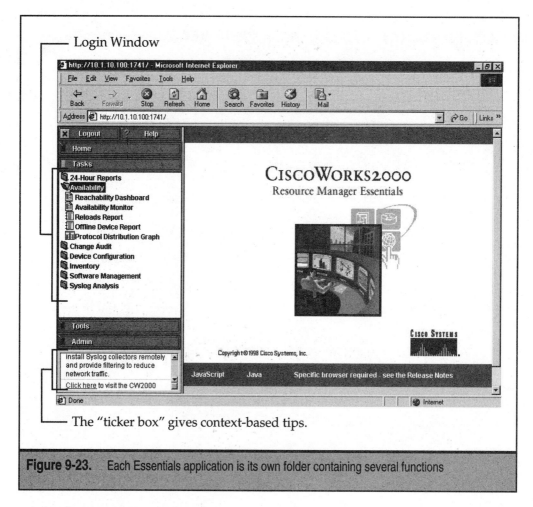

Login Window

The "ticker box" gives context-based tips.

Figure 9-23. Each Essentials application is its own folder containing several functions

Adding Devices to Essentials

Even with everything installed properly, Essentials is of no use until network devices are loaded into its database. This is usually done by importing them from other applications, such as HP OpenView, Castle Rock Computing's SNMPc, a CiscoView database, or even an earlier version of CiscoWorks. Importing is the preferred method because inputting dozens or hundreds of network devices by hand is laborious and error prone. For illustration purposes, Figure 9-24 shows the Essentials screen for entering a device record by hand. The User Fields can be used for whatever items the network team wishes to store on a device—in this example, the contact person, the asset number, and the serial number.

Figure 9-24's screen is followed by others for inputting SNMP community strings and TACACS+ passwords (TACACS+ is a security application covered in the next chapter). Notice that Essentials uses the Start | Next | Finish paradigm you know from the Install Programs Wizard in the Microsoft Windows Control Panel. Essentials uses a three-step

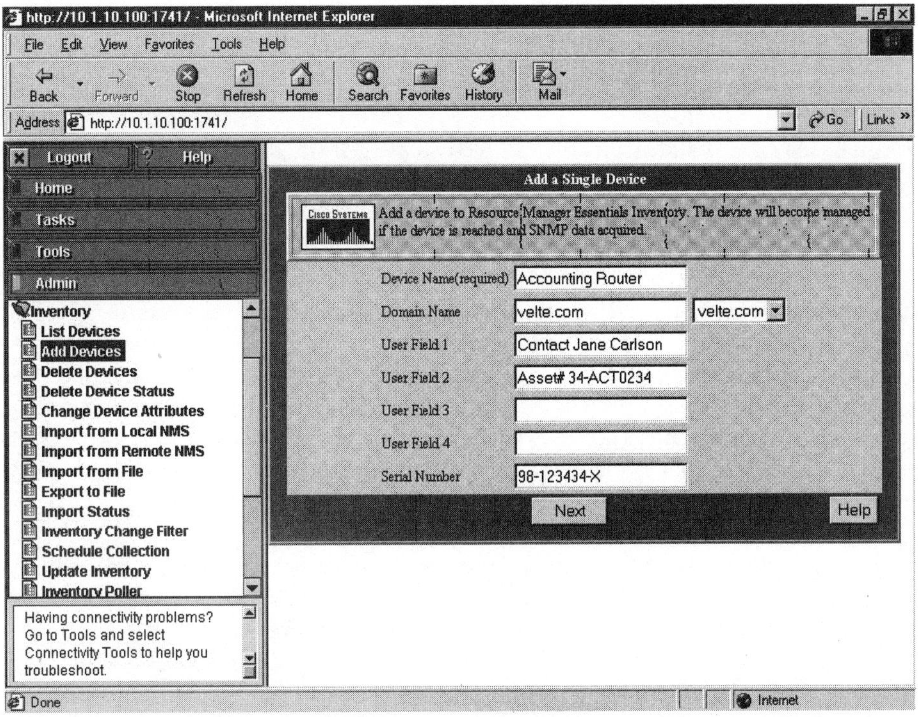

Figure 9-24.   A device inventory database must be built before the network can be managed

routine to do things: select the application option, select the devices to report on, and then display the reported information. Sometimes the output is displayed in the right pane; for other reports, a separate browser instance is started.

CiscoView: The Tool for Managing Individual Devices

Cisco's most basic management tool is CiscoView. It comes packaged with Essentials; but it isn't browser based, so it's not an option in the Essentials login window and must be started as a separate Windows application.

CiscoView is the tool used to work with individual Cisco devices. It's a sophisticated RMON-based monitoring application that communicates to the NMS through the SNMP communications channel. A real-time image of the device is presented, displaying two kinds of information:

▼ **Configuration**   The CiscoView interface can be used to configure the device.

▲ **Performance**   Real-time monitoring information is displayed to help with device management.

CiscoView, also incorporated into CWSI Campus, is the place to go to check on the status of a Cisco device. For example, if you suspect that a particular router is causing a network performance bottleneck, open a CiscoView image of that device and click around with your mouse to check its operating status. The other major role of CiscoView is to set RMON thresholds.

When CiscoView is started, a small window called the Main Menu appears, as shown in Figure 9-25. The Main Menu is the stopping-off point from which you can move among managed devices.

The Main Menu's layout adheres to standard Windows conventions. There is a menu bar across the top containing six menus: File, View, Configure, Monitor, Options, and Help. The menus having to do with a specific device—View, Configure, and Monitor—remain grayed out until a device is opened.

To open a device, select File | Open Device and enter the device's IP address or symbolic name. This will bring up the CiscoView Open Device dialog box, shown in Figure 9-26, in which you must enter the SNMP community strings. These are the shared passwords given to SNMP managed devices. They're called shared because a single set of strings is issued for a group of devices, and members of the network team have access to them.

The Write community string must be entered if you want to change any settings. Often, managers limit distribution of Write community strings to select members of the network team, limiting other team members to read-only capability.

The CiscoView Interactive Device Image

Once a device is opened, CiscoView presents a color image of it, as shown in Figure 9-27. The image isn't just a pretty picture, it's interactive. In other words, the administrator can point at and click the image and enter commands into the individual device's config file.

The contents of the image reflect the current situation within the device—only the modules that are actually installed on the device are shown. For example, the device image in Figure 9-27 depicts a Cisco 4500 router that's accurate right down to the configuration, such as the four serial ports and two Token Ring interfaces installed. Remove a

Figure 9-25.   When CiscoView is opened, the first stop is the Main Menu window

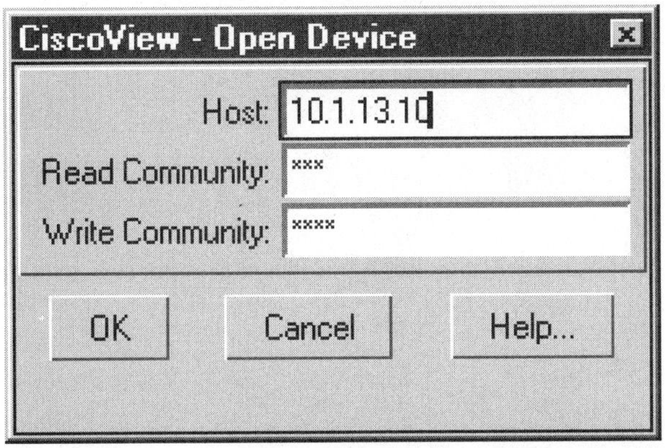

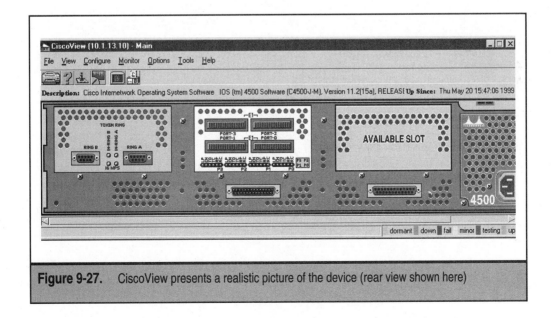

Figure 9-26. CiscoView uses SNMP community strings to restrict access to a device

module and it will be deleted from the CiscoView image of that device because objects in the image are updated each SNMP polling cycle.

It's hard not to like CiscoView, not only because it's neat to look at, but also because the interface is so intuitive. The interface is a natural way to work with devices because it's like being physically present with them—even though you might be hundreds of miles away. Actually, in some ways CiscoView is better than the real thing because of the

Figure 9-27. CiscoView presents a realistic picture of the device (rear view shown here)

intelligence added to the display. For example, the status of each port in the device is reported by presenting the ports in one of five coded colors:

▼ **Green**   The link is up.

■ **Magenta**   The link is being tested.

■ **Brown**   The link is administratively down (it's there, but was taken offline on purpose).

■ **Yellow**   There is a problem—an SNMP policy is violated and an alarm was sent.

▲ **Red**   There is no status reported.

CiscoView supports most Cisco routers, switches, access servers, and hubs. As you might suspect, all actions taken from the CiscoView image are executed by operating equivalent commands in the device's IOS command line. In other words, selecting something on a CiscoView menu executes an IOS command in the background.

NAVIGATING A DEVICE VIA CISCOVIEW   The image display is the equivalent of using the **show** command in the IOS command-line interface. But it's a lot more powerful, because it shows many parameters instead of just one at a time. This makes for better monitoring and troubleshooting because at a glance you can check the status of most components in the device.

Double-click on a component to see details about it. A dialog box will appear displaying information about the component's status and configuration. The example in Figure 9-28 details the TokenRing1 interface of our example Cisco 4500 router. All this information is gathered from the router via SNMP polling.

The dialog box reports the interface's operating status, speed, MAC address, and so on. Clicking the Interface button in Figure 9-28 will bring up a different dialog box that details what's happening on the LAN connected to the interface (in Figure 9-28's example, the TokenRing1 LAN). In either of these dialog modes, CiscoView lets you manually turn things on and off; for example, you can bring an interface administratively down, restart the network, and so on.

CiscoView provides a dashboard from which to monitor current device operations. Each MIB variable being managed on the device is displayed in its own pane. Figure 9-29 shows an example with statistics kept on seven variables.

The example variables displayed in Figure 9-29 are the "deep" objects that can only be monitored using Cisco's NMS. Usually, physical readings on device air temperature and voltages require using a private MIB—in this example, Cisco's private MIB.

SETTING SNMP EVENT THRESHOLDS   The place in CiscoView to make config file settings is the Threshold Manager application. Network administrators use events to monitor

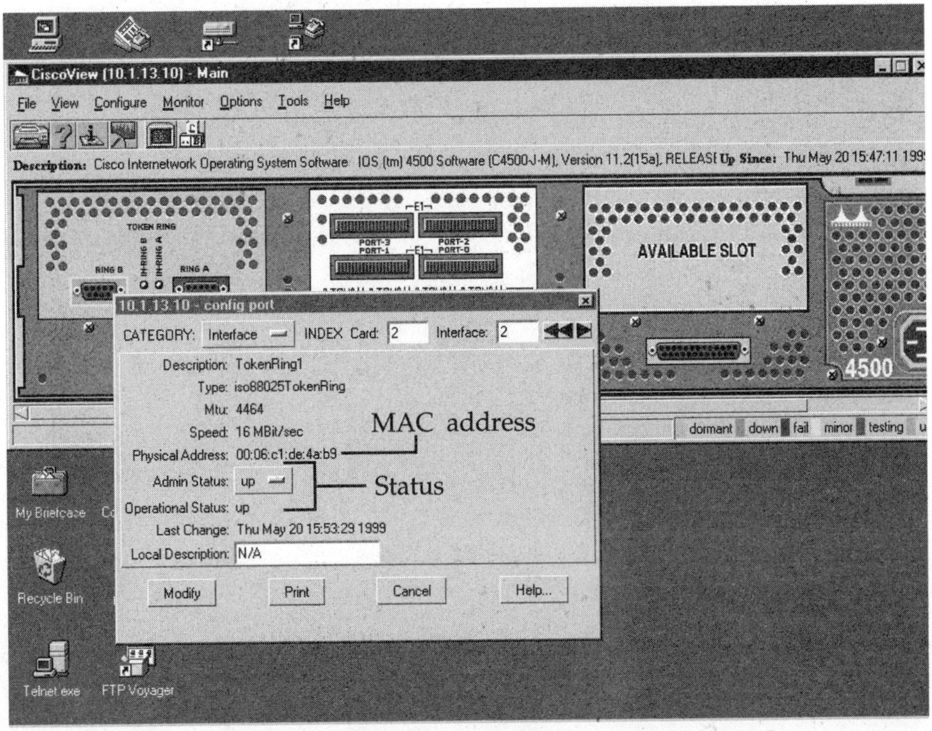

Figure 9-28. You can drill down for details on an object's configuration and status

what's going on inside the device. Setting thresholds tells the SNMP agent software what you consider noteworthy. The agent keeps statistics on the managed object for each time interval, and it reports when polled. However, once the statistic crosses the threshold, an event is said to have taken place, and the agent can take proactive measures, such as triggering an alarm. Essentials uses the RMON alarm and event groups to operate.

Select Tools | Threshold Manager from the menu bar to open the Config Thresholds tab, as shown in Figure 9-30. This is where tolerances are set for SNMP events.

The upper pane in the Configure Thresholds dialog box lists all policies in effect for the device. You can create new policies and modify existing ones from here. The Policies pane displays all threshold policies in effect for that managed device. Beneath that is the Settings pane with the threshold settings.

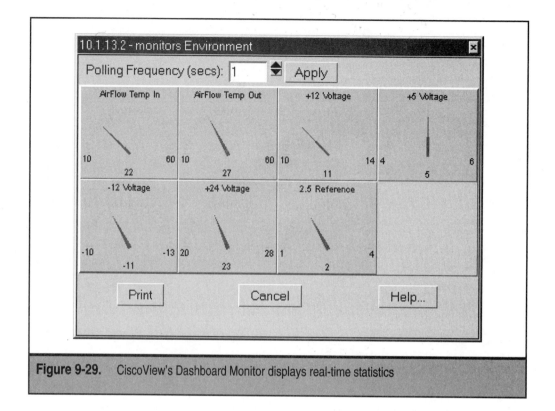

Figure 9-29.   CiscoView's Dashboard Monitor displays real-time statistics

Double-click on a threshold in the Policies pane to modify a threshold through the dialog box shown in Figure 9-31.

Sliders are used to set thresholds for the sampled statistic. The Interval setting is the time period for which the total is counted. Notice at the bottom of Figure 9-31 that you can set whether the event should trigger an alarm or just be logged to an events file for later review.

Earlier in this chapter, Figure 9-13 depicted how rising and falling thresholds define an acceptable operating range to monitor events. Event monitoring is the basis for deciding what gets monitored and reported via SNMP. A threshold setting is a value for the "sampled statistic" of a managed object's variable, such as input interface utilization, runt packets, fragmented packets, and so on. When the current sampled value of the statistic is greater than or equal to the threshold value, a single event is generated. A *falling threshold* is a technique to make sure only one event is generated. After a rising threshold is crossed, a new event for that object cannot be generated until its sampled value falls below the falling threshold. In other words, things must return to normal for the managed

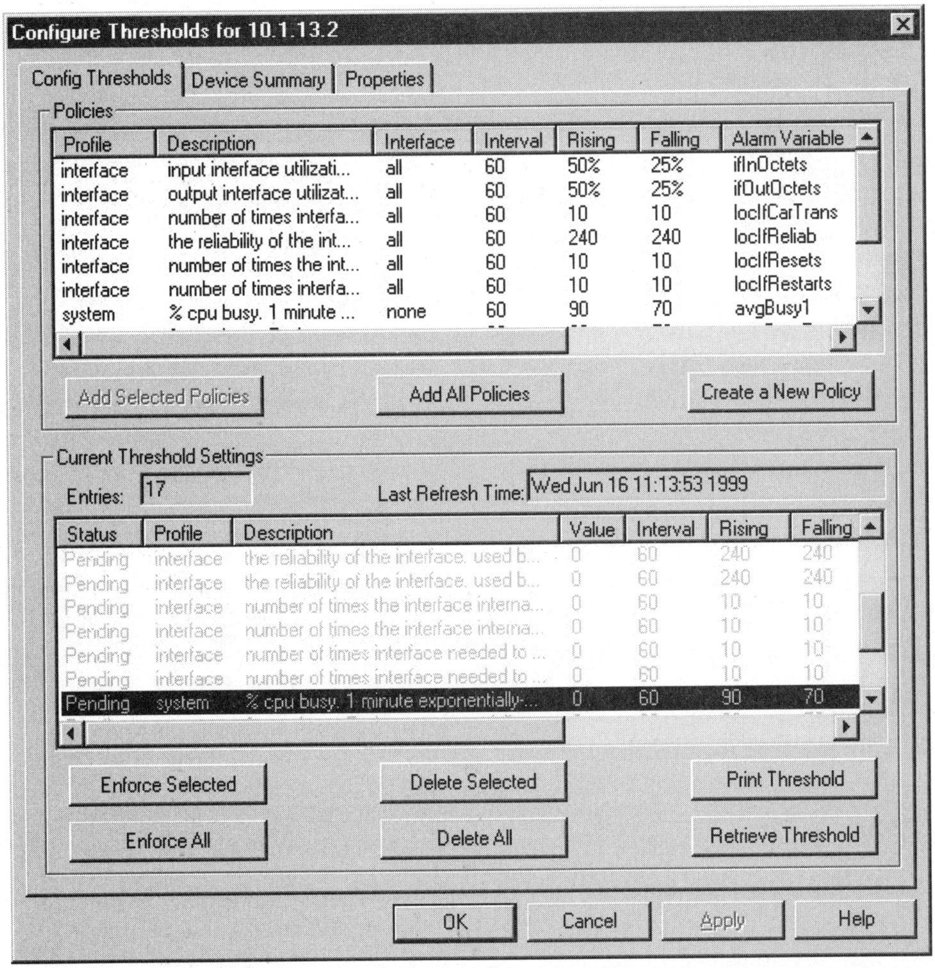

Configure Thresholds for 10.1.13.2

Config Thresholds | Device Summary | Properties

Policies

Profile	Description	Interface	Interval	Rising	Falling	Alarm Variable
interface	input interface utilizati...	all	60	50%	25%	ifInOctets
interface	output interface utilizat...	all	60	50%	25%	ifOutOctets
interface	number of times interfa...	all	60	10	10	locIfCarTrans
interface	the reliability of the int...	all	60	240	240	locIfReliab
interface	number of times the int...	all	60	10	10	locIfResets
interface	number of times interfa...	all	60	10	10	locIfRestarts
system	% cpu busy. 1 minute ...	none	60	90	70	avgBusy1

[Add Selected Policies]   [Add All Policies]   [Create a New Policy]

Current Threshold Settings

Entries: 17   Last Refresh Time: Wed Jun 16 11:13:53 1999

Status	Profile	Description	Value	Interval	Rising	Falling
Pending	interface	the reliability of the interface. used b...	0	60	240	240
Pending	interface	the reliability of the interface. used b...	0	60	240	240
Pending	interface	number of times the interface interna...	0	60	10	10
Pending	interface	number of times the interface interna...	0	60	10	10
Pending	interface	number of times interface needed to ...	0	60	10	10
Pending	interface	number of times interface needed to ...	0	60	10	10
Pending	system	% cpu busy. 1 minute exponentially-...	0	60	90	70

[Enforce Selected]   [Delete Selected]   [Print Threshold]

[Enforce All]   [Delete All]   [Retrieve Threshold]

[OK]   [Cancel]   [Apply]   [Help]

Figure 9-30.   SNMP event thresholds tolerances are set to monitor operations

object before a new abnormal report—event—can take place. Otherwise, an unlimited number of events would be generated during the time the sampled statistic is above the threshold value.

An event causes a trap message to be sent. You have an option to either log a type of event to a file or trigger an alarm on the NMS console.

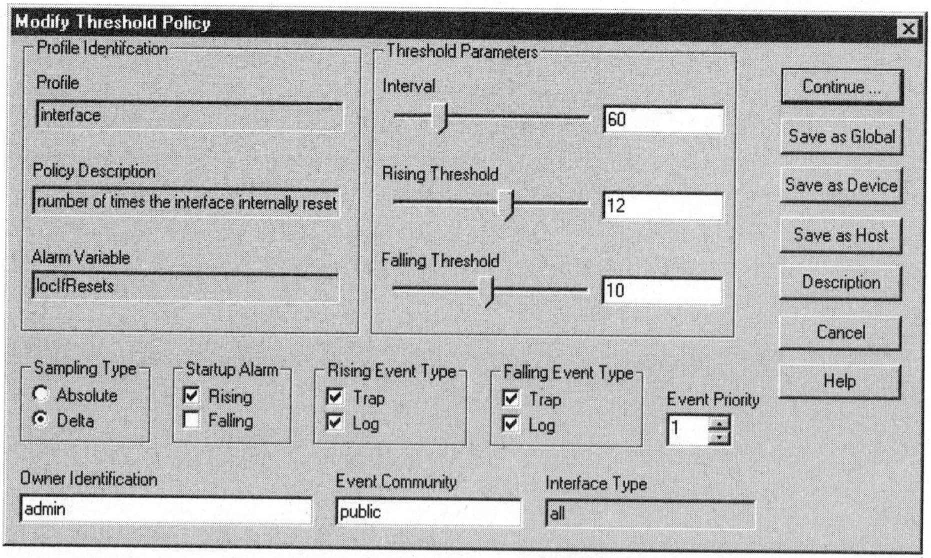

Figure 9-31. Event thresholds are the basis for most network management

HOW CISCO IMPLEMENTS SNMP Cisco implements SNMP and RMON in a three-tier arrangement. At the top is the profile, in the middle are threshold policy files, and at the bottom are the actual policies.

A *profile* is a group of threshold policy files covering the community of managed devices. Threshold Manager supports three types of standard profiles:

▼ **System** Threshold policy files to track system-level information, such as CPU capacity events, available memory, buffer failures caused by lack of memory, and so on.

■ **Interface** Threshold policy files specific to an interface, such as the number of connections, internal resets, and so on.

▲ **Ethernet statistics** Threshold policy files to collect operational totals, such as Ethernet collisions detected, fragmented packets, and so on.

A policy file is a collection of one or more policies that define threshold values for specific MIB variables. Cisco ships 18 standard policy files that cover the most commonly monitored variables. They come with default threshold values, but can be customized if desired. Table 9-2 lists the standard policy files and shows the kinds of issues network administrators deal with on a daily basis. (Going back to Chapters 4 and 5, you'll recognize the *if* mnemonic as standing for interface.)

Threshold Policy File	Description	Default Threshold
avgBusy5	Average CPU utilization during last five minutes	90%
avgBusy1	Average CPU utilization during last minute	70%
etherStatsOctets	Ethernet segment utilization (RMON Ethernet statistics group)	50%
freeMem	Free DRAM memory	Falling 500K
ifInOctets	Utilization of input bandwidth on an interface	50%
ifOutOctets	Utilization of output bandwidth on an interface	50%
locIfCarTrans	Number of carrier transitions on an interface	10/minute
locIfReliab	Reliability of an interface expressed as a score within a defined worst-to-best range of values	Falling 240
locIfResets	Number of resets on an interface	10/minute
locIfRestarts	Number of restarts on an interface	10/minute
bufferFail	Buffer allocation failures	5/half-minute
bufferNoMem	Buffer creation failures	5/half-minute
etherStatsPkts	Ethernet packets	500/second
etherStatsCRC-AlignErrors	Ethernet segment alignment errors (RMON Ethernet Statistics group)	50/minute
etherStats-Collisions	Ethernet segment collision errors (RMON Ethernet Statistics group)	50/minute
etherStats-UndersizePkts	Ethernet segment size too small errors (RMON Ethernet Statistics group)	50/minute
etherStats-Oversize Pkts	Ethernet segment size too large errors (RMON Ethernet Statistics group)	50/minute
etherStats-Fragments	Fragmented packet errors (RMON Ethernet Statistics group)	50/minute

Table 9-2. Cisco Ships Devices with 18 Default Event Threshold Policy Files

Resource Manager Essentials Applications

Six applications are packaged with Essentials:

▼ **Availability**   A device's recent track record for availability and response time

■ **Change Audit**   What was changed in a config file, who made the change, when it was made, and from which management application

■ **Device Configuration**   Tools to centrally search and manage config files

■ **Inventory**   Central repository of all data stored on every device in the network, updated automatically

■ **Software Management**   Tools for managing and upgrading IOS images and other Cisco software products

▲ **Syslog Analysis**   Tools used to keep a running history of network events, and to sort and analyze them in order to diagnose problems

The inventory database is the key to everything. This is where a central record is kept on everything having to do with an individual device: its serial number, what cards it has installed, who's responsible for it, where it is, its IOS version, and so on. Hundreds of data items are stored on every piece of equipment. All CiscoWorks2000 applications revolve around the inventory database.

> **NOTE:**   Essentials has a feature called Report Filters. A *filter* is a reusable format that tells the application what fields to report, and in what order. Filters are used to customize the data that is collected for reports. Instead of specifying the information you want every time you generate a report, a filter can be reused.

Availability Manager

Availability Manager keeps statistics on device reachability and response time. Availability Manager can monitor current status or give an availability history for one or more selected devices. The Reachability Dashboard shows current device availability status down to the interface level. The Protocol Distribution Graph depicts the device as a bar chart or pie chart showing level-3 protocol packet types going through a device—a useful feature because most large internetworks are multiprotocol. The Availability Monitor, shown in Figure 9-32, gives reachability and response time track records for a device.

This report is handy for troubleshooting. When there is a problem in part of an internetwork, the administrator looks at devices in that area for likely suspects. Knowing a device's recent availability track record is usually a pretty good clue.

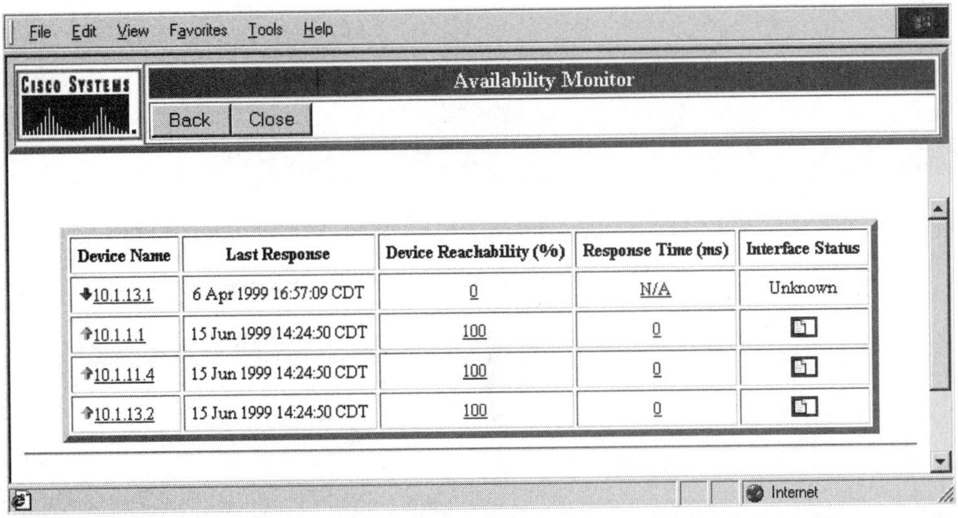

Figure 9-32. A device's track record for reachability and response time can be shown

Configuration Manager

Managing a good-sized internetwork means keeping track of hundreds of config files, and keeping track of parameter settings in that many devices can be a nightmare. Configuration Manager keeps an active archive of config files in all managed devices. *Active* means the database can be updated automatically. Administrators use this application as a search tool and reporting tool. The most popular report is comparing configurations. For example, if a router is having problems, it makes sense to compare its running config file against one that you know is good, to highlight parameter settings that might be causing the trouble.

Change Audit

Essentials automatically maintains a running record of who changed what in a config file. Change Audit is a valuable management tool in big network teams where it can be hard to keep track of things. When something comes up with a config file, before you change it, you want to make sure you're not breaking something that was put in there for a reason of which you're not aware. Change Audit is the place to check before making a change. Figure 9-33 shows the audit history screen.

Even in smaller network teams, it's useful to have a record of something that was done in the past. A busy administrator works on so many devices that it's not possible to remember the reason every setting was made.

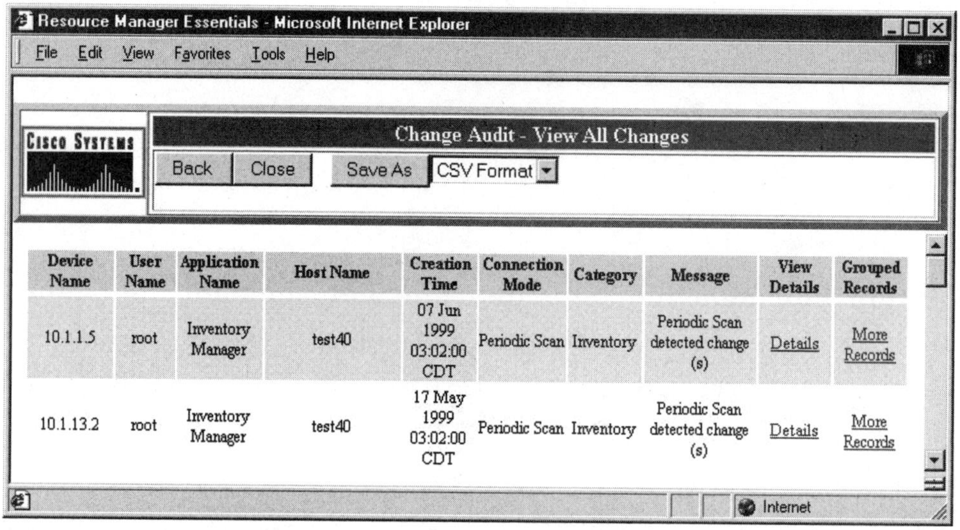

Figure 9-33. A running record is maintained of changes made to config files

Inventory Manager

Inventory Manager is the foundation of CiscoWorks2000. It acts as the central repository for information about devices. Closely related to the Software Manager and Configuration Manager applications, Inventory Manager produces reports and graphs that give the big picture about the devices making up a topology. For example, the Chassis Summary Graph tallies utilization by type of router—a good thing to look at when setting routing protocol metrics to steer traffic through various parts of the topology. Figure 9-34 shows the kinds of basic inventory facts maintained on device inventory.

Inventory Manager can generate reports and graphs by device type, IOS version, domain name, and so on. Cisco leverages its private MIB to report device configurations right down to the chassis slot level.

Inventory data is collected by periodically scanning the network for new devices and changes in existing devices. The scans are usually scheduled to avoid disrupting traffic during business hours. Scanning a big internetwork can take hours and consumes a lot of bandwidth.

Software Manager

Software Manager handles IOS upgrades and troubleshooting. It's not unusual for several version levels of IOS to be in use in an internetwork at the same time. Things are

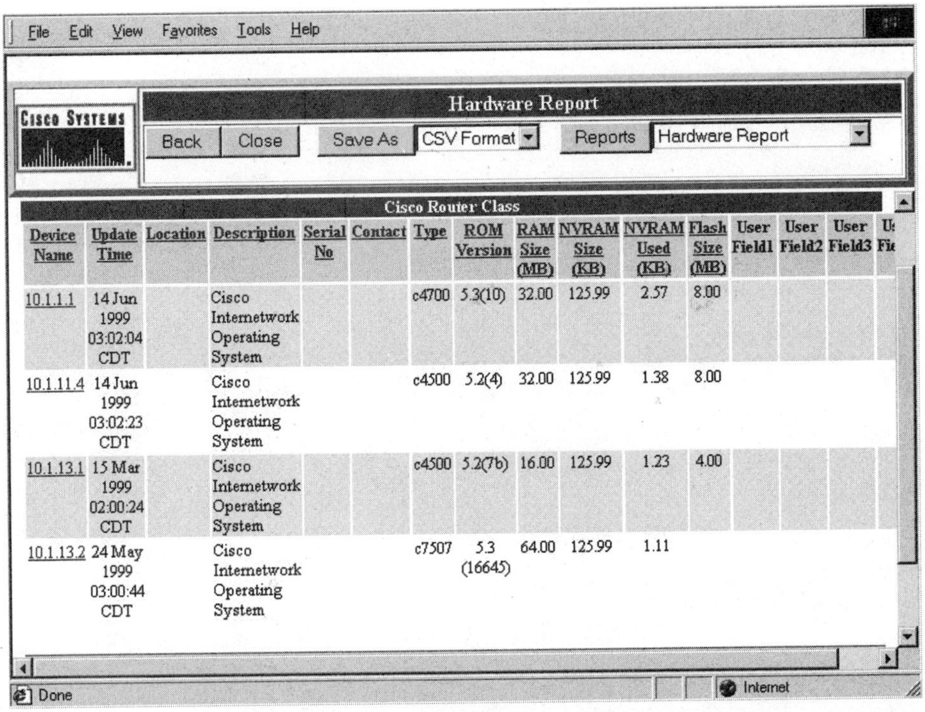

Figure 9-34. Inventory Manager automatically tallies data about network devices

made more complicated by the fact that individual devices are configured with different IOS feature sets. Software Manager performs two main functions:

▼ Analyze IOS images for conflicts both within and between devices.

▲ Maintain a library of IOS software images for downloading and installing onto devices.

Figure 9-35 shows the screen for setting up distribution jobs. Software Manager can deploy an image on more than one device in a single job.

Because of interdependencies, administrators work to keep IOS versions synchronized throughout the network. Because IOS has so many features and options, keeping everything straight can be an enormous job. Software Manager performs dependency checks to make sure the software will work with the hardware on which it's being installed.

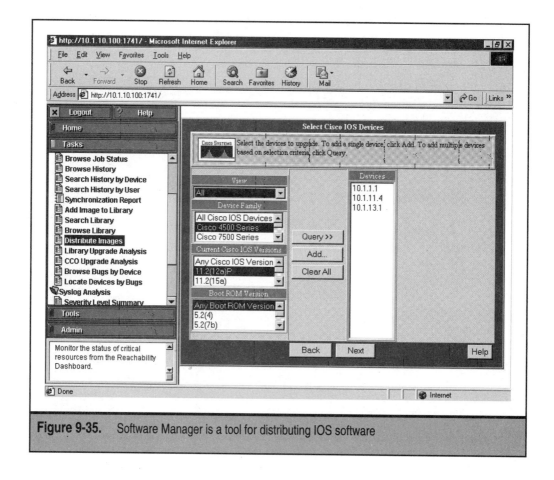

Figure 9-35.   Software Manager is a tool for distributing IOS software

Cisco offers an online upgrade analysis from its Web site. (Again, CCO stands for Cisco Connection Online, the name of the cisco.com site.) Registered customers of CCO can have a device's IOS image analyzed for necessary patches or upgrades. Like any computer company, Cisco releases minor fixes to its operating system on an almost daily basis, and CCO helps customers keep up with changes. For example, if a major bug is found in a certain type of IOS image, CCO Tools can be used to tell where to install the code patch Cisco released as a fix.

Syslog Analyzer

Almost every Cisco device logs unusual events to a system file. Syslog Analyzer automatically collects error messages from devices and uploads them to the Essentials database on the NMS. Syslog Analyzer lets you selectively filter events—such as a link-down or a device reboot—by type and severity level. There are six severity levels, ranging from informational to emergency.

Syslog Analyzer is configurable. For example, you can define how long a device stores error messages, how frequently a remote collector uploads syslog files to the NMS, and so on.

CiscoWorks Switch Internetworks (CWSI)

CiscoWorks for Switched Internetworks is the part of CiscoWorks2000 used to manage switched networks. It's a sister management suite to Essentials. In fact, before you can install CWSI, Essentials must already be installed on the same computer.

Why a separate management suite just for switched networks? Because—as discussed in Chapter 6—a switched network's behavior is fundamentally different from network behavior in normal LANs, which run on truly shared LAN media. This is not so on a switched network where, at any given instant, the medium is shared only between a pair of MAC addresses. If you monitor a routed network, the traffic making up all the logical connections (sessions) are visible to the SNMP agent. On a switched network, sessions are visible only for a series of tiny instants, making them harder to detect. These RMONs provide the sensor instrumentation necessary to monitor switched bandwidth.

CWSI Campus is actually a product from a company called NetScout Systems, and Cisco resells it. Cisco packages it to work closely with Cisco devices by implementing private Cisco MIB and RMON objects into the data discovery process. When CWSI Campus discovers a device configuration or status, it's able to look deeper into the device and measure such things as whether the cooling fan is running, what the air temperature is within the device, and so on. Like Essentials, CWSI Campus uses proprietary protocols to track things: Cisco Discovery Protocol to find hardware, Virtual Trunk Protocol to identify VLANs, and others.

CWSI Campus is an end-to-end solution for switched internetworks that lets network teams monitor switch traffic and view VLANs as they exist atop physical topologies. Also, because it monitors at layer 2—where it sees frames instead of packets—CWSI Campus can monitor ATM (Asynchronous Transfer Mode) transmission media—the network specification of choice for most high-speed backbones.

CWSI Management Applications

CWSI Campus comes in the form of three Director applications:

▼   **VLAN Director**   An interactive tool to display, modify, and manage VLANs.

■   **Traffic Director**   An application that provides usage monitoring for troubleshooting performance problems.

▲   **ATM Director**   Used to work with ATM switches, this application discovers switches, physical links, and virtual circuits, and monitors performance and analyzes traffic within RMON-enabled Cisco ATM switches.

CWSI Campus comes packaged with CiscoView for inspecting individual devices. But the CWSI Campus Map shows the big picture and serves as the interface through which the Director applications are operated.

NOTE: As a reminder, LANE (for LAN Emulation) is a technology that allows an ATM network to function as a LAN backbone. Remember, ATM is a networking specification equivalent to Ethernet or Token Ring, but fundamentally different in its use of fixed-size packets (called *cells*), instead of dynamically sized packets. For ATM to work with another technology, such as Ethernet, it must perform address mapping (MAC-to-ATM) and adapt to the other protocol's most essential conventions (such as Ethernet's rules for managing virtual or permanent circuits).

CWSI CAMPUS MAP   The CWSI Campus Map diagrams switched networks in an interactive color graphical display. Figure 9-36 shows the map as it appears after CWSI Campus has been started and it has completed the network device discovery process. A key function of CWSI Campus is to discover and document all Cisco devices in the network topology. Remember, discovery goes beyond the whole device level to detail individual cards, interfaces, RMONs, and even software. These things constantly change, so network teams rely on tools like CWSI Campus and Essentials to keep things up-to-date.

The CWSI Campus Map can pan, zoom, refresh its contents, drill down into individual devices, and use other navigation techniques. The key to the CWSI interface, however, is filtering. You can see the device and link filters in the Map Highlighting pane to the right of the map. Click the check box next to a type, and that kind of device or link is incorporated into the map. This is good for finding resources. For example, if you're trying to decide where to locate a server that will consume a lot of bandwidth, you might want to filter out all devices except Catalyst 5000 switches to find the throughput power necessary to avoid a bottleneck. In the Map Highlighting window to the right, "C" stands for Catalyst and "LS" for LightStream.

Notice that the list of device types in the upper right-hand corner includes Cisco router model numbers. This is because switched internetwork topologies generally include routers to augment switching intelligence. As covered in Chapter 6, multilayer switching (MLS) is an advanced technique in which routing tables are used to dynamically identify and verify a new optimal path and then "bump" nearby switches to place that path at the top of its MAC address table for use. To configure and monitor a switched network, then, you must be able to view and configure routers in addition to the switches. (In case you're wondering, only the Cisco 4000 and 7000 Series routers currently support MLS.)

The CWSI Campus Map uses filters to control its contents. Five filters are available to select what will be included in the topology:

▼ **Device and link filters**   Displays a specific set of devices or network links, such as all Token Ring networks

■ **VLAN management filter**   Displays a specific VLAN by highlighting it in color on the map

■ **LANE management filter**   Same as the VLAN filter, but displays a specific ATM VLAN by highlighting it in color on the map

■ **Multilayer switching filter**   Displays multilayer switching devices—layer-3 routing devices that act in conjunction with switched networks

▲ **Discrepancy filter**   Displays configuration discrepancies in the network

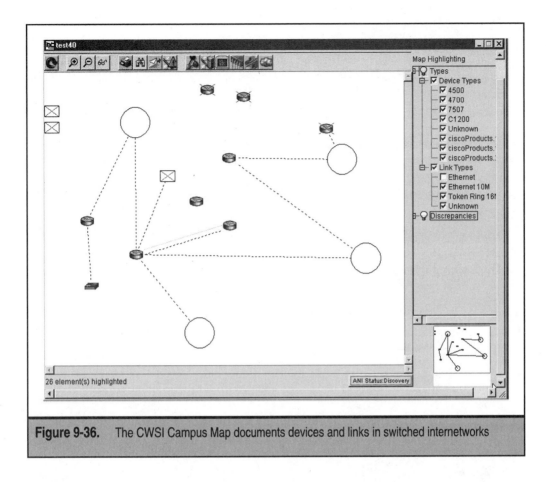

Figure 9-36.   The CWSI Campus Map documents devices and links in switched internetworks

When the VLAN Director application is started, the LANE management and VLAN filters are automatically turned on in the map display. In essence, each Director application takes ownership of the map and populates the diagrammed topology from its perspective.

TRAFFIC DIRECTOR   Traffic Director is a console providing 14 functions. The console, shown in Figure 9-37, is divided into three parts. Hardware can be analyzed by device and even down to the port level. Indeed, many Traffic Director functions—such as App Monitor—*must* have ports selected. Data also can be gathered from a specific RMON agent or a group of agents. In Figure 9-37's example, HTTP traffic is being analyzed for port 04 on switch2900x1. Functional analysis can be performed for a number of things, such as application traffic now or over a historical period, conversations (sessions), and what's called TopN talkers. *TopN* is for the host pair that talked the most during the most recent sampling interval.

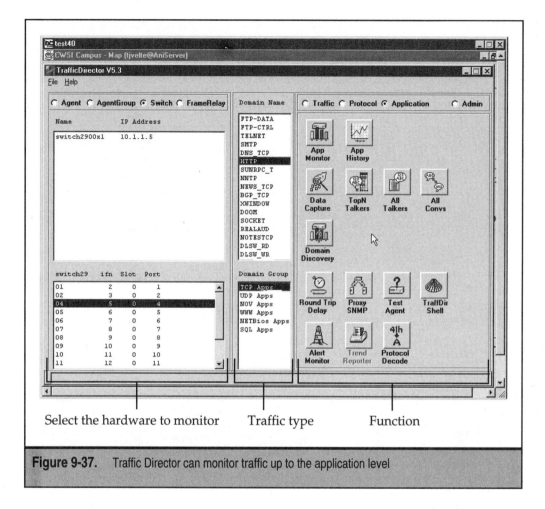

Select the hardware to monitor   Traffic type   Function

Figure 9-37.   Traffic Director can monitor traffic up to the application level

Traffic Director can look at traffic by application, network protocol, and as raw traffic. The buttons in the top half of the Traffic Director console change, depending on which mode is selected. In traffic mode, the App Monitor button shown in Figure 9-37 changes to the Traffic Monitor button—sorting traffic by TCP, UDP, or other low-level traffic types instead of by network application type. In protocol mode, Traffic Director's console changes to let you sort traffic statistics by network protocols such as IP, IPX, AppleTalk, and others.

VLAN DIRECTOR   VLAN Director is used to configure and manage VLANs. Remember, a virtual LAN is not defined by a shared medium such as a hub. It is instead defined by a network administrator, who assigns users VLAN memberships according to enterprise policy. A VLAN cannot be seen by looking at a physical topology map, so a key benefit of CWSI Campus is VLAN Director's ability to discover and display VLAN topologies on the map.

VLAN Director performs the gamut of tasks that must be done to manage virtual LANs: assign membership, look up VLAN switch device statistics, and track movement of end users.

When VLAN Director is on, the map displays Spanning-Tree Protocol (STP) configurations. STP is the control protocol that uses an algorithm to stop loops from appearing as MAC address tables are exchanged between neighbor switches (the equivalent of routing loops, but in a switched internetwork). When performance slows in a switched internetwork, frequently the cause is a looping MAC address that is causing connections to be made over bad paths. When this happens, the network administrator can view the STP information and tweak the settings to steer traffic back in the right direction.

ATM DIRECTOR   ATM Director is used to configure, display, and monitor ATM topologies by displaying virtual channels in the same way VLAN Director displays virtual LANs. Because switched networks are less intelligent than routed ones, network administrators often intercede and manually *merge* or *separate* ATM groupings in order to steer traffic. Figure 9-38 shows ATM Director's dialog box for building a group or fabric of ATM switches.

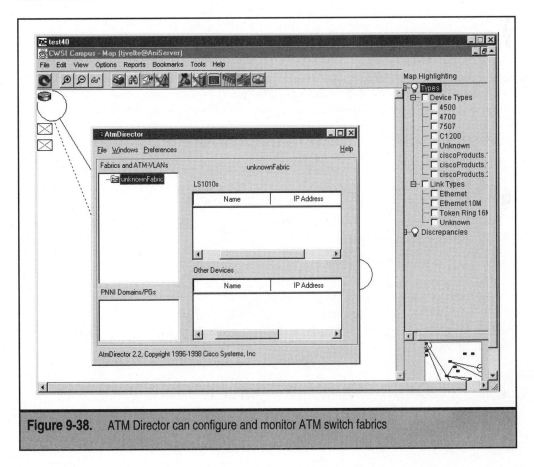

Figure 9-38.   ATM Director can configure and monitor ATM switch fabrics

ATM Director also can be used to assign circuits within fabrics. Remember that in a switched network, a connection (session) is normally made dynamically in the form of a switched virtual circuit, or SVC. But sometimes a permanent virtual circuit (PVC) should be configured. For example, if a pair of communicating hosts exchange heavy traffic over an ATM backbone, a PVC should be configured because it's always busy.

VLANs can be configured and managed using ATM Director. It lets you specify hosts and interfaces to run the LAN Emulation (LANE) translation process. Once configured, LANE clients then talk to a LANE server that provides joining, address resolution, and address registration for the clients in the ATM-VLAN.

NetSys Baseliner

Cisco NetSys Baseliner is a network modeling application used to design and analyze internetworks. A *baseline* is a detailed snapshot taken of an internetwork's configuration at a given point in time. Baselines are used as a starting point from which to model proposed configuration changes. Baselining tools have become popular because configurations can be checked for mistakes prior to actually implementing them.

How Baseliner Differs from Essentials and CWSI

There's a good deal of overlap in functionality with other CiscoWorks2000 applications. For example, Baseliner keeps a history of config file changes much like Change Audit, maintains a device inventory, has an interactive network topology map, and so on. Indeed, it seems that Cisco will, over time, integrate Baseliner more fully into Essentials, where the two share a common map GUI, inventory database, and application functions that are now redundant.

But redundancy aside, Baseliner differs from Essentials in two fundamental ways:

▼ **Config file–based discovery** Baseliner builds a relational database of topologies directly from all device config files, yielding a more complete picture than the one possible via SNMP polling.

▲ **Traffic mapping** The Baseliner topology map displays traffic from different perspectives, such as by routing protocol, network protocol, type of data, and so on.

Baseliner automatically generates a topology map from a database built by using device config files, as shown in Figure 9-39.

After it's built, the baseline can be updated via periodic config file scans and SNMP polling (Baseliner supports the Cisco MIB). The ability to characterize traffic is useful for measuring how efficiently network resources are being utilized. Once a problem area is identified, you can test what-if scenarios by reconfiguring devices in the Baseliner database as if they were actually changed in the physical configuration. Baseliner will "run" the traffic over the modeled configuration and simulate the effect on performance.

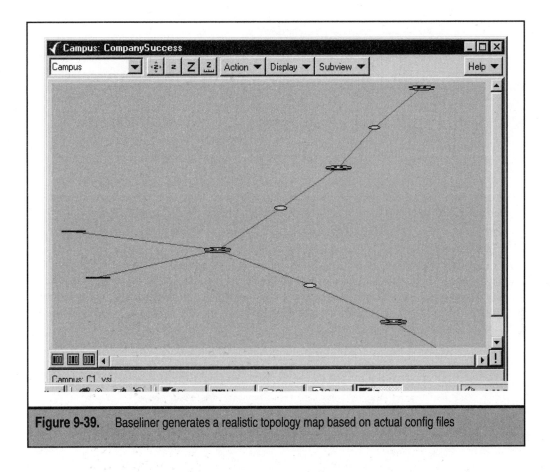

Figure 9-39.   Baseliner generates a realistic topology map based on actual config files

NOTE: To explain the name, Cisco acquired NetSys Technologies a few years ago. Baseliner is just now being integrated into the CiscoWorks2000 suite. It's actually a stand-alone application, although NetSys reports can be accessed from the Essentials Configuration Manager. Like CiscoView and CWSI Campus, Baseliner is not browser based.

Once the baseline is built, Baseliner uses RMON probes and IOS device accounting to instrument network traffic. This enables features to help understand traffic characteristics. For example, reports can be generated identifying high-traffic locations, host pairs that generate the most traffic, and other information. Thanks to its detailed configuration database and heavy instrumentation, Baseliner is able to monitor information at a level not possible using other CiscoWorks2000 applications.

How Baseliner Collects config Files

Collecting config file information is a three-step process. The first task is to physically upload all config files from the topology—using Essentials Inventory Manager's scan function, if you have the CiscoWorks2000 NMS. Then copy the config files into a single directory that Baseliner NMS workstation can access. Finally, start the data acquisition program in Baseliner to read the files into its relational database. The dialog box reporting such collection logs is shown in Figure 9-40.

Using config file data, Baseliner builds a logical representation of the entire network topology. A key benefit of this is that Baseliner can perform integrity checking. It compares the config files and validates their consistency as a whole, and looks for any internal inconsistencies within config files. Baseliner's software targets the common configuration mistakes, greatly reducing the time it takes to isolate and fix problems.

Benefits of Baseliner's Richer Topology Database

Baseliner can do more because it keeps a database built from whole config files instead of SNMP polling. The most obvious benefit of this is that a baseline of an existing network topology's config files makes it possible to model proposed changes, done by altering the config files of preexisting devices and adding new config files to represent devices to be added to the topology.

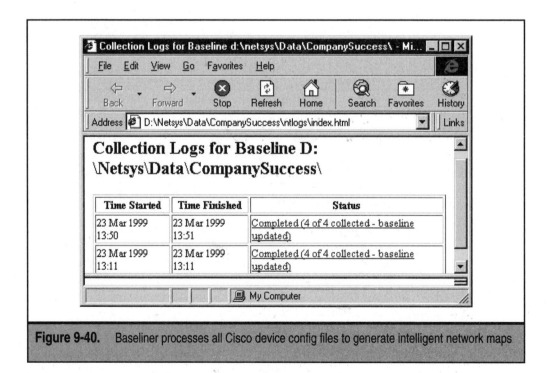

Figure 9-40.   Baseliner processes all Cisco device config files to generate intelligent network maps

Cisco claims that over half of all network problems result from about 100 configuration errors, and Baseliner has built-in logic to automatically identify them. Because it has a complete database of information to work with, Baseliner is able to spot problems by scanning all config files in its database and looking for likely conflicts.

Baseliner can trace connections end-to-end—even into subnets and VLANs, where many topology-mapping tools stop. This means that Baseliner can see beyond the router's subnet mask and all the way to the subnetted host. In other words, Baseliner has sufficient information and intelligence to translate the subnet mask address, find the device, and display it on the topology map.

Perhaps Baseliner's greatest single benefit is its ability to depict routing protocol domains. As discussed in the previous chapter, an internetwork's ability to self-regulate is what makes internetworking possible. But routing protocols themselves must be managed. Baseliner visualizes routing domains and is thereby able to judge how efficiently available bandwidth is being utilized. The value of this is that when a poorly performing link is identified, routing metrics can be tuned to make better use of the resource.

CHAPTER 10

Cisco Security

You may have noticed that Chapter 9's review of management consoles barely mentioned security. That's because network management applications focus strictly on topology design, device configuration, and network performance—not policing bad guys. In fact, network security is so important that it's still handled separately. The industry has never had a chance to really integrate security applications into NMS suites such as HP OpenView or IBM Tivoli.

But network security has a natural conflict with network connectivity. The more an autonomous system opens itself up, the more risk it takes on. This, in turn, requires that more effort be applied to security enforcement tasks. The Computer Security Institute reports that security staff budgets rose 100 percent over the past seven years, and it forecasts similar growth in the foreseeable future. Three trends have increased the bite that security takes out of the IT department's overall budget:

▼ Internetworks are getting bigger and more complicated.

■ New threats are always emerging.

▲ The typical network security system is usually not a system at all, but is a patchwork of vendor-specific tools (sound familiar?).

Network security is so pervasive a consideration that even network management consoles raise concerns. As mentioned in the preceding chapter, some worry about whether the SNMP infrastructure itself is secure enough. After all, stealing the right SNMP community string would give a hacker a road map to an entire internetwork's configuration. And, unless you've been living in a cave, you know about computer viruses spreading in various forms: e-mail bombs, Trojan horse Java applets, denial-of-service attacks, and other worrisome new threats to computer security. Suffice it to say that a lot of time, money, and effort go into network security.

In Chapter 7, we reviewed Cisco's Internet access products. The focus there was mainly on how firewalls and even routers monitor internetwork traffic at the packet level to provide security. Traffic-based security runs on firewalls and routers, and deals mainly in IP addresses.

But a second kind of security operates at the *people* level. This kind of security, called *user-based security*, employs passwords and other login controls to authenticate users' identities before they are permitted access. There are two basic types of user-based security:

▼ End-user remote access to servers, in which employees dial into their enterprise internetworks and subscribers dial into their Internet service providers (ISPs)

▲ Network administrator access to network devices, in which technicians log into IOS on various kinds of network devices in order to work on them

Security is the third major control system in internetworking, along with network management systems and routing protocols. Although the three control systems have distinct missions, as we cover CiscoSecure you'll see a familiar pattern:

▼ **Embedded commands** Application commands built directly into IOS that are used to configure individual devices to participate in a larger network control system

■ **Dedicated control protocol** A communications protocol that coordinates the exchange of messages needed to perform the network control system's tasks

▲ **Server and console** A server to store the messages and a workstation to provide the human interface through which the network control system is operated

Figure 10-1 illustrates the common architecture shared by network control systems. Looking at the figure, you see two new names listed next to SNMP—TACACS+ and RADIUS. These are the protocols used for security, not management, as is SNMP, but they're analogous in how they operate: data is gathered from network devices and stored in a central database, and a console is used to configure devices from a central management workstation. Network management and security systems differ in what they do, but are basically the same in how they work.

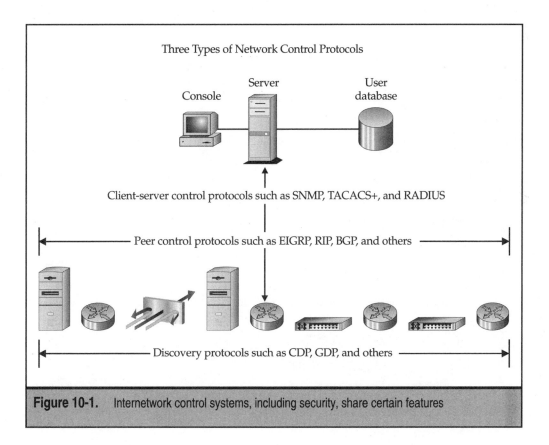

Figure 10-1. Internetwork control systems, including security, share certain features

The third internetwork control system, routing protocols, differs sharply. Routing protocols don't use servers because the information—route tables—is transient and doesn't need to be stored on disk. And they don't use consoles because they are largely self-operating.

The structural similarities between network management and security will make it easier to understand network security technology. Just swap in new names for protocols (TACACS+ and RADIUS) and consoles (CiscoSecure), and you understand the general setup.

OVERVIEW OF NETWORK SECURITY

There are two kinds of network security. One kind is enforced as a background process not visible to users; the other is in your face:

▼ **Traffic-based security**   Controls connections requested by a network application, such as a Web browser or an FTP download

▲ **User-based security**   Controls admission of individuals to systems in order to start applications once inside, usually by user and password

One kind of traffic-based security is the use of firewalls to protect autonomous systems by screening traffic from untrusted hosts. The other kind of traffic-based security is router access lists, used to restrict traffic and resources within an autonomous system. User-based security is concerned with people, not hosts. This is the kind of security with which we're all familiar—login-based security that asks you for a username and password.

The two types complement one another yet operate at different levels. Traffic-based security goes into action when you click a button in a Web browser, enter a command into an FTP screen, or use some other application command. User-based security asserts itself when an individual tries to log into a network, device, or service offered on a device.

Traffic-Based Security

Traffic-based security is implemented in a Cisco internetwork by using firewalls or router access lists. This style of security—covered in Chapter 7—focuses mainly on source and destination IP addresses, application port numbers, and other packet-level information that can be used to restrict and control network connections.

Until recently, firewalls have focused strictly on guarding against intruders from outside the autonomous system. However, they're now coming into use in more sophisticated shops to restrict access to sensitive assets from the inside. Access lists have been the traditional tool used to enforce intramural security.

Access List Traffic-Based Security

Routers can be configured to enforce security in much the same way firewalls do. All routers have access lists, and they can be used to control what traffic may come and go through the router's network interfaces, and what applications may be used if admitted. What exactly an access list does is left to how it's configured by the network administrator.

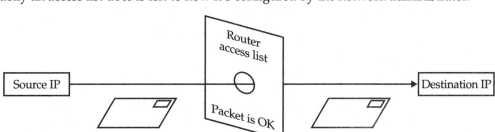

Mostly, access lists are used to improve network performance by isolating traffic in its home area. But a heavily configured access list can pretty much behave like an internal firewall, restricting traffic among departments.

Firewall Traffic-Based Security

Firewalls are basically beefed-up routers that screen processes according to strict traffic management rules. They use all sorts of tactics to enhance security: address translation to hide internal network topology from outsiders; application layer inspection to make sure only permitted services are being run; even high/low counters that watch for any precipitous spikes in certain types of packets to ward off denial-of-service attacks such as SYNflood and FINwait.

Harking back to Chapter 7, remember that firewalls intentionally create a bottleneck at the autonomous system's perimeter. As traffic passes through, the firewall inspects packets as they come and go through the networks attached to its interfaces.

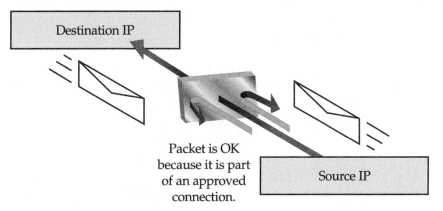

Firewalls read source and destination host addresses, port numbers (for example, port 80 for HTTP), and establish a context for each permitted connection. The context comes in the form of a session, where packets with a certain address pair and port number must belong to a valid session. For example, if a user tries to connect to a Web server to download a file, the firewall will check the user's source IP address and the application service requested before permitting the packets to pass.

Think of traffic-based security as being like those "easy pass" automated tollbooths now going into use on major toll roads. Vehicles are funneled through a gateway where a laser reads each electronic ID, barely slowing the flow of traffic.

User-Based Security

User-based security evokes a different picture—this one of a gate with a humorless security guard standing at the post. The guard demands to know who you are and challenges you to prove your identity. If you qualify, you get to go in. More sophisticated user-based security systems also have the guard ask what you intend to do once inside and issue you a coded visitor's badge giving you access to some areas, but not others.

Thus, user-based security is employed where a person must log into a host, and the security comes in the form of a challenge for your username and password. In internetworking, this kind of security is used as much to keep bad guys from entering network devices such as routers or switches, as it is to restrict access to payload devices, such as servers.

Unlike firewalls, however, user-based security is nearly as concerned with insiders as outsiders. That security guard at the gate has colleagues on the inside, there to make sure nobody goes into the wrong area. You know the routine—there are employee badges and there are visitor badges, but the employee badges let you go more places.

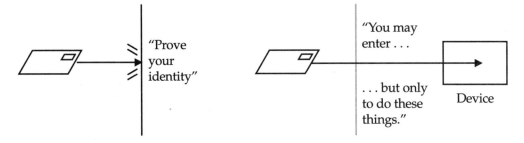

Login/password points are generally placed on every network device and all servers. Because user-based security mechanisms are software, not hardware, they can be deployed at will within an internetwork with little impact on performance or budget. The trade-off is how much inconvenience you're willing to put network users through, having to log in to gain access to various services. User-based security has four major applications:

▼ To grant remote employees access to the enterprise internetwork

■ To grant on-site employees access to protected hosts and services within the internetwork

■ To let network administrators log into network devices

▲ To let ISPs grant subscribers access to their portals

Because most user-based security involves remote dial-in connections, WAN technologies play an important role. The two most important pieces in WAN connections are access servers and dial-in protocols.

Access Servers

Entering an internetwork via a dial-in connection is almost always done through an access server. The access server is a dedicated device that fields phone calls from remote individuals trying to establish a connection to a network. *Access servers* are also called *network access servers* or *communication servers*. Their key attribute is to behave like a full-fledged IP host on one side, but like a modem on the other side. Figure 10-2 depicts the role access servers play in dial-in connections.

When you connect to an internetwork's host from the enterprise campus, you usually do so over a dedicated twisted-pair cable that is connected to a hub or a switch. To make that same connection from afar, you usually do so over a normal telephone line through an access server—a device that answers the phone call and establishes a network connec-

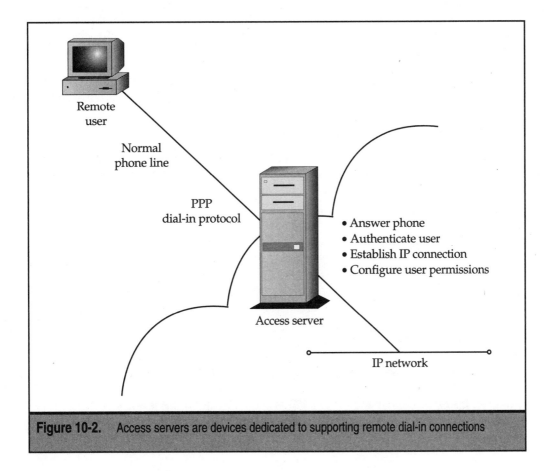

Figure 10-2. Access servers are devices dedicated to supporting remote dial-in connections

tion. Besides making connections for remote dial-in users, access servers can also be used to connect remote routers; we'll cover this in the next chapter.

USER-BASED SECURITY FOR LOCAL CONNECTIVITY   When you turn on your PC and log in at work, you're not dealing with TACACS+ or RADIUS. The username and password prompts are coming from your local server. Most LAN servers run Novell NetWare, UNIX, or Windows NT platforms. They have security subsystems and user databases of their own to authenticate and authorize users. RADIUS isn't used because it's a dial-in password protocol. TACACS+ isn't used because it controls entry into the Cisco network devices themselves—routers, switches, and access servers—in addition to providing dial-in security much like RADIUS.

In this chapter, discussions of local or "in-network" connections refer to network administrators logging into IOS to work on a Cisco network device.

USER-BASED SECURITY FOR REMOTE CONNECTIVITY   Small office and home office users tap into their enterprise internetworks via an access server, making it perhaps the most basic device in any wide area network. Low-end access servers are inconspicuous desktop devices resembling a PC without a monitor. When you dial into your ISP to get into the Internet from home, the call is also answered by an access server. As you might imagine, an ISP's computer room is jammed with rack-mounted high-density access servers to handle connections made from thousands of subscribers. (As a reminder, *high density* means many ports per device.)

Access servers are intelligent devices that handle other tasks in addition to making a line connection. They provide special services to accommodate configurations frequently encountered in enterprise internetworks:

▼ **Routing service**   Run by access servers called *access routers*, this makes it seem as if the dial-in user is sitting directly on the campus network. The key feature of access routers is dial-on-demand routing (DDR), which makes it possible to route traffic from a remote LAN to the main network over low-cost dial-up phone lines.

■ **Terminal service**   Many WAN connections still use terminal protocols. For that reason, most access servers support terminal protocols such as IBM's TN3270, UNIX rlogin, or Digital Equipment's Local-Area Transport (LAT). A PC could run terminal emulation software to make such a connection.

▲ **Protocol translation**   A remote user may be running a virtual terminal protocol and then connect to a system running another virtual terminal protocol. Most access servers still support protocol translation.

As computing infrastructure improves, terminal service and protocol translation are declining in use. In contrast, access routers are increasing in popularity as small offices build LANs of their own and turn to DDR for convenience and savings.

Dial-in Protocols

As you've learned by now, there's a protocol for just about every major internetworking task. Making dial-in network connections work properly presents special problems because most telephone company infrastructure was designed to handle voice, not high-speed data. Dial-in protocols exist to handle the point-to-point dial-in connections over normal telephone lines.

- ▼ **PPP**   The Point-to-Point Protocol is the de facto standard for remote dial-in connections to the IP networks; virtually all dial-in connections to the Internet use PPP. Most PPP connections are over asynchronous lines, but a growing number are made over ISDN in areas where it's available.

- ■ **SLIP**   The Serial Line Internet Protocol is also used to make point-to-point dial-in connections to IP networks from remote sites. SLIP is the predecessor to PPP, but is still in use in some quarters. You may also encounter a SLIP variant called CSLIP, the Compressed Serial Line Internet Protocol.

- ▲ **ARAP**   The AppleTalk Remote Access Protocol is Apple's tool for dial-in connectivity to remote AppleTalk networks.

In the old days, to make a remote connection, you dialed into a PBX to connect to a mainframe or minicomputer as a dumb terminal. With the rise of internetworking, network-attached terminal servers took over the job of taking dial-in calls. As demand for remote computing grew still more, simple terminal connections were replaced by those made using the SLIP protocol. By that point, many desktops had PCs instead of terminals, but they emulated terminals in order to make dial-in connections. The boom in demand for Internet connectivity drove the market to replace SLIP with PPP, a protocol even more capable of computer-to-computer communications over phone lines. For our purposes, we'll assume PPP as the dial-in protocol unless otherwise noted.

AUTHENTICATION, AUTHORIZATION, AND ACCOUNTING (AAA)

The framework for user-based security is called authentication, authorization, and accounting (AAA), pronounced *triple-a*. The AAA framework is designed to be consistent and modular in order to give network teams flexibility in implementing the enterprise's network security policy.

NOTE: Network security systems like CiscoSecure control access to LAN segments, lines, and network applications such as HTTP and FTP. Network access devices—usually access servers and access routers—control access to these network-based services. But an additional layer of security is sometimes configured into the server platform once it is reached. For example, an IBM mainframe will enforce security policy using its own mechanisms. Security for computer platforms and major application software packages is still performed using self-contained security systems resident in the application server, in addition to the network access device security measures covered in this chapter.

Overview of the AAA Model

AAA's purpose is to control who is allowed access to network devices and what services they are allowed to use once they have access. Here is a brief description of the AAA model's three functional areas:

▼ **Authentication** Validate the user's identity as authentic before granting the login.

■ **Authorization** Grant the user the privilege to access networks and commands.

▲ **Accounting** Collect data to track usage patterns by individual user, service, host, time of day, day of week, and so on.

Thankfully, the acronym makers put the three functions in sequential order, making the AAA concept easier to pick up: first, you're allowed to log in (your identity is authenticated); then you have certain privileges to use once you're in (you have predetermined authorizations); and finally, a running history is kept on what you do while logged in (the network team keeps an account of what you do).

The philosophy is to let network teams enforce security policy on a granular basis. Most AAA parameters can be put into effect per LAN segment, per line (user), and per protocol—usually IP.

AAA is a clearly defined security implementation framework that everybody can understand. The architecture is defined down to the command level. Indeed, the AAA concepts are actual IOS commands. Starting an AAA process on a Cisco device involves using the **aaa** prefix followed by one of the three root functions, such as **aaa authentication**. A whole AAA command line might read **aaa authentication ppp RemoteWorkers tacacs+ local**, for example. The purpose of AAA is to provide the client-side command structure on which CiscoSecure relies.

AAA Modularity

A security policy is a set of principles and rules adopted by an enterprise to protect system resources, confidential records, and intellectual property. It's the network manager's responsibility to implement and enforce the policy. But in the real world, security policy can get dragged down into the mire of office politics, budget constraints, and impatience. An end-user manager can have a lot of clout as to how the policy will be conducted on his or her turf. After all, the company, not the IT department, funds the network. Consequently, there can be a lot of variance among security policies—even within an enterprise's internetwork.

This means that security policies must be highly adaptable. CiscoSecure tries to satisfy this need with modularity—the ability to separately apply security functions by secured entity, independent of how they are applied to other resources. The AAA architecture gives you the option to implement any of the three functions independent of the other two. This includes whether they're activated on a device, which security protocol is used, and what security server or user database is accessed.

AUTHENTICATION CONTROLS   The **aaa authentication** command validates a user's identity at login. But once you're authenticated, exactly what can you access? That depends on the type of access being made:

▼ If you're a network administrator logging into a switch to tweak its config file, the authentication gets you into that switch's IOS command prompt.

■ If you're an employee sitting inside the enterprise and you were authenticated by a router, you get into a protected host to run Windows or browser-based internetwork client-server applications.

■ If you're a telecommuter and you were authenticated by an access server, you're admitted to your enterprise's internetwork to run the same client-server applications.

▲ If you dialed into the Internet from home, as a member of the general public, you were authenticated by one of your ISP's many access servers, and you enter the World Wide Web.

Security must protect three destination environments: the Internet, the internetwork, and most of all the internal operating system of the devices over which internetworks run. Figure 10-3 illustrates access types and destination environments.

The scenario of the network administrator logging into IOS devices is unique. In Cisco internetworks, that type of access is usually authenticated using TACACS+. Other types of access open into a Windows- or HTTP-based application service. Network administrators access a device's IOS environment in order to perform device maintenance tasks.

Users also require different dial-in services. Although almost everybody uses PPP nowadays, there still can be different requirements. Depending on the local network from which the call is made, different PPP services may be required, such as IP, IPX, NetBUI, or just a plain terminal connection.

Whatever the issues may be, different requirements often call for a variety of authentication methods to be used in the same internetwork. CiscoSecure lets the network manager employ any of the major dial-in protocols and authentication techniques. In addition, it supports the ability to apply these different tools by network interface or line—even on the same device.

AUTHORIZATION CONTROLS   AAA authorization limits services to the user. In other words, if authorization has been activated on a secured entity using the **aaa authorization** command, users must be explicitly granted access to it.

The person's user profile is usually stored in the security server and sometimes also in the device's local user database. When the administrator logs into the device and his or her user profile is checked, the device configures the authorizations to know what commands to allow the administrator to use during that session. Commands can be authorized by IOS command mode (the **MyRouter>** versus **MyRouter#** prompts) or by specific commands within a mode. Figure 10-4 lays out some of the various forms authorizations can take.

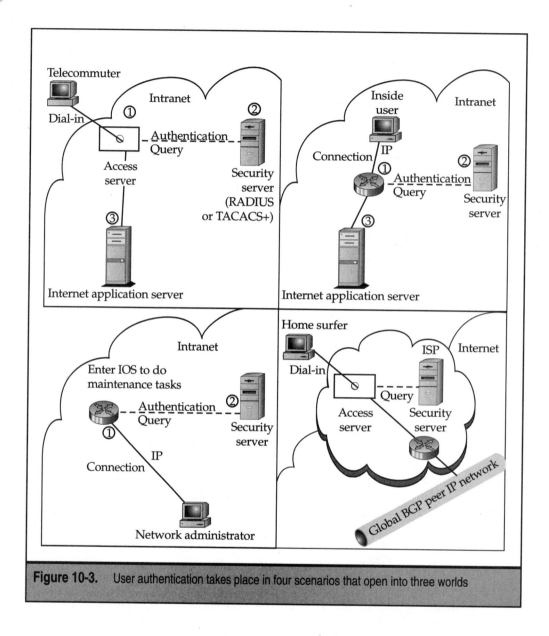

Figure 10-3. User authentication takes place in four scenarios that open into three worlds

Authorization can be more complicated than authentication. After you've been authenticated, the security server must supply the access device configuration information specific to the user—for example, which networks the user may access, which applications may be run, which commands are OK to use, and so on. Without centralized maintenance of authorization information, it wouldn't be practical to assign authorizations by user (it's hard enough just to keep usernames and passwords up-to-date).

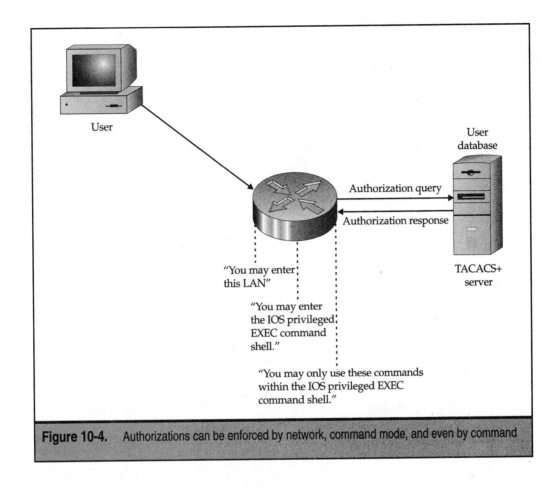

Figure 10-4. Authorizations can be enforced by network, command mode, and even by command

NOTE: In the context of AAA network authorization, a *network* is a LAN segment and a *line* is a virtual connection made to a device's operating system, usually through a so-called VTY—virtual terminal—line.

MODULAR ACCOUNTING CONTROLS Accounting doesn't permit or deny anything, but instead keeps a running record of what users do. AAA accounting is a background process that tracks the person's logins and network use. Figure 10-5 shows how AAA security accounting tracks resource usage.

AAA accounting reflects events as they take place in entering systems and using services. Thus the accounting commands more or less mirror the others. For example, accounting tasks can be enabled by system, command mode, network device interface, protocol, and connection—just like authorization commands.

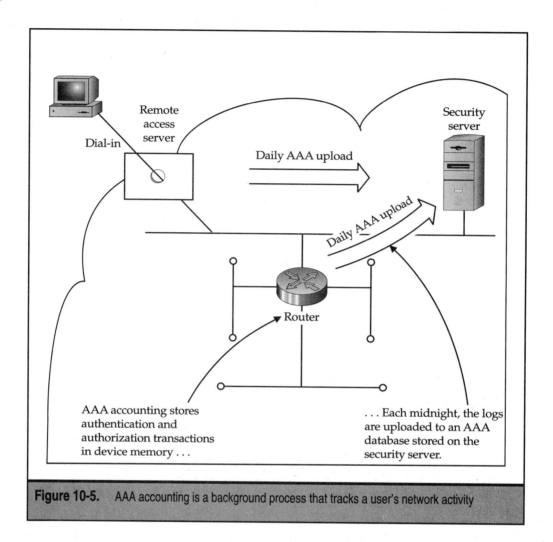

Figure 10-5. AAA accounting is a background process that tracks a user's network activity

---

NOTE: By default, AAA defines IOS as having two command modes: the user EXEC mode (sometimes also called Shell) and the privileged EXEC modes. The IOS **level** command can be used to further divide things in up to 16 command levels (numbered 0–15), so access to commands can be authorized on a more fine-grained basis.

Trends Leading to Client-Server Security Systems

As with most network control systems, AAA uses the client-server model to manage security. In other words, there is a central security server holding the user profile information used by client access devices to enforce security. When a user makes a request to connect to a network, line, or service, the client device queries the server to check if it's

OK. Centralization is necessary because it's no longer feasible to administer security one access device at a time; there are simply too many of them to keep track of.

In the 1970s, a natural by-product of remote users dialing into central mainframes was that user security profiles (accounts, passwords, and authorizations) were stored right there on the same computer where all the services sat. This made it easy for the security system to check on user permissions. Then, in the 1980s, departmental minicomputers became popular, spreading computers out into the organization. Terminal servers were invented to provide the additional entry points the distributed topologies required, but user databases were now spread across many access devices—making it much tougher to maintain the security system. By the time IP-based networking took off, it became apparent that security information had to be centralized. Figure 10-6 depicts this trend.

The rise of internetworking demands that an enterprise offer dial-in access throughout the organization. Doing so presents problems for enforcing consistent security controls across so many access servers. The AAA architecture is Cisco's game plan for meeting theses challenges.

AAA's Two Security Protocols: TACACS+ and RADIUS

It's possible to use AAA security on a stand-alone basis, with no central security database. In the real world, few do this because it would require the extra effort of maintaining security parameters on a device-by-device basis—a labor-intensive and mistake-prone proposition. IOS supports stand-alone security because in some cases a security server is unavailable, for example, in a very small internetwork or during the period of time when a security server is being implemented but is still not operable.

AAA configures access devices as clients. Client devices include access servers, routers, switches, and firewalls. The clients query one or more security servers to check whether user connections are permitted. To do this, a protocol is needed to specify rules and conventions to govern the exchange of information. AAA security can use two protocols to handle client-server security configurations:

▼ **RADIUS** A security protocol used mainly for authentication. RADIUS stands for Remote Dial-in User Service. RADIUS is an industry standard under the auspices of the IETF.

▲ **TACACS+** A proprietary Cisco protocol that is largely the equivalent of RADIUS, but with stronger integration of authorization and accounting with authentication. Cisco has submitted TACACS+ to the IETF for consideration as a security protocol standard.

NOTE: There is a third security protocol called Kerberos. Developed at MIT, Kerberos is an emerging open standard for secret-key authentication that uses the Data Encryption Standard (DES) cryptographic algorithm. Although more difficult to implement and administer, Kerberos is gaining in popularity in internetworks more sensitive to security. Its key benefits are that it can function in a multivendor network like RADIUS, but it doesn't transmit passwords over the network (it passes so-called *tickets* instead). IOS includes Kerberos commands in its AAA framework.

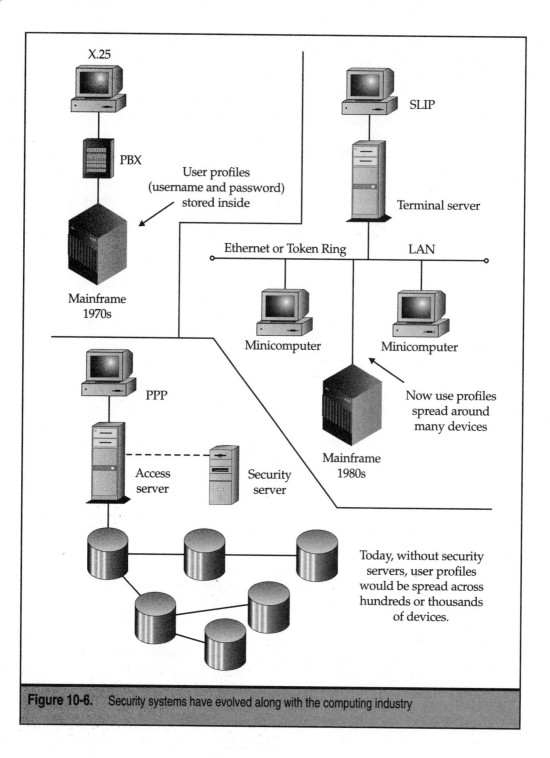

Figure 10-6. Security systems have evolved along with the computing industry

How AAA Works

AAA is the security infrastructure of IOS devices. AAA commands are located in the IOS privileged EXEC mode. Each client device is configured for security using the AAA commands from global configuration mode. Properly configured, the device can then make use of the CiscoSecure server via either the TACACS+ or RADIUS security protocols—or both.

In fact, AAA commands can be used stand-alone to secure a device. In other words, the device can use a local user database stored in NVRAM on the device itself, instead of one on a RADIUS or TACACS+ server. However, this is rarely done because it entails maintaining and monitoring user security data in hundreds or even thousands of device config files instead of in a single database.

TACACS+ and RADIUS are client-server network protocols used to implement client-server security over the network. In that sense they are the equivalent of what SNMP is to network management.

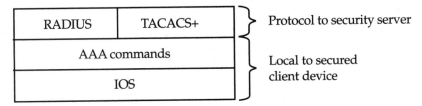

A user database changes every time users are added or deleted, passwords are changed, or authorizations are modified. Separating the user database from device config files reduces the number of places updates must be made. Most internetworks use a primary server and one or two alternate security servers, leaving only a few places in which user profile databases need to be updated.

Ensuring that the user databases contain identical data is called *database synchronization*. This can be done automatically by using Replication Partners in CiscoSecure. In the scenario with three security servers, the three user databases would be configured as replication partners, and the CiscoSecure ACS would automatically synchronize user profile records between the three on a daily basis.

The AAA Approval Process

AAA works by compiling attributes that specify a user's permissions. In the AAA context, an *attribute* is an entity (or object) to which the person may have access. For example, an authentication attribute might be a specific LAN segment to which the person is permitted access. An authorization attribute might be the limit on concurrent connections the person may have open at one time.

When a user attempts to connect to a secured service, the access device checks to see if the user has clearance per the security policy. It does so by sending a query to the server database to look for a match. The secured access device knows what to query for based on its config file parameter settings. The query is to verify that the user has permission to do whatever is being attempted.

ATTRIBUTE-VALUE PAIRS The query contains the attributes that are mandatory for the requested service, as defined in the access device's config file. The server processes the query by searching for the same attributes in the user's profile in the user database. The search is for so-called attribute-values. An attribute, called an *attribute-value pair* (or AV pair) in TACACS+ terminology, is a fancy term for a network entity that is secured.

For example, in someone's user profile the password is an attribute, and the person's actual password, *iamreallyme,* is the value paired with it. When the user enters the password, the access device handling the login first knows to check for a password because to do so is set as a parameter in the device's config file. By checking the person's user profile, it looks for a match between the value entered into the password prompt and what's on file in the user database for the username the person entered. Figure 10-7 shows the AAA procedure for handling a user's request for a connection.

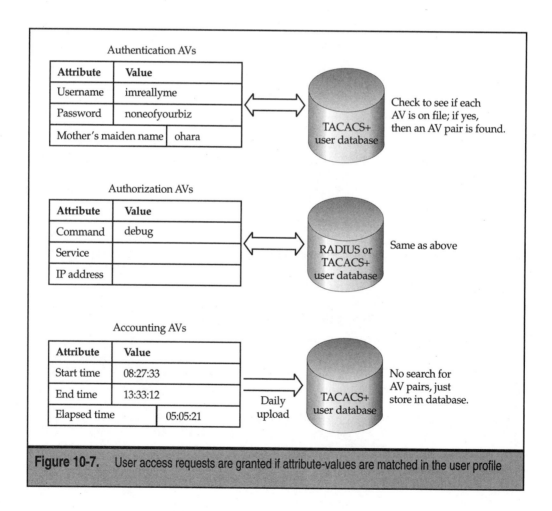

Figure 10-7.   User access requests are granted if attribute-values are matched in the user profile

HOW AAA HANDLES AUTHENTICATION TRANSACTIONS   When the connection is established, the access device contacts the security server to obtain a user prompt and displays
it to the user. The user enters the information (usually just a username and password),
and the protocol (RADIUS or TACACS+) encrypts the packet and sends it to the server.
The server decrypts the information, checks the user's profile, forms and encrypts the response, and returns the response to the access device.

The rules of AAA approval are fairly simple: If an ACCEPT is returned, the requested
connection is made. If a REJECT is returned, the user's request-for-connection session is
terminated. But if an ERROR is returned and the access device is configured for multiple
security servers, the query is then forwarded to an alternate server. If that server also fails
to return a response, the process continues until the query runs out of servers. At that
point, if the access device has been configured with a second method, it will iterate
through the process again, first trying for approval with a query to the primary security
server, and so on. If the access device exhausts authentication methods, it terminates the
user's request-for-connection session.

The CONTINUE response is another optional configuration parameter that prompts
the user for additional information. The prompts can be anything the network administrator arbitrarily defines. For example, prompting users for their mother's maiden name
is a common challenge.

> **NOTE:**   A *daemon* (pronounced either with long *e* or long *a*) is a process that runs on a server to per-
> form a predefined task, usually in response to some event. The term comes from Greek mythology, in
> which daemons were guardian spirits. Daemons are called system agents in Windows parlance. A
> TACACS+ daemon sits on the security server and fields authentication or authorization queries from
> client access devices. It does so by searching the user database for required AV pairs and returning
> the results to the client in TACACS+ packets.

AUTHORIZATION TRANSACTIONS   If the user is authenticated, the daemon is contacted to
check for authorization attributes on a case-by-case basis. Figure 10-8 depicts how authentication and authorization work together.

Authorization attributes can be issued for such services as connection type (login,
PPP, etc.); IOS command modes (user EXEC or privileged EXEC); and various connection
parameters, including host IP addresses, user timeouts, access lists, and so on. Authorization is by nature more sophisticated than authentication. More information than just
username and password is involved, and the attributes have a state. For example, the
Maximum-Time attribute requires the server to keep tabs on how long the user has been
connected, and to terminate the session when the value (number of seconds) for the user
has been exceeded.

Authentication Protocols

CiscoSecure supports a number of authentication mechanisms. Also called *password configurations* or *password protocols*, authentication protocols make sure you are who you say

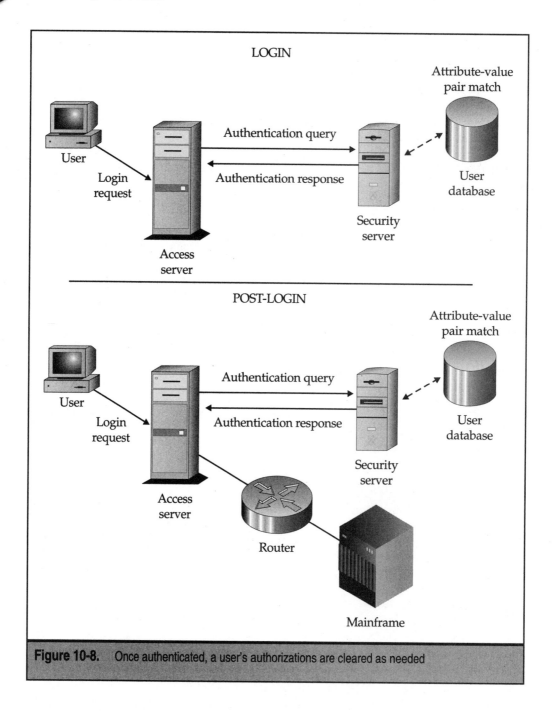

Figure 10-8.   Once authenticated, a user's authorizations are cleared as needed

you are when logging into a system. Here are four major authentication mechanisms supported by AAA:

▼ **ASCII**   American Standard Code for Information Interchange is the oldest authentication protocol. ASCII is a machine-independent technique for representing English characters and has many other uses besides authentication. ASCII authentication requires the user to type in a username and password to be sent in clear text (that is, unencrypted) and matched with those in the user database stored in ASCII format.

■ **PAP**   Password Authentication Protocol is used to authenticate PPP connections. PAP passes passwords and other user information in clear text. You know PAP as a protocol that lets you store your username and password in the dialog box so you don't have to type it during each login.

■ **CHAP**   Challenge Handshake Authentication Protocol provides the same functionality of PAP, but it is much more secure, as it avoids sending the password and other user information over the network to the security server. Figure 10-9 depicts how challenge-response works.

▲ **Token-card**   This authentication technique uses one-time passwords. A token-card is an electronic device a bit larger than a credit card. The card is used to generate an encrypted password that must match one filed for the user in the token-card database residing on the security server. The encrypted password is good for only one use; thus the name *token*. Token-card authentication systems provide the best access security.

AAA also supports NASI (NetWare Asynchronous Services Interface), an authentication protocol built into Novell LANs. Another vendor-specific password protocol is ARAP (AppleTalk Remote Access Protocol), with a double challenge-response authentication mechanism that goes CHAP one better by making the security server authenticate *itself* to the client as well. In addition, there are subtle variations in how the PAP protocol works with Windows NT.

Security comes at a cost—mostly in the form of increased inconvenience to users, but there's also additional expense to deploy and administer security measures. For example, CHAP requires some extra hardware and expertise, and token-cards are cumbersome to deploy. Can you imagine the giant Internet service provider AOL mailing token-cards to every new user and administering a token database of one-time passwords? The added expense and logistical complexity of advanced authentication protocols have discouraged their adoption.

PAP is by far the most widely used authentication protocol because it's simple for users and inexpensive for network operators. When you log into the Internet from home,

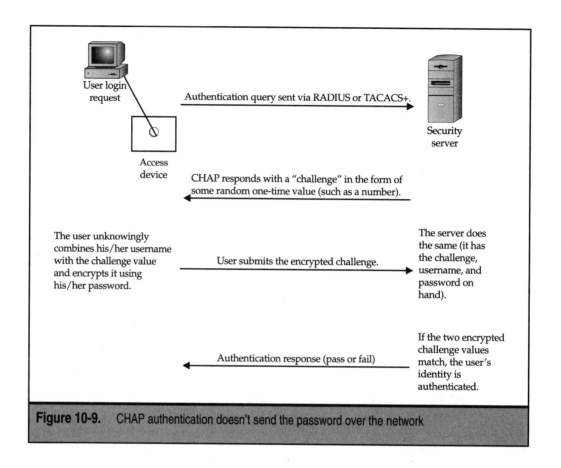

User login request

Authentication query sent via RADIUS or TACACS+.

Security server

Access device

CHAP responds with a "challenge" in the form of some random one-time value (such as a number).

The user unknowingly combines his/her username with the challenge value and encrypts it using his/her password.

User submits the encrypted challenge.

The server does the same (it has the challenge, username, and password on hand).

Authentication response (pass or fail)

If the two encrypted challenge values match, the user's identity is authenticated.

Figure 10-9. CHAP authentication doesn't send the password over the network

you're almost certainly going through a PAP mechanism. Corporate internetworks are more likely to use CHAP. Token-cards are mainly used to protect high-security networks in the military, R&D, or banking. From an ISP's standpoint, preventing a hacker from gaining free Web access isn't worth the trouble and expense of replacing PAP with a better authentication technology.

Methods and Types

Certain pieces must be put in place before security can be enforced. As you just saw, the access device must be configured to query one or more security servers for authentication and authorization, and the user database must have profiles containing attributes that define what the user is permitted to do on the network. But what exactly happens when the query hits the TACACS+ or RADIUS database? What steps are taken to verify the user's identity and figure out what services that person is permitted?

AAA command statements in an access device's config file tell the device what to do when a user tries to log in. The root AAA commands **authenticate**, **authorization**, and **ac-**

counting are used in conjunction with various keywords to code config file instructions on how connection attempts are to be handled. As mentioned earlier, these instruction parameters are modular in that they can be applied per user and per service. The instructions are implemented in the access device's config file using methods and types.

▼ A *method* is a prepackaged computer program that performs a specific function. For example, **radius** is a method to query a RADIUS server.

▲ A *type* is the entity to which the method applies. For example, a **radius** method is applied to a **ppp** type so that when a user attempts to make a connection using the PPP protocol, the access device queries its RADIUS server to authenticate the person's identity.

Because there are almost always multiple security parameters set for a device, AAA configurations are referred to as *named method lists*. They're called *named* methods because they are named by the administrator in the device config file and applied to one or more specific secured entity types. Figure 10-10 shows how named method lists and types work together to enforce security.

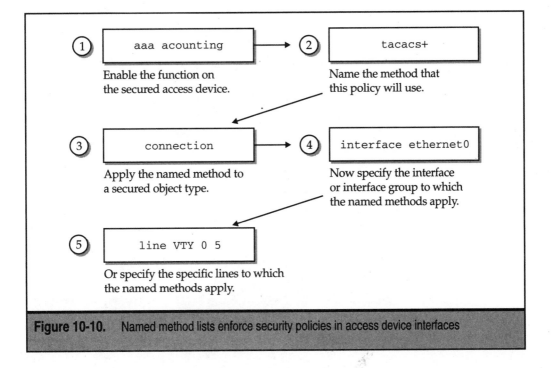

Figure 10-10.   Named method lists enforce security policies in access device interfaces

NOTE: There are unnamed methods in the form of the default method list. If an interface or line has no named method list configured, a default method list is automatically put into force for it. To have no AAA security, you must explicitly configure as such using the **none** method. Cisco makes it hard to have no security in force.

Named method lists are entered into the config file of the access device being secured—usually an access server or a router. IOS applies methods in the sequence in which they appear in the configuration, initially trying the first method and then turning to the following ones until an ACCEPT or REJECT is returned. Figure 10-11 explains a typical named method list.

The last part of the AAA configuration in Figure 10-11 specifies lines because authentication deals with individual users. Traffic-based security can be applied on the interface level because the firewall or router monitors information in the header of each packet—a process that is done either to all or none of the packets passing through an interface. By contrast, user-based security controls individuals as they make a remote network connection via an access server, or log into IOS inside a router or switch within the network. Each of these two scenarios involves using a line.

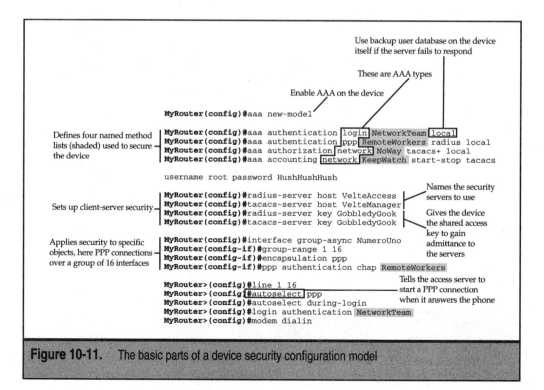

Figure 10-11. The basic parts of a device security configuration model

AAA AUTHENTICATION METHODS AND TYPES   AAA has several methods to authenticate user identity. Only one method may be used per user line (except when the Local method is configured as backup to one of the three client-server methods). Table 10-1 lists Cisco's authentication methods.

The list of AAA methods in Table 10-1 varies slightly according to the password mechanism being used. Remember that AAA is an architectural model that must be adapted to differences in the way other vendors design their products. For example, AAA supports Guest and Auth-Guest methods for the password protocol in Apple's ARAP.

It's possible to configure different authentication methods on different lines within the same access device. For example, you might want to configure PPP connections to query the user database on a RADIUS server, but to check the local user database for login connections made from the console or AUX ports.

CONNECTION TYPES   Because authentication is applied to user lines, named authentication methods are applied to connection types. A *connection type* is the communications protocol used to make a connection. To explain, remote connections to ISPs and internetworks nowadays are usually PPP connections. But when a network administrator logs into IOS in order to work on a device, that connection is via a Telnet session (if

IOS Command Keyword	AAA Authentication Method
RADIUS	Authenticate using the RADIUS protocol and user database.
TACACS+	Authenticate using the TACACS+ protocol and user database.
Krb5	Authenticate using the Kerberos 5 protocol and user database. (Note: Kerberos can only be used with the PAP password protocol.)
Local	Authenticate using a user database stored in memory in the access device, or for backup if the security server does not respond.
Enable	Authenticate using Enable Secret passwords in the access device's config file.
If-needed	Do not require authentication if the user has already been authenticated on a VTY or TTY line.
None	Use no authentication.

Table 10-1.   Authentication Methods in IOS

over the network) or a terminal emulator (if over the console or AUX port). Table 10-2 explains the authentication types.

The following example statement illustrates a serial interface on an access server being configured to use TACACS+ to authenticate persons making PPP network connections:

```
MyAccessServer(config)#aaa new-model
MyAccessServer(config)#aaa authentication ppp MyNamedMethods tacacs+ local
MyAccessServer(config)#interface serial0
MyAccessServer(config-if)#ppp authentication pap MyList tacacs+ local
MyAccessServer(config-if)#tacacs-server host 10.1.13.10
MyAccessServer(config-if)#tacacs-server key DoNotTell
```

The **aaa new-model** command activates (enables) the AAA inside the device's IOS software. The **interface serial0** command points the configuration to all lines on the access server's serial network interface named serial0. The **ppp authentication pap MyList tacacs+ local** specifies that the PAP password protocol be used for PPP connections and applies the named method list **MyList** to be used as the test. Then the statement specifies that a TACACS+ security protocol be used and that the local user database should be used if the TACACS+ server fails to respond.

The next statement specifies that the TACACS+ server resides on the host computer at IP address 10.1.13.10. The next line specifies that the encryption key **DoNotTell** be used for all communications between the security server and the client access device being configured here. The shared encryption key also must be configured on the security server(s) with which the client access device will communicate.

IOS Command Keyword	AAA Authentication Type
Login	Line connections made to Ethernet or Token Ring network interfaces using Telnet, or to console or AUX ports using virtual terminal (VTY)
PPP	Dial-in line connections made to serial network interfaces using the Point-to-Point Protocol
SLIP	Dial-in line connections made to serial network interfaces using the Serial Line Internet Protocol
ARAP	Dial-in line connections made to serial network interfaces using the AppleTalk Remote Access Protocol

Table 10-2. Entity Types Secured by AAA Authentication Methods

> **NOTE:** Three types of protocols play a major role in AAA: dial-in protocols such as PPP, security protocols such as RADIUS, and password protocols such as CHAP. Dial-in protocols are network protocols that handle signals over phone lines, keeping the IP packets together between the access server and the remote user. Security protocols provide the client-server messaging system to the centralized user database. Password protocols are relatively simple mechanisms to deal with the person logging in. Some dial-in protocols incorporate their own password protocol—ARAP, for example.

AAA AUTHORIZATION METHODS AND TYPES   AAA has five methods for authorization. There are actually six, but the **none** method is a request not to do any authorization procedure. Table 10-3 explains the AAA authorization methods. Each method is a keyword for use as an argument with the root **aaa authorization** command. These, in turn, are applied to secured entity types.

As mentioned, RADIUS and TACACS+ can coexist on the same access device. Depending on the connection being attempted and how the device is configured, the client will query either the RADIUS or the TACACS+ servers, which are separate user databases.

The **if-authenticated** command waives authorization if the user has already been authenticated elsewhere. This is important, because during a single session a user may make dozens of connections to entities secured by AAA authorization (such as IOS command

IOS Command Keyword	AAA Authorization Method
TACACS+	Send a message requesting authorization information from the TACACS+ server.
RADIUS	Send a message requesting authorization information from the RADIUS server.
If-authenticated	Allow access to the requested function if the user has already been authenticated (*if* here is the word *if*, as in "depending on," not the mnemonic IOS uses for network interface in the config prompt).
Local	Use the local user database to execute the authorization program.
Krb5-instance	Use an instance defined in the Kerberos instance map.
None	Do not execute any authorization methods on this access device.

Table 10-3.   AAA's Six Named Methods for User Authorization

modes), and it would be unwieldy for the client device to query the TACACS+ or RADIUS server each time.

Generally, a device's local user database contains only usernames and passwords. Remember that network devices don't have hard disks, and they must store permanent information in NVRAM memory, already burdened with storing a boot image of IOS and even daily AAA accounting logs. For this reason, local user databases generally do not hold authorizations for users. Therefore, if a security server were unavailable when a user logged in, that person would likely be unable to access any services configured to require authorization. Figure 10-12 shows how a local user database coexists with the server database(s).

If no authorization is to be executed on a secured entity, this should be explicitly configured by using the **none** command. Otherwise, the IOS software will automatically put the default authorization methods into force. The four types of secured objects to which AAA authorization methods can be applied are explained in Table 10-4.

The four authorization entity types can be broken down into two pairs:

▼ The EXEC and Command methods each deal with access to IOS commands.

▲ The Network and Reverse Access methods both deal with connections, but going in different directions.

On Cisco access devices, the **aaa authorization config-commands** command is enabled by default. That way the device has security right out of the box, in case the administrator installs it without configuring security. The following example statement

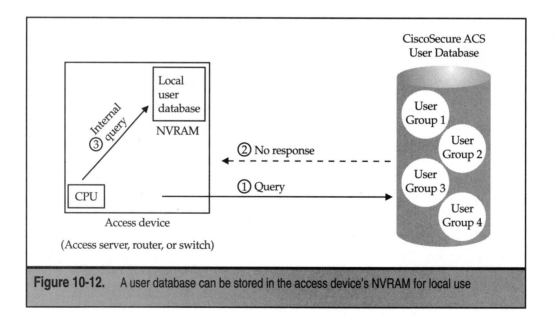

Figure 10-12. A user database can be stored in the access device's NVRAM for local use

Type	AAA Authorization Type
Network	Applies method to network-related service requests, including direct Login connections (via console or AUX), Telnet connections (via IP or IPX), or dial-in connections (via PPP, SLIP, or ARAP).
Reverse Access	Applies method to Telnet sessions in which the user is attempting to connect outbound from the secured access device to another host—a common maneuver by a hacker who has broken into a network device.
EXEC	Applies method to sessions at the user EXEC command mode and can be applied by user, date, and start and stop times.
Commands	Applies method to restrict access to specific commands. Command methods must be applied to an IOS command level group. There are two default groups, numbers 0 and 15 (user EXEC and privileged EXEC modes, respectively). The Command method can be applied by user, date, and start and stop times.

Table 10-4.   IOS's Four Authorization Types

illustrates a router being configured to require authorization for any type of network connection. This would apply, for example, whether the connection was being made via a console TTY login, a Telnet VTY login, or a PPP dial-in login.

```
MyRouter(config)#aaa new-model
MyRouter(config)#aaa authorization network NetTeam tacacs+ local
```

The preceding command specifies that the TACACS+ security protocol be used to check users against the NetTeam named method list, and to use the local user database for backup. By default, this authorization is applied to all network interfaces on the device (as opposed to authentication methods, which must be applied to specific lines).

But, as mentioned earlier, sometimes having authorizations stored on the device itself isn't practical. To accommodate this, the restriction could be loosened using the **none** command to allow a network connection if the TACACS+ server fails to respond:

```
MyRouter(config)#aaa authorization network NetTeam tacacs+ none
```

In the preceding command, the user's identity must have already been authenticated with a password to get this far into the AAA configuration. The **none** command goes into effect only when the TACACS+ server failed to respond. The following code statement configures a somewhat more sophisticated authorization:

```
MyRouter(config)#aaa authorization commands SeniorTechs
MyRouter(config)#line vty 0 5
MyRouter(config-line)#authorization commands 15 SeniorTechs
```

The preceding statement shows an example of configuration by line, as opposed to network interface. Here, the six virtual terminal (VTY) lines are secured. In this example, the named method list SeniorTechs is declared as necessary for an administrator to use IOS command level 15 in this device. We mentioned earlier that the IOS **level** command can be used to authorize the use of a group of commands. By default, all privileged EXEC mode commands are grouped into level 15, and all user EXEC mode commands are grouped into level 0. Therefore, the preceding code snippet specifies that only administrators with user profiles configured with the SeniorTechs attributes will be permitted to use the privileged EXEC commands.

ACCOUNTING METHODS AND TYPES   AAA accounting methods configure user activities to track within a secured access device. Accounting methods gather data from TACACS+ and RADIUS packets and log it into a file stored on the access device. The security server comes around each day and collects the data into a central AAA accounting database. Table 10-5 explains how the two work.

Notice that the only accounting methods are the security protocols themselves. This is because accounting data is, by default, collected for the entire device. The reason for the two methods is that the accounting data must travel either in TACACS+ or RADIUS packets to the server (AAA accounting isn't done without servers).

AAA has five accounting secured entity types, slightly different from those for authorization. Table 10-6 explains them.

The **system** accounting keyword only collects a default set of variables. It cannot be configured to collect only certain events. The reason for this is that a system event simply happens—a user does not request permission to cause it. An example system event

Command Keyword	AAA Accounting Method
TACACS+	Logs accounting information on TACACS+ in the CiscoSecure ACS database
RADIUS	Logs accounting information on RADIUS in the CiscoSecure ACS database

Table 10-5.   AAA Accounting Uses One Method per Security Protocol

Command Keyword	AAA Accounting Type
Network	Applies method to network connections, usually a PPP connection, but methods can also be named for logins, SLIP, or ARAP connections.
EXEC	Provides information on all user EXEC mode terminal sessions within the access device's IOS environment. EXEC accounting information can be collected by user, date, and start and stop times.
Commands	Provides information on any commands issued by users who are members of an IOS privileged EXEC mode. Command accounting information can be collected by user, date, and start and stop times.
Connection	Provides information on all outbound connections attempted from the secured access device in sessions made using the Telnet, rlogin, TN270, PAD, and LAT terminal protocols.
System	Provides information about system-level events, such as reboots.

Table 10-6.   AAA Accounting Can Track Asset Usage for Five Secured Entity Types

would be a network interface going down at 11:32:28 Tuesday March 11, 1999. AAA accounting does not automatically associate the system event with a security transaction. But comparing accounting and authorization logs for that date and time would make it easy for a system administrator to figure out who the culprit was.

Like authorization, AAA accounting named method lists must be applied to all network interfaces they are meant to secure, and then applied to an indicated accounting type. For example, the **MyRouter(config-if)#aaa accounting network ppp** command configures IOS to keep track of all PPP connections made over a network interface.

But accounting is a little more complicated in how it tracks requests. AAA accounting relies on so-called accounting notices to gather data. An *accounting notice* is a special packet notifying the accounting method of an event. This information is recorded in the accounting log file for upload to the appropriate security server. One of three AAA accounting keywords must be used to specify exactly when during the service request process the notices are to be sent. The terminology can get a bit confusing, but Figure 10-13 will help you visualize how the three work:

▼ **Stop-only**   For minimal accounting. Has RADIUS or TACACS+ send a stop recording accounting data notice at the *end* of the requested service. Stop-only accounting is good only for tracking who went where—important information for security purposes.

■ **Start-stop**   For more accounting. Has RADIUS or TACACS+ send a start accounting notice at the *beginning* of the requested service and a stop accounting notice at the end of the service. Start-stop accounting yields elapsed times of a connection.

▲ **Wait-start**   For maximum accounting. Has RADIUS or TACACS+ wait until the start notice is received by AAA accounting *before* the user's request process begins. Most regard wait-start as overkill and an inconvenience to users, so its use is limited to very sensitive services.

To select a method, include any one of the three keywords as arguments to the root **aaa accounting** command in the configuration statement. The three options give differing levels of accounting control. For example, if an administrator requests entry into a secured device's user EXEC mode, the stop-only process records only the end of the administrator's session within user EXEC mode. The start-stop process records the beginning and the end of the session. The wait-start process ensures that no connection is made prior to the accounting notice having been received and acknowledged.

The following example shows a AAA accounting configuration. Lines 2, 3, and 4 show all three AAA functions being configured together, the normal practice in the real world.

```
MyAccessServer(config)#aaa new-model
MyAccessServer(config)#aaa authentication login NetTeam local
MyAccessServer(config)#aaa authentication ppp RemoteWorkers tacacs+ local
MyAccessServer(config)#aaa authorization network NetTeam tacacs+ local
MyAccessServer(config)#aaa accounting network WeWillBillYou
MyAccessServer(config)#
MyAccessServer(config)#tacacs-server host BigUnixBox
MyAccessServer(config)#tacacs-server key JustBetweenUs
MyAccessServer(config)#
MyAccessServer(config)#interface group-async 1
MyAccessServer(config-if)#group-range 1 16
MyAccessServer(config-if)#encapsulation ppp
MyAccessServer(config-if)#ppp authentication chap RemoteWorkers
MyAccessServer(config-if)#ppp authorization NetTeam
MyAccessServer(config-if)#ppp accounting WeWillBillYou
```

The accounting commands are woven in with the others, to give you an idea of how statements really look. As configured here, full start-stop accounting records will be

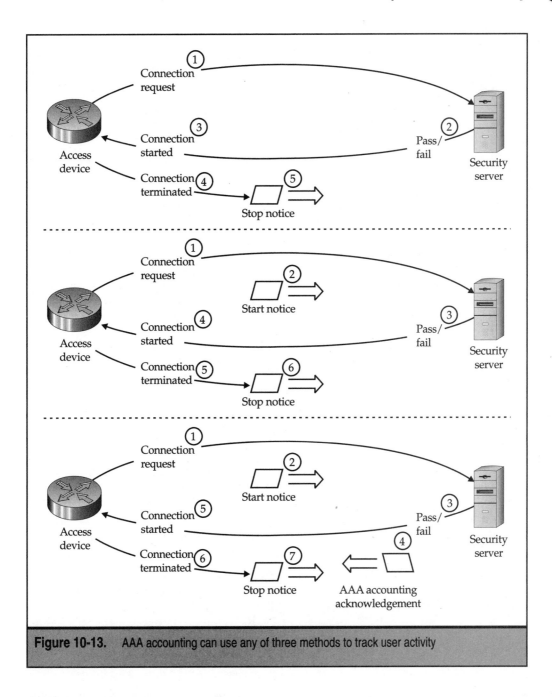

Figure 10-13. AAA accounting can use any of three methods to track user activity

logged for all network connections made by the network team through any of the 16 asynchronous ports on the device MyRouter.

Exactly what gets logged depends on how the named method list WeWillBillYou is configured. Most network managers at a minimum would use the **network** command to account for connection times. Generally speaking, the command-oriented parameters **exec** and **commands** are useful only for security audits.

RADIUS and TACACS+ Attributes

A security protocol is largely defined by the attributes it supports. After all, they define the raw material used to operate the user-based security system. RADIUS and TACACS+ are separate protocols packaged into the AAA command structure within IOS. The major differences between the two come into play inside the user database, where each user has a security profile containing attributes that define what that person may do. As separate technologies, RADIUS and TACACS+ have their own attributes.

RADIUS is an open standard under the auspices of the IETF and defines nearly 60 attributes. We won't list them all here, but Table 10-7 shows several to help you see what's involved in user-based security.

Seventeen RADIUS attributes are so-called vendor-proprietary attributes. These are items that vendors can customize to extend functionality within their products. Table 10-8 shows a few Cisco extensions to give you an idea of what vendors like to customize.

RADIUS Attribute	Description
User-Name	The name of a person's user profile account. For example, Deborah Johnson's username might be "johnsonde."
User-Password	The secret pass code created by the person.
CHAP-Password	The encrypted value returned during the challenge-handshake exchange. This is the username mixed with a random number called a *challenge*.
NAS-IP Address	IP address of the access server requesting authentication. (Recall that NAS stands for network access server, the same thing as an access server.)
NAS-Port	The physical port number on the access server. This includes the various types of interfaces possible, including asynchronous terminal lines, synchronous network lines, ISDN channels, and other types of interfaces.
Service-Type	The service requested or granted; for example, an administrator might request the **enable** command in IOS in order to enter the privileged EXEC command mode.

Table 10-7.   RADIUS Attributes Used to Enforce User-Based Security

RADIUS Attribute	Description
Login-Port	The TCP port with which the user is to be connected; for example, port 80 for HTTP Web browsing.
Acct-Session-Id	A unique accounting identifier used to match start and stop notices in an accounting log file.
Acct-Session-Time	The number of seconds the user remained connected.
Acct-Authentic	The way the user was authenticated, whether by RADIUS, the local user database, TACACS+, or Kerberos.

Table 10-7. RADIUS Attributes Used to Enforce User-Based Security *(continued)*

TACACS+ has over 50 attributes (attribute-value pairs). While TACACS+ and RADIUS both support the three AAA functions, TACACS+ is more sophisticated. For example, it has attributes such as Tunnel-Id to help secure VPN connections. This is why internetworks that use RADIUS for authenticating dial-in users will frequently use TACACS+ for authorization and accounting. Table 10-9 shows example TACACS+ attributes to give you a feel for the protocol.

The sampling of AV pairs in Table 10-9 shows two areas in which TACACS+ is stronger than RADIUS. First, TACACS+ offers stricter internal security than RADIUS by locking down commands and access lists. The first thing a hacker would do upon breaking into an IOS device would be to make new entries into its access lists, which makes file transfers possible. These AV pairs not only help to stop hackers, they also let the network

Cisco-Specific RADIUS Attribute	Description
Password-Expiration	Specifies a time interval or event that forces the user to create a new password.
IP-Direct	The Cisco device will bypass all routing tables and send packets directly to a specified IP address. For example, IP-Direct might be used to make sure a user's WAN connection goes through a firewall.
Idle-Limit	Specifies the maximum number of seconds any session may be idle.

Table 10-8. Cisco Extensions to the RADIUS Standard

TACACS+ AV Pair	Description
service=x	Specifies the connection service to be authorized or accounted. For example, **aaa authorization service=ppp** would be used to authorize a person to make a remote PPP connection to a device. Another example would be **service=shell** to let an administrator get into a device's privileged EXEC command mode.
protocol=x	A protocol is a subset of a service. For example, a PPP connection might use TN3270, VINES, Telnet, or other protocols. A key protocol nowadays is VPDN (Virtual Private Dialup Network). The AV pair **protocol=vpdn** would let a remote dial-in user establish an encrypted connection to the enterprise's VPN network.
routing=x	Specifies whether routing updates may be propagated through the interface used for the connection.
priv-lvl=x	Specifies the IOS command mode the person may use. For this to work, commands must first be grouped using the **level** command.
acl=x	Restricts connection access lists on a device. Connection access lists are also called *reflexive access lists*, used to track sessions.
inacl=x, inacl#=x, outacl=x, outacl#=x	Four AV pairs restricting access to per-user inbound and outbound access lists placed on an interface.
tunnel-id	Specifies a username for establishing remote VPN connections.
gw-password=x	Specifies the password placed on the home gateway into the VPN. Must be used where **service=ppp** and **protocol=vpdn**.

Table 10-9. TACACS+ Authentication and Authorization AV Pairs

manager specify which devices, IOS commands, or access lists individual administrators may work with. Locking out certain team members helps avoid configuration errors.

The second area where TACACS+ is stronger is protocol support. For example, TACACS+ has AV pairs to enhance security of VPNs, which are exploding in popularity. As would be expected, TACACS+ also has accounting attributes to go along with the areas where it expands beyond RADIUS. For example, the **cmd=x** AV pair lets you keep track of which IOS commands an administrator used while working on a device—useful information for diagnosing how a configuration error was made.

CISCOSECURE ACS

CiscoSecure ACS is a package of several components (ACS stands for *Access Control Server*). CiscoSecure is composed of three major parts:

▼ The NT or UNIX server platform on which the user database resides

■ The user database(s) that contain the AV pairs in user profiles, used to perform authentication and authorization queries, and to store AAA accounting logs

▲ The CiscoSecure software console from which network security is centrally managed

The CiscoSecure console can be used to configure network security on Cisco access servers, routers, switches, and the Cisco PIX Firewall. In other words, instead of typing the source code directly into the access device's config file—as shown thus far in this chapter—most parameters can be centrally set from the CiscoSecure console. The CiscoSecure console is limited to entering typical AAA command statements. Specialized or fancy AAA command statements must still be entered directly through the access device's command-line interface. Indeed, experienced Cisco network administrators prefer working directly through IOS to configuring via the CiscoSecure console.

CiscoSecure ACS Architecture

The CiscoSecure ACS client-server architecture is intended to give customers choices as to server platforms, database platforms, security protocols, and other configuration elements. It's meant to be a centralized platform that can integrate disparate network subsystems under the umbrella of a single security console. How the CiscoSecure ACS acts as a common platform for various services is depicted in Figure 10-14.

CiscoSecure relies on service modules to deliver services. Modularity means that interdependencies are minimized between the major portions of the system. This allows some parts to be turned off while others run, or for various parts to be distributed across different databases and even server platforms.

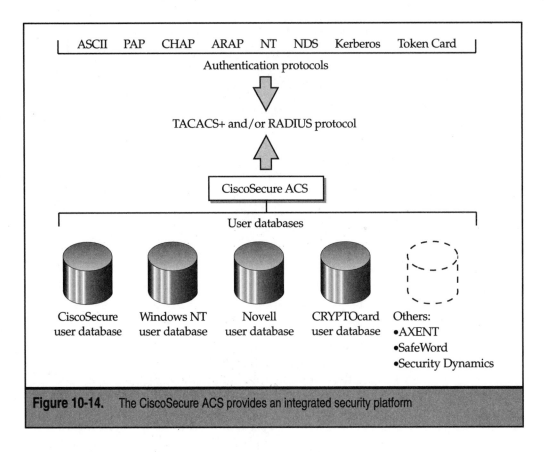

Figure 10-14. The CiscoSecure ACS provides an integrated security platform

CiscoSecure ACS Service Modules

CiscoSecure ACS has six service modules, each of which can be started and stopped independent of the others ("CS" stands for CiscoSecure):

▼ **CSAdmin** Service for the CiscoSecure ACS integral Web server. An external Web server such as Microsoft's IIS is not required to run CiscoSecure; it has its own.

■ **CSAuth** Service for authentication and authorization. CSAuth is used both to configure and enforce user privileges.

■ **CSTacacs** Protocol used to communicate between the CSAuth module and the access device requesting user authentication or authorization from a TACACS+ server.

■ **CSRadius** Protocol used to communicate between the CSAuth module and the access device requesting user authentication or authorization from a RADIUS server.

■ **DBSync**   Service used to archive user database information for use in recovery from system failure or database corruption.

▲ **CSLog**   Service to capture data from TACACS+ and RADIUS packets and log them into CSV files located in a directory on the CiscoSecure ACS platform. CSV stands for comma-separated value—a crude but effective format that uses commas to separate records. CSLog is mostly used to store AAA accounting records. CSV files are most commonly used to import data into Microsoft Excel, for example. Administrators frequently export CiscoSecure data into spreadsheets for analysis and presentation.

With these service modules, the network manager can choose to implement and operate only those parts of CiscoSecure that are needed. (Many software packages require that most or all modules be operated because of interdependencies.)

RADIUS and TACACS+ Coexistence in AAA and CiscoSecure

A prime feature of AAA is that it can run RADIUS and TACACS+ within an integrated platform and manage them through a single interface. These two security protocols make central control of network security possible, but they have other benefits beyond centralization. For example, RADIUS and TACACS+ both encrypt PAP and even ASCII passwords. Table 10-10 shows how Cisco positions the RADIUS and TACACS+ protocols relative to one another.

Table 10-10 also shows why an enterprise with tighter security needs might want to select TACACS+. TCP is more reliable because it's a full-duplex, connection-oriented transport, while UDP is connectionless. This means that TACACS+ packets will be deliv-

TACACS+	RADIUS
TCP is used as the transport protocol for TACACS+ packets.	UDP is used as the transport protocol for RADIUS packets.
Supports full packet encryption.	Only up to 16 bytes of data can be encrypted (the password is encrypted first).
Is an independent, full-featured AAA.	Has good authentication, some authorization, no accounting.
Has very powerful AAA configuration capabilities for Cisco routers.	Not useful for router security management on Cisco or anybody else's routers.

Table 10-10.   TACACS+ vs. RADIUS Features

ered with greater reliability. Encryption is becoming almost mandatory in sophisticated internetworks, because it secures the data itself. A third advantage of TACACS+ is stronger network accounting, both for security audits and general network management.

So everybody's using TACACS+, and RADIUS is fading from use, right? That's what Cisco would like to see happen, but RADIUS is stronger than ever. Vendors and the IETF have big plans to continue its development as a standard. RADIUS is a powerful draw because it gives a common software platform that device makers and security software companies can use. Understandably, vendors are always uneasy about developing products that depend on a proprietary product like TACACS+. If Cisco didn't have such a dominant share in the router market, RADIUS would be even more ubiquitous.

> **NOTE:** Encryption—the translation of data into a secret code—provides the best data security. To access an encrypted file, you must have a key that lets you decrypt it. Unencrypted data is called *clear text* or *plain text*, and encrypted data is sometimes referred to as *cipher* text. The use of encryption to secure data is called *cryptography*.

Using the CiscoSecure ACS

Three things must be in place for an access device to be placed under the control of the CiscoSecure ACS:

▼ First, the necessary AAA security parameters must be set within the individual access device's config file. This can be done either through the CiscoSecure console, or directly inside the device's IOS command-line interface (as shown thus far in this chapter).

■ Second, a user database must be built so the CiscoSecure ACS can respond to queries sent by access devices. The user database is composed of user profiles that contain attribute-value (AV) pairs specifying what each person is permitted to do.

▲ Third, a security protocol must be selected to let the client access device use the CiscoSecure ACS for authentication, authorization, and accounting services.

As mentioned, server configurations vary. Larger internetworks often have two or more tiers of network security servers, hierarchically configured into a master server. Also, files (user profiles, accounting logs, etc.) are usually imported and exported between the security server and other systems by CSV files.

The CiscoSecure ACS Console Interface

As an application, CiscoSecure ACS uses a browser-based GUI. The example screen shown in Figure 10-15 is taken from CiscoSecure ACS 2.1 for Windows NT. The icon-bearing buttons stacked on the left are used to enter CiscoSecure applications. The stack of buttons represents CiscoSecure's eight applications (plus an online help system).

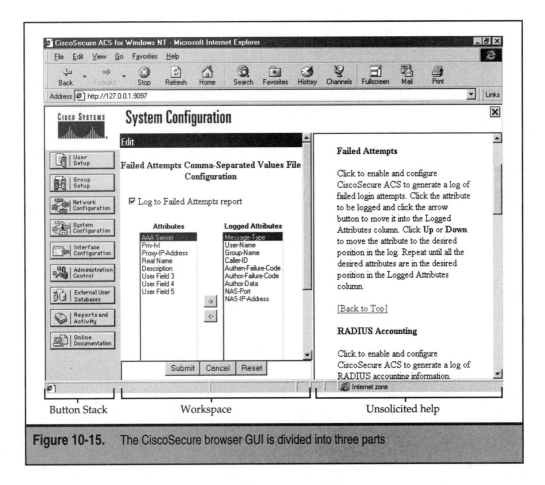

Figure 10-15. The CiscoSecure browser GUI is divided into three parts

Another thing to notice is the Submit button. Because this is a browser interface, settings must be submitted over the network in order to be input inside the access device's config file.

In the previous chapter, we said that CiscoView's GUI was easy to like. But the same can't be said of CiscoSecure's user interface. Looking at Figure 10-15, one must question why fully 40 percent of precious screen space is dedicated to unsolicited onscreen help—especially given the fact that an entire help subsystem is available at the click of a button. With almost half the screen displaying unsolicited help, the actual workspace—the middle panel—is so skinny that the user must do a lot of vertical scrolling to get to fields.

CiscoSecure User Database Choices

CiscoSecure can use either its own CiscoSecure ACS User Database (packaged with the product) or an external user database. External user databases are used where one or more larger databases already store user profile information. For example, if an enterprise has dozens of Novell NetWare servers, it makes sense to use the user profiles already stored in the NDS Tree user databases instead of maintaining duplicate user information in the CiscoSecure ACS User Database.

Also, you must use a specialized external user database for token-card authentication. The external user databases supported by CiscoSecure are shown in Figure 10-16.

NDS stands for NetWare Directory Services, a product from Novell that stores user profiles. Windows NT and NetWare are the predominant network operating system platforms. Notice that there are several token-card user databases. This list represents the top vendors slugging it out in the token-card authentication market right now. If computer industry history is any indication, this list will probably be shorter in a few years as the market sorts itself out.

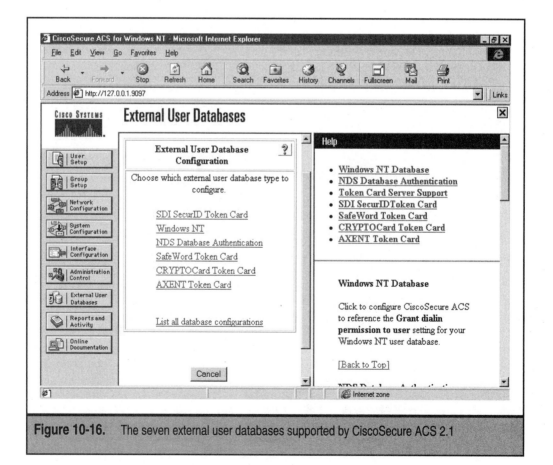

Figure 10-16.   The seven external user databases supported by CiscoSecure ACS 2.1

User Database Technologies

The CiscoSecure ACS User Database can use either a so-called hashed-indexed flat file or a relational database management system (RDBMS) from Sybase or Oracle. Most use the indexed flat file version because it's less expensive and faster.

A *flat file* works by what's called sequential searching. It starts searching through records at the top of the file and works its way down until it finds the record it needs. A hashed-indexed file builds an indexed tree structure that makes it possible to locate a record in fewer steps. Indexed flat files are ideal for uses in which the information is relatively simple and speedy response time is paramount. Figure 10-17 compares flat files with indexed flat files and relational databases.

As you can see, relational databases are quite different even from indexed flat files. They have separate tables for each aspect of a record. An RDBMS user database stores entries into separate tables for username, password, authorization attributes, and accounting logs. To read this data, the server must dynamically "join" the information gleaned from these tables in order to read the entire user profile record in memory (thus the name *relational*). By contrast, an indexed flat file stores all the information in one place, making searches much quicker than with an RDBMS.

Relational databases are necessary to handle complicated data and have become standard technology for most business applications. But user security databases aren't complicated; they're composed of only three or four categories of data. This is why most network managers prefer to use indexed flat files instead of taking on the unnecessary processing overhead of an RDBMS.

> **NOTE:** So, what does the term *database* mean, exactly? Strictly speaking, a database is a file that uses separate hierarchical tables to store information on various aspects of an entity. A database record is more logical than physical, with its information spread across dozens of tables. But the term *database* is frequently bastardized and used to refer to flat files as well, where all information on an entity is stored inside a single place. Indexed flat files aren't true databases, but as long as the industry refers to them as "user databases," we will, too.

Setting Up the User Databases

To get things started, the CiscoSecure ACS needs a population of users to secure. This means that you must somehow get records into your user database. This can be done any of three ways:

▼ Typing user profiles directly into the CiscoSecure ACS User Database

■ Importing user profile records from an external source

▲ Using an external user database, a common practice in larger internetworks

Figure 10-18 shows the screen used to tell CiscoSecure to check external databases. This example shows two external user databases to be queried if the CiscoSecure ACS User Database fails to authenticate a user. This is what's called "sophisticated unknown

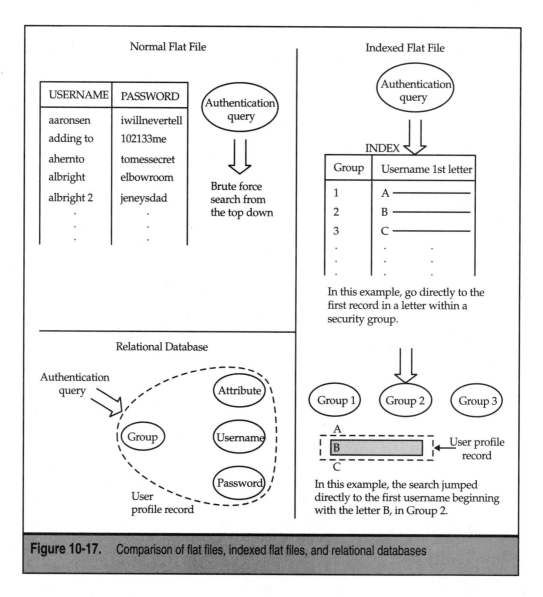

Figure 10-17. Comparison of flat files, indexed flat files, and relational databases

user handling." In big internetworks, it's common for the primary security server to be unaware of a user while a related server has the person in its user database. The example in Figure 10-18 shows two external databases that could be configured as alternate references.

If authentication succeeds on one of the alternate databases, a record of that person's user profile is automatically entered into the CiscoSecure ACS User Database. In this way, the primary user database self-updates such that the next time the user attempts a login, it won't be necessary to search the alternate external databases.

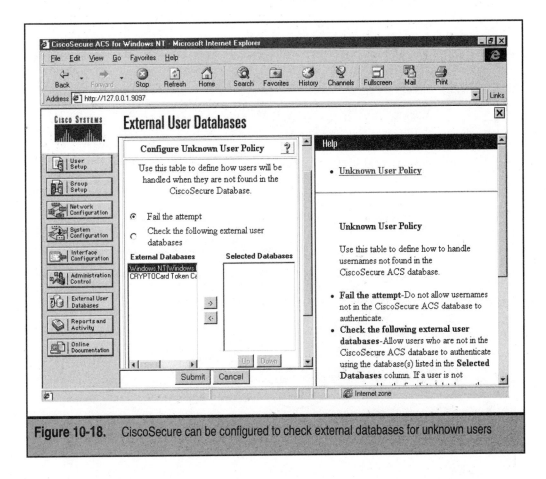

Figure 10-18. CiscoSecure can be configured to check external databases for unknown users

The trade-off in using external databases is that they can slow security transactions. It makes sense to try to catch nearly all users in the primary user database (the CiscoSecure ACS User Database in Figure 10-18's example) so that users will seldom have to endure waiting while CiscoSecure queries other servers trying to validate their security profiles.

Group Setup

It would be unwieldy to customize security permissions for each user, one at a time. That would mean configuring the same attribute-value pairs hundreds of times over. Assigning rights to users by group eases the administrative burden. The Group Setup screen shown in Figure 10-19 is used to do this. The example shown is to set time-of-day usage restrictions for security Group 1. The AV pairs for time-of-day access are then automatically entered into the user profile record of each person assigned to Group 1.

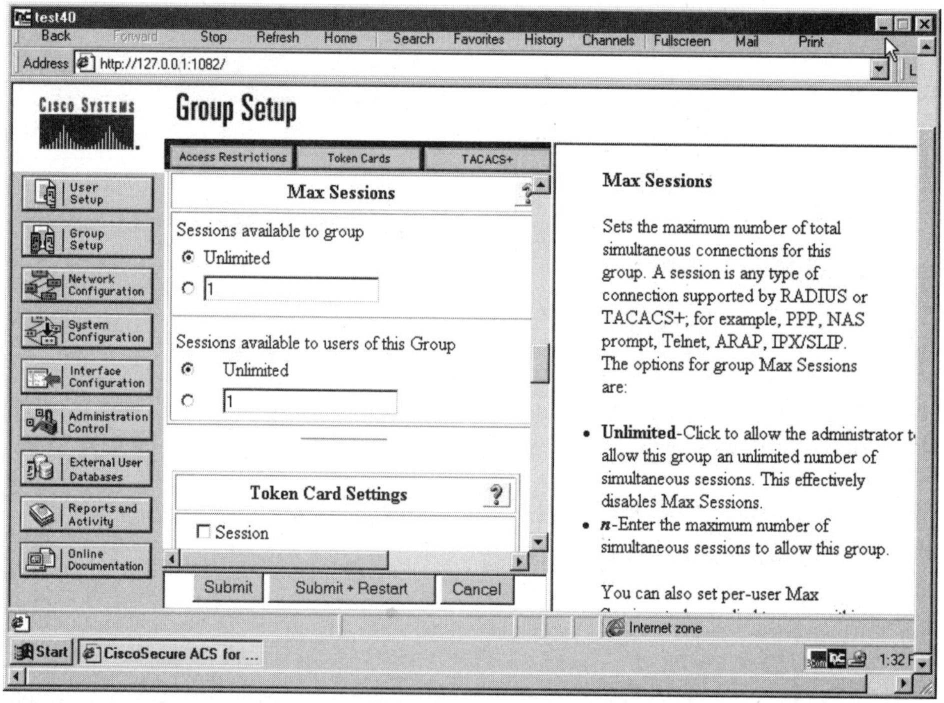

Figure 10-19. Security parameters are set by groups of users, not individuals

Up to 100 groups may be defined in CiscoSecure. Several attributes can be set en masse for users who are members of a security group:

▼ **Time-of-day access** Set time blocks during which the group's users are not permitted network access. This is sometimes used to limit peak-load traffic.

■ **Network access restrictions** Set locations (phone numbers) from which the group's users may dial into the access server. This technique uses caller ID to help thwart unauthorized access by hackers.

■ **Token-card settings** Set parameters for token caching.

■ **TACACS+ settings** Set attributes for TACACS+, the most common being whether to allow the administrator within the user EXEC command mode, to restrict access using a declared access control list, and so on. Session parameters can also be set, such as maximum idle time or the timeout interval.

▲ **RADIUS attributes** Set attributes for RADIUS connections.

We've shown that access to commands can be permitted or denied by IOS command modes. But even more fine-grained control can be exerted by individual commands. Figure 10-20 shows CiscoSecure being used to specify the root command **debug** and keyword argument combinations to either permit or deny.

Checking the Permit field configures users in the group as authorized to use the specified commands. Taking the opposite approach, check the Deny field to explicitly forbid group members from using a command. An unlimited number of commands can be set by repeatedly using the GUI shown in Figure 10-20. Two contrasting strategies are used to control access to IOS commands. One is to set users at level 0 and then add permissions to use commands on a case-by-case basis. The other approach is to set users at level 15 and deny permission to use specific commands.

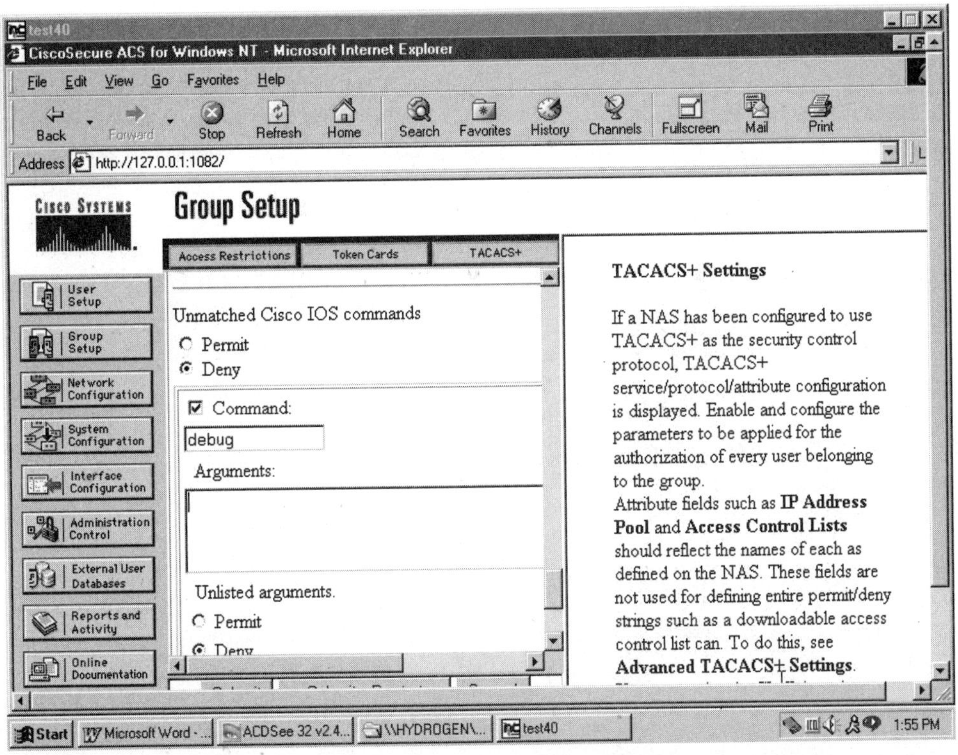

Figure 10-20. Specific IOS commands can be authorized or denied to group members

Network Configuration

As with CiscoWorks2000, CiscoSecure needs a device inventory to operate. Figure 10-21 shows the fields describing individual access devices to the CiscoSecure ACS database—this example being an access server. Again, records can be imported en masse from a network management server's device inventory database.

The CiscoSecure ACS needs general information such as the access server's host name and IP address. Perhaps the most important setting on the screen is the choice of security protocol to use for user authentication.

A valid shared encryption key must be entered so the access device can be a client to CiscoSecure ACS servers holding the same key. The shared encryption key must be configured directly into the access device's config file through the IOS command-line interface, as this example shows:

```
MyAccessServer(config)#tacacs-server key LooseLipsSinkShips
```

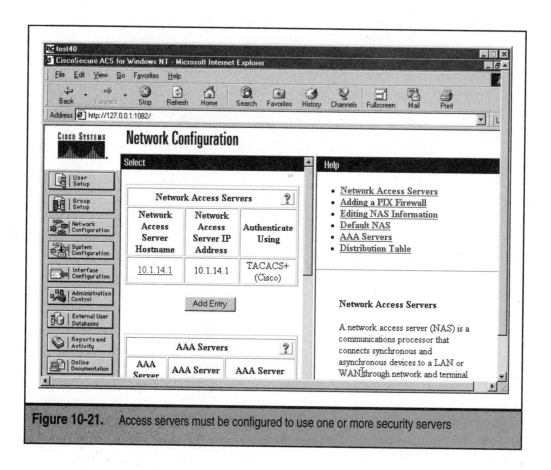

Figure 10-21.   Access servers must be configured to use one or more security servers

Without this precaution, individual devices would be more susceptible to breaking and entering by hackers. The shared key keeps all security packets invisible to the average hacker. Until it's set up by hand on the client side, no packets can be sent between it and the CiscoSecure ACS.

System Configuration

Many AAA accounting attributes are "system level" in that they apply to the entire access device, not to a particular interface or line. Figure 10-22 shows the System Configuration screen, used to select which accounting attributes to log to the server in accounting uploads. To configure settings, the administrator selects attributes from the left vertical selection box in the workspace area and clicks them over into the right box.

You have the option of configuring CiscoSecure to record failed attempts to log into the network. This is an indicator of potential security breaches and is one focus of security

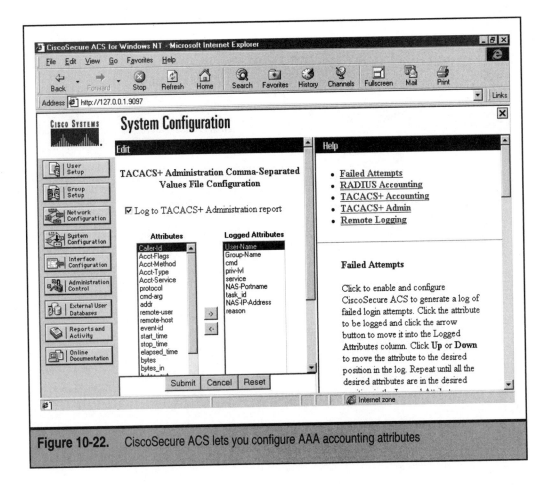

Figure 10-22. CiscoSecure ACS lets you configure AAA accounting attributes

audits. Notice also that the option is given to use either the TACACS+ or RADIUS security protocol for accounting. This demonstrates the modularity discussed earlier. You can use different security protocols for each AAA function.

Interface Configuration

Most access security is enforced at the network level. And, as with users, it makes sense to set named access lists for networks en masse—in other words, by groups of interfaces. Figure 10-23 shows the Interface Configuration screen, used to set parameters for network interfaces. Now you can see the relationship between interface parameters and group settings. At the interface level, you turn the parameter on. At the group level, you define what specifically is permitted for that parameter. Figure 10-23 sets the Max Sessions attribute; Figure 10-19 sets the value for the attribute. That makes an attribute-value pair.

Several other restrictions can be set by network interface. For example, time-of-day user access restrictions can be set for a group—a good way to limit traffic during peak network usage hours.

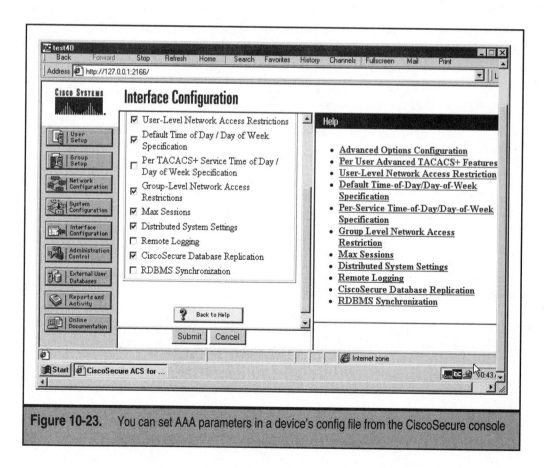

Figure 10-23. You can set AAA parameters in a device's config file from the CiscoSecure console

Administration Control

As mentioned, every network manager's worst nightmare is a hacker gaining administrative control over a network device. Yet at the same time it's not practical for administrators to physically go to each device and work on it individually. The solution is to restrict the IP addresses from which the device can take connections, as shown in Figure 10-24.

This precaution makes it harder for imposters to log into a device as the authorized network administrator because the hacker must now not only steal an administrator's username and password, but also show a preapproved source IP address before gaining entry.

Reports and Activity

Like network management, the hard part of network security is capturing data and controlling events. Once the data is stored, a raft of reports can be generated for use in identifying events or analyzing trends. Figure 10-25 shows CiscoSecure's reporting menu.

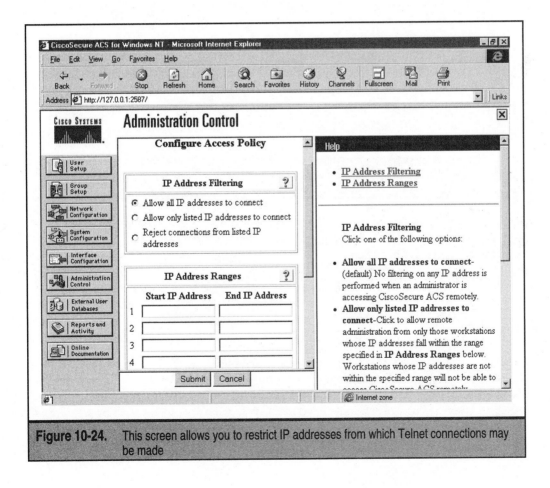

Figure 10-24.   This screen allows you to restrict IP addresses from which Telnet connections may be made

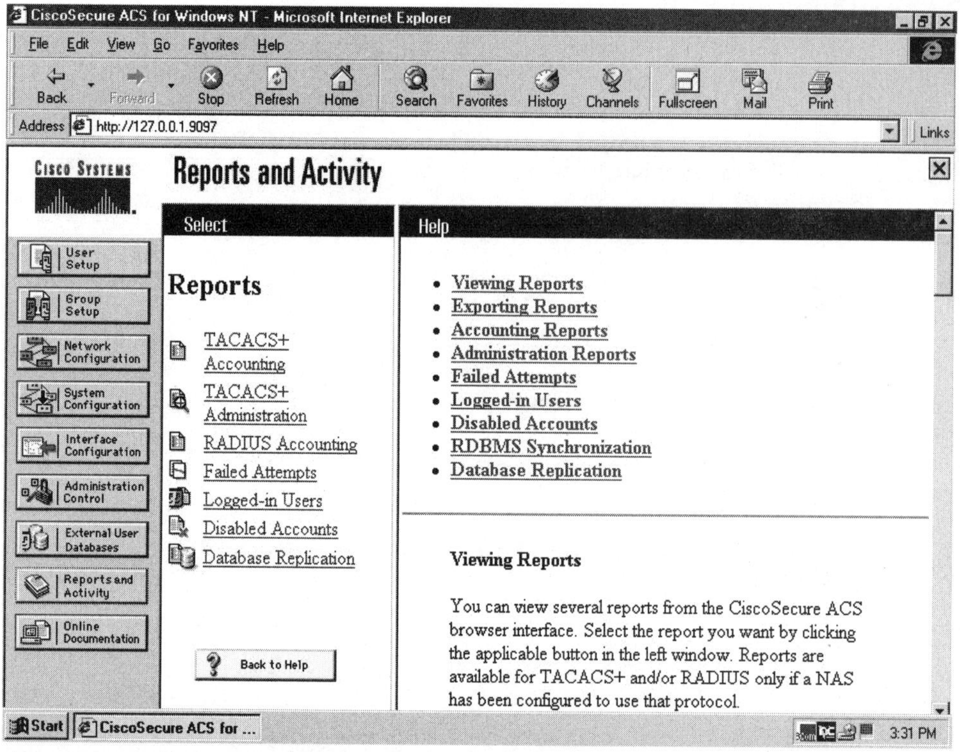

Figure 10-25.   A battery of reports can be generated from the CiscoSecure console

As you can see, events such as failed login attempts can be viewed. For analysis, reports can be generated based on the AAA accounting logs. The accounting logs are by far the richest source of data generated by CiscoSecure. This information can be used to track user activities through time—a great way to audit and plan network security.

DYNAMIC ACCESS LISTS

Access lists are normally used to filter traffic at the packet level. In other words, when a connection is attempted through a router interface, packet headers are inspected for prohibited IP addresses or application port numbers, and traffic is passed or blocked. These are called extended access lists, discussed in Chapter 7. To review, such access lists are *extended* in that they can filter based on network application port numbers instead of just addresses. They're also called *static* extended access lists, because the **permit** and **deny** commands are blindly enforced, regardless of user. To make an exception for a particular person, an administrator would need to go into the router's config file and edit the list for that interface.

Dynamic access lists are configured using so-called lock-and-key commands. Using them, a user who would otherwise be blocked can be granted temporary access to a network or subnet via a Telnet session over the Internet.

The Telnet session is opened to a router configured for lock-and-key. The dynamic access list prompts the user for authentication information. As with other user-based security protocols, lock-and-key can be configured to check against a user database on the router itself (local), or against a user database maintained on a TACACS+ or RADIUS server. If authenticated, the user is automatically logged out of the Telnet session and can start a normal application such as a browser.

Lock-and-Key Using a Local User Database

The following sequence of code snippets shows how lock-and-key could be configured on a router using a locally maintained user authentication file. To start, a particular network interface on the router is declared along with a subnetted IP address. The **ip access-group** command places the just-named interface and networks under the control of access list 103:

```
MyRouter(config)#interface ethernet1
MyRouter(config)#ip address 209.198.208.30 255.255.255.0
MyRouter(config)#ip access-group 103 in
```

The keyword **in** specifies that access control be applied only to inbound connections (lock-and-key can also be used to restrict outbound connections).

In the following statement, the first entry of access list 103 allows only Telnet connections into the router. The second entry of access list 103 is ignored until lock-and-key is triggered whenever a Telnet connection has been established in the router. The keyword **dynamic** defines access list 103 as a dynamic (lock-and-key) list.

```
MyRouter(config)#access-list 103 permit tcp any host 209.198.207.2 eq telnet
MyRouter(config)#access-list 103 dynamic InCrowd timeout 60 permit ip any any
```

This is the key juncture. So configured, an attempted Telnet connection to the router causes it to check against its local user database to see if the user and password are valid for lock-and-key access to the router. If validated, the **timeout 60 permit ip any any** statement gives the user 60 minutes to use the router as a connection between any two IP addresses.

Finally, an **autocommand** statement creates a temporary inbound access list entry (named InCrowd in the previous statement) at the network interface Ethernet1 and line 0 on the router. The temporary access list entry will timeout after five minutes.

```
MyRouter(config)#line vty 0
MyRouter(config)#login local
MyRouter(config)#autocommand access-enable timeout 5
```

The temporary access list entry isn't automatically deleted when the user terminates the session. It will remain configured until the timeout period expires.

Dynamic access lists can also be configured to authenticate users against a user database maintained on either a TACACS+ or RADIUS server. This, in effect, turns a router into an access server through which a user can gain entry into an internetwork, but only by logging in via a Telnet session.

CHAPTER 11

Building Cisco Networks

W e've now covered the components that make up an internetwork. In this chapter, we'll put this knowledge to work by examining the network design process and configuring networks to fit various design scenarios.

As you've seen, there is no shortage of technologies and products to choose from—even in Cisco's product line alone. You've also seen how there is no free lunch in networking: every design move brings a trade-off of one kind or another. Trade-offs can come in the form of reduced bandwidth to carry payload traffic, increased complexity, additional expense, or other disadvantages. When designing a network, you need to know not only what the options are, but also how to juggle them to strike the best possible balance.

Each year brings so many technology advances and new products that just keeping the acronyms straight is difficult. In this chapter, we'll sort things out a bit by applying Cisco's array of products to real-world problems. Looking at internetwork configuration problems will help put things into perspective and bring those critical trade-offs into sharper focus.

INTERNETWORK DESIGN BASICS

Internetworking is geographical by nature, so most design practices have to do with matching topology to needs. (Recall from Chapter 6, a topology is a map of an internetwork's physical layout.) The layout of an internetwork largely dictates how it will perform and how well it can scale. In networking, *scale*, or *scalability*, means how much an internetwork can grow without having to change the basic shape of its topology (that is, without having to replace or excessively reconfigure existing infrastructure).

Internetworking Basics Reviewed

One last run-through of what we've learned thus far is in order. Doing so is especially important here, because in this chapter we'll be looking at the variety of design factors and options. To do that, one should be clear on the various components that make up an internetwork.

LAN Segments

Hubs and switches form LAN segments, the basic building block of every internetwork. A LAN segment could be a departmental LAN or a high-speed LAN backbone servicing dozens of other LAN segments within an enterprise.

NOTE: To refresh, a LAN segment is a physical medium shared among a group of devices. Most LAN segments are formed by hubs or switches. Strictly speaking, a LAN segment is a LAN. Usually, though, the term *LAN* is used to refer to a local network consisting of many LAN segments.

Collision and Broadcast Domains

A collision domain is a shared network medium in which Ethernet packets are allowed to collide; a broadcast domain is the area within which messages may be sent to all stations using a so-called broadcast address. Collision domains should be kept small because collisions limit the use of bandwidth. The more hosts that are connected to a LAN segment, the slower the traffic moves.

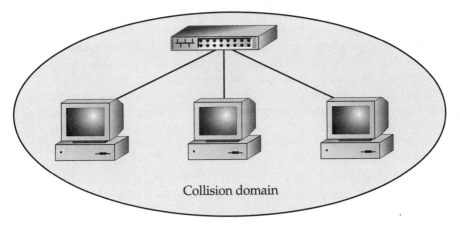

Collision domain

Most collision domains are formed by hubs that connect host devices to the internetwork. Hubs are the functional equivalent of the Ethernet cable segments used in the early days of local area networking.

A broadcast domain is the network area in which broadcast messages are forwarded. To refresh, broadcasts use the reserved dotted decimal IP number 255; therefore, a message to be forwarded to every device within network 298.92.182 would be addressed 298.92.182.255. Some broadcasts are useful, but too many can bog down a network in useless overhead traffic—an unwelcome phenomenon called a *broadcast storm*. Broadcast domains are, by default, the same as a network's collision domain for shared media (i.e., hubs), but the scope of broadcast addresses can be made smaller than a collision domain using switches. Routers normally limit broadcasts, but a broadcast domain can be extended by configuring a router to let broadcast messages pass.

Shared Bandwidth vs. Switched Bandwidth

Switches also connect hosts to networks, but in a fundamentally different way. A switch "time slices" network access among its attached hosts in such a way that each switch port forms a channel with a collision domain of one. This is called *switched bandwidth*, as opposed to the *shared bandwidth* of hubs. Switched networks are estimated to be ten times faster than shared networks over the same medium.

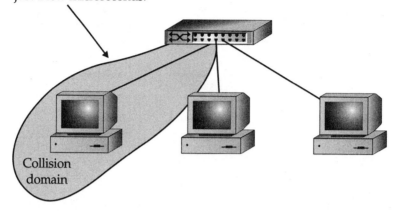

While transmitting or receiving, the host has 100% of the switch's reported throughout. This could be just a few microseconds.

Collision domain

Moreover, switched networks support virtual LANs (VLANs), enabling administrators to group users rationally instead of being forced to group them according to the hub to which host devices are attached. Therefore, a hub shared by two or more hosts forms a collision domain; a switch does not.

In addition to forming them by connecting hosts, larger switches connect LAN segments to form internetworks. To avoid confusion, the two types of switches are sometimes called access switches and LAN (or backbone) switches.

Routers Control Internetworks

The third basic device in internetworking is the router. Routers connect LAN segments instead of hosts, as do hubs and access switches. Routers are used to isolate intramural traffic and to provide internal security. In addition, they can extend broadcast and multicast domains to specified LAN segments, to help bind those networks into a functional unit.

Routers are deployed both inside internetworks and at the edge of autonomous systems. Inside routers are sometimes called internal routers or access routers. Routers that concentrate on communicating with the outside are called edge, or gateway, routers. For example, an Internet service provider (ISP) will use gateway routers to connect to the Internet. By contrast, a big company will place at least one internal router at each of its major sites to help manage in-house traffic.

Routers are more intelligent than hubs and switches because they are able to interpret network addresses. They read network addresses in order to filter traffic, control access to networks or services, and choose the best path to reach a destination. Routers bring internetworks to life. It's no coincidence that the three most basic devices in internetworking operate at different levels of the seven-layer OSI reference model, as illustrated here:

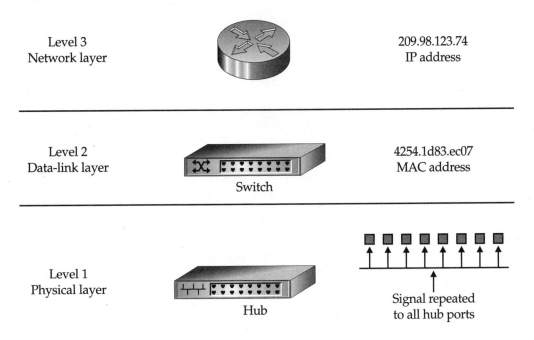

Routers operate at the network layer (layer 3). Today, most internetworks use IP network addresses—all Internet routers do. But many internal routers must still use legacy desktop protocols such as IPX, AppleTalk, or DECnet. For that reason, Cisco and its competitors have invested heavily in engineering multiprotocol products to allow legacy LANs to interoperate with IP. Cisco's IOS feature sets exist mostly to give network designers options in purchasing system software that fits their network protocol needs.

Routers Use Layer-3 Network Addresses

Whether IP or a legacy layer-3 protocol, network addresses are inherently hierarchical. As a router works its way rightward through an IP address, it zeros in on the LAN segment to which the destination host is attached. Over long-haul routes, moves through the address are manifested in hops between routers. A one-hop route would require only finding the LAN segment on which the destination resides.

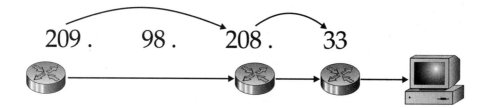

Routes are often summarized before being shared with other routers. This improves performance by greatly reducing the number of address entries carried inside a router's route table. Route summarization, called *route aggregation*, works by relying on a gateway router to know the target LAN segment's full address, allowing interim routers to carry fewer entries in their respective routing tables, thereby improving performance. Address translation is also frequently used, where internal addresses are either altered or grouped into a global address in packets sent outside an internetwork. Mechanisms such as Port Address Translation (PAT) and Network Address Translation (NAT) are used at edge routers or firewalls to make these translations in the packet address fields in both directions.

Switches Use Layer-2 MAC Addresses

Switches operate at the data-link layer (layer 2), dealing in MAC addresses instead of network addresses. A MAC address is a long number that uniquely identifies physical hardware devices. MACs combine a manufacturer code with a serial number. Even routers use MAC addresses for a message's last step—resolving an IP address to the physical MAC address to locate the destination host within the LAN segment.

MAC addresses are topologically flat. The logical profile of a MAC address appears as if all hosts are connected to the same cable; it offers no clue as to where hosts are located because it's basically a serial number. Switched networks, therefore, must operate by brute force, flooding broadcasts of MAC addresses to all ports when a destination MAC is unknown.

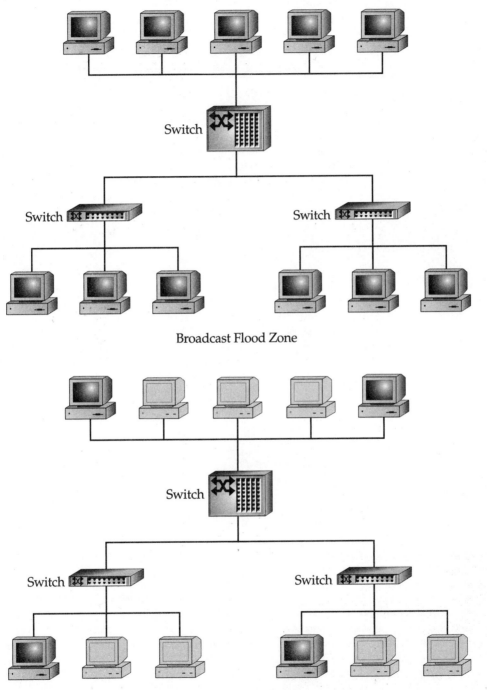

Broadcast Flood Zone

VLAN Broadcast Flood Zone

VLANs give switched networks hierarchy by limiting broadcasts to discrete groups of users. This combines the speed of switched bandwidth with the hierarchical topology heretofore available only in shared bandwidth networks. In addition, VLANs flexibly assign users to logical workgroups instead of having to group users by hub.

Path Optimization

Internetworks use control protocols to route messages. There is so much dynamic change in internetworks—through growth, changing traffic patterns, a device going down, and the like—that they must self-operate to some degree by constantly updating device routing tables. Routed networks rely on routing protocols to keep track of paths through internetworks. For example, many small internetworks use RIP 2; most large ones use EIGRP or OSPF (EIGRP is Cisco proprietary, OSPF is an open standard). These trade in lists of routes, mostly within an autonomous system, and are used to connect LAN segments. BGP trades in lists of autonomous systems and is used to connect the Internet.

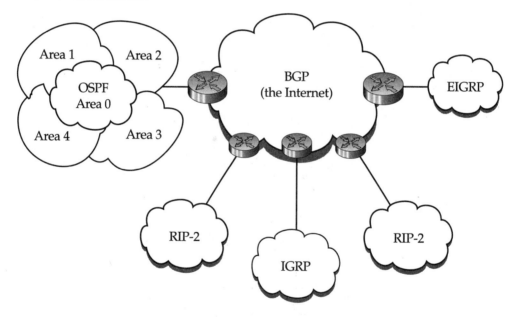

As you've learned, internetworks maintain a degree of self-awareness by way of discovery protocols, which find new devices and keep checking the status of known ones. These protocols—Cisco Discovery Protocol (CDP) is an example—are the supporting cast to routing protocols. When an event takes place, it's discovered and the news is passed around until the device population converges on a new list of routes. Sometimes loops appear, where a suggested route turns back toward its source device, creating nonsensical routes that can slow or even crash an internetwork. Routing protocols use metrics to tune internetworks. RIP uses only hop count, but the more sophisticated protocols use several metrics that can be combined into a weighted matrix to steer traffic along desired links.

Switched networks aren't so sophisticated. Switches exchange only lists of MAC addresses, with the most recently used MACs toward the top, the highest one being the first choice. Switched networks use the Spanning Tree Protocol (STP) to prevent loops.

Internetwork Architectures and Applications

In just the past few years, the design requirements of the typical enterprise have changed radically. These changes have occurred at opposite ends of the topology. At the bottom, segmentation using hubs and access switches has greatly increased the number of LAN segments and, therefore, the amount of traffic to go over the backbone between segments. At the top, whole new computing architectures are becoming standard, with Web-based intranets replacing traditional client-server management systems, extranets transforming traditional electronic data interchange (EDI) systems, and virtual private networks (VPNs) replacing leased-line wide area networks (WANs).

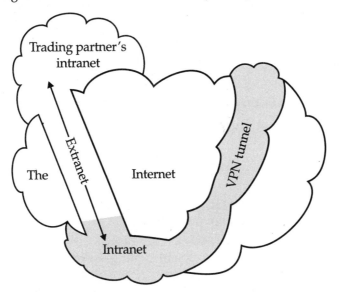

Driving even more change is the fact that new network applications have changed traffic characteristics. For example, videoconferencing is becoming popular, increasing the need for configurations optimized to handle multicasts—where a single copy of a message is forwarded to a subset of destination hosts.

The Three-Layer Hierarchical Design Model

Hierarchical topologies are inherently better than flat ones for a number of reasons, the main one being that hierarchy contains traffic to its local area. The rule of thumb designers use is that broadcast traffic should not exceed 20 percent of the packets going over each link—the implication being that segmentation will naturally boost throughput by isolating traffic to its most likely users. This rule of thumb applies only to the amount of broadcast packets in the traffic mix, and is not to be confused with the 80/20 rule. The 80/20 rule states that 80 percent of all traffic stays home and only 20 percent goes beyond the local area.

A flat topology—one in which each device does more or less the same job—increases the number of neighbors with which an individual device must communicate. This increases somewhat the amount of payload traffic the device is likely to carry and greatly increases overhead traffic. For example, each time a router receives a broadcast message, its CPU is interrupted. For many small internetworks, a flat topology is sufficient, and the added expense and complexity that hierarchy requires isn't warranted. But it doesn't take many LAN segments to hurt an internetwork's performance and reliability, with devices and hosts bogged down in unnecessary traffic.

This is why the industry adheres to a classical hierarchical design model. The model has three layers: the access, distribution, and core layers. This separates local traffic from high-volume traffic passing between LAN segments and areas, and lets network devices at each layer concentrate on doing their specific job. The hierarchical model is depicted in Figure 11-1.

Hierarchy is made possible by segmentation—the practice of dividing hosts into smaller LAN segments. Fifteen years ago, most LAN segments were actual cable spans running through walls and ceiling plenums; today most are formed by "cable-in-a-box" hubs and access switches. Segmentation and hierarchical topology yield several benefits:

▼ **Performance**   Traffic is isolated to source areas, thereby narrowing Ethernet packet collision domains and speeding throughput.

■ **Reliability**   Most faults are isolated to the segment from which the problem originated.

■ **Simplicity**   By separating dissimilar areas, network elements can be replicated as needed throughout the internetwork.

■ **Scalability**   Modular design elements can be added as the internetwork grows over time, with minimal disruption of existing networks.

▲ **Security**   Access can be controlled at well-defined junctures between the layers.

Internetworks naturally tend toward a two-level hierarchy. Hubs and switches connect host devices into LAN segments, and the backbone connects the segments into a local network, whether within a floor, building, office campus, or even a metropolitan area. This is a relatively flat topology in the sense that, even though collision domains are limited, excessive broadcast traffic still chews into available bandwidth. This makes the distribution layer the key. By isolating traffic, the distribution layer also isolates problems and complexity.

Hierarchy also helps reduce costs. By dividing hosts and traffic, variations are limited to fewer LAN segments, or even a single segment. Variations include such things as desk-

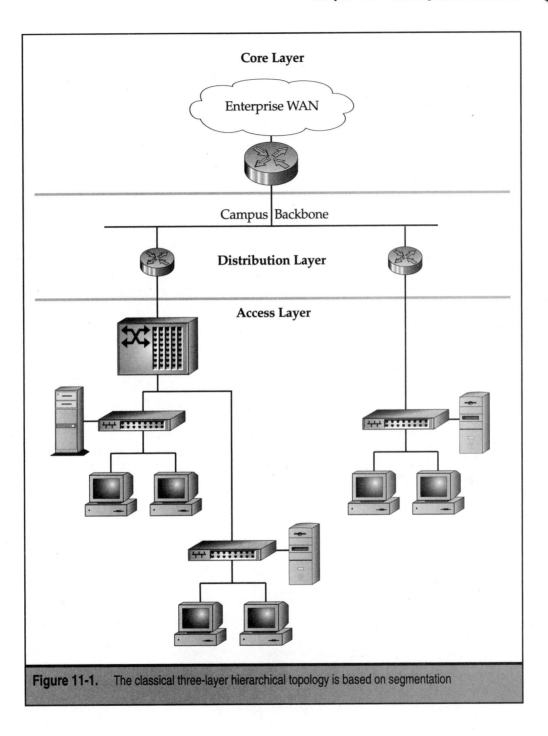

Figure 11-1.   The classical three-layer hierarchical topology is based on segmentation

top protocols (IP, IPX, AppleTalk), traffic volumes (workgroup vs. backbone), and traffic type (big graphical files, e-mail, HTTP). Hierarchy allows the network designer to tune the configuration for the particular job at hand. Adjustments are made in the model of network device purchased and in how it is configured in terms of memory, modules, software, and config file parameter settings.

The Access Layer

The access layer is made up mostly of hubs and switches, which serve to segment host devices such as PCs and servers into many LAN segments made up of either shared or switched bandwidth. This is where MAC-layer filtering can take place.

If an internetwork has remote sites, such as branch offices or home offices, the access layer would also include access servers. WANs must use some type of long-distance transmission medium. There is a wide selection of media now, such as leased digital T1 or T3 lines and Frame Relay public digital networks. Dial-in remote users employ analog modem lines and, in certain areas, higher-bandwidth technologies such as Digital Subscriber Line (DSL) and Integrated Services Digital Network (ISDN). Figure 11-2 shows access-layer functionality.

In large internetworks, the access layer can include routers. These internal routers serve mostly to isolate overhead, control traffic, and enhance internal security. The access layer encompasses a mix of technologies in most internetworks. Dial-on-demand routing (DDR) has become popular for remote connections because it keeps a link inactive except when traffic needs to be sent, thereby reducing telecommunication costs.

Most enterprises have legacy technologies that are being gradually phased out as new ones are implemented. For example, many big companies still use their leased-line T1 WANs alongside growing VPNs, substituting shared network usage for dedicated leased lines. From a practical standpoint, this is necessary because the routers must be upgraded along each VPN link.

The Distribution Layer

The distribution layer is made up mostly of routers. They're used to separate slow-speed local traffic from the high-speed backbone. Traffic at the access layer tends to be bandwidth intensive because that's where most LAN and host addresses reside. Network overhead protocol traffic for discovery protocols, SNMP, routing protocols, and other network control systems is heavier at the access layer.

Because routers are intelligent enough to read network addresses and examine packets, they also improve performance by sending traffic as directly as possible to its destination. For example, distribution-layer routers define broadcast and multicast domains

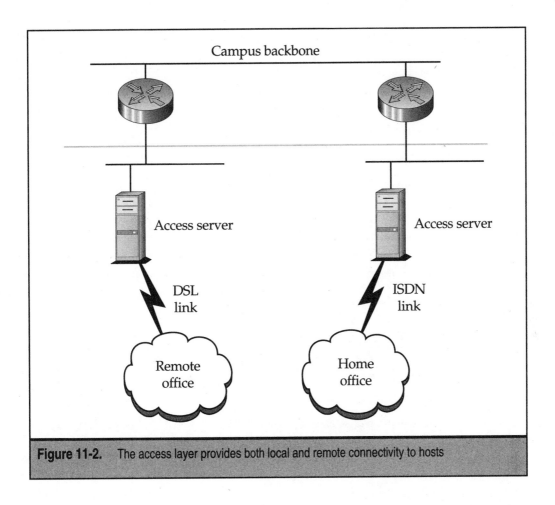

Figure 11-2. The access layer provides both local and remote connectivity to hosts

across LAN segments. Domains are, by default, limited to LAN segments; routers can extend domains across segments as the hierarchy design dictates. Figure 11-3 depicts distribution-layer functionality.

In configurations using multilayer switches, distribution-layer devices route messages between VLANs. *Multilayer switching* is a relatively new technology in which packets are filtered and forwarded based on both MAC and network addresses. The Catalyst 5000 is perhaps the best example of a multilayer switch, incorporating route switch modules (RSMs) in addition to those with typical switch electronics.

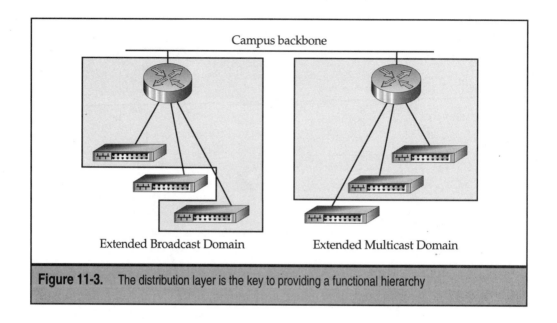

Figure 11-3. The distribution layer is the key to providing a functional hierarchy

Most value-added services are provided by devices at the distribution layer. Address translation takes place at this layer, usually on a gateway router or a firewall (itself a type of router). Address aggregation also takes place here, as well as area aggregation if the internetwork is running OSPF routing domains. Other services are also performed on distribution-layer routers: translation between protocols such as IPX and IP; encryption for VPN tunneling; traffic-based security using access lists and context-based firewall algorithms; and user-based security using security protocols such as RADIUS, TACACS+, and Kerberos.

The Core Layer

The core layer is the backbone layer. In large internetworks, the core incorporates multiple backbones, from campus backbone LANs up through regional ones. Sometimes special backbone LANs are configured to handle a specific protocol or particularly sensitive traffic. Most backbones exist to connect LAN segments, usually those within a particular building or office campus. Figure 11-4 depicts how the core layer might look in a typical large enterprise internetwork.

To run fast, a backbone LAN should be configured to experience a minimum of interruptions. The goal is to have as many backbone device CPU cycles as possible spent transferring packets among segments. The distribution layer makes this possible, by connecting workgroup LAN segments and providing value-added routing services. A minimum of packet manipulation should occur at this level. This is why most newer backbones are switched LANs. The need for address interpretation at the core is mini-

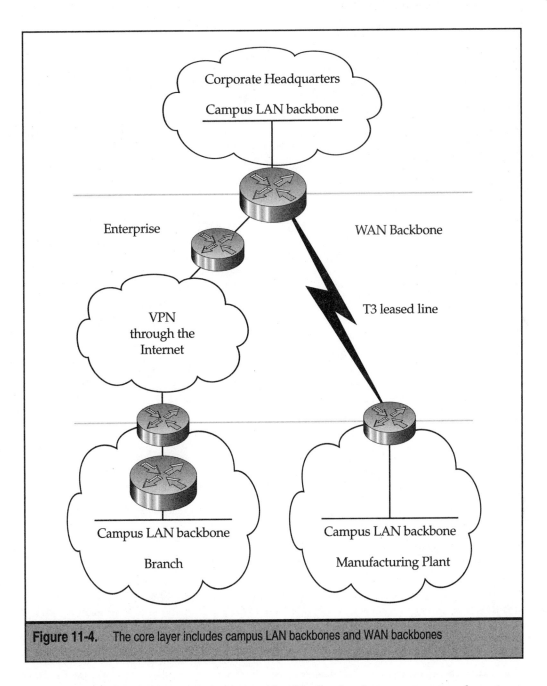

Figure 11-4. The core layer includes campus LAN backbones and WAN backbones

mized by the processing already performed by distribution-layer routers, so why not use switching technology to move data over the backbone much faster?

ATM (Asynchronous Transfer Mode) and Gigabit Ethernet are doing battle to become the switched backbone technology of choice. ATM has an edge for multimedia applications because it uses fixed-sized cells instead of Ethernet's variable-length packets. The obvious advantage of Gigabit Ethernet switched backbones is easier compatibility with the millions of Ethernet LANs already installed throughout the world.

ATM is an international cell relay standard for service types such as video, voice, and data. The fixed-length 53-byte cells speed data transfer by allowing processing to occur in hardware. Although ATM products exist to take data all the way to the desktop, the technology is optimized to work with high-speed transmission media such as OC-48 (2.5 Gbps), T3 (45 Mbps), and T3's European counterpart, E3 (34 Mbps).

Design Methods

Over the years, the networking industry has developed a set of concepts and best practices for use in internetwork design. Most internetworks are works in progress; very few are designed from a clean sheet of paper. As internetwork topologies evolve through time and circumstance, it becomes difficult to maintain a rigorous hierarchical network design—especially in large enterprises with distributed management structures, or in shops that have high personnel turnover in their network teams.

Redundancy and Load Balancing

Redundancy is the practice of configuring backup equipment. This is done to provide fault tolerance, where traffic will shift to the backup device if the primary unit fails, a process called *failover*. For example, most high-speed backbones have dual-configured switches at each end in case the primary switch goes down. Another common safeguard is to have redundant power supplies within a device, so that if one fails, the device keeps running.

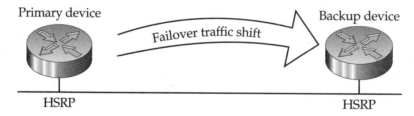

Cisco's technology to support redundancy is the Hot Standby Router Protocol (HSRP), a suite of commands in IOS. *Hot standby* is a computer industry term meaning that the backup unit is always up and running, thereby allowing automatic failover in the event of a failure. HSRP works by creating a group of backup routers, with the IP address of the primary router used to process traffic. The primary router is monitored by others in the group, and should it fail, the backup router's address will take over traffic processing duties. Failovers are achieved with no human intervention and are generally accomplished in a few seconds.

Because redundant configurations are expensive, fault-tolerant configurations are usually limited to critical devices. Redundancy is most commonly configured into backbone devices and firewalls, where device failure would have the broadest effect on the overall network.

Load balancing is a configuration technique that shifts traffic to an alternative link if a certain threshold is exceeded on the primary link. Load balancing can be achieved through various means, such as tuning routing metrics in router config files within routing protocol domains.

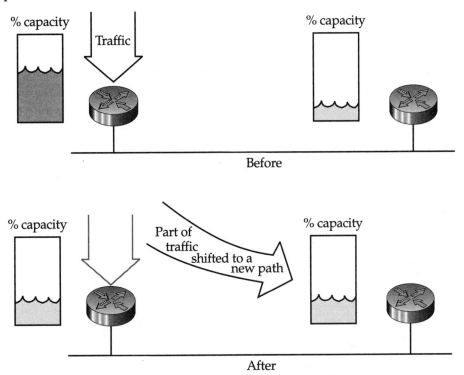

Load balancing is similar to redundancy in that an event causes traffic to shift directions, and alternative equipment must be present in the configuration. But in load balancing, the alternative equipment isn't necessarily *redundant* equipment that only operates in the event of failure.

Topology Meshing

A good design will incorporate a meshed topology to achieve redundancy and load balancing. A *mesh* is where two network devices—usually routers or switches—are directly connected. In a fully meshed topology, all network nodes have either physical or virtual circuits connecting them to every other node in the internetwork. You can also have a partially meshed topology, in which some parts of the topology are fully meshed, but some nodes are connected only to one or two other nodes. Figure 11-5 depicts the two.

At first blush, all meshing seems to be an inherently good thing. Looking at the example in Figure 11-5, you can readily see the benefits in the full-mesh topology:

▼ **Performance**   It's only a single hop to any network attached to one of the other routers, and the fewer the hops the faster the speed.

■ **Availability**   Having redundant paths means that if any one router goes down, one or more alternate routes is always available.

▲ **Load balancing**   Alternate paths can also be used for normal operations, where routing parameters can be configured to use alternate paths if a preset traffic load is exceeded on the primary router.

The partially meshed internetwork on the bottom of Figure 11-5 doesn't have these advantages. For example, to go from router A to C takes two router hops, not one. If routers on both sides of router F go down, it will be unable to communicate with the rest of the internetwork. Also, fewer mesh connections reduce opportunities for load balancing. However, although meshing can bring benefits, it must be used carefully; it comes at a cost:

▼ **Expense**   Every router (or switch) interface dedicated to meshing is one that can't be used to connect a LAN segment. Meshing consumes hardware capacity.

■ **Overhead traffic**   Devices constantly advertise their services to one another. The more mesh links a device has, the more advertisement packets it broadcasts, thereby eating into payload bandwidth.

■ **Vulnerability**   Meshing makes it more difficult to contain problems within their local area. If a misconfigured device begins propagating indiscriminate broadcast messages, for example, each element in a mesh will cause the broadcast storm to radiate farther from the source.

▲ **Complexity**   Additional connections make it more difficult to isolate problems. For example, it would be harder to track down the device causing the broadcast storm in a fully or heavily meshed internetwork, because there would be so many trails to follow.

For these reasons, few internetworks are fully meshed. The general practice is to fully mesh the backbone portion of topologies to provide fault tolerance and load balancing along these critical links, but only partially mesh the access- and distribution-layer topologies.

Backdoor and Chain Configurations

Circumstance sometimes dictates deviating from the strict hierarchical model. The two most common topology deviations are so-called backdoors and chains. A *backdoor* is any direct connection between devices at the same layer, usually the access layer. A *chain* is the addition of one or more layers below the access layer. Figure 11-6 depicts the two.

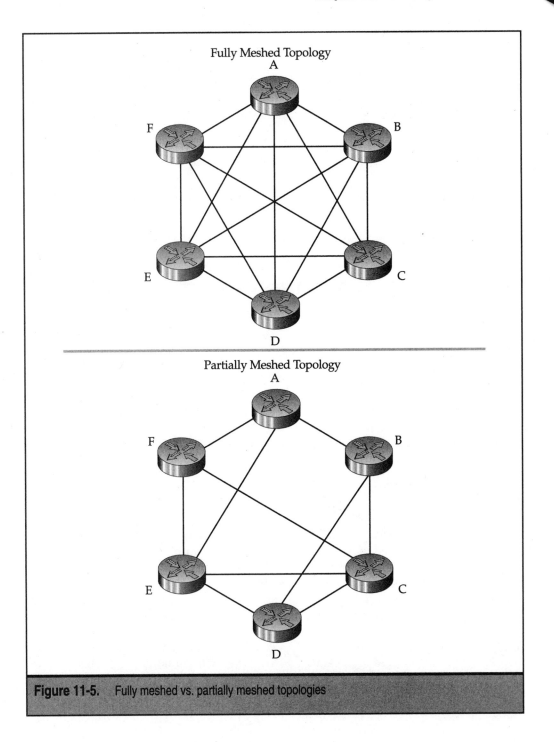

Fully Meshed Topology

Figure 11-5.   Fully meshed vs. partially meshed topologies

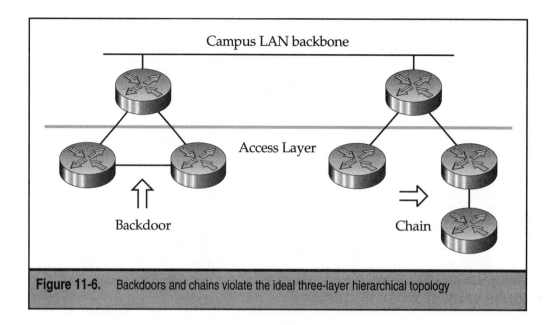

Figure 11-6.   Backdoors and chains violate the ideal three-layer hierarchical topology

Sometimes it makes sense to configure a backdoor. For example, you might want to directly link two remote sites if the links to the distribution-layer routers are costly or slow. Backdoors also provide a degree of redundancy: if the backdoor link goes down, the two remote sites can failover to the distribution-layer router and keep communicating. More often than not, however, backdoors and chains emerge because of poor network planning or a renegade manager who installs networking equipment without involving the network team.

DESIGNING TO FIT NEEDS

You'd be surprised how many internetworks—even big sophisticated ones—have grown haphazardly. Unmanaged network growth occurs for any number of reasons. The most common one is that things simply happened too fast. Keep in mind that realities we now take for granted—client-server computing, intranets, the Web, extranets—were mere concepts until the last decade. This left many IT managers unprepared to formulate well-researched, reasoned strategic network plans for their enterprises.

In many cases, a plan wouldn't have done much good. Management fads come and go, but one fad that stuck is the credo "if I pay, then I have the say." The management trend has been toward flat organizational structures, with minimum layers between the CEO and worker. Most IT departments are now "budgeted" by individual divisions, groups, or even departments. In other words, IT decisions are increasingly being made from the bottom up by the entity that owns the budget, not the central IT department.

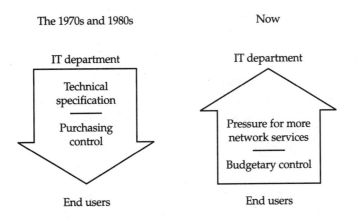

This kind of distributed decision making has been magnified by the slowness of many IT departments to respond to emerging customer demands driven by such things as business process reengineering, mergers, acquisitions, and trading partner cooperatives. So it got to the point where many end-user managers simply threw out the corporate technical architecture, picked up the phone, and ordered new networks on their own.

The trend over the last several years has been for IT departments to break off networking into a separate group called *infrastructure*. Separate the chip heads from the wire heads, so to speak. This is being done because internetworking has simply become too big and too complicated to be left to a manager who, say, has a background in COBOL and mainframe software project management. Networking is its own game now. It is fast becoming its own discipline with its own set of best practices—some of which we'll review in the remainder of this chapter.

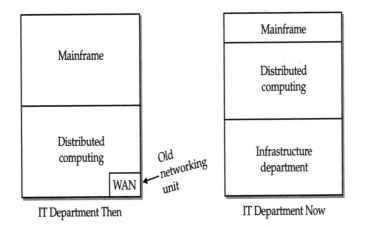

Methodologies have been developed to help bring network planning under control. Not surprisingly, these bear a strong resemblance to data processing methodologies. First and foremost, of course, is to fit the solution to the business needs through some form of needs assessment—both present and future.

Understanding Existing Internetworks

As mentioned earlier, few network designs start from scratch. Although it would be nice to work from a blank sheet of paper, most designs must accommodate a preexisting network. Most are incremental redesigns to serve more users or to upgrade bandwidth capacity, or both. A common upgrade, for example, is to insert a layer of routers between the LAN backbone and the layer at which hosts access the network. This is being done in many enterprises to improve performance and accommodate projected growth. Whatever the change, the preexisting infrastructure must be thoroughly analyzed before even considering a purchase.

The next section describes methods for network planning and design. They focus on establishing a baseline of how the network will look upon implementation. To refresh on the subject, a baseline is a network's starting point, as expressed in traffic volumes, flows, and characteristics. Allowances are made for margins of error and projected growth over and above the baseline.

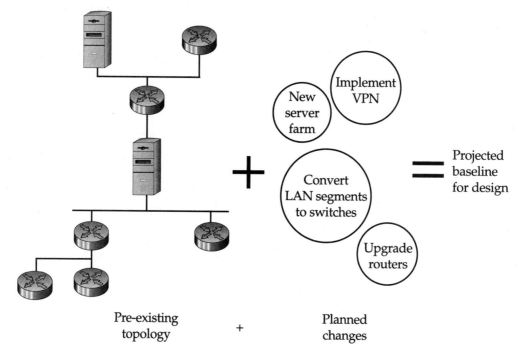

Pre-existing topology	+	Planned changes

If designing an entirely new network area, you must arrive at a design baseline based on well-researched assumptions, often derived from paperwork or other non-networked data traffic already in place. If an existing network topology is being upgraded, the baseline is taken by measuring its characteristics. If the design scenario encompasses non-networked and networked elements, then the two must be compiled together. Whatever the case, the principles and methods of good network design remain the same.

Characterizing Networks

There are several methods for understanding an internetwork well enough to formulate a proper design. These methods apply whether it's an existing internetwork or a topology to be built from scratch. As you might expect, the methods focus on geography and traffic—in other words, where network nodes are and what travels between them. A network node is any device in the topology, including network devices such as routers and payload hosts such as servers. For our purposes, when designing a network from scratch, a node could be a noncomputer entity such as a desk or a file cabinet. The point is to identify where the users are and what they're using.

Quality of Service (QoS)

Characterizing networks is good for managing as well as designing. The industry is pushing the concept of quality of service (QoS)—an approach largely based on characterizing traffic. QoS is the technique of assuring throughput for traffic through an internetwork. QoS is more sophisticated than just guaranteeing that a certain link will run at a certain throughput level. Most QoS guarantees are associated with a particular type of traffic, say, prioritizing video multicasting for distance learning over e-mail and other less critical traffic.

Some regard QoS as more high-concept marketing hype than actual product. And to some extent they're right, given that full realization of QoS is still a few years off. But there is a suite of powerful QoS commands up and working in the current release of IOS, most of which have to do with traffic queuing (a fancy term for prioritization).

As you might imagine, QoS policy implementation relies heavily on information gathered via SNMP and RMON and presented through NMS consoles such as Resource Manager Essentials and CWSI Campus. Like those console applications, QoS uses the client-server model by storing a QoS database, and it implements policies through purpose-built applets such as Policy Manager, Distribution Manager, and Cisco Assure.

Cisco Policy Manager creates abstract commands that group individual IOS commands to perform a task from the Cisco Policy Manager GUI. As with other NMS console applets, when you push a button, one or more commands are put to use on the client network device being configured. Some QoS subcommands are generic IOS commands (the **interface** command, for example); others are QoS specific. The major QoS abstract commands are as follows:

▼ **WFQ** Stands for *weighted fair queuing*. Combines the **interface** and **fair-queue** commands to let network managers prioritize how a mix of traffic types will flow through certain areas of the topology. For example, e-mail might be given a higher priority on Lotus Notes servers, but not elsewhere.

■ **WRED**   Stands for *weighted random early detection*. Combines the **interface** and **random-detect** commands (**random-detect** accepts a weight value to represent the relative importance of a traffic type). WRED tries to control traffic congestion as it begins to emerge.

▲ **CAR**   Stands for *committed access rate*. CAR is the fundamental QoS bandwidth control technology. CAR uses a sophisticated RMON MIB to recognize traffic types, set priorities, and limit packet rates as needed.

QoS techniques are mostly applied at the network interface level, and make heavy use of access control lists to filter packets. The idea is to differentiate traffic types within topology areas and influence network behavior—a technique dubbed *traffic shaping*. The goal of traffic shaping is to guarantee minimum levels of end-to-end service for various types of traffic. There are several other QoS abstract commands dealing with special areas such as Frame Relay links and Fast EtherChannel bandwidth aggregation. But, for now, many operational areas don't yet have meaningful QoS infrastructure in the form of commands and RMONs. Many hope that QoS will come to fruition with IP's next major release, IP version 6.

Understanding Traffic Flow

Understanding and documenting traffic flow is the first step in network design. Drawing an analogy to highway design might seem too obvious, but the two are remarkably similar. A road designer must know where the roads should be, how wide, covered with what type of surface, and what traffic control rules are to be applied. All these things are largely a function of traffic flow.

Traffic characteristics are largely a matter of directionality, symmetry, packet sizes, and volumes. A unidirectional flow does most communicating in one direction; a bidirectional flow communicates with roughly the same frequency in both directions of a connection. An asymmetrical flow sends more data in one direction than the other; a symmetrical flow sends roughly equal amounts of data back and forth. For example, an HTTP session's flow is bidirectional and asymmetric because a lot of messages are sent both ways, but data is mostly downloaded from the Web server to the browser client.

IDENTIFYING TRAFFIC SOURCES   To understand traffic flow, you must know its sources. This is done by identifying groups of users, not individual persons. In the parlance of computer methodology, a group of users is often called a *community* (probably because the obvious term, *user group*, is already used by customer associations, for example, the Cisco User Group).

An inventory of high-level characteristics, such as location and applications used, should be gathered. This isn't to say that one would go around with a clipboard gathering the information. Most network designers would pull this information off a database from such tools as Resource Manager Essentials or NetSys Baseliner. The following example shows a form that might be used to gather user information:

Community	# Persons	Locations	Applications	Host Type
Accounting	27	St. Louis	AR, AP, GL	AS/400
Customer Service	200	Minneapolis	Call Center	Windows NT 4.0

You can gather whatever information you want. For example, you might not want to document the type of host the group uses if everybody has a Pentium PC. On the other hand, if there's a mix of dumb terminals, thin clients, PCs, and souped-up UNIX workstations, you might want to know who has what. This information can help you more accurately calculate traffic loads.

If you're analyzing an existing network, this information can be gathered by turning on the record-route option in IOS. This information can also be gathered using Resource Manager Essentials, CWSI Campus, NetSys Baseliner, or many third-party tools.

IDENTIFYING DATA SOURCES AND DATA SINKS   Every enterprise has major users of information. The experts identify these heavy data users as *data sinks* because it's useful to trace back to the data sources they use to help identify traffic patterns. The most common sources are database servers, disk farms, tape or CD libraries, inventory systems, online catalogs, and so on. Data sinks are usually end users, but sometimes servers can be data sinks. The following illustration shows information to gather on data sinks:

Data Sink	Locations	Applications	User Communities
Server farm 3	St. Louis	AR, AP, GL	Accounting
CCSRV	Denver	Call Center	Customer Service

Documenting which communities use each data sink enables you to correlate traffic. You can now begin connecting user desktop hosts to data sink servers. Combining the information in the preceding two illustrations lets you begin drawing lines between client and server. Correlate every user community to every data sink, and an accurate profile of the network's ideal topology begins to emerge.

IDENTIFYING APPLICATION LOADS AND TRAFFIC TYPES   Most network applications generate traffic with specific characteristics. For example, FTP generates unidirectional and asymmetric traffic involving large files. Table 11-1 is a sampling of typical message types and their approximate sizes. Obviously, sizes can vary widely; but these are industry rules of thumb useful for estimating traffic loads.

Beyond traffic loads, it's also useful to know the traffic type. Traffic types characterize the kinds of devices connected and how traffic flows between them:

▼ **Client-server**   Usually a PC talking to a UNIX or NT server, this is the standard configuration today. In client-server types, traffic is usually bidirectional and asymmetrical.

Message Type	Approximate Size
Web page	50K
Graphical computer screen (such as a Microsoft Windows screen)	500K
E-mail	10K
Word processing document	100K
Spreadsheet	200K
Terminal screen	5K
Multimedia object (such as videoconferencing)	100K
Database backup	1MB and up

Table 11-1.   Typical Message Sizes for Estimating Traffic Loads

- **Server-to-server** Examples include data mirroring to a redundant server backing up another server, name directory services, and so on. This type of traffic is bidirectional, but the symmetry depends on the application.

- **Terminal-host** Many terminal-based applications run over IP, even IBM terminal connections to mainframes. Another example is Telnet. Terminal traffic is unidirectional, but symmetry depends on the application.

▲ **Peer-to-peer** Examples include videoconferencing and PCs set up to access resources on other PCs, such as printers and data. This type of traffic is bidirectional and symmetric.

Understanding what types of traffic pass through various links gives a picture of how to configure it. The following illustration shows information used to identify and characterize traffic types.

Application	Traffic Type	User Community	Data Sinks	Bandwidth Required	QoS Policy
Web browser	Client-server	Sales	Sales server	350 Kbps	CAR
TN3270	Terminal	Purchasing	AS/400	200 Kbps	WRED

Frequently, a link is dominated by one or two traffic types. The Bandwidth Required column in the preceding illustration is usually expressed as a bit per second estimate and could be Mbps or even Gbps. Once all the applications in an internetwork are identified and characterized, the designer has a baseline from which to make volume-dependent configuration decisions. Traffic typing is especially useful for knowing where and how to set QoS policies. In other words, you must identify which applications go through a router before you can properly set QoS parameters in its config file.

Understanding Traffic Load

After the user communities, data sinks and sources, and traffic flows have been documented and characterized, individual links can be more accurately sized. The traffic flow information in the following illustration ties down the paths taken between sources and destinations.

	Destination 1	
	Link	**Mbps**
Source 1: Accounting	Frame Relay	0.056
Source 2: Call Center	Point-to-Point	1.54

	Destination 2	
	Link	**Mbps**
Source 1: Accounting	Frame Relay	0.256
Source 2: Call Center	Frame Relay	1.54

	Destination 3	
	Link	**Mbps**
Source 1: Accounting	Frame Relay	0.256
Source 2: Call Center	Frame Relay	0.512

Designing internetworks to fit needs is more art than science, though. For example, even after having totaled the estimated bandwidth for a link, you must go back and pad it for soft factors such as QoS priorities, anticipated near-term growth, and so on.

CISCO NETWORK DESIGNS

Designing networks is largely a matter of making choices. Most of the choices have to do with selecting the right technologies and products for the job. Even design elements over which you have no control may still leave choices to make. For example, if the company's art department uses AppleTalk and has no intention of changing, you must decide whether to run it over multiprotocol links or break it off into one or more AppleTalk-only LAN segments.

Once the present and future needs of the enterprise have been researched and documented, the next step is to choose technologies for various functional areas:

▼ **Backbone technology selection** A variety of backbone LAN technologies exist, chosen mostly based on the size of the internetwork and its traffic characteristics.

■ **Protocol selection** It's assumed here that IP is the network protocol, but choices remain as to which routing and other network control protocols to use.

▲ **Access technology selection** A mix of hubs and switches is usually configured to best fit the needs of a workgroup or even a particular host.

After the underlying technologies are chosen, specific products must be configured to run them. After that step, more design work must be done to implement the configuration. For example, an IP addressing model must be configured, a name services subsystem must be set up, routing metrics must be tuned, security parameters must be set, and so on.

Internetwork design takes place at two levels: the campus and the enterprise. Campus designs cover the enterprise's main local network, from the desktop up to the high-speed backbone to the outside. The enterprise level encompasses multiple campus networks and focuses on WAN configurations—whether a private leased-line WAN or an Internet-based system tunneled through the Internet.

Logical Network Design

An internetwork design is defined by both a physical and a logical configuration. The physical part deals with topology layout, hardware devices, networking software, transmission media, and other pieces. Logical configuration must closely match the physical design in three areas:

▼ **IP addressing** A plan to allocate addresses in a rational way that can conserve address space and accommodate growth

■ **Name services** A plan to allow hosts and domains to be addressed by symbolic names instead of dotted-decimal IP addresses

▲ **Protocol selection** Choosing which protocols to use, especially routing protocols

Internetwork design should always start with the access layer, because higher-level needs cannot be addressed until the device and user population are known. For example, estimating capacity is virtually impossible until all hosts, applications, and LAN segments have been identified and quantified, and most of these elements reside in the access layer.

From a practical standpoint, the three logical design elements of addressing, naming, and routing are good first steps in nailing down how the physical hardware should be laid out. Each of the three requires forethought and planning.

IP Addressing Strategies

The number of available addresses is called *address space*. Enterprises use various addressing schemes to maximize address space within the block of IP addresses they had assigned to them by their ISPs. Various addressing strategies have been devised, not only to maximize address space, but also to enhance security and manageability.

PRIVATE IP ADDRESS BLOCKS   An enterprise receives its public IP address from the Internet Assigned Numbers Authority (IANA). The IANA usually only assigns public addresses to ISPs and large enterprises, and then as a range of numbers, not as a single IP address. In actual practice, the majority of enterprises receive their public IP addresses from their ISP. When designing IP, the IETF reserved three IP address ranges for use as private addresses:

▼   10.0.0.0 through 10.255.255.255

■   172.16.0.0 through 172.31.255.255

▲   192.168.0.0 through 192.168.255.255

These three IP address blocks were reserved to avoid confusion. You may use addresses within any of these reserved blocks without fear of one of your routers being confused when it encounters the same address from the outside, because these are private addresses that never appear on the Internet.

Private IP addresses are assigned by the network team to internal devices. Because they'll never be used outside the autonomous system, private addresses can be assigned at will as long as they stay within the assigned range. No clearance from the IETF or any other coordinating body is required to use private addresses, which are used for these reasons:

▼   **Address space conservation**   Few enterprises are assigned a sufficient number of public IP addresses to accommodate all nodes (hosts and devices) within their internetwork.

■   **Security**   Private addresses are translated via PAT or NAT to the outside. Not knowing the private address makes it tougher for hackers to crack into an autonomous system by pretending to be an internal node.

■ **Flexibility**   An enterprise can change ISPs without having to change any of the private addresses. Usually, only the addresses of the routers or firewalls performing address translation need to be changed.

▲ **Smaller routing tables**   Having most enterprises advertise just one or perhaps a few IP addresses helps minimize the size of routing tables in Internet routers, thereby enhancing performance.

This last item perhaps explains why the IETF settled on a 32-bit IP address instead of a 64-bit design. Doling out infinitely greater address space would discourage the use of private addresses. The use of global IP addresses would be rampant, engorging routing tables in the process. This would create the need for routers to have faster CPUs and lots more memory. Back when IP was designed, during the 1970s, network devices were in their infancy and were very slow and underconfigured by today's standards.

OBTAINING PUBLIC IP ADDRESSES   Registered IP addresses must be purchased from the nonprofit IANA, which is responsible for ensuring that no two enterprises are assigned duplicate IP addresses. But few enterprises obtain their IP addresses directly from the IANA; most get them indirectly through their ISP.

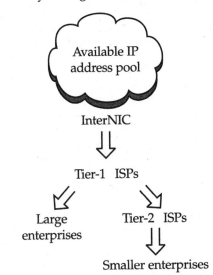

For example, Tier 1 ISPs such as UUNET or Sprint secure large blocks of IP addresses from the IANA. They in turn dole them out to Tier 2 ISPs (there are probably dozens in your town alone), who in turn assign them to end-user enterprises. Most large companies deal directly with Tier 1 ISPs. IP addresses are doled out in blocks. The bigger your enterprise, the larger the range of IP addresses you should obtain.

DYNAMIC ADDRESSING   Dynamic addressing is a technique whereby end-system hosts are assigned IP addresses at login. Novell NetWare and AppleTalk have had built-in dynamic addressing capabilities from the beginning. That's not the case with IP, though. Remember, desktop protocols such as NetWare IPX were designed with client-server in mind, while IP was originally designed to connect a worldwide system, the Internet. IP dynamic addressing came to the fore only in the mid-1980s to accommodate diskless workstations that had nowhere to store permanent IP addresses.

A couple of earlier dynamic IP address assignment protocols led to the development of the Dynamic Host Configuration Protocol (DHCP). DHCP, now the de facto standard, uses a client-server model in which a server keeps a running list of available addresses and assigns them as requested. DHCP can also be used as a configuration tool. It supports automatic permanent allocation of IP addresses to a new host and is even used for manual address assignments as a way to communicate the new address to the client host. Figure 11-7 depicts DHCP's processes.

Dynamic allocation is popular because it's easy to configure and conserves address space. DHCP works by allocating addresses for a period of time called a *lease*, guaranteeing

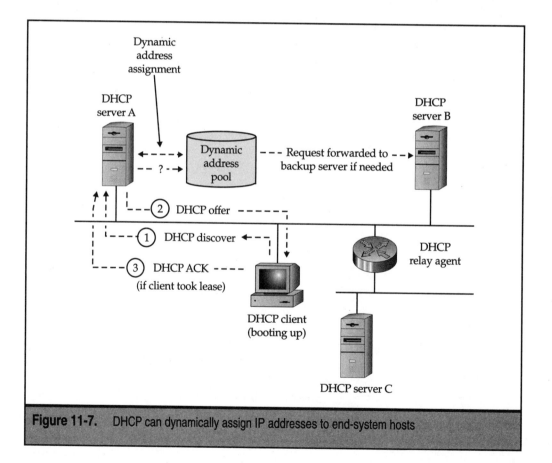

Figure 11-7.   DHCP can dynamically assign IP addresses to end-system hosts

not to allocate the IP address to another host as long as it's out on lease. When the host logs off the network, the DHCP server is notified and restores the address to its available pool.

To assure service, multiple DHCP servers are often configured. When the host logs in, it sends a DHCP discover message across the network to the server specified by the DHCP identifier field of the message. The DHCP server responds with a DHCP offer message or passes the discover request to a backup server. The client accepts the offer by sending the server a DHCP ACK message as acknowledgment.

If the offer is accepted, the server locks the lease in the available address pool by holding the assignment in persistent memory until the lease is terminated. Lease termination occurs when the client logs off the network (accomplished usually by the user turning off his or her PC at the day's end). If the identified DHCP server is down or refuses the request, after a preset timeout period the client can be configured to send a discover request to a backup DHCP server. If the server isn't on the same subnet, a router can be configured as a DHCP relay agent to steer the request message to the LAN segment on which the server resides.

Domain Name System

As discussed in our review of internetworking fundamentals in Chapter 2, people almost always reach network nodes by name, not by address. Think about it—how many times have you typed a dotted-decimal IP address into the address field in your browser? In most cases, you type in a URL instead, or simply click one sitting beneath a hypertext link on a Web page.

The service used to map names on the Internet is called the Domain Name System (DNS). A DNS name has two parts: host name and domain name. Taking toms.velte.com as an example, *toms* is the host (in this case a person's PC), and *velte.com* is the domain. At this writing, domain names must be registered with InterNIC (which stands for Internet Network Information Center), a U.S. government agency. However, by the year 2000 this responsibility will be transferred to several private companies, taking the government out of the URL business.

The IETF has specified that domain name suffixes be assigned based on the type of organization the autonomous system is, as listed in Table 11-2.

There are also geographical top-level domains defined by country. For example, .fr for France, .ca for Canada, .de for Germany (as in Deutschland), and so on.

For domain names to work, they must at some point be mapped to IP addresses so routers can recognize them. This mapping is called *name resolution*—a task performed by name servers. Domain Name Systems distribute databases across many servers in order to satisfy resolution requests. A large enterprise would distribute its DNS database throughout its internetwork topology. People can click their way around the Internet because their DNS databases are distributed worldwide. Figure 11-8 depicts the name services process.

When a client needs to send a packet, it must map the destination's symbolic name to its IP address. The client must have what's called *resolver software* configured in order to do this. The client's resolver software sends a query to a local DNS server, receives the

Domain	Autonomous System Type
.com	Commercial company
.edu	Educational institution
.gov	Governmental agency
.org	Nonprofit organization
.net	Network provider

Table 11-2.   Top-Level Domains Are Specified for Five Types of Autonomous Systems

resolution back, writes the IP address into the packet's header, and transmits. The name-to-IP mapping is then cached in the client for a preset period of time. As long as the client has the mapping for a name in cache, it bypasses the query process altogether.

NAME SERVER CONFIGURATION   Many internetworks have multiple DNS servers for speed and redundancy, especially larger autonomous systems on which hosts frequently come and go. Usually, name services are handled from the central server within the internetwork. For example, NT networks have so-called primary domain controller (PDC) servers, which are responsible for various housekeeping duties, including logon requests.

Besides DNS, the other two major naming services are the Windows Internet Name Service (WINS) and Sun Microsystems' Network Information Service (NIS). While DNS is optimized for Internet mappings, WINS and NIS manage name services at the internetwork level. WINS servers use DHCP to field requests, because DNS doesn't lend itself to handling dynamic names (it wants them stored permanently). NIS performs similar duty among UNIX hosts.

DNS is an important standard. You're able to click between hosts throughout the world because there are hundreds of thousands of DNS servers across the globe, exchanging and caching name mappings across routing domain so that it takes you a minimum of time to connect to a new Web site.

Campus Network Designs

The term *campus network* is a bit of a misnomer. What's meant is any local internetwork with a high-speed backbone. For example, the local network of a company's headquarters located entirely in a skyscraper is an example of a campus network. The term has had such heavy use in computer marketing that it's stuck as the term for medium-to-large local networks. Whatever it's called, a number of models have been developed for how to configure campus networks. We'll review them here.

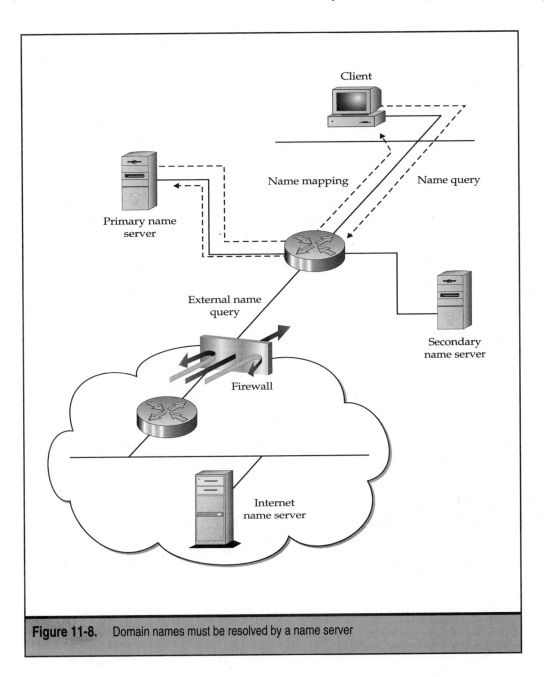

Figure 11-8. Domain names must be resolved by a name server

The Hub-Switch-Router Configuration

The so-called hub-switch-router configuration covers the access and distribution layers of the three-layer hierarchical network design model. The two layers are considered together because the distribution routers are generally located in the same building as host devices being given network access.

ACCESS-LAYER CONFIGURATION   The access layer of the three-layer hierarchical model is largely a function of the so-called hub-switch-router configuration. The major exception to this is remote access, covered later in this chapter (see "Connecting Remote Sites"). Configuring the access layer is largely a matter of wiring together hosts in a department or floor of a building. As far as physical media, we'll assume that Category 5 unshielded twisted-pair (UTP) cable is used to wire hosts into access devices. Two basic choices must be made when configuring the access and distribution layers:

▼ **Network type**   Most access-layer LAN segments being designed today run over Fast Ethernet specification, the 100 Mbps variant of the Ethernet standard. Token Ring has by all appearances lost the standards war to Ethernet, its use limited to IBM-dominated customer enterprises.

▲ **Bandwidth type**   A growing number of access-layer LAN segments run over switched bandwidth instead of shared hub bandwidth. However, switches as a rule of thumb are generally between 30 and 40 percent more expensive than hubs, causing switch ports to be used selectively in most enterprises.

These decisions dictate what Cisco products to configure and to some extent how to lay out your topology.

SELECTING ACCESS-LAYER TECHNOLOGY   Nowadays, if you have a choice, it's pretty much a given that you'll use Fast Ethernet for the access layer. It's fast, cheap, and the talent pool of network administrators knows this LAN specification best. If you have Token Ring or 10 Mbps Ethernet, your choices are somewhat more limited. You also must be careful that any existing cable plant meets the physical requirements specified by the LAN technology.

Exactly how you lay out the access layer is a little more complicated. If you've gathered the needs analysis information discussed earlier, that data will go a long way toward telling you two important things:

▼ **Workgroup hierarchy**   Large homogenous workgroups lend themselves to flat switched networks. For example, large customer service departments or help desks tend to connect to a fairly consistent set of hosts to run a limited set of applications. These shops are great candidates for flat (non-VLAN) switched networks.

▲ **Traffic loads**   If traffic volumes will be heavy and QoS policies stringent, you might want to look at a VLAN switched network, or at least high-bandwidth routed network configurations.

As you answer these two questions for various areas across the topology, the configuration begins to take shape. Quite often, this process is iterated floor by floor and building by building. This shouldn't surprise you. After all, networking isn't the only field of endeavor geographical in nature. So is operations management; it usually makes sense for managers to group certain types of workers and/or certain types of work tasks into one physical location.

PHYSICAL LAYOUT   The classical access-layer topology is the data closet–MDF layout. A *data closet* (also called a *wiring closet* or *phone closet*) is a small room housing patch panels connecting hosts to hubs or access switch ports. The patch panel is where networks start. A patch panel is a passive device with rows of RJ-45 jacks similar to the RJ-11 jacks for telephones. The host device's unshielded twisted-pair (UTP) cable plugs into one jack, and a cable from another jack plugs into the hub or switch port. This modular arrangement gives flexibility in moving devices between ports.

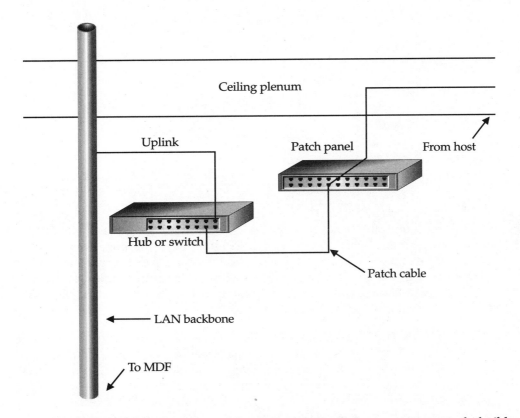

Signals go through the hub or switch by going out its uplink port to connect to the building's riser. *Riser* refers to the bundle of individual cables running from each floor down to a termination point. An *uplink* connects the hub or switch "up" in the logical sense, in that the riser is headed toward a larger piece of equipment—usually a router or a LAN switch.

MDF stands for *main distribution facility*—usually a room in a secure location on the building's first floor. The MDF serves as the termination point for the wiring emanating from the data closets, often equipment for both voice and data. The trend has been to locate the MDF in the enterprise's computer room if there's one in the building. Depending on the building's setup, the backbone travels either through holes punched through the floors or through the elevator shaft.

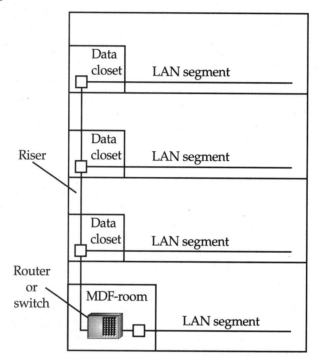

A riser's medium is almost always fiber-optic cable in larger buildings. The main reason for using fiber is that it can carry data more than 100 meters and is unaffected by electrical noise in buildings. But there's also a physical reason: because a riser hangs, over time the inexorable force of gravity will pull the twists out of a twisted-pair cable by causing the copper wire strands to unwind, deteriorating its electrical properties. Fiber-optic glass won't suffer that fate because it isn't twisted.

THE HUB-SWITCH CONFIGURATION   Various rules of thumb are applied when configuring the access layer. UTP cable can span up to 100 meters from the data closet. This is almost always more than enough on the horizontal plane (few work areas are wider than a football field is long). If the data closet is located at the center of a floor, the effective span would be 200 meters. As shown in Figure 11-9, not all buildings are vertical. Many are large horizontal structures of one or two floors, such as manufacturing plants and warehouses. For very large floors, the practice is to place data closets on either side.

From a logical standpoint, it doesn't make sense to place a router or LAN switch on every floor. Doing so would be prohibitively expensive and, just as important, would waste precious IP address space, because each LAN segment must have a unique IP address. The strategy, then, is to minimize the number of router interfaces servicing a given number of hosts. Hubs and switches fulfill this.

Figure 11-9 shows a configuration for a medium-sized company holding a few hundred employees in a building. To connect users on each floor, at least one Cisco FastHub 400 is placed in each data closet. FastHub 400 models connect 12 or 24 hosts per unit and

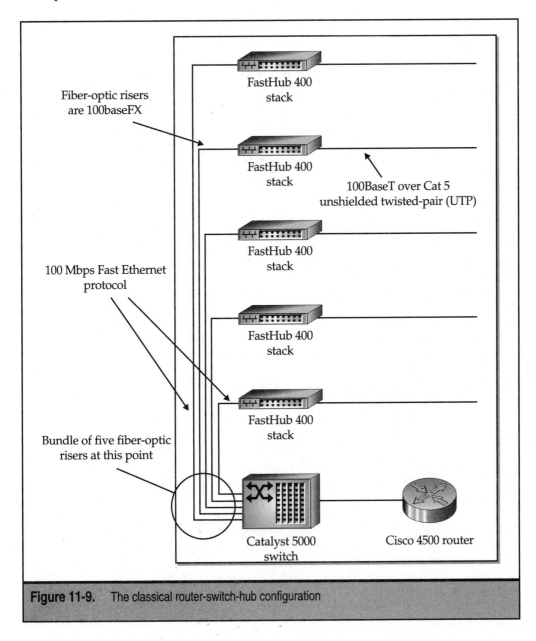

Figure 11-9.   The classical router-switch-hub configuration

are stackable up to four units per stack. The size of the stack depends on the number of employees on the floor. Which particular FastHub 400 model you use depends on the population density: some models support 12 ports for a stack density of 48 ports, and others support 24 ports for a density of 96 ports. If the population goes beyond 96, simply put another stack in the data closet to increase the number of ports.

The bottom left of Figure 11-9 shows how a riser is not a backbone in the proper sense of the term. The uplink running out of the FastHub 400 on the ground floor expands the riser bundle to a total of five fiber cables, which are essentially long wires used to avoid having to put a terminating device on each floor. Think of riser cables as "feeder wires" instead of as a backbone.

The LAN technology throughout the example building is Fast Ethernet, which runs at 100 Mbps. That speed is plenty for connecting most individual host devices. In practical terms, this means our riser is heading into MDF with 500 Mbps raw bandwidth; so a fast device is needed to handle the connections. We've configured a Cisco Catalyst 5000 switch for the job. With a 1.2 Gbps backplane, the Catalyst 5000 has plenty of horsepower to maintain satisfactory throughput for traffic from the five LAN segments. This box has five module slots, but a single 12-port 100FX card will handle all five LAN segments, leaving plenty of room for growth. A second slot is used to connect to the outside, leaving three open slots.

Figure 11-9 draws out the inherent advantages of LAN switching. You'll remember from Chapter 6 that a switch is roughly ten times quicker when it has a MAC address in its switching table. Our example company has 300 employees, and the Catalyst 5000 has more than adequate memory and backplane speed to handle a switching table of that size (it can handle thousands). Because the switch is talking to all 300 hosts, it has their MAC addresses readily available, so why go through the relatively slow process of processing their IP addresses in a router?

THE ACCESS SWITCH CONFIGURATION   We've mentioned that most people think eventually hubs will give way to switches. What they're talking about here is *access switching*, as opposed to the LAN switching example in Figure 11-9. An access switch does the same thing as a hub—it connects hosts to a LAN segment. This extends switched bandwidth all the way out to the desktop or server. Figure 11-10 shows a typical access switch configuration.

It wouldn't be practical to run a fiber-optic cable all the way down to the MDF for every switched host. As Figure 11-10 shows, an interim step can be configured using an access switch such as the Cisco Catalyst 1912, able to connect up to 12 devices. A lower-end switch such as a Cisco MicroSwtich isn't used here because it doesn't have an FX port for connecting to a fiber-optic riser.

The hierarchical model discourages connecting hubs into switches. Doing this makes for easy connectivity to the backbone, but amounts to a chain configuration (as described earlier). Yet the reality is that hub-switch connections are routinely used in internetwork designs because it's an easy way to add connection ports to a topology.

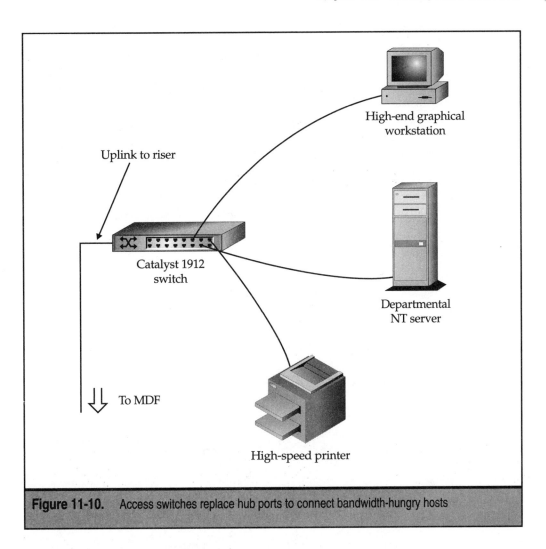

Uplink to riser

High-end graphical
workstation

Catalyst 1912
switch

Departmental
NT server

To MDF

High-speed printer

Figure 11-10.   Access switches replace hub ports to connect bandwidth-hungry hosts

It should be pointed out that in high-density environments, users are faced with either configuring high-end Catalyst switches in the data closet or running riser cables to the MDF.

THE SWITCH-ROUTER CONFIGURATION   To be able to internetwork, users need to be routed at some point. The standard practice is to configure a local router in the MDF room. That way, users inside the enterprise are connected to the enterprise internetwork for intramural communications, and to the firewall to access the Internet.

Figure 11-11 zooms in on our example company's MDF room. A Cisco 4500 router is configured in this situation because it has three module slots that can accommodate LAN or WAN modules. One slot is filled with a one-port 100BaseTX LAN module to connect the Catalyst 5000 switch; the other houses a one-port T1 WAN module, connecting the building to the outside world.

If you're thinking that with all the bandwidth floating around the building, a mere 1.544 Mbps pipe to the outside might not provide sufficient capacity, you're catching on. A T1 link indeed might not be enough, depending on how much of the local traffic load flows to the outside.

THE NEW 80/20 RULE   Remember the 80/20 rule discussed earlier in the chapter (see "The Three-Layer Hierarchical Design Model")? The traditional dictum has been that only 20 percent of the traffic goes to the outside. But things have changed. Now the gurus are talking about the "new 80/20 rule," where as much as 80 percent of traffic can go to the outside as users reach into the Internet to download files, talk to other parts of the enterprise intranet, or even deal with trading partners via an extranet.

The single biggest driver turning the 80/20 rule on its head is e-commerce, where networked computers are taking over traditionally human-based sales transactions. Web

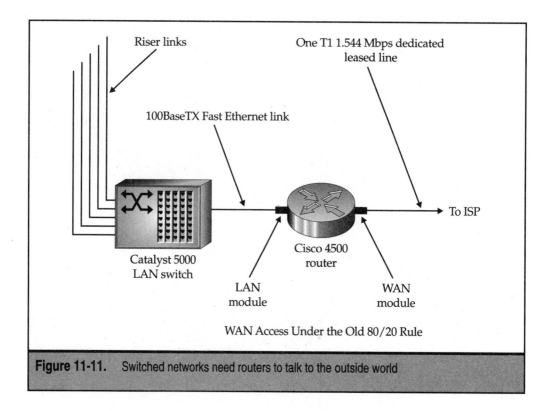

Figure 11-11.   Switched networks need routers to talk to the outside world

sites such as Amazon.com and E*Trade are famous for cutting out the middleman, but electronic business-to-business trading—called electronic data interchange (EDI)—is generating more IP traffic with each passing day.

Assuming the new 80/20 rule holds for our example enterprise, the MDF room might be configured along the lines of Figure 11-12, where a much fatter pipe is extended to the outside in the form of a T3 line—a 43 Mbps leased-line digital WAN link medium.

Now the router is bigger and the switch is smaller. If the users are talking to the outside 80 percent of the time, there's less need to switch traffic within the building. We've configured a Cisco Catalyst 3000 switch instead of the Catalyst 5000 because there's less LAN switching work to do. The high-end Cisco 7205 router is configured for greater throughput capacity, with a faster processor and a five-slot chassis.

At 45 Mbps, T3 runs nearly 30 times faster than a T1 line. More and more enterprises are turning to T3 to make the point-to-point connection to their ISPs. Few, however, need all that capacity, so most ISPs resell a portion of the bandwidth to individual customers according to their needs, a practice called *fractionalizing*, in which the customer signs up for only a fraction of the link's capacity.

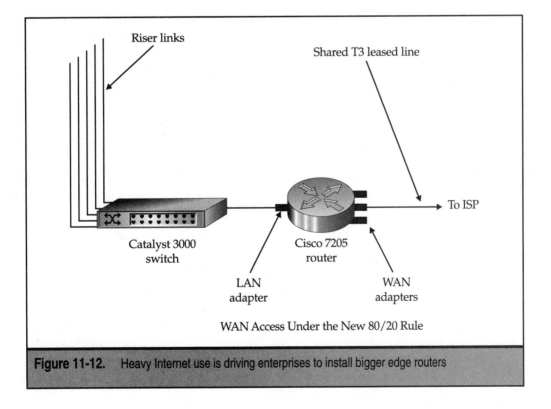

Figure 11-12.   Heavy Internet use is driving enterprises to install bigger edge routers

Choosing a High-Speed Backbone

Backbones are used to connect major peer network nodes. A backbone link connects two particular nodes, but the term *backbone* often is used to refer to a series of backbone links. For example, a campus backbone might extend over several links.

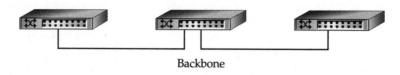

Backbone

Backbone links move data between backbone devices only. They don't handle traffic between LAN segments within a site. That's done at the distribution layer of the three-layer hierarchical model by LAN switches and routers. Backbones concentrate on moving traffic at very high speeds over a geography.

Campus backbones obviously cover a short distance, usually via underground fiber-optic cabling. WAN backbones—used by big enterprises and ISPs—move traffic between cities. Most WAN backbone links are operated by so-called Internet backbone providers, although many large enterprises operate their own high-speed long-distance links. WAN links run over high-speed fiber-optic cable links strung underground, on electrical pylons, and even under oceans. Satellite links are also becoming common. Regardless of transport medium, and whether it's a campus or WAN backbone, they share these characteristics:

▼ **Minimal packet manipulation**   Such processing as access control list enforcement and firewall filtering are kept out of the backbone to speed throughput. For this reason, most backbone links are switched, not routed.

■ **High-speed devices**   A relatively slow device like a Cisco 4500 would not be configured onto a high-speed backbone. The two ends of a backbone link generally operate over a Catalyst 5000 link or faster.

▲ **Fast transport**   Most high-speed backbones are built atop transport technology of 1 Gbps or higher.

The two main backbone technologies now are ATM and Gigabit Ethernet. FDDI is more widely installed than either, but with a total capacity of only 100 Mbps, few new FDDI installations are going into high-speed backbones.

ATM BACKBONES   Asynchronous Transfer Mode (ATM) uses a fixed-length format instead of the variable-length packets Ethernet uses. The fixed-length format lends itself to high-speed throughput because the hardware always knows exactly where each cell begins. For this reason, ATM has a very positive ratio between payload and network control overhead traffic. This architecture also lends itself to QoS—a big plus for operating critical backbone links.

Figure 11-13 shows a campus backbone built over ATM. The configuration uses Catalyst 5000 LAN switches for the outlying building and a high-end Catalyst 8500 Multiservice switch router to handle traffic hitting the enterprise's central server farm.

A *blade* is an industry term for a large printed circuit board that is basically an entire networking device on a single module. Blades plug into chassis slots. For a Catalyst switch to talk ATM, the appropriate adapter blade must be configured into the chassis. The LightStream 1010 blade is used here because it's designed for short-haul traffic—there are other "edge" ATM blades for WAN traffic. One reason for this is to allow Cisco to support different technologies in a single product.

Cisco ATM devices use the LAN emulation (LANE) adapter technology to integrate with campus Ethernet networks.

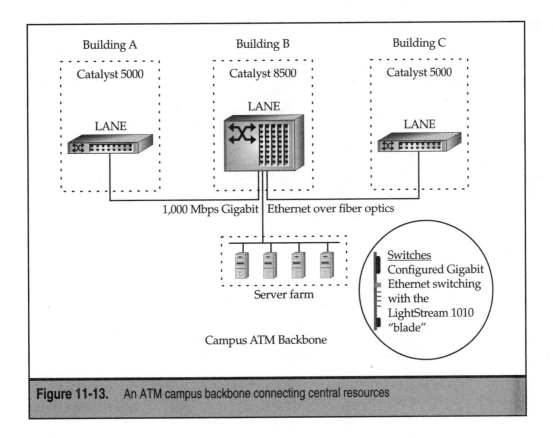

Figure 11-13.   An ATM campus backbone connecting central resources

Switched WAN backbones run over very high-speed fiber-optic trunks running the SONET specification. Most new trunks being pulled are OC-48, which run at about 2.5 Gbps. OC stands for Optical Carrier, and SONET stands for Synchronous Optical Network. This is a standard developed by Bell Communications Research for very high-speed networks over fiber-optic cable. The slowest SONET specification, OC-1 runs at 52 Mbps—about the same speed as T3. OC SONET is an important technology because it represents the higher speed infrastructure "pipe" the Internet needs to continue expanding. We mention this here because ATM and Gigabit Ethernet R&D efforts are carried out with the SONET specification in mind, and it's the presumed WAN link transport.

GIGABIT ETHERNET BACKBONE Although Gigabit Ethernet is a much newer technology than ATM, many network managers are turning to it for their backbone needs instead of ATM. Figure 11-14 shows that a Gigabit Ethernet backbone can be configured using the same Catalyst platforms as for ATM. This is done by configuring Gigabit Ethernet blades

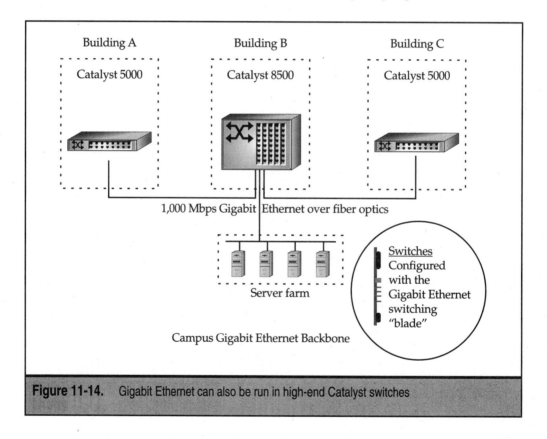

Figure 11-14. Gigabit Ethernet can also be run in high-end Catalyst switches

instead of ATM blades. Note, also, that the same fiber-optic cabling can be used for Gigabit Ethernet, but the adapters must be changed to those designed to support Gigabit Ethernet instead of ATM.

As you might imagine, the technology-specific blades and adapters represent the different electronics needed to process either variable-length Ethernet packets or fixed-length ATM cells.

Connecting Remote Sites

There are two kinds of remote locations: the branch and the small office/home office (SOHO). The defining difference between the two is the type of connection. Because they have only one or two users online at any given moment, SOHO sites use dial-in connections, while branch sites use some form of a dedicated circuit. Three major remote connection technologies are configured here. You might want to flip back to Chapter 2 to refresh on how these respective technologies work.

FRAME RELAY   Frame Relay is ideal for "bursty" WAN traffic. In other words, dedicated leased lines such as T1 or T3 only make economic sense if they're continually used. Frame Relay solves that problem by letting users share WAN infrastructure with other enterprises. Frame Relay can do this because it's a packet-switched data network (PSDN), in which end-to-end connections are virtual. You only need to buy a local phone circuit between your remote site and a nearby Frame Relay drop point. After that point, your packets intermix with those from hundreds of other enterprises.

Normally, a device called a FRAD is needed to talk to a Frame Relay network. FRAD stands for Frame Relay Assembler/Disassembler, which parses data streams into proper Frame Relay packet format. But using a mere FRAD only gets you connected and offers little in the way of remote management, security, and QoS. Cisco has built Frame Relay capability into many of its routers to provide more intelligence over Frame Relay connections. Figure 11-15 shows a typical Frame Relay configuration using Cisco gear.

Because Frame Relay uses normal serial line connections, no special interfaces need be installed in a router to make it Frame Relay compatible. The Cisco 2600 router is a cost-effective solution for the stores in Figure 11-16's example, because they have sufficient throughput capacity to handle traffic loads these remote locations are likely to generate.

INTEGRATED SERVICES DIGITAL NETWORK (ISDN)   ISDN can be used for either dial-in or dedicated remote connections. It provides much more bandwidth than normal analog modem telephone connections, but must be available from a local carrier to your premise. ISDN has channel options called BRI and PRI. BRI has two so-called B-channels to deliver 128 Kbps bandwidth and is usually used for dial-in connections from home or small offices. PRI packages 23 B-channels, for about 1.48 Mbps bandwidth, and is generally used for full-time multiuser connections.

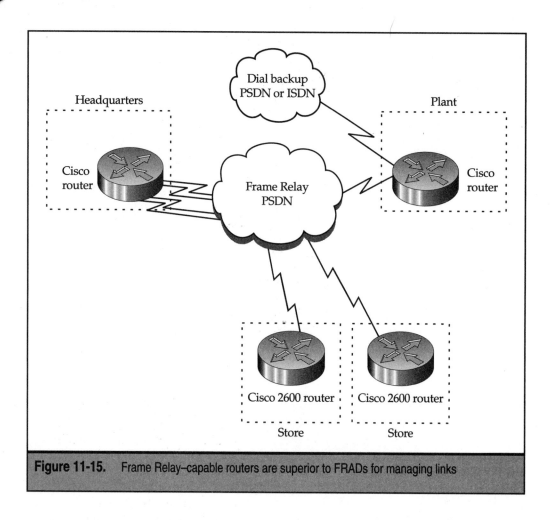

Figure 11-15.   Frame Relay–capable routers are superior to FRADs for managing links

Figure 11-16 shows a typical Cisco ISDN configuration. The Cisco 800 series router is targeted to connect ISDN users. The 804 has four ports, and the 801 has one port. If, however, VPN connection is required, the Cisco 1720 Access Router must be configured. It's more costly, but it has the electronics and software to handle encryption/decryption that VPN networking requires.

DIGITAL SUBSCRIBER LINE (DSL)   DSL is competing with ISDN for the small office/home office market. To use DSL, you must be serviced by a local telephone switch office that

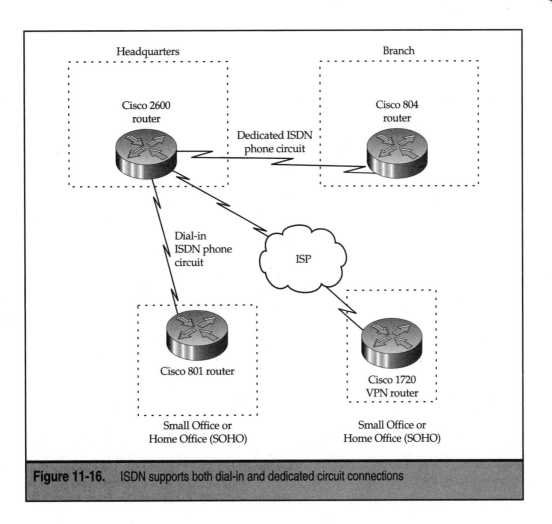

Figure 11-16.   ISDN supports both dial-in and dedicated circuit connections

supports DSL and be within a certain distance of it—usually a few miles. DSL is characterized by asymmetrical data rates, where more data comes down from the phone company than the user can send back up. This means that DSL should be selectively used where traffic characteristics match this constraint—in other words, where the user does a lot of downloading but not a lot of uploading. This is the case with most Internet users, though, and DSL has become very popular where the phone companies offer it.

The configuration in Figure 11-17 shows a Cisco 675 Speedrunner ADSL router (ADSL stands for asymmetric digital subscriber line). The Speedrunner looks like a fat radar detector, but has an Ethernet interface on the back to connect local users.

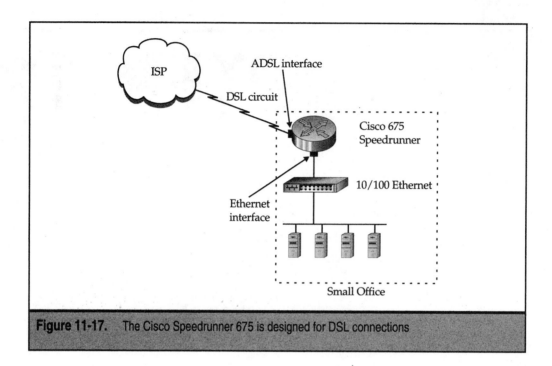

Figure 11-17.   The Cisco Speedrunner 675 is designed for DSL connections

CHAPTER 12

Troubleshooting
Cisco Networks

Keeping an internetwork going is a full-time job. As you saw earlier, problems emerge with such frequency that the industry invented routing protocols to deal with them automatically, not even waiting for a network administrator to intervene. And they do a pretty good job—at least with problems that can be ameliorated by detouring to a new route. But changing routes is only a temporary solution. In order for a network to run effectively, all its components must be kept up and running properly as much of the time as possible. After all, delivering available bandwidth to users under normal circumstances is hard enough, without having a LAN segment out of commission or a router at partial capacity.

For this reason, a big part of a network team's time is spent troubleshooting. Problems range from a single user unable to access a service to an entire LAN segment crashing. Troubleshooting isn't just a matter of finding and fixing broken parts; much of it is dedicated to fixing performance bottlenecks. When a problem emerges, the network administrator often has no idea which device is causing the trouble. And once the problem device is identified, the cause of the problem must be diagnosed. Then decisions must be made on how to fix the situation.

A methodical approach should be taken to troubleshooting; otherwise, a lot of time can be wasted trying to figure out what's causing the problem. Like a doctor, the troubleshooter must recognize the symptoms, associate them with a set of probable causes, and then progressively narrow down the list until the culprit is finally identified. From there, a proper action plan must be devised and implemented. That's troubleshooting.

In this chapter, we'll review how to troubleshoot problems in a variety of Cisco configurations by running through some troubleshooting scenarios. For simplicity's sake, we'll assume IP as the network protocol and the Microsoft Windows platform as the host. Although the terminology can vary, networking problems are largely the same regardless of the protocol or host environment. We'll also restrict the examples to troubleshooting routers, which is where most of the action is.

THE MECHANICS OF NETWORK TROUBLESHOOTING

In internetworks, trouble is caused either by failing device hardware or a configuration problem. The location of most problems can be identified remotely, and to some extent the problems can also be diagnosed and even fixed remotely (but the hardware must still be running for that). By *remote* here, we mean without walking over and actually looking at and touching the device; we don't necessarily mean being geographically removed. If, say, an enterprise's campus internetwork is experiencing a problem, network administrators usually do most troubleshooting tasks without even leaving their desks.

In Cisco environments, remote work can be done through a network management console or by logging directly into a device's IOS command-line environment via Telnet. As you learned, the Cisco NMS consoles—Resource Manager Essentials, CWSI Campus, and NetSys Baseliner—use their graphical interfaces to indirectly manipulate IOS commands inside the remote device. Thus, most of the real troubleshooting work takes place inside the device's IOS environment. Here are the major IOS commands used to perform most troubleshooting tasks:

▼ **ping**   Indicates whether "echo" packets are reaching a destination and returning. For example, if you enter **ping 10.1.1.1**, IOS will return the percentage of packets that echoed back from the 10.1.1.1 interface.

■ **trace**   Reports the actual path taken to a destination. For example, if you enter **trace ip 10.1.1.1**, IOS will list every hop the message takes to reach the destination 10.1.1.1 interface.

▲ **show**   Reports configuration and status information on devices and networks. For example, the **show memory** command displays how much memory is assigned to each network address and how much is free.

The source of problems must be in either device or network media (cabling, connectors, and so on). Even if the trouble is in a cable, the way to it is through IOS. The **ping** and **trace** commands are used to locate problems. If the device is still running, the **show** and **debug** commands can be used to diagnose them. Actual fixes are done by changing either the hardware or its configuration. The **debug** command is similar to **show**, except it generates far more detailed information on device operations—so much so that running **debug** may greatly slow device performance.

Network Troubleshooting Methods

Problems are usually brought to a network administrator's attention by users. They want to know why they can't access a service within the enterprise's internetwork, or complain that performance is slow. The location and nature of the complaint are themselves strong clues as to what's causing the problem. Many times the administrator immediately knows what's wrong and how to fix it. But oftentimes an investigation must be launched to figure out which device is the source of the trouble, what's causing it, and what is the best way to fix it. The network administrator must find answers by methodical troubleshooting. As you might imagine, troubleshooting largely works by the process of elimination.

▼ **What are the symptoms?**   Usually this boils down to users not being able to reach a destination. Knowing both endpoints of a network problem—the source and destination addresses—is the base information in most troubleshooting situations.

■ **Where do I start looking?**   Does the scenario fit a known pattern that suggests probable causes? For example, if a server isn't responding to service requests from a client, there could be a problem with the server or the client itself. If the server is working OK for other clients, then it might be the client device. If not that, then the problem must reside somewhere between the two.

■ **Where do I start?** There are rules of thumb that short-list what's most likely causing a certain type of symptom. The administrator should diagnose "best-candidate" causes first. For example, if a server accessed via a WAN link seems slow to remote dial-in users, the link could be going bad, usage could be up, there could be a shortage of buffer memory in the router interface servicing the link, or the hosts could be misconfigured. One of these probable causes will explain the problem 95 percent of the time.

▲ **What's the action plan?** Finding the exact cause of a problem in a malfunctioning device means dealing with one variable at a time. For example, it wouldn't make sense to replace all network interface modules in a router before rebooting. Doing so might fix the problem, but it wouldn't define the exact source or even what fixed it. In science this is called changing one variable at a time. The best practice is to zero in on the source by cutting variables down one by one. That way the problem can be replicated, the fix validated as a good one, and the exact cause recorded for future reference.

Most internetwork problems manifest themselves as either seriously degraded performance or as "destination unreachable" timeout messages. Sometimes the problem is widespread; other times it's limited to a LAN segment or even to a specific host. Let's take a look at some typical problems mapped to their probable causes. Table 12-1 outlines problems with host connectivity (hosts are usually single-user PCs, but not always).

Unfortunately, most internetwork problems aren't limited to a single host. If a problem exists in a router or is spread throughout an area, many users and servers are affected. Table 12-2 outlines a couple of typical network problems that are more widespread.

Symptoms	Probable Causes
Host can't access networks beyond local LAN segment.	Misconfigured settings in host device, such as bad default gateway IP address or bad subnet mask. The gateway router is malfunctioning.
Host can't access certain services beyond local LAN segment.	Misconfigured extended access list on a router between the host and the server. Misconfigured firewall, if the server is beyond the autonomous system.

Table 12-1. Typical Host Access Problems and Causes

Symptoms	Probable Causes
Most users can't access a server.	Misconfigured default gateway specification in the remote server. Misconfigured access list in the remote server.
Connections to an area can't be made when one path is down.	Routing protocol not converging within the routing domain. All interfaces on router handling alternative path not configured with secondary IP addresses (discontinuous addressing).

Table 12-2. Sometimes the Remote Host or Meshed Path Redundancy Is Misconfigured

Many times, networks and services are reachable, but performance is unacceptably slow. Table 12-3 outlines factors that can affect performance within a local network. It doesn't address WAN links. They're covered separately later in this chapter because serial lines involve a slightly different set of technologies and problems.

Symptoms	Probable Causes
Poor server response; hard to make and keep connections.	Bad network link, usually caused by malfunctioning network interface module or LAN segment medium. Mismatched access lists (in meshed internetwork with multiple paths). Congested link, overwhelmed by too much traffic. Poorly configured load balancing (routing protocol metrics).

Table 12-3. Campus LAN Performance Problems and Their Causes

Troubleshooting Host IP Configuration

If a user is having trouble accessing services and the overall network seems to be OK, a good place to start looking for the cause of the problem is inside that person's computer. There are a couple of things that could be misconfigured in the user's host computer:

▼ **Incorrect IP information**   The IP address or subnet mask information could be missing or incorrect.

▲ **Incorrect default gateway**   The default gateway router could be misconfigured.

To refresh on the subject, every host has a default gateway specified in the host's network settings. A *default gateway* is an interface on a local router that is used for passing messages sent by the host to addresses beyond the LAN. A default gateway (also called a *gateway of last resort*) is configured because it makes sense for one router to handle most of a host's outbound traffic in order to keep an updated cache on destination IP addresses and routes to them. A host must have at least one gateway, and a second one is often configured for redundancy in case the primary gateway goes down.

Checking the Host IP Address Information

Misconfigured network parameters in desktop hosts are usually attributable to a mistake by the end user. Keep in mind that—on Windows 9x computers, at least—any user can easily access and modify network settings. To check the host's configuration (in our Windows PC example), click the Start button on the menu bar and click Control Panel | Network | Configuration to go to the Network Configuration tab in Windows 9x. In the Network tab's list box, double-click the component that connects the host to the network. In Windows NT (renamed Windows 2000 in its next incarnation), click on the Protocols tab and then TCP/IP Properties. This will allow you to set the IP address and default gateway.

The component will usually be a network interface card (NIC) connecting the host to the LAN, as is the case with the TCP/IP Ethernet PC card highlighted in Figure 12-1. (If the host dials into the internetwork, the dial-up adapter should be selected instead.)

Once you're pointed at the right NIC, start by making sure that the host is identifying itself correctly to the network. To do that, click Network | IP Address to review the settings in the IP Address tab. The example in Figure 12-2 shows a statically defined IP address and subnet. These must match what's on file for the host in the config file of the router serving as the default gateway. If the "Obtain an IP address automatically" selection is checked, the host's IP address is dynamically assigned by a server—a Dynamic Host Control Protocol (DHCP) server. If DHCP or an equivalent is in use, misconfigured host IP information is less likely, but the troubleshooter could check the situation at the address server.

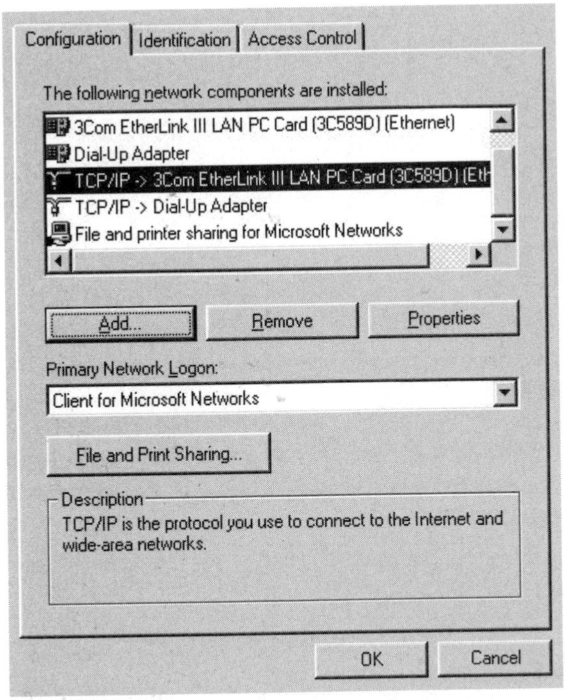

Figure 12-1. To troubleshoot a host, the place to start is the network interface card

Next, make sure the host's declared IP address is the right one by logging into its gateway router and entering the **show arp** command. You'll remember that ARP stands for Address Resolution Protocol, a utility that maps the physical device's media access control (layer 2) address to its assigned IP (layer 3) address in order to handle the final stage of delivery between the gateway router and the host. Figure 12-3 shows the ARP table in the config file of our example gateway router. The shaded line shows that the Ethernet interface indeed has an address 10.1.13.12 on file, as was declared in the host's IP Address tab. The host itself is uniquely identified by the MAC address of its NIC.

Another potential host problem is the config settings for the default gateway itself. In other words, you have to make sure the host has the correct IP address configured as its default gateway router. To do that, click the Gateway tab in the Network dialog box, shown in Figure 12-4.

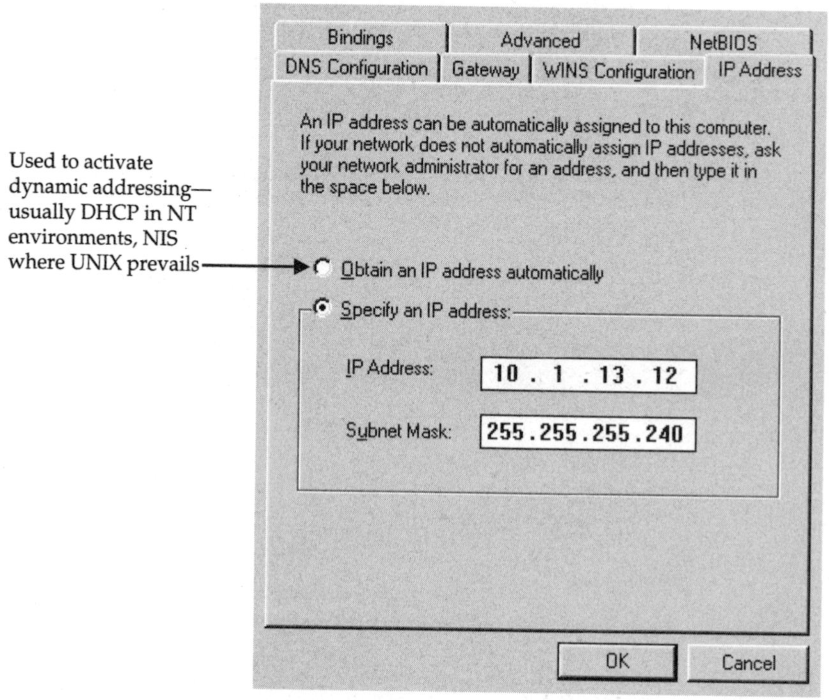

Used to activate
dynamic addressing—
usually DHCP in NT
environments, NIS
where UNIX prevails

Figure 12-2.   The host's IP address settings and those in the default gateway router must match

MAC address

```
vsigate#show arp

Protocol   address      Age (min)   Hardware Addr    Type    Interface
Internet   10.1.13.11      0         0050.0465.395c   ARPA    Ethernet1
Internet   10.1.11.1      12         0060.3eba.a6a0   SNAP    TokenRing0
Internet   10.1.13.12      9         00a0.c92a.4823   ARPA    Ethernet1
Internet   10.1.11.2       -         0006.f4c5.5f1d   SNAP    TokenRing0
Internet   10.1.11.3     190         0006.c1de.4ab9   SNAP    TokenRing0
Internet   10.1.12.3       -         0006.f4c5.5fdd   SNAP    TokenRing1
Internet   10.1.13.12     15         0050.04d7.1fa4   ARPA    Ethernet1
```

Figure 12-3.   The host's IP address must match the one for the gateway router in the ARP table

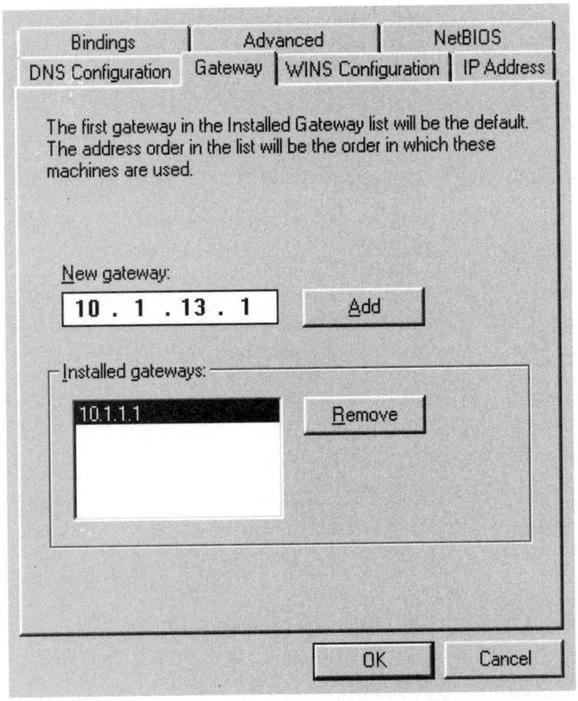

Figure 12-4. Check to make sure the correct default gateway IP address is configured

The host's default gateway IP address must match the one set for the network interface module on the gateway router. To check that this is the case, go to the gateway router and enter the **show interfaces** command, as shown here:

```
MyRouter#show interfaces
 .
 .
 .
interface Ethernet1
 ip address 10.1.13.1 255.255.255.240
 ip accounting output-packets
 ip nat inside
 ip ospf priority 255
 media-type 10BaseT
 .
 .
 .
```

As you can see, our example interface Ethernet1 is indeed addressed 10.1.13.1, as declared in the host's Gateway tab.

This is also where you can check to make sure the host's declared subnet mask matches the one on file in the gateway router. Mask 255.255.255.240 is also correct, because it matches the one declared in the host's IP Address tab.

Obviously, if any of the host's network settings are incorrect, the administrator should adjust them to match the gateway router's settings, reboot the PC, and try to make a network connection. On the other hand, if the PC's settings are OK, the troubleshooter must work outward from the operable host to identify the source area of the problem.

Isolating Connectivity Problems

Most network problems have to do with the inability to connect to a desired host or service. Connectivity problems—also called "reachability problems"—come in many forms, such as attempted HTTP connections timing out, attempted terminal connections getting no response from the host, and so on. As just outlined, the troubleshooter should first make sure the host reporting the problem is itself properly configured, then work outward. To draw an analogy, the troubleshooter must work the neighborhood door to door, much like a cop searching for clues.

Checking Between the Host and Its Gateway Router

If the host's network settings are configured properly, the next step is to work outward from the host to the gateway router. This should be done even if the host's problem is failing to connect to a remote server. Before working far afield, the best practice is to first check the link between the host and its gateway router.

USING THE PING COMMAND   The easiest way to check a link is to use the **ping** command. This command sends ping packets to a specific network device to see if it's reachable. In technical terms, **ping** sends its packets via the ICMP transport protocol instead of via UDP or TCP. It actually sends several packets, as shown here:

```
MyRouter>ping 10.1.1.100

Type escape sequence to abort.
Sending 5, 100-byte ICMP Echos to 10.1.1.100, timeout is 2 seconds:
!!!!!
Success rate is 100 percent (5/5), round-trip min/avg/max = 1/1/1 ms
MyRouter>
```

Host computers and network devices both have **ping** commands. The preceding example was taken from a Cisco router, and the ping successfully reached the destination. But one could just as well use the **ping** command available in the command line of the host. We're using a Windows host for our examples, but other platforms—such as Macs, the various UNIX platforms, IBM's OS/400, and other proprietary server architectures—all have **ping** and other basic network commands built into their operating systems.

Usually, the first ping test from a host is the link to its gateway router. On a Windows machine, check this by clicking the Start button in the menu bar and choosing Programs | MS-DOS Prompt to get to the DOS command line. Then check to see if the gateway router is responding by entering the **ping** command, as shown in the following code snippet:

```
Microsoft(R) Windows NT(TM)
(C) Copyright 1985-1996 Microsoft Corp.

C:\>ping 10.1.13.1

Pinging 10.1.13.1 with 32 bytes of data:

Request timed out.
Request timed out.
Request timed out.
Request timed out.

C:\>
```

The preceding example shows that four ping packets were sent to the gateway router, which failed to respond. This tells the troubleshooter a few things:

▼ The host PC's NIC is good; otherwise, MS-DOS would have generated an error message when the card failed to respond to the **ping** command.

■ The Ethernet LAN segment might be down—a condition often referred to as a "media problem" (the shared medium is apparently not working).

▲ The network interface module on the gateway router might be faulty.

If the host checks out OK, the troubleshooter must move outward. As mentioned, the investigation should start with the link to the gateway router.

USING THE SHOW INTERFACES COMMAND   To check on whether the problem is the gateway router's interface or the LAN segment's medium, log into the gateway router, and enter the **show interfaces** command to obtain the following report:

```
MyRouter>show interfaces
Ethernet1 is up, line protocol is down
   Hardware is MyRouter, address is 0060.2fa3.fabd
(bia 0060.2fa3.fabd)
   Internet address is 10.1.13.1/28
   .
   .
   .
```

In the preceding example, the router reports both that the Ethernet1 network interface module is up and the line protocol is down. The term *line protocol* denotes both the cable into the router and the LAN protocol running over it. A line protocol reported as down probably indicates that the LAN segment's shared medium—a hub, an access switch, or a cable—is faulty. From there you would physically check the medium to identify the hardware problem (how to do that is covered later in this chapter under "Troubleshooting Cisco Hardware").

Another potential condition could be that a network administrator has turned off either the interface or the line, or both. This is routinely done while a piece of equipment is being repaired, upgraded, or replaced. Notifying IOS that a piece of equipment is down for maintenance avoids having needless error messages generated by the router. The following example shows the report when a network interface module is administratively down:

```
MyRouter>show interfaces
Ethernet1 is administratively down, line protocol is down
  Hardware is MyRouter, address is 0060.2fa3.fabd
(bia 0060.2fa3.fabd)
  Internet address is 10.1.13.1/28
    .
    .
    .
```

Whether a piece of equipment is down by design or because of a malfunction, it still stops traffic. So it's important to know when a piece of equipment is being worked on in order to make sure an alternative path is available to handle traffic.

If both the gateway router interface and line protocol are up and running fine, the cause of the connectivity problem probably resides in a link to another network.

Troubleshooting Problems Connecting to Other Networks

Things get a little more complicated beyond the home LAN segment. If the host can't connect beyond the gateway router, there are at once both more potential sources and more types of trouble to check out. What's meant by potential problem *sources* here is that many more hardware devices must be considered as potential causes of the reachability problem. What's meant by potential problem *types* is that such things as access lists, routing protocols, and other factors beyond hardware must now also be considered.

USING THE TRACE COMMAND TO PINPOINT TROUBLE SPOTS   Instead of pinging outward from the host one link at a time, the route between the host and the unreachable server can be analyzed all at once using the "trace route" command. In our example Windows host, do this by clicking Start | MS-DOS Prompt to get into the host's DOS prompt. Once there, enter the **tracert** command, Microsoft's version of the trace route command. The example in Figure 12-5 shows the route being traced from the host PC to www.PayrollServer.AcmeEnterprises.com, which is an internal server several hops away. It's optional to use either the domain name or the IP address. Each line in the **tracert** command represents a hop along the path to the destination.

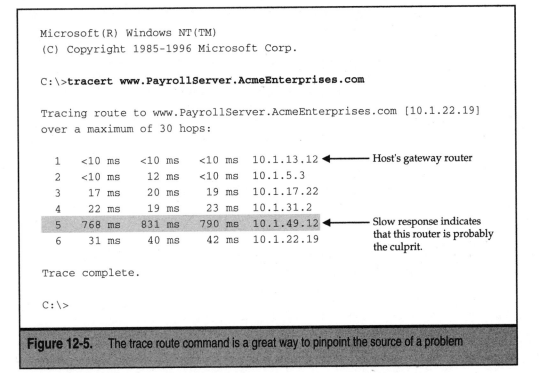

```
Microsoft(R) Windows NT(TM)
(C) Copyright 1985-1996 Microsoft Corp.


C:\>tracert www.PayrollServer.AcmeEnterprises.com

Tracing route to www.PayrollServer.AcmeEnterprises.com [10.1.22.19]
over a maximum of 30 hops:

    1    <10 ms    <10 ms    <10 ms   10.1.13.12 ◄──────── Host's gateway router
    2    <10 ms     12 ms    <10 ms   10.1.5.3
    3     17 ms     20 ms     19 ms   10.1.17.22
    4     22 ms     19 ms     23 ms   10.1.31.2
    5    768 ms    831 ms    790 ms   10.1.49.12 ◄────── Slow response indicates
    6     31 ms     40 ms     42 ms   10.1.22.19          that this router is probably
                                                          the culprit.

Trace complete.

C:\>
```

Figure 12-5.   The trace route command is a great way to pinpoint the source of a problem

In TCP/IP internetworks, trace route commands work by sending three trace packets to each router three times and recording the echo response times. As with the **ping** command, trace packets use the ICMP transport protocol. However, trace packets differ from ping packets in that they have a time-to-live (TTL) field used to increment outward from the host one step at a time. The TTL field causes the packet to die when the counter hits zero. The trace route command uses the TTL field by sending the first trace packet sent to the nearest router with a TTL of 1, to the next router with a TTL of 2, and so on. This process is repeated until the destination host is reached—if it's reachable. The network administrator can put a limit on how many hops the trace may take, to automatically stop the process if the destination proves unreachable.

The *ms* readings are milliseconds, and you can see that nearby routers naturally tend to echo back faster. Under 10 ms is fast; anything over 100 ms or so is getting slow—but one must always adjust the timings according to how many hops removed the router is. As you can see, the router in the shaded line in Figure 12-5 is the likely suspect for the slow service because of its slow response times. The probable explanation is that the router's interface or the LAN segment attached to it is either congested or experiencing hardware faults. The next step would be to Telnet into router 10.1.49.12 (if possible) and diagnose the system, the involved network interface, and so on. If making a Telnet connection isn't possible, the troubleshooter must go in through the Console or AUX port, which of course requires that somebody be physically present at the device, unless a dial-in maintenance solution has been configured beforehand.

Sometimes a trace route will locate a node that's stopping traffic altogether. An example of this is shown in Figure 12-6, where 10.1.49.12 now is dropping trace packets instead of merely returning them slowly. The asterisks indicate a null timing result because nothing came back, and the message "request timed out" is inserted. Take note that this does not necessarily mean the entire router is down. It could be that only the network interface or LAN segment that connects the suspect router may be down, or configured not to respond to pings.

If possible, first try to Telnet into the router through one of its other interfaces. If this doesn't work, the next move depends on the router's proximity. If it's nearby, go to it and log in through the Console or AUX port. If it's remote, you should contact the person responsible for dealing with it and walk that person through the diagnosis steps.

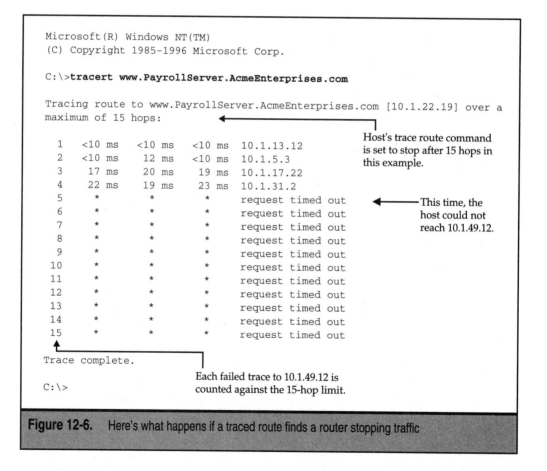

Figure 12-6. Here's what happens if a traced route finds a router stopping traffic

NOTE: Troubleshooting almost always takes place within the enterprise's internetwork. This is because the network team can control events only within its autonomous system. The trace route command is a good example of this. If you traced a route through the Internet—say, to troubleshoot a VPN connection—most lines between your gateway router and the destination node will return asterisks instead of timings, and "request timed out" messages instead of IP addresses. This is because almost all edge routers are configured by their network teams not to respond to trace routes. This is done as a security precaution. The point here is to highlight the trade-off a VPN must incur: loss of control is exchanged for very low cost WAN links; you can't troubleshoot somebody else's network.

USING THE SHOW INTERFACES COMMAND   Once the suspect network interface module has been identified, the troubleshooter must diagnose what's causing the problem. The best way to do that is to run the **show interfaces** command and review the latest statistics on the interface's operations. Remember, this information not only reflects on the interface module itself, but also gives a rich set of clues as to what's happening out on the network.

An example **show interfaces** report is given in Figure 12-7. Don't let its size and cryptic terminology intimidate you. There is indeed a lot of information in it, but nothing that takes a rocket scientist to understand.

This report is a snapshot of the interface at a particular instant in time. To check for trends, the troubleshooter must run the **show interfaces** command intermittently to look

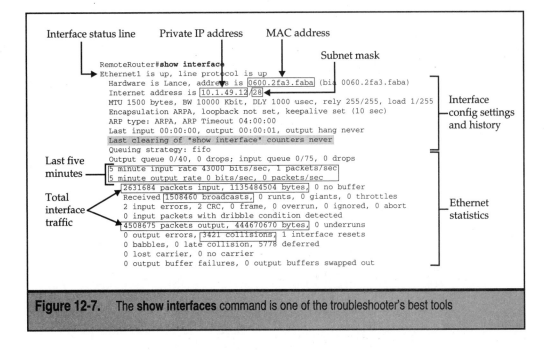

Figure 12-7.   The **show interfaces** command is one of the troubleshooter's best tools

for changes. The interface is identified by private IP address 10.1.49.12/28. Remember, usually only routers on the edge of an autonomous system—firewalls, Web servers, FTP servers, and the like—use public Internet addresses. The /28 notation lets other routers know that LAN segments attached to RemoteRouter are subnetted using the 255.255.255.240 subnet mask. The notation uses "28" because the 255.255.255.240 mask has 28 bits available for network addressing (as opposed to hosts). As mentioned earlier, mismatched subnets often cause problems.

The first thing to look at is the seventh line of the **show interfaces** report that reads "Last clearing of show interfaces counters never" (highlighted in Figure 12-7). The example states that nobody has reset the report's counters to zero since the last time the router was rebooted. The length of time since the statistics were last cleared is very important because most of the statistics are absolute numbers, not relative values such as percentages. In other words, the longer IOS has been compiling the totals, the less weight the statistics should be given. For example, ten lost carriers in a day is a lot, but the same total over six months is not. To see when the last reboot was, use the **show version** command, as shown here:

```
RemoteRouter>show version
Cisco Internetwork Operating System Software
IOS (tm) 4500 Software (C4500-IS-M), Version 11.2(17),
RELEASE SOFTWARE (fc1)
Copyright (c) 1986-1999 by cisco Systems, Inc.
Compiled Mon 04-Jan-99 18:18 by ashah
Image text-base: 0x600088A0, data-base: 0x60604000

ROM: System Bootstrap, Version 5.3(10) [tamb 10],
RELEASE SOFTWARE (fc1)
BOOTFLASH: 4500 Bootstrap Software (C4500-BOOT-M), Version 10.3(10),
RELEASE SOFTWARE (fc1)

RemoteRouter uptime is 2 weeks, 3 days, 13 hours, 32 minutes
System restarted by power-on
    .
    .
    .
```

The second-to-last line in the preceding example shows that the router has been up for about two and a half weeks. Knowing this lets the troubleshooter more accurately judge whether certain error types are normal or excessive.

The exception to this sampling window are the two lines sitting in the middle of Figure 12-7. These report input and output to the interface over the five minutes prior to the report having been run. A troubleshooter trying to discern a trend in traffic patterns would periodically generate the **show interfaces** report and look at these numbers.

Statistics differ on what constitutes excessive. For example, Ethernet arbitrates media access control by collisions, so it's normal for them to occur to some degree. The count of 3421 collisions in Figure 12-7's example is OK for a period of two weeks or so, but a figure of 50,000 would indicate congested bandwidth. Broadcast packets are also normal, because they perform positive functions such as alerting routers of topology changes and providing other useful updates—again, within limits. There are over one and a half million in Figure 12-7's report, which might be excessive. What's excessive is subject to so many variables that it must be left to the judgment of the troubleshooter. That's where experience comes into play.

But many statistics should ideally be very low or even at zero (depending on the time period reported). For example, *runts* and *giants* are malformed packets sometimes caused by a poorly functioning network interface card. In a WAN link, lost carrier events probably indicate a dirty line or a failing telecommunications component.

Table 12-4 defines many of the items reported using the **show interfaces** command. Knowing the items will help you understand how they can be used to diagnose problems.

Statistic	Explanation
Five-minute rates (input or output)	The average number of bits and packets passing through the interface each second, as sampled over the last five-minute interval.
Aborts	Sudden termination of a message transmission's packets.
Buffer failures	Packets discarded for lack of available router buffer memory.
BW	Bandwidth of the interface in kilobits per second (Kbps). This can be used as a routing protocol metric.
Bytes	Total number of bytes transmitted through the interface.
Carrier transitions	A carrier is the electromagnetic signal modulated by data transmissions over serial lines (like the sound your modem makes). Carrier transitions are events where the signal is interrupted, often caused when the remote NIC resets.
Collisions	The number of messages retransmitted due to an Ethernet collision.
CRC	Cyclic redundancy check, a common technique for detecting transmission errors. CRC works by dividing the size of a frame's contents by a prime number and comparing the remainder with that stored in the frame by the sending node.

Table 12-4.   Definitions of Some Ethernet Statistics

Statistic	Explanation
DLY	Delay of the interface's response time, measured in microseconds (µs), *not* milliseconds (ms).
Dribble conditions	Frames that are slightly too long, but are still processed by the interface.
Drops	The number of packets discarded for lack of space in the queue.
Encapsulation	The encapsulation method assigned to an interface (if any). Works by wrapping data in the header of a protocol to "tunnel" otherwise incompatible data through a foreign network. For example, Cisco's Inter-Switch Link (ISL) encapsulates frames from many protocols.
Errors (input or output)	A condition in which it is discovered that a transmission does not match what's expected, usually having to do with the size of a frame or packet. Errors are detected using various techniques such as CRC.
Frame	The number of packets having a CRC error and a partial frame size. Usually indicates a malfunctioning Ethernet device.
Giants	Packets larger than the LAN technology's maximum packet size—1518 bytes or more in Ethernet networks. All giant packets are discarded.
Ignored	Number of packets discarded by the interface for lack of available interface buffer memory (as opposed to router buffer memory).
Interface resets	When the interface clears itself of all packets and starts anew. Resets usually occur when it takes too long for expected packets to be transmitted by the sending node.
Keepalives	Messages sent by one network device to another to notify it that the virtual circuit between them is still active.
Last input or output	Hours, minutes, and seconds since the last packet was successfully transmitted or received by the interface. A good tool for determining when the trouble started.
Load	The load on the interface as a fraction of the number 255. For example, 64/255 is a 25% load. This counter can be used as a routing protocol metric.

Table 12-4.   Definitions of Some Ethernet Statistics *(continued)*

Statistic	Explanation
Loopback	Whether loopback is set to on. *Loopback* is where signals are sent from the interface and then directed back toward it from some point along the communications path; used to test the link's usability.
MTU	Maximum transmission unit for packets passing through the interface, expressed in bytes.
Output hang	How long since the interface was last reset. Takes its name from the fact that the interface "hangs" because a transmission takes too long.
Overruns	The number of times the router interface overwhelmed the receiving node by sending more packets than the node's buffers could handle. Takes its name from the fact that the router interface "overran" the sender.
Queues (input and output)	Number of packets in the queue. The number behind the slash is the queue's maximum size.
Queuing strategy	FIFO stands for first in, first out, which means the router handles packets in that order. LIFO stands for last in, first out. FIFO is the default.
Rely	The reliability of the interface as a fraction of the number 255. For example, 255/255 is 100% reliability. This counter can be used as a routing protocol metric.
Runts	Packets smaller than the LAN technology's minimum packet size—64 bytes or less in Ethernet networks. All runt packets are discarded.
Throttles	The number of times the interface advised a sending NIC that it was being overwhelmed by packets being sent, and to slow the pace of delivery. Takes its name from the fact that the interface asks the NIC to "throttle" back.
Underruns	The number of times the sending node overwhelmed the interface by sending more packets than the buffers could handle. Takes its name from the fact that the router interface "underran" the sender.

Table 12-4. Definitions of Some Ethernet Statistics *(continued)*

Now that we're introduced to the various statistics compiled in the **show interfaces** report, let's review how to read it. Figure 12-8 shows the Ethernet statistics portion of the report, this time with some of the more important variables highlighted. These are the variables an experienced network administrator would scan first for clues.

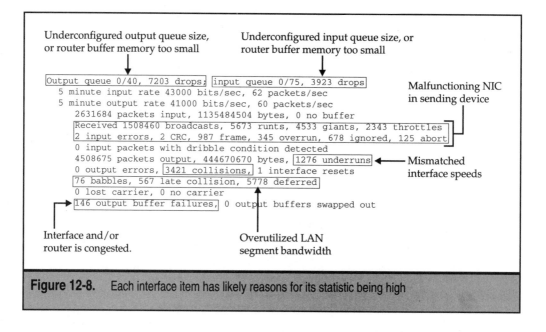

Undercorfigured output queue size,
or router buffer memory too small

Undercorfigured input queue size, or
router buffer memory too small

```
Output queue 0/40, 7203 drops;  input queue 0/75, 3923 drops
    5 minute input rate 43000 bits/sec, 62 packets/sec
    5 minute output rate 41000 bits/sec, 60 packets/sec
    2631684 packets input, 1135484504 bytes, 0 no buffer
    Received 1508460 broadcasts, 5673 runts, 4533 giants, 2343 throttles
    2 input errors, 2 CRC, 987 frame, 345 overrun, 678 ignored, 125 abort
    0 input packets with dribble condition detected
    4508675 packets output, 444670670 bytes, 1276 underruns
    0 output errors, 3421 collisions, 1 interface resets
    76 babbles, 567 late collision, 5778 deferred
    0 lost carrier, 0 no carrier
    146 output buffer failures, 0 output buffers swapped out
```

Malfunctioning NIC
in sending device

Mismatched
interface speeds

Interface and/or
router is congested.

Overutilized LAN
segment bandwidth

Figure 12-8.   Each interface item has likely reasons for its statistic being high

More often than not, connectivity problems are caused by some type of configuration problem, not by a piece of failing equipment. Depending on the Ethernet statistic that's high, the interface may be overwhelmed by incoming traffic, have insufficient queue size configured, have insufficient buffer memory, or be mismatched with the speed of a network sending input.

CHECKING ACCESS LISTS FOR PROPER CONFIGURATION   The classic example of a device malfunctioning even though its hardware is running fine is the misconfigured access list. You'll recall that access lists are used to restrict what traffic may pass through a router's interface, thereby cutting off access to the LAN segment attached to it. The basic access list does this by inspecting for source and destination IP addresses—a way of controlling who may go where. The extended access list also uses application layer port numbers, to further restrict which applications may be run once you're admitted. Indeed, access lists are the most rudimentary form of internetwork security, used as a kind of internal firewall. Not all use of access lists has to do with security; sometimes they're used to steer traffic along certain routes in order to "shape" traffic to best fit the internetwork's resources.

The first step in checking for access list problems is to determine whether a suspect router—or a suspect interface on a router—is even configured with an access list. To find this out, log into the router and enter the **show access-lists** command to see if all the access lists are configured:

```
RemoteRouter#show access-lists
Extended IP access list 100
    deny    ip any host 206.107.120.17
    permit ip any any (5308829 matches)
Extended IP access list 101
access-list 101 permit tcp any host 209.98.208.33 established
access-list 101 permit udp host 209.98.98.98 host 209.98.208.59
access-list 101 permit icmp any host 209.98.208.59 echo-reply
access-list 101 permit tcp any host 209.98.208.59 eq smtp
access-list 101 permit tcp any host 209.98.208.59 eq pop3
access-list 101 permit tcp any host 209.98.208.59 eq 65
access-list 101 permit tcp any host 209.98.208.59 eq telnet
access-list 101 permit tcp host 209.98.208.34 host 209.98.208.59
access-list 101 permit tcp any 209.98.208.32 0.0.0.15 established
access-list 101 permit icmp any 209.98.208.32 0.0.0.15 echo-reply
    .
    .
    .
```

Looking at the preceding example, access list 100 explicitly denies traffic to a certain IP address. This is frequently done to stop outbound traffic to a known undesirable IP address, or some other type of router that could allow hackers a crack at the enterprise's edge router. Access list 101 is more sophisticated, with a series of permit rules to control which applications may be used between hosts. The application's IP port is defined behind each **eq** modifier, such as **eq smtp** for e-mail or **eq 65** for TACACS+ database service. (Certain ports can be identified by acronym, others must be identified by number.) Also note that access list 101 has only permit rules. This is possible because if a packet's request for service isn't explicitly permitted, it will be denied by the "implicit deny" rule when it reaches the bottom of the access list.

It could be that the inadvertent deny rule or lack of a permit rule is causing the problem. The troubleshooter would scan the access lists for any rules that might be causing the problem at hand. For example, if a person can't connect to the mail server, the troubleshooter would look for statements containing **eq smtp** or the mail server's IP address. The next step would be to go to the interface connecting the network experiencing the problem to see if the **access-group** command was used to apply the questionable access list to it. To do this, you must enter privileged EXEC mode and go into configure interface mode pointed to the interface in question, as shown here:

```
MyRouter>enable
Password:
MyRouter#write terminal
 .
 .
 .
interface Ethernet1
 ip address 10.1.13.1 255.255.255.240
 ip access-group 101 in
 ip access-group 100 out
 .
 .
 .
```

If the questionable access list is in force, temporarily disable it to see if traffic can pass the router without it. There are two access lists in our example, so we would disable them both to see if the problem is being caused by access lists. Disable access lists on the interface as follows:

```
MyRouter(config)#interface ethernet1
MyRouter(config-if)#no ip access-group 100 in
MyRouter(config-if)#no ip access-group 101 out
```

In case you forgot, the **in** modifier at the end of each access-group statement configures the access lists to be applied to inbound packets only. An **out** modifier would do the opposite; the absence of a modifier applies the list to both inbound and outbound traffic.

Once the access lists are disabled, attempt to make the connection between the host and the server reported as nonresponding. If the traffic goes through with the access lists disabled, then a statement somewhere in one of the access lists is probably the cause. The next step is to see which list contains the problem by reenabling one of the two. Access list 101, with all its rules, is the most likely culprit. To find out if this is the case, put it back into force with the following command:

```
MyRouter(config-if)#ip access-group 101 out
MyRouter(config-if)#
```

Now try to connect to the server again. If the problem has returned, you've established that the problem resides somewhere inside access list 101.

To debug the access list, carefully review it to find the offending rule. It could be a misplaced deny rule, but a missing TCP or UDP port in a permit rule could also be the problem. Remember, each access list rule must declare to which IP transport protocol it applies: TCP, UDP, or ICMP. Most often, however, offending application ports are the source of the problem, simply because there are so many of them and network applications being used change so much. For example, if users are having a problem making a connection to a Web server, look to make sure that HTTP port number 80 is permitted between the host and server addresses.

It's also possible that the traffic is being denied before getting to the permit rule designed to let it through. Remember that access control lists read from the top down until a match is found. If this is the case, the sequence in which rules are listed should be adjusted accordingly by putting the priority rules nearer the top.

REDIRECTING TRAFFIC FROM CONGESTED AREAS   Sometimes traffic becomes congested in a particular router. This could be the result of new hosts having been added in the area, new network applications coming online, or other causes. When this happens, log into the congested router and enter the **show ip route** command to generate the following report:

```
MyRouter#show ip traffic
IP statistics:
  Rcvd:  7596385 total, 477543 local destination
         0 format errors, 0 checksum errors, 96 bad hop count
         0 unknown protocol, 1 not a gateway
         0 security failures, 0 bad options, 0 with options
  Opts:  0 end, 0 nop, 0 basic security, 0 loose source route
         0 timestamp, 0 extended security, 0 record route
         0 stream ID, 0 strict source route, 0 alert, 0 cipso
         0 other
  Frags: 0 reassembled, 0 timeouts, 0 couldn't reassemble
         0 fragmented, 0 couldn't fragment
  Bcast: 53238 received, 280 sent
  Mcast: 205899 received, 521886 sent
  Sent:  738759 generated, 6113405 forwarded
         13355 encapsulation failed, 374852 no route
.
.
.
```

In addition to reporting IP traffic, the **show ip traffic** command reports traffic generated by transport protocols, routing protocols, ARP translation requests, and even packet errors. The report also breaks out broadcast and multicast messages. It's a quick way to understand the loads being put on a router and what options you might have to lighten the load.

For example, if broadcast traffic seems excessive, you might look into tightening restrictions in the access lists governing the surrounding routers. But, if it appears that all or most of the heavy traffic is legitimate, traffic affecting neighbor routers should also be analyzed. If there is an inequity in loads between routers of similar power, perhaps load balancing is in order. In most cases, this makes more sense than buying more powerful hardware.

One way to balance traffic loads between routers is to log into the congested router and enter config-router mode by calling up the routing protocols; then set individual distance metrics for each router to steer traffic away from the congested router to its less congested neighbor. Let's take an IGRP example:

```
MyRouter(config)#router igrp 3
MyRouter(config-router)#distance 255
MyRouter(config-router)#distance 120 10.1.13.1 0.0.0.255
MyRouter(config-router)#distance 80 10.1.14.1 0.0.0.3
MyRouter(config-router)#
```

As covered in Chapter 8, routing protocols choose best routes based on theoretical cost. The **distance** commands in the preceding code snippet make routes through 10.1.13.1 more costly than those using 10.1.14.1 by boosting its administrative distance relative to its neighbor.

To explain, the **router igrp 3** statement places the router into config-router mode in order to set parameters for the router's behavior within IGRP routing protocol domain number 3. The **distance 255** statement, by having no IP address, instructs the router to ignore all routing updates from routers for which no explicit (nondefault) administrative distances have been set. Then, the statement **distance 120 10.1.13.1 0.0.0.255** sets the congested router's distance metric to 120. (Cisco routing protocols use inverse masks, thus the **0.0.0.255** modifier.) Finally, the **distance 80 10.1.14.1 0.0.0.3** statement sets the neighboring router's distance metric to 80, making it one-third "cheaper" to use than the congested router. This routing metric tweak will automatically steer traffic away from 10.1.13.1 toward 10.1.14.1.

Troubleshooting WAN Links

Troubleshooting WAN problems entails using a slightly different set of tools. This is because most connections into WAN links must go through a serial line. To refresh on the subject, a serial line connects a CSU/DSU unit to a router. Telephone networks don't transmit signals using a data-link layer (layer 2) network technology such as Ethernet. Routers aren't telephone switches, so the transitions between the two technologies must somehow be made. The CSU/DSU–to–serial-line interface gives the router signals it can understand.

NOTE: A CSU/DSU is like a modem, but it works with digital lines instead of analog ones. CSU stands for *channel service unit*, an interface connecting to a local digital telephone line such as a T1 (instead of a modem connecting to an analog phone line). DSU stands for *data service unit*, a device that adapts to the customer end of the connection, usually into a router or LAN switch.

Serial links have an obvious importance because they extend internetworks beyond the office campus to remote locations. A remote link of any size requires using a digital telephone circuit of some kind, ranging from a fractional T1 up to a full T3 (DS3) line.

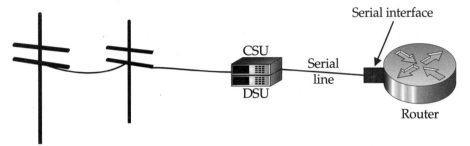

Even though a serial line is only a short run of cable, it provides a window through which its entire WAN link can be diagnosed. In other words, not only can you analyze the serial line and its interfaces, but by looking at the traffic it carries, you can also diagnose the digital phone loop and, to some extent, what's happening at the remote end of the link.

Differences in the show interfaces serial Report

Cisco provides a special tool for troubleshooting serial links in the **show interfaces serial** command. It's largely the same as the normal **show interfaces** command, but with some important differences, as highlighted in Figure 12-9.

One way serial links differ is that encapsulation must be used over digital telephone loops. The High-Level Data-link Control (HDLC) encapsulation protocol is indicated in the top shaded box in Figure 12-9. Encapsulation is necessary to maintain Ethernet packets over the digital telephone link. Sometimes encapsulation may have been inadvertently turned off, so the Encapsulation field should be checked.

Another difference is that conversations (sessions) are reported in the **show interfaces serial** report. WAN links have less bandwidth than local shared media. To wit, a T1 (DS1) circuit has a data rate of 1.544 Mbps, and a T3 (DS3) has 45 Mbps. Most enterprises use fractional T1 or T3 by purchasing channels within them (T1 has 24 channels, T3 has 672). WAN bandwidth therefore is limited compared to, say, a 100 Mbps LAN segment, and sometimes a particular user session takes more than its share. Therefore, when troubleshooting a WAN link, it helps to know how many conversations are going on. In case you're wondering, the Reserved Conversation field has to do with the Resource Reservation Protocol (dubbed RSVP). RSVP is an emerging industry standard designed for use in QoS tools to help guarantee service levels.

The box at the bottom of the figure shows a third difference in the **show interfaces serial** report. These five fields are the same as the blinking lights you may have noticed on external modems. For example, DTR stands for Data Terminal Ready, an EIA/TIA-232 (née RS-232) circuit that is activated to notify the data communications equipment at the other end that the host is ready to send and receive data. DCD stands for Data Carrier

```
RemoteRouter>show interface serial0
Serial0 is up, line protocol is up
  Hardware is HD64570
  Internet address is 10.1.14.1/30
  MTU 1500 bytes, BW 1544 Kbit, DLY 20000 usec, rely 255/255, load 217/255
  Encapsulation HDLC, loopback not set, keepalive set (10 sec)
  Last input 00:00:00, output 00:00:00, output hang never
  Last clearing of "show interface" counters never
  Input queue: 0/75/390 (size/max/drops); Total output drops: 54920
  Queueing strategy: weighted fair
  Output queue: 0/1000/64/12921 (size/max total/threshold/drops)
     Conversations  0/1/256 (active/max active/max total)
     Reserved Conversations 0/0 (allocated/max allocated)
  5 minute input rate 39000 bits/sec, 52 packets/sec
  5 minute output rate 36000 bits/sec, 48 packets/sec
     26405 packets input, 1977458 bytes, 0 no buffer
     Received 12385 broadcasts, 0 runts, 0 giants, 0 throttles
     1294 input errors, 0 CRC, 0 frame, 0 overrun, 0 ignored, 397 abort
     4783008 packets output, 2510565558 bytes, 0 underruns
     0 output errors, 0 collisions, 9172 interface resets
     0 output buffer failures, 0 output buffers swapped out
     12 carrier transitions
     DCD=up  DSR=up  DTR=up  RTS=up  CTS=up
```

Figure 12-9. Most WAN links still use serial lines to connect routers to phone loops

Detect, which is important because it senses the actual carrier signal (the modem noise you hear when making a modem connection). The five modem circuits are included in the **show interfaces serial** report for troubleshooting serial links that run over analog/modem lines instead digital lines.

Key Diagnostic Fields in the show interfaces serial Report

Serial links differ by nature from LAN segments, so diagnosing them takes a different focus. Certain things that are to some extent taken for granted in LAN segment links are often the cause of performance problems or even failures in serial links. Figure 12-10 highlights the items that troubleshooters look at first in a serial interface.

As you can see, troubleshooting serial links emphasizes looking at errors and line activity. This is natural, given that the middle part of a WAN link—the telephone circuit—is basically invisible to networking equipment.

Looking at Figure 12-10, we see a case in which input traffic seems to be going OK, but a lot of output packets are being dropped. Given that the serial line is being pushed hard, running at about 80 percent of available bandwidth, we can conclude that the drops are being caused by overuse, not faulty hardware in the link.

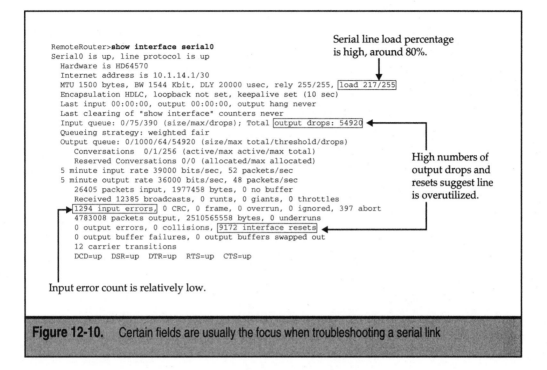

```
RemoteRouter>show interface serial0
Serial0 is up, line protocol is up
  Hardware is HD64570
  Internet address is 10.1.14.1/30
  MTU 1500 bytes, BW 1544 Kbit, DLY 20000 usec, rely 255/255, load 217/255
  Encapsulation HDLC, loopback not set, keepalive set (10 sec)
  Last input 00:00:00, output 00:00:00, output hang never
  Last clearing of "show interface" counters never
  Input queue: 0/75/390 (size/max/drops); Total output drops: 54920
  Queueing strategy: weighted fair
  Output queue: 0/1000/64/54920 (size/max total/threshold/drops)
     Conversations  0/1/256 (active/max active/max total)
     Reserved Conversations 0/0 (allocated/max allocated)
  5 minute input rate 39000 bits/sec, 52 packets/sec
  5 minute output rate 36000 bits/sec, 48 packets/sec
     26405 packets input, 1977458 bytes, 0 no buffer
     Received 12385 broadcasts, 0 runts, 0 giants, 0 throttles
     1294 input errors, 0 CRC, 0 frame, 0 overrun, 0 ignored, 397 abort
     4783008 packets output, 2510565558 bytes, 0 underruns
     0 output errors, 0 collisions, 9172 interface resets
     0 output buffer failures, 0 output buffers swapped out
     12 carrier transitions
     DCD=up  DSR=up  DTR=up  RTS=up  CTS=up
```

Serial line load percentage is high, around 80%.

High numbers of output drops and resets suggest line is overutilized.

Input error count is relatively low.

Figure 12-10. Certain fields are usually the focus when troubleshooting a serial link

TROUBLESHOOTING SERIAL-LINE INPUT ERRORS One of the most common causes of serial-line problems is input errors—in other words, data inbound from the remote site. Probable causes of serial-line input errors, with suggested actions, are outlined in Table 12-5.

TROUBLESHOOTING SERIAL-LINE OUTPUT ERRORS Another clue to serial-line problems is a trend of increasing dropped packets at the interface. A *drop* occurs when too many packets are being processed in the system and insufficient buffer memory is available to handle the packet. This applies to both input and output drops, as outlined in Table 12-6.

Drops taking place in one direction but not the other (input versus output) can point the troubleshooter toward the problem's source. If they're happening both ways, the router or its serial interface is probably the culprit.

TROUBLESHOOTING SERIAL LINKS Most of us have used modems long enough to know that sometimes an established connection can falter, or even be broken. This goes for serial lines, too, usually because of interface resets or carrier transitions, as outlined in Table 12-7.

Input Error Symptoms	Probable Causes and Suggested Actions
Input errors along with CRC or frame errors	A dirty line, where electrical noise interferes with data signal. Serial cable exceeds maximum length specified for the type of phone circuit. Serial cable is unshielded. The phone circuit itself may be malfunctioning. **Actions:** Reduce cable length. Install shielded cable. Check phone loop with a line analyzer. Clocking jitter in line where data signal varies from reference timing positions, or clocking skew where device clocks are set differently. **Actions:** Make sure all devices are configured to use a common line clock.
Input errors along with aborts	The transfer of a packet terminated in midtransmission. Usually caused by an interface reset on the router being analyzed. Can also be caused by a reset on the remote router, a bad phone circuit, or a bad CSU/DSU. **Action:** Check local hardware, then remote hardware. Replace faulty equipment.

Table 12-5.   Dirty Lines, Clocking Problems, or Bad Hardware Can Cause Input Errors

Packet Drop Symptoms	Probable Causes and Suggested Actions
Increase in dropped input packets	Input drops usually occur when traffic is being routed from a local interface (Ethernet, Token Ring, FDDI) that's faster than the serial interface. The problem usually emerges during periods of high traffic. **Actions:** Increase the interface's input hold queue size in the router's config file.

Table 12-6.   Packets Are Usually Dropped During High Traffic Periods

Packet Drop Symptoms	Probable Causes and Suggested Actions
Increase in dropped output packets	Output drops happen when no system buffer is available at the time the router is attempting to hand the packet off to the transmit buffer during high traffic. **Actions:** Increase the interface's output hold queue size. Turn off fast switching. Implement priority queuing.

Table 12-6. Packets Are Usually Dropped During High Traffic Periods *(continued)*

Although they're not LAN segments per se, serial links are integral to geographically distributed internetworks. Don't forget to consider them even when a serial-line problem is not initially apparent. For example, when evaluating performance problems, it could be that a faulty serial link is shifting traffic loads elsewhere within the internetwork.

Line Error Symptoms	Probable Causes and Suggested Actions
Increasing carrier transitions	Interruption in the carrier signal. Usually due to interface resets at the remote end of the link. Resets can be caused by external sources such as electrical storms, T1 or T3 overuse alerts, or faulty hardware. **Actions:** Use breakout box or serial analyzer to check hardware at both ends. Then check router hardware. Replace faulty hardware as necessary. No action required if problem was due to external cause.
Increasing interface resets	Interface resets result from missed keepalive messages. They usually result from carrier transitions, lack of buffer, or a problem with CSU/DSU hardware. Coincidence with increased carrier transitions or input errors indicates a bad link or bad CSU/DSU hardware. **Actions:** Use breakout box or serial analyzer to check hardware at both ends. Contact leased-line vendor if hardware is OK.

Table 12-7. Carrier Transitions or Resets Can Interrupt or Disconnect Serial Links

TROUBLESHOOTING CISCO HARDWARE

When the probable location of the problem has been identified, the first step is to physically examine and test the suspect device. This will identify the problem's cause in a surprising number of troubleshooting situations. Sometimes the problem is caused by something as simple as a loose component; other times, something is damaged.

Inspecting Devices

Once a suspect device is identified, it should be physically inspected. This is routine procedure; even when a suspect or troubled device is in a remote location, a contact person is sent to make an inspection. Earlier, we stated that most troubleshooting tasks are done from the administrator's desk, and that's true. Most tasks are done from the administrator's PC or an NMS console. However, there's no substitute for actually looking at a device to see what's going on. The two parts of inspecting a device are reading its LEDs and inspecting the device's components.

Reading Device LEDs

If the device is still online, the first thing to do is to read the LEDs (light-emitting diodes). You probably recognize LEDs as those blinking lights on the front of many electronic devices. Virtually all network devices have LEDs to assist in troubleshooting. The LED bank arrangement follows the device layout:

▼ Access devices with a bank of ports on the front, with a twisted-pair cable plugged into each port using an RJ-45 phone-style jack. Products from the Cisco FastHub 400 to the Catalyst 5000 Switch fit this description. There is usually one LED per port.

■ Motherboard-based routers with LAN segments plugged into the back, usually via twisted-pair cable, but also fiber-optic cables for uplinks. The Cisco 4500 Router fits this description. LEDs on these devices appear behind smoked-glass panels on the front of these boxes.

▲ High-end routers and switches of the bus-and-blade configuration, again with networks plugged into the back, both fiber-optic and twisted-pair cable. The Cisco 7500 Router and Catalyst 6000 Switch fit this description. LEDs on these devices appear both behind smoked-glass panels on the front and on the blades (card modules) themselves on the back (remember, a blade is basically an entire router or switch on a board).

LEDs are also called *activity lights*. Each LED on an access device represents a host. Router and LAN switch LEDs represent entire LAN segments.

LEDs blink and change colors according to the port's status. Green means OK, and orange means the port is coming up. If the port is down, its LED goes dark. The port's LED blinks when packets are passing through it. A common practice is to press Reset to see what happens. LEDs temporarily go orange or even red if they encounter trouble during the power cycle. They will eventually go green, but the temporary error condition may indicate a nonfatal configuration error.

The rule is that if an activity light is green, the line is good and the problem must stem from some type of configuration problem. If the light is orange, the line is operating but malfunctioning. If the activity light is off, the line is down.

Physically Inspecting Devices

The next step is to physically inspect the device itself. Start by making sure the device is offline, and then remove the cover from the top of the device chassis and inspect the interior, looking for the following:

▼ **Loose connections**   Look for any loosely attached card (module) or cable. Reseat any that are found.

■ **New cards**   If you know any card to be new, reseat it into its connection several times. New cards are more prone to oxidation or carbon film buildup on their backplane connections.

■ **Burned or damaged parts**   Look for any burned wires, ribbon cables, or cards. Also look at the backplane to see if it's OK. Closely inspect the wires leading to the device's power supply. Also look for any crimped wires.

▲ **Dirty device interior**   If the device has dust and lint in the interior, turn off the device and clean it. Devices can accumulate a lot of foreign substances from the air in dusty or dirty environments, which sometimes can affect performance.

After completing the inspection, try rebooting the device to see if power-cycling it will fix the problem. One important caution: Don't change anything in the configuration. Doing so before rebooting can make it very difficult to determine the problem's source afterward; it only adds more variables to the mix.

The Reboot Test

If no severe problem was found inspecting the device, the next step is to try a power-cycle test to see how it responds. *Power-cycle* means to turn a device off and then turn it on again, which you probably know as the cure-all for Microsoft Windows. As we saw in Chapter 4, rebooting devices can tell a lot about the status of a device, and in some cases, it even makes the problem go away.

When you reboot, if the configuration in memory is mismatched with the hardware, a variety of problems can ensue. Ports might hang, bus timeout errors may occur, and so on. If the device reboots and prompts for a password, the circuitry and memory are working properly. Some major symptoms and probable causes are outlined in Table 12-8.

Reboot Symptom	Probable Causes
No response	Bad power supply, blown fuse, bad breaker, bad power switch, bad backplane
Won't reboot	Bad or miswired power supply, bad processor card (or poorly seated), bad memory board, bad IOS image in NVRAM, shorted wires
Partial or constant reboot	Bad processor, controller, or interface card; bad backplane; bad power supply; bad microcode
No cards show up in boot display	Bad processor, controller, or interface card; bad backplane; cards not seated in backplane; bad power supply

Table 12-8.   Typical Reboot Problems and Their Probable Causes

When hardware problems this extreme are encountered, it's time to call in support from Cisco or a third-party maintenance organization with which your enterprise has contracted. Typically, devices are shipped into the maintenance center for bench repair. Only end-user enterprises with spare parts, Cisco-trained personnel, and proper instruments attempt to repair networking hardware devices in-house.

Remember, however you attack a troubleshooting problem, the goal is to "follow the wire" and track the source of the problem down to the end.

APPENDIX A

Configuring Switches and Hubs

If you're sitting in an office, that wire running out of the network interface card on the back of your PC almost certainly plugs into either a hub or a switch. These two types of devices form the basic building blocks of network topologies: LAN segments. They swallow up cabling from servers, PCs, and printers and put them into a shared network medium.

▼   Hubs form a simple LAN-in-a-box. Switches are more powerful devices. As the cost per switch ports gradually drops nearer the cost per hub port, switched networks are replacing traditional hub-based networks.

▲   Switches narrow the size of the collision domain (the group of hosts that share network bandwidth by sharing message traffic). Switches squeeze more bandwidth out of a network medium and make it possible to configure virtual LANs (VLANs), in cases where selected users from one or more LANs are part of a shared broadcast domain.

How LANs are formed is fundamental to internetworking. This appendix shows the user interfaces provided by Cisco to install and manage its switches and hubs: Hub Management Console and Visual Switch Manager (VSM) software. VSM is particularly interesting because it is used to manage the various protocols that make switched networks work. Switching is eclipsing hubs at the low end and is partly taking over from routers at the high end.

Flip through the screens of VSM and Hub Management Console in this appendix to get a feel for how LAN topologies are set up.

VISUAL SWITCH MANAGER

Visual Switch Manager Software

Visual Switch Manager (VSM) is a Web browser–based tool used to work with Cisco Catalyst switches. VSM presents real-time information measuring activity in a switch while it runs. This information is used to monitor and manage a switch. More important, the tool is also used to modify switch configuration.

VSM operates by talking to a switch through the HTTP protocol. HTTP is the IP protocol used to support Web browser–based applications. As a browser application, VSM overlays the switch's image of Cisco IOS software and runs IOS commands.

Initial switch installation is done while running a terminal session through the switch's Console port (not Visual Switch Manager). Notice that both Telnet and Visual Switch Manager are options in Figure A-1. It is only after the switch is made a member of a LAN that management activity can begin through VSM.

The home page also provides access to other tools besides VSM. For example, clicking the Telnet hyperlink lets you log into the IOS command-line interface. Other hyperlinks connect to Cisco resources, such as Cisco's Web page and Technical Assistance Center.

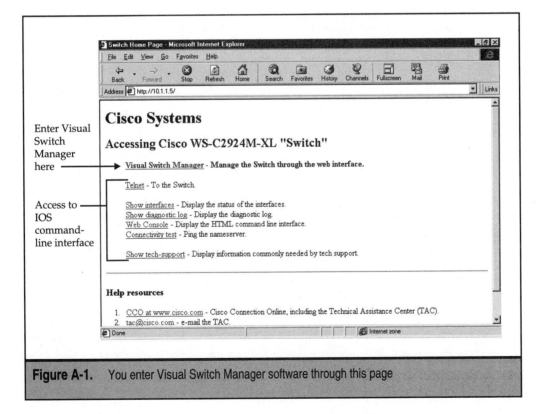

Figure A-1.   You enter Visual Switch Manager software through this page

The Visual Switch Manager Home Page

Basic housekeeping tasks are handled in the VSM home page. This is where the switch is given a name, where a network administrator responsible for the switch is assigned, where passwords are maintained, and so forth. Notice that the IP address and Cisco IOS Software version fields are display only. They are defined elsewhere and cannot be input from this page.

Switches are almost always administered from inside the enterprise's private network. Figure A-2 shows a private IP address (http://10.1.1.5) as opposed to a public address (such as http://209.98.86.52). For security reasons, administrative access to a switch from outside the private network is rare.

For a parameter change to take effect in the switch's running-configuration file, the Apply button must be clicked. This causes the parameter change to be uploaded to the switch and updated in the device's memory. The Revert button reverts switch parameter settings to what they were before the last change.

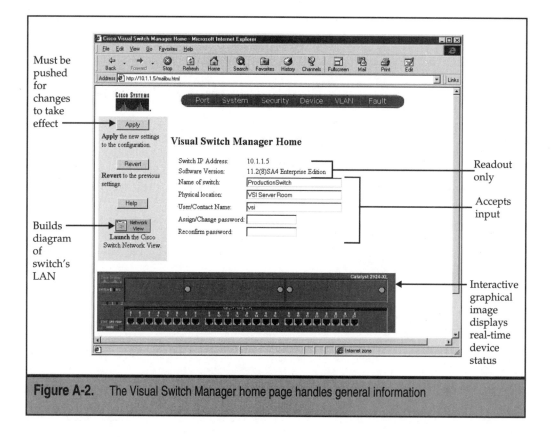

Figure A-2.   The Visual Switch Manager home page handles general information

The Interactive Device Graphic in Visual Switch Manager

Visual Switch Manager takes its name from the interactive graphical image of a switch at the bottom of the home page. The image is of the actual switch device. The example in Figure A-2 is logged into a Cisco Catalyst 2924-XL. The switch image is "live" in that status information displayed reflects what's currently happening on the device. Each switch port is lighted up in one of three colors to indicate current device status:

▼ **Green**   The link is up.

■ **Blue**   No link is reported.

▲ **Red**   The link is either faulty or disabled.

The switch image does more than just report status. It's an interactive interface through which you can change configuration parameters. If you've already read this book, you'll recognize the switch image as the same interactive graphical device interface used in CiscoView. CiscoView (covered in Chapter 9) is a superset of VSM in that it handles all Cisco devices, not just switches.

The dialog box in Figure A-3 comes up after the user clicks the FastEthernet0/8 port in the switch image in Figure A-2. This input dialog is specific to the port that is clicked.

The port's basic parameters are set here. The Enable check box turns the switch port on or off. The status below the Enable check box is a readout indicating whether connection to the LAN is working properly (up or down). Figure A-3's example indicates UP.

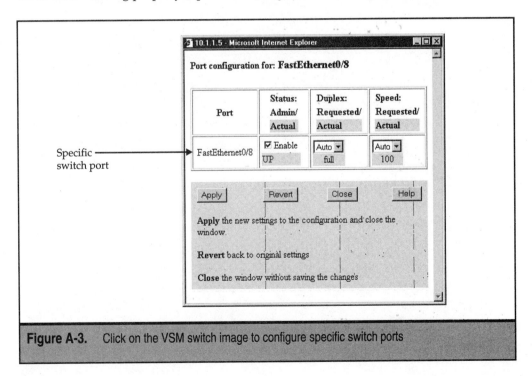

Figure A-3.   Click on the VSM switch image to configure specific switch ports

Network View

The Network View feature is an application that discovers and diagrams surrounding network topology. Network View diagrams *only* Cisco devices. Network View provides reports on network devices and links, and can be used as an interactive interface to change device configuration parameters. Network View diagrams include these features:

▼ **Visual Stack**   Use this to display a switch image of one or more members of a switch stack.

■ **Switch Manager**   Click the right mouse button on a switch in the image to show a pop-up menu with two options: to see a report on the switch, or to launch a management software application that can be used to reconfigure the LAN.

■ **Link Report**   Click the right mouse button on a link (the line connecting devices in the diagram) to see that link's IP addresses, operating mode, VLANs, and other operating parameters.

▲ **Toggle Labels**   Use this to change device labels in the diagram from IP addresses to the Cisco device model numbers (for example, from IP address 10.1.1.5 to model number 2924M-XL) and to label network links (lines). Link labels contain the name of the device interface through which the link is running (for example, Ethernet1).

Be careful before launching Network View, though. It can be slow, because it uses CDP (Cisco Discovery Protocol) to find other devices. For example, it took over 20 minutes to generate the diagram in Figure A-4.

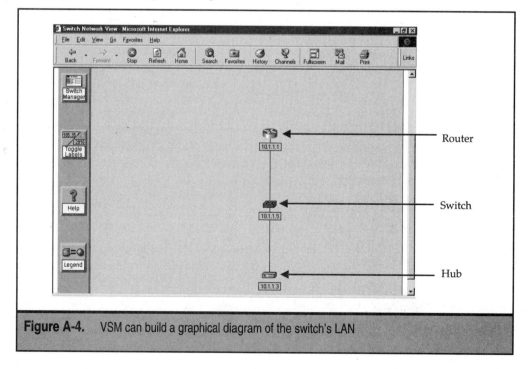

Figure A-4.   VSM can build a graphical diagram of the switch's LAN

Switch Port Configuration

A port is where stations physically connect to the switch. Ports on switch devices are called *switch ports* or *switched ports*. They are the connections into which twisted-pair cables from hosts (such as PCs, servers, or printers) are plugged. Other network devices, such as hubs, routers, and other switches, also connect to switch ports.

Switch ports have both administrative status and actual status, shown in Figure A-5. Administrative status is set to enabled mode by default. The Enable setting means the port is ready for work. Actual status can be either Up or Down. It's possible for a port's administrative status to be enabled and its actual status to be Down. This would indicate that the port is operationally ready but is not at work (Down), because nothing is plugged into it.

Two parameters can be set to affect a switch port's effective operating speed: duplex mode and transmission speed.

The Duplex parameter can be set so it automatically recognizes and sets either full duplex or half duplex. Duplex mode is whether transmission is one-way or two-way. If devices connected at both ends of a link have full-duplex capability, the Auto setting will automatically set to it, in effect doubling transmission speed. Unless configured otherwise, VSM always autonegotiates full-duplex mode when possible.

In switches with 10/100 autosensing, the Transmission Speed Requested parameter is usually set to Auto. The term 10/100 refers to the capability of a switch to automatically sense whether the device at the other end of a link is running 100 Mbps (Fast Ethernet) or 10 Mbps (plain Ethernet). Unless configured otherwise, VSM always autonegotiates a 100 Mbps connection when possible. Network administrators will override Auto and specify one speed over the other when the switch is having trouble correctly sensing a link's speed.

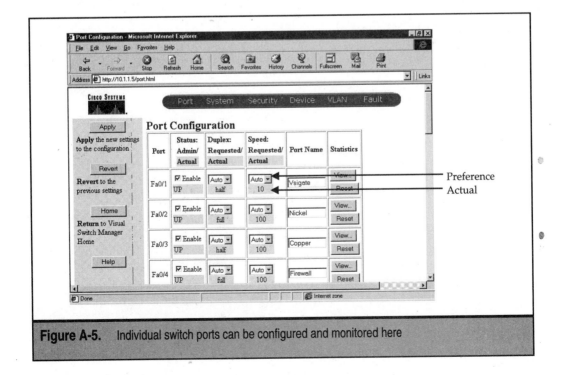

Figure A-5.   Individual switch ports can be configured and monitored here

Port Grouping

Port groups are logical high-speed connections between switches. They are configured for either Fast EtherChannel or Gigabit EtherChannel connections. Port groups create redundant links between switches so that if there's a failure with one link in the group, its traffic will automatically move to the other links (an automatic process called *fail-over*). EtherChannel is discussed in Chapter 6.

A port group is treated as a single logical port. Forming port groups simplifies management and reporting. For example, configuration changes for a port group need to be made in just one place instead of for each individual port. Figure A-6 shows the interface for forming port groups.

All ports in the group must belong to the same set of VLANs (Virtual LANs) and must all be source based or destination based. *Source-based* switching is when the port group makes switching decisions based on the source MAC addresses (a Media Access Control address is a device's physical address as opposed to its IP address). In *destination-based* switching, switching decisions are based on the destination MACs. It's OK to configure both source-based and destination-based port groups on the same switch, but not in the same group.

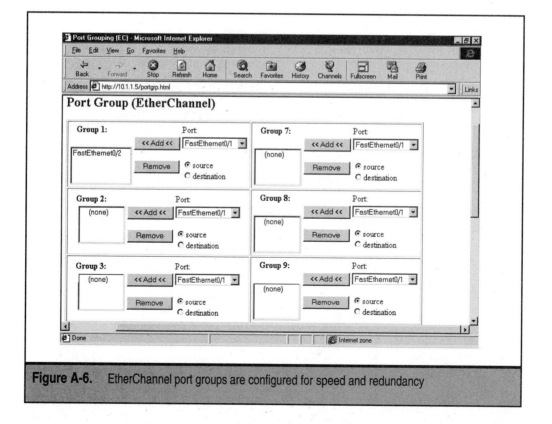

Figure A-6.   EtherChannel port groups are configured for speed and redundancy

Port Monitoring (SPAN)

SPAN stands for Switched Port ANalyzer. SPAN gathers real-time information for monitoring switch ports and diagnosing problems. The purpose of SPAN is to concentrate port activity information into a single port—the SPAN port—dedicated to troubleshooting. A SPAN port functions as a test instrument probe, but in the form of a dedicated switch port instead of separate hardware from an external test device.

SPAN operates by mirroring traffic from one or more switch ports to the SPAN port. If the ports being monitored are members of a VLAN, the SPAN port must be a member of the same VLAN. Figure A-7 shows that three ports on the example switch are being monitored.

The SPAN port runs RMON probe software. *RMON* (for Remote Monitoring) is specialized probe software that tracks port performance statistics, traffic patterns, and alarms. Usually, a Network Management Module (NMM) card is inserted into the switch to provide electronics dedicated to monitoring and diagnosing problems. Sometimes a Network Management Station reads data from the port instead of an NMM. Network Management Stations are usually PCs or UNIX workstations. Having this type of information available across a switched network helps network administrators anticipate and solve network problems. Without SPAN, port network management in switched networks would require more time and effort.

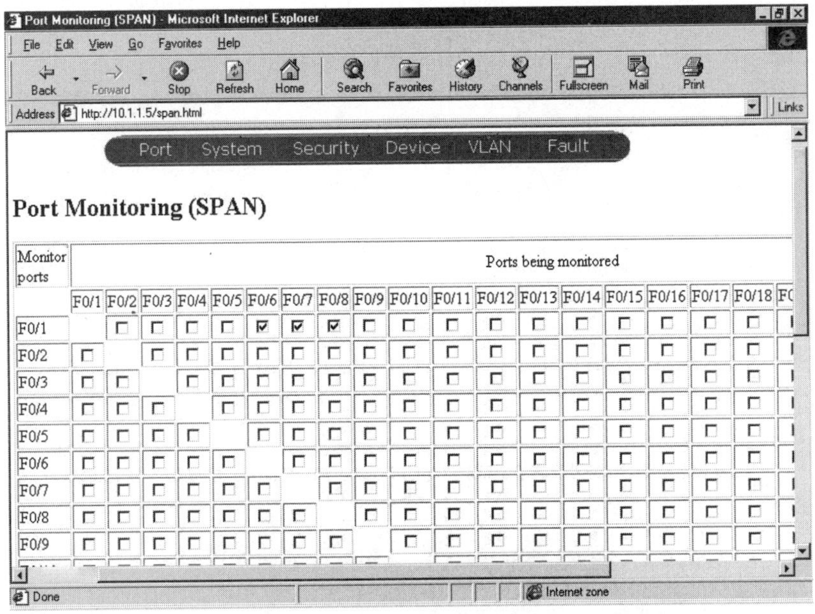

Figure A-7.   Individual switch ports can be selected for real-time monitoring

Flooding Controls/Network Port

Flooding is when traffic received in one switch port is passed out all other ports. Switches flood when they receive messages with unknown destination addresses. Flooding is necessary in switched networks because they rely on MAC (Media Access Control) addresses of physical devices, not logical IP addresses, as do routers. Without flooding in switched networks, a message would be dropped by the first network, unaware of its destination MAC address, effectively terminating the transmission.

But controls are necessary to ensure against a switch being drowned in a glut of flooded messages. The potential for flooding is made worse by the fact that messages are passed by a switch to all VLANs in which it has membership (switches are frequently multi-VLAN). Figure A-8 shows the Flooding Controls page.

Flooding controls block the forwarding of unnecessary flooded traffic by one of the following techniques:

▼ Sending all flooded messages to a single port (the *network port*) so only that port gets flooded.

■ Enabling *broadcast storm thresholds* to limit how many flooded messages a port will accept.

▲ Blocking the forwarding of unicast (one-to-one) and broadcast (one-to-all) messages, shown in the Receive Unknown MACs field in.

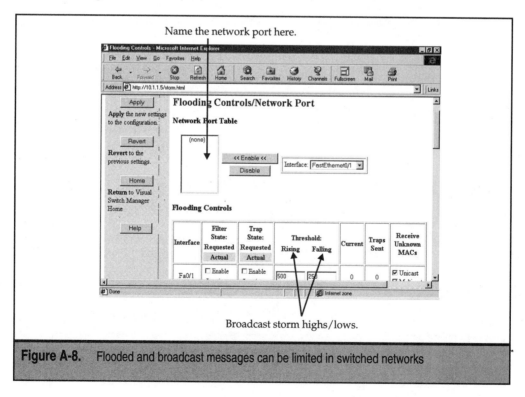

Figure A-8. Flooded and broadcast messages can be limited in switched networks

System Configuration

Cisco switches run a full-blown image of the IOS software optimized for switching. An IOS config file must be created and maintained for the switch. The startup-config file tells it how to reconfigure itself when it reboots. Figure A-9 shows the System Configuration page. It's used to maintain basic setup information on the IOS image running on the switch.

NVRAM stands for nonvolatile random access memory. NVRAM buffer size tells the switch how many bytes to allocate for storing the startup-config file. The Boot Loader Flags field tells the switch to perform an extended self-test during reboot.

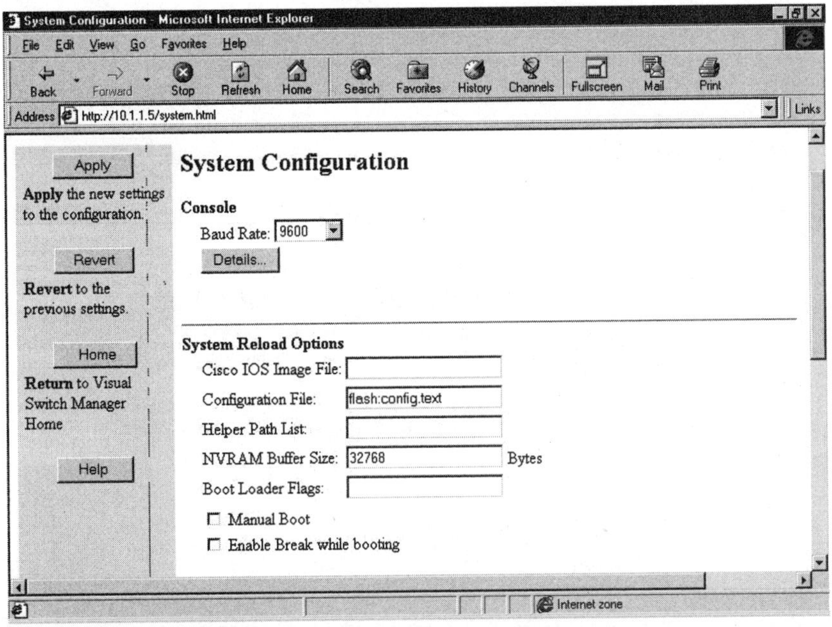

Figure A-9.   The System Configuration page is where the config file is maintained

IP Management

For a switch to become operable on a network, it must have several IP addresses assigned. The IP Management page shown in Figure A-10 is used to administer and update IP information. Three mandatory IP addresses are

▼ **IP address**   A 32-bit address assigned to hosts using TCP/IP, written as four octets separated with periods (for example, 209.98.86.52).

■ **IP subnet mask**   A mask overlaying a full IP address to indicate the bits of the full IP address used to address the local subnetwork, often simply called the *mask*. The mask is always some portion of the left side of the overall IP address (for example, 255.255.255.248). Refer to the blueprints section in the center of this book for an explanation of subnet masking.

▲ **Default gateway**   The switch sends traffic to an unknown IP address through the default gateway. When a message is sent outside the local network, it's routed through the default gateway, which has one or more external addresses. The default gateway address is frequently an Internet Service Provider (ISP).

Notice that the Management VLAN is read-only in this page. That's because the IP Management page controls only what goes into the config file of the individual switch device being managed. The Management VLAN that the device is a part of is specified in the config file of a higher-level device called the Network Management Station (NMS). The NMS—usually a PC or UNIX workstation—is the master console used by the network management team.

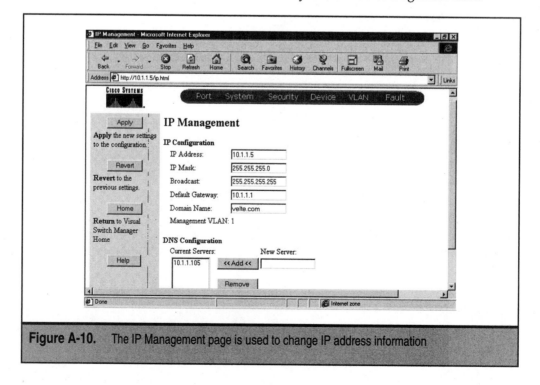

Figure A-10.   The IP Management page is used to change IP address information

SNMP Configuration

SNMP (Simple Network Management Protocol) is an IP application used to administer and troubleshoot network devices from a so-called Network Management Station (NMS). SNMP is an industry standard, not a proprietary Cisco protocol. The interface shown in Figure A-11 is of course Cisco's, but the paramters set via this page enable the creation of generalized SNMP information that can be used by any SNMP software product, not just Cisco's. You have the option of not enabling SNMP management for the switch. Disabling SNMP prevents SNMP-based network management applications from being able to monitor or reconfigure the switch.

SNMP works by setting up *agents* on a device. These agents are small software programs that observe activity on the switch and send alerts called *traps* to the NMS, informing it of significant events. A *community string* is a text string that acts as a sort of group password used to authenticate messages sent between the NMS and the devices it manages. The community string is sent in every packet between the manager and the SNMP agent. Refer to Chapter 9 to read about various Cisco products incorporating SNMP functionality.

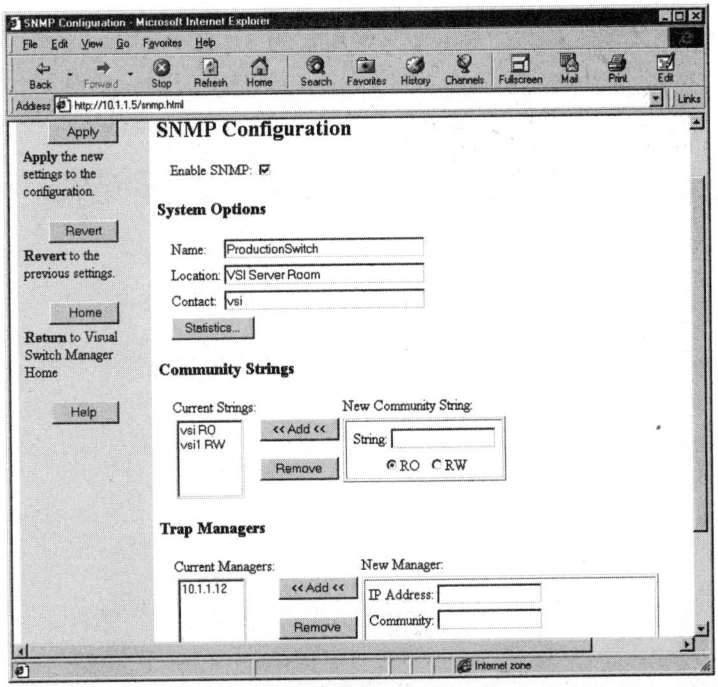

Figure A-11.   This page is used to configure a Cisco switch for SNMP management

ARP Table

ARP stands for the Address Resolution Protocol, which is an industry standard protocol for mapping IP addresses to MAC addresses. MAC stands for Media Access Control, which is a unique address for a physical device (MACs are sometimes also referred to as *physcial addresses*).

Translating addresses is necessary because when a message reaches its destination LAN, it must resolve the logical IP address to a physical MAC address in order to know which physical host device to communicate with. In ARP tables inside Cisco switches, the IP address is on the left and the MAC address it is associated with is on the right.

Addresses are dynamically added to the ARP table as messages pass through the switch. To prevent infinite growth of the table, the ARP Cache Timeout Value field limits how long entries stay in the table prior to being dropped. The ARP table ages off of addresses that go unused for that specified period of time *except* those that were added to the table manually. In the example in Figure A-12, the aging period is set for 14,400 minutes (4 hours).

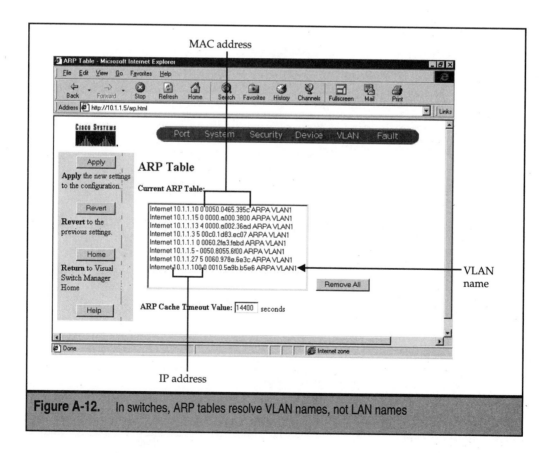

Figure A-12. In switches, ARP tables resolve VLAN names, not LAN names

Address Management

The address table (also called the address management table) is used by switches to decide where to forward incoming messages. The address table associates a list of MAC addresses with specific switch ports. Unlike IP addresses, MAC addresses are a sort of network serial number identifying physical network devices (usually the network interface card). Address tables are the centerpiece of switched network architecture because they guide messages to their destinations. MAC addresses do in switched networks what IP addresses do in router-based networks. There are three kinds of address tables:

▼   **Dynamic address table**   Built by the switch by associating each message's incoming port number and source MAC address. See Figure A-13.

■   **Secure address table**   A secure address has only one destination port; they're manually entered and don't age.

▲   **Static address table**   Like a secure address in that they're manually entered and don't age, but a static address applies to the entire switch instead of just a single port.

Most ports in switched networks use dynamic addressing, because that way the network can help operate itself without human intervention. Static addressing is used for port grouping. Secure addressing is used to protect valuable network resources and proprietary data.

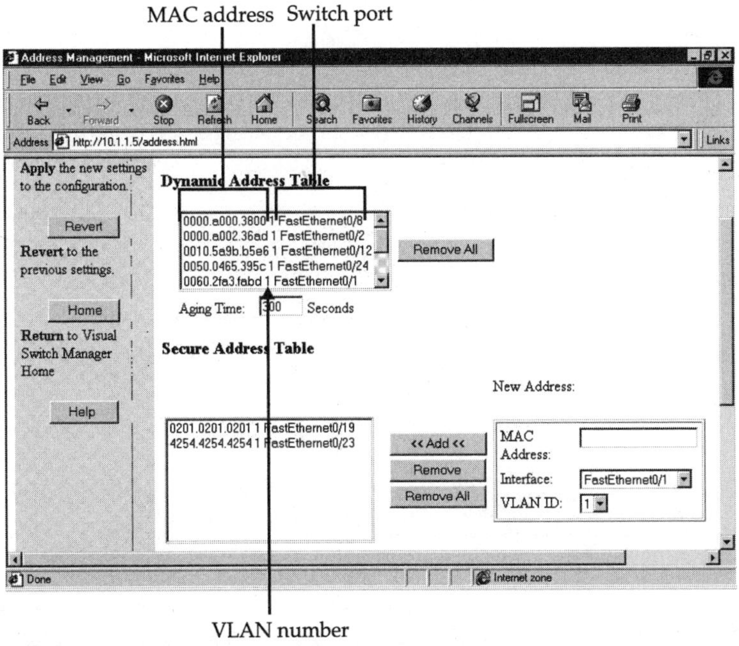

Figure A-13.   The address table is the key to how switched networks operate

Port Security

A *secure port* is created by creating a list of one or more source MAC addresses that may send traffic to it. In this sense, a secure port is a form of static-access port. Port security should not be mixed up with SNMP alerts and other security applications. Port security works by restricting access to a port to explicitly named links. This is often done as much for performance reasons as for data security. Figure A-14 shows the Port Security page.

The advantages of securing a port are that unknown devices cannot connect to the port without your knowledge. It's also a good way to dedicate the port's bandwidth by setting the size of the port's address table to 1, thereby making available all the port's bandwidth to that device. A port is secured by checking the box in the Security column, and one or both of the Trap and Shutdown fields. Port security cannot be enabled on a multi-VLAN port.

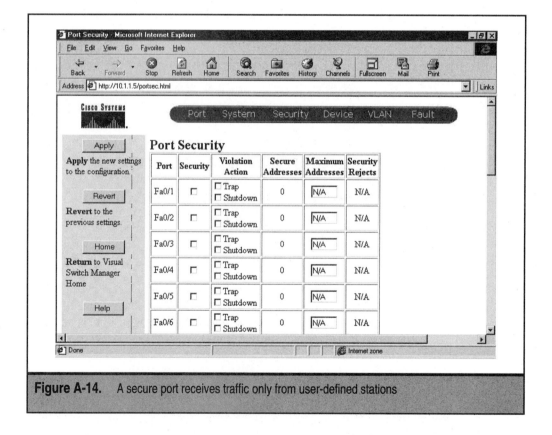

Figure A-14. A secure port receives traffic only from user-defined stations

Cisco Discovery Protocol

Cisco Discovery Protocol (CDP) is a proprietary Cisco protocol that automatically finds other Cisco devices on the same network. CDP is a low-level protocol that is independent of higher-level networking protocols such as IP or NetWare's IPX. In this way, it can draw an accurate picture of Cisco devices in a LAN—regardless of what protocols each is running. CDP enables various Web-based management software tools—including Visual Switch Manager's Network View application—to graphically diagram networks as they exist in real time.

Packet Hold Time is the number of seconds a neighboring device will retain the CDP neighbor information it receives (set to 180 seconds in the example in Figure A-15). CDP can be enabled by individual port, which is a common practice done in order to conserve bandwidth or for security reasons.

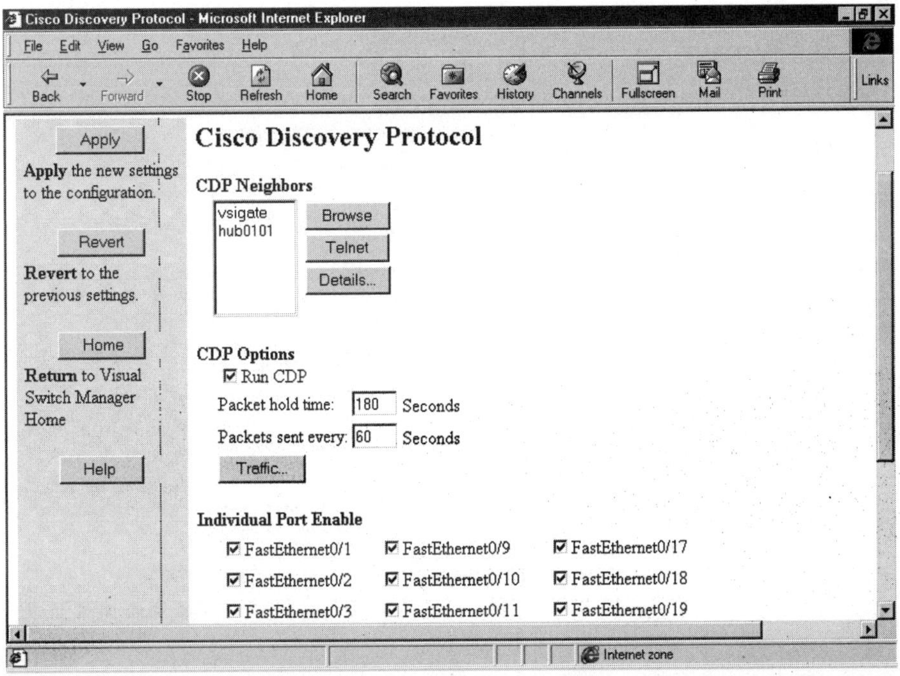

Figure A-15. CDP is used to dynamically discover and document neighboring devices

Cisco Group Multicast Protocol

CGMP (Cisco Group Multicast Protocol) is a proprietary Cisco protocol used to limit the forwarding of IP multicast (one-to-many) packets in a network. For example, a switch might sign up to receive multicasts advertising new MAC addresses from networks outside the intranet. CGMP is sort of a subscription processing service in which hosts enroll in a group that receives certain kinds of multicasts. Hosts issue *join* messages to join a multicast group and *leave* messages to quit. Like most table-building protocols, CGMP ages off of unused subscriptions to limit table size. The Router Hold Time parameter (set to 300 seconds in the example in Figure A-16) removes an entry after a user-specified time period.

The CGMP table is maintained on a router. For CGMP to work, therefore, a switch must have a connection to a router that is running both CGMP and IGMP (Internet Group Management Protocol). IGMP is used by IP hosts to report their multicast group memberships to an adjacent multicast router. When the router receives an IGMP request (leave or join) from a client, it forwards this information to the switch in a CGMP packet. The switch uses this information to alter its forwarding behavior.

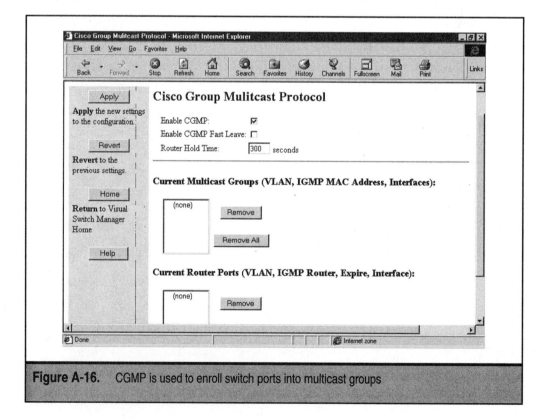

Figure A-16.   CGMP is used to enroll switch ports into multicast groups

Spanning-Tree Protocol

STP (Spanning-Tree Protocol) is an industry-standard technique for preventing loop-back paths in switched networks. Switched networks use MAC addresses in lieu of logical IP addresses. They work by forwarding a message to any switch containing the desired MAC address. Without STP, switched networks are susceptible to using paths that double back to the switch that sent the message—causing slow delivery and generating unnecessary traffic.

STP works by identifying redundant paths and blocking at least one of them. The Spanning-Tree Protocol page, shown in Figure A-17, is used to enable a switch for STP and to define a root switch for each VLAN. Having a root switch for a VLAN helps the STP algorithm figure out which paths are best to block or not block. STP uses a *path costing* system not unlike the routing protocols discussed in Chapter 8. A lower path cost represents higher-speed (for example, an STP cost value of 100 for 10 Mbps versus 4 for 1 Gbps). The Hello Time parameter sets the number of seconds between STP messages. The Max Age parameter (set to 20 seconds in Figure A-17) sets how long the switch should wait between STP messages before reconfiguring STP on its own.

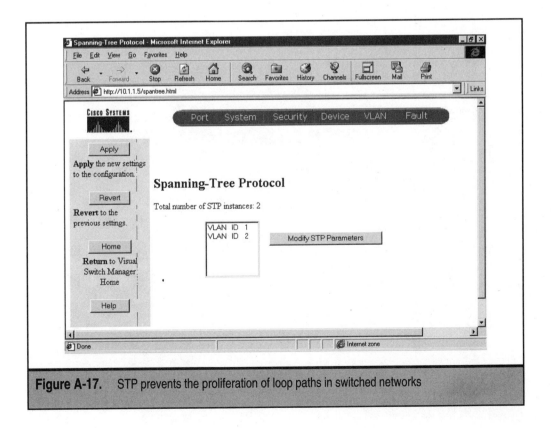

Figure A-17.   STP prevents the proliferation of loop paths in switched networks

VLAN Membership

VLAN membership is a simple matter of assigning a switch port to one or more virtual LANs. The maximum number of VLANs a port may belong to is a function of the switch model. The example switch in Figure A-18 is a Cisco Catalyst 2924-XL, which supports up to 64 VLANs per port. VLAN membership modes are as follows:

▼ Static-access VLAN membership mode

■ Multi-VLAN membership mode

■ Dynamic-access VLAN membership mode

▲ ISL trunk VLAN membership mode

ISL, which stands for Inter-Switch Link, is a proprietary Cisco protocol for interconnecting multiple switches and maintaining VLAN information as traffic goes between them. ISL provides VLAN capabilities while maintaining high performance on Fast Ethernet links in full- or half-duplex mode.

Special IOS software feature sets are required on a switch for it to operate advanced VLAN modes such as multi-VLAN and dynamic-access VLAN.

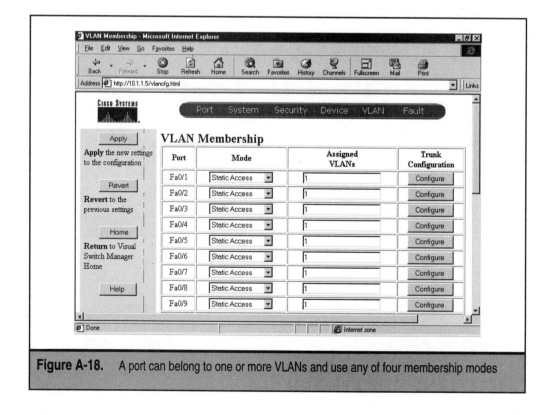

Figure A-18. A port can belong to one or more VLANs and use any of four membership modes

VTP Management

VTP (VLAN Trunk Protocol) enables network administrators to make configuration changes on a single switch and automatically communicate those changes to all the other switches in the network. Central configuration limits a number of problems, such as duplicate VLAN names, incorrect VLAN-type specifications, and security violations. VTP works by sending advertisements over the switched network as a way to maintain VTP trunk memberships and transmit other VTP configuration changes. VTP configuration is maintained as a VLAN database stored in the NVRAM of member switches. A switch can be in any one of three VTP modes:

▼ **Client VTP mode**   A switch that is enabled for VTP; can send advertisements but cannot configure VLANs

■ **Transparent VTP mode**   A switch that is disabled from using VTP; cannot send its own advertisements but can receive and forward them to and from other switches

▲ **Server VTP mode**   A switch that is enabled for VTP; can send advertisements and can configure VLANs

As shown in Figure A-19, the VTP Management screen displays VTP status information at the top and inputs configuration parameter changes at the bottom.

ISL works by encapsulating frames going through a switch with an ISL header, letting other switches on the trunk filter through ISL encapsulated messages as "native" to the trunk. The IEEE 802.1Q tagging format, an open standard that is not proprietary to Cisco, supports simultaneous tagged and untagged traffic on a switch port.

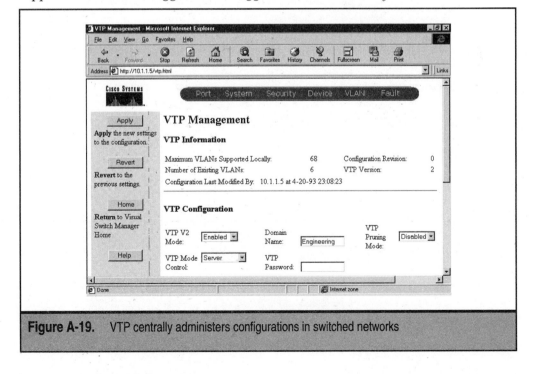

Figure A-19.   VTP centrally administers configurations in switched networks

VMPS Configuration

VMPS (VLAN Membership Policy Server) dynamically assigns switch ports to VLANs based on the MAC address of the device connected to the port. When a host is moved from a port on one switch in the network to a port on another switch in the network, it's automatically assigned to the proper VLAN. A VMPS maintains a database that maps the MAC addresses of VMPS-enabled ports to VLANs. It's downloaded from the server via TFTP (Trivial File Transfer Protocol).

VMPS is useful in enterprises in which users move about between locations and use their laptop computers to jack into the intranet from wherever they are. The VMPS Configuration page (Figure A-20) is used to set the VMPS server, and to add or remove VLANs and set a VLAN as the primary VLAN.

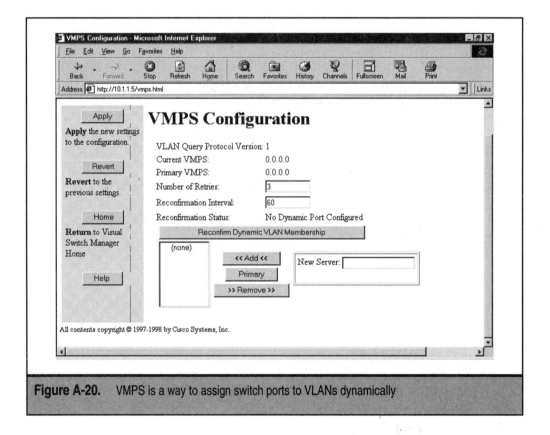

Figure A-20.   VMPS is a way to assign switch ports to VLANs dynamically

VTP/VQP Statistics

VTP (VLAN Trunk Protocol) and VQP (VLAN Query Protocol) gather VLAN policy statistics. A switch transmits advertisement messages on all its trunk ports after a VLAN configuration changes, and transmits periodic summary advertisements on any trunk port for which it has not sent or received an advertisement for the last five minutes. By hearing these advertisements, other switches in the same management domain learn about new VLANs configured in the transmitting switch.

VTP statistics summarize advertisement messaging; VQP statistics summarize message results such as number of query messages, bad messages, changes, denied responses, and other totals, as shown in Figure A-21.

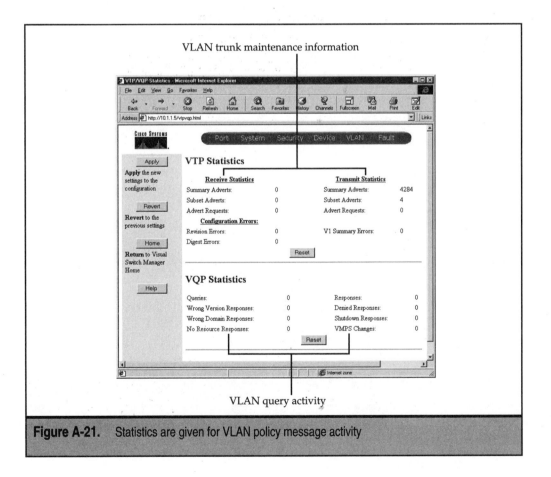

Figure A-21.   Statistics are given for VLAN policy message activity

Logging Configuration

Switches log activity records as they operate. They do so by severity levels when network or switch events occur. You can display log information about switch activity on a console or write log messages to a buffer, to a file, or to the UNIX syslog facility.

The Logging Configuration page (Figure A-22) configures how these things are done for a switch. The Logging Level field is where you select the minimum severity level you want reported. The options are as follows:

Emergencies	Alerts	Critical
Errors	Warnings	Notifications
Informational	Debugging	

The user cannot define which switch events belong to the severity levels. Cisco IOS software correlates events to severity-level category.

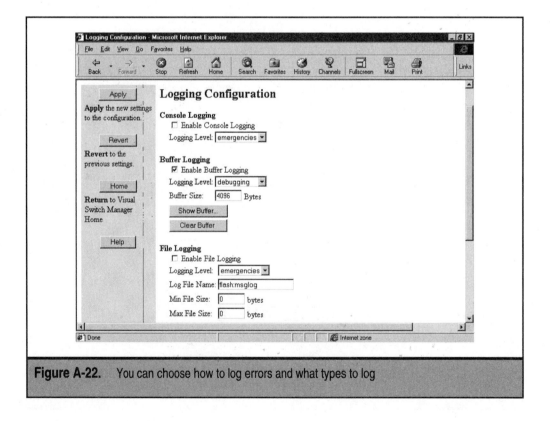

Figure A-22.   You can choose how to log errors and what types to log

HUB MANAGEMENT CONSOLES

Hub Management Console Main Menu

Cisco's Management Hub Console software runs through a menu-driven interface. Cisco hubs run a cut-down version of the Cisco IOS software, so only menu-driven input is possible. A full-fledged command-line interface, as in Cisco MicroHub routers and other devices, is unavailable on Cisco hubs. And the low-end MicroHubs don't even have the menu-driven interface. Users can't log into MicroHubs at all; they are self-configuring.

When customers purchase a Cisco FastHub, they first must log into the hub via the Console port and make the hub part of a LAN. Once the hub is part of a network, the interface shown in Figure A-23 can be used to further configure the device.

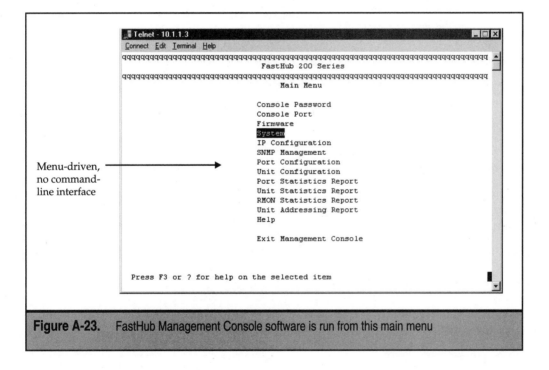

Figure A-23.   FastHub Management Console software is run from this main menu

Console Password Screen

The Console Password screen is used to set parameters for the Line password, restricting access to the hub. A "Password intrusion threshold" tells the Hub Management Console software how many failed login attempts to allow before terminating the connection, as seen in Figure A-24.

"Silent time upon intrusion detection" tells how long to keep the Hub Management Console software unavailable after the password intrusion threshold has been exceeded.

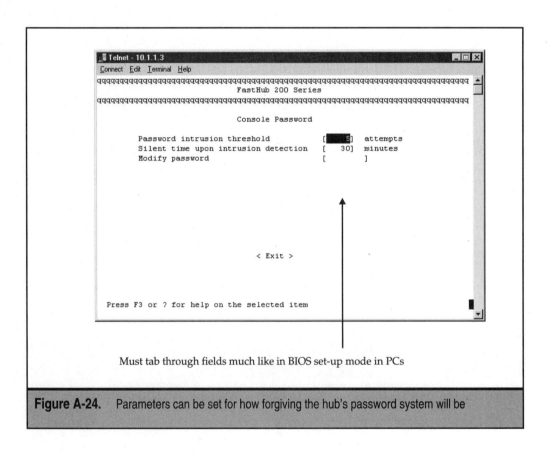

Must tab through fields much like in BIOS set-up mode in PCs

Figure A-24.   Parameters can be set for how forgiving the hub's password system will be

Console Port Screen

The Console Port screen is used to set up modem communications between the network management console and the hub. Without setting the Console Port screen's parameters (shown in Figure A-25), the network manager will not be able to log into the hub remotely. In that event, performing configuration or management tasks for the hub would require a technician to be physically present at the hub and to access the Hub Management Console interface directly through the Console port on the back of the hub.

The Hub Management Console interface works much like a PC BIOS setup interface, in which one must tab between fields one by one.

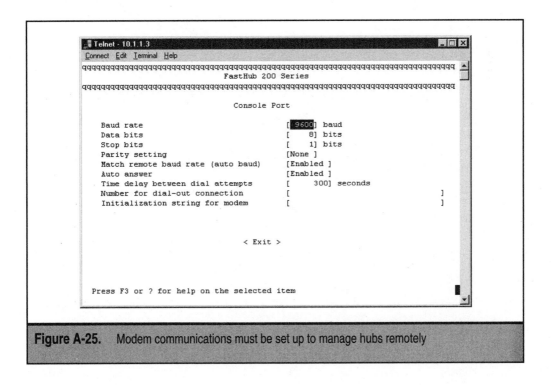

Figure A-25.   Modem communications must be set up to manage hubs remotely

Firmware Screen

Firmware is executable software code stored in read-only memory (ROM). In Cisco hubs, there are two types of firmware: one to manage the device bootstrap and the other to run the management software. Hub firmware is updated from TFTP servers. TFTP is a stripped-down version of the FTP application commonly used over the Internet. A TFTP server is a computer used to download updates to hubs and other devices, and to receive backup files uploaded from the devices. As shown in Figure A-26, the Firmware screen displays firmware upgrade status, the IP address of the TFTP server, and whether the upgrade was completed successfully.

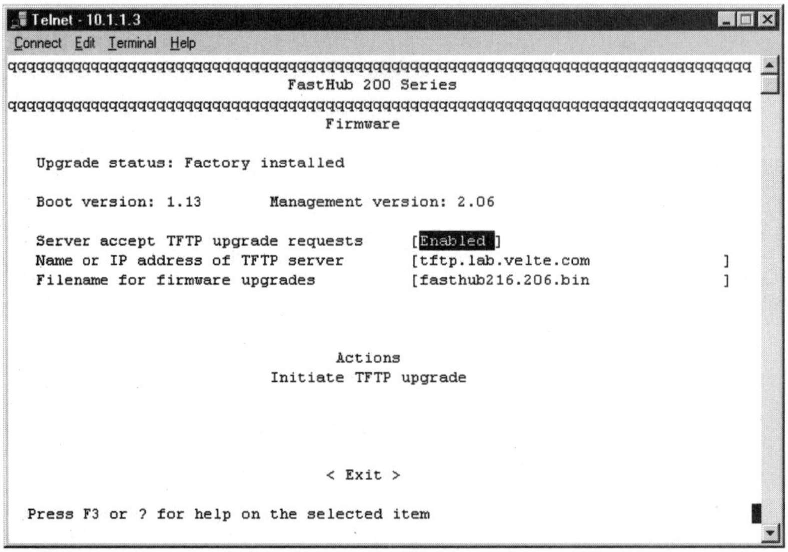

```
 Telnet - 10.1.1.3                                                    _ □ ×
Connect  Edit  Terminal  Help
qqqqqqqqqqqqqqqqqqqqqqqqqqqqqqqqqqqqqqqqqqqqqqqqqqqqqqqqqqqqqqqqqqqqqqqqqq ▲
                            FastHub 200 Series
qqqqqqqqqqqqqqqqqqqqqqqqqqqqqqqqqqqqqqqqqqqqqqqqqqqqqqqqqqqqqqqqqqqqqqqqqq
                                 Firmware

   Upgrade status: Factory installed

   Boot version: 1.13       Management version: 2.06

   Server accept TFTP upgrade requests      [Enabled ]
   Name or IP address of TFTP server        [tftp.lab.velte.com          ]
   Filename for firmware upgrades           [fasthub216.206.bin          ]



                               Actions
                         Initiate TFTP upgrade



                              < Exit >

   Press F3 or ? for help on the selected item                         █
                                                                       ▼
```

Figure A-26.   Firmware upgrades can be loaded into hubs from remote servers

System Screen

The System screen is used to configure basic settings for the hub. This is where the hub is given a name (for example, Accounting Dept. Hub). The name of the person to contact should the hub fail can also be stored in the System screen. The fields in brackets in Figure A-27 can accept input needed. Fields that are not in brackets are readout fields that cannot accept input. The screen displays how long the hub has been up and how long it will maintain a management communications link before timing out due to inactivity.

Perhaps the most important task in the System screen is whether to enable Cisco Discovery Protocol for the hub. CDP is discussed in Chapter 5.

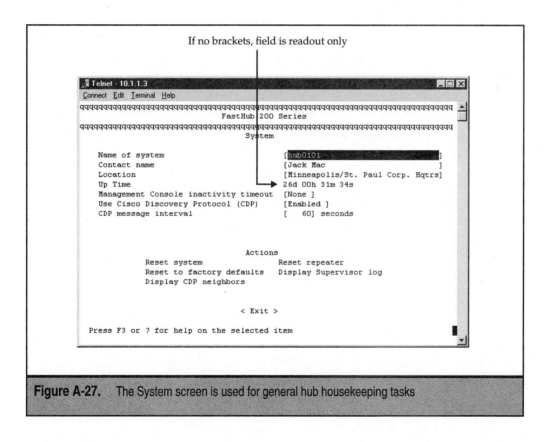

Figure A-27. The System screen is used for general hub housekeeping tasks

IP Configuration Screen

IP addresses are usually the first parameters to set for a hub. This is because they configure the hub into the network by giving the hub a series of IP addresses, shown in Figure A-28. The IP address of the system is the hub's unique address on the network. The subnet mask identifies the subnetwork on which the hub is located. The default gateway is the address of the router port to which the hub forwards messages with unknown destination addresses.

Domain Name System addresses are also input in the IP Configuration screen, as is the hub's resident domain name. Setting these parameters makes it possible for routers to translate between domain names (like *velte.com* in Figure A-28) and the corresponding IP address. An important task in this screen is whether to enable RIP (Routing Information Protocol) for the hub. RIP "listens" to the network to automatically discover new IP gateways for the hub to use. Routing protocols are discussed in Chapter 8.

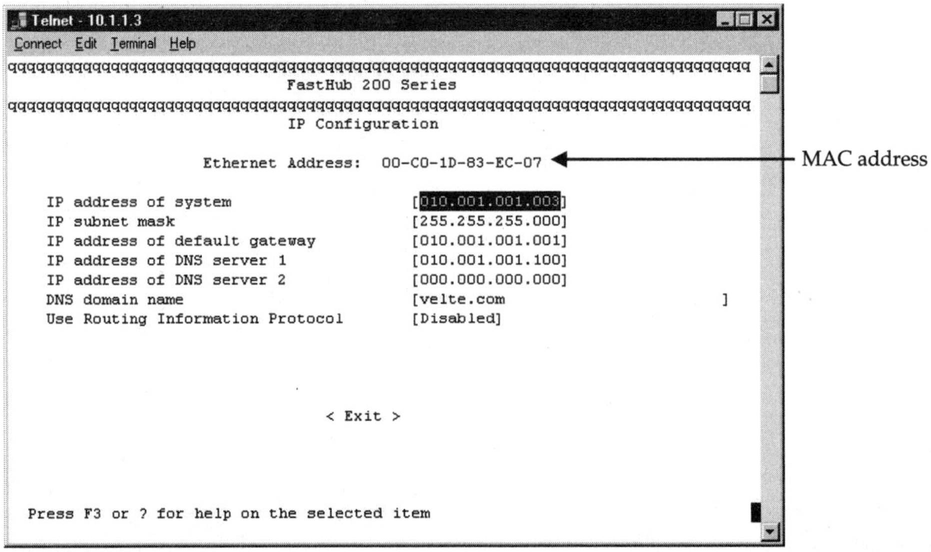

Figure A-28. IP addresses must be configured before the hub can operate

SNMP Management Screen

Also called the SNMP Configuration screen, the SNMP Management screen is where the administrator defines what Simple Network Management Protocol information the hub will maintain. The IP addresses in Figure A-29 are the addresses of Network Management Stations (NMSs) with which the hub will conduct SNMP communications.

Traps are alerts that a predefined SNMP event has occurred or threshold has been exceeded. A Write Manager is an NMS enabled to change SNMP settings on the hub. An *authentication trap* alerts a management workstation of SNMP requests that do not carry a valid read (Get) or write (Set) community string. Recall from earlier in this appendix that community strings are a kind of shared password used to authenticate messages. SNMP is covered in Chapter 9.

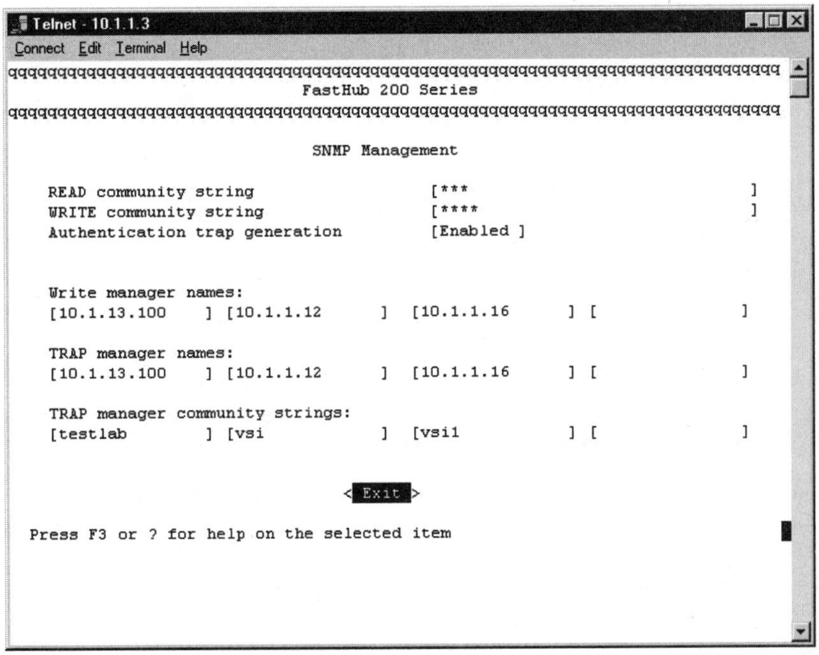

```
 Telnet - 10.1.1.3                                                    _ □ ×
Connect  Edit  Terminal  Help
qqqqqqqqqqqqqqqqqqqqqqqqqqqqqqqqqqqqqqqqqqqqqqqqqqqqqqqqqqqqqqqqqqqqqqqq
                         FastHub 200 Series
qqqqqqqqqqqqqqqqqqqqqqqqqqqqqqqqqqqqqqqqqqqqqqqqqqqqqqqqqqqqqqqqqqqqqqqq

                           SNMP Management

        READ community string               [***                       ]
        WRITE community string              [****                       ]
        Authentication trap generation     [Enabled ]


        Write manager names:
        [10.1.13.100    ] [10.1.1.12    ]  [10.1.1.16    ] [           ]

        TRAP manager names:
        [10.1.13.100    ] [10.1.1.12    ]  [10.1.1.16    ] [           ]

        TRAP manager community strings:
        [testlab        ] [vsi          ]  [vsi1         ] [           ]


                           ◄ Exit ►

        Press F3 or ? for help on the selected item
```

Figure A-29.   The type of SNMP information the hub will maintain is specified here

Port Configuration Screen

The Port Configuration screen is where operating parameters for individual hub ports are set. A *linkbeat* (also called a *link pulse*) is a periodic check to see that a link is still running over the port—in other words, that it still has a "heartbeat." (The example in Figure A-30 indicates "No-linkbeat," which means that port's link is dead.)

A hub port must be enabled for it to operate on the network. "Last source address" is the MAC address of the host that sent the most recent message received by the hub port.

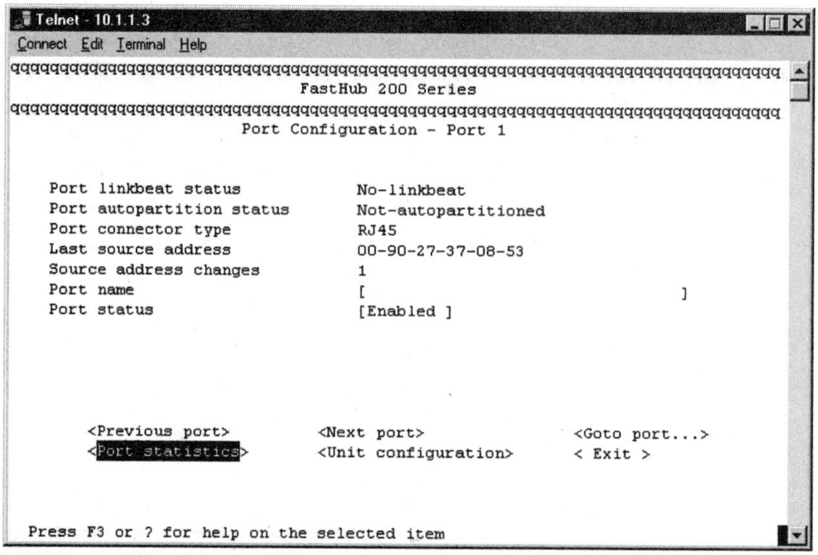

```
Telnet - 10.1.1.3                                                    _ □ ×
Connect  Edit  Terminal  Help
qqqqqqqqqqqqqqqqqqqqqqqqqqqqqqqqqqqqqqqqqqqqqqqqqqqqqqqqqqqqqqqqqqqqqqqqqqqqqqq
                          FastHub 200 Series
qqqqqqqqqqqqqqqqqqqqqqqqqqqqqqqqqqqqqqqqqqqqqqqqqqqqqqqqqqqqqqqqqqqqqqqqqqqqqqq
                      Port Configuration - Port 1


         Port linkbeat status           No-linkbeat
         Port autopartition status      Not-autopartitioned
         Port connector type            RJ45
         Last source address            00-90-27-37-08-53
         Source address changes         1
         Port name                      [                           ]
         Port status                    [Enabled ]



             <Previous port>       <Next port>           <Goto port...>
             <Port statistics>     <Unit configuration>  < Exit >


      Press F3 or ? for help on the selected item
```

Figure A-30.   Individual hub ports can have their own settings

Unit Configuration Screen

Certain configuration parameters are, by nature, hubwide. As shown in the example in Figure A-31, these parameters have to do with hardware configuration. RPS stands for remote power supply.

A hub can operate using either an internal power supply or a remote one. The version numbers on this screen indicate the version of the hub's main processor board and the currently loaded bootstrap and management firmware.

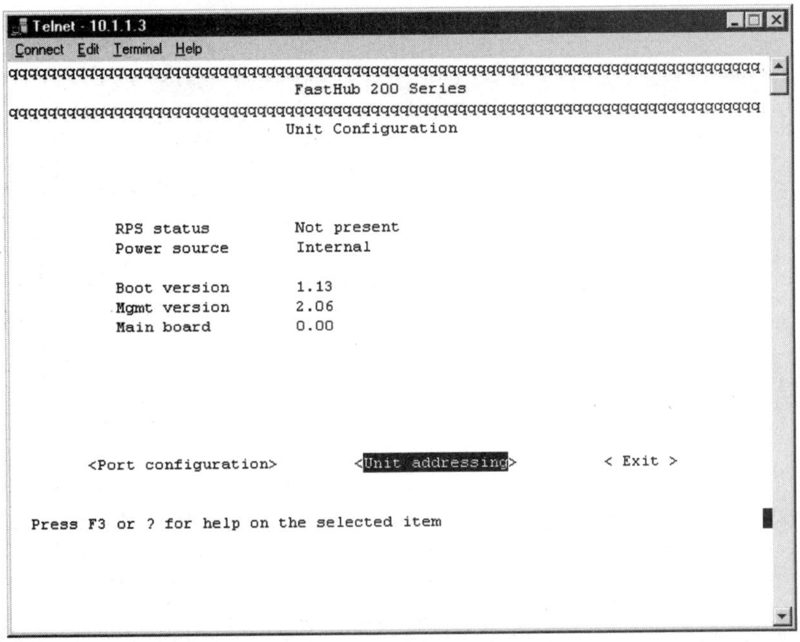

```
Telnet - 10.1.1.3                                                    _ □ ×
Connect  Edit  Terminal  Help
qqqqqqqqqqqqqqqqqqqqqqqqqqqqqqqqqqqqqqqqqqqqqqqqqqqqqqqqqqqqqqqqqqqqqqqqqqqqqqqq
                              FastHub 200 Series
qqqqqqqqqqqqqqqqqqqqqqqqqqqqqqqqqqqqqqqqqqqqqqqqqqqqqqqqqqqqqqqqqqqqqqqqqqqqqqqq
                              Unit Configuration



            RPS status        Not present
            Power source      Internal

            Boot version      1.13
            Mgmt version      2.06
            Main board        0.00




        <Port configuration>        <Unit addressing>        < Exit >


    Press F3 or ? for help on the selected item
```

Figure A-31.   Unit configuration parameters apply to the entire hub, not just one port

Port Statistics Report

The Port Statistics Report shows totals and error totals for a specific port on the hub. These totals reflect frame transmit and receive counts for the measures shown in Figure A-32. FCS stands for frame check sequence, a technique that adds extra characters to a frame (packet) and uses them to check for out-of-sequence frames. *Runts* are packets with missing data, a condition usually caused by collisions. *Jabber* is an error condition in which a network device continually transmits random, meaningless data onto the network.

The statistics here are read-only; data cannot be input here. The statistics on the Port Statistics Report are compiled automatically by the hub's management software.

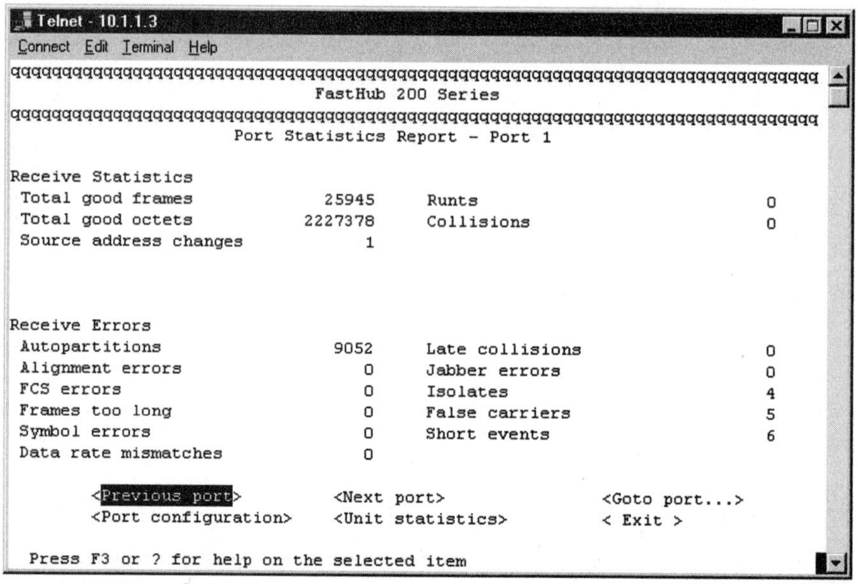

```
Telnet - 10.1.1.3                                                    _ □ ×
Connect  Edit  Terminal  Help
qqqqqqqqqqqqqqqqqqqqqqqqqqqqqqqqqqqqqqqqqqqqqqqqqqqqqqqqqqqqqqqqqqqqqqqqqqq
                           FastHub 200 Series
qqqqqqqqqqqqqqqqqqqqqqqqqqqqqqqqqqqqqqqqqqqqqqqqqqqqqqqqqqqqqqqqqqqqqqqqqqq
                     Port Statistics Report - Port 1

Receive Statistics
  Total good frames            25945    Runts                     0
  Total good octets          2227378    Collisions                0
  Source address changes           1



Receive Errors
  Autopartitions                9052    Late collisions           0
  Alignment errors                 0    Jabber errors             0
  FCS errors                       0    Isolates                  4
  Frames too long                  0    False carriers            5
  Symbol errors                    0    Short events              6
  Data rate mismatches             0

          <Previous port>          <Next port>            <Goto port...>
          <Port configuration>     <Unit statistics>      < Exit >

  Press F3 or ? for help on the selected item
```

Figure A-32.   Frames (layer-2 messages) sent and received are profiled here

Unit Statistics Report

The Unit Statistics Report measures the same things as the Port Statistics Report, except that it totals the information for all ports on the hub. As can be seen in Figure A-33, no individual port subtotals are given.

The statistics here are read-only; data cannot be input here. The statistics on the Unit Statistics Report are compiled automatically by the hub's management software.

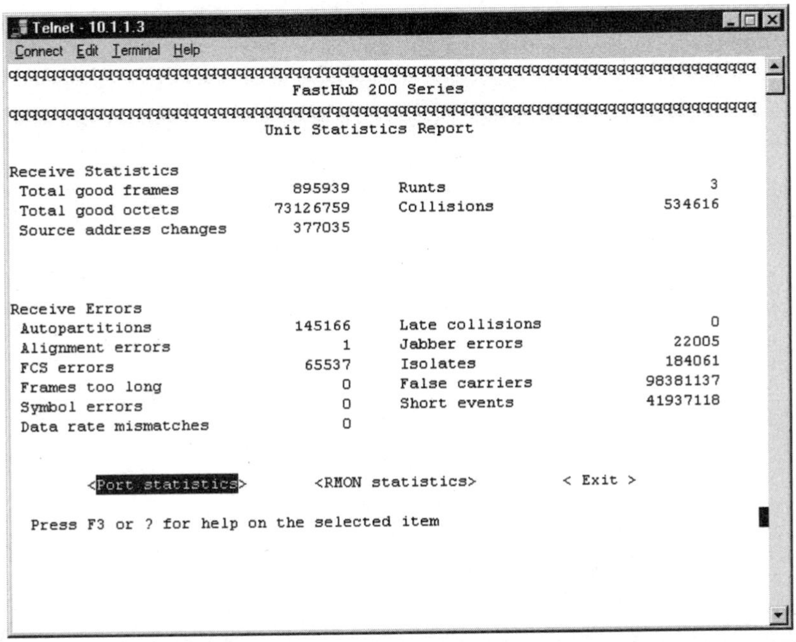

Figure A-33. Unit statistics are for the entire hub, not particular ports

RMON Statistics Report

Comparing Figure A-34 with Figure A-33 shows that the RMON Statistics Report is similar to the Unit Statistics Report. The difference is that the RMON Statistics Report reflects the information the RMON agent is storing in the SNMP management information base (MIB) for the hub. RMON stands for remote monitor. It's a hardware/software capability incorporated into a hub to actively gather and store information in SNMP MIBs. A management information base is stored for a certain subject SNMP is configured to manage. Without RMON, SNMP would have to poll the hub's MIBs in an ongoing manner. By storing MIB information in RMON, the information can be uploaded to the SNMP network management console on an as-needed basis, which lowers network overhead traffic.

The statistics here are read-only; data cannot be input here. The statistics on the RMON Statistics Report are compiled automatically by the hub's management software.

```
Telnet - 10.1.1.3                                                    _ □ ✕
Connect  Edit  Terminal  Help
qqqqqqqqqqqqqqqqqqqqqqqqqqqqqqqqqqqqqqqqqqqqqqqqqqqqqqqqqqqqqqqqqqqqqqqqqqqq
                              FastHub 200 Series
qqqqqqqqqqqqqqqqqqqqqqqqqqqqqqqqqqqqqqqqqqqqqqqqqqqqqqqqqqqqqqqqqqqqqqqqqqqq
                          RMON Statistics Report

Total frames          1572485        Good broadcast frames        63815
Total octets        119132600        Good multicast frames       766925
Runts                       3        Total collisions                0
Errors:
 FCS errors             65537        Oversize frames                 0
 Alignment errors          12        Undersize frames                0
 Jabber errors              0

         Size (bytes)       Number of frames      Distribution
            64                   721637              45.89 %
            65 -   127           795287              50.57 %
           128 -   255            31619               2.01 %
           256 -   511            23354               1.48 %
           512 -  1023              465               0.02 %
          1024 -  1518              120               0.00 %

       <Port statistics>    <Unit statistics>  <Clear statistics>  < Exit >

       Press F3 or ? for help on the selected item
```

Figure A-34.   These are the unit statistics stored by RMON, which is an SNMP facility

Unit Addressing Report

The Unit Addressing Report lists the addresses of stations connected to each port on the hub. The Port field in Figure A-35 indicates the port number on the hub itself. The Source Address field contains the source MAC address of the host or device connected to that port.

The information here is read-only; addresses cannot be input here. The addresses on the Unit Addressing Report are compiled automatically by the hub's management software.

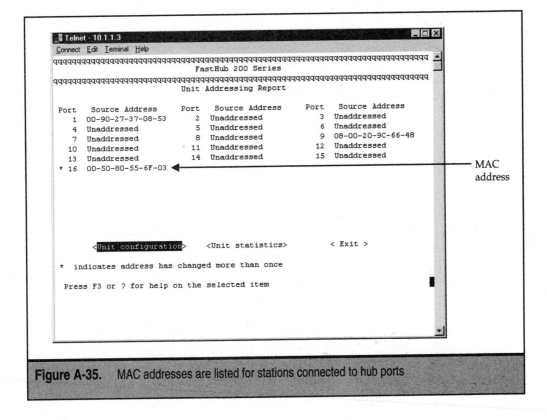

Figure A-35. MAC addresses are listed for stations connected to hub ports

Index

S